POLICE SERGEANT

EXAMINATION

FOURTH EDITION

by

Donald J. Schroeder, Ph.D.
Adjunct Professor,
John Jay College of Criminal Justice

Senior Partner,
S & L Company, National Police Consultants

Former Commanding Officer,
81st Police Precinct, New York City Police Department

Frank A. Lombardo
Deputy Inspector (Retired)
New York City Police Department

Adjunct Professor,
John Jay College of Criminal Justice

Former Commanding Officer,
30th Police Precinct, New York City Police Department

BARRON'S

We dedicate this book to the heroes of law enforcement
who performed their last tour of duty on 9/11/01. May
your spirit of service to the community live on and shed
light on the paths that lead us to the future.

All inquiries should be addressed to:
Barron's Educational Series, Inc.
250 Wireless Boulevard
Hauppauge, New York 11788
http://www.barronseduc.com

Library of Congress Catalog Card No. 2003057774

International Standard Book No. 0-7641-2360-2

Library of Congress Cataloging-in-Publication Data
Schroeder, Donald J.
  How to prepare for the police sergeant examination / by Donald J. Schroeder, Frank A.
Lombardo.—4th ed.
    p. cm.
  ISBN 0-7641-2360-2
    1. Police—United States—Examinations, questions, etc. I. Title: Police sergeant
examination. II. Lombardo, Frank A. III. Title.

HV8142.S37 2004
363.2′2′076—dc22

                                                                            2003057774

PRINTED IN THE UNITED STATES OF AMERICA

9 8 7 6 5 4 3 2

CONTENTS

Preface

In preparing the fourth edition of *How To Prepare for the Police Sergeant Examination*, we have included a new chapter on the latest approach to policing—that is, community policing, which is recognized as the philosophy that will dominate attitudes in policing as we move ahead into the twenty-first century.

No longer will quick response to calls for service along with handling such incidents as separate isolated occurrences be acceptable. Under community policing merely making arrests and clearing cases as separate incidents will not be sufficient. Not only must criminal actions be addressed, but their root causes must also be identified and eliminated. This moves police work, and the officers that act as supervisors under community policing, toward the realization that the police must of necessity become involved in matters that traditional policing saw as outside its sphere of responsibility.

As part of addressing the police response now known as community policing, we recognize the police managerial tool commonly known as Compstat. More and more, the statistics brought to the foreground through Compstat have enabled police to become proactive and to achieve the mainstay of community policing, namely problem solving in partnership with the community.

Recognizing that supervisors more than ever must demonstrate an ability to interpret and apply such data, the text continues to include a chapter that deals with data interpretation through graphs and charts.

The fourth edition text continues to cover other topics added in the third edition, such as police science, as well as to offer information and exercises dealing with assessment center style examinations. Candidates have found these practice exercises extremely helpful in preparing for such assessment-style examinations.

As in the past, we continue to champion commitment and endurance as a requirement for promotion. The candidate who is truly committed to competing successfully on promotional examinations is quick to realize that studying for promotion is the result of being committed to the goal of getting promoted and is married to the related act of endurance. Studying for promotion is not a one shot or quick fix kind of process. Simply stated, it takes time and being able to stick to your goal.

Both your authors began as police officers and followed a successful trail to higher police ranks. While the trail was certainly difficult, it was most certainly worth it. Follow the advice and strategies we offer in this text and stay committed to your goal. Good luck in your efforts.

Donald J. Schroeder
Frank A. Lombardo

PART ONE:
GENERAL INFORMATION

CHAPTER 1

About the Police Sergeant Examination

Almost without exception throughout the United States, candidates for the rank of Police Sergeant are already police officers or detectives. This is so since lateral entry into police departments is very rare, except at the entry-level rank and also at the highest rank in the department. Therefore, we, the authors, assume that those using this book are police officers or detectives, although certain portions of the material would be helpful for those studying for higher ranks in a police department. In any case, we realize that the great majority of our readers are sworn law enforcement officers. Hence, we have geared our writing accordingly and have based this book on our combined fifty years' experience preparing for and taking such examinations, our subsequent writing and scoring of such examinations, and our coaching of thousands of students preparing for them. Since you, the reader, have taken the initiative to acquire this book, you are probably properly motivated. We would like at the outset to fuel this motivation by sharing with you some of our findings concerning promotion to sergeant and the sergeant's examination itself.

Basic Ideas

SACRIFICE IS NECESSARY

Success on police promotion examinations is a matter of endurance more than anything else. As a general rule, every police officer has the potential to become a sergeant, but not every police officer is willing to make the sacrifice required to compete successfully on the sergeant's examination.

YOU SHOULD BE STUDYING FOR CAPTAIN

The sergeant's rank is the most difficult to attain. For some reason, after promotion to sergeant, many officers are content and cease studying. This means that for the officer who is willing to continue his/her studying efforts after becoming a sergeant, the competition actually is not as great. For this reason, we suggest you adopt the mental posture that you are "studying for the captain's test"; passing the Sergeant Examination is merely a step along the way.

HAVE A GAME PLAN AND FOLLOW IT

Far too many police officers waste their studying efforts by completely ignoring a very important area of concentration. Allow us to explain by the following:

Learn about your examination. The first and most important step in your studying efforts is to ascertain what type of examination is involved in your jurisdiction and to get a good idea of the scope of the content matter on which you will be tested. In most jurisdictions the type of examination will be multiple choice, but this is beginning to change, as we will discuss later. The second part of this first step, however, is critical. Understanding what content matter you will be responsible for knowing is essential. This is where wasted time enters the picture. If you are not studying the right material, you are obviously wasting your time. Later in this chapter we will explain the steps you can and should take to guard against this happening to you.

Develop test-taking strategies. Far too many police promotion students concentrate almost exclusively on learning the content matter involved and ignore test-taking strategy. This is a grievous error. Different types of examinations require different test-taking strategies. For this reason, we emphasize strategy in every section of this book. In the final analysis, if you fail to recognize the importance of test-taking strategy and fail to work on it as much as you can, you are hurting your chances for success on the examination.

Who Takes the Examination, and Why?

As a general rule, every eligible police officer takes the sergeant's test. A good student must realize, however, that most candidates are hoping for a minor miracle. We know of very few instances in which candidates who didn't prepare were successful. So, in terms of raw numbers, the odds against your being successful if you do not study are relatively high. However, the odds are in favor of those who prepare adequately. Many others are taking the examination on the outside chance that their native intelligence will see them through; you, the prepared student, are merely expecting the examination results to reflect the effort you put into preparation. All this is being said to convince you even more to sacrifice your time now so you can reap the rewards of your sacrifice later.

Meaning of Test Validity

There are many kinds of test validity. Scores of books have been written on the subject. Complete understanding by the police officer student of this very complex concept is not at all necessary. But to guide you in your study efforts, you should have a basic understanding of test validity.

SERGEANT'S EXAMINATION MUST BE "JOB RELATED"

In any examination, if it is to be valid, the candidate can only be tested for the requisite knowledges, skills, and abilities needed by an incumbent in the position for which the examination is being held. In other words, the test must relate to the job. A simple example should make this clearer. If a person is being tested for a job as a typist, the test shouldn't require the candidate to understand shorthand or take dictation. Therefore, any valid test for the rank of Sergeant in a police department must limit itself to testing for knowledge, skills, and abilities actually needed by a police sergeant working in the department in which the candidate is working. It would not suffice if an examination were constructed based on the sergeant's job in one department—the New York City Police Department, for example—and given to sergeant's candidates in another jurisdiction— the San Francisco Police Department, for example. Therefore, the examiner constructing the examination must have a good idea of just what an incumbent actually does in the position being tested for. It is the job analysis for the position that the examiner uses in the development of the test.

IMPORTANCE OF VALIDITY

The necessity for an examination to be valid, or job related, is one of great concern to the examiner. This is so since an examination adjudged to be nonvalid or non-job-related would, if challenged, be invalidated by the courts. Many a jurisdiction has learned this lesson the hard way during the last ten years. Nowadays, however, most jurisdictions understand their responsibility to construct valid examinations. A good student will recognize this and take advantage of it, as explained below.

Job Analysis

The job analysis is a comprehensive statement of duties and responsibilities of a given job. It is developed primarily through in-depth interviews with incumbents coupled with periods of observation during which the job analysis developer actually observes an incumbent doing the job being analyzed. The completed job analysis is then given to the test developer, who uses it to write the examination. What does all of this mean to the promotion candidate? In plain language, it means that, legally, when you take the examination for promotion to sergeant, you can only be asked questions related to the duties and responsibilities of a sergeant in your department. These duties and responsibilities must also be reduced to a job analysis, which is often available for public inspection. If you can get a copy of the job analysis for your jurisdiction, use it to help direct your study efforts.

Emerging Format of the Police Sergeant Examination

Primarily because of the federal requirement to administer job-related examinations, the format of the police sergeant's examination has been undergoing significant changes. Currently, the typical sergeant's examination consists of one or more of the following components:

1. Technical skills and/or

2. General (or generic) skills and/or

3. Assessment exercises

TECHNICAL SKILLS COMPONENT

This part of your examination includes that professional material a police sergeant must know to perform successfully in your particular department. It typically includes the following areas.

Department rules and regulations. This includes those policies and procedures that must be followed by and enforced by the sergeant. Since patrol sergeants are supervisors, they must know those rules and regulations that pertain to the supervisor's job, as well as the procedures that must be followed by anyone under the direct supervision of the sergeant. It follows, therefore, that sergeants must know the rules, regulations, and procedures that have to be adhered to by the police officer on patrol.

Department orders, memos, policies, and so on. This includes those written orders that control the job in the particular department involved.

Law. This area includes constitutional law, both federal and state, the criminal law and procedural law for the jurisdiction concerned, and various other local laws and ordinances, including traffic regulations.

GENERAL SKILLS COMPONENT

This part of your examination contains general material that should be known by all police sergeants in every jurisdiction. The content matter doesn't change from department to department as is the case with the technical skills component. That is, although technical material may differ greatly among police jurisdictions, the material in the general skills component is exactly the same. Included in this component of the typical sergeant's examination are such topics as

1. Principles of supervision

2. Training and safety

3. Principles of management and administration

4. Community relations

5. Patrol operations

6. Report writing and record keeping

7. Data interpretation

8. Police science principles

PRACTICAL ASSESSMENT EXERCISES

This is the newest and, in fact, still emerging component of the police sergeant's examination. When properly constructed and administered, assessment exercises are quite job related. Although there are great variations in the form of these exercises, the basic concept is simple. You are put into an artificial situation that resembles a real-life situation from the workday of a sergeant. You are then given some sort of job to perform that is reflective of what a typical sergeant working in your jurisdiction actually has to perform, as determined from a job analysis. You are then scored based on how you perform in this artificially constructed work situation. This may sound difficult or complex, but once you understand the process, it is actually simple. In Part Three, we devote considerable time to help you understand the process. For now, keep in mind the identification of the more common forms of assessment exercises: (1) in-basket exercises, (2) oral interviews, and (3) fact-finding and problem-solving exercises.

Importance of the Examination Announcement

One of the most important factors in preparing for the sergeant's examination is understanding, insofar as possible, the material that will be covered on the examination: technical skills material or general skills material, or both, and also understanding what type of examination you will be given—multiple-choice, in-basket, oral examination, or some combination of these formats. One way of finding this out is by obtaining and studying the examination announcement published by the agency administering the examination. The examination announcement usually includes the scope of the examination and often includes a bibliography. It is a very important document and should be studied by the serious police promotion student.

OTHER WAYS TO FIND OUT ABOUT YOUR EXAMINATION

We cannot emphasize enough the importance of properly directing your study efforts toward what will actually be asked on the sergeant's examination in your own particular jurisdiction. In addition to the examination announcement, other ways of learning what to expect on your test are as follows.

Look at previous examinations, if they are available. Be careful, however, since nowadays examination formats are changing, especially in jurisdictions that have experienced successful court challenges to previous examinations.

Ask those who have been successful in your department. It has been our experience that successful test takers empathize with serious students and enjoy helping them. Do not, however, for obvious reasons, rely on advice from unsuccessful candidates.

Consult a coaching school. We will have more to say about coaching schools in the next chapter. For now, however, we would suggest that a good coaching school usually has an accurate understanding of both the content matter you should study and the format of the examination you will be given.

What This Book Covers

This book touches on all of the content matter you can expect to find on a typical sergeant's examination, except it does not deal with technical skills. Our reasons for not including any material on technical skills are as follows. Technical skills material varies so greatly from jurisdiction to jurisdiction that we believe we could not comprehensively and accurately deal with all of the material involved in any one text. We did, however, include a section in Chapter 2 that offers some very valuable tips for dealing with the technical skills component.

More importantly, and you must understand this, technical skills material changes so frequently and so quickly that any text attempting to adequately deal with technical skills is usually outdated six months after it is published. For example, all it would take is one significant United States Supreme Court decision in a given technical skills area to change the material in that area completely.

With respect to the general skills and the assessment exercise components, this book should prove to be of great value to you. However, before you begin to study the material included in the various chapters, we strongly suggest that you read Chapter 2, especially the sections Developing Good Study Habits and How to Use This Book Effectively.

CHAPTER 2

How to Maximize Your Test Score

This chapter covers a number of very important matters vital to scoring high on the police sergeant examination. The topics include

> Developing good study habits
> Ten rules for studying more effectively
> Strategies for handling multiple-choice questions
> Value of study groups
> Tips for dealing with the technical skills component
> Importance of understanding the test format for your jurisdiction
> Value of coaching schools
> How to use this book effectively

Because all these items are so important, it would be best for you to review this chapter periodically as you study for your examination. At the very least, you should review this section prior to taking each of the full-length multiple-choice examinations included in this book.

Developing Good Study Habits

Many students for police promotion incorrectly believe that the amount of time spent studying is the most important factor in test preparation. This is not so. Effective study habits are in fact the key to successful test preparation. Of course, all else being equal, the amount of time you devote to your studies is a critical factor. But spending time reading is not necessarily studying. If you want to retain what you read, you must develop a system. For example, a person who devotes sixty minutes a day to uninterrupted study in a quiet, private area will generally retain more than someone who puts in twice that time by studying five or six times a day for fifteen to twenty minutes at a time.

Ten Rules for Studying More Effectively

We have listed a number of rules for you to follow to increase study time efficiency. If you abide by these rules, you will get the most out of this book.

1. **MAKE SURE YOU UNDERSTAND THE MEANING OF EVERY WORD YOU READ.** Your ability to understand what you read is the most important skill needed to pass the test. Therefore, starting now, every time you see a word that you don't fully understand, make certain that you write it down and make note of where you saw it. Then, when you have a chance, look up the meaning of the word in the dictionary. When you think you know what the word means, go back to the reading material that contained the word and make certain that you fully understand the meaning of the word.

   Keep a list of all words you don't know and periodically review them. Also, try to use these words whenever you can in conversation. If you do this faithfully, you will quickly build an extensive vocabulary that will be helpful to you not only when you take the police sergeant examination, but for the rest of your life.

2. **STUDY UNINTERRUPTEDLY FOR AT LEAST 30 MINUTES.** Unless you can study for an uninterrupted period of at least thirty minutes, you should not bother to study at all. It is essential that you concentrate for extended periods of time. Remember, the actual examination takes anywhere from three to eight hours to complete, with the average four hours. You must concentrate just as hard in the final portion of the test as you did in the first hour. Therefore, as the examination approaches, study for more extended periods of time without interruption. And later on when you take the practice examinations, do a complete examination in one sitting, just as you must do at the time of the actual examination.

3. **SIMULATE EXAMINATION CONDITIONS WHEN STUDYING.** Study under the same conditions as those of the examination, as much as possible. Eliminate as many outside interferences as you can. And if you are a smoker, refrain from smoking while studying since you will not be allowed to smoke in the classroom on the day of your examination.

4. **MAKE CERTAIN WHAT YOU ARE STUDYING IS JOB RELATED.** Don't waste time studying non-job-related material. See our suggestion in Chapter 1 to help you determine what to study.

5. **MAKE SURE YOU UNDERSTAND THE ANSWERS TO EVERY QUESTION IN THIS BOOK.** Every answer is accompanied by an explanation. Whenever you get a question wrong, be sure that you

understand why you missed it so you won't make the same mistake again. However, it is equally important to make certain that you have answered a question correctly for the right reason. Therefore, study the answer explanation to every question in this book as carefully as you study the question itself.

6. **ALWAYS FOLLOW THE RECOMMENDED TECHNIQUE FOR ANSWERING MULTIPLE-CHOICE QUESTIONS.** In the next section of this chapter we provide an invaluable technique for answering multiple-choice questions. Make sure you use it.

7. **ALWAYS TIME YOURSELF WHEN DOING PRACTICE QUESTIONS.** Running out of time on a multiple-choice examination is a tragic error that is easily avoided. Learn, through practice, to move to the next question after a reasonable period of time spent on any one question. Therefore, when you are doing practice questions, always time yourself and always try to stay within the recommended time limits. The correct use of time during the actual examination is an integral part of the technique that will be explained later in this chapter.

8. **CONCENTRATE YOUR STUDY TIME IN THE AREAS OF YOUR GREATEST WEAKNESS.** The diagnostic examination contained in this book is designed to identify the most difficult question types for you. Although you should spend most of your time improving yourself in these areas, do not ignore the other types of questions.

9. **EXERCISE REGULARLY, AND STAY IN GOOD PHYSICAL CONDITION.** Students who are in good physical condition have an advantage over those who are not. It is a well-established principle that good physical health improves the ability of the mind to function smoothly and efficiently, especially when taking examinations of extended duration, such as the police sergeant examination.

10. **ESTABLISH A SCHEDULE FOR STUDYING, AND STICK TO IT.** Do not put off studying to those times when you have nothing else to do. Schedule your study time, and try not to let anything else interfere with that schedule. If you feel yourself weakening, remind yourself of why you would like to become a police sergeant.

Strategies for Handling Multiple-Choice Questions

Listed below is a very specific test-taking strategy valuable for a multiple-choice examination. Study the technique, and practice it; then study it again until you have mastered it.

1. **READ THE DIRECTIONS.** Do not assume that you know the directions without reading them. Make sure you read and understand them. Note particularly whether the directions are different from one section of the examination to another.

2. **MAKE SURE YOU HAVE THE COMPLETE EXAMINATION.** Check the examination page by page. Since examination booklets have numbered pages, simply make certain that you have all the pages and that all words are legible.

3. **TAKE A CLOSE LOOK AT THE ANSWER SHEET.** Some answer sheets are numbered vertically and some horizontally. The answer sheets in your practice examinations are typical of those you will see on your examination. However, do not take anything for granted. Review the directions on the answer sheet carefully, and familiarize yourself with its format. Never make extraneous marks on an answer sheet. The sheets are usually machine scored, and the machine might interpret an extraneous mark as a wrong answer.

4. **BE CAREFUL WHEN MARKING YOUR ANSWERS.** Be sure to mark your answers in accordance with the directions on the answer sheet. Be extremely careful that

   ● You mark only one answer for each question.

   ● You do not make extraneous markings on your answer sheet.

   ● You completely darken the allotted space for the answer you choose.

   ● You erase completely any answer you wish to change.

5. **MAKE ABSOLUTELY CERTAIN YOU ARE MARKING THE ANSWER TO THE RIGHT QUESTION.** Many multiple-choice tests have been failed because of carelessness in this area. All it takes is one mistake. If you put down one answer in the wrong space, you will probably continue the mistake for a number of questions until you realize your error. We recommend that you use the following procedure when marking your answer sheet.

   ● Select your answer, circle that choice on the test booklet, and ask yourself what question number you are working on.

   ● If you select choice C as the answer for question 11, circle choice C on the test booklet, and say to yourself, "C is the answer to question 11."

   ● Then find the space on your answer sheet for question 11, and again say, "C is the answer to question 11" as you mark the answer.

- Although this might seem rather elementary and repetitive, after a while it becomes automatic. If followed properly, it guarantees that you will not lose valuable points because of a careless mistake.

6. **MAKE CERTAIN THAT YOU UNDERSTAND WHAT THE QUESTION IS ASKING.** Read the stem of the question (the part before the choices) very carefully to make certain that you know what the examiner is asking.

7. **ALWAYS READ ALL OF THE CHOICES BEFORE YOU SELECT AN ANSWER.** It is the examiner's intent when writing "distractor choices" (incorrect choices) to make at least one of them sound very much like the correct choice. Therefore, you must read all the choices to make sure you do not fall into the examiner's trap and select a distractor choice as the correct answer before you get to the correct choice.

8. **BEWARE OF KEY WORDS THAT OFTEN TIP OFF THE CORRECT AND INCORRECT ANSWERS.**

    Absolute words are usually a wrong choice
    (They are generally too broad and difficult to defend):

never	always	only
none	all	any
nothing	everyone	
nobody	everybody	

    Limiting words are usually a correct choice:

usually	sometimes	many
generally	some	often
few	possible	
occasionally		

9. **NEVER MAKE A CHOICE BASED ON FREQUENCY OF PREVIOUS ANSWERS.** Some students pay attention to the pattern of answers when taking an examination. Always answer the question without regard to what the previous choices have been.

10. **CROSS OUT CHOICES YOU KNOW ARE WRONG.** As you read through the choices, put an X through the letter designation of any choice you know is wrong. After reading through all the choices, you only have to reread those you did not cross out the first time. If you cross out all but one of the choices, the remaining choice should be the answer. Read the choice one more time to satisfy yourself, put a circle around its letter designation in the test booklet (if you still believe it is the best answer), and transpose it to the answer sheet.

(See the procedure given under rule 5.) If you cross out all but two choices when you read through the first time, you only have to reread the two remaining choices and make a decision.

Many times, the second time you read the remaining choices, the answer is clear. If that happens, cross out the wrong choice, circle the correct one, and transfer the answer to the answer sheet. If more than two choices are still not crossed out, reread the stem of the question and make certain you understand the question. Then go through the choices again. (Keep in mind the key words mentioned in rule 8, which may give you a hint of the correct answer.)

11. **SKIP OVER QUESTIONS THAT GIVE YOU TROUBLE.** The first time through the examination, be certain not to dwell too long on any one question. Simply skip the question after putting a circle around the number of the skipped question on the test booklet (to keep your answers from getting out of sequence), and go to the next question. Do not guess at this point if you do not know the answer. Remember, when recording an answer on the answer sheet after you skipped a question, to use the strategy from step 5 to make certain you do not answer questions out of sequence.

12. **RETURN TO THE QUESTIONS YOU SKIPPED AFTER YOU FINISH THE REST OF THE EXAMINATION.** Once you have answered all the questions you were sure of on the entire examination, check the time remaining. If time permits (and it should if you follow our recommendations), return to each question you did not answer and reread the stem and the choices that are not crossed out. It should be easy to find the questions you have not yet answered because, as per the instructions in rule 11, all of them will have their number designation circled on the test booklet. If the answer is still not clear and you are running out of time, then make an educated guess between those choices you have not already eliminated. When making an educated guess, follow the guidelines presented in rule 15.

13. **NEVER LEAVE QUESTIONS UNANSWERED UNLESS THE INSTRUCTIONS INDICATE A PENALTY FOR WRONG ANSWERS.** In almost all police sergeant examinations, you do not lose credit for wrong answers. In this case, guess at any questions you are not sure of.

However, in rare instances, a penalty is assessed for wrong answers on multiple-choice examinations. Since this would have to be explained in the instructions, be sure to read them carefully. If this is the case on your examination, weigh how certain you are about each question before answering. Note that this almost never happens on police sergeant examinations.

14. **CHECK YOUR TIME PERIODICALLY.** At the very beginning of your examination, very often before the test actually begins, you will be told the amount of time allowed and the number of questions involved. Your job is to manage your time efficiently throughout the examination by determining the average time you should spend on each question. Then periodically throughout the test you should check to make sure you are on schedule. Far too many students only become concerned about time toward the end of the examination, when very often it is too late to make adjustments. Don't make this mistake.

Suppose you are taking a multiple-choice test with 100 questions you have to complete in three-and-a-half hours. Under these circumstances, you will have no trouble at all with time if you average about one-and-a-half minutes per question. In other words, take about fifteen minutes for every ten questions. Check yourself after every ten questions to make sure you are not taking too long. Never spend more than two minutes on any question. In that way, you will have plenty of time at the end of the examination to go back to the questions you skipped the first time through. (Always schedule your time to leave at least a half-hour at the end of the examination to go back to the questions that you skipped.)

In any case, the key to successful time management is to establish a schedule at the beginning of the test and check your progress periodically from the very beginning. Don't wait until it is too late into the examination to adjust.

15. **RULES FOR MAKING AN EDUCATED GUESS.** Your chances of picking the correct answer to questions you are not sure of will be significantly increased if you use the following rules.

- Never consider answer choices that you have already eliminated. (See rule 10.)

- Be aware of key words that give you clues as to which answer might be right or wrong. (See rule 8.)

- The answer choice that has significantly more or significantly fewer words in it than the other choices is very often the correct choice.

- If all else fails, and you have to make an outright guess at more than one question, guess the same lettered choice for each question. The odds are that you will pick up some valuable points.

- If two choices have a conflicting meaning, one of them is probably the correct answer. And if two choices are too close in meaning, probably neither is correct. Consider the following question:

EXAMPLE

John's complaint about the weather was that:
(A) It was too hot.
(B) It was too cold.
(C) It varied too much.
(D) It was unpredictable.

In this example, choices C and D are so close together in meaning that neither is likely to be the correct answer. Choices A and B, on the other hand, are quite opposite each other, and one of them is most likely the correct answer.

Many times, two choices are worded so that combined they encompass all the possibilities. In these cases, one of them has to be the correct choice.

EXAMPLE

Which of the following is the most accurate statement about John?
(A) John is guilty of murder.
(B) John is not guilty of murder.
(C) John is guilty of arson.
(D) John is guilty of assault.

In this rather obvious example, John is either guilty of murder or he is not guilty of murder. The correct choice will be one of these two. The other choices will be wrong because questions are not intended to have more than one right answer.

Perhaps another example would help.

EXAMPLE

How old is John?
(A) Seven years old or less
(B) Six years old
(C) Over seven years old
(D) Fourteen years old

In this example, a correct answer has to be either choice A or C, because if John is not seven years old or less (choice A), then he must be over seven years old (choice C). Please note that even if he is fourteen years old (choice D), choice C is still correct. His age must fit into either choice A or choice C.

16. **BE VERY RELUCTANT TO CHANGE ANSWERS.** Unless you have a very good reason, do not change an answer once you have chosen it. Studies have shown that all too often people change an answer from the right one to the wrong one.

Value of Study Groups

We are frequently asked to comment on the value of a study group to the candidate for police promotion. Our response is that, if used properly, a study group can be of great value, but if used improperly, a study group can be counterproductive.

REVIEW GROUPS

The first problem with "study groups" is that they are improperly named. In fact, they should be called *review* groups because the members of the group should come together periodically to collectively review material they have learned individually. This is critical to the success of such a group. *You study best when you study alone.* Meeting with other serious students on a regular basis to go over material everyone is already familiar with is quite beneficial for the following reasons. It "forces" you to study the material before the scheduled group meeting. It is every group member's responsibility to come to the review session fully prepared to discuss the material. Members who are chronically unprepared should be dropped from the group.

It also provides an opportunity to make sure you understand the material. If there is disagreement over interpretation of certain material, discussion is healthy and informative, but prolonged debate is damaging and self-defeating. Make a note about the conflict, and table the matter pending research and/or conferral with an informed source, such as someone from a coaching school or a police training academy.

SUGGESTION FOR RUNNING A REVIEW GROUP

Review groups must be well organized, and the members must be equally motivated if they are to be successful. If a group is structured in accordance with the following suggestions, it can be mutually beneficial to all members and a very useful component of your overall examination preparation effort.

Optimum group size is from three to five serious, dedicated students.

Meetings should be held weekly.

Meetings should not become social gatherings; food and drink should *not* be served.

At the first meeting, agreements should be reached concerning the content matter to be studied.

At each weekly meeting, at the end of the session, the group should agree on the material to be discussed at the next weekly session. Then, each member is *obligated* to study the assigned material before the date of the next meeting.

During the meeting, group members should alternate as discussion leaders, in accordance with a predetermined schedule. In this way each week it is the added responsibility for each member to be prepared to lead a discussion of a portion of that week's assignment.

All members must understand that they will be expected to be prepared for the meeting; discussion leaders must be especially well prepared.

Tips for Dealing with the Technical Skills Component

As previously mentioned, this book will not deal directly with technical skills material that might be included on your test, such as statutory law, case law, and department procedures. Since this material varies greatly from jurisdiction to jurisdiction and because it is amended so often, technical skills material is not included in this book. Nonetheless, you must include technical skills material in your test preparation effort if it is indeed to be included on your test. When studying technical skills material, we recommend the following procedures.

Make sure your material is up to date. As we have already pointed out, technical skills material changes so much that you must be certain what you are studying is current.

When studying procedures, concentrate on the responsibilities of the sergeant and those of the subordinates who are supervised by the sergeant.

When studying the law, concentrate on those crimes that are most often dealt with by the police, such as robbery, burglary, and assault, and stay away from crimes the police rarely become involved with, such as insurance fraud, or frauds on creditors.

As a general rule, you shouldn't be too concerned about distinguishing between degrees of various crimes. Understanding the basic elements of each crime is usually sufficient. Check previous examinations from your jurisdiction to verify this rule.

Study case law as well as the "black letter" law. Examiners often use actual cases to frame questions.

Study procedural law, especially cases involving individual rights, such as those contained in the Fourth, Fifth, Sixth, and Eighth Amendments to the United States Constitution. Concentrate on decisions of the United States Supreme Court and the highest court of the state in which you work.

Importance of Understanding the Test Format for Your Jurisdiction

Knowing what material will be covered on your test is extremely important—vital, in fact, to success. Therefore, as we explained in Chapter 1, you should read the examination announcement very carefully, study the job analysis if it is available, and understand what was covered in previous examinations. As important as knowing what material will be covered on your examination, however, is knowing what the format of your examination will be. In other words, what kind of test you will have to take. Will it be a multiple-choice test, which is the most common format, or will you be given some form of practical assessment exercise, such as an in-basket examination? Perhaps you will be given some form of oral interview. And there is always the possibility that you will be given some combination of these formats. In any case, our book will help you since we cover all the most common test formats.

Coaching Schools

Quite often we are asked by our students for our opinion on the value of the so-called coaching schools. Our response is that coaching schools can be helpful if used to supplement your own studying efforts. In a sense, a coaching school is like a review group, in that you should not depend on it to learn material but rather to test your understanding of material you have already studied. In other words, a coaching school, like a review group, should be a supplement to your personal preparation effort.

BENEFITS OF COACHING SCHOOLS

A good coaching school offers the following advantages.

Availability of experts to interpret complex areas. When you are having difficulty understanding something, such as a procedure of a law, you can get clarification from an instructor at the school.

Defining the content matter and format for your examination. A coaching school lives or dies on its ability to help students get promoted. Consequently, it is important for the school to keep current with the content matter and format for your particular examination. Therefore, coaching schools are excellent places to obtain this kind of information.

Practice test taking. As we do in this book, all good coaching schools offer students the opportunity to take practice examinations under simulated test conditions. This is perhaps the primary reason all good students should attend a coaching school.

Evaluation of your progress. Attending a coaching school allows students to evaluate their own progress by comparing the level of their knowledge to that of other students. Remember, however, that those who attend coaching schools are usually better prepared students than the general candidate population.

CAVEATS CONCERNING COACHING SCHOOLS

Beware of the following caveats concerning coaching schools.

Don't rely exclusively on the school. Your principal preparation must be your own.

Don't attend more than one school. Students who spend all their time running from one school to another are wasting their time. Pick a good school with a good track record, and stay with it. However, if there is more than one good school, find another student, perhaps a member of your review group, and make a deal. You go to one school, your colleague goes to the second school, and you share the material.

Choose your school carefully. The best way to do this is to ask someone who has been promoted for a recommendation. Attend only a school that specializes in police examinations.

How to Use This Book Effectively

If your examination is of the multiple-choice format and its content matter includes supervision, administration, and community relations, among other topics, follow steps 1 through 9.

1. Read and understand the material in Chapter 1.

2. Take the diagnostic test in this book to evaluate your strengths and weaknesses. Please note that the diagnostic test includes a diagnostic chart to help you to analyze your strong and weak areas, based on your performance on the diagnostic examination. Also note that each practice test in Part Two includes a diagnostic procedure.

3. Study all the material in Part Two, giving special emphasis to those chapters covering areas in which you were diagnosed as being weak when you took the diagnostic test.

4. A very important feature in Part Two is the section called Examatopics. Here you will find statements that have all been used in one form or another in previous police tests; many of them have been used a number of times. In other words, they are topics that often appear on examinations; hence the word *examatopics.* The examatopics do not always repeat information covered in the narrative part of the text but often introduce new "bits" of information gleaned from past examinations. Therefore, the examatopics should be carefully studied and frequently reviewed. Concentrate on them.

5. Take Practice Examination One, after you complete studying Chapters 4 through 12. When taking practice examinations, make sure you simulate actual examination conditions. You are cheating yourself if you take these examinations on a piecemeal basis. You must become mentally and physically prepared to take an examination that lasts several hours. The only way to do this is actually to take practice examinations of comparable duration.

6. Evaluate the results of your performance on Practice Examination One by using the diagnostic procedure included in the chapter. Based on this evaluation, go back and study the chapters in which you have a demonstrated weakness. Bear in mind, however, that not all the material on the practice tests is specifically covered in the chapters. In these cases, we added additional explanatory information in the Answer Explanations section. Therefore, the answer explanations should also be carefully studied and frequently reviewed.

7. Repeat steps 5 and 6 for Practice Examinations Two and Three.

8. Constantly review the Examatopics in Chapters 4 through 12.

9. From time to time, review Chapters 1 and 24.

10. About one week before your examination, reread Chapter 24.

USING THE BOOK FOR ASSESSMENT EXERCISES

If your examination includes an assessment center exercise as described in Chapter 1, take the following steps.

1. Read and understand the explanatory information contained in Chapter 16.

2. Study the portion of Chapter 16 that explains how assessment exercises are scored. If you understand what behavioral dimensions are being tested, you will be in a much better position to obtain a very good score.

3. Chapters 17 through 20 cover the assessment exercise you will be taking. Study the particular chapter, or if you know you will be taking some form of assessment exercise but you are not sure which type, study all four chapters.

4. Take the appropriate practice exercise found in Chapters 21 through 23.

5. Follow steps 9 and 10.

IT'S TIME TO GET TO WORK

You are now ready to begin your quest for promotion. Develop a schedule for studying, and stick to it. It's easy to find reasons to skip some study time. Remember, however, that the more you study, the better your chances are to get that first promotion, which incidentally is the hardest to get. Good luck.

PART TWO:
GENERAL SKILLS

Answer Sheet
Diagnostic Examination

Follow the instructions given in the text. Mark only your answers in the ovals below.

Warning: Be sure that the oval you fill is in the same row as the question you are answering. Use a No. 2 pencil (soft pencil).

Be sure your pencil marks are heavy and black. Erase completely any answer you wish to change.

Do *not* make stray pencil dots, dashes, or marks.

1 Ⓐ Ⓑ Ⓒ Ⓓ	2 Ⓐ Ⓑ Ⓒ Ⓓ	3 Ⓐ Ⓑ Ⓒ Ⓓ	4 Ⓐ Ⓑ Ⓒ Ⓓ	5 Ⓐ Ⓑ Ⓒ Ⓓ	6 Ⓐ Ⓑ Ⓒ Ⓓ
7 Ⓐ Ⓑ Ⓒ Ⓓ	8 Ⓐ Ⓑ Ⓒ Ⓓ	9 Ⓐ Ⓑ Ⓒ Ⓓ	10 Ⓐ Ⓑ Ⓒ Ⓓ	11 Ⓐ Ⓑ Ⓒ Ⓓ	12 Ⓐ Ⓑ Ⓒ Ⓓ
13 Ⓐ Ⓑ Ⓒ Ⓓ	14 Ⓐ Ⓑ Ⓒ Ⓓ	15 Ⓐ Ⓑ Ⓒ Ⓓ	16 Ⓐ Ⓑ Ⓒ Ⓓ	17 Ⓐ Ⓑ Ⓒ Ⓓ	18 Ⓐ Ⓑ Ⓒ Ⓓ
19 Ⓐ Ⓑ Ⓒ Ⓓ	20 Ⓐ Ⓑ Ⓒ Ⓓ	21 Ⓐ Ⓑ Ⓒ Ⓓ	22 Ⓐ Ⓑ Ⓒ Ⓓ	23 Ⓐ Ⓑ Ⓒ Ⓓ	24 Ⓐ Ⓑ Ⓒ Ⓓ
25 Ⓐ Ⓑ Ⓒ Ⓓ	26 Ⓐ Ⓑ Ⓒ Ⓓ	27 Ⓐ Ⓑ Ⓒ Ⓓ	28 Ⓐ Ⓑ Ⓒ Ⓓ	29 Ⓐ Ⓑ Ⓒ Ⓓ	30 Ⓐ Ⓑ Ⓒ Ⓓ
31 Ⓐ Ⓑ Ⓒ Ⓓ	32 Ⓐ Ⓑ Ⓒ Ⓓ	33 Ⓐ Ⓑ Ⓒ Ⓓ	34 Ⓐ Ⓑ Ⓒ Ⓓ	35 Ⓐ Ⓑ Ⓒ Ⓓ	36 Ⓐ Ⓑ Ⓒ Ⓓ
37 Ⓐ Ⓑ Ⓒ Ⓓ	38 Ⓐ Ⓑ Ⓒ Ⓓ	39 Ⓐ Ⓑ Ⓒ Ⓓ	40 Ⓐ Ⓑ Ⓒ Ⓓ	41 Ⓐ Ⓑ Ⓒ Ⓓ	42 Ⓐ Ⓑ Ⓒ Ⓓ
43 Ⓐ Ⓑ Ⓒ Ⓓ	44 Ⓐ Ⓑ Ⓒ Ⓓ	45 Ⓐ Ⓑ Ⓒ Ⓓ	46 Ⓐ Ⓑ Ⓒ Ⓓ	47 Ⓐ Ⓑ Ⓒ Ⓓ	48 Ⓐ Ⓑ Ⓒ Ⓓ
49 Ⓐ Ⓑ Ⓒ Ⓓ	50 Ⓐ Ⓑ Ⓒ Ⓓ	51 Ⓐ Ⓑ Ⓒ Ⓓ	52 Ⓐ Ⓑ Ⓒ Ⓓ	53 Ⓐ Ⓑ Ⓒ Ⓓ	54 Ⓐ Ⓑ Ⓒ Ⓓ
55 Ⓐ Ⓑ Ⓒ Ⓓ	56 Ⓐ Ⓑ Ⓒ Ⓓ	57 Ⓐ Ⓑ Ⓒ Ⓓ	58 Ⓐ Ⓑ Ⓒ Ⓓ	59 Ⓐ Ⓑ Ⓒ Ⓓ	60 Ⓐ Ⓑ Ⓒ Ⓓ
61 Ⓐ Ⓑ Ⓒ Ⓓ	62 Ⓐ Ⓑ Ⓒ Ⓓ	63 Ⓐ Ⓑ Ⓒ Ⓓ	64 Ⓐ Ⓑ Ⓒ Ⓓ	65 Ⓐ Ⓑ Ⓒ Ⓓ	66 Ⓐ Ⓑ Ⓒ Ⓓ
67 Ⓐ Ⓑ Ⓒ Ⓓ	68 Ⓐ Ⓑ Ⓒ Ⓓ	69 Ⓐ Ⓑ Ⓒ Ⓓ	70 Ⓐ Ⓑ Ⓒ Ⓓ	71 Ⓐ Ⓑ Ⓒ Ⓓ	72 Ⓐ Ⓑ Ⓒ Ⓓ
73 Ⓐ Ⓑ Ⓒ Ⓓ	74 Ⓐ Ⓑ Ⓒ Ⓓ	75 Ⓐ Ⓑ Ⓒ Ⓓ	76 Ⓐ Ⓑ Ⓒ Ⓓ	77 Ⓐ Ⓑ Ⓒ Ⓓ	78 Ⓐ Ⓑ Ⓒ Ⓓ
79 Ⓐ Ⓑ Ⓒ Ⓓ	80 Ⓐ Ⓑ Ⓒ Ⓓ	81 Ⓐ Ⓑ Ⓒ Ⓓ	82 Ⓐ Ⓑ Ⓒ Ⓓ	83 Ⓐ Ⓑ Ⓒ Ⓓ	84 Ⓐ Ⓑ Ⓒ Ⓓ
85 Ⓐ Ⓑ Ⓒ Ⓓ	86 Ⓐ Ⓑ Ⓒ Ⓓ	87 Ⓐ Ⓑ Ⓒ Ⓓ	88 Ⓐ Ⓑ Ⓒ Ⓓ	89 Ⓐ Ⓑ Ⓒ Ⓓ	90 Ⓐ Ⓑ Ⓒ Ⓓ
91 Ⓐ Ⓑ Ⓒ Ⓓ	92 Ⓐ Ⓑ Ⓒ Ⓓ	93 Ⓐ Ⓑ Ⓒ Ⓓ	94 Ⓐ Ⓑ Ⓒ Ⓓ	95 Ⓐ Ⓑ Ⓒ Ⓓ	96 Ⓐ Ⓑ Ⓒ Ⓓ
97 Ⓐ Ⓑ Ⓒ Ⓓ	98 Ⓐ Ⓑ Ⓒ Ⓓ	99 Ⓐ Ⓑ Ⓒ Ⓓ	100 Ⓐ Ⓑ Ⓒ Ⓓ	101 Ⓐ Ⓑ Ⓒ Ⓓ	102 Ⓐ Ⓑ Ⓒ Ⓓ
103 Ⓐ Ⓑ Ⓒ Ⓓ	104 Ⓐ Ⓑ Ⓒ Ⓓ	105 Ⓐ Ⓑ Ⓒ Ⓓ	106 Ⓐ Ⓑ Ⓒ Ⓓ	107 Ⓐ Ⓑ Ⓒ Ⓓ	108 Ⓐ Ⓑ Ⓒ Ⓓ
109 Ⓐ Ⓑ Ⓒ Ⓓ	110 Ⓐ Ⓑ Ⓒ Ⓓ	111 Ⓐ Ⓑ Ⓒ Ⓓ	112 Ⓐ Ⓑ Ⓒ Ⓓ	113 Ⓐ Ⓑ Ⓒ Ⓓ	114 Ⓐ Ⓑ Ⓒ Ⓓ
115 Ⓐ Ⓑ Ⓒ Ⓓ	116 Ⓐ Ⓑ Ⓒ Ⓓ	117 Ⓐ Ⓑ Ⓒ Ⓓ	118 Ⓐ Ⓑ Ⓒ Ⓓ	119 Ⓐ Ⓑ Ⓒ Ⓓ	120 Ⓐ Ⓑ Ⓒ Ⓓ
121 Ⓐ Ⓑ Ⓒ Ⓓ	122 Ⓐ Ⓑ Ⓒ Ⓓ	123 Ⓐ Ⓑ Ⓒ Ⓓ	124 Ⓐ Ⓑ Ⓒ Ⓓ	125 Ⓐ Ⓑ Ⓒ Ⓓ	126 Ⓐ Ⓑ Ⓒ Ⓓ
127 Ⓐ Ⓑ Ⓒ Ⓓ	128 Ⓐ Ⓑ Ⓒ Ⓓ	129 Ⓐ Ⓑ Ⓒ Ⓓ	130 Ⓐ Ⓑ Ⓒ Ⓓ	131 Ⓐ Ⓑ Ⓒ Ⓓ	132 Ⓐ Ⓑ Ⓒ Ⓓ
133 Ⓐ Ⓑ Ⓒ Ⓓ	134 Ⓐ Ⓑ Ⓒ Ⓓ	135 Ⓐ Ⓑ Ⓒ Ⓓ	136 Ⓐ Ⓑ Ⓒ Ⓓ	137 Ⓐ Ⓑ Ⓒ Ⓓ	138 Ⓐ Ⓑ Ⓒ Ⓓ
139 Ⓐ Ⓑ Ⓒ Ⓓ	140 Ⓐ Ⓑ Ⓒ Ⓓ	141 Ⓐ Ⓑ Ⓒ Ⓓ	142 Ⓐ Ⓑ Ⓒ Ⓓ	143 Ⓐ Ⓑ Ⓒ Ⓓ	144 Ⓐ Ⓑ Ⓒ Ⓓ
145 Ⓐ Ⓑ Ⓒ Ⓓ	146 Ⓐ Ⓑ Ⓒ Ⓓ	147 Ⓐ Ⓑ Ⓒ Ⓓ	148 Ⓐ Ⓑ Ⓒ Ⓓ	149 Ⓐ Ⓑ Ⓒ Ⓓ	150 Ⓐ Ⓑ Ⓒ Ⓓ

Diagnose Your Problem

CHAPTER 3

A Diagnostic Examination

There are 120 questions on this diagnostic examination, and you should finish the entire examination in four hours. For maximum benefit, it is strongly recommended that you take this examination in one sitting as if it were an actual test.

The answers to this examination and their explanations begin on page 67. By completing the Diagnostic Chart, you can get an idea of which question types give you the most difficulty. You can devote most of your time to those areas.

Before You Take the Examination

Before taking this examination, you should have read Chapters 1 and 2. Be sure you employ the recommended test-taking strategy outlined in Chapter 2 while taking this examination.

Remember to read each question and related material carefully before choosing your answers. Select the choice you believe to be the most correct, and mark your answer on the answer sheet provided at the beginning of this chapter. This answer sheet is similar to those used on most actual examinations. The answer key, diagnostic procedure, and answer explanations appear at the end of this chapter.

The Test

DIRECTIONS: Select the best answer for each of the following questions.

1. The kind of direction or order given by a supervisor often tells something about the supervisor. A weak supervisor would be one who relied excessively on which of the following kinds of orders?
   A. Implied orders and calls for volunteers
   B. Implied orders and direct orders
   C. Direct orders and calls for volunteers
   D. Requests and calls for volunteers

2. Police Officer Skylark is considered by his supervisor Sergeant Hardy to be a less than dedicated worker. In directing Officer Skylark, the sergeant finds one type of order especially effective. Which of the following kinds of orders is generally recommended for use when dealing with a lazy or indifferent employee?
   A. An implied order
   B. A request
   C. A call for volunteers
   D. A direct order

3. Different situations call for the use of different types of orders. In addition, different types of orders should be used when dealing with employees with different personality types. A police sergeant should be aware that calling for volunteers as a mode of order giving is best for:
   A. An experienced worker
   B. A sensitive worker
   C. Distasteful assignments
   D. Routine assignments

4. While discussing possible alternate methods for conducting an investigation, Sergeant Nolan notices that two of his detectives disagree on how to proceed. Sergeant Nolan should recognize that as a general rule:
   A. Disagreement is bad because it never leads to clarification of issues.
   B. Disagreement is good because it gives the sergeant an opportunity to properly show authority.

C. Disagreement is bad because it blocks meaningful communication.
D. Disagreement is good because it can be vital to discovering facts.

5. No two supervisors are exactly alike; nor do any two supervisors use the same exact style of supervision. However, certain supervisors, because of specific actions they consistently take, fit into general categories. The police supervisor who operates on a "leave things alone" basis, is said to be utilizing the:
A. Authoritarian style of leadership
B. Laissez-faire style of leadership
C. Democratic style of leadership
D. Participative style of leadership

6. Virtually every police sergeant wants to be recognized as a good supervisor by both superiors and subordinates. This is, however, not an easy task. One key in reaching this goal is recognizing that a primary key to supervisory success is:
A. Treating each person as an individual
B. Always holding production needs as paramount
C. Never delegating the authority to do a job
D. Handling all problems without seeking assistance

7. Police Officer Ryan comes to Sergeant Brown, his immediate supervisor, with a problem concerning his work. In this situation, the sergeant's best course of action would be to:
A. Tell the officer to try and see if he can come up with the solution to his own problem
B. Ask probing questions that might assist the officer in finding his own solution to the problem
C. Give the officer the benefit of his experience by providing a solution to the problem
D. Postpone the conversation in the hope that the officer will find a solution of his own in the interim

8. Consider the following statements concerning leadership.
   (1) The only good leaders are those born with special leadership abilities.
   (2) The art of leadership cannot be learned.
   (3) Leadership is determined, to a large degree, by a person's position in an organization.
   Based on the above, which of the following is most accurate?
   A. Only statement 1 is accurate.
   B. Only statement 2 is accurate.
   C. Only statement 3 is accurate.
   D. All the statements are inaccurate.

9. Sergeant Kegler is an experienced police sergeant. She offers the following advice to Sergeant Brown, who is a newly promoted sergeant. She tells Sergeant Brown that at times subordinates will want to talk about themselves, their own problems, and even their personal hopes and fears. Sergeant Kegler would be correct in her advice if she stated that, in these instances, Sergeant Brown should:
   A. Allow the discussion to take place but clearly indicate a reluctance to do so in order that such discussions are discouraged in the future
   B. Be polite but steadfastly refuse to engage in such discussions
   C. Recommend that such talks would be best conducted with an officer of a rank higher than sergeant because of the sergeant's ambivalent role
   D. Exhibit a willingness to discuss such matters when they are initiated by the subordinate

10. Consider the following statements concerning police morale.
    (1) It is important to praise an employee for any job he/she may do.
    (2) Morale depends to a fair degree on personal relationships and everyday working conditions.
    (3) A supervisor who is fair and impartial is a positive impetus toward high morale.
    Regarding the above statements, which of the following is most correct?
    A. Only statements 1 and 3 are accurate.
    B. Only statements 1 and 2 are accurate.
    C. Only statements 2 and 3 are accurate.
    D. All the statements are accurate.

11. You are told by the station house clerk that a police officer wants to speak to you. You ascertain it is Police Officer Clark, and you arrange to have him see you. Police Officer Clark complains to you, his squad sergeant, that you have unfairly turned down his request for a day off. Your best action to take at this point would be to:
    A. Refer the officer to the commanding officer
    B. Refer the officer to his union representative
    C. Explain the reason for your actions in this instance
    D. Provide documentary proof of your objectivity in handling similar requests

12. Sergeant Doe is approached by one of the police officers in her squad. The officer has a grievance and relates it to the sergeant. After hearing the grievance once, Sergeant Doe asks the officer to repeat the grievance while the sergeant takes notes. This practice is:
    A. Good, because it will indicate to the officer that the sergeant is taking the complaint seriously
    B. Bad, because more than likely the officer just wanted to "let off some steam" and now the sergeant has forced the officer to proceed
    C. Good, because in this way the officer cannot alter his story later on
    D. Bad, because writing down someone's grievance always seems to hinder the free flow of information

13. Consider the following statements concerning the disciplinary process.
    (1) Supervisors should never lose their tempers.
    (2) The disciplinary interview should be kept private.
    (3) The transfer of an employee is never the answer to a disciplinary problem.
    After considering these statements, which of the following is most accurate?
    A. All statements are correct.
    B. Only statements 2 and 3 are correct.
    C. Only statements 1 and 2 are correct.
    D. All statements are incorrect.

14. A police officer you supervise has a small vegetable garden in his home. During a conversation you mention how fond you are of tomatoes. A short time thereafter, he places a few tomatoes on your desk and from time to time continues this practice. Other sergeants in the command, however, tell you that some of the other officers you supervise are saying that the officer is getting special privileges from you. Your best action would be to:

A. Tell the officer to cease at once without any explanation

B. Confront the other officers and ask for proof of their allegation of favoritism

C. Explain to the officer that your professional relationship with him is being damaged and request him to cease

D. Disregard the comments of the other officers as long as you know there is no favoritism being shown

15. Although it is true that a certain amount of change is required when getting promoted to a new rank in a police department, probably the greatest change occurs when a police officer is promoted to sergeant. This is true mainly because the newly promoted sergeant:

A. Has to learn new duties

B. Must show that he/she can do all phases of the job better than the officers he/she supervises

C. Has more authority in the new position

D. Is responsible for the first time for the work of someone else in the same work group

16. Sergeant Martin delegates to his subordinates the authority to make decisions in routine matters. In addition, the sergeant also insists that full responsibility be assigned to these same subordinates if they make errors in handling these routine matters. This procedure is:

A. Proper, since the sergeant is developing subordinates

B. Improper, since the sergeant cannot delegate away full responsibility to subordinates

C. Proper, since the sergeant realizes responsibility must be commensurate with authority

D. Improper, since the sergeant will be creating individuals who will only seek to gain even more authority

17. It is often suggested that praise be mixed with criticism. Sergeant Nolan has the practice of praising an officer only when he is about to criticize him. Such a practice is:
   A. Good, because praise should be mixed with criticism
   B. Good, because it shows that the sergeant is not solely a negative force
   C. Bad, because praise should follow, not precede criticism
   D. Bad, because the tendency will be for the praise not to be heard as the expected criticism is awaited

18. Some police departments claim that their officers are self-disciplined. This self-discipline will not occur under certain conditions. Specifically, self-discipline on the part of police officers is not likely to occur when:
   A. The requirements of the position are fair
   B. The police officers participated in the development of the regulations of the department
   C. The reasons for the regulations of the department are explained
   D. The supervisors take a totally objective view in giving out the penalties to those who violate the regulations of the department

19. The "exception principle" basically states that the head of an organization should not act on each matter under his/her jurisdiction. Instead, he/she should act only on exceptional matters that require personal attention. The key to the successful application of the exception principle is best indicated by which of the following?
   A. Delegation of authority
   B. Proper selection standards for department members when initially recruited into the agency
   C. Training in the matter to be handled by the subordinate
   D. Having authority commensurate with responsibility

20. Sergeant Corey completes giving a police officer instructions in a new police procedure. The police officer makes no comment during or after the instructions. It would be most proper for Sergeant Corey to:

A. Assume that the procedure will be followed by the officer in the future

B. Assume that the officer will probably not follow the new procedure in the future

C. Ask the officer what if any objections he/she may have to the new procedure and to have the officer restate the new procedure in his/her own words

D. Dismiss the officer but indicate that failure to follow the new procedure could result in disciplinary action

21. Consider the following statements concerning the principles of learning and training.
    (1) Training of police is a well-justified expense for the public, who will profit from a well-trained police department.
    (2) Failing to learn a certain part of a job will motivate a student to try harder.
    (3) Self-defense techniques is a good area for which to provide refresher training.
    Which of the following choices best separates these statements into those that are true and those that are not true?
    A. All of the statements are true.
    B. All of the statements are false.
    C. Only one statement is true.
    D. Only one statement is false.

22. The impact of recruit training on the newly hired police officer is recognized by all police supervisors. There must be a constant effort to ensure that the content matter meets the needs of the department. How is this best accomplished?
    A. Ensure proper testing procedures are followed during the recruit training.
    B. Select the kind of recruit who will properly respond to the recruit training.
    C. Examine on a regular basis the role and function of the police officer on the street.
    D. Test the recruit after he/she has been exposed to field work.

23. Sergeant Hartman is directed by his commanding officer, Captain Gorden, to evaluate the precinct training programs. Which of the following is the best question to ask in evaluating the training programs from the viewpoint of the agency?

A. Have the attitudes, skills, and knowledge of each individual trainee been affected by the training programs?
B. Has the training been applied to the actual work of each employee who was trained?
C. Were the latest teaching techniques used in instructing the trainees?
D. Do the employees now continue training efforts on their own time?

24. All police agencies claim to have training programs. The actual worth of the individual programs is another matter. A valuable training program must have all the following characteristics, except which?
A. It should consist of mostly formal training sessions.
B. It should assist in raising morale.
C. It should be designed to reduce waste and error in the work process.
D. It should help to minimize punitive damage awards resulting from civil actions against the agency and its employees.

25. Consider the following statements concerning training.
(1) A lack of questions on the part of trainees may indicate they are intimidated by the instructor.
(2) The first step in developing a formal training program is the selection of a suitable training site.
(3) In determining training needs, the opinions of the employees to be trained are of minimal value.
Which of the following most accurately classifies these statements into those that are accurate and those that are not?
A. Statement 1 is accurate; 2 and 3 are not.
B. Statement 2 is accurate; 1 and 3 are not.
C. Statement 3 is accurate; 1 and 2 are not.
D. None of the statements is accurate.

26. Consider the following statements concerning safety in the workplace.
    (1) A safety and accident prevention program should include a written policy outlining management's position in the matter.
    (2) The department's formal personnel evaluation procedures should include a component that measures an employee's safety and accident prevention performance.
    (3) Employees should be formally recognized for outstanding contributions in safety and accident prevention.
    Which of the following most accurately classifies these statements into those that are accurate and those that are not?
    A. All the statements are accurate.
    B. All the statements are not accurate.
    C. Only one of the statements is accurate.
    D. Only two of the statements are accurate.

27. There are several steps to the instruction process. They are:
    (1) Presentation
    (2) Application
    (3) Preparation
    (4) Testing
    Which of the following best indicates the correct sequence of these steps?
    A. 1, 2, 3, and 4   C. 3, 1, 4, and 2
    B. 3, 1, 2, and 4   D. 1, 3, 2, and 4

28. A trainee's rate of learning is affected by a number of factors. One of these factors is known as the trainee's apperceptive base. Which of the following most clearly describes a trainee's apperceptive base?
    A. It is a trainee's ability to memorize important facts.
    B. It is a trainee's ability to reason logically.
    C. It represents a trainee's overall motivation for the particular training being given.
    D. It represents a trainee's past training and experience.

29. When a specialized training unit is established in a police department, there are several advantages. However, there are also some disadvantages. Which of the following best describes one of these disadvantages?

A. Supervisors not assigned to the training unit believe that training is no longer one of their functions.

B. The subject matter taught by the training unit has no bearing on the actual field operations.

C. Supervisors assigned to the training unit no longer see supervision as part of their function.

D. Such training units are staffed by former patrol personnel, who are not qualified as instructors.

30. Consider the following statements concerning training in police-community relations:

(1) The trainer can safely assume that all officers have the attitude needed to deal with the public.

(2) The trainer should recognize that communications skills, including body language, are an important part of the training.

(3) The trainer should be aware that instruction in telephone courtesy would be a proper part of the training.

Which of the following most accurately classifies these statements into those that are accurate and those that are not?

A. All the statements are accurate.

B. Only statements 1 and 2 are accurate.

C. Only statements 1 and 3 are accurate.

D. Only statements 2 and 3 are accurate.

31. Sergeant Ford always prepares his officers for instructions when conducting training sessions. Which of the following is not a valid reason for preparing the officers for instruction?

A. It puts the officers at ease.

B. It creates interest in the instruction.

C. It shows some personal advantage to the individual officers in learning the new material.

D. It allows the individual officers to make errors in a practice session.

32. Police department X utilizes different types of training modes. One of these training modes is known as the understudy system. The understudy system of training is best described as a system whereby:

A. Sergeants select certain qualified police officers of one unit to learn the jobs of certain police officers of another unit
B. A selected group of sergeants learn their own duties as well as those of the lieutenant at the next higher rank
C. Highly motivated sergeants study a specialized operation under the direct supervision of an expert in the operation
D. A lieutenant selects a group of sergeants to perform the duties of certain police officers under their supervision for a specified time period

33. After experiencing many reported instances of problems with the report writing of the police officers in her squad, Sergeant Norbert decides to conduct a training session. In conducting a training session in report writing, the sergeant should recognize which of the following as a key?
A. The individual police officer too often views the department's reporting requirements as red tape.
B. The limited writing skills of those who chose police work as an occupation.
C. No one likes to write.
D. Police work is so dynamic that reporting requirements are constantly changing.

34. There is a philosophy of training that postulates that when a student fails, the teacher also fails. According to experts in the field of training, the most important single cause of teacher ineffectiveness is:
A. A lack of instructor competency
B. The presence of irrelevant material in the teaching plan
C. Oversimplification of complex material
D. Aimlessness created by an illogical presentation

35. Training is not an easy matter. During the multistep process of training, an instructor must use imagination. Which of the following steps in the instructional process most taxes the imagination of the instructor?
A. Introduction   C. Application
B. Presentation   D. Testing

36. For an employee evaluation system to be effective, certain circumstances must exist. An employee evaluation system will be relatively ineffectual unless:
    A. The form is simple
    B. The rater is trained
    C. The ratee is willing to listen
    D. The employee understands the form

37. Sergeant Connors keeps a little notebook in his desk at the precinct. Every time a budgetary need arises, the sergeant makes a note in his notebook, thus recording information about the need. This practice is generally considered to be:
    A. Good, mainly because it will provide documentation and reference for future financial allotment requests
    B. Bad, mainly because it could be embarrassing to the department if the notebook fell into the wrong hands
    C. Good, mainly because it would ensure that any requests for funds would be approved
    D. Bad, mainly because the sergeant's supervisors would become suspicious of the sergeant's actions

38. The placement of those officers who are charged with the responsibility for the department's budget preparation is an issue that requires careful consideration. Often the choice is made to place such officers in the department's planning unit. The most logical reason for this is:
    A. A budget is a fiscal plan
    B. Planning and budgeting are solely staff responsibilities
    C. Both planning and budgeting personnel require the direct supervision of the chief of the department
    D. No one other than those members with a high level of expertise should be involved in the planning and budgeting process

39. Consider the following statements concerning inspections.
    (1) An advantage of requiring line officers to conduct inspections is that they force the line officer to examine conditions that might otherwise be neglected.

(2) A staff inspection is not reliable because the staff officer may never have performed the task being inspected.

(3) When a staff officer conducts an inspection of a line function, the staff officer should never report the results of the inspection directly to the line unit.

Based on the above, which of the following is most accurate?

A. Statement 1 is true; statements 2 and 3 are false.

B. Statement 2 is true; statements 1 and 3 are false.

C. Statement 3 is true; statements 1 and 2 are false.

D. All the statements are false.

40. Control is a necessary part of a sergeant's job. Through which of the following techniques are the best control results obtained?

A. Personal observations of the sergeant

B. Inspection of field logs of police officers

C. Perusal of reports submitted by police officers

D. Analysis of the results of staff inspections

41. Different types of plans are for different purposes and uses. Of the various types of plans utilized by the typical police department, which of the following types of plans best describes a plan to process traffic summonses?

A. Procedural plan

B. Tactical plan

C. Operational plan

D. Auxiliary plan

42. If properly conducted, planning can reap many rewards for a police agency. It is, however, often a difficult process with many steps. Which of the following most accurately identifies the most difficult component of the planning process?

A. Gathering the data needed to formulate the plan

B. Isolating and clarifying the problem that brought about the need for the plan

C. Gaining concurrences for the plan

D. Implementing the plan

43. At times the skills of certain members of a police department may cause changes to be made in the organizational structure of the department. These changes are more properly made:
  A. At the top of the organization because of the skills or limitations of the higher level officers
  B. At the bottom of the organization because of the skills or limitations of the lower level officers
  C. At the middle of the organization because of the skills or limitations of the middle managers
  D. Anywhere in the organization, but only if the entire structure of the organization is re-shaped

44. Captain Gray consults Sergeant Leary about a pending reorganization of the department. The captain wants to know the sergeant's feeling about specialization in a police agency. Which of the following would be the most accurate comment for the sergeant to make about specialization in a police agency?
  A. It should not be done if it will reduce patrol efficiency.
  B. It should not be done because it is so difficult to find qualified personnel to staff the specialized units.
  C. It should be done because it usually raises the morale and esprit de corps of the entire department.
  D. It should be done only if the department can grant extra compensation to the specialists.

45. Consider the following statements concerning organizational charts.
  (1) Organizational charts are seldom up to date.
  (2) Organizational charts do not show the informal networks of authority.
  (3) Organizational charts can be properly used as a training aid.
  Based on the above, which of the following is most accurate?
  A. All the statements are true.
  B. All the statements are false.
  C. Only two of the statements are true.
  D. Only one of the statements is true.

46. In organizing the line duties of a police agency, the need for staff assistance is a factor that must be considered. Staff supervisors, however, often think that relationships between them and line supervisors are less than adequate. Which of the following does not accurately describe a criticism of line supervisors by staff supervisors?
    A. Line supervisors do not know how to use staff assistance.
    B. Line supervisors have a tendency to assume the authority of staff supervisors.
    C. Line supervisors resist new ideas.
    D. Line supervisors often ignore the advice of staff supervisors.

47. Some raters do not rate employees fairly. When a rater rates all employees about average, which rating error is being committed?
    A. Central tendency error
    B. Association error
    C. Contrast error
    D. Error of leniency

48. Officer Smart is a graduate of a large ivy-league college. Sergeant Harding, his supervisor, knows of the college and is impressed by its high academic standing. The sergeant consistently gives the officer high personnel evaluations when in reality the officer's performance just about meets standards. Which of the following rater errors is the sergeant committing?
    A. Contrast error
    B. Association error
    C. Halo effect error
    D. Central tendency error

49. Sergeant Sardone has the practice of making an entry in a small notebook whenever a police officer under her supervision performs a job exceptionally well or well below standards. The sergeant is asked about this practice by one of the police officers. The sergeant truthfully tells him that the notebook serves as the basis of future evaluation reports. The practice of the sergeant is:
    A. Good, since she should not rely on memory when preparing evaluation reports
    B. Bad, since none of the police officers will be sure of what is in the notebook

C. Good, since it will keep the police officers on their toes
D. Bad, since it may be misplaced and fall into the wrong hands

50. Sergeant Palumbo delegates a rather complex task to a police officer. The task is one the police officer has never done before. In this case the sergeant should, when communicating this complex task to the police officer:
A. Repeat it twice, since the police officer will then surely understand
B. Tell the officer to check with the sergeant if he has any problems
C. Accompany the original oral instructions with some written directives explaining the steps to be taken
D. Let the officer start the job, and then check on him when the sergeant's schedule permits

51. Sergeant Gordon is unsure of whether or not to pass a certain piece of information to his supervisor, Lieutenant Rodriguez. In this case, the sergeant should:
A. Pass the information on to the lieutenant
B. Not pass the information on to the lieutenant
C. Ask one of the lieutenant's peers if it would be a good idea to pass the information on to Lieutenant Rodriguez
D. Leave the information on the lieutenant's desk in the form of an unsigned written note

52. Consider the following statements concerning the communications process in a police department.
(1) It provides administrators with the information they need to monitor and control the job.
(2) It has the potential to totally eliminate the grapevine.
(3) It allows for employee input into policies and procedures governing their jobs.
Which of the following statements most accurately classifies the above statements into those that are true and those that are false?
A. Statements 1 and 2 are true; 3 is not.
B. Statements 1 and 3 are true; 2 is not.
C. Statements 2 and 3 are true; 1 is not.
D. All the statements are true.

53. Supervisors must talk with their subordinates and vice versa. Regarding the communications process, status differences or the difference in rank in a police agency:
   A. Is always helpful since a subordinate will automatically respect and therefore listen to a supervisor.
   B. Is always a hindrance since both participants are distances apart in the rank structure of the agency.
   C. Can be a help or a hindrance.
   D. Never plays a role in the communications that take place in a police agency.

54. Many police administrators strongly maintain that the success of the efforts of a police department in the overall attainment of the goals of the department depends heavily upon how well the first-line supervisor does his/her job. Which of the following best describes the reason for this opinion?
   A. The first-line supervisor has the final responsibility for all the tasks at the level of operations.
   B. Because of his/her experience, the first-line supervisor can usually perform the operational tasks better than anyone in the department.
   C. To be successful, police work requires teamwork, and the first-line supervisor transforms the policies of the administrator into successfully accomplished tasks.
   D. In the final analysis, the first-line supervisor will take disciplinary action against police officers who resist the policies of the administrator.

55. There is no doubt that there is a true need for selective enforcement in police work. All the following are justifications offered by the police as to why the police engage in selective enforcement, except:
   A. Lack of manpower
   B. No one in the criminal justice system truly wants strict enforcement by the police
   C. There is no sufficient community financial support for strict enforcement of the laws
   D. Most laws are worded so loosely that strict enforcement is virtually impossible

56. Public relations does at times assist community relations. Which of the following is one of the situations whereby public relations can aid community relations?
   A. In explaining the success of a newly purchased crime information computer system
   B. In a recruitment campaign geared toward recruiting minorities
   C. In dramatically reporting a decrease in complaints against the police that were found to be unsubstantiated
   D. In explaining the necessity for raising the legal drinking age

57. Sergeant Russo is in charge of a group of officers at the scene of a potentially forceful demonstration. She is advised by a trustworthy veteran police officer that in the past the citizens of this particular community take offense to seeing large numbers of police officers policing demonstrations in their neighborhood. More pointedly, the citizens see it as a direct provocation. Which of the following is the sergeant's best course of action?
   A. Make sure no officer carries a nightstick or wears a helmet.
   B. Find a community leader and ask how many police would be acceptable to the community in policing the demonstration.
   C. Simply tell the appropriate members of the demonstration how many officers are assigned and indicate why.
   D. Keep a portion of the officers as a reserve group, at a location away from the demonstration.

58. There are several roles the police can adopt in their work, but traditionally they have placed major emphasis on one of them. Which role is that?
   A. Service model role
   B. Law enforcement role
   C. Order maintenance role
   D. Peace-keeping role

59. Although motorized patrol has made police patrol more efficient and therefore police service more available, it has not escaped criticism by members of the community. They believe that police of-

ficers ride by their streets and have become strangers to them. One way that this problem has been effectively dealt with is through:

A. Elimination of motorized patrol and reintroduction of foot patrol

B. Having police officers park their patrol cars and walk a beat from time to time

C. Expansion of police-community relations units

D. Use of storefront centers

60. Police-community relations means many things to many people. Basically, however, it is most dependent on which of the following?

A. Efforts of the department to convince the public of the quality of police service through a clear one-way communications channel

B. Policies and procedures developed at the highest levels of the department

C. Individual contacts each police officer has with each member of the community he/she serves

D. Ability of a specially created unit to deal with police-community relations problems

61. Which of the following best describes what sound police-community relations should emphasize?

A. Specific job requirements of a specialized police-community relations unit

B. Policies of the chief administrator of the department

C. Need for sufficient supervisory effort by the first-line supervisor

D. A way of viewing the responsibilities of the police toward the public

62. The question has been raised in police work as to who must support community relations to make it successful. Although certainly it must have the support of many, which of the following, not supporting community relations, would certainly cause its doom?

A. Key political figures of the minority community

B. Police officer on post

C. Chief of the department

D. Youth of the community

63. Good community relations can result in many benefits to a police agency. Which of the following is a benefit that accrues to the police through good community relations but is looked upon with disfavor by the community itself?
    A. Reduction of job stress for police officers
    B. Increase in the ability of the agency to recruit minority members
    C. Increased capacity to prevent crime
    D. Increased ability to gather intelligence information

64. Police officers often exhibit a reluctance to get involved in community relations. All of the following are reasons for this reluctance except:
    A. Promotions are usually based on law enforcement activities, not community relations activities
    B. Not much peer approval is obtained from community relations activities
    C. Recognition from the media for community relations activities is negligible
    D. Very little internal satisfaction to be gained from community involvement

65. The attitude of the citizenry impacts on the ability of the police to do their job. Who among the following has the greatest direct impact on the citizen attitudes?
    A. First-line supervisor by his/her style of supervision
    B. Chief of police whose policies mold the actions of each member of the department
    C. Community relations officer whose efforts revolve totally around police-community relations
    D. Patrol officer who responds to calls for police assistance

66. The benefits of a good police-community relations program are many, but great care must be taken to ensure its effective operation. In order for a police-community relations program to operate effectively, it must contain which of the following?
    A. Support of the elected representatives of the minority community
    B. Totally nonpolice participant civilian complaint review board

C. Mutual exchange of ideas and other communications between the public and the police
D. Constant effort on the part of the police to build their image in the eyes of the community

67. Sergeant Cabrera tells the police officers in his squad not to enforce a certain law. In exchange, the sergeant has received a promise from the community that the police will be supported in most other important police issues. In this case, the sergeant's actions were:
A. Good, mainly because the officers will undoubtedly be able to make more important arrests
B. Bad, mainly because a potential for the loss of integrity in the minds of the community has been created
C. Good, mainly because the police have time to deal only with the more important issues
D. Bad, mainly because there will be a great deal of confusion and disharmony when the sergeant is transferred or retires

68. Consider the following statements concerning community relations.
(1) Law enforcement is not the only service the police offer the public.
(2) Public cooperation must be one of the subordinate goals of the police.
(3) Community relations in the final analysis should be viewed as a finite program.
Based on the above, which of the following statements is accurate?
A. All the statements are true.
B. All the statements are false.
C. Only two of the statements are true.
D. Only two of the statements are false.

69. At times, the police, for a variety of compelling factors, become involved in a drive to combat public morals violations. When they do, several events occur. Which of the following is not one of these events?
A. Usually a large commitment of police officers is required.
B. The potential for police corruption arises.
C. Tension between the police and the community is reduced.
D. The police help to create criminality.

70. The debate over whether policing is truly a profession is ongoing. What is clear, however, is that if the police are to grow in a professional sense, then which of the following is crucial?
    A. More minorities find their way into the ranks of the police.
    B. The media, especially the press, actively support the police.
    C. The top police administrators be recruited from other fields.
    D. The public openly accepts the concept of police discretion.

71. Different police agencies engage in different roles or models of policing. The order maintenance model of policing would have which of the following characteristics?
    A. Wide discretion
    B. Heavier use of patrol cars then foot patrol
    C. Required quotas expecting a high number of arrests to be effected
    D. Full enforcement of laws dealing with public disorders

72. While assigned to desk duty, Sergeant Chevrons receives a telephone inquiry from the press about a police matter. The sergeant has the information but is not sure if he should give the information to the press. His best action would be:
    A. Not give the information to the caller
    B. Give the information to the caller but make a record of it
    C. Give the information to the caller after receiving assurances he will not be directly quoted
    D. Tell the caller he does not have the information

73. Sergeant Gomez often assigns police officers to enforcement of speeding regulations. The sergeant usually recommends that the officers position themselves behind a large billboard or some other obstruction so that motorists cannot detect their presence. The sergeant's recommendation is:
    A. Good, mainly because the officers will apprehend more violators by using that tactic
    B. Bad, mainly because most gains obtained from enforcement actions will be outweighed

by the ill feelings created in the minds of the public that a quota system exists

C. Good, mainly because anytime motorists see a billboard, they will think the police are behind it and will comply with the law

D. Bad, mainly because it provides too much temptation for the officers for inattention to duty because they are concealed from view

74. One of the disadvantages of motorized patrol is that police officers assigned to this type of patrol cannot maintain a close contact with the public they serve. Which of the following, however, has been the most important in reducing this disadvantage?
A. Community council meetings
B. The walkie talkie radio
C. Mandating that police officers drive more slowly while on routine radio motor patrol
D. Citizen ride-along programs

75. Having overcome resistance from a variety of sources, the use of dogs on patrol is growing throughout police departments across the country. It is recognized that the success of police dogs is based on several factors. Which of the following is not one of these factors?
A. Proper selection of the dog
B. Proper selection of the handler
C. Avoiding the release of any advance notice to the public that might reduce the psychological deterrent of the dog
D. Ensuring that a proper relationship is established between the dog and the handler

76. While on radio motor patrol, police officers at times become involved in vehicle pursuits. Often, it is the job of the patrol sergeant to determine whether the pursuit should be continued or called off. In making this decision, the sergeant should base the decision on which of the following?
A. The seriousness of the offense that the suspect has committed
B. The kind of vehicle the suspect is driving
C. If the danger created by the pursuit outweighs the suspect's danger to the community
D. Whether other officers are available to lend assistance

77. It is generally recognized that responding to an emergency with the emergency siren in the "constant position" is not a good patrol practice. This is mainly true because of all of the following, except which?

A. It tends to blur the radio transmissions from the patrol car.

B. It blots out the sound of other responding emergency vehicles.

C. It tends to draw large crowds to the scene of an incident.

D. It makes it difficult for other vehicles to determine from which direction the patrol car is coming.

78. A police sergeant in charge of a detail of police officers assigned to crowd control must have a good working knowledge of crowd behavior. Of the following, the recommended way of dealing with a crowd that has just become polarized is to:

A. Attempt to divert the attention of the crowd with the use of a bullhorn

B. Attempt to identify everyone in the crowd by covertly taking photographs

C. Attempt to bring the crowd together by focusing their attention on a common object or event

D. Attempt to locate the leaders of the crowd and separate them from the crowd

79. Sergeant Marks responds to an incident in which Police Officer Jones has been called to the scene of a dispute. The sergeant finds that the focus of the dispute has shifted from the two civilian disputants to the police officer, with all participants, including the police officer, becoming quite excited. A large crowd has gathered and is watching. Other officers also respond. The sergeant directs that Officer Jones be removed from the scene while the dispute is being handled. In this instance, the sergeant's actions are:

A. Correct, since an officer is never expected to become excited

B. Incorrect, since Police Officer Jones will undoubtedly lose face with the crowd

C. Correct, since it removes the potential of Police Officer Jones' feeling of excitement being communicated to the crowd

D. Incorrect, since it will make the other officers responding to the scene think that Officer Jones is incompetent

80. Under certain limited circumstances, police agencies establish "fixed posts" to deal with ongoing police hazards. The major criticism of the use of fixed posts is that they:

A. Result in a heavy drain on overall police effectiveness

B. Almost guarantee inattention to duty on the part of the assigned officer because of the high level of boredom involved

C. Usually receive little or no supervision by the patrol supervisor because of the inherent difficulties of supervising an officer on a fixed post

D. Create an impression of favoritism in the general community, which results in numerous requests for additional fixed posts

81. A certain sergeant is outlining the steps of a preliminary investigation to the police officers under his supervision. Regarding a preliminary investigation, who has the responsibility for conducting it?

A. First supervisor on the scene

B. First detective on the scene

C. First sworn member of the department on the scene

D. Officer assigned to the post

82. Some police departments assign their patrol force to permanent shift assignments. All of the following are valid reasons for such shift assignments except which?

A. It provides a supervisor with a disciplinary tool by transferring an officer to a less desirable shift.

B. It facilitates an officer's becoming familiar with conditions on a shift.

C. It provides a supervisor with a promotional device by being able to transfer a deserving officer to a more desirable shift.

D. It facilitates an officer's becoming familiar with conditions on a post.

83. In choosing between automobile patrol and foot patrol, the characteristics of the area to be patrolled often influence the choice. Which of the following best describes an area that should be patrolled in an automobile?
    A. An area in which inspectional duties take up most of the patrol officers' time
    B. An area that contains large numbers of people congregating about, such as an amusement park
    C. A downtown business area, where many commercial premises are located
    D. A residential area, where police mobility is a critical factor

84. The prevention of criminal acts is an accepted role of the police. This role is often performed by the patrol force. Which of the following is an accurate description of a method used by the patrol force to prevent crimes?
    A. Patrolling in such a way that the potential criminal's desire to engage in criminal conduct is eliminated
    B. Attempting to create a belief in the minds of criminals of the omnipotence of the police
    C. Maintaining proper contacts with the citizens in the community, which helps develop attitudes that reduce criminal activity
    D. Helping citizens by such activities as the return of stolen property

85. Dogs have a variety of uses in many facets of police work, such as routine patrol, investigations, and bomb and drug detection. Of the following, it is generally accepted that the greatest value of the use of dogs on patrol is that:
    A. They have a keen sense of smell and hearing, which has proven to be infallible
    B. Their presence has a definite psychological effect on many would-be offenders
    C. Their speed facilitates the apprehension of fleeing felons
    D. Their presence is an excellent community relations asset

86. In police department X, it is the practice to have patrol officers assist in finding solutions to patrol problems on their posts. This practice is:
   A. Good, mainly because the officers will be more motivated to do a good job
   B. Bad, mainly because any gains in discovering solutions will be offset by the costly expenditure of time spent in this process
   C. Good, mainly because the answers to all patrol problems lie with the officers on patrol
   D. Bad, mainly because this would result in a definite erosion of hierarchal authority, thereby causing disciplinary problems

87. During roll call, a certain police sergeant is asked by a group of newly assigned recruits, about the best method of patrolling their posts. The sergeant would be most correct if she advised the recruits to:
   A. Patrol all areas of your posts frequently in a regular manner so that the people on your posts can always reach you for help
   B. Patrol your posts in a conspicuous and regular manner so that a supervisor may always reach you if necessary
   C. Patrol your posts in an irregular manner while conspicuously covering all areas as frequently as possible
   D. Find out where the troublesome locations are, and spend all your time patrolling those areas

88. Sergeant Smith is the patrol supervisor in a certain precinct. Several streets in the precinct are efficiently patrolled by special security guards who are employees of a highly reputable security firm. The local residents of these streets privately pay for this service. The sergeant has directed that police officers under his supervision are not to patrol these streets routinely and they are not even to be in the area unless specifically called in by someone or unless they have knowledge of a crime occurring there. In this instance, the sergeant's direction is:
   A. Proper, mainly because the police should not interfere if private citizens choose to have their streets protected by private security officers
   B. Improper, mainly because the police cannot give up one of their major duties regardless of

the efficiency of the private security officers involved

C. Proper, mainly because a confrontation could occur between the police officers and the private security officers if they patrol the same areas

D. Improper, mainly because this situation offers the police an excellent opportunity to show the local residents how unnecessary the private security officers are

89. Distribution of the patrol force by police departments remains a subjective issue from department to department. It is not, however, performed without guidance. This guidance comes in the form of weighted factors that are measured and evaluated in arriving at the proper distribution levels for patrol personnel. One of these factors is the existence of tangible hazards. Which of the following is not representative of a tangible hazard?

A. An amusement park frequented by disorderly youths

B. A team of burglars casing a warehouse for a future burglary

C. An area where pimps and prostitutes congregate

D. A park used by senior citizens who are the victims of street robberies

90. Before any meaningful traffic law enforcement can occur, its primary objective must be identified. Which of the following most accurately describes the primary objective of traffic law enforcement?

A. Punishment of offenders

B. Income generation

C. Deterrence of violators

D. Issuance of traffic citations

91. During a roll call briefing, the sergeant tells the police officers that random stops of private citizen vehicles are not to be made. A police officer at the roll call asks the sergeant if there was any particular reason for this prohibition against randomly stopping cars. The sergeant would be most correct if he/she replied by stating which of the following reasons for the prohibition against the random stopping of automobiles?

A. Random vehicle stops are a nuisance to the public and yield limited results.
B. Unnecessary traffic congestions via "rubbernecking" result from random stops.
C. Officers are much too lax and have been seriously injured by oncoming motorists during random stops.
D. The courts have held that random stops leave too much discretion to the individual police officer.

92. Consider the following statements concerning motorcycle patrol.
   (1) A two-wheel motorcycle is less maneuverable than a two-wheel motor scooter.
   (2) Two-wheel motorcycle patrol is less expensive than automobile patrol because of the gas savings.
   (3) The two-wheel motorcycle has limited use during adverse weather conditions.
   Which of the following most accurately classifies these statements into those that are accurate and those that are not?
   A. Only one statement is accurate.
   B. Only two statements are accurate.
   C. All the statements are accurate.
   D. None of the statements are accurate.

93. The captain of the precinct has asked you, a sergeant, to answer a letter from a community group that has requested permission to close a street for twenty-four hours for a block party. The location of the intended block party, however, is a main thoroughfare and would cause undue hardship to the rest of the community. The captain believes it is a violation of local laws and wants to deny the request. The best way to begin your letter is by:
   A. Mentioning the good work the group has done in the community
   B. Clearly indicating that unfortunately their request cannot be granted
   C. Quoting the laws involved
   D. Recommending another location for the block party

94. Sergeant Sands is instructing a new investigator in preparing investigative reports. The sergeant should instruct the investigator that when preparing investigative reports, the main focus should be on:
    A. Opinions   C. Facts
    B. Conclusions   D. Quotes

95. Information is not synonymous with intelligence records. Only after a series of procedural steps does information become intelligence. One of the steps is an evaluation of the information. Basically, what takes place during this step is that:
    A. It is determined if an arrest can be made based on the information
    B. The past reliability of the source of information is examined
    C. It is decided who might be interested in the information
    D. The true meaning of the information is established

96. In police department X, the policy is that each unit maintains its own records; none are kept centrally. Sergeant Simpson makes a recommendation that the policy be changed and most records be kept in a central location. In supporting her recommendation, the sergeant should offer which of the following as the principal disadvantage of a decentralized record-keeping system?
    A. Decentralized records might not represent an accurate accounting of police work.
    B. There is less coordination of the department's records when they are kept at many decentralized locations.
    C. The response for information contained in records is slower in a decentralized system.
    D. The expertise of record-keeping specialists is prevented when many individuals are charged with responsibility of record keeping.

97. In order for the police to better utilize their limited resources to deal with incidents requiring their immediate attention, many police departments have adopted a "mail-in" reporting system. Under this system, a form is mailed to a complainant in cases involving certain minor offenses

and the complainant is required to complete the form and return it in the mail. The chief drawback of such a system is that:

A. The form may be lost in the mail
B. Because of the lack of personal police attention, most citizens do not respond, thereby resulting in an inaccurate crime picture
C. The form cannot uncover other, possibly more serious offenses that police officers do uncover when they respond and personally interview complainants
D. The form alerts neighbors that the complainant is communicating with the police

98. The "rough sketch" of an investigator made at a crime scene should provide all the details necessary to allow the investigator to complete a finished sketch at a later time. Regarding this rough sketch, all of the following statements are accurate, except which?

A. The rough sketch may be required to be introduced as evidence in court.
B. The rough sketch should include all important objects at the crime scene.
C. The rough sketch should be drawn to scale.
D. No changes or additions should be made to the rough sketch once the investigator leaves the scene.

99. Sergeant Nolan prides himself in being familiar with and properly utilizing all the records systems in the precinct. Which of the following is the least likely result of his actions?

A. The activities of subordinates will be able to be reviewed, thus improving the level of supervision.
B. The understanding and cooperation of the community can be obtained in certain instances.
C. The deployment of subordinates can be more effective.
D. The current records can be used to predict future statistics for the next year exactly.

100. The value of reports to a police agency cannot be overstated. One particularly valuable report to the police is the Uniform Crime Reports, which is

published by the Federal Bureau of Investigation. Which of the following most accurately describes the Uniform Crime Reports?

A. It is a report that precisely indicates how much crime was committed in the United States in any given year.

B. It is a report that presents an annual compilation of the amount of crime reported to the police in the United States.

C. It is a report that represents the total number of arrests made against the total number of crimes that occurred in the United States on a yearly basis.

D. It is a report that analyzes actual crimes reported, convictions obtained, and penalties imposed for eight very serious crimes, known as Index Crimes.

Answer questions 101-110 based on the following data.

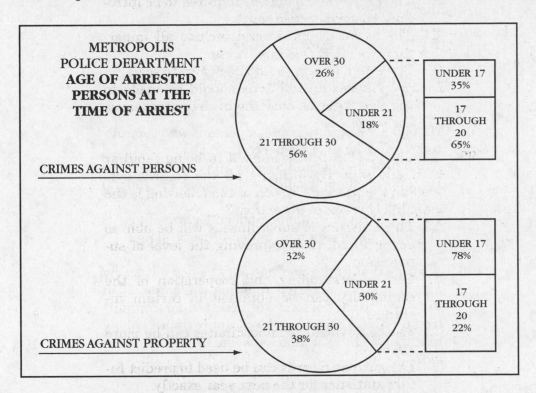

101. What percentage of persons arrested by the Metropolis Police Department for violent crimes are between 21 and 30 years of age?

A. 56%   B. 38%

C. 32%   D. It cannot be determined.

102. Of all of the persons who have been arrested for committing crimes against persons, the majority of them are:
A. under 21
B. between 21 and 30
C. over 30
D. of an age that cannot be determined from the data

103. Of all the persons under 21 who are arrested for committing a crime against a person, most of them are:
A. under 17
B. 17 through 20 years of age
C. 18 years old
D. of an age that cannot be determined from the data

104. Of all the persons under 21 who are arrested for committing a crime against property, most of them are:
A. under 17
B. 17 through 20 years of age
C. 16 years old
D. of an age that cannot be determined from the data

105. If 1000 arrests were made of persons who committed a crime against property, then about:
A. 320 of them would be over 30 years of age
B. 560 of them would be between 21 and 30 years old
C. 180 of them would be under 21 years of age
D. 63 of them would be under 17 years of age

106. Assume that in the coming year the percentage by age of persons arrested remains the same. If in that year 1000 persons are arrested for committing a crime against a person, approximately how many of them would be between 17 and 20 years old?
A. 180
B. 300
C. 117
D. 63

107. What percentage of all persons arrested for committing a crime against a person are over 21 years of age?
    A. 56%
    B. 26%
    C. 82%
    D. It cannot be determined.

108. Which of the following is the most accurate statement concerning the age of persons arrested by the Metropolis Police Department?
    A. Most are over 30.
    B. Most get convicted.
    C. Most are being arrested for the first time.
    D. Most are over 21.

109. Which of the following is the most accurate statement concerning arrests made by the Metropolis Police Department?
    A. The actual number of people arrested for crimes against persons is greater than those arrested for crimes against property.
    B. The actual number of people arrested for crimes against property is greater than those arrested for crimes against persons.
    C. The actual number of people arrested for crimes against persons is approximately equal to those arrested for crimes against persons.
    D. There is not enough data to determine the actual number of people arrested for either crimes against property or crimes against people.

110. Assume that 1000 persons were arrested by the Metropolis Police Department and charged with committing a crime against property. The majority of those arrested would be:
    A. under 17
    B. 21 through 30
    C. over 30
    D. 17 through 20

111. A certain child has been the victim of a sex crime committed by a neighbor. In interviewing the child all the following are recommended except:
    A. allowing the child to move around the room
    B. permitting the child to color while being interviewed

C. allowing as many interruptions as possible in recognition of the child's short attention span

D. permitting the presence of a parent whom the child wishes to be present

112. Sergeant Walls is supervising the interview of a seven-year-old female who was sexually assaulted by a male stranger in an abandoned house. In such a situation the sergeant should NOT permit which of the following to be asked or stated by the interviewer?
   A. Was it nighttime or daytime?
   B. I need to know what the man did.
   C. Why did you go into the house?
   D. Did the man say it was a secret?

113. At the scene of a hostage negotiation situation after the situation has been stabilized, which of the following captors is the easiest to deal with?
   A. A professional criminal who has had his escape blocked while committing an independent crime
   B. A terrorist
   C. An emotionally disturbed person who is hearing voices telling him what to do
   D. A religious fanatic

114. Consider the following statements concerning hostage negotiations.
   (1) Members of a hostage negotiation team should appear mature in order that they may be perceived as persons of authority by the captor.
   (2) The actual negotiator should portray himself as the ultimate decision maker.
   (3) Generally the more time a captor spends with his/her captives, the less likely the captor is to kill the captives.
   Which of the following choices best classifies the above statements into those which are accurate and those which are inaccurate?
   A. Statement 1 is inaccurate; statements 2 and 3 are accurate.
   B. Statement 2 is inaccurate; statements 1 and 3 are accurate.
   C. Statement 3 is inaccurate; statements 1 and 2 are accurate.
   D. All of the statements are accurate.

115. Which of the following is not generally considered to be a basic fingerprint pattern?
    A. Arches
    B. Ridges
    C. Loops
    D. Whorls

116. Evaluate the following statements concerning bloodstains:
    (1) A bloodstain begins to dry at the center of the stain and the process continues toward the edges of the stain.
    (2) Blood stains dry faster on rough and non-absorbent surfaces.
    Which of the following is most accurate concerning the statements above?
    A. Only statement 1 is correct.
    B. Only statement 2 is correct.
    C. Both statements 1 and 2 are correct.
    D. Neither statement 1 nor 2 is correct.

117. The lands of the rifling found in a firearm are actually raised ridges that cut into the surface of a bullet that is being fired and give the bullet its rotational motion. Regarding these impressions made on a fired bullet by the lands of a firearm, it would be most accurate to state that such land impressions:
    A. always slant to the right
    B. always slant to the left
    C. may slant to the left or right
    D. slant neither to the left nor right but stand upright

118. Regarding extractor marks found on the shell of a fired bullet, such marks would be least likely to be found on the shell of a bullet fired from:
    A. an automatic pistol
    B. a revolver
    C. an automatic rifle
    D. a lever action rifle

119. The dark blue discoloring that can be seen on the parts of a dead body which are closest to the ground is known as:
    A. rigor mortis
    B. post-mortem lividity
    C. cadaveric spasm
    D. putrefaction

120. At the scene of a burglary it becomes evident that a window and the wood and metal surrounding it have been pried or jimmied open. In connection with such an incident, it would be most accurate to state that any tool marks which may be positively identified as having been made with a particular tool would best be found:
A. on the metal
B. on the wood
C. either on the metal or the wood
D. on neither the metal nor the wood

Answer Key

1. C	25. A	49. A	73. B	97. C
2. D	26. A	50. C	74. B	98. C
3. C	27. B	51. A	75. C	99. D
4. D	28. D	52. B	76. C	100. B
5. B	29. A	53. C	77. C	101. D
6. A	30. D	54. C	78. A	102. B
7. B	31. D	55. D	79. C	103. B
8. D	32. B	56. B	80. A	104. A
9. D	33. A	57. D	81. C	105. A
10. C	34. D	58. B	82. D	106. C
11. C	35. A	59. B	83. D	107. C
12. A	36. B	60. C	84. C	108. D
13. C	37. A	61. D	85. B	109. D
14. C	38. A	62. C	86. A	110. B
15. D	39. A	63. D	87. C	111. C
16. B	40. A	64. D	88. B	112. C
17. D	41. A	65. D	89. B	113. A
18. D	42. B	66. C	90. C	114. B
19. C	43. A	67. B	91. D	115. B
20. C	44. A	68. D	92. B	116. D
21. D	45. A	69. C	93. B	117. C
22. C	46. B	70. D	94. C	118. B
23. B	47. A	71. A	95. B	119. B
24. A	48. C	72. A	96. A	120. A

Diagnostic Chart

Insert the number of correct answers you obtained in the blank space for each section of the examination. The scale in the next column indicates how you did. The information at the bottom indicates how to correct your weaknesses.

SECTION	QUESTION NUMBERS	AREAS	YOUR NUMBER CORRECT	SCALE
1	1–18	Principles of supervision		17–18 right—excellent 15–16 right—good 14 right—fair Under 14 right—poor
2	19–36	Safety and training		17–18 right—excellent 15–16 right—good 14 right—fair Under 14 right—poor
3	37–54	Management		17–18 right—excellent 15–16 right—good 14 right—fair Under 14 right—poor
4	55–72	Community relations		17–18 right—excellent 15–16 right—good 14 right—fair Under 14 right—poor
5	73–92	Patrol operations		19–20 right—excellent 17–18 right—good 16 right—fair Under 16 right—poor
6	93–100	Report writing		8 right—excellent 6–7 right—good 5 right—fair Under 5 right—poor
7	101–110	Data interpretation		9–10 right—excellent 7–8 right—good 6 right—fair Under 6 right—poor
8	111–120	Police science		9–10 right—excellent 7–8 right—good 6 right—fair Under 6 right—poor

If you are weak in Section 1, then concentrate on Chapter 5.
If you are weak in Section 2, then concentrate on Chapter 6.
If you are weak in Section 3, then concentrate on Chapter 7.
If you are weak in Section 4, then concentrate on Chapter 8.
If you are weak in Section 5, then concentrate on Chapter 9.
If you are weak in Section 6, then concentrate on Chapter 10.
If you are weak in Section 7, then concentrate on Chapter 11.
If you are weak in Section 8, then concentrate on Chapter 12.

Note: Consider yourself weak in a section if you receive other than an excellent rating in it.

Answer Explanations

1. **C** The excessive direct order giver relies on his/her authority too much, and the excessive call for volunteers indicates the supervisor's unwillingness to do his/her job, which includes giving orders.

2. **D** The direct order is needed in this situation. A no-nonsense and to-the-point attitude must be taken with this kind of employee. Using other than a direct order with a lazy or indifferent worker is quite risky since the job might not get accomplished.

3. **C** A call for volunteers may also be proper when there is a dangerous assignment, but only if time permits. In emergencies, in which time is of the essence, direct orders are required.

4. **D** Disagreement can lead to the discovery of facts and to the clarification of issues. It is not unhealthy when it is controlled. When, however, disagreement is uncontrolled, it tends to cloud issues and results in digression from the original issues.

5. **B** Laissez-faire usually leads to low morale because of the supervisor's message to "leave things alone." It is the least effective leadership style.

6. **A** Treating workers as individuals shows that each individual involved is a special person. This is the key to supervisory success. (Also, as a test-taking drill, can you pick out the absolute words in the wrong choices?)

7. **B** The sergeant should listen to the worker and help him to find his own solution, but the sergeant should resist telling the officer exactly what to do.

8. **D** Statements 1 and 2: Most leaders are not "born," and a person can learn to be a good leader by applying certain proven principles of leadership. Statement 3: There are many informal yet strong leaders in the rank and file.

9. **D** Conversations with subordinates about their personal problems are proper when brought up by the worker or if personal matters are affecting the employee's work performance.

10. **C** Statement 1 tells us that praise is to be given for any job. What about an improperly performed job? Make sure you are identifying those absolute words, such as "any" or "all." Statements 2 and 3 are accurate as stated.

11. **C** When an employee presents a sergeant with a grievance, the sergeant should not refer it away, nor should he/she try to deal with it by bringing in evidence of fair treatment in other similar cases.

12. **A** It is extremely important that the grievance be properly received and the employee be made to understand that serious consideration will be given to a grievance. Having the officer repeat the grievance twice and writing it down the second time it is told indicates that the sergeant is in fact taking the grievance seriously. After the grievance is reduced to writing, the sergeant should read it back to the grieving officer.

13. **C** Transfer of an employee might be proper in the limited situation in which a supervisor and employee personally cannot get along and this has led to disciplinary problems.

14. **C** The sergeant's ambivalent role requires him to be part of the work group while maintaining a certain distance from the group.

15. **D** Part of the ambivalent role of the sergeant is responsibility for the work of others in the work group while being part of the same work group.

16. **B** While delegated authority must be commensurate with responsibility, the final full responsibility always rests with the subordinate's supervisor.

17. **D** The officer will be conditioned to "wait for the other shoe to drop." When the officer hears praise, he will ignore it and wait for the negative part.

18. **D** In giving out penalties a supervisor should be subjective and deal with each case separately. In determining penalties, consideration should be given to such things as the employee's past discipline record and work performance. Choices A, B, and C specify conditions under which self-discipline is likely to occur.

19. **C** Only trained personnel could be expected to handle assignments under the exception principle. Although it is true that proper delegation of authority to deal with responsibilities given to subordinates is necessary under the exception principle, only subordinates trained in the delegated task could realistically be expected to perform the task properly.

20. **C** It is important to ensure that the officer understands the procedure and to identify any objections that could lead to improving the procedure. This also stimulates conversation through which the trainer can get a better picture of the officer's understanding and acceptance of the new procedure.

21. D Only statement 2 is false. Nothing succeeds or is encouraging like success. The instructor should realize that a learner is encouraged by success in the learning attempt and learning one point is essential before moving on to the next. Regarding refresher training, self-defense is an appropriate topic, because although it is not used frequently, it is imperative that it is known when, in fact, it is needed.

22. C The purpose of recruit training is to prepare the recruit for field work. Therefore, the training must be based on an accurate and up-to-date assessment of the job in the field. This is accomplished through the development of a job analysis.

23. B If the answer here is *yes,* then the training is successful. The point is that, in order for training to be successful, what is learned must be applied on the job.

24. A A valuable training program does not have to be a mostly formal one. It should consist of an appropriate blend of formal and informal efforts.

25. A Statement 2: The first step in the development of a formal training program is identification of training needs (not selection of site). Statement 3: The opinions of the employees are extremely valuable (not of minimal value) in determining training needs. Statement 1: A lack of questions could also indicate a lack of interest and/or a lack of understanding.

26. A All three statements are accurate and should be part of any real safety program.

27. B Note that, with the testing step, follow-up is sometimes included.

28. D A trainee's apperceptive base is influenced by past training and experience and has a definite influence on the rate of future training.

29. A The truth is training always remains part of a supervisor's job even though a specialized training unit is formed. Note that, anytime a specialized unit is formed, the danger exists that the rest of the department tends to believe that the functions performed by the specialized unit no longer need to be performed by anyone else.

30. D The trainer should know that proper attitude is something that is not always present but can be developed through training in community relations.

31. D Actually, in the preparation phase of training, the employee does not engage in any actual practice operation. This comes later, in the application phase.

32. **B** The value of an understudy system lies in its ability to provide promotional replacements. It occurs when a certain rank must learn its own duties and the duties of the next higher rank.

33. **A** When the "why" of reporting is made clear, the information system is more accurate and productive. For this reason it is important that all required reports are indeed necessary.

34. **D** Aimlessness as a cause of ineffective teaching comes from a lack of planning and illogical organization of the material to be taught.

35. **A** It is imperative that the introduction place the learner in a state of readiness by having the student attentively focused on the subject. It is in the introduction step that the student's interest must be raised. If the instructor fails in this step, the remaining steps of presentation, application, and testing lose their value.

36. **B** Although all the choices are important, if the rater is not aware of the objectives of the rating program and the common pitfalls of rating, the results can be devastating. Training of the rater can ensure that this does not occur.

37. **A** Keeping records to act as a reference and as documentation is a good idea. In this way, when it is time to submit budget requests, a cumulative file is available for use.

38. **A** A budget is no more than a plan expressed in financial terms. Budget preparation, therefore, requires planning expertise.

39. **A** Inspections force line officers to look at things they ordinarily would not look at. Further, staff inspections of line tasks are actually quite reliable because the staff officer has no particular bias toward the results of the inspection. The results of a staff inspection of line functions should, with the possible exception of very large departments, be given directly to the line unit. This is done to save time in getting the line unit to correct the discrepancy, which is, after all, the goal of an inspection.

40. **A** As the saying goes, one picture is worth a thousand words. Through first-hand, direct observation the sergeant is better able to determine if policies are being followed and if resources are being properly used.

41. **A.** Procedural plans usually relate to standardized procedures, such as how to process summonses after they have been served.

42. **B** Too often police agencies analyze the symptoms of a problem instead of isolating and clarifying the problem that highlighted the need for a plan. Therefore, plans are improperly created to deal with the symptoms of a problem instead of the problem itself.

43. **A** Organizational changes can be made at the top of the organization to allow for the skills or limitations of the top brass. Changes are usually not made anywhere else in the organization for this purpose. That is, the organization can be changed at the top to fit the worker, but at any other level lower than the top, the worker should be fit into the organization because there are more jobs as one descends the levels of the organization.

44. **A** No specialization should occur that damages the patrol effort. Personnel can usually be identified for special units with little trouble, and it does not usually require the lure of extra compensation since it is the specialized unit, not the entire department, that enjoys a high esprit de corps.

45. **A** The typical police organization is so dynamic that it constantly changes. Organization charts are seldom current and never show the informal lines of authority. These charts can be used, however, to show formal lines of communication and authority and are therefore good training aids.

46. **B** Actually, the opposite of that stated in choice B is true. Line supervisors often criticize staff supervisors for having a tendency to assume the authority of line supervisors. The criticisms in choices A, C, and D are often criticisms heard of line supervisors made by staff supervisors.

47. **A** Rating everyone as average usually happens when the supervisor doesn't know the workers well. In these cases, the supervisor should make every effort to get to know the employee's performance level during the time before the actual formal evaluation. If the present supervisor is recently assigned, he/she should confer with the previous supervisor about the employee and indicate this conferral on the evaluation form.

48. **C** The sergeant is impressed by something that gives him an overall impression about the officer but has nothing to do with the evaluation process. This is an example of the rating error known as the "halo effect."

49. **A** It assists the sergeant in evaluating objectively and being able to document the evaluation. There is also nothing wrong with letting subordinates know they are constantly being evaluated. Actually, the good worker welcomes an honest and objective evaluation.

50. **C** When communicating something complex, some written instructions should accompany the verbal directions. In an examination, anytime you get a question in this area and the examiner describes the communication as "complex," your antennae should rise. Look for an answer that states that further explanation is available, such as written instructions. Choice A suggests more explanation, but the use of the word *surely* makes it a wrong choice.

51. **A** If there is any doubt about whether to pass information on to a supervisor, the doubt should always be resolved in favor of passing the information on.

52. **B** The phrase "totally eliminate" in statement 2 is too absolute. No matter how effective a department's communications system, it will never be able to eliminate the grapevine. By supplying facts on key issues, however, it can minimize employee use of the grapevine.

53. **C** Status can be a help or a hindrance to effective communication. Generally, if the person with status is respected, the status can aid the communication process. If the person with status is feared, the status can be a hindrance.

54. **C** In police work, there is an overwhelming need for teamwork. The first-line supervisor takes a policy or procedure, explains it to those at the level of operation, and ensures that the workers do their individual parts of the total job.

55. **D** It is not the wording of the law that creates the need for selective enforcement as much as the reasons stated in Choices A, B, and C.

56. **B** A good public image, created by a good public relations program, helps to attract minority applicants to the police service. This in turn aids community relations, since "minority recruitment" is a must for developing good relations with the minority community.

57. **D** It is obviously not a wise decision to advise the demonstration leaders about the exact strength of the detail assigned or to let community leaders make command decisions. Nor is it wise to relieve officers of equipment they might need for safety purposes. Choice D is an accepted police strategy at demonstrations with "potential" to erupt.

58. **B** Police officers prefer to think of themselves as crime fighters, not as social workers, although they spend a majority of their time performing activities of a service nature. This conflict of roles often creates tension among police officers.

59. **B** Such programs as park-walk-and-talk have gone a long way toward reintroducing the police to the public. There are many advan-

tages that accrue when an individual citizen has a personal acquaintance with the "neighborhood cop."

60. **C** Police-community relations is the job of every member of the department.

61. **D** Actually, police-community relations is a proper attitude of the police toward their responsibility of providing service.

62. **C** Although community relations is everyone's job, the chief sets the tone and makes community relations a real program.

63. **D** Police officers see no problem with using community relations activities to gather intelligence information, but the community in general frowns upon the practice as being akin to spying. It is a different story, however, when a community member voluntarily comes forward with intelligence information. What the community resents are covert attempts to use community relations as a pretext for obtaining intelligence information.

64. **D** It is unfortunately true that promotions are very rarely given for community relations activities, that peer recognition is lacking, and that the media gives little attention to community service activities. However, internal satisfaction is one of the primary reasons that police officers interact with the community.

65. **D** The patrol officer most influences the attitude of the public because of the large amount of contact patrol officers have with the public.

66. **C** If this is not at the core of the program, it is doomed.

67. **B** The integrity of the police must be maintained at a very high level if community relations are to be effective. However, the sergeant in this question, depending on the nature of the law involved, could pursue a nonenforcement policy through official channels.

68. **D** Statement 2 is false; it must be the primary goal of the police. Statement 3 is false since community relations is more than a program; it is a policy and a process that reaches all parts of police work.

69. **C** Tension increases when the police become involved in an attempt to legislate morality. Regarding the creation of criminality, this is so because in most public morals crimes the laws being violated are *mala prohibita,* or illegal because someone has said so. A large number of police officers must be dedicated, and the potential for corruption rises when enforcing these crimes because their enforcement involves the wide use of discretionary authority.

70. **D**   As in all professions, discretion and its acceptance must exist before an occupation can truly be considered a profession. For example, the public must fully understand that a policy of full enforcement of all laws is not attainable.

71. **A**   The order maintenance model of policing requires wide discretionary authority because full enforcement of the laws is not a desired goal. Therefore, alternative action is often taken when crimes, especially minor ones, are committed.

72. **A**   All doubts are to be resolved in favor of withholding the information. It can be given later, but once given it is next to impossible to retrieve.

73. **B**   This practice is not recommended. Community relations is a part of the difficult job of traffic duty.

74. **B**   This has allowed officers to leave their cars and patrol on foot.

75. **C**   It has been found that the public should be advised of the intent to use dogs on patrol to obtain increased public acceptance of the use of dogs.

76. **C**   If the danger created by the pursuit outweighs the danger to the community created by allowing the suspect to remain free at this time, then the pursuit should be terminated.

77. **C**   Any police siren, whether or not it is on the "constant position," would tend to draw crowds to the scene of a police incident. Use of the constant siren position is not recommended because of the reasons stated in choices A, B, and D.

78. **A**   Remember, a polarized crowd is a group of people whose attention has been focused on a common event or object. The idea is to divert attention away from the point of interest.

79. **C**   Emotional upset or excitement on the part of a police officer is easily communicated to the more excitable members of the crowd, thereby worsening the situation.

80. **A**   Remember, it takes five officers for each fixed post on a twenty-four hours a day, seven days a week basis. Choice B: boredom is a real problem with fixed posts but can be dealt with by rotation of assignment. Choice C: fixed posts are generally very easy to supervise; either the assigned officer is at his/her fixed location, or he/she is not there. In addition, because a fixed post is so expensive, the need for the assignment must be carefully analyzed before the post is established.

81. **C** The first sworn police member has this task, and he/she must do whatever is possible to protect the crime scene. Once evidence is lost or adulterated, its value is destroyed forever. A tainted crime scene can only yield tainted evidence.

82. **D** This question was asked to test your ability to carefully read the stem of the question. Remember, in our test-taking strategy outlined in Chapter 2, we emphasized the importance of understanding what you are being asked. In this question you are being asked about advantages of steady *shift* assignments, not about steady *post* assignments. Choice D is not a valid reason for permanent shift assignments, although it is a valid reason for permanent post assignments. Read carefully, and underline.

83. **D** When mobility is important, motorized patrol is the answer. Choices A, B, and C accurately describe areas where foot patrol is recommended.

84. **C** The patrol officer does not attempt to remove the desire for criminal conduct but can help set a tone in the community that criminal acts will not be tolerated, either by the police or by the community. Choice B: when attempting to prevent crime, the police strive to create a feeling of police omnipresence.

85. **B** Choice B spells out the primary value of dogs on patrol. Choice A: they are not infallible; Choice D: in some areas the community might object to their presence.

86. **A** Although patrol officers may not have the answers to all problems, their adherence to procedures they have had a part in formulating will be greatly increased by this practice.

87. **C** Routine patrol, unless otherwise specified, is preventive patrol. Preventive patrol requires a conspicuously attired (uniformed) officer to patrol in an irregular manner but as frequently as possible. Remember, the patrol must be highly visible but unpredictable.

88. **B** Although it should not personally bother the police that certain citizens choose to pay for additional security, that private security officers patrol a given area in no way relieves the police of their sworn duty to patrol in that area.

89. **B** There is no way to identify the burglars casing the warehouse as criminals or potential criminals. They would actually be an intangible hazard, one that cannot be measured or counted. The other choices, which represent more visible hazards, are all tangible hazards. Remember, intangible hazards are combatted via routine patrol.

90. C Through deterrence, traffic accidents, with their resulting injuries, deaths, and property damage, can be reduced. And when one considers that about 50,000 people a year die in automobile accidents, the importance of deterrence is put into its proper perspective.

91. D Choice D restates what the Supreme Court of the United States has held concerning random vehicle stops. However, this does not rule out a vehicle stop made for "articulable and reasonable suspicion" or in cases when a violation of law has been observed.

92. B Motorcycle patrol is more expensive than automobile patrol because of the high incidence of disability resulting from accidents involving motorcycles. Only statement 2 is not accurate.

93. B The group should be immediately and politely made aware of the decision not to grant their request.

94. C Facts are the essence of any good investigative report.

95. B During evaluation, the question is asked about how good this souce has been or whether this is the first time this source has been used.

96. A All the choices spell out disadvantages of a decentralized record-keeping system, but the greatest danger lies in the possibility of less than honest record reporting and keeping when records are not kept on a decentralized basis.

97. C There is no substitute for the personal appearance of a trained police officer to interview a complainant. More information can be obtained via face-to-face interviews or interrogations than by using any other method.

98. C The finished sketch prepared later on should be drawn to scale. While at the scene, it is only necessary to draw the rough sketch in proportion, not necessarily to scale.

99. D There is obviously no vehicle to predict accurately the future, although last year's experience is often used to forecast this year's workload. Be careful of absolute words like *exactly*.

100. B The Uniform Crime Reports are simply a compilation of crimes reported to the police. It is not, therefore, a measurement of the actual number of crimes committed. And remember, estimates of the amount of unreported crime run very high.

101. D A favorite ploy of exam writers is to ask data interpretation questions that cannot be answered due to a lack of specific data.

Here the question asked about violent crimes while the chart speaks only about crimes against the person and crimes against property. Notice also that all of the choices involve percentages that appear on the chart. Nonetheless, the answer is D since the data are not specific enough to yield an answer.

102. **B** 56% of those arrested for committing crimes against persons are between 21 and 30 years of age. A majority is more than half.

103. **B** 65% of those under 21 who are arrested for a crime against a person are between 17 and 20 years of age. Since *most* means more than half, choice B is the answer. Concerning choice C, there is no way of determining from the data any specific information about persons who are 18 years of age. 18-year-old arrested persons are included in the overall category of 17 through 20.

104. **A** 78% of those persons under 17 who are arrested for committing a crime against property are under 17.

105. **A** Choices B, C, and D would all be correct if the category involved was crimes against persons. However, the category was crimes against property. In the over 30 age group for the category crimes against property, 32% of arrested persons are over 30. 1000 new arrests multiplied by .32 (32% in decimal form) equals 320, as indicated in choice A.

106. **C** This is a difficult question since it involves making two calculations. You must first determine the approximate number of persons arrested for committing crimes against persons who are under 21. This is accomplished by multiplying 1000 (the total number of new arrests) by .18 (the decimal equivalent of 18%). By doing this you determine that the number of newly arrested persons under 21 charged with committing a crime against a person is 180. Of that number, 65% of them are between 17 and 20 years old. This means that 117 of them are between 17 and 20 years old (180 multiplied by .65, the decimal equivalent of 65%).

107. **C** To determine the answer to this question, all you had to do was to pick the answer off of the graph. Over 21 includes two categories, 21 through 30 and over 30. Since, in the category of crimes against persons, 56% are between 21 and 30 and 26% are over 30, simply add the two percentages to arrive at the answer, which is 82%.

108. **D** 82% of those arrested for committing crimes against persons and 70% of those arrested for committing crimes against property are over 21.

109. **D** The pie chart involved deals only with percentages. The missing data are the actual number of people arrested.

110. **B** If you picked choice A because of the high percentage (78%) indicated on the chart for that age group, you overlooked the fact that those arrested who were under 17 were 78% of the 30% who were arrested for crimes against property. Therefore, if 1000 people were arrested for crimes against property, then 380 of them would be 21 through 30 (1000 $\times$ .38), but only 234 of them would be under 17 (1000 $\times$ .30 $\times$ .78).

111. **C** Interruptions tend to divert the aim of the interview and distract a child who by virtue of his/her age already has a short attention span. The actions in choices A, B, and D are recommended in such an interview.

112. **C** The interview statements and questions indicated by choices A, B, and D assist in the investigation by helping to establish the answers to when, what, and the type of coercion that took place. However, choice C really seeks to answer the question "Why?" These kinds of questions should be avoided because they tend to sound accusatory and, of course, should not because the child here is a victim and not a perpetrator.

113. **A** The professional criminal is more likely to rationally assess the odds against him/her and come to terms with the situation.

114. **B** Statement 2 is inaccurate because the actual negotiator should not portray himself as the ultimate decision maker in order to be able to defer decisions and buy more time when the captor makes demands.

115. **B** The basic fingerprint patterns are arches, loops, and whorls.

116. **D** A bloodstain begins to dry at its outer edges and continues to dry toward the center. Also, bloodstains dry faster on smooth, nonabsorbent surfaces.

117. **C** They may slant to the left or right and correspond to the direction of the twist in the bore of the firearm.

118. **B** Extractor marks are typically formed when the fired case is drawn from the chamber by the extractor. Obviously in a revolver the fired case remains in the cylinder.

119. **B** It usually occurs in about two hours after death.

120. **A** Impressions found in the wood might be able to indicate the size of the tool, but not the exact tool. However, marks made in the metal could possibly identify a particular tool.

Correct Your Weaknesses

CHAPTER 4

Community Policing

In General

We have chosen community policing as the beginning of our treatment of areas that are consistently tested on examinations for Police Sergeant. The reason for this is simple. In today's modern police organizations, the general concepts associated with community policing permeate the entire organization. Consequently, what follows in subsequent chapters should be viewed as action parts of an overall process of policing that is consistent with and subsumed by the concept of community policing. Therefore, it is clear that community policing is not one single program. It is a combination of many programs geared to deal with problems facing the community with a goal of improving the overall quality of life of such community. Hence, community policing is a mind set or a philosophy followed by all members of a police department.

Regarding such a philosophy, the police must see the community as both necessary and critical in solving the problems of the community. The community in turn must see, understand, and support the mission and role of the police. This requires a departure from many of the previous tenets that police departments followed. Specifically, police have traditionally operated as semimilitary organizations, in which actions had to be approved and, in many cases, orchestrated by the top of the organization. Under community policing, however, the officer on the beat has increased discretion and responsibility for dealing with the concerns of the community he/she serves.

In community policing the mission of the police is to improve the quality of life of the community the police serve. The major objectives of a community policing program include:

1. Preventing and controlling conduct that poses a threat to life and property, with emphasis on the reduction of quality of life crimes, such as disorderly conduct and loitering

2. Establishing and maintaining a sense of security in the community through the reduction of the fear of crime

3. Uncovering and dealing with problems in the community that are, or may become, serious problems for the police or government in general

To meet these major objectives, the police assign the same patrol officers to the same posts or beats on a permanent basis. The thinking being that such deployment of personnel will enhance both an officer's knowledge of local conditions and his/her feeling of responsibility toward the area assigned. Typically such officers are known as community patrol officers and these officers seek to accomplish the objectives of community policing by:

1. Establishing direct lines of communication with the community. Such communication takes place on an ongoing and regular basis.

2. Getting the community to assist in determining its law enforcement concerns and then making such concerns a police priority.

3. Convincing the community to increase its involvement in community-based law enforcement programs.

4. Solving problems by using nontraditional strategies as a part of the police response in solving such problems.

5. Acting as coordinators of police service from other units in the police department, from other governmental agencies, and from resources of the private sector of the community.

Community Policing
Problem Solving

Key to effective community policing is the fact that the community patrol officer, in conjunction with the community, must engage in problem solving.

The steps in such problem solving involve:

1. Clearly identifying the problem. If the problem is not accurately identified, then no amount of effort can hope to solve the problem.

2. Examining the problem. So that the problem can be properly addressed, each facet of the problem must be analyzed.

3. Drafting the answer to the problem. Questions such as "Who will do what, when will they do it, and how much will they do?" should be answered here.

4. Putting the answer to the problem to work. The community policing officer not only must coordinate the efforts of all the problem solvers but must also set up channels to get feedback to determine if the problem is being solved.

5. Measuring the answer. Here the results may range from the problem has been completely solved to a new plan is required and the problem must be more clearly identified and reexamined.

EXAMATOPICS ABOUT COMMUNITY POLICING

1. If some type of immediate action is required, community policing officers are authorized to take such action as an interim measure pending further analysis of the problem.

2. Community policing has been found to be particularly effective when dealing with conditions that effect an entire community.

3. Community policing seeks to establish security in a neighborhood by removing conditions that are seen as disorder by the community itself.

4. Brainstorming, a process that calls upon those concerned with a problem to come up with answers to the problem, is a favorite technique of community policing.

5. When examining a problem, everything from the physical environment of an affected area to social problems in the area are considered by a community policing officer.

6. Although community policing requires radical change, such change must, of necessity, occur over a period of time and not overnight.

7. Empowerment, which results when the officer on the beat receives increased discretion to carry out his/her duties, must occur if community policing is to be effective.

8. Management must recognize that community policing entails taking risks and must also be aware that honest mistakes will be made as a result of such risk taking.

9. Under community policing, police are more proactive and do not merely react to incidents after they occur.

10. Community policing should not be seen as a one-shot, quick-fix cure-all for all the concerns of a community.

11. With community policing, the police become a central part of the community's way of life, and the community helps the police to fix priorities and obtain needed resources.

Supervision Under Community Policing

The police sergeant operating in a department subscribing to community policing must deviate from traditional methods of supervision. He/she must be aware that incidents that typically take up a great deal of an officer's time can better be dealt with by dealing with the fundamental problem(s) that brought about such an incident.

It is the supervisor's job to make clear the intentions of upper management and through the officer on the beat to make them happen. In accomplishing this task, the sergeant must be available to advise and coach the officer on post to enable that officer to make good decisions. Also part of the sergeant's job is to help subordinates obtain the resources needed to achieve their goals. At times, the sergeant must ensure that other units of the department are cooperating with the officer on the beat.

Obtaining assistance must not be exclusively limited to the assistance that the resources of the agency bring. If the assistance of other agencies is needed, the sergeant should periodically check to determine if the beat officer is in fact obtaining such assistance.

The community policing sergeant should consider the old saying, "Consider the turtle, if he does not stick his neck out, he does not get anywhere." Here the sergeant must realize that community policing encourages risk taking, and as such, the sergeant must be prepared to encourage subordinates to take risks in dealing with the concerns of the community they serve. Therefore, the sergeant must also be prepared to tolerate those mistakes that subordinates will honestly make when engaging in actions that are neither traditional nor previously attempted.

IS DISCIPLINARY ACTION NECESSARY UNDER COMMUNITY POLICING?

While the traditional authoritarian style of supervision is usually inappropriate under community policing, the sergeant must realize that not all officers are willing to embrace the tenets of community policing voluntarily. The sergeant must be ready to bring such officers around by motivating them to accept community policing. This motivation is best achieved by showing such officers how community policing can help them, specifically by showing them how it can make their role more of that of a professional. Nonetheless, community policing does not advocate the acceptance of inferior work by unwilling subordinates. The supervisor is still responsible for the accomplishment of tasks by his/her subordinates. As such, disciplinary action is not abandoned under community policing. However, it should be noted that, in certain instances, such disciplinary action may take the form of positive discipline or training, which is discussed in a subsequent chapter.

RESPONSIBILITIES OF THE FIRST LINE SUPERVISOR

In a police department practicing community policing, the first-line supervisor is expected to conduct daily briefings with subordinate officers. During such briefings, he/she will discuss such things as personnel problems, deal with scheduling requirements and, most importantly, stay abreast of the efforts of subordinates, and carry forward subordinates' requests for resources to higher levels in the agency. He/she should allow subordinate officers enough discretion to accomplish their tasks. Once again, the supervisor should maintain the attitude that honest failures are what drive the forward progress of the agency since lessons learned from such honest attempts will obviously pay future dividends. When something goes wrong, the incident and not the person should be examined and judged with an eye toward future improvement.

THE PROBLEM-SOLVING MEETING

One of the tools a police sergeant has to assist subordinate officers in solving problems is the problem-solving meeting. Such a meeting is useful when a problem affects an entire unit, such as lack of cooperation from an outside agency or errors in completing certain paperwork. It is not to be used to deal specifically with an employee's poor performance. Nor is it to be used as a substitute for the supervisor making his/her own administrative decisions. The aim of a problem-solving meeting is to arrive at a solution to a problem that seems to affect all members under the sergeant's supervision.

The supervisor who will chair the problem-solving meeting should prepare before the meeting. Such preparation is critical. This preparation includes:

1. Establishing a clear definition of both the problem and aim of the meeting

2. Choosing those who he thinks should attend the meeting

3. Limiting the number of attendees to fifteen, including the chairperson

4. Providing each attendee, before the meeting, a copy of the agenda for the meeting, along with a description of the problem and any data that might help in dealing with the issues involved

Note that the chairperson's agenda must not influence nor bias the thinking of attendees. It is their thoughts that should be brought to the meeting.

Those who are invited to attend should prepare for the meeting by:

1. Reviewing the agenda

2. Clarifying anything that is not understood

3. Gathering before the meeting any necessary information and data an attendee needs if such attendee is expected to make a presentation.

While at the meeting, the supervisor as chairperson should seek to involve everyone present. The discussions should consistent of three phases: the opening, the discussion of issues, and the summary.

During the opening the chairperson greets those in attendance and ensures that everyone knows the identity and assignment of everyone else who is present.

The chair should begin by reviewing the reason for the meeting and outlining the procedure to be followed in conducting the meeting. The best way to get the discussion started is for the chairperson to direct a question to the group or a specific individual.

During the meeting, the supervisor acting as the chairperson should keep the discussion flowing by involving each person in the discussion. He should not allow any one individual to monopolize the discussion or have the discussion stray from the subject agenda. From time to time the chairperson should summarize what has been said to keep the discussion on point. An error usually made by an inexperienced chairperson is to pass immediate judgment on remarks made by an attendee. Ideas should not be criticized during the idea-generation stage. It inhibits thinking and also tends to put a drag on the discussion and limit the ideas that are generated.

At the conclusion of the discussion, the supervisor acting as the chairperson should assist the group in coming to a consensus on what has been decided. The chairperson has the task of making sure that no misunderstanding exists.

EXAMATOPICS ABOUT THE SERGEANT'S ROLE

1. The old supervisory style of fixed and imminent supervision is not the recommended supervisory style of community policing.

2. Under community policing, supervisors are to act as mentors, motivating and helping beat officers acquire the resources needed to solve community problems.

3. Supervisors help officers by providing assistance in identifying and solving community problems.

4. In community policing, teamwork takes the place of authority-oriented supervision, honest errors are tolerated, and risk taking and creative ways of solving problems are encouraged.

5. A police sergeant should spend the majority of his/her work time in the neighborhood actually with officers.

6. The police sergeant is the individual who is in the middle of changes required to bring about true community policing by a police department.

7. When more than fifteen people attend a problem-solving meeting, it becomes too difficult to manage the group, and discussions often wander off track.

8. The community policing sergeant strengthens communication between his/her subordinates and other members of the agency, individual citizens, community groups, and other agencies both public and private.

9. When analyzing a problem, the sergeant should emphasize the importance of obtaining external information such as that from outside the agency.

10. A community policing sergeant recognizes that community policing is a combination of problem solving, crime prevention, and community engagement as opposed to traditional random visible patrol.

11. Under community policing, the role of the sergeant shifts from being the one in charge to being a facilitator.

Compstat

As has already been recognized, so much of what community policing is all about is problem solving. Also noted is that proper identification of the problem is key in problem solving. If the problem has not been properly identified, then an appropriate solution to the problem cannot be obtained. A clear aid in properly identifying problems is information about what crimes are actually occurring in the community. A method for doing this, which has evolved and spread from the New York City Police Department to other law enforcement jurisdictions, is known as Compstat. This method basically holds commanders accountable for dealing with crime patterns developing in areas under their command.

HOW COMPSTAT WORKS

Compstat was originally known as crime meetings or computer-statistics meetings. This method operates as follows: At what is usually a monthly meeting attended by top brass and individual unit commanders, significant statistics for a geographic area of responsibility, such as a precinct, are listed by year on large computer monitors. These significant statistics should include such things as crimes committed, cases cleared, and domestic violence cases, with the corresponding increases and decreases being highlighted.

Each unit commander then discusses the statistics for the area under his/her command. Note that the agency head or his/her representative who is present already has these statistics. The individual commander is expected to demonstrate his/her awareness of conditions and indicate strategies to deal with them. In short, he/she must show how to solve the emerging problem indicated by the statistics. Commanders are not faulted for not immediately coming up with the correct strategy or for the fact that crime has risen in their areas of responsibility. They are criticized and even removed from command assignments, however, if they are totally unaware of the crime or have no strategy to deal with it.

To reiterate, risk taking and a kind of failure management that recognizes honest mistakes are employed in community policing. However, once again, not identifying a problem or not dealing appropriately with an already identified problem is considered inferior work and is not tolerated.

COMPSTAT WORKS AT ALL LEVELS

Compstat maintains a policy of inclusion whereby commanders are given the trust of the agency and the authority to do the job and then held accountable for the successful accomplishment of the goals of the job.

There can be several levels of Compstat. For example, a chief of police first empowers and then interrogates a command-level supervisor, forcing him/her to come up with a plan to attack the problem that has been surfaced by Compstat. This command-level supervisor then empowers and interrogates his/her platoon commander who, in turn, repeats this procedure with his/her sergeants (e.g., What are we doing on this shift to address the condition that has been identified by Compstat?). Each sergeant involved then repeats the process with his/her subordinates (e.g., Officer Green, tell me about the car thefts on your post).

Some supervisors do not do well with Compstat; others do. It has sometimes been referred to as Police Darwinism, where the fittest survive. Compstat, similar to the breadth of community policing, involves patrol but is also used with all units of a police agency.

As in community policing, Compstat is guided by partnership, problem solving, and prevention. And like community policing, it demands community involvement, innovative tactics, and assertive policing. It emphasizes reducing crime as well as preventing crime. It is obvious, therefore, that the problem solving called for by Compstat is an integral component of a modern law enforcement agency and is to be used by the law enforcement supervisor engaging in community policing.

EXAM ATOPICS ABOUT COMPSTAT

1. Under Compstat, the sentiment exists that an arrest, in and of itself, is not enough of an answer to a crime problem.

2. Under Compstat, an answer is consistently sought to the question, "How can we eradicate the problem?"

3. The Compstat method can be utilized through several levels of a police agency and is not restricted to the upper levels of management.

4. A key aspect of Compstat is empowerment whereby considerable discretion to solve problems is given to those who are to be held responsible for solving the problems that Compstat has surfaced.

Typical Duties of Community Policing Police Officers

A police sergeant supervising police officers in a police department committed to community policing would ensure such police officers engage in some or all of the following:

1. Creating beat profiles which identify critical problems connected to the beat or post being patrolled

2. Working with community members to create a methodology for solving identified critical problems

3. Jointly with community members, identifying the resources needed to solve critical problems

4. Fully using the agency's resources when solving community problems

5. Collaborating with other public and private agencies in solving community problems

6. Acting as a catalyst when helping to solve problems that have traditionally not been seen as falling under the sphere of responsibility traditionally assigned to the police

7. Taking risks that are bound to exist when implementing innovative solutions to problems

8. Assessing results of problem-solving efforts

EXAMATOPICS ABOUT TYPICAL DUTIES OF COMMUNITY POLICING POLICE OFFICERS

1. Officers on foot patrol are expected to respond to nonemergency calls for service (e.g., minor fires, aided and accident cases).

2. A series of calls or incidents are seen as being related when there are similarities in behavior complained of, locations, persons involved, or victims.

3. People, locations, or behaviors that generate frequent calls for service are targeted with the goal of eliminating the underlying cause of the call for service.

4. Under community policing, specialty units, such as detectives, are not eliminated but instead become part of the beat community police officer's problem-solving effort.

5. Community police officers engaging in problem solving should use resources external to his/her agency when analyzing community problem.

6. The last step of a community police officer's problem-solving effort should always be assessing or evaluating the result of his/her problem-solving effort.

Practice Exercises

You are now ready to do some practice questions. Always try to answer the questions in the allotted time. After completing each of the three groups of questions, make sure you thoroughly review the explanations for each answer before going to the next set of questions. This includes reviewing the explanation for all questions, those you answered correctly and those you answered incorrectly. This is done to ensure that you always arrive at the correct choice for the right reasons. Remember, now is the time to make mistakes. If you understand why you made a mistake, you should not make the same mistake on the examination, when it really counts.

GROUP ONE—10 QUESTIONS—15 MINUTES

1. In community policing, the mission of the police is to
   A. Make as many arrests as possible through strict enforcement of all statutes
   B. Increase enforcement of all traffic regulations
   C. Improve the quality of life of the community
   D. Remove any responsibility for a safer community from the community and place it entirely on the shoulders of professional police officers

2. Which of the following least accurately describes a major objective of a community policing program?
   A. Preventing and controlling conduct that poses a threat to life and property, with emphasis on the reduction of quality of life crimes, such as disorderly conduct and loitering
   B. Establishing and maintaining a sense of security in the community through the reduction of the fear of crime
   C. Uncovering and dealing with problems in the community that are, or may become, serious problems for the police or government in general
   D. Faster and faster response to isolated 911 calls for service to ensure that rapid response to such calls remains the yardstick used to measure effective policing

3. Under community policing, the same patrol officers should be assigned to the same posts or beats. This statement is:
   A. True, mainly because community policing should be performed by only a select group of officers of a department
   B. False, mainly because continuous assignment of an officer to one area will cause an officer to become too close to the community in that area, and, thus, the officer will not be able to carry out his/her duties impartially
   C. True, mainly because such deployment of personnel will enhance both an officer's knowledge of local conditions and his/her feeling of responsibility toward the area assigned
   D. False, mainly because such an assignment policy thwarts the overall development of personnel

4. In connection with community policing, evaluate the following statements:
   (1) In accomplishing the objectives of community policing, an officer should establish direct lines of communication with the community.
   (2) Under community policing, professional police officers, who are able to determine on their own what the law enforcement concerns of a community should be, are developed.
   A. Both statements are accurate.
   B. Both statements are inaccurate.
   C. Only statement 1 is accurate.
   D. Only statement 2 is accurate.

5. Consider the following actions that should be taken by community policing patrol officers in accomplishing the objectives of community policing.
   (1) Convincing the community to increase its involvement in community-based law enforcement programs.
   (2) Solving problems by using nontraditional strategies as part of the police response in solving such problems
   (3) Acting as coordinators of police service required by the community from other units in the police department.

A. Actions 1 and 2 are accurate; action 3 is inaccurate.

B. Actions 1 and 3 are accurate; action 2 is inaccurate.

C. Actions 2 and 3 are accurate; action 1 is inaccurate.

D. All the statements are accurate.

6. Under community policing, police officers must, in conjunction with the community, engage in problem solving. In taking such action, which of the following is generally recognized as being the first step in such problem solving?
   A. Analyzing the problem
   B. Identifying the problem
   C. Coming up with a possible answer to the problem
   D. Coordinating the efforts of those involved to solve the problem

7. If problem solving is to be part of community policing, then it should be acknowledged that problem solving is a process with very definite steps. Which of the following should most likely be the last step in any such problem-solving process?
   A. Putting the answer to the problem to work
   B. Measuring the answer
   C. Identifying the problem
   D. Determining who should be doing what to solve the problem

8. Under community policing which of the following actions is most likely to occur?
   A. Requiring strict adherence to a hierarchical structure in connection with any decisions made by community patrol officers
   B. Requiring an increase in the use of radio motor patrol
   C. Allowing community policing officers to be authorized to take some type of immediate action as required
   D. Paying less attention to matters outside the direct purview of the police

9. As used in community policing, the process of brainstorming calls upon which of the following to come up with answers to a problem?
   A. Only the police
   B. Those concerned with the problem
   C. Exclusively, specifically chosen experts who have solved problems similar to the one currently presenting itself to the community
   D. Only the community

10. Community policing should be considered mainly as:
    A. The ability to understand and deal with all concerns of the community without any input from the police
    B. A function that is to be carried out only by certain specially trained officers who would belong to an elite unit in the department
    C. A type of policing that will reduce crimes that the department has unilaterally determined to be most upsetting to the community it serves
    D. A mindset or philosophy that permeates the entire department and is carried out by every member of the agency

GROUP TWO—10 QUESTIONS—15 MINUTES

11. In constructing an understanding of community policing, which of the following would be least likely to apply?
    A. Community residents and the police work jointly together.
    B. Resources outside the police department can be used in solving problems.
    C. The needs and concerns of the community must be considered by the police in formulating its actions.
    D. The police who are professionally trained solely determine the causes of crime affecting the community.

12. Which of the following least accurately indicates an appropriate reward to officers that engage in community policing?
    A. More emphasis and reliance on the regulatory function of an officer's arrest and citation powers
    B. Greater control over the work they perform
    C. More autonomy
    D. Increased responsibility

13. A community policing sergeant should recognizes that community policing is a combination of all of the following except:
    A. Problem solving
    B. Crime prevention
    C. Community engagement
    D. Random visible patrol

14. In order to achieve the objectives of a community policing program, community policing stresses:
    A. Centralization
    B. Decentralization
    C. Neither centralization nor decentralization
    D. Both centralization and decentralization

15. Sergeant Neil Bailes is a first-line supervisor in a police department operating as a community policing agency. He is planning a problem-solving meeting to deal with a certain issue. In connection with such a problem-solving meeting, which of the following actions would be most appropriate for Sergeant Bailes to take?
    A. Avoid issuing an agenda before the meeting so as not to have attendees arrive with biased positions on the issues to be discussed
    B. Be prepared during the meeting to immediately silence suggestions and recommendations he feels are not feasible
    C. Be prepared at the end of the meeting to assist the group to come to a consensus on what has been decided
    D. Recognize that during the meeting he should not summarize what has been said so as to avoid giving the impression of favoring any of the suggestions or recommendations

16. At a problem-solving meeting, the maximum number of attendees, including the chairperson, should be no more than:
    A. Ten
    B. Twelve
    C. Fourteen
    D. Fifteen

17. In planning a problem-solving meeting with subordinate members of her squad, a certain community policing supervisor is contemplating what issues would be appropriate for consideration at the problem-solving meeting. In connection with this situation, which of the following issues would be least appropriate for discussion at such a problem-solving meeting?
    A. A rise in the number of pocketbook snatches occurring in the area patrolled by the squad
    B. A particular personnel problem caused by one of the members of the squad
    C. Difficulties created by the inception of a new department form, which is required to be prepared by all members of the department
    D. A safety problem that has been surfaced by various members of the squad concerning a new bullet-proof vest issued by the department

18. Sergeant Neil Bailes is training a group of newly assigned police officers on community policing. As such he begins by explaining what community policing is all about. In his explanation, Sergeant Bailes would be correct if he stated that community policing involves all the following except:
    A. A strong law enforcement focus that utilizes proactive problem solving
    B. A partnership between the police and the community that recognizes the need for mutual respect and support
    C. Police officers being assigned on a permanent basis to posts and beats
    D. An incident-driven and immediate response-oriented approach

19. Concerning supervision under community policing, evaluate the following statements:
    (1) When something goes wrong, the person and not the incident should be examined and judged by the community policing supervisor with an eye toward future improvement.
    (2) A community policing sergeant must realize that community policing discourages risk taking.
    A. Both statements are accurate.
    B. Both statements are inaccurate.
    C. Only statement 1 is accurate.
    D. Only statement 2 is accurate.

20. As a police sergeant appropriately supervising under community policing, Sergeant Joe Funcheon realizes that the primary ingredient of community policing is:
    A. The problem-solving effort participated in jointly by both the police and community
    B. The use of routine services to determine the needs of the community
    C. Paying close attention to conditions in the community that are fear inducing
    D. Deploying police officers under his supervision in closer proximity to the community they serve by establishing permanent post and beat assignments for such officers

GROUP THREE—10 QUESTIONS— 15 MINUTES

21. Consider the following statements concerning Compstat:
    (1) The goal of Compstat is to motivate police commanders and, in turn, their supervisors to get those under their management and supervision to make as many arrests as possible.
    (2) The exclusive use of Compstat is to examine incidents of crime and the clearance of such crimes.
    (3) Compstat is proactive policing, which permits a police department to conduct a critical analysis of data, to foresee or rapidly identify rises in areas of concern, and to react appropriately.

A. Statements 1 is accurate; statements 2 and 3 are inaccurate.
B. Statements 2 is accurate; statements 1 and 3 are inaccurate.
C. Statements 3 is accurate; statements 1 and 2 are inaccurate.
D. All the statements are inaccurate.

22. Similar to community policing, Compstat is guided by all the following except:
A. Political intervention
B. Prevention
C. Problem solving
D. Partnership

23. When the New York City Police Department first began using Compstat, all the following resulted except:
A. Information became available in a clear and easy-to-understand format
B. Local commanders, eligible for retirement, delayed their retirement due to Compstat, which made their jobs less demanding
C. The sharing of information became more widespread
D. Quality of life issues were dealt with through an appropriate deployment of resources at the operational level

24. Evaluate the following statements regarding Compstat:
(1) Under Compstat, policy decisions can be made on hard data.
(2) Compstat forces police commanders and supervisors to restrict their efforts to traditional and previously accepted methods of combating crime.
A. Both statements are accurate.
B. Both statements are inaccurate.
C. Only statement 1 is accurate.
D. Only statement 2 is accurate.

25. Which of the following most accurately indicates what is generally considered inferior work according to the standards set forth by Compstat?
A. The fact that crime has risen in a supervisor's area of responsibility
B. Failing to deal with an already identified problem

C. Failure of a strategy created by a supervisor to correct a condition previously identified by the supervisor

D. A supervisor not immediately coming up with the correct strategy to deal with a spike in crime in such supervisor's area of responsibility

26. During a coffee break, Sergeant Don Ginty hears the following statements made by subordinate officers under his supervision concerning community policing:

(1) Officer Funcheon states, "Under community policing, the police organize the community, protect the community, and, under the proper circumstances, are advocates for community members."

(2) Officer Bailes states, "Problem solving is a big part of the job under community policing."

(3) Officer Sunshine says, "In a police department that practices community policing, the police and the community agree on the causes of crime."

Sergeant Ginty would be most correct if he made which of the following determinations concerning the statements made by his subordinate officers.

A. Officer Funcheon and Officer Bailes are accurate; Officer Sunshine is inaccurate.

B. Officer Funcheon and Officer Sunshine are accurate; Officer Bailes is inaccurate.

C. Officer Bailes and Officer Sunshine are accurate; Officer Funcheon is inaccurate.

D. All the officers are accurate.

27. Which of the following should be considered to be in the middle of changes required to bring about true community policing in a police agency?

A. The police sergeant or first-line supervisor

B. The community policing beat officer

C. The chief of the police agency

D. Individual members of the community

28. Which of the following least accurately describes an attribute of a police sergeant properly acting as a first-line supervisor in a department engaged in community policing?

A. Acting like a facilitator

B. Being able to motivate subordinates

C. Being able to manipulate subordinates

D. Acting like a coach

29. In which of the following actions should a community policing police sergeant engage?
   A. Empower subordinates by allowing subordinates expanded discretionary powers in making decisions
   B. Keep the efforts of patrol beat officers and specialized units, such as detectives, separate and apart in order to more readily identify deficiencies and derelictions of duty
   C. Understand that community policing requires radical departures from traditional methods of policing and must happen instantaneously
   D. Personalize failures at the operational level to identify the officer(s) responsible for such failures in order to identify training needs more accurately

30. Sergeant Joseph Funcheon is training Community Policing Police Officer Bailes in problem solving. As such, the sergeant would be most correct if he named which of the following as the last action in a problem-solving effort?
   A. Verifying that the problem has been accurately identified
   B. Analyzing all facets of the problem
   C. Implementing the solution to the problem
   D. Evaluating the solution to the problem

Answer Key

1. **C**	7. **B**	13. **D**	19. **B**	25. **B**
2. **D**	8. **C**	14. **B**	20. **A**	26. **D**
3. **C**	9. **B**	15. **C**	21. **C**	27. **A**
4. **C**	10. **D**	16. **D**	22. **A**	28. **C**
5. **D**	11. **D**	17. **B**	23. **B**	29. **A**
6. **B**	12. **A**	18. **D**	24. **C**	30. **D**

Answer Explanations

GROUP ONE

1. **C** Under community policing, the responsibility for a safer community is shared between the police and the community. Thus the community has responsibility for a safer community. Further, community policing goes beyond simply making arrests and issuing traffic tickets. In community policing, the mission of the police is to improve the quality of life of the community by solving community problems. Strict enforcement of all statutes and traffic regulations is not always the best approach to solve a community problem.

2. **D** Choices A, B, and C are major objectives of a community policing program. Choice D is not. Mere rapid response to calls for service is not a yardstick for measuring effective policing under community policing. Responding to an incident and handling it without attention to a possible underlying problem is not what community policing is all about. Under community policing, the police address underlying problems and their causes. And this is not always attained by faster and faster response to isolated calls for service.

3. **C** Under community policing, an officer should become close to the community served. Any possibility of partiality would be overcome by professional conduct standards required of officers working in a department engaged in community policing.

4. **C** Statement 1 is accurate, and such communication should take place on an ongoing and regular basis. Statement 2 is inaccurate in that under community policing, the community assists police officers in determining what the law enforcement concerns of a community should be.

5. **D** Actions 1, 2, and 3 are recognized methods of accomplishing the objectives of community policing.

6. **B** The first step in such a problem-solving effort is to identify the problem. If the problem is not accurately identified, then no matter how much effort is put into the process, and no matter how well it is carried out, it will not be effective simply because the wrong problem is being solved and the real problem remains.

7. **B** Whether referred to as assessing the efforts made to solve the problem or evaluating the results of the problem-solving effort or, as indicated in choice B, *measuring the answer,* the essence of the last step in problem solving remains the same. It is to see if what has been done to solve the problem has really worked.

8. **C** Under community policing, the power and discretion of community policing patrol officers on the beat are increased so much so that these officers are authorized to take such kind of immediate actions as interim measures pending further analysis of the problem. All decisions are not strictly to be cleared first as they might be under a hierarchical structure. Also, foot patrol is increased under community policing. Finally, under community policing, the police pay attention to problems that concern the community even if such problems traditionally fall outside the reach of the police.

9. **B** Under community policing, a favorite technique is to involve those concerned with a problem to come up with the answers. It is not otherwise restricted to only the community, or to only the police, or to some type of panel of experts.

10. **D** Community policing recognizes the concerns of the community and jointly with the community goes about improving the quality of life in the community it serves. Hence it is a mindset or philosophy that permeates the entire department and is carried out by every member of the agency.

GROUP TWO

11. **D** Notwithstanding the professional training of the police, the causes of crime must be agreed upon by the police and the community, which means that any unilateral determination of the causes of crime should not be part of community policing.

12. **A** Choices B, C, and D indicate an appropriate reward to officers who engage in community policing. In addition, such officers will experience a greater amount of involvement in the decision-making process due to their increased participation in solving the problems of the community they serve. Choice A does not indicate a reward to officers who engage in community policing since such officers will be encouraged to use a full range of options when solving community problems and not to rely more on arrest and citation powers.

13. **D** Instead of random visible patrol, community policing uses tailor-made strategies that are arrived at with the assistance of the community so that a more proactive policing style can be developed to more effectively solve problems and prevent crime.

14. **B** Community policing stresses decentralization through geographical assignments such as beats, posts, sectors, areas, or zones, with each officer having territorial responsibility for the area being served.

15. **C** The sergeant must be prepared at the end of the meeting to help the group come to a consensus on what has been decided. He will do this because the chairperson has the task of making sure that no misunderstanding exists. Choice A is incorrect because those invited to attend should give some thought to the issue(s) to be discussed and thus be able to come to the table with suggestions and recommendations. Choice B is incorrect because to do so will stifle further discussion by those in attendance. Choice D is incorrect because he should summarize from time to time to keep the discussion on point.

16. **D** Attendance by more than fifteen creates separate and independent discussions between groups, which creates distractions and makes the overall regulation of the meeting more difficult for the supervisor acting as the chairperson.

17. **B** A problem-solving meeting is useful when a problem affects an entire unit. It is not to be used to deal with specific personnel problems. It is not to be used as a substitute for the supervisor making his own administrative decisions. The aim of a problem-solving meeting is to arrive at a solution to a problem that seems to affect all members under the sergeant's supervision, such as those illustrated in choices A, C, and D.

18. **D** Community policing is not incident driven. Traditional policing, which calls for responding to, and holds as most important, individual 911 calls for service, is incident driven. Under community policing, the underlying problems creating the calls for service are identified and ultimately sought to be solved. You should not be confused regarding choice A in that community policing is not soft on

crime and has a strong law enforcement focus; however, it seeks to go beyond merely responding to the incident at hand. It is a more proactive type of policing that attempts to prevent the need for future calls for service concerning the incident at hand by identifying and eliminating the cause of the call.

19. **B**   Statement 1 is inaccurate because, under community policing, when something goes wrong, the incident and not the person should be examined and judged by the community policing supervisor with an eye toward future improvement. Statement 2 is inaccurate because a community policing sergeant must realize that community policing encourages risk taking. The sergeant must be prepared to encourage subordinates to take risks in dealing with the concerns of the community they serve. Therefore, the sergeant must be prepared to experience a certain share of mistakes that subordinates will honestly make when engaging in actions that are neither traditional nor previously attempted. However, such risks will pay future dividends as they lead to innovative responses to problems and can then be shared with other officers confronted with similar problems.

20. **A**   Although choices B, C, and D all appropriately reflect ingredients of community policing, choice A is the primary ingredient of community policing.

GROUP THREE

21. **C**   Statement 3 accurately describes Compstat and indicates what Compstat is intended to accomplish. Statements 1 and 2 are inaccurate because Compstat's goal is to eradicate the problem, not just to make arrests, since even though crime clearance is achieved, such action may not be able eradicate and solve the underlying problem.

22. **A**   Choices B, C, and D all correctly identify the guiding factors of Compstat. Choice A does not. In actuality, Compstat brings hard data to the forefront, and that is what drives and guides Compstat.

23. **B**   Actually such commanders retired more and more, and they claimed the pressure to reduce more and more unfavorable incidents occurring in their areas of responsibility became unbearable.

24. **C**   Statement 2 is inaccurate because Compstat encourages flexibility and creativity in responding to identified conditions. Statement 1 is accurate in that the hard data available to commanders and supervisors is what they are encouraged to be familiar with and share. Thus, it is the fabric of decisions creating policy.

25. B Commanders and supervisors are criticized and even removed from command assignments if they are totally unaware of the crime or have no strategy to deal with it. Compstat is not a tool for punishing commanders and supervisors who are taking risks and engaging in actions intended to deal with an identified condition appropriately. Nor are such personnel held responsible for rises in crime, which as a fact of police work will occur from time to time. Once again, it is the commander or supervisor who fails to take action, or is not even aware of what is taking place in his/her area of responsibility, who will be faulted.

26. D The statements made by all three officers are correct concerning community policing.

27. A It is the police sergeant who is in the middle of changes required to bring about true community policing by a police agency. No matter what the agency's top brass may intend, if the first-line supervisor, the sergeant, does not translate their intentions for change for those at the operating level, such changes will not occur.

28. C Choices A, B, and D are attributes of a police sergeant acting as a first-line supervisor in a department engaged in community policing. Such attributes all share the intent of supervisory assistance for subordinates doing their jobs. Choice C, however, connotes more of an exploitation of, rather than assistance to, subordinates, which is not the intention of true community policing supervision.

29. A Choice B is inaccurate because the efforts of patrol officers and specialized units need to be coordinated so that beat officers can be afforded proper assistance from these specialized units. Choice C is inaccurate because although radical departures from traditional methods of policing are required, such changes cannot happen instantaneously. The process will be gradual but constant. Choice D is inaccurate because operational failures should be depersonalized by judging overall incidents rather than the actions of specific persons. Choice A is accurate because the subordinates must be encouraged to take innovative actions and thereby given the expanded discretionary powers needed to take such actions.

30. D Generally, in order, the steps in problem solving, which is a large part of community policing, are:
1. Identifying the problem
2. Verifying that the problem has been accurately identified
3. Analyzing the problem
4. Implementing a solution to the problem
5. Evaluating the solution to the problem to determine whether the results are a product of the actions taken, acceptable, and sufficient to eradicate the problem, as well as whether such actions are still required to keep the condition from reoccurring

CHAPTER 5

Principles of Supervision

In General

To fully grasp the principles of supervision one must first be able to distinguish a supervisor from other categories of workers. And it is important for police personnel to understand that the principles of supervision apply mostly to all work settings, not just to a police organization. Many of the same supervisory techniques that are effective for auto workers on the assembly line in Detroit work equally well for police officers on the streets of New York or Chicago.

WHO ARE SUPERVISORS?

The key element in the supervisory process is a relationship with people. The basic tools of a supervisor are the workers under his/her supervision. And like all tools, they work best when they are used properly. The principles of supervision, therefore, are guidelines that, when followed, enable a supervisor to use his/her workers properly.

Many experts in the field prefer to explain a supervisor's role by comparing it with two other roles found in a typical operations-level police unit. In every such unit, the following three classifications of personnel can always be found.

Managers. It is generally agreed that it is at the rank of Lieutenant in police departments that workers first assume managerial responsibilities. We believe, however, that sergeants assigned as desk officers also function as managers. The basic task of a manager is to coordinate all the available resources in an attempt to attain the goals of an organization. It should be noted that the managerial function doesn't necessarily require interaction with people, although, as in the case of the desk lieutenant, it often does involve a direct relationship with people. One final point: managers do not establish department policy. They implement policy that has been set at the administrative and executive levels of an organization. Remember also that sergeants can and do perform managerial functions via the delegation process.

Supervisors. As mentioned above, the supervisory function invariably involves an ongoing relationship with people. As opposed to managers, supervisors are often present at the scene where workers build their product or deliver their service. In a police department, the key supervisory rank is Sergeant. And as all police officers know, it is the sergeant who is often on the scene with them when they do their job.

Workers. The worker who actually does the work justifies the organization's existence. In police departments, the police officers and detectives are the workers; they are the ones who accomplish the basic goals of the organization.

WHAT ARE THE BASIC INGREDIENTS OF THE SUPERVISOR?

Are there some common elements in the job of all supervisors? Yes; it is generally agreed that all supervisors share the following responsibilities.

Direction. Directing people means much more than using authority to order them around. For example, a good supervisor knows how to get workers to do things through positive discipline and leadership.

Creation of a suitable working climate. A major responsibility of all supervisors is the building of a work environment conducive to efficient and effective work performance. It is a well-established fact that a suitable work climate encompasses much more than physical considerations, such as new buildings and up-to-date equipment. More importantly, it means an atmosphere in which workers are treated like individuals, not like drones or robots.

Employee development. Every progressive organization has a responsibility to develop its employees to their maximum potential. The first-line supervisor shares a major portion of this responsibility. The best example of this is the training role that must be performed by the supervisor. Police officers must be trained on an on-going basis, and the police sergeant is in the best position to deliver this training.

Self-development. To remain effective, a supervisor must remain abreast of developments in his/her field. This is especially true in a profession as dynamic as police work. Laws change frequently, for example, and drastic consequences are possible when a police supervisor doesn't know the law. For one thing, the United States Supreme Court has held that police officers are liable if they enforce laws that have been ruled unconstitutional.

Ambivalent Role of the Supervisor

The most difficult adjustment an individual has to make as he/she ascends the promotion ladder in a police department is going from the Police Officer rank to the rank of Sergeant. This is so for a number of reasons. One of the most compelling factors is the ambivalent nature of the police sergeant's role.

CLOSE TIES DEVELOP WITH WORKERS

Because the first-line supervisor is constantly in contact with the work group, he/she readily identifies with that group and develops loyalty toward it. Very often the personal need to be included in the work group as a social unit results in close ties between workers and their supervisors. These ties are often strengthened by the obligation of the supervisor to defend the interest of the work group before management.

THE SUPERVISOR ALSO REPRESENTS MANAGEMENT

Sergeants develop close ties with those they supervise. Why does that pose a problem? The answer to this lies in the reality that the supervisor also has an obligation to represent the interests of management. Supervisors are expected to implement, interpret, uphold, support, and even defend the policies of management.

CONFLICT ARISES

This dual role that the supervisor must play quite often leads to conflict in the mind of the supervisor. It is not easy to "walk the tightrope" between these two roles. The best way for a supervisor to deal with this conflict is through constant exercise of objectivity. Subjective action can damage the supervisor in the eyes of the worker or from the perspective of management, or both.

Leadership

For a long time it was assumed that leaders were born and could not be made and that leadership ability was determined by a person's position in an organization. We now know that both these assumptions are false. It is now generally accepted that leadership can be learned and that there are certain principles of leadership that, when followed, can improve one's leadership ability.

LEADERSHIP DEFINED

There are many different definitions of leadership. The one that we believe applies best to a police sergeant is as follows.

> Leadership is that process by which an individual can influence others in an organization to willingly make their best effort to achieve the goals of the organization.

It is erroneous to believe that those persons who have been put in positions of authority in an organization can automatically influence workers to "willingly" make their best effort to achieve department goals. Although it is true that those in authority are not totally without power to make workers perform up to minimal standards, this should not be confused with leadership. The key words in the above definition are *willingly* and *best effort*. Only a leader can influence a person to willingly make his/her best effort.

LEADERSHIP STYLES

It is generally agreed that there are three readily identifiable styles of leadership, as follows.

Authoritarian style. This style of leadership is exemplified by the boss who is akin to a dictator. Individual initiative is discouraged, and great reliance is placed on formal authority. Please do not assume that this style of leadership cannot work well. If those in authority, especially the chief in a police department, are very competent and always make the right decisions and do the right thing, the job can get done. However, there are many negative side effects that spring from authoritative leadership, not the least of which is a lack of individual growth within the organization.

Laissez-faire style. This is clearly the least effective leadership style. *Laissez-faire* is French for "to leave alone" or "do nothing." A laissez-faire leader interferes very little with workers. This results in confusion in the work force and fosters a disorganized work group. Productivity and morale suffer, and unofficial leaders emerge to fill the void.

Democratic style. Over the long haul, this is the best and most effective leadership style. It occurs when the leader stresses teamwork and encourages participation in decision making. Rather than adopting a "do what I say" attitude, as the authoritarian leader does, or a "leave them alone" posture, as the laissez-faire leader does, the democratic leader adopts an attitude of "let's work this out together." The importance of the individual to the organization is stressed. A democratic leader attempts to have power conveyed from below, rather than relying on authority formally granted from above. A mandate is associated with the democratic leadership style. It requires a leader with good human relations skills.

ATTRIBUTES OF A GOOD LEADER

The police leader is responsible for accomplishing the mission of the police department. For a long time, experts searched for a leadership type that is most successful. The idea was to identify a certain type of person who most often made a good leader and then select only that type of person for key leadership positions. The effort proved fruitless. Great leaders were found to have vastly different individual traits. However, more recently, it has been discovered that police leaders who effectively discharge their major responsibilities have certain work practices in common, as follows.

1. They manage their time effectively.

2. They delegate matters that do not require their personal attention.

3. They are results oriented.

4. They know their own strengths and the strengths of those who work for them. More importantly, they build on these strengths.

5. They do *not* spread themselves too thin. They concentrate on a few areas in which outstanding results can be obtained.

6. They are effective decision makers. They realize that decision making is a matter of following a proven system.

EXAMATOPICS ABOUT LEADERSHIP

1. Good leaders do not necessarily always back up their subordinates. It depends on the circumstances. If a subordinate is in the right, however, a good leader gives that worker full support.

2. A good supervisor creates the proper work climate when he/she balances the responsibility to treat workers as individuals with the proper concern for achieving the goals of an organization.

3. A good leader develops subordinates who willingly do their job in the absence of the leader.

4. Leadership by personal example is the best type of leadership. A "don't do as I do, do what I say" attitude is a definite sign of a poor leader.

5. Leadership is an art that can be learned.

6. Counseling does not mean telling a person what to do. It means helping a person find his/her own solution to a problem.

7. Good supervisors always find time to get to know their subordinates.

Discipline

Discipline is among the most misunderstood concepts in the typical work setting. Most police officers entertain only negative thoughts when the term "disciplinary action" is mentioned. Discipline and punishment are thought of as interchangeable. This, of course, is completely erroneous. In truth, discipline is a two-sided coin. The primary aim of discipline is to train. The term itself is related to the word *disciple*, meaning a follower or student.

POSITIVE DISCIPLINE

There are actually two general types of discipline, positive and negative. It must be understood that police officers who violate a department policy or procedure might do so for either of the following reasons:

1. They might not realize that the conduct involved is prohibited.

2. They might be intentionally violating the policy or procedure involved.

Gaining compliance through positive discipline means convincing an employee through nonpunitive measures to comply willingly.

Positive discipline usually takes the form of

1. Formal training

2. On-the-job training

3. Corrective interviews or

4. Counseling

Quite naturally, positive discipline is the preferred way to achieve compliance with department policies and procedures. Positive discipline works best when the requirements of a job are fair, communicated clearly to all employees, accompanied by a rationale, so workers understand why they are expected to comply, and insofar as possible, established via a participative process.

It is also well established that discipline is maintained at a higher level when employees are the subject of performance evaluations on a periodic basis.

NEGATIVE DISCIPLINE

In every department, regardless of the quality of positive discipline efforts, the need for negative or punitive discipline will always arise. It must be remembered that discipline, both positive and negative, is crucial to employee morale and effective performance. The general rule, however, should be that positive discipline should always be given first consideration when an employee goes astray. If it is determined that negative discipline is required and deserved, punishment should be applied as quickly as possible.

It is often stated that, to maintain the appearance of fairness, all similar violations should be dealt with via equal punishments. This is fallacious reasoning. Each case must be judged on its own merits. No two incidents are ever exactly the same.

FORMS OF NEGATIVE DISCIPLINE

Negative discipline can take any of the following forms, which are presented in ascending order of severity:

1. Oral reprimand or warning

2. Written reprimand

3. Loss of assignment

4. Loss of accrued time

5. Suspension without pay

6. Suspension without pay followed by a probationary period

7. Fines

8. Demotion

9. Termination

10. Judicial prosecution

Oral Reprimands

The most often used form of negative discipline is the oral reprimand. A police sergeant should follow the following steps when giving an oral reprimand.

1. Be certain that the reprimand is deserved; get all the facts before acting.

2. Bear in mind that the purpose of the reprimand is to train the officer to perform properly.

3. Treat the officer as an individual.

4. Keep an even temper; never lose your temper.

5. Praise in public, but discipline in private.

6. Always offer the officer a chance to respond.

EXAMATOPICS ABOUT DISCIPLINE

1. The first-line supervisor who is out on the street with the police officers, where most problems occur, is the key figure in the disciplinary process.

2. It is a police sergeant's responsibility to look for weaknesses in subordinates and to take appropriate disciplinary action, positive or negative, when discovered.

3. Punishment does not have to be severe to be effective. However, it must be swift and certain.

4. As a general rule, the use of a transfer as a means of dealing with a problem employee is not recommended. It is not good personnel policy to transfer a problem police officer to another supervisor without good cause.

Order Giving

Order giving is a very important part of a police sergeant's job. The supervisor's task is to get the job done through subordinates. If the subordinates are not sure of what is expected of them, there is no chance of success. In the quasi-military world of the police, the term "order giving" is readily accepted. In other less military oriented occupations, the term used is "direction." In any case, whether you call it giving orders or directing others, it is a special communications problem that must be mastered if a supervisor is to be effective.

TYPES OF ORDERS

The first concept a newly promoted sergeant must grasp is that different situations require different types of orders. It is generally accepted that all orders can be classified as

1. Commands or direct orders

2. Requests

3. Implied orders

4. Call for volunteers

COMMANDS OR DIRECT ORDERS

A command or a direct order is a very precisely worded statement that clearly conveys that a subordinate is absolutely required to do exactly as told. It is not a good practice to overuse the direct order. Its best use is in emergency situations when time is of the essence and close coordination plus swift and definite action is required. Direct orders are also recommended for use when dealing with lazy or uncooperative employees. The use of direct orders in situations in which they are not needed is a sign of a weak leader who relies too much on official authority.

REQUEST ORDERS

A request order is just what its name suggests. It is an order framed as a request. It is a good tool to use on most employees since it de-emphasizes the superior-subordinate relationship and helps to develop a participative climate in which teamwork is very important. The request order is excellent for use with very sensitive workers or for workers who are older than the supervisor. Obviously, it is inappropriate for use in an emergency or when dealing with lazy or uncooperative workers. And it must be pointed out that framing an order in the form of a request always leaves the door open for a refusal. When and if that occurs, if the order was in fact given as a request, no retaliatory action can be taken. However, unless sufficient extenuating circumstances were present, the refusing officer should thereafter be the subject of direct orders.

IMPLIED ORDERS

An implied order is really a suggestion that something should be done. It is a useful tool for identifying willing workers. It is also helpful in developing the initiative, ability, and judgment of subordinates. It must be remembered that an implied order leaves the method of accomplishment up to the doer. Therefore, when something has to be done in a certain way, an implied order would not suffice.

CALL FOR VOLUNTEERS

This method of getting things done can be a two-edged sword. When used sparingly, it can be very helpful. However, overuse of the call for volunteers method of direction is indicative of a weak leader who is trying to avoid responsibility. Overuse is also very unfair to the willing workers and beneficial to the lazy subordinate who never volunteers. The call for volunteers is often recommended for tasks that are generally thought of as unpleasant. Although for obvious reasons it should never be used in emergency situations, when speed of action is imperative, a call for volunteers promotes the process of participation and can increase job satisfaction for officers who volunteer.

MAKING SURE THE ORDER IS UNDERSTOOD

It is the responsibility of the order giver to make sure the order receiver understands the order. It is a mistake for a supervisor simply to ask a subordinate if an order is understood. When this occurs, most workers feel a certain pressure to respond in the affirmative rather than appear incompetent. In addition, most workers feel that the boss expects them to say they understand. The recommended way to check comprehension of an order is to have the order receiver repeat the order in his/her own words. One final note: except in emergency situations, when prompt obedience is essential, it is always a good idea to explain to the worker the "why" of an order. Giving the rationale for an order very often assures greater acceptance of the order. In the same manner, insofar as possible, a worker should be allowed a voice in deciding how an order should be carried out. This technique tends to build enthusiasm, provide for individual growth, develop a desired participative climate, and interest the worker in the success of the endeavor.

IMPORTANCE OF FOLLOW-UP

Following up after an order has been given is essential. Follow-up begins when, as recommended above, the supervisor makes sure the subordinate understands the order. The essence of follow-up is making sure the order has been carried out. The extent of the follow-up process depends on the importance of the task and the ability, attitude, and experience of the doer.

EXAMATOPICS ABOUT ORDER GIVING

1. As a general rule, the type of order given to an individual will depend on the situation and on the attributes of the individual.

2. Overuse of the command or direct order weakens the value of that type of order in an emergency situation.

3. In nonemergency situations, a recommended way of assigning unpleasant tasks is via a call for volunteers.

4. All important orders, including long-standing procedural orders, should be put in writing.

5. A supervisor who issues an order and ascribes responsibility for them to a higher authority jeopardizes the proper execution of the order. In addition, continued use of this practice will earn the supervisor a reputation as a weak leader.

6. The sequential steps in the process by which written orders are published are as follows: (a) recognition of the need for the order; (b) development of the objectives of the order; (c) data collection; (d) framing the details of the order; (e) obtaining concurrences for the order; (f) gaining the necessary approval of the order; and (g) publishing the order.

7. It is a bad practice to preface orders by saying they are being given "for the record." The main weakness of this practice is that subordinates won't know if they should or should not comply with the order.

8. Using an implied order on an inexperienced officer is unfair and not recommended since it places a responsibility on him/her that he/she might want to discharge but is incapable of so doing.

9. The use of the implied order on an unreliable worker is folly.

Handling Employee Grievances

It is as natural to expect employee grievances in a police department as it is to expect that spring follows winter. The first-line supervisor, the sergeant in a police department, plays a very important role in the handling of employee grievances. An employee whose legitimate grievance is satisfied experiences a sense of gratification and, in many cases, becomes a more productive and loyal worker. On the other hand, an employee whose grievance is ignored, even if it is a minor grievance, but certainly if it is a serious one, becomes disenchanted and unproductive. The grievance then tends to take on greater significance. In some cases, a police officer with an unresolved grievance becomes something like a crusader with a holy cause. His/her attention is on the grievance, not on the job. And in most cases, early and appropriate intervention can lead to satisfying resolution of grievances. It must be remembered, however, that police officers will, as a general rule, only bring their grievances to supervisors they perceive as approachable and concerned with their well-being.

FORMAL VERSUS INFORMAL GRIEVANCE PROCEDURE

Most progressive police departments have formal grievance procedures, although, in truth, many formal grievance procedures were born over a negotiating table, having been put there by police line organizations. Despite the existence of this formal machinery, a police sergeant should understand that it is best to resolve grievances on an informal basis before they become formal grievances. This is so for the following reasons: (1) the processing of formal grievances is expensive; (2) the formal grievance procedure fosters a divisive "us against them" climate; and (3) officers who have their grievances satisfactorily handled by their first-line supervisor tend to develop a loyalty toward the supervisor and the department.

HOW SHOULD GRIEVANCES BE HANDLED?

The way a supervisor handles a grievance is extremely important. Regardless of the merits of the grievance, it is imperative that a police sergeant receiving a grievance from a police officer convince the officer that the problem will be given serious consideration. Sometimes an officer is aggrieved by an incident that the supervisor believes is minor or unimportant. To convey this feeling to the grieving officer would be quite damaging. If a person is upset enough to raise the issue, it is indeed important and serious in the mind of that person. In fact, to make certain that all grievances are taken seriously, a standardized four-step approach is recommended:

1. Receive the grievance properly.

2. Gather the necessary facts.

3. Make a decision, and implement it.

4. Take follow-up action.

RECEIVING THE GRIEVANCE

This is a very critical stage of the process. An employee with a grievance must be convinced the supervisor is interested in the problem. To accomplish this, it is necessary to tell the story without any outside interference or interruption. After hearing the details of the grievance, the supervisor should repeat the story to the employee to make sure the supervisor's understanding of the facts is accurate. In some cases, such as very common, often-repeated grievances, the supervisor can give an immediate decision. In most cases, however, the supervisor has to obtain additional information. It is very important in these instances that the employee be told approximately when an answer or decision can be expected.

GATHERING THE NECESSARY FACTS

This is a very important step in the handling of grievances. The supervisor is looking for facts that support the employee making the grievance as well as facts supportive of management. If the facts support a decision that favors the employee, then so be it. The supervisor must be objective when gathering facts. Remember, if the grievance becomes formal, the supervisor's decision will be reviewed a number of times. The employee has a right to appeal the decision, and the appeals board wants to see decisions based on documentable facts.

In gathering the necessary facts, a supervisor should remember to include all the following areas in the investigation:

1. Related portions of any existing collective bargaining agreement

2. Statements from witnesses

3. Any official files or records that might shed light on the issue

4. Results of similar grievances, if any, to see if any precedents might apply

5. The service record of the grieving officer and other officers involved

6. The viewpoint of the immediate supervisor of the officer making the grievance

MAKING AND IMPLEMENTING A DECISION

The supervisor must remember that mere words do not correct grievances. If an employee was justified in grieving, action must be taken to prevent any recurrence. If necessary, supervisors must be made to change their behavior. Ideally, this can be handled through training. If, on the other hand, the investigation clearly indicates the employee was wrong, the employee must not simply be told he/she was wrong. The worker is entitled to a full and complete explanation of the decision. Although the supervisor should endeavor to satisfy the employee to avoid appeals, this does not mean the supervisor should base a decision on any consideration other than the facts of the case. If the employee expresses dissatisfaction with the decision and decides to use the appeals process, the supervisor should not hold a grudge against the employee. An employee is entitled, without prejudice, to take advantage of the appeals process.

FOLLOW-UP

The fact that action has been taken to resolve a grievance doesn't mean the matter is closed. The supervisor implementing remedial action must follow up to make certain that planned action has indeed been carried out. Failure to follow up is the major cause for repeated grievances from the same source.

EXAMATOPICS ABOUT HANDLING EMPLOYEE GRIEVANCES

1. Supervisors who are successful in defending their decisions in grievance cases are those who base their decisions on the facts in the case and are able to show they treated the employee fairly.

2. No matter how trivial a grievance may appear to a supervisor, it must be treated seriously since it is very important in the mind of the worker.

3. Even "imagined" grievances must be treated seriously, since they are "real" in the mind of the grieving employee.

4. Physical factors in the work setting account for a large percentage of employee grievances.

5. Courts have consistently ruled that an employee cannot be punished for inappropriate conduct unless it can be shown that the conduct is related to official duties and impaired efficiency; some of the most difficult cases to justify are those involving the off-duty conduct of an employee.

6. Transfer might be an appropriate solution in some instances, but more often than not a transfer doesn't solve the problem.

7. Most grievances that aren't based on a collective bargaining agreement can be resolved by the first-line supervisor.

8. Processing and resolving formal grievances is an expensive undertaking.

9. Inconsistent supervision is a prime instigator of employee grievances.

10. Many grievances are caused by rules and regulations that are believed by workers to infringe on their rights as individuals, but the manner in which the rules and regulations are enforced by supervisors is a more significant concern.

11. Supervisors who almost never have work problems or grievances brought to them are probably thought by the workers to be unapproachable.

12. A supervisor can and should be aware of the most common causes of grievances and try to deal with them, thereby preventing further grievances.

Delegation of Authority

The principle of delegation is a topic that police examiners never overlook. It is an area in which you should be very well versed. In essence, delegating is the process of turning over an activity to the care of another. It is a poor supervisor who doesn't delegate when appropriate. However, there are some matters that shouldn't be delegated under any circumstances. And it must always be remembered that it is impossible to delegate away complete responsibility.

ADVANTAGES OF DELEGATION

Supervisors who delegate wisely:

1. Free themselves from many routine tasks, which, in turn, enables them to engage in more important activities, such as planning.

2. Provide opportunity for subordinates to grow in their jobs: In other words, delegation is an excellent way to increase subordinates' skills and knowledge by allowing them to perform new tasks.

3. Counter feelings of insecurity in some workers by demonstrating confidence in them.

4. Engage in a process that is highly cost effective.

5. Help to identify possible training needs.

6. Enable better evaluation of subordinates and early identification of future leaders.

CAVEATS CONCERNING DELEGATION

Delegation can, however, lead to certain problems:

1. Many supervisors erroneously believe they can avoid accountability for results simply because they have delegated a responsibility to a worker. It must be remembered that a supervisor cannot avoid responsibility through delegation.

2. Much harm can be done if a supervisor delegates to subordinates tasks that are beyond the present capacity of the employee to perform properly.

3. Supervisors should never delegate tasks that should only be performed by the supervisor. For example, administering negative discipline is simply not something that should be delegated.

EXAMATOPICS ABOUT DELEGATION OF AUTHORITY

1. The process of delegation is an excellent tool for developing workers for positions of greater responsibility.

2. The general rule for delegation is that all tasks in an organization should be delegated to the lowest level in the organization in which the ability to perform the tasks properly exists.

3. Continued willingness to perform delegated tasks depends to a large degree on the supervisor giving credit to the worker for a job well done.

4. Follow-up on all delegations of authority is vital since the process of delegation loses its value as a supervisory device if inspections aren't made to check on the results of delegations.

5. Delegations can take the form of simple oral directions or can be made via complex written instructions, depending on the degree of complexity of the delegated task.

6. It is very important for a supervisor to include in all delegations clear and comprehensive instructions. If this is not done, it is not possible to hold a subordinate responsible for performing the delegated task.

7. Authority should always be commensurate with responsibility.

8. The principle of completed staff work requires that the person to whom work has been delegated complete the delegation. All the delegator has to do is to approve the work.

Building and Maintaining Morale

Morale is a much misunderstood concept. Contrary to popular belief, morale is distinct from job satisfaction. A person can have high job satisfaction but low morale, and vice versa. To understand how this can be, let's start with a working definition of morale, as follows.

Morale is a state of mind which reflects the degree to which a member of an organization has confidence in the organization and the other members of his work group; morale is also a reflection of the degree to which a worker believes in the objectives of the organization, and desires to accomplish them.

FACTORS THAT AFFECT MORALE

Morale can be thought of as a commitment to the efforts of the group. It is a shared feeling, but it is also a fluctuating condition. It might be high today and low tomorrow, and it is impacted on by a wide variety of stimuli. The kinds of things that affect morale are:

1. Quality of leadership

2. Salary levels and other remuneration received by workers, including fringe benefits

3. Level of discipline in the organization

4. Quality of supervision received

5. Opportunity for individual growth and promotion

6. Working conditions in general

CRITICAL FACTOR IN MORALE

For a long time it was believed that salary and working conditions were the most important determinants of productivity. However, the now famous Hawthorne Western Electric Plant study in 1927 gave the first indication that factors not related to working conditions affected productivity. More specifically, it was determined that morale and motivation were so important to productivity that they overshadowed the influence of working conditions on productivity. This finding led to a comprehensive effort to determine what exactly determines the level of morale in an organization, which in turn resulted in the above listing of factors that affect morale. It is very important to note, however, that it is now generally agreed that the critical factor in the development of employee morale is the quality of supervision received.

HOW IS MORALE MEASURED?

Since morale is dependent on a number of somewhat independent factors, it is difficult, if not impossible, to measure the exact level of morale at any given time in an organization. This is especially true when you consider that one ill-conceived act of supervision or some other act of unfairness can adversely affect the level of morale almost immediately. Just the same, morale can be measured in a broad framework, and the measuring criteria include the following:

1. Quality and quantity of work performed

2. Absentee rates

3. Volume of negative disciplinary actions taken

4. The number of grievances reported

5. Group cohesiveness

6. General appearance of personnel

7. Accident rates

8. Attitudes toward the leadership and goals of the group

HOW THE SERGEANT CAN BUILD MORALE

Remember, we stated above that the critical factor in the development of employee morale is the quality of supervision. The sergeant in a police department, therefore, plays a major role in building and maintaining morale. Following are some strategies the sergeant can utilize to fulfill this role.

1. Administer discipline in a fair and impartial manner.

2. Praise workers in public, and criticize them in private.

3. Always recognize good performance.

4. Provide employees with an opportunity for individual growth.

5. When possible, explain the reasons for department policies and procedures.

6. Distribute work fairly and equitably.

EXAMATOPICS ABOUT MORALE

1. Workers with low job satisfaction can still share in high group morale if they believe their interests are compatible with those of the group.

2. Morale is dependent on day-to-day working conditions.

3. A supervisor's ability to be objective, fair, and impartial is closely related to the ability to build and maintain high morale.

4. A supervisor should be constantly aware that all workers have the need for recognition, opportunity, belonging, and security.

5. A supervisor should not become involved in the private problems of subordinates unless so requested or unless the problems interfere with the quality of the subordinate's job performance.

6. A supervisor must consider the needs of the group as well as those of the individual.

7. Extremely close supervision of routine tasks inhibits the exercise of independent thought and action.

8. The major advantage of "job enlargement" is that it increases a worker's job satisfaction.

9. The most effective method of building morale in a new employee is to give sincere praise whenever possible; however, high praise for mediocre performance is damaging in the long run.

Practice Exercises

You are now ready to do some practice questions. Always try to answer the questions in the allotted time. After completing each of the three groups of questions, make sure you thoroughly review the explanation for each answer before going to the next set of questions. This includes reviewing the explanations for all questions, those you answered correctly and those you answered incorrectly. This is done to ensure that you always arrive at the correct choice for the right reasons. Remember, now is the time to make mistakes. If you understand why you made a mistake, you should not make the same mistake on the examination, when it really counts.

GROUP ONE—10 QUESTIONS—15 MINUTES

1. There is a fairly standardized approach to handling grievances. Of the following four steps in a typical approach to handling of grievances, which of the following would be the second step?

A. Follow-up action
B. Obtaining the facts
C. Receiving the complaint
D. Action phase

2. Supervisory actions often include the delegation of tasks to others. Supervisors with certain leadership styles delegate more freely than those with different styles. In which of the following styles of leadership would a police sergeant be most likely to delegate freely to subordinates?
A. Laissez-faire
B. Authoritarian
C. Autocratic
D. Democratic

3. Sergeant Nolan has the practice of praising officers only whenever he is about to criticize them. Such a practice is:
A. Good, because praise should be mixed with criticism
B. Good, because it shows that the sergeant is not solely a negative force
C. Bad, because praise should follow, not precede criticism
D. Bad, because praise will tend not to be heard as the expected criticism is awaited

4. Experts in the field of administration have debated the differences between supervision and management. Perhaps the most marked distinction between supervision and management is that supervision:
A. Is more directly involved with a profit motive
B. Is only concerned with people
C. Has people as its major concern
D. Has to coordinate tasks between major units of the organization

5. Police administrators are constantly striving to identify the determinants of good police morale. It has been suggested that many factors bring about good employee morale. Which of the following is usually seen as the most important factor in determining employee morale?
A. The proper supervision of the work force
B. Higher pay
C. Liberal fringe benefits
D. Formal grievance machinery

6. Consider the following statements concerning order giving in a police department.
   (1) One of the main reasons for establishing rules and procedures in a police agency is to ensure uniform practices and increase efficiency.
   (2) When a sergeant indicates that an order is "just for the record," the police officers receiving the order will be uncertain about whether to carry it out.
   (3) Sergeants who constantly call for volunteers are not carrying out one of their major responsibilities.

   Based on the above, which of the following is most correct?
   A. Only one of the statements is correct.
   B. Only two of the statements are correct.
   C. All the statements are correct.
   D. All the statements are incorrect.

7. When supervisors are caught between representing the work group they supervise and representing the management, it is recommended that the supervisors act objectively. If the supervisors act subjectively, it is believed that they:
   A. Will be damaged but only in the eyes of the work group
   B. Will be damaged but only in the eyes of management
   C. Will be damaged in the eyes of the work group or management but never over the same incident
   D. Could be damaged in the eyes of both the work group and management at the same time over the same incident

8. A certain police sergeant makes the following statement to subordinates during a training session: "Authority should be commensurate with responsibility when an employee is given a job to do." This statement is:
   A. Correct, because if employees will be held responsible for their actions, they should have the authority to do the job
   B. Incorrect, because a sergeant should never give up any authority

C. Correct, because there are times when the sergeant will delegate all authority and responsibility to an employee
D. Incorrect, because to do so over a sustained period will cause an erosion of the sergeant's official position

9. When Sergeant Norris goes on patrol she takes along a memorandum book. Anytime it becomes necessary to give a strong reprimand to a police officer, the sergeant makes a notation in the book a short time afterward. This practice is:
A. Good, since the police officers will work harder to keep out of the sergeant's book
B. Bad, since the police officers could come to resent this practice
C. Good, since the sergeant will have documented information that can be utilized for making disciplinary decisions in the future
D. Bad, since the book could be lost and fall into the wrong hands

10. Although the police sergeant has a definite responsibility to take necessary disciplinary action against subordinates, it goes a little farther than that. Actually, part of the sergeant's job is to try to reduce the number of formal disciplinary cases. Experts have stated that all the following are factors that can reduce formal disciplinary cases, except which?
A. Continual on-the-job training
B. A formal, on-going personnel evaluation system
C. Transfer of employees with disciplinary problems
D. Counseling employees who indicate they require assistance

GROUP TWO—10 QUESTIONS—15 MINUTES

11. In most police agencies, assignments to supervisory positions are made from within the agency through various selection procedures. The most difficult adjustment an individual has to make in ascending the promotion ladder in a police department is going from the rank of:

A. Police officer to sergeant, because of the ambivalent role of the sergeant
B. Police sergeant to lieutenant, because a lieutenant is responsible for other supervisors
C. Police lieutenant to captain, because the captain is usually responsible for entire precincts or districts
D. Police captains to higher ranks, because the interaction with the community becomes more complex

12. A certain police department has a policy of not allowing their supervisors to delegate authority. This policy is not without consequence. The failure to delegate authority in a police agency will most probably result in:
   A. Bringing an inordinate number of small problems to the higher levels of the department for resolution.
   B. Preventing officers from performing any of their routine functions
   C. An increase in the decision-making process at the level of operations
   D. Impeding the flow of information

13. Consider the following statements as they relate to police discipline.
   (1) Discipline grows from the bottom of an organization upward to the top.
   (2) A newly promoted sergeant should realize that discipline, unfortunately, is always negative in nature.
   (3) The most important link in any disciplinary system is the commanding officer of the unit.
   Based on the above, which of the following choices is most accurate?
   A. All the statements are false.
   B. Only statements 1 and 2 are false.
   C. Only statements 2 and 3 are false.
   D. Only statements 1 and 3 are false.

14. Sergeant Lotto is in charge of a group of uniform police officers. A certain police officer in his squad tells the sergeant that she, the officer, does not agree with a procedure the sergeant has indicated should be followed in performing a specific task. The sergeant should tell the officer that:

A. The procedure involved has been in place for many years and has worked successfully

B. The officer is obligated to follow specific instructions in the same manner as the sergeant

C. He will look into the officer's comments and get back to her at a later date

D. Police work is best carried out in the framework of a semimilitary organization in which directives are not questioned

15. A police officer whom you supervise comes to you complaining that some unknown officers in his squad play practical jokes on him while he is at work. In this case you should as sergeant:

A. Write a memo directing that this practice stop immediately

B. Bring the matter to the attention of the commanding officer

C. Not get involved since it is apparently strictly a personal matter

D. Attempt to ascertain who is responsible for these actions and ascertain if possible disciplinary action is needed

16. In the police supervisory process, there is one key element. Which of the following most closely indicates that element?

A. A good grasp of substantive and procedural law

B. A firm understanding on the part of subordinates that a supervisor is not afraid to back them in any instance

C. A good relationship with people

D. The ability to get a job done at any cost

17. A supervisor must be aware that motives and incentives influence an employee's performance. In a supervisor's role of dealing with subordinates, he/she must recognize the difference between motives and incentives. Which of the following best describes the relationship between them?

A. Motives are narrower than incentives and not related.

B. Incentives are narrower than motives and not related.

C. Motives are related to incentives but are broader.

D. Incentives are related to motives but are broader.

18. In making a comparison of first-line police supervisors with first-line supervisors in a non-police agency, certain findings are evident. A first-line police supervisor compared to a counterpart in private industry is:
   A. More dependent on the ability to motivate workers
   B. Less dependent on the ability to motivate workers due to the quasi-military nature of police agencies
   C. Equally dependent on the ability to motivate workers
   D. Woefully lacking when one considers the police supervisor's ability to motivate workers

19. Raising the morale of an individual often requires change on the part of the individual. In bringing about this change in the individual, it would be most accurate to state that the change:
   A. Must be sparked by a system of rewards and punishments
   B. Must involve increasing some facet of technical knowledge
   C. Must be seen as important by the individual
   D. Will be most lasting if carefully maneuvered by the supervisor

20. Much of the work of a police department is accomplished through order giving at the level of operation. Concerning order giving, at the point when a police sergeant gives an order to a police officer, the sergeant's job is:
   A. Completed, since it is the police officer's role to actually do the job
   B. Not completed, since the sergeant must now follow up to ensure the job is done correctly
   C. Completed, as long as the order was clear and concise
   D. Not completed, but only if the police officer is newly appointed to the agency

GROUP THREE—10 QUESTIONS—
15 MINUTES

21. When a police officer is promoted to the rank of sergeant, the newly promoted sergeant learns of the ambivalent role of a police supervisor. Actually, more than any other police supervisor, the police sergeant has this ambivalent role. This is so because the police sergeant:
    A. Has a personal and professional life
    B. Has political views that may differ from the organization's political policies
    C. Wants to be personally recognized while recognizing the need for organizational teamwork
    D. Personally wants to be a member of the work unit while simultaneously having to supervise that group

22. Sergeant Cotter is conducting a formal course for police officers who are about to be promoted to sergeant. Cotter warns the trainees of certain errors made by newly promoted sergeants. For example, one of the most common errors made by newly appointed sergeants is the tendency to delegate:
    A. Too much authority and expect the officers under their supervision to do too much
    B. Too little authority and try to do everything themselves
    C. All assignments and fail to follow up properly
    D. Work to others of equal rank in an attempt to establish lateral cooperation

23. One of the responsibilities a supervisor cannot delegate is in the area of discipline. A supervisor should have a complete understanding of the disciplinary process. Which of the following should a police sergeant recognize as most correct concerning the issue of discipline?
    A. If discipline is not severe, it serves little or no purpose.
    B. A supervisor should act immediately in a disciplinary situation even if the supervisor is angry.

C. Sometimes discipline should be delayed so that it will have a greater impact on the violator.
D. The reason an employee is disciplined should be made clear.

24. In a certain police department, there exists a strong police union. In that same department, the sergeants are generally characterized as strong supervisors. The most likely explanation for this is that:
A. Employee input into the decision-making process is limited
B. The chief of the department probably always backs the sergeants
C. The sergeants must be prepared to stand behind their positions in a face-to-face exchange of views
D. Most of the sergeants used to be part of the police union as police officers

25. Sergeant Orgin maintains an "open door" policy with the officers in his squad. This practice is:
A. Good, because the officers will like him better
B. Not good, because it is too time-consuming
C. Good, because it has the potential of nipping supervisory problems in the bud
D. Not good, because it encourages frivolous complaints

26. One of the needs of a worker is security in the belief that the supervisor supports him. A certain police sergeant always backs his officers in any situation. The sergeant's actions are:
A. Correct, since he will always receive the support of the officers in return
B. Incorrect, since there are times when he should not back his officers
C. Correct, since the officers will be more productive because of their recognition of the sergeant's support
D. Incorrect, since it is not ever the job of a sergeant to back his officers

27. Sergeant Smith has been given an unpopular directive by the captain to be read to the police officers at roll call. Sergeant Smith should:
    A. Not read the directive and advise the captain that the directive is unpopular
    B. Read the directive as if it emanated from himself/herself
    C. Read the directive but make a point that it comes from the captain
    D. Not read the directive but put it on the bulletin board

28. Understanding the causes of and results gained from good morale in the workplace can aid the police supervisor in obtaining, retaining, and utilizing good morale. A police sergeant should recognize that a squad of police officers with high morale would most likely have all of the following characteristics, except:
    A. Total satisfaction with their individual assignments and tasks
    B. Group cohesiveness
    C. Positive views of leadership
    D. Positive attitudes toward the continuation of the group

29. The amount of explanation of details that should accompany an order is most influenced by which of the following?
    A. Complexity of the job and the previous experience of the employee
    B. Complexity of the job and the previous experience of the supervisor
    C. Employees' feelings toward being told exactly what to do
    D. Morale of the officer receiving the order

30. Captain Pulver tells Sergeant Evers that the sergeant is to select a police officer assigned to the sergeant's squad to perform some task. The task must be completed as soon as possible. Sergeant Evers issues an order that requires prompt obedience. Which type of order should he issue?
    A. Implied order
    B. Direct order
    C. Quick call for volunteers
    D. Request

Answer Key

1. B	7. D	13. A	19. C	25. C
2. D	8. A	14. C	20. B	26. B
3. D	9. C	15. D	21. D	27. B
4. C	10. C	16. C	22. B	28. A
5. A	11. A	17. C	23. D	29. A
6. C	12. A	18. A	24. C	30. B

Answer Explanations

GROUP ONE

1. **B** The correct order of the four-step procedure to handle grievances is as follows. (1) Receive the complaint; (2) Obtain the facts; (3) Take remedial action as part of an "action phase"; (4) Follow up.

2. **D** Delegation more common with the democratic style of leadership. A democratic leader also encourages subordinates to participate more in the decision-making process.

3. **D** Officers will be conditioned to wait for the "other shoe" to drop if the only time they are praised is when they are about to be criticized. Remember, however, that when praise is deserved, it should be given. And as a general rule you "praise in public and criticize in private."

4. **C** The major, but not the only, concern of supervision is people, and this is probably the biggest distinction between supervision and management.

5. **A** There is no substitute for proper supervision. It is the most important factor in bringing about good morale.

6. **C** All the statements are correct. A sergeant should not consistently ask for volunteers; it is the supervisor's job to direct people to do the job. Also, a boss who says, "This is just for the record," confuses the worker, who is then unsure if the order should or should not be followed.

7. **D** Both management and the work group sincerely expect the supervisor to be objective. When the supervisor fails, he/she could disappoint both groups.

8. **A** Although the sergeant is still accountable for the completion of the job, the employee needs the tools (the authority) to get the job done.

9. **C** In any disciplinary action facts are vital, and properly recording the facts to document the necessity for future actions is a recommended strategy.

10. **C** The only possible time when a transfer should be considered as a resolution of a disciplinary matter is when a personal conflict between a supervisor and an employee has led to the disciplinary problem.

GROUP TWO

11. **A** The sergeant has ties to the work group and subordinates and also represents the interests of management.

12. **A** If an employee does not have the authority to make decisions because he/she was not delegated that authority, then the decisions must be made at the higher levels of the department, even those decisions relating to small problems. The other results of failure to delegate are that routine jobs continue to get done and information would still flow, but there would not be widespread decision making.

13. **A** Discipline grows from the command level downward, but the sergeant or first-line supervisor is key since he/she is at the level of operations where policies are put into action. Also, discipline can be positive or negative. Therefore, all the statements are false.

14. **C** The complaint of the officer should be examined. Aside from showing interest in the officer's suggestion, looking into it might also result in a real gain for the agency.

15. **D** The sergeant should recognize that he should try to handle this grievance and that it is not strictly a personal matter because it is happening at work.

16. **C** A supervisor certainly must know the law but is not expected to back improper conduct. Also, a job should be done not at any cost but efficiently and economically. A good relationship with people is the true key element of supervision.

17. **C** Motives are related to incentives but are much broader. Incentives are specific ways of satisfying motives. If a police officer was motivated to become a detective, an incentive for that officer would be an opportunity to attend an investigative course.

18. **A** The increased dependency on motivation stems from the limited awards a police supervisor can give an employee in a civil service system. The most obvious example is in the area of salary. Quite often, supervisors in private industry control salary scales. In civil service positions, salary is a negotiated item and is relatively the same for all police officers in the same department.

19. **C** People will not change unless they see the need for it.

20. **B** Follow-up, although to a lesser degree, is needed for veterans as well as new recruits. Without follow-up, the sergeant cannot be sure if he/she met the final responsibility to make sure the job was done.

GROUP THREE

21. **D** The police sergeant's ambivalent role refers to the fact that the sergeant works with the officers and yet represents management to the officers while at the same time representing the officers to management.

22. **B** The tendency of newly promoted sergeants is to delegate too little authority and try to do everything themselves. As they mature, they learn to delegate. However, not all assignments can be properly delegated. Certain functions, such as planning, are inappropriate for delegation. Also, work cannot be delegated to peers.

23. **D** Discipline need not be severe. Although it should be sure and swift, it is not advisable to take disciplinary action while you are angry. On the other hand, too much of a delay before taking action lessens the impact on the violator. Actually, the employee tends to forget why he/she is being disciplined, which underlies the principles that, when disciplining a worker, the supervisor should make clear the reason for the action.

24. **C** This would obviously take place in an agency where the police officers are strongly represented by a police union; that is, the sergeants would have to be prepared to defend the positions and actions they take against union grievances.

25. **C** An open-door policy keeps the lines of communication open and free flowing, which is essential to prevent problems and eliminate those that do occur promptly.

26. **B**   A sergeant cannot always back the officers. An example would be when an officer engages in misconduct. The sergeant would not be expected to support misconduct.

27. **B**   The sergeant should support the captain since, although the directive is unpopular, it may not be improper. If, prior to the establishment of a policy or a procedure, a sergeant believes something is wrong with it, then he/she should communicate these views through the chain of command. Once, however, a decision is made to implement the policy or procedure, despite the sergeant's objections, the sergeant is obligated to support it as if it emanated from himself/herself.

28. **A**   Morale and job satisfaction are not always present together. A police officer could have high morale and low job satisfaction with an individual assignment and task. The reverse is also true; an officer can have low morale but be quite satisfied with the job.

29. **A**   These two combined factors more than any others will dictate the amount of explanatory details required in an order: that is, how complex is the job, and what is the previous experience of the employee.

30. **B**   Direct orders require prompt obedience. In a police department, which is a quasi-military organization, there are times when prompt obedience is a necessity. These are the times when direct orders must be used.

CHAPTER 6

Training and Safety

In theory, any job-related problems are an indication that management has failed to provide adequate training. The importance management attaches to the training function, the quality and extent of a police department's training program, and the ability of first-line supervisors to meet their training responsibilities are all excellent barometers of the potential for police misconduct and of the quality of service delivered to the community. It has been demonstrated time and again that highly productive employees receive more and better training, and the type of training they receive impacts on their sense of personal worth. As mentioned previously, when employees are allowed to engage in activities they perceive as contributing to their personal development, the agency also benefits.

What Is Training?

A typical definition of training is as follows:

> *Training* is a process by which employees are aided by their employing agency to become more proficient at their jobs through the development of proper attitudes, required skills, and necessary knowledge.

It must be noted, however, that unless the attitude, skills, and knowledge developed by an agency's training program are utilized by employees after their development, then training is not taking place. In other words, for training to be effective, there must be a transfer of attitudes, skills, and knowledge developed by the training to the actual working environment. It is also important to note that training must include agency involvement; unaided self-improvement efforts by individual employees is not training. Furthermore, the newly acquired attitudes, skills, and knowledge must be required by the employer. If there is only a slight chance that the training will be helpful on the job, then the training has little if any value. Training must be job related. Otherwise, it is counterproductive.

WHO IS THE KEY FIGURE IN THE TRAINING PROCESS?

Without question, the most important person in the training process is the first-line supervisor. In a police department this is, of course, the sergeant. The police sergeant has a grave responsibility to train subordinates. Inherent in this responsibility is the need to become familiar with the principles of learning and teaching that have been so successfully developed by professional educators as well as psychologists. These principles are addressed later in this chapter. Remember, it is well established that the success of a training effort is rarely dependent on the efforts of the learner alone. The instructor must assume a major portion of that responsibility. Supervisors are obligated, therefore, to make themselves proficient trainers. For all of these reasons, a police sergeant should look upon teaching and training as normal supervisory activities.

IS TRAINING A CONSTANT PROCESS?

There is literally no end to the need for training. It is a continuous process that should permeate all officer-sergeant encounters. To think of training as something that occurs only in a formal setting is inaccurate thinking. Training is an informal as well as a formal process. The need for constant training is found in the extremely dynamic nature of the police profession. Laws, for example, change much more frequently than the average person supposes. A single significant Supreme Court decision, and there are many each term, requires that the nation's hundreds of thousands of police officers be retrained. The requirement to keep pace with the constitutional law is heightened by a court ruling that individual officers are required to be current concerning procedural and substantive law. Ignorance of the law does not exempt police officers from civil liability. The law is only one example of the changing nature of police work. It has become axiomatic that the need for training of police officers is as great as the need for police officers.

EXAMATOPICS ABOUT THE MEANING AND PURPOSE OF TRAINING

1. The best training takes place when employees actively participate in the training process.

2. Training must be useful in an employee's present or planned work assignment.

3. The aim of training programs is to improve attitudes, develop skills, and impart knowledge.

4. Training is more effective when the actual learning phase is followed by an application phase.

5. A supervisor should recognize the wants and interests of subordinates and attempt to satisfy them whenever possible.

6. Morale benefits when workers realize that their supervisor cares enough about them to train them properly.

7. Training reduces the necessity for direct orders to subordinates, thereby facilitating the supervisor's job.

8. Supervisors must constantly attempt to create an appropriate "climate" for learning.

9. Training failures can often be traced to neglect by management to impart to supervisors the importance of the training function through actions rather than words; far too often, when fiscal problems appear, the training function is the first to suffer.

10. Supervisors need training in the art of training.

11. A good training program, over the long haul, is a cost-effective venture since it can raise morale, prevent waste and errors, and, very importantly, minimize punitive damages from civil actions.

Types of Police Training

As mentioned above, the need for police training is never ending. It follows, therefore, that on-the-job training is an important ingredient in the overall training process. On the other hand, a police agency that relies exclusively on the *ad hoc* training that takes place in the street between the sergeant and the police officer is evading training responsibilities. Throughout their careers, police officers should be subjected to a blend of formal and informal training, which can range from attending a college credit course at an accredited university to receiving instructions from a sergeant in a street situation.

Most police experts agree that there are six distinct types of police training:

1. Recruit training

2. Formal in-service training

3. Roll call training

4. On-the-job training

5. Specialized training

6. Supervisory and management training

RECRUIT TRAINING

It is widely accepted that nothing in the entire selection process has a greater impact on the newly hired police officer than the content and conduct of recruit training. Unfortunately, some recruit training curricula do not realistically prepare the rookie police officer for street duty. The cause for this is that far too many police departments allow the recruit training process (and other training as well) to become static. The content matter of all training programs, especially recruit training, needs continual re-examination. The best way to assume that the content matter taught in recruit school meets the needs of the department is to examine the role and function of operational police officers on a regular basis. The idea is to perform a thorough job analysis and then determine what attitudes, skills, and knowledge are needed to perform the police officer's job successfully. Once identified, these are the attitudes, skills, and knowledge that must be identified during recruit training.

FORMAL IN-SERVICE TRAINING

We like to differentiate between formal in-service training programs and roll call training. Technically they both qualify as in-service training, but each has a different objective. Formal in-service training programs are often held away from the patrol officer's base of operations—either in a classroom setting or at the police firing range. Proactive planning should be used when determining the subject matter of formal in-service training programs. And although everyone in a department may need on a regular basis certain in-service training, such as firearms training and first aid refresher courses, not everyone needs exactly the same in-service courses. Officers working in different capacities, such as patrol, investigations, and traffic, have different training needs.

ROLL CALL TRAINING

Roll call training and on-the-job training are the two areas in which the police sergeant serves as the primary instructor. Typically, as the name implies, roll call training is held at the beginning of a tour when the roll is called. It generally lasts for about five to twenty minutes. One constant element in all roll call training is the briefing of the ongoing platoon concerning current problems, recent procedural changes, new laws, and other matters. A wise supervisor, however, in keeping with the principle of repetition, should use some roll call training time to review long-standing, but important, procedures, policies, and laws. It is also very important to remember that, although roll call training has great value, it must be supplemented by a program of formal in-service training.

ON-THE-JOB TRAINING

This type of training, unfortunately, is improperly named. It should be called on-the-job-site training. The great majority of police training takes place when on duty or on the job, but this type of training is one-on-one training given by the first-line supervisor while the job is actually being performed. This is the area in which a conscientious police sergeant can make the greatest impact. If training is to be effective it must be continuous, and it is on-the-job training that allows training to be continuous. The sergeant must remember, however, that teaching is a form of positive discipline and as such should be performed in a positive manner. There should be no negative connotations involved with correcting a field officer's mistakes if they are not intentional.

SPECIALIZED TRAINING

Certain skills are needed by all police departments, but not frequently enough to train more than a few "specialists." Besides, specialized training is usually very expensive, so expensive that these specialists are usually not found in smaller police departments. Instead, these smaller departments usually "borrow" or contract for the services from larger departments, usually the state police. A good example of an area in which specialized training takes place is the forensic sciences.

SUPERVISORY AND MANAGEMENT TRAINING

Progressive police administrators now realize that good street cops do not automatically make good supervisors or managers. Therefore, all police agencies need some form of management training to properly equip newly promoted officers to function effectively in their new rank. The smaller departments seek this training from outside agencies; larger departments develop an internal supervisory or management training capacity.

1. Police administrators are recognizing the importance of training supervisors to make early identification of problem employees, such as the drinker or the drug user.

2. Police supervisors need training in counseling and human relations.

3. In-service training should be people oriented and based on observed needs.

4. Many police agencies have incorporated an assessment center into their personnel practice.

5. The assessment center approach provides a very good measurement of required attitudes and skills.

Discovering Training Needs

The first step in the development of any formal training program is the identification of training needs. Far too often this step is ignored or neglected, and the standard training courses are given on a continual basis, without regard to need. This, of course, is not the recommended strategy. For formal training to be fully cost effective, it must be given in areas of demonstrated needs.

It is generally agreed that the identification of training needs is a two-stage effort, as follows.

IDENTIFICATION OF GENERAL PROBLEMS

The first step in the identification of training needs is to find out what general problems exist in the overall operation of the unit, command, or department, whatever the case may be. An important tool in identifying these general problems is the inspections process, which is discussed in Chapter 7. Other ways to uncover general problem areas are

1. Supervisory observations

2. Methods analysis

3. Review of records and reports

4. Interviews with workers

DETERMINATION OF SPECIFIC NEEDS

Once areas are identified in which there are general problems, the second step in determining training needs is to find out specifically what is causing the general problems in each of the areas uncovered in the first step. This is accomplished in the following manner:

1. Find out what attitudes, skills, and knowledge are needed to successfully accomplish the task or tasks being examined. In other words, just what is necessary for the employee to perform effectively.

2. Determine what portion of the task the employees can perform at present in a satisfactory manner.

The difference between steps 1 and 2 is the training need. Written in formula equation, it would appear as follows:

Training needs = attitudes, skills, knowledge needed
− attitude, skills, knowledge possessed

EXAMATOPICS ABOUT DISCOVERING TRAINING NEEDS

1. When attempting to discover training needs, the opinions of employees are invaluable.

2. When determining the requirements of a job, consider the overall objectives of the job.

3. When evaluating employees' present abilities, observe them perform; test them, if necessary; and review the employees' personnel folders and past experience.

Planning Training Programs

Once a specific training need is identified, effective planning for a formal training program to meet the identified need includes the following steps.

Stating the objectives of the training. This is no more than a specific written declaration of what the results of the training are expected to be.

Selecting the instructor. It is not true that expertise is the only factor to consider when selecting an instructor. A good teacher must be familiar with the recognized techniques of instruction. Although training is an integral part of every supervisor's job, not all supervisors perform the function equally well. A formal training program, with its concomitant expenditure of time and resources, however, requires careful selection of the most qualified instructor.

Selecting the participants. Unless universal training is required, the selection of the trainees should be done carefully. It is very important to consider availability of expertise. Since policing is a twenty-four-hour-a-day occupation, care must be taken to select trainees so that the expertise developed is available when needed. So, for example, personnel from all shifts must be trained if it is determined that the need is present on all shifts. Also, expertise should be spread among a number of officers, rather than concentrated in a few. It is not wise to intentionally develop a small cadre of indispensable workers if it can be avoided. When selecting personnel for extensive training, consideration must be given to the likelihood that the trainees will stay with the organization. Those at or close to retirement age, for example, should not be selected unless they agree to remain for a certain minimum period of time.

Availability of alternatives to department training. Before committing department resources to large-scale formal training, consideration should be given to finding a suitable alternative method of delivering the needed training. Regional training sites, state police training, university-level training, and federal training institutions should all be considered.

Selecting the proper location. The training environment should be conducive to learning. The site should be free of distractions and interruptions. Naturally, the physical conditions, such as lighting and ventilation, should be adequate.

Time of training. As a general rule, training should be conducted during working hours and during periods when the demand for police service is minimal.

Testing. Some mechanism should be developed to ensure that the trainees have acquired the desired attitudes, skills, and knowledge the training program was designed to impart.

Evaluation. The trainees should always be given the opportunity to evaluate formal training programs with an eye toward continuous improvement.

Follow-up. No formal training program should be planned without a follow-up to ensure that the expertise developed during the program is actually used on the job. Unless this occurs, the training was wasted.

1. In-service training programs are needed primarily because personnel must be kept abreast of changes in the law and changes in policies and procedures.

2. An absence of questions from the trainees during a training session does not necessarily indicate understanding; instead, it may be indicative of a lack of understanding and/or interest, or it could be a sign of intimidation.

3. Someone with considerable expertise in a subject does not necessarily have the ability to transfer that expertise to others in the capacity of a teacher or trainer.

4. A demonstrated desire to attend a training session is preferred over mandatory attendance.

5. As a general rule, ordering employees to attend training sessions is not recommended; this is so because optimum learning occurs only with highly motivated students.

Understanding the Learning Process

As previously mentioned, the first-line supervisor is the most important cog in a police department's training machinery. Expertise alone is not enough, however. To fulfill training responsibilities adequately, a police sergeant must study the learning process.

LEARNING IS CHANGE

We often train employees to change their old way of doing things in favor of more effective methods. However, people resist change. This is so in part because there is a certain degree of social condemnation associated with change. Another reason is that it requires effort to change and the reason for a change is often not apparent. For this reason, a supervisor performing his/her training function should understand that many workers view change as threatening. Therefore, it is important to explain thoroughly the need for the change. Ideally, prior concurrences concerning the need for change were obtained from the work group when the training need was discovered. In any case, it is vital that the reason for any change be thoroughly explained and, when possible, adequately documented. If the employee can be convinced that change is needed, the learning process is significantly aided.

PRINCIPLE OF READINESS

Learning occurs most efficiently when the trainee has an attitude that is favorable to learning. This is why volunteers are preferred over students who are compelled to attend training programs. One of the primary responsibilities of a trainer in any setting, including a police sergeant in a one-on-one street situation with an officer who needs instruction, is to create, insofar as possible, the proper climate for learning. More than anything else this means stimulating or motivating learners so that they will want to learn. One way of doing this is by emphasizing personal gains that could result from increased expertise.

PRINCIPLE OF EFFECT

When learning takes place and the learners feel they are in fact learning, the potential for additional learning is enhanced. Success in learning is, to many, very pleasing and satisfying. On the other hand, failure to learn causes unpleasant feelings and tends to stifle the learning process. For this reason, it is recommended that, whenever possible, learning take place in stages. Each separate task in an operation, for example, should be taught in its proper sequence and understood before going on to the next task. In this way, the learner can experience a sense of achievement, which should in turn create a desire for even more success, which is then translated into more learning.

PRINCIPLE OF REPETITION

This is a principle that not only applies in a classroom session but also has application for all supervisors when they perform their daily training function. The principle of repetition provides that

1. Repetition builds habits.

2. Good habits lead to success.

3. Success causes a feeling of satisfaction.

4. The feeling of satisfaction leads to a desire to engage in repetition, which takes us back to step 1.

A good supervisor or instructor will be guided, therefore, by the age-old Latin adage, *repetitio est marcus studiorum* (Repetition is the soul of learning). Patrol sergeants should realize, however, that everyone forgets in varying degrees with the passage of time. Therefore, it is imperative that the patrol officers under their supervision be periodically exposed to vital training material.

EXAMATOPICS ABOUT THE LEARNING PROCESS

1. A teacher should always relate new material with material already learned: Relate the unknown to the known.

2. A trainee's learning rate is affected by a number of factors, principal among which are the learner's past experience and training, which is known in textbooks as the learner's *apperceptive base*.

3. The learning process involves communicating with all five senses; however, sight and hearing are the most useful senses in the learning process.

4. Demonstration is not enough to ensure learning although it is an effective technique.

5. Training is more effective when the trainee is given an opportunity to relate back to the trainer what has been learned.

6. Sometimes, a teacher's expertise makes it difficult to see the training material from the learner's point of view.

7. A trainer is often faced with the difficulty of keeping pace with the fast learners while meeting the needs of the slow learner.

8. A good teacher has different teaching strategies to deal with various situations. Sometimes being very demanding, for example, works well. In other situations it is not effective.

9. Patience and understanding are essential qualities of a competent instructor.

10. A good training technique in the development of a manual skill is repeated practice.

11. Trial-and-error training is ineffectual and expensive.

12. Training is ineffective if it does not provide for a transfer of attitudes, skills, and knowledge to the job situation. Knowing is not enough; application is required for success.

13. Training is a continuous process.

Methods of Instruction

Once a supervisor or instructor decides on or is assigned a subject for presentation in a formal in-service training environment, specific and general objectives must be developed. Specific objectives are the milestones along the way to the general objectives. They are goals to be reached in the various segments of the overall presentation or lesson. All of the specific objectives are designed to obtain the general or overall objectives of the training. General objectives, therefore, relate to the bottom-line reasons for the training. Or put another way, the general objective of any training program is to deal with a specific training need, which has already been identified.

THE LESSON PLAN

All formal in-service training sessions should be based on written lesson plans. Lesson plans, although necessary, do not have to be complex. Instead, they need only be simple sequential listings of the instructional steps to be followed. It is important that the lesson plan be arranged in a logical manner. Experienced instructors understand the value of "interest arousers" and "tricks of the trade" and insert them liberally into the lesson plan. Also included in a lesson plan should be a number of practical examples to fortify more academic points. Any procedure that provides for student participation in the lesson is usually beneficial. It is important to note that a lesson plan should not be a verbatim recitation of information. The plan should be a guide to what will be said in the form of a series of notes. Finally, there is no one correct form for a lesson plan to take. It is a matter of individual choice and need.

THE FOUR-STEP METHOD OF INSTRUCTION

The four-step method of instruction is very valuable since it is appropriate for any type of instruction. This orderly procedure for imparting knowledge is equally effective in the street as in the classroom. The four steps of the classic procedure are

1. Preparation

2. Presentation

3. Application

4. Test and follow-up

PREPARATION

This first stop in this four-step instructional process is perhaps the most critical. If the learner is not properly prepared to learn, what follows is seldom productive. The preparation step is closely related to the learning principle of readiness, already discussed. That principle, in effect, says that if the learner's mind is receptive to learning, then learning will in fact take place. Remember, one of the surest ways of creating learner interest is to convince the student that learning the particular lesson involved represents a personal benefit for him/her. Other ways to effectively prepare a trainee to learn are as follows:

1. Put the trainees at ease; assure them that the lesson can be mastered.

2. Relate personal or practical examples to emphasize the importance of the lesson.

3. Get the students involved in the discussion from the beginning.

4. Relate the task being learned to the entire operation.

PRESENTATION

In this step the objective is to impart new attitudes, skills, and knowledge or to refresh a student's memory about those already learned (remember the importance of the principle of repetition). Every attempt should be made to relate new materials to material already known. During the presentation it is important to achieve all of your specific objectives. Explain, demonstrate (if only by example), and question. Definitely don't do all the talking. Bear in mind that understanding the "why" of a policy, procedure, or law assists the learning process greatly. Adjust your pace to accommodate the varying needs of the group.

APPLICATION

Remember that people learn by doing. In this stage of the process, the learner is presented with a real or simulated opportunity to apply what has been learned. Role playing is an excellent method to employ in the application phase of the instruction process. So is problem solving. Errors and omissions should be corrected as they occur. When correcting errors, remember:

1. Avoid criticism.

2. Compliment before you correct.

3. Don't overdo correction.

4. Self-correction by the learner is ideal.

5. Errors could just as well emanate from poor teaching as from anything else.

Most teachers know enough to criticize and correct mistakes. Too few teachers understand the very positive aspects of complimenting successful performance. Compliments encourage further learning, if they are sincere. Don't just compliment perfection; improvement also merits recognition.

TEST AND FOLLOW-UP

The fourth and last step in the instructional process is the test or follow-up stage. This step is not to be confused with the evaluation phase of the training process explained below. The "test" step requires an immediate evaluation of the learner's progress. Test questions should be related to more important aspects of the lesson. The test phase of the process is necessary because it lets the teacher know if the general and specific objectives of the training program are being met. Remember also that tests measure not only the learner's progress, but also the effectiveness of the teacher.

EXAMATOPICS ABOUT METHODS OF INSTRUCTION

1. The greater the interest of the learner, the easier it is to train.

2. A two-way discussion results in greater learning than a lecture.

3. Understanding the "why" of something accelerates the learning process.

4. People learn well when they learn by association. The more new material can be connected to things students already know, the more students will retain.

5. Quite often a teacher assumes that students know more than they actually do know.

6. It is a grave mistake to feign competency in front of in-service personnel; the truth is bound to come out.

7. The lecture method of teaching is overused and often ineffective.

8. A lack of questions does not always indicate that learning is taking place.

9. It is not unusual for students to think they understand even when they don't.

10. Instructional aids can be very useful but they should not be used instead of teaching; they should complement teaching.

Safety and the Police Supervisor

A significant training responsibility of police sergeants, especially when they are functioning as patrol supervisors, is to develop a safety consciousness among subordinates. It is well established that a concerted effort on the part of management can many times reduce the number of accidents involving not only the police but also the public. A positive concern for the safety of subordinates has a number of benefits, principal among which are:

1. Reduction of accidents, with their concomitant loss of life, injury, and property loss

2. Reduction of sick time and disability retirements

3. Increase in employee morale and motivation by virtue of the concern shown by the supervisor

4. A reduction in the number of court awards in negligence cases instituted against the agency

RECOMMENDED SAFETY PROGRAM

It is not enough to talk in vague terms about safety. A progressive police department should have a structured safety program, which should include the following:

1. A clearly worded written policy statement indicating management's position regarding safety and accident prevention.

2. A definite commitment by management to engage in an ongoing training and education effort to reduce accidents, which must include a defensive driving component.

3. Specific accountability for safety should be established. The commander in charge of personnel or training should have a major share of the responsibility.

4. A rating or evaluation system that includes a safety component is essential, especially for line personnel at the level of operations, plus their immediate supervisors, and most especially for line commanders.

5. A comprehensive reporting system that mandates investigations and recommendations whenever an accident occurs involving department personnel. Also required is in-depth analysis of all such reports.

6. A provision for employee input into the department's safety program. This strategy should include formal recognition for outstanding contributions.

EXAMATOPICS ABOUT SAFETY AND THE SUPERVISOR

1. Supervisors are obligated to set the proper climate for safety consciousness via personal example.

2. Accident investigations must always result in a cause of the accident being identified.

3. The primary objective of an accident investigation should not be to determine *who* caused the accident, but to ascertain *what* caused the accident and how a recurrence can be prevented.

Evaluating Training Programs

The real degree of success of a training program can't be measured until some time after the training has ended. This is so even if all the trainees have demonstrated that they absorbed the material taught. It is also true even if the trainees evaluated the program in glowing terms. Why is this so? Because gaining new attitudes, skills, and knowledge is just half the battle. In order for a training program to be successful, there must be a transfer of the newly acquired attitudes, skills, and knowledge to the work setting. Training is wasted if it doesn't have a positive impact on an employee's performance. Therefore, any attempt to evaluate the effectiveness of a training program without a follow-up field evaluation component is incomplete. Many times this evaluation can be made a part of the staff inspection function, which is covered in Chapter 7.

MORE EXAMATOPICS ABOUT TRAINING

1. Corruption control lends itself well to training. Specific examples of corruption, with the accompanying tragic aftermaths, can be presented in a workshop setting, such as an ethical awareness workshop.

2. A police officer who specializes in working with juveniles might require the most intensive training of all officers.

3. Considerable training resources should be expended to prepare police officers for the various human relations tasks they will be performing.

4. Training in communication skills should include a segment on understanding body language.

5. Police officers should be made aware of the extent of their liability in high-speed vehicle pursuit cases.

6. It is essential to have constant training concerning the lawful use of force and the law of arrest.

7. The public should be trained in crime prevention strategies.

8. Training for investigators should include a classroom component and field experience.

9. Untrained or under-trained jail personnel create a potentially dangerous condition.

Practice Exercises

You are now ready to do some practice questions. Always try to answer the questions in the allotted time. After completing each one of the three groups of questions, make sure you thoroughly review the explanation for each answer before going to the next set of questions. This includes reviewing the explanations for all questions, those you answered correctly and those you answered incorrectly. This is done to ensure that you always arrive at the correct choice for the right reasons. Remember, now is the time to make mistakes. If you understand why you made a mistake, you should not make the same mistake on the examination when it really counts.

GROUP ONE—10 QUESTIONS—15 MINUTES

1. Many police departments have what they believe is a safety program for their employees. How well it works is another issue. A good safety program should include all of the following except:
   A. A clear policy statement regarding safety on the part of management
   B. A designation of a department safety officer
   C. Fixed responsibility for safety solely as a function of a specialized staff unit
   D. An ongoing training and education program in safety

2. Although personnel management has come to be seen as a legitimate and necessary function in police departments, not all aspects of personnel management have received sufficient attention. One of the most frequently neglected areas of personnel management is:
   A. Budget management
   B. Evaluation procedures
   C. Safety and accident prevention
   D. Labor relations

3. In the learning process, lag periods or plateaus often occur. During these periods, it seems that little progress is made. Recognizing this, a trainer should:
   A. Attempt to schedule easier material during these periods
   B. Simply warn the learner that these periods do exist for all learners
   C. Attempt to encourage the learner during these periods
   D. Arrange the various training sessions so that these periods can be avoided

4. Different students learn at different rates depending on various conditions. An instructor would be recognizing a student's apperceptive base by engaging in which of the following actions?

A. Recognizing that a person's physical makeup affects learning

B. Understanding that the personality of an instructor is perceived differently by different students, who react to the instructor according to their own personalities

C. Repeating important points in a manner that firmly fixes main points in the student's mind

D. Linking new knowledge to old since the apperceptive base of the student represents the trainee's past training and experience

5. Different trainers use a variety of training modes. Which of the following is an accurate statement concerning the "sink or swim" method of training?

A. It is efficient since no scheduling time is expended for formal training.

B. It is quick since each person finds his/her method of performing each task.

C. It is inexpensive since no instructors are needed.

D. Its use sometimes indicates an area in which formal training should be given.

6. It is well understood that instruction is not totally a verbal effort. However, an instructor who wishes to draw a diagram while giving a lecture should be careful because of which of the following?

A. Most people do not draw well.

B. Everyone in the class may not have a clear view of the drawing.

C. It may tend to take away from the presentation.

D. Diagrams work well only if the audience has prior knowledge of the material.

7. A skilled instructor employs a variety of teaching techniques when instructing. Which of the following is the name of the technique that takes a question asked by one student and directs that same question to another student?

A. Overhead questions

B. Relay questions

C. The reverse question

D. The direct question

8. A certain sergeant has invited a group of officers to a training session at which the officers will be able to direct questions to a panel of experts. Which of the following is a disadvantage of such an arrangement?
    A. Not all of the officers will ask questions, and unless everyone participates, the session will not be cost effective.
    B. It is a costly training method and it tends to drift.
    C. It always results in one officer monopolizing the questioning process.
    D. The content matter of the training is limited to the information given out by the panel in response to questions asked.

9. Because lectures are used so often in training, police sergeants should be thoroughly familiar with the lecture method of training. Which of the following statements is the least accurate concerning the pure lecture method of training?
    A. Sometimes it is erroneously assumed that all attendees progress at the same rate.
    B. One long lecture is better than several short lectures.
    C. The lecture should be supplemented by some teaching aids.
    D. Some showmanship assists the lecture at times.

10. Sergeant Jones is giving a talk about the techniques of defensive driving. He would be most correct if he proceeded according to which of the following teaching sequences?
    A. From the safe to the hazardous areas of the subject
    B. From the hazardous to the safe areas of the subject
    C. In any sequence that best interests the audience
    D. In any sequence that is best for the sergeant's style of instruction

11. Training is not without its costs. If, however, the training is effective, the costs are worthwhile. Which of the following is most reflective of an effective training program?
    A. Increase in knowledge on the part of the learner in the subject taught
    B. Increase in the learner's ability to do the job being taught
    C. Change in the worker's attitude reflected by a change in work habits
    D. Feedback to the instructor so that future teaching efforts incorporate the true needs of the workers

12. Consider the following statements regarding police training.
    (1) A police sergeant who knows a job extremely well may not be qualified to teach the job.
    (2) An instructional aid, such as a statistical chart, should not be displayed to students until it is to be used in the training session.
    (3) Individual employees receive their most meaningful training at formal training sessions.
    Which of the following most accurately classifies the above statements into those that are accurate and those that are not?
    A. Only one of the statements is accurate.
    B. Only two of the statements are accurate.
    C. All of the statements are accurate.
    D. None of the statements is accurate.

13. Recruit training is often criticized by senior police officers. This stems from the fact that at times the best police student at a police academy does not become the best police officer in the field. This is mostly because of which of the following?
    A. People learn nothing about a job unless they actually do it.
    B. The job of a police officer cannot be taught at all in a formal setting.
    C. It is next to impossible to duplicate operating field situations in the classroom.
    D. Academics are overrated when it comes to police work.

14. A new procedure is to be established in a certain police department. It will be the job of each sergeant to instruct subordinates in this new procedure. In conducting the training, it would be most important for each sergeant to do which of the following as a first step in delivering this training?
   A. Present the material to the student.
   B. Prepare the student for training.
   C. Have the student attempt to apply the subject matter to field operations.
   D. Demonstrate the actual operation to be learned.

15. A sergeant in a certain police department has decided to train newly appointed police officers separately from experienced officers, even though the subject matter is the same. This practice is:
   A. Good, since in all likelihood different emphasis must be given to the subject matter for each group
   B. Bad, since it creates an artificial barrier between the two groups
   C. Good, since the newly appointed officers are probably better educated and are more receptive to training
   D. Bad, since the veteran officers' experience cannot be shared with the newly appointed officers

16. Police work, because of its dynamic and fast-changing nature, requires continuous training for the police. One vehicle used to provide this continuous training is in-service training. Ideally, in-service training in a police department should be:
   A. Proactive, production oriented, and based on individual need
   B. Reactive, people oriented, and based on the needs of the entire department
   C. Proactive, people oriented, and based on individual need
   D. Reactive, production oriented, and based on the needs of the entire department

17. From chief to recruit, all police personnel usually agree that officers should be trained in community relations. The disagreement arises over the issue of what should be part of this training. Ac-

cording to experts, which of the following should not be a component of a training course in police-community relations?

A. The geographic characteristics of the area
B. Exclusive use of police personnel as trainers, preferably those with field experience who can establish credibility with the officers
C. Talks by members of groups who may be seen as antipolice by police officers
D. Lectures by handicapped persons geared to better understand the problems of the handicapped

18. Becoming an effective trainer is a product of several factors. A supervisor desiring to become an effective trainer should understand that all of the following are essential to effective training except:

A. The trainer's general understanding of the steps in the learning process
B. A desire on the part of the trainer to improve training skills
C. How well the trainer knows the subject
D. Elaborate teaching aids

19. What is to be taught often determines how it is to be taught. Sergeant O'Neil is teaching a group of police recruits a complicated and lengthy operation. How should he teach the operation?

A. As a whole, in the same sequence as it will be performed in the field
B. As a whole, but with the hard steps first
C. In small steps with the hard steps first
D. In small steps in the same sequence as it will be performed in the field

20. In-service police training serves many purposes. However, the main purpose or reason for in-service police training is to:

A. Ensure that the police officers have not forgotten what they learned in their recruit days
B. Keep pace with the rapidly changing field of police work
C. Find out the officers' needs with respect to training
D. Identify those police officers who have promotional potential

GROUP THREE—10 QUESTIONS—
15 MINUTES

21. Consider the following statements concerning training in a police department.
    (1) An employee who has been trained well remains trained forever.
    (2) During training, a mistake should be corrected as it is made.
    (3) The best motivation for learning is self-interest.
    Based on the above, which of the following is most accurate?
    A. Only statement 1 is not accurate.
    B. Only statements 1 and 2 are not accurate.
    C. Only statements 2 and 3 are not accurate.
    D. Only statement 3 is not accurate.

22. Much has been said and written concerning the sergeant's role and responsibility in the training function of police departments. In which of the following situations can a police sergeant have the greatest impact on the department's training function?
    A. As a lecturer in a course given to a class of police recruits
    B. During on-the-job training encounters with individual police officers
    C. During roll call training
    D. As a commentator on a proposal for formal department-wide training

23. In conducting a training session, Sergeant Colt indicates that officers should not cock their revolvers when they are involved in a situation that may call for the use of their firearms. Which of the following is the principal reason for the sergeant's statement?
    A. An officer can shoot a revolver more accurately when firing double action.
    B. An accidental discharge might occur if the revolver is cocked.
    C. It takes up valuable time to cock one's revolver.
    D. The chances for misfire are lessened by not cocking one's revolver.

24. Because information must often be given to large numbers of police officers, police supervisors constantly search for the best method of giving a maximum of information to large groups of police officers. Which of the following is the most efficient method of accomplishing this purpose?
    A. The conference method
    B. "Hands-on" practical demonstrations
    C. The lecture method
    D. Group discussion of information that has been disseminated ahead of time

25. Sergeant Tosk is in charge of a group of police officers who are very well trained in their job. It should be recognized, therefore, that the need for direct orders to the officers from the sergeant:
    A. Is low, because the officers understand the goals of the department and the various ways of reaching them
    B. Is high, because well-trained officers know the detailed requirements of the job and the sergeant must therefore be very specific when giving instructions
    C. Has no relationship to the amount of training received by the police officers but instead relies solely on the job satisfaction of the police officers
    D. Would be low only if the police officers were performing routine tasks

26. A certain supervisor is giving a training lecture to a group of police officers. The supervisor senses that a few of the officers look bored and give him the feeling that he is moving through the material too slowly. The supervisor would be most correct if he:
    A. Increased the pace of the lecture so as not to bore these officers
    B. Kept the pace of the lecture the same
    C. Slowed the pace of the lecture to see if this has any effect on the rest of the group
    D. Stopped the lecture and asked the few officers who appear bored if he is in fact going too slowly

27. A training program does not end when the last student has left the classroom. The knowledgeable supervisor realizes there is more. Therefore,

a sergeant should always evaluate the results of training programs. The primary reason for this evaluation is indicated by which of the following?

A. The training ability of instructors can be measured.

B. The need for future training can be identified.

C. How training programs are conducted is a primary measure of a supervisor's success.

D. Feedback from the participants guarantees that future programs will be meaningful.

28. Which of the following choices best describes what a police training program should include?

A. Preparation of recruits to conform with the high standards expected of them

B. The development and maintenance of skills in seasoned officers

C. Providing supervisors and command level officers with the skills and knowledge necessary to function effectively

D. All of the above

29. Police training has made great strides since the early days of policing in the United States. Unfortunately, not all areas of police service have received the attention they deserve. Which of the following is thought to be one of the most neglected aspects of police training?

A. Recruit training

B. Supervisory training

C. Firearms training

D. Self-defense training

30. A training program to be successful should be carefully planned. Which of the following is the least accurate statement concerning the planning of a training program?

A. Trainers often assume a learner possesses more knowledge about the subject than the learner actually does

B. Technical proficiency in a job ensures that the trainer is a good instructor

C. A failure to plan and organize the teaching material usually confuses the student about the aim of the training

D. Sufficient training time must be allotted to prepare the student to learn prior to the presentation of the material

Answer Key

1. C	7. B	13. C	19. D	25. A
2. C	8. D	14. B	20. B	26. B
3. C	9. B	15. A	21. A	27. B
4. D	10. A	16. C	22. B	28. D
5. D	11. C	17. B	23. B	29. B
6. C	12. B	18. D	24. C	30. B

Answer Explanations

GROUP ONE

1. **C** Responsibility for a safety program should be given to all operating divisions, not made the sole responsibility of a staff unit. Getting line units involved shows that the program is real and everyone's concern. The program does not just belong to some distant staff unit.

2. **C** The area of safety and accident prevention, unfortunately, takes the shape of lip service and a variety of poster drives. In this area, the rank and file take their cues from the supervisory staff of the department. If the supervisors do not consider safety important, neither will the police officers.

3. **C** These periods cannot be avoided, and simply warning the learner is not enough. Encouragement is needed to get the trainee through this period.

4. **D** An instructor associates new material with the student's past experiences, through the student's apperceptive base.

5. **D** The sink or swim method, also known as the trial-and-error method, if used extensively in an area usually indicates a need for formal training in that area. The sink or swim method is actually expensive and inefficient because so much time is spent by a learner groping for the best method to perform some job. In police work it also can cause injury and other unnecessary losses.

6. **C** Distraction from your presentation is a constant foe of any instructor. An instructor must be careful that the diagram used to illustrate a point does not totally subsume the point. Diagrams can work well, even when the audience has no prior knowledge of the material, but a diagram is just a means to an end, not the end itself.

7. **B** When directing the question asked by one student to another student for an answer, care must be taken not to embarrass the student who has been asked to respond to the relay question. Questions should never be asked to embarrass a student or the instructor will lose that student forever.

8. **D** In such a training mode, in which students ask questions of a panel of experts, the instructor does not have total control. It is, however, particularly useful where there is some confusion among the students and they wish to receive direct answers from qualified sources.

9. **B** If at all possible, it is better to give several short lectures than one long one. Short lectures should begin with a brief review of the most important points of the previous lecture and should progress logically. The student will absorb the subject more readily, especially if there are no extensive time periods between each lecture.

10. **A** In teaching defensive driving, it is best to move from the safe to the hazardous so that safe maneuvers can be emphasized and hazardous areas can be contrasted with the safe procedures, with which most of the officers are probably familiar. Remember, when teaching, it is always a good idea to go from the known to the unknown.

Group Two

11. **C** Training is given to an employee to improve the work setting. That is what makes it truly effective. The key to effectiveness, however, is the application of what is learned. A change in negative work habits must occur for training to be effective.

12. **B** Only statement 3 is inaccurate. The most meaningful training of an individual employee can take place in a one-to-one situation in an informal setting. If the rapport between the trainer and the trainee is good, the chance for open and free-flowing discussion is greater than in a formal setting.

13. **C** Police work is a science, but it is also an art that must be performed in a real-world setting. This real-world setting cannot be totally duplicated in a classroom.

14. **B** Before any actual training, the officer or student must first be made ready to learn by having his/her interest in the subject raised.

15. **A** In training, different groups require different approaches or emphasis. This is especially pronounced in the area of in-service training.

16. **C** When it comes to in-service training, C best describes its characteristics—that is, proactive, people oriented, and based on individual need. In this way it will serve to recognize and improve an agency's most important resources—its workers.

17. **B** In a police-community relations training program, there should be trainers who are not part of the agency in addition to police personnel because they can present the community point of view.

18. **D** Teaching aids need not be elaborate. The instructor is more important than the teaching aids, as is knowledge of the subject and desire to improve his/her skills as an instructor. A good instructor should also understand the learning process.

19. **D** When teaching a complicated and lengthy operation, the instructor should move in small steps in the same sequence as the operation will actually be performed in the field.

20. **B** Police work is dynamic, and in-service training is one of the best vehicles to stay abreast of changes in the field.

GROUP THREE

21. **A** Statement 1 is not accurate; officers need continual training to remain proficient in an area. No one remains trained forever.

22. **B** Although there is some impact in all the situations listed, the greatest impact occurs in on-the-job training situations because of one-on-one contacts and the frequency of contacts.

23. **B** Cocking a revolver is a safety hazard that should be avoided.

24. **C** The lecture method is the most efficient (cost effective) when a lot of information has to be given to a large number of officers.

25. **A** When officers are well trained, they are aware of the choices available to them in a given situation. They can act more on their own, thereby lessening the need for direct orders.

26. **B** It is better to move at a pace that is too slow rather than too fast and risk confusing the majority of the group. In this item, the key is that there are only a few officers who appear bored. Rather than change the pace of the lecture, the instructor should attempt to bring the "bored" officers into the classroom give and take.

27. **B** Training is a never-ending process, and the results of past effort serve as direction markers for future programs. Realistically, the success of a training program cannot be known until some time after the training is completed by inspection of the work of those who attended the training session.

28. **D** Choices A, B, and C combine to form what should be included in an effective police training program—that is, recruit training, ongoing in-service training, and command and supervisory training. (We also asked this question to see if you are considering all the choices before choosing an answer. Since choice A is a correct statement with respect to what a police training program should include, if you selected A without reading all the choices, you would not have determined that, in fact, all the choices are correct.)

29. **B** Some agencies erroneously believe that the passing of a civil service examination in itself qualifies one to act as a supervisor and that no supervisory training is required.

30. **B** There is no guarantee that a person who is technically proficient in a subject will be a good instructor in that subject.

CHAPTER 7

Principles of Management and Administration

It is generally agreed that the major responsibilities of a police sergeant differ from those of higher ranks, including the police chief, only in degree, not in kind. Said another way, a police sergeant performs the same functions as other ranking officers in a police department. The only difference is how often each function is performed. For example, a police sergeant and a police captain both engage in planning, but the captain probably does more planning than the sergeant and certainly plans on a different scale. Nonetheless, they both engage in the administrative function of planning. This is true of all the administrative and management functions. Although the supervisor's job as stated earlier deals primarily with people, the supervisor must be concerned with other non-people-related conditions within the agency, such as those managerial and administrative functions in the now-famous acronym POSDCORB created long ago by Luther Gulick. POSDCORB is derived from the initials of those activities engaged in by all managers and administrators, including the police sergeant.

1. Planning

2. Organizing

3. Staffing

4. Directing

5. Coordinating

6. Reporting

7. Budgeting

Although it is true that many of these functions are more appropriately the responsibility of those in the higher ranks, they become the responsibility of subordinates via the process of delegation of authority.

EXAMATOPICS ABOUT PRINCIPLES OF MANAGEMENT AND ADMINISTRATION

1. The major portion of a police sergeant's job can be subdivided into the three general areas of leading, directing, and controlling those in the work group.

2. Supervision is an activity performed by all ranks in a police department, with the exception of the entry-level rank, that of the police officer.

3. In theory, over the long haul, the interests of management are the same as the interests of the worker.

4. A supervisor should be thoroughly familiar with the workings of the local government, as well as the workings of the other agencies in the criminal justice system.

5. A supervisor can develop leadership ability by learning the principles involved and by emulating other successful leaders.

6. The job of the first-line police supervisor is of great importance because of the overwhelming need for teamwork in police work.

The Communications Process

Many police experts believe that the single most important skill of a police supervisor is the ability to communicate clearly and effectively with superiors, peers, and subordinates. One of the major reasons for the importance of communication in a police department (or other similar organizations) lies in the group-life aspect of the occupation. Since group life requires cooperation and conflict interrupts cooperation, effective communication is required to resolve or control conflict. Another important reason for the importance of clear lines of communication in a police agency is the importance of coordination of effort. Unless there is clear communication, there can be no coordination. Without coordination, it is not possible to maintain a constructive organization.

WHAT IS COMMUNICATION?

Basically, communication is a social process by which information is shared among individuals and organizations. It is the passage of information from a sender to a receiver. A number of different systems of communications make social life possible, and of course, language is the most prominent of these systems. Other systems involve digital signs, as in sign language for the hearing impaired, formal signs and codes, such as we see more and more of on our highways and other public areas, and, of course, machine language for computers.

FUNCTIONS OF COMMUNICATION IN GROUP LIFE

Communication functions in different ways in different situations. In group-life situations, as in a police department, formal communication serves the following functions.

It provides subordinates with the information they need to do the job.

It provides management with the feedback they need to monitor and control the job.

It provides for employee input into the job and encourages creative thinking via conferences, brainstorming sessions, and so on.

It clears up employee expectations and perceptions.

It satisfies natural curiosity and prevents overreliance on informal communication systems, such as the grapevine (explained below).

GUIDELINES FOR EFFECTIVE COMMUNICATION

A police supervisor should strive to become a better communicator. This can be done since the ability to communicate well is a skill that can be improved upon by adhering to the following guidelines for effective communication.

Determine the objectives of the communication. Before communicating, clarify your ideas in your own mind. If you are not sure what you want to communicate, how can you expect others to grasp your meaning? Therefore, the first step in communicating is to systematically analyze the matter to be communicated.

Empathize with the recipients of the communication prior to communicating. Except in emergency situations, a supervisor should carefully consider the feelings and viewpoints of the targets of communication before it occurs. When possible, the communication process should consider the impact the message will have on its receivers and try to soften any negative impact.

When possible, consult with others prior to communicating. There is no doubt that directives receive greater acceptance if those affected are permitted to participate in planning their development. Besides increasing probable support for the communication, advance conferral can often result in added insight, objectivity, and effectiveness.

Remember, there is more to communicating than the spoken word. The content matter of any spoken message can be greatly altered by such things as body language, tone of voice, and facial expressions. Also important is the way in which the sender receives the listener's response to the communication.

If possible, include a positive portion in all of your communications. A good supervisor tries to convey something of value to the receiver in every communication that lends itself to this strategy. This process is facilitated by using empathy, as explained in the second point.

Practice what you preach. The need to be consistent must be understood if supervisors want their communications to be persuasive. Dual standards, especially one for supervisors and another for subordinates, destroy the communications process. In this regard it is important to note that many experts believe the most convincing communications involve what is done, not what is said.

Include a follow-up component in your communications. It has been said that following up on communications, also known as obtaining feedback, is the best way for supervisors to determine if they are communicating effectively. Feedback can be obtained verbally by asking questions and encouraging receiver responses, or it can be obtained through such nonverbal techniques as follow-up inspection and/or a review of records and reports. Concerning the feedback process, remember that it is normal for subordinates, in good faith or otherwise, to shield the supervisor from negative information. This shielding process is known as "filtering." The supervisor should be aware that filtering will occur and try to minimize its frequency and impact.

Understanding others is as important as being understood yourself. Nothing impacts more negatively on a communication attempt between a supervisor and a subordinate than a failure by the supervisor to listen to what the subordinate has to say. Although a subordinate's failure to listen is indeed harmful, the supervisor has the authority to "compel" the subordinate to listen, at least to the point that the subordinate can be questioned concerning the communication. The subordinate has no such officially sanctioned recourse when the supervisor fails to listen. Remember, true learning results from listening, not from talking. Listening includes paying attention to implicit meanings, such as body language and facial expressions, as well as paying attention to the verbal content of the message.

BARRIERS TO EFFECTIVE COMMUNICATION

Some of the barriers to effective communication are merely a negative restatement of the above guidelines for effective communication, but they are the subject of so many official examination questions that we will list them below.

Failure to listen. Many believe that the biggest barrier in the communications process is the inability or unwillingness to listen carefully to another person.

Defensiveness. The penchant of many individuals to defend their own ideas or their strongly held beliefs is a very common barrier to effective communication. Also in this category is the natural inclination to resist new ideas.

Hierarchical created differences. Generally speaking, the greater the difference in status or rank between two communicators, the greater is the probability for ineffective communication. This is also true when there is an appreciable difference in prestige between two communicators.

The upward communication. Communications travel more easily and quickly downward in an organization than they travel upward in the same organization.

Filtering of information. As mentioned, filtering refers to the intentional or unintentional withholding of information as it is passed from one communicator to another. Unintentional filtering occurs most often as a result of a subordinate's reluctance to tell bad news to the supervisor. This type of filtering is often the result of a supervisor's communicated preference not to hear disagreeable news. A supervisor whose attitude clearly indicates not wanting to be troubled with bothersome information will soon be operating in a vacuum. In the final analysis, when subordinates withhold information from a supervisor, they are doing the supervisor a tremendous disservice and exposing the supervisor to great danger because important decisions will be made in the absence of all the available information.

Jumping to conclusions. A supervisor who reaches immediate decisions based on a quick, gut reaction to a not yet completed communication not only is engaging in ineffective communications, but is inviting the resentment of subordinates. Trying to talk to someone who doesn't seem to want to listen is an experience most people will try to avoid once it has occurred. The obvious result of this is that no communication will take place.

Too much communication. This is the opposite side of the coin from filtering. Some supervisors insist on being told everything, and this too can cause resentment because it is indicative of a lack of trust. It is up to the supervisors to set the guidelines concerning the quality of the messages they receive, and the byword should be reasonableness. The rule of thumb should be that when a subordinate is doubtful of the importance of a message, it should be passed on to a supervisor.

THE GRAPEVINE

No discussion of communications in an organization would be complete without mention of the organization's informal communications system, known as the grapevine. When the organization's official communications system fails to satisfy the reasonable and natural curiosity of its members, rumors are born. Rumors are created, and they can grow when the following two conditions exist:

1. The content matter of a grievance is of importance to both the teller and the receiver.

2. The official facts or the truth in the matter is uncertain.

After rumors are started, they travel about an organization via the grapevine. It is important to note that, although the growth of rumors can be minimized by sufficient official information, it is not realistic to believe that the grapevine can be eliminated. In fact, wise supervisors can, when necessary, use the grapevine to release information they believe workers should know. However, it would be unwise to overuse this strategy since the grapevine almost always distorts all but the most simple of messages.

EXAMATOPICS ABOUT THE GRAPEVINE

1. It is unreasonable to expect that organizations can satisfy the informational needs of all their members.

2. The remedy for rumor is truth.

3. Supervisors have a responsibility to keep their subordinates as well informed as possible.

WRITTEN COMMUNICATIONS

Clarity of meaning is even more important in written communications than it is in oral communications. This is so because readers do not have the face-to-face opportunity to clarify meanings that listeners have in a two-way oral exchange. For this reason, clarity of meaning is essential in written communications. Despite this shortcoming, however, written communications are extremely valuable when

1. Permanency is an important consideration

2. A standard procedure is to be followed by many officers

3. Documentation of receipt is an important factor

TYPES OF WRITTEN ORDERS

Many police departments utilize some form of the following types of written orders.

General orders. These are orders that establish policy.

Special orders. These are orders that implement policy. They are, of necessity, more specific and more detailed than general orders.

Operations orders. These are orders that dictate operational procedures at a particular event or occurrence. Tactical operations orders are for events that will occur infrequently, perhaps only once, such as a visit by a foreign dignitary. Strategic operations orders are for repeating events, such as an annual parade or searches for missing persons.

EXAMATOPICS ABOUT COMMUNICATIONS

1. Information that travels on the grapevine is usually distorted significantly.

2. Communication is one of the most difficult tasks of a police sergeant; it is also one of the most important functions.

3. A communicator who has status will be either helped or hindered by that status, depending upon the reputation of the communicator; for an unapproachable person with status, status is a hindrance to effective communication.

4. A supervisor who has a habit of editorializing about or otherwise evaluating every comment or opinion made by a subordinate will hamper the free flow of communications.

5. When the purpose of a communication is explained to its receivers, the communication is much more likely to be understood and accepted.

6. Supervisors are evaluated to a large degree by how well they communicate, both orally and in writing.

7. To the extent possible, rumors should be countered with facts.

8. Misunderstood oral communications are quite often the result of poor listening skills.

9. Good communications skills can be learned, just as leadership skills can be learned.

Evaluation Process

Nonprofit, service agencies, such as police departments, have a difficulty in evaluating or rating their personnel that profit-making agencies do not experience. The difficulty lies in the fact that there is no wholly objective yardstick to determine if a worker is doing a good job. A police officer cannot be fairly evaluated by numbers alone, that is, the number of arrests made, summonses issued, or other tasks. A good police officer performs many intangible functions that a less than effective officer doesn't perform. What makes matters worse is that police officers at the level of operations spend over ninety percent of their working day in an unsupervised capacity. Despite all of these problems, however, a police supervisor can most effectively utilize the most important and expensive resource, entry-level workers, by knowing the capabilities of these workers. Therefore, an evaluation process is a necessity to assess employee performance against desired norms.

WHAT IS A PERFORMANCE EVALUATION?

Performance evaluations are know by a variety of names including service rating, personnel evaluations, merit ratings, and annual evaluations. Regardless of what they are called, all ratings are judgments of the quality of a person's work made by that person's supervisor. Since they are judgments, they must of necessity by somewhat subjective, which is the source of most of the problems involving performance evaluations. The accuracy of the rater's judgment when making evaluations depends on many factors, including the following.

Tangibility of the traits being measured. For example, if the trait being considered is "times late" and the agency has a solid procedure for determining and recording lateness, the accuracy of this judgment is likely to be high. If the trait involved is "personal appearance," however, judgment is certainly subjective.

Clarity with which the trait is defined. A trait that is defined in precise terms, even if it is intangible, is likely to be judged more objectively and accurately than the same trait that is loosely defined.

Amount of contact between the rater and the ratee. If the rater and the ratee work closely together a great deal of the time, the judgment is more likely to be accurate than one made when a rater and a ratee do not normally have much personal contact. As already pointed out, police sergeants rarely work closely with any of the officers under their supervision.

Skill of the rater. Judgments made by untrained raters are obviously likely to be less accurate than those made by trained raters.

WHY DOES RATING TAKE PLACE?

Performance evaluation systems have a very stormy history. Very few rating systems receive widespread employee acceptance. Yet, they live on. The most common reasons that police organizations rate their employees are to

1. Satisfy the requirements of a local or state law

2. Improve employee morale by giving recognition to those who deserve it

3. Maintain a reasonable level of performance in the organization

4. Determine training needs

5. Award merit pay increases, or to withhold such increases

6. Select personnel for tenure and promotion

COMMON RATER ERRORS

In the final analysis, rating systems can only succeed if the raters as well as those being rated really want them to succeed. Just the same, even if everyone involved is properly motivated, a number of common rating errors must be recognized and dealt with by those in control of the rating system. The best way to deal with these errors is through training. The most commonly occurring errors are as follows.

LENIENCY

The most common rating error is leniency, which is of course the tendency of the rater to evaluate personnel more favorably than deserved. Leniency in evaluating personnel stems from the following.

1. A supervisor's natural tendency to avoid unpleasant interactions with subordinates. Since a well-designed rating system requires a face-to-face review of the rating between the rater and the ratee, a great majority of supervisor-raters, especially untrained ones, take the easy alternative and rate all or most subordinates "above standards" without too much consideration for reality.

2. A rater's desire to be seen as a friend of the worker.

3. A perception by the rater that the evaluation system has very little value.

4. The subjective nature of most rated traits, which makes it possible to justify almost any rating.

5. The widespread recognition among supervisors that "everyone else" rates leniently.

HALO EFFECT

This error represents a widespread tendency to allow a general impression of a worker to affect each specific trait being rated. For example, a supervisor who values punctuality tends to assign a high rating to workers who are always prompt, regardless of the trait being considered. So punctual workers could get high ratings on such traits as judgment or job knowledge, based not on judgmental ability or knowledge of the job but based instead on the favorable impression created by their punctuality. It also works in reverse; tardy workers get low ratings on other specific traits because of lateness.

ERROR OF CENTRAL TENDENCY

This error reflects a tendency to group all workers around the central rating scale of "average" or "meets standards." It occurs very often when a supervisor is not very familiar with each individual in the work group.

CONTRAST ERROR

This error occurs when supervisors compare workers to themselves or their own expectations and aspirations. The actual error is either of two ways:

1. Rating a worker on a specific trait in the opposite direction from yourself because you believe the worker is not like you, hence the name "contrast" error

2. Rating a worker on a specific trait as you would rate yourself on the trait because you believe the worker is like you

ASSOCIATION ERROR

As its name implies, this error occurs when a supervisor associates certain traits on the evaluation form with one other in his/her own mind and then assigns similar ratings to these traits, in a manner that indicates the supervisor is grouping the traits together. It should be noted that supervisors often associate traits that are adjacent to each other on the rating form.

EXAMATOPICS ABOUT PERFORMANCE EVALUATIONS

1. Every competent police supervisor rates subordinates on a continuous basis even if there is no formal rating system in the agency.

2. Since personnel evaluations often impact significantly on a police officer's career, supervisors must understand that careless errors can have serious consequences.

3. Intangible, vague rating traits should be minimized because of their subjectivity.

4. Unless a police agency takes active steps to strengthen the personnel evaluation system, such as explaining its purpose and dealing with common errors, the system will be disliked by supervisors and workers.

5. The absence of a formal rating system gives rise to "spot ratings," which are apt to be inaccurate compared with a formal procedure.

6. The most accurate and fair evaluations are those based on day-to-day recorded observations of good or poor performance.

7. Rating traits must be job related if they are to have any validity.

8. Bias in rating occurs when a supervisor has a predetermined inclination to rate in one direction or another. When this bias is completely unreasonable, it amounts to prejudice and represents a serious deficiency in the system.

9. A worker's immediate supervisor is the key figure in the evaluation system.

10. The primary aim of a personnel evaluation system should be to improve employee performance, which is why ratings should be discussed with ratees.

11. A worker's previous evaluation should not be a factor in a current performance evaluation.

12. A rating system helps an agency to better control the activities of the agency by determining if the employees are performing their jobs properly.

Planning

All supervisors must forecast potential needs and problems for the specific work group and develop plans to deal with them. A conspicuous difference between plans formulated at the higher levels of a police department and those prepared by a first-line supervisor is that the plans developed by the supervisor must be more detailed and precise than those prepared by administrators.

TYPES OF PLANS

Plans are often classified according to their purpose. The major types of plans are as follows.

Policies. Policies are plans that are very broad in nature and meant to guide personnel in their day-to-day activities. When confusion exists concerning the application of a policy, a supervisor should take whatever steps are required, including a request to the commanding officer for an interpretation, to clarify the meaning of the policy. Policies are not always reduced to writing since they often result from the experiences of an organization.

Rules and regulations. A police department's rules and regulations are, in fact, plans to deal with the daily conduct and performance of its employees. Some rules and regulations have department-wide application, and others are developed for specific commands. Similarly, some rules and regulations are prepared by administrators, and others are developed by first-line supervisors for a particular work group. To remain effective, rules and regulations must be constantly reviewed and amended, if appropriate. This review and amendment process depends to a great extent on the cooperation of first-line supervisors.

Procedural plans. These are plans that outline standard operating procedures to be followed when engaging in such ongoing activities as issuing summonses and appearance tickets, processing summary arrests, and handling domestic disputes.

Operational plans. These are the plans that assist operating personnel perform their normal duties, such as engaging in high-speed vehicle pursuits and responding to the scene of a crime in progress. They usually include several structured steps.

Tactical plans. Plans developed to deal with seldom occurring police emergencies are known as tactical plans. An example of a tactical plan would be a plan for dealing with a major disaster.

WHY IS PLANNING NECESSARY?

The work of a police agency is dynamic: it is always changing. Such changes require amending the way things are done. Without advance planning, chaos would rule. Problems must be anticipated and plans made to deal with the problems when they occur. Of course, this is not always possible. Insofar as it is possible, however, it should be done. It is said that you deal with the unexpected by planning for the expected. Some other reasons that planning is necessary are as follows.

It is the responsibility of all supervisors, managers, and administrators to obtain the most efficient use of police resources. Without planning, this cannot be done.

Planning assists the supervisor in a number of ways. It negates the need to engage in trial and error. It makes the job easier. Developing standard plans makes the supervisor's training job easier.

PLANNING PROCESS

Planning should take place after the need for a plan is established. Once the need for a plan is established, there is a recognized and accepted method of engaging in the planning process with which every police supervisor should be familiar and should utilize. It is a four-step process, as follows.

Determination of objectives. A plan cannot achieve its purpose unless that purpose is very clearly identified by the planner. Performing this initial step accurately is very important because it impacts on all work processes that must occur before the plan is implemented, including budgeting and training.

Deciding what resources are required. After the objectives of the plan have been determined, the next issue involves the expenditure of resources. In these days of fiscal austerity, this step takes on increased importance. In a service agency, such as a police department, personnel expenditures are usually the most expensive component of any plan. Therefore, careful consideration must be given to the most efficient utilization of labor.

Determination of methods to be used. This step in the process, for all practical purposes, is performed simultaneously with the preceding step. This is so since method and resources are interdependent. If the objective of a plan is to reduce the incidence of burglaries in a given location, the methods employed might be foot patrol, motor patrol, anti-crime patrol, or a combination of them all. From this example, the relationship between methods and resources is obvious.

Determination of control mechanism. A procedure must be included in every plan to monitor its progress with respect to its stated objectives. Ideally, the monitoring device can be objective in nature.

EXAMATOPICS ABOUT PLANNING

1. Plans are useless if they are not accurately conveyed to the implementors of the plans.

2. The planning process and the morale of workers are interrelated. Good planning helps to raise employee morale. This is accomplished by having employees feel more secure in seeing that the organization has and follows specific courses of action in obtaining its goals.

3. Not all plans need to be reduced to writing.

4. A patrol supervisor must prioritize work in order to plan patrol assignments properly.

5. Involving workers in the planning process is a good way to ensure the success of the plan. This is sometimes referred to as "gaining needed concurrences" and should not be overlooked.

6. Planning is an important responsibility of all line units even if there is a staff unit responsible for planning in the department.

7. A good plan will answer the following questions: when, where, who, what, how, and why.

8. The need for a plan can be recognized at any level of the department.

Coordinating

Coordination is a vital function of management since it ensures that all organizational subdivisions work toward a common goal with a minimum expenditure of resources. Coordination of effort must be provided for at all levels of the department. As an organization increases in size and complexity, however, the necessity to coordinate activities increases.

HOW IS COORDINATION DEFINED?

Coordination can be equated with the efficient implementation of the action portion of a plan. It cannot be performed in a vacuum since it very often requires harmonizing the activities of other units, including, in some cases, agencies outside the police department. The best way to coordinate activities is through direct communication. It is very unwise to attempt to coordinate by mandate. It just won't work. Another coordination problem occurs if all concerned aren't pursuing common objectives. This problem is seen when the members of a specialized unit pursue the goals of their own unit instead of those of the entire department.

GUIDELINES FOR EFFECTIVE COORDINATION

Conscientious police supervisors will make it their business to cultivate friendly relations with supervisors of other units, especially those performing related functions. This is a big help when the situation arises that requires coordinating the efforts of these related units. Supervisors can also facilitate the coordination process by creating a climate in the unit that is conducive to mutual cooperation. Other suggestions for achieving effective coordination are as follows.

1. A supervisor should avoid excessive personal intervention in the coordination process. The supervisor's job is to create the potential for effective coordination and then let it happen.

2. Be aware that coordinating is a complex and neverending process.

3. Poor planning and organization are very often the cause when certain activities constantly need extensive coordination efforts.

EXAMATOPICS ABOUT COORDINATION

1. Coordinating requires a constant striving to prevent duplication of effort and resources.

2. The interchange of personnel between units for a temporary period of time facilitates the coordination process.

3. High-quality management performance in the areas of planning, organizing, directing, and controlling will result in few coordination problems.

4. A simple definition of coordinating is that it is the logical and orderly arrangement of the efforts of a group to provide unified action while pursuing a common goal.

5. As an agency becomes larger in size or more specialized units appear, coordination becomes more difficult. This is due to the increased number of relationships and because the specialist and generalist fail to recognize each other's role in the agency.

Controlling

Controlling is the process of ensuring quality in an organization. Like planning, evaluation, training, and coordinating, it is an ongoing process. The essence of the control function is determining if there is individual and group compliance with the objectives, policies, and procedures of the organization and evaluation of the use of department resources.

SUPERVISOR'S ROLE IN THE CONTROL PROCESS

Control is not strictly a function of top management and staff units. It is also an important responsibility of the first-line supervisor, who is in a position in the agency to exercise the control function at the level of operations. A primary control responsibility of the patrol supervisor is to see that all activities are conducted with honesty and integrity. A first-line supervisor normally exercises the control function in the following ways.

Exercising control over the quality and quantity of work performed. This is, perhaps, the police supervisor's primary control duty. No one in the agency is in a better position than the patrol supervisor to exercise control over the work of police officers on patrol.

Properly allocating work assignments among the police officers. This control function is important because an even distribution of work is important for morale purposes and essential to effective operations.

Monitoring the expenditure of resources. The patrol supervisor plays a key role in controlling wasteful expenditures of resources.

Prioritizing and scheduling work. The control function of the patrol supervisor is meant to eliminate or at least minimize unnecessary work and duplication of effort.

HOW DOES THE SUPERVISOR EXERCISE CONTROL?

It is generally agreed that there are three vital elements involved in the control process. An individual who is not in a position to adequately perform all of these three components cannot exercise effective control. The three elements are:

1. The person exercising control over work must have a very good working knowledge of the goals and objectives to be accomplished by the work.

2. The control person must be in a position to obtain accurate information concerning the progress being made toward the achievement of the goals and objectives being pursued.

3. The control person must be able to follow up to correct any problems uncovered by step 2.

EXAMATOPICS ABOUT CONTROL

1. The principal vehicle of control in a police agency are: personal observation by supervisors, reports, records, and inspections.

2. Controlling is a necessary component of effective and efficient management of an organization.

3. The development and refinement of control devices was caused primarily by the problem of police misconduct in police departments.

4. Reports from subordinate commands assist top administrators in exercising control over the organization.

5. The control function measures how well the agency implements its policies and follows its procedures.

Organizing

Organizing involves grouping people who do not necessarily have common or even similar interests and values into functional work groups. An organizational structure is created, and the various work groups are artificially fitted into the overall organizational structure. An organizational structure is a mechanical method of indicating the relationships that exist among the various workers, work groups, and functions within an organization. An organizational chart is nothing more than a pictorial statement that shows these relationships. A principal feature of an organizational chart is that it indicates graphically the lines of authority and responsibility and working relationships among the work groups in the organization.

TYPES OF ORGANIZATIONAL STRUCTURES

There are only a handful of organizational structures in existence today, and even the most progressive modern-day structures are offshoots of these few recognized structural arrangements. The most common types of organizational structures are as follows.

LINE ORGANIZATION

This type of organization, which is quite often referred to as the military type of organization, is the oldest and most simple organizational structure. It is found to exist in only the smallest of police departments. As its name implies, the only type of authority that exists in a line organization is line, or direct, authority. Commanders or supervisors who have line authority can make command decisions on their own initiative; commanders or supervisors who have only staff authority cannot make command decisions. Staff authority is limited to offering advice to a line commander, who has final decision-making authority. Therefore, a "staff" unit is a specialized work group that makes its expertise available to line commanders. Examples are training units or intelligence units. In a straight-line organization, therefore, there is no staff authority, since all units are line units. This means, of course, that commanders and supervisors of the units in a line organization often have to perform the duties of specialists because there are no staff personnel with special expertise available to advise them.

FUNCTIONAL ORGANIZATION

This type of organization is rarely found in police departments today. It might possibly be found near the top of the very largest of police departments, but not throughout the agency. A functional organization divides authority and responsibility among a number of specialists who are then responsible for their specialized function wherever it is performed in the agency. For example, the traffic commander in a functional organization is responsible for traffic control and enforcement throughout the entire department, regardless of who in the department performs the function. The major disadvantages of this type of organizational structure are as follows.

1. Coordination of effort is extremely difficult.

2. Administration of discipline is difficult.

3. Lines of authority and responsibility are unclear.

LINE AND STAFF ORGANIZATION

This is the type of organization found in almost all police agencies in the United States. As its name implies, it combines line and staff authority, thereby providing line commanders and supervisors with the expertise of specialists. Very simply stated, in a line and staff organization staff personnel are responsible for "innovative thinking" but they leave the "doing" up to line personnel. To work properly, it is important for line supervisors to remember that staff advice is a command that must be followed. Unfortunately, failure to adhere to these line and staff relationships is the biggest and most frequently occurring problem in a line and staff organization since it makes coordination so difficult.

DIVISION OF WORK

To obtain each of the overall objectives of a police agency, all the various types of work that have to be performed must be logically apportioned among the various units in the department. Insofar as possible, homogeneous work should be assigned to the same unit. Any unit whose workers have to perform too much divergent functions will probably not be an efficient or effective operation. Work in an organization is usually divided by using one of the following bases.

Purpose. This involves dividing work according to the purpose of the work. In the organizational structure of a municipality, the police department has the primary responsibility for work whose purpose it is to prevent criminal activity.

Process. This involves dividing work according to how it is to be done. For example, the officers in a mounted unit in a police department perform their work on horseback.

Clientele being served. When work is grouped on the basis of the characteristics of the persons being served, it is said to be based on *clientele*. The most common example of this type of division of work in a police department is the juvenile unit because it uses the age of the clientele served as the basis of the grouping.

Area being served. It is a very common practice in larger police departments to divide work according to geographic areas, often called precincts.

Function being performed. Functional work grouping is used when the work involved is highly specialized. A very good example is the providing of forensic science services via the police laboratory.

Time. Division of work by time is necessary in a police agency because of the necessity to provide police service on a twenty-four-hour-a-day, seven-days-a-week basis. Most police agencies operate on a three-shift basis.

PRINCIPLES OF ORGANIZATION

Supervisors must be aware of and follow certain principles of organization. Disregard of these principles, except in certain limited situations, is counterproductive. The three most important principles of organization are as follows:

1. Unity of command

2. Span of control

3. Authority commensurate with responsibility

UNITY OF COMMAND

The principle of unity of command requires that every employee be under the direct command and supervision of only one ranking officer. If this principle is violated without justification, it results in confusion among workers and the possibility of conflicting direction being given. Violation of unity of command also often results in duplication of effort and loss of control. The two instances that justify a ranking officer's violation of the principle of unity of command are

1. In an emergency situation when prompt action is a necessity and following the principle would result in delayed action.

2. When the reputation of the department is at stake, such as when an employee is engaged in a gross deviation of the rules of conduct and the worker's immediate supervisor is not readily available to intervene.

SPAN OF CONTROL

The principle of "span of control" refers to the number of workers that can be effectively supervised by one supervisor. The span of control is very narrow at the top of an organization, where it ranges from three to five subordinates to each ranking officer, and broadens somewhat as one travels down the hierarchy. There is no optimal span of control at the operations level in a police agency since a supervisor's effective span of control is affected by so many variables that the ideal span must almost be determined on a case-to-case basis. Some of the factors that affect a supervisor's span of control are as follows.

Abilities of the supervisor. A supervisor with well-developed physical and mental facilities can, of course, handle a broader span of control than a less capable supervisor.

Abilities of those supervised. Naturally, the greater the abilities of the employees being supervised, the easier it is to supervise them, provided they are properly motivated.

Geographic working area. A supervisor who has very little difficulty supervising twelve employees in an office would have a much more difficult time supervising the same twelve workers if they were spread out over a large geographic area, as is the case when a police sergeant supervises police officers on patrol. Therefore, a supervisor's effective span of control tends to decrease as the geographic distance between the supervisor and the subordinates increases.

Nature of the work being performed. If employees are performing simple, routine tasks, then their supervisor's job is not difficult and a larger span of control is possible. Conversely, if the job being performed is complex, the span of control of the supervisor tends to decrease.

Nature of the supervisor's job. If the supervisors in a police department are required to do productive work themselves, such as community relations or public relations work, they have less time available for supervisory responsibilities and, consequently, have a narrower span of control than if they had more time for their supervisory duties. This is also true in agencies that rely heavily on the first-line supervisor for the training of newly appointed police officers.

AUTHORITY COMMENSURATE WITH RESPONSIBILITY

The principle of delegation of work, covered in detail in the chapter on the principles of supervision relates to the process of transferring responsibility for a certain activity to a subordinate. It allows a supervisor to carry an increased span of control since the delegation process frees the supervisor to engage in supervisory responsibilities. The principle of authority and responsibility mandates that, when responsibility for a task is delegated, sufficient authority to perform the task effectively must also be delegated. This principle of organization stems from the understanding that workers do not want to be held responsible for accomplishing work when they don't have the tools necessary to accomplish the work.

ORGANIZATIONAL CHARTING

As previously mentioned, an organization chart is a graphic representation of the hierarchical chain of command. An important value of an organization chart is that it enables a supervisor to tell at a glance when major breaches occur in the command coordination process. Other uses of the organizational chart are as follows.

1. It can be used to understand the command relationships in the organization.

2. It helps employees to better understand their role and position in the organization.

3. It can be used as a training aid.

The limitations on the use of an organizational chart are as follows.

1. It cannot show the informal relationships that exist and that are so important in an agency.

2. It often is out of date because of the constantly changing nature of a formal organization.

SPECIALIZATION

As police work becomes more and more complex, specialization within police departments generally increases. In many instances this development is quite appropriate and proper. However, specialization should never occur if the patrol force is able to handle the task that is about to be specialized, and even more emphatically, it should never occur if the patrol force will be weakened by the loss of personnel to the newly created specialized unit. Otherwise, what occurs is a spiraling effect that damages the department's patrol efforts, which as we have already pointed out a number of times is the most important police function. The whole problem is exacerbated by the fact that usually the best and most experienced patrol officers are recruited for the specialized units. The point is that specialization should be resisted if it damages the patrol force. It would be better to make adjustments in the patrol force to handle the situation if at all possible.

ADVANTAGES OF SPECIALIZATION

1. Training is facilitated, since only a few need training in the specialized task.

2. The morale of those assigned to the specialized unit is raised because they enjoy being associated with what they consider to be an "elite" unit.

3. Responsibility is fixed for the accomplishment of the specialized tasks.

4. Expertise in the specialized task is increased.

DISADVANTAGES OF SPECIALIZATION

1. Specialization might weaken the patrol function, as discussed above.

2. The remainder of the department is not trained in the task of the specialist and consequently knows very little about the task.

3. Compartmentalization and exclusion occur. Compartmentalization is the feeling shared by members of a specialized unit who only see the goals of their unit as important. They no longer see the department's

overall objectives as having anything to do with them. Exclusion is the feeling that tends to develop in the ranks of the patrol force because they no longer feel responsible for the tasks of the specialized unit. They have "excluded" the specialized task from their responsibilities. The patrol supervisor should be constantly vigilant to minimize the adverse effects of compartmentalization and exclusion.

4. Members of the patrol force tend to resent the elitist attitude of the specialists, and friction often develops.

5. Coordination of activities is, as mentioned earlier in this chapter, made more difficult.

EXAMATOPICS ABOUT ORGANIZING

1. Quick decisions are very possible in a straight-line organization because of the very direct lines of authority in such an organization.

2. Coordination of effort is relatively easy to obtain in a straight-line organization, compared with a functional organization or a line and staff organization.

3. The process of organizing involves the grouping of people, which is accomplished to a large extent by an artificial process that fits workers into a prefabricated structure.

4. Staff authority is quite different from line authority. A staff unit supervisor does not have direct command authority over line personnel, except in emergency situations or when the reputation of the department is at stake.

5. Supervisors of staff units exercise line command over the personnel in their own units.

6. Span of control is increased in an organization when a level of supervision is eliminated, and it is decreased when a supervisory level is added.

7. The number of employees a supervisor can effectively supervise is dependent upon the authority and willingness of the supervisor to delegate work.

8. Communications, both verbal and written, in an organization must follow the chain of command; that is, they must pass through the sender's immediate supervisor.

Inspections

Inspection is an administrative process that provides for the collection of facts about an organization. These collected facts are then used to judge the efficiency and effectiveness of the organization in its attempt to obtain its objectives. The facts collected in the inspections process relate to all facets of the organization's activities, including people, actions, and conditions. The facts are obtained by means of observation, analysis of reports and records, and inquiry. There are two types of inspections that are used in all but the smallest of police departments:

1. Line inspection

2. Staff inspection

LINE INSPECTION

Line inspections are inspections made by those who have the authority to require that corrective action be implemented immediately. Said differently, line inspections are those made by line personnel who have line authority over the unit being inspected. The responsibility to perform line inspections exists in every police department regardless of its size. Every police supervisor must, as a command responsibility, engage in the inspections process. Unfortunately, however, although line inspections are a valuable control mechanism, they have serious limitations. The most serious weakness is the natural tendency to avoid self-criticism. Remember, in a line inspection, the person doing the actual inspection is the same person who is responsible for the condition of the unit being inspected. Therefore, an incompetent supervisor or, worse yet, a corrupt supervisor can conceal deficiencies via an inadequate or inept inspections process. It is primarily for this reason that the staff inspection is a more reliable process and a major control device in most police departments.

STAFF INSPECTION

A staff inspection is one conducted by personnel who are neither responsible to the commanding officer of the unit being inspected nor responsible for the performance of the employees who are being inspected or whose work is being inspected. The theory is that personnel performing staff inspections can perform more objective inspections without fear of repercussion upon uncovering negative findings.

Budgeting

Budgeting is a planning process whereby a police department's total program is created for a given period of time, usually one year. A department's budget sets goals and objectives and indicates the portion of the total resources of the department to be used to meet these goals and objectives.

TYPES OF BUDGETS

Although it is true that, in many jurisdictions, the first-line supervisor has very little to do with budget preparation or execution, competent supervisors should have a working knowledge of the various types of budget most often used in police departments, as follows.

Operating budget. This is the financial plan that pays, for example, salaries, equipment, and services necessary to run the operation of the department for the period of time involved, usually one year.

Capital budget. This is the financial plan that sets aside resources on a periodic basis, usually one year, to pay for planned capital improvements, such as a new police headquarters or a new precinct station house. Note, however, that capital budget projects for the current year are executed via the operating budget after a transfer of funds from the capital budget.

EXAMATOPICS ABOUT BUDGETING

1. Supervisors function as economists when they perform the very important supervisory task of making maximum use of the resources under their control.

2. A supervisor is obligated to notify the commanding officer when available resources are insufficient to do the job.

3. There are three steps involved in the budgeting process: the preparation phase, when administrative planning takes place; the adoption phase, when the completed budget is presented to the legislation for approval; and the execution phase, when the budget is used, or executed.

4. A logical starting point for the preparation of a new budget is last year's budget.

5. Police supervisors are obligated to be cost conscious.

6. Approximately ninety percent of the operating expenses of police departments are for personnel services costs; the remaining ten percent is for other than personnel services costs (OTPS).

7. A budget is nothing more than a plan in fiscal terms.

Total Quality Management—A Nontraditional Management Technique

Total Quality Management (TQM) is a management style or philosophy that stresses quality at all levels of an agency. In TQM all members of the agency are to control and continuously improve how the work is done. Mostly credited to W. Edwards Demming, TQM has found its way into many police agencies.

TQM is fundamentally different from traditional management. It holds that management is more a journey than a destination. This is because emphasis is given to the *constant and continuous* improvement of the resulting product, which in the case of a police agency is the resulting police service the community receives. Agencies are seen as systems that are made up of processes, and such processes are made up of elements or steps. For example, in a police agency, one process would be the hiring of new police officers. Elements of the hiring process might begin with a job analysis, which in turn might lead to the element of creating a job description and ultimately end with the element of getting the approval to hire a rookie officer. Other related work processes made up of their own elements join together and thus make up systems, which are what make up agencies. Systems are, in short, the essence of agencies.

In TQM, when what the agency seeks to provide (e.g., in a police agency service to the community) falls below the intended level of quality, management is to examine the work systems instead of the individual performance of its members. If the job of managers is to produce work systems, then according to TQM even though *some* problems of a work system might be caused by the mistakes of individual employees, *most* problems are caused by the work systems management has created to get the work done.

EXAMATOPICS ABOUT TOTAL QUALITY MANAGEMENT

1. Under TQM, the police service is to be determined by the consumer (i.e., community) and not the "expert specialists" of the agency. Despite meeting certain levels of police performance, if the performance does not meet the needs of the community, then total quality has not been achieved.

2. Traditionally, management inspects things after they have been produced. It relies on after-the-fact audits by specialists using some type of predetermined measurement and is ready to devote resources to re-doing some of the work. In TQM, the emphasis is on improving the process that produces the service to the point that the process is free of errors and has minimal waste of resources.

3. TQM believes in empowering front-line managers and workers alike. Empowerment means allowing such front-line managers and workers to make decisions. Quality control and quality assurance in the workplace is accomplished by empowering these managers and workers.

4. Under TQM, workers are an important resource to be developed rather than controlled.

5. Even though technology and its resulting breakthrough advances are to be utilized under TQM, it holds steady and continuous quality improvement by ongoing gains each workday as being more important.

6. The reasons for and sources of variations in performance must be determined and understood by TQM managers.

7. In sum, TQM must begin at the top of a police agency; it calls for an examination of the agency's leadership, participation by all its members, and knowledge of how to measure the quality of results accurately.

8. As a final note, implementation and use of TQM by police agencies is not without problems:

   a. Even though employees are encouraged to constantly improve the quality of their performance because police agencies operate under civil service rules, there are limitations on the rewards that can be given for superior quality performance.

   b. Concerning community satisfaction with police service, demands for limited public resources often leave some segment of the community less than fully satisfied.

   c. It is difficult to assess the quality of some police actions. For example, how should the quality of handling a domestic dispute be measured?

   d. When the quality of life in a neighborhood improves, it is inevitably the result of the actions of several public agencies (e.g., sanitation, housing, police). How then can the efforts of a police agency be separated from those of other public agencies?

Practice Exercises

You are now ready to do some practice questions. Always try to answer the questions in the allotted time. After completing each one of the three groups of questions, make sure you thoroughly review the explanation for each answer before going to the next set of questions. This includes reviewing the explanations for all questions: those you answered correctly and those you answered incorrectly. This is done to ensure that you always arrive at the correct choice for the right reasons. Remember, now is the time to make mistakes. If you understand why you made a mistake, you should not make the same mistake on the examination when it really counts.

GROUP ONE—10 QUESTIONS—15 MINUTES

1. Consider the following statements concerning personnel evaluations.
   (1) Some sergeants leniently rate police officers because the sergeants desire to be seen as a friend of police officers.
   (2) Some sergeants leniently rate police officers because the sergeants believe the evaluation system is of great value.
   (3) Some sergeants believe that all other sergeants rate employees leniently so they rate in the same manner.

   Which of the following most accurately classifies these statements into those that are accurate and those that are not?
   A. Statements 1 and 2 are not accurate.
   B. Statements 1 and 3 are not accurate.
   C. Only two of the statements are accurate.
   D. All of the statements are accurate.

2. The effectiveness of communications is often a function of the direction of the communications. In general, which of the following statements is most accurate concerning two-way communications?
   A. They are faster than one-way communications.
   B. They are less accurate than one-way communications.
   C. They leave no room for feedback.
   D. They may be used in systems involving informal channels of communications.

3. Sergeant Holly frequently prefaces orders by saying, "The lieutenant told me to tell you ...." This practice is bad because:
   A. The lieutenant might not have made the statement
   B. It may appear to the police officers that the sergeant is after the lieutenant's job
   C. The police officers might believe that the sergeant does not really support the order
   D. It would be impossible for the sergeant to conduct any follow-up

4. The question is often asked, Do staff supervisors ever exercise line authority? The most accurate answer to this question is:
   A. No. The staff officer is involved in assisting the line supervisor and never has direct authority over line officers.
   B. Yes. The staff supervisor can exercise line authority but only in emergency situations or when the reputation of the department is at stake.
   C. No. A staff supervisor who exercised line authority would cease to be a staff supervisor.
   D. Yes. When supervising members of the staff unit, the staff supervisor exercises line authority.

5. A short police organization has been defined as one that has short administrative distances between the chief of police and the operating police officers. There are only a few layers of bureaucracy in a short organization. The chief weakness of this type of organization is:
   A. Elitist groups of specialists are developed
   B. An excessive amount of filtering of the communications process takes place
   C. It tends to be a less humane organization
   D. It can lead to an erosion of authority

6. Having the ability to resort to the correct plan called for by a situation is something a police sergeant should possess. A plan that guides the police in the deployment of personnel when searching for suspects is a (an):
   A. Procedural plan
   B. Tactical plan
   C. Operational plan
   D. Auxiliary services plan

7. Sergeant Harris has been recently assigned to a planning unit. The sergeant is told by her supervisor that the work she submits should be in the form of completed staff work. Which of the following statements is most accurate concerning the concept of completed staff work?

A. It refers to any assignment the staff member views as being completed.
B. It refers to work completed in such a way that all the head of the unit has to do is to approve it.
C. It refers to any assignment after it has been signed off on by the head of the unit.
D. It refers to the responsibility to do an assignment in strict accordance with the directions received by the staff unit commander.

8. Sergeant Toner is designated the planning officer for the precinct. The sergeant should recognize that the first step in planning is:
   A. The gathering of needed data
   B. Gaining concurrences from units that will be affected
   C. Establishing the need for the plan
   D. Evaluating the plan's chances for success

9. Sergeant Miller gives Police Officer Weiser an order. For Sergeant Miller to effectively hold Police Officer Weiser responsible for properly executing the order, Sergeant Miller must engage in some form of:
   A. Organization   C. Coordination
   B. Control   D. Planning

10. Approximately what percentage of the typical police department's budget is allocated for cost related to personnel?
    A. Fifty   C. Sixty
    B. Ninety   D. Eighty

GROUP TWO—10 QUESTIONS—15 MINUTES

11. Conducting evaluations is a task subject to many errors. Which of the following is the most common error made by supervisors when rating employees?
    A. Halo effect
    B. Central tendency effect
    C. Leniency error
    D. Error of related traits

12. Consider the following statements concerning evaluations.
    (1) A diagnostic postevaluation interview between the rater and the ratee should not focus on who is wrong.
    (2) Ratings should be discussed with employees with a view toward future improvement of performance.
    (3) The immediate supervisor of an employee is the key figure in any evaluation process.
    Based on the above, which of the following choices is most accurate?
    A. All of the statements are accurate.
    B. All of the statements are inaccurate.
    C. Only two of the statements are accurate.
    D. Only one of the statements is accurate.

13. Sergeant Nolan receives certain information from his subordinates. Some of the information contains some "bad news." The sergeant filters this bad news when communicating with his supervisor. This practice is:
    A. Good, since the sergeant will be seen as a decision maker by subordinates
    B. Bad, since the subordinates will not be sure when the sergeant is filtering information from them
    C. Good, since the sergeant's supervisor does not want to be overly burdened
    D. Bad, since the sergeant may be filtering out important information

14. There are several ways to organize a police department. Depending on how a department is organized, the need to delegate authority varies. A knowledgeable patrol supervisor recognizes that the need to delegate authority is most critical when organization is based on:
    A. Clientele being served
    B. Area being served
    C. The time the services are being delivered
    D. The process by which the service is being delivered

15. Of the various types of organizational structures, one type places an expert in charge of a function regardless of where in the agency that function is performed. What is this type of organizational structure called?

A. Line organization
B. Functional organization
C. Staff organization
D. Line and staff organization

16. A police sergeant should be familiar with the different types of plans called for by different situations. Which of the following situations would best be handled by a tactical plan?
A. Processing arrest warrants
B. Dealing with a civil disorder
C. Deployment of police officers to search for lost persons
D. Conducting a recruitment campaign

17. It is sometimes recommended that the planning and inspection responsibilities of a police department be combined and assigned to one unit. Which is the main reason for this recommendation?
A. One product of inspections is the discovery of a need for a plan, which is the first step in the planning process.
B. Both functions are only performed by staff personnel.
C. Neither function is a line responsibility.
D. Both inspections and planning require a high degree of writing expertise.

18. The police sergeant at times is required to plan and implement procedures to deal with police problems. Often the plan will cause resentment among the troops because it will be a departure from current procedures and therefore call for a change in routine. Change is something that most employees resist. For the sergeant, the best way to lessen this resistance is to:
A. Make sure that any plan he/she devises conflicts as little as possible with existing procedures
B. Downplay the parts of the plan that call for change when explaining it
C. Simply announce the plan and deal with any resistance as it develops
D. Attempt to gain compliance by announcing and explaining the need for the plan before putting it into effect

19. A certain police department has recently reorganized. It now has a high degree of specialization in many newly created specialized units. Which of the following administrative responsibilities is most likely to become more difficult in this department?
A. Staffing
B. Coordination
C. Training
D. Reporting

20. Consider the following statements concerning inspections.
(1) Although inspections may be necessary, they invariably lower morale.
(2) Inspections may be carried out by line or staff personnel.
(3) Police officers must expect to be inspected since most police service is performed by police officers.

Based on the above, which of the following is most accurate?
A. Statements 1 and 2 are true; statement 3 is false.
B. Statements 1 and 3 are true; statement 2 is false.
C. Statements 2 and 3 are true; statement 1 is false.
D. All of the statements are true.

GROUP THREE—10 QUESTIONS— 15 MINUTES

21. Evaluations are conducted for many reasons. Which of the following is most often identified as the primary reason for employee evaluations?
A. Identify potential candidates for promotion.
B. Weed out those employees not suitable for the agency.
C. Improve employee performance.
D. Identify supervisors who are willing to make the hard choices.

22. The rating process should be a very careful and deliberate process. A sergeant who rates a police officer on a general mental impression of the officer instead of the specific traits being evaluated is committing the rating error known as the:

A. Leniency error
B. Associated traits error
C. Central tendency error
D. Halo effect error

23. In a certain police department, the sergeant becomes aware of the existence of an extensive grapevine. Which would be the sergeant's best action?
   A. Identify the leaders of the informal communications network and immediately discipline them.
   B. Identify the rumors being spread on the grapevine, and counter these rumors with the facts.
   C. Identify the leaders of the informal communications network and tell them that in the future they will be fully informed on all issues.
   D. Ignore the existence of the grapevine and after a while it will eliminate itself.

24. Communication should usually follow the chain of command. At times this principle may be violated. Which of the following least accurately describes when this principle is allowed to be violated?
   A. During an emergency
   B. When the reputation of the department is at stake
   C. When a staff officer conducts an inspection
   D. When a sergeant gives orders to police officers not under his/her direct supervision to save time

25. Span of control refers to the number of subordinates a supervisor can effectively supervise. Generally, as one ascends a police hierarchy, the span of control:
   A. Increases
   B. Decreases
   C. Fluctuates unpredictably
   D. Remains the same

26. A police organization is structured by dimensions just as any other organization is structured. Which of the following most accurately describes the dimensions of a police organization?
   A. Vertical and horizontal only
   B. Horizontal and lateral only
   C. Vertical and lateral only
   D. Horizontal, vertical, and lateral

27. Consider the following statements concerning planning.
    (1) Planning is the responsibility of a sergeant because it assists in obtaining the most efficient utilization of police resources, which is a primary concern of the sergeant.
    (2) Planning can make the supervisor's training job easier.
    (3) Planning can make the trial-and-error method of job accomplishment more efficient.
    Which of the following most accurately classifies the above statements into those that are accurate and those that are not?
    A. All of the statements are accurate.
    B. None of the statements are accurate.
    C. Only two of the statements are accurate.
    D. Only one of the statements is accurate.

28. It is a well-established administrative principle that a plan should be developed only when clear need for the plan exists. Where in the typical police agency does this recognition of need usually take place?
    A. Mainly at upper levels of the department
    B. Only at the middle levels of the department
    C. Mainly at the lower levels of the department
    D. At any level of the department

29. As the size of an organization increases, some of the administrative responsibilities are influenced. Which of the following best describes what happens to the process of coordination when an organization grows in size?
    A. Coordination gets harder.
    B. Coordination remains about the same.
    C. Coordination gets easier.
    D. Coordination changes only if the overall number of line units increases.

30. Consider the following statements concerning the control function in a police department.
    (1) One of the primary causes of the present-day control mechanisms found in police departments has been police misconduct.
    (2) One of the purposes of control is to evaluate the use of department resources.
    (3) There is no substitute for a thorough analysis of a well-written report to aid a supervisor in the control function.

Which of the following most accurately classifies these statements into those that are accurate and those that are not?
A. All of the statements are accurate.
B. None of the statements is accurate.
C. Only two of the statements are accurate.
D. Only one of the statements is accurate.

Answer Key

1. C	7. B	13. D	19. B	25. B
2. D	8. C	14. C	20. C	26. D
3. C	9. B	15. B	21. C	27. C
4. D	10. B	16. B	22. D	28. D
5. D	11. C	17. A	23. B	29. A
6. C	12. A	18. D	24. D	30. C

Answer Explanations

GROUP ONE

1. **C** Sergeants, like other supervisors, rate leniently because they want to have the workers as friends, because they believe other supervisors are rating leniently, and also because they believe the evaluation process holds very little real value. Therefore, only statement 2 is not accurate.

2. **D** The traits of two-way communications are that they are slower than one-way communications, so choice A is not accurate; they are more accurate than one-way communications, so choice B is not accurate; and they allow for considerable feedback, so choice C is not accurate. Informal channels of communication involve both one-way and two-way communications, so choice D is accurate.

3. **C** In communicating directives, a supervisor should appear to be supportive of the directive.

4. **D** This is a tricky question. Normally, staff supervisors do not exercise line authority. They are not charged with the responsibility for the accomplishment of a line function. However, in an emergency situation, when a line supervisor is not available, a staff supervisor could exercise line authority over line personnel. For example, at the scene of a serious accident, a staff supervisor in the absence of a line supervisor could supervise the activities of line officers assisting any injured persons. Also, if a line officer engages in

conduct that could cause embarrassment to the department or damage to the reputation of the department and the line supervisor is not available, the staff supervisor could take action. These are *not* the *only* situations in which staff supervisors exercise line authority. They also exercise line authority over the subordinates assigned to the staff unit by engaging in such normal supervisory activities as regulating attendance and punctuality. (The only reason choice B isn't the correct answer is because of the absolute word *only* in the wording of the choice.)

5. **D** Because of the greater potential for the supervisors and workers to socialize, because of the closeness involved, authority is sometimes weakened in agencies with few hierarchical levels.

6. **C** Operational plans serve to guide the police in these instances, such as searching for suspects. Operational plans have, obviously, structured steps, which are to be followed and usually require minimal modifications at the time of execution at the scene.

7. **B** In completed staff work, all the details have been worked out and all that is left to be done is for the unit head to make a decision.

8. **C** If no need exists, then why plan? The planning process should only be invoked in response to an identified need.

9. **B** A supervisor engaged in control makes sure that policies or procedures are followed or that department resources are properly used.

10. **B** About ninety percent of a police department's budget is for salaries and personnel benefits.

Group Two

11. **C** The leniency error is caused by the supervisor's desire to be popular. Rating in this manner is actually a disservice to the employee since the evaluation then has little meaning.

12. **A** The post evaluation interview should focus on what is wrong and how performance can be improved. It should not focus on who is wrong. In any discussion of ratings, the intent is to improve future work. The immediate supervisor observes the work, does the evaluation, and explains it to the employee, and therefore is key in the rating process.

13. **D** It is part of the supervisor's job to accurately and comprehensively report information to his supervisor, who will then be better equipped to make decisions.

14. **C** A commander who works during business hours of necessity must delegate authority for decision making to those subordinates who work at a time when the commander does not work.

15. **B** In the functional organizational structure, a specialist is responsible for a function no matter where it takes place in the organization. This type of organization has the following problems: coordination is difficult, disciplinary systems are difficult to administer, and lines of authority and responsibility are unclear.

16. **B** These tactical plans are usually flexible and can be modified as the need arises, as in a civil disorder when conditions may change rapidly. Plans for major disasters are another example of tactical plans. Remember also that tactical plans are for rare situations.

17. **A** Planning and inspections, which are often performed by both line and staff personnel, can be made the specific responsibility of one unit because the results of a good inspection often reveal a need for planning.

18. **D** When employees understand the need for a plan, they resist it less and support it more.

19. **B** Specialists tend to see the goals of their units as paramount, and often they do not view the goals of the department as having anything to do with them. On the other hand, the tendency is for the generalists in the department to lose a sense of responsibility for the areas that have been specialized. Consequently, coordination becomes more difficult.

20. **C** Most police service is a direct result of the actions of police officers. These officers should and do expect to be inspected either by line or staff personnel, so much so that many officers actually welcome an inspection. It is those officers who are performing their jobs efficiently whose morale is lifted by the inspectional process. Therefore, statement 1 is false and statements 2 and 3 are true.

GROUP THREE

21. **C** Although evaluations may help in the areas indicated in choices A, B, and D, choice C identifies the main reason for employee evaluations, which is to improve an employee's performance.

22. **D** The halo effect occurs when the rater's overall impression of a ratee influences each specific trait being evaluated. This general impression often comes from an isolated trait the employee displays, which the rater either likes or dislikes. The result, then, is often an overall rating based on an isolated trait.

23. **B** Rumors are reduced only by supplying the facts. Remember, in very selected instances supervisors can benefit from the existence of the grapevine by using it to release information. They must be very careful in these instances, however, since the grapevine tends to distort all but the simplest of messages.

24. **D** Choices A, B, and C are examples of when the chain of command need not be followed while communicating. They are in an emergency, when the reputation of the department would be damaged or embarrassed and when the staff function of the department is being inspected. Merely saving time is not an acceptable reason for violating the chain of command.

25. **B** In the typical pyramidal structure of a police agency, with its broad base and apex at the top, the supervisor nearer the top directly supervises fewer people than the supervisor nearer the bottom. Therefore, as one ascends the hierarchy of a typical police organization, the span of control decreases.

26. **D** The vertical dimensions represent the rank-ordering structure, such as the lieutenant is superior to the sergeant. The horizontal dimension represents relationships between employees with the same authority and similar relationships, such as two sergeants working in the same command. The lateral dimension represents employees with the same authority but with different responsibilities, such as a sergeant from patrol interacting with a sergeant from investigations.

27. **C** Two of the statements are accurate. Statement 3 is not an accurate statement. Planning tends to eliminate the need for trial-and-error job accomplishment. Good planning does make the sergeant's training function easier, and it also assists in the proper use of police resources.

28. **D** Recognizing that a plan is needed can be done by the chief's inspectional unit, a middle manager, or a police officer on patrol. Anyone in the department can recognize or uncover the need for a plan.

29. **A** It stands to reason that as more units and personnel are added to an organization, the more difficult it becomes to coordinate the efforts of all employees to a common goal.

30. **C** Statement 3 is false since the best way to control is through personal observation. Statements 1 and 2 are correct. Many of the control mechanisms in existence today were made necessary by police misconduct, and controlling does evaluate the use of police resources.

CHAPTER 8

Community Relations

The need to strengthen the relationship between the police and the community they serve is critical. There is no doubt that crime is not solely a police problem; it is a community problem. If there is to be a lasting solution to the crime problem, it must come from a cooperative effort involving all segments of the public and private sector, including the community in general. Simply acknowledging the need for mutual cooperation, however, is only the first step toward the establishment of effective police-community relations, although it is a necessary first step if progress is to be made. It is the responsibility of the police to take the initiative in this process. The police must make the effort, and it must be a continuing effort. The police will be one of the beneficiaries of a sound police-community relations program because their job will become easier. The community will also benefit greatly because better relations between the police and the community means an almost certain reduction in crime and an increase in arrested offenders.

What Is Community Relations?

Community relations, or more appropriately, police-community relations, is a broad concept that emphasizes that the police are not separate from the community but, rather, an important part of the community. Properly understood, police-community relations is a total concept that must permeate an entire police department to be effective. It is not and cannot be the responsibility of one unit or a few individuals. In fact, the single most important factor in any police-community relations program is the conduct of every police officer who comes into personal contact with citizens. What the chief of the department has to say about police-community relations means little if the cop on the street doesn't put the chief's policies into action, although final responsibility for community relations rests with the chief. In short, police-community relations is the two-way exchange of information and services between the police and the community, designed to produce a mutually beneficial result. Most often, the partnership formed between the police and the community via community relations concerns itself with how common problems can be resolved.

EXAMATOPICS ABOUT COMMUNITY RELATIONS

1. The concept of police-community relations has the objective of preventing or minimizing community problems through the joint efforts of the police and the community.

2. The best way for the police and the rest of the criminal justice system to control crime is to work with the community to reduce the number of people entering the criminal justice system by the use of practices that divert people from crime.

3. The patrol officer who responds to calls for police assistance has the greatest impact on citizens' attitudes toward the police.

4. A big problem in community relations is that, in the United States, there is no general agreement on the meaning of law or on just exactly what constitutes order.

5. Law enforcement is not the only service that the police perform for the community.

6. Public cooperation must be the primary or superordinate goal of the police.

7. Community relations is not one program; it is both a policy and a process.

8. Police-community relations is a proper attitude of the police; it is a way of viewing the responsibilities of the police toward the public.

9. To be effective, police-community relations must emphasize two-way communications.

Importance of Community Relations

The existence of a good relationship between the police and the community is important for a number of reasons. It must be remembered that police departments are specifically charged with the social control of our populace. To achieve this goal, the police have unusual powers in two areas:

1. They have a legal monopoly on the use of force in the United States.

2. They have the authority to arrest on probable cause. This means that they can err in the arrest process if the mistake is a reasonable one.

Because of the official charge to engage in social control, as well as the authority to make arrests and use force, the public, and unfortunately some police personnel, have the erroneous idea that the police are the exclusive agents of social control in our society. Actually, many experts refer to the police as the social control agency of last resort, since the primary social control agencies, such as the family, the school, the church, and the community, all usually have an opportunity to control the conduct of citizens before the police get their chance. Many times, unfortunately, when the police get involved with an individual, it is already too late.

CITIZEN INVOLVEMENT IN POLICE ACTIVITIES

The real importance of community relations, therefore, is that it is the vehicle by which the police can earn the support and cooperation of the public. The really important word in the last statement is the word "earn." You can't earn public support except via the two-way, give-and-take process known as community relations. Through public relations, discussed later, public support can be temporarily obtained, but unless a police department engages in the constant process known as community relations, it cannot maintain support over an extended period of time. As stated by a past President's Commission on Law Enforcement, no lasting improvement can be made in law enforcement unless and until public confidence and cooperation is secured. This is what community relations is all about. Getting citizens involved in law enforcement is the beginning of a partnership that must be formed if the police are to successfully do their job. Listed below are some immediate benefits of citizen involvement in police matters.

1. More crime will be reported, and the reports will be made more quickly.

2. More witnesses to crime will come forth.

3. More police officers will be spared from injury because of timely citizen intervention via calls for assistance.

4. More citizens will actively engage in crime prevention.

5. The quality of life in many areas will improve considerably.

1. If police officers are to be effective in a given neighborhood, they absolutely must understand and make adjustments to the culture of the people in that neighborhood.

2. The police often have to provide social services to people because of the failings of traditional social service agencies.

3. Police administrators have to deal with the attitude on the part of many police officers that social work is not the province of the police; actually, statistics show that about ninety percent of the police officer's job involves the delivery of services and not the enforcement of law.

4. In order for a police-community relations program to operate effectively, it must contain a mutual exchange of ideas and other communications between the public and the police.

5. Certain conditions, such as a large number of arrests for disorderly conduct and resisting arrest, could cause a conflict with the community when they occur in a densely populated area.

Police Roles and Community Relations

What is the main thrust of a police officer's job? This question has traditionally prompted much discussion in police circles. It is, however, a most important question, since the role that the police assume in a given jurisdiction impacts on police-community relations to a significant degree. The way the police behave or the actions they take very often differ from jurisdiction to jurisdiction, even if both jurisdictions are in the same relative geographic area. (Remember, there are over 40,000 police agencies in the United States.) For example, some police agencies deal with minor violations of law principally by use of the arrest process; other agencies would not treat the matter by applying sanctions but rather via a process of education by using official warning and admonitions. In such situations, the determining factor is the role of the police officer involved, which is, of course, established for the officer by the department. As a result of an extensive study of police departments around the country, the noted criminologist James Q. Wilson determined that there are three general styles of policing in use in the United States:

1. Watchman or caretaker style

2. Legalistic or enforcement style

3. Service or assistance style

Before we discuss the role assumed by the officer as a result of the style of policing involved, we will first briefly review the kinds of tasks police officers throughout the country perform, without regard to the manner in which they perform them.

WHAT DO THE POLICE DO?

Contrary to popular belief, the police spend very little of their time "fighting crime." Most studies indicate that only about ten percent of the police officer's time is engaged in law enforcement activities. The great majority of a police officer's time on duty is spent dealing with other issues. To attempt to catalog a complete listing of the tasks performed by the police would be unrealistic.

WHY DO THE POLICE PERFORM SUCH DIVERSE TASKS?

A listing of the activities of the police would of necessity have to include tasks that are responsibilities of other municipal agencies, of the courts, of corrections, and so on. Why is this so? Actually, there is a logical reason that the police over the years have become the quintessential representative of municipal government. The police perform so many diverse tasks primarily because they are mobile and they are available twenty-four hours a day. They are never off duty. This is true even for officers who are not working. There are other reasons, of course, such as their investigative ability and their legal authority to use force, but they are not as important as continuous availability. What is important, however, is to recognize that the way the police perform their myriad tasks has a significant impact on community relations, and the way they perform their tasks is largely a product of the role emphasized for them by their particular agency. There is general agreement that the police assume three distinct major roles, as follows:

1. Peacekeeping role

2. Community service role

3. Crime-fighting role

Remember, these roles are basically a product of the function of the police work involved. For example,

Police officers maintaining order assume the peacekeeping role.

Police officers delivering a service assume the community service role.

Police officers enforcing the law assume the crime-fighting or law enforcement role.

PEACEKEEPING ROLE

It is interesting to note that, although most people view crime fighting as the principal occupation of the police, the first officially sanctioned role of the police in the United States was that of preserving the peace. A nonpolice person might reason that it would be relatively easy for a police officer to slide back and forth from one role to another, but this is not the case, although some role switching can and does take place. The reason that roles are largely predetermined for an officer is that the overall function that the particular department wants to emphasize, such as maintaining order or enforcing the law, is facilitated by such things as existing organizational structure and the amount of discretion the department is willing to give to its officers. Since these kinds of things cannot be easily changed, a department must make a choice. If they choose the "maintenance of order" function, they are emphasizing the peacekeeping role for their officers. The maintenance of order function is facilitated by department policies and procedures that provide for

1. Wide discretionary authority

2. A de-emphasis of the importance of arrest and an absence of arrest quota

3. The development of a close working relationship between police officers and the community through the increased use of foot patrol, for example

4. Decentralized command authority

CRIME-FIGHTING ROLE

This is the role the police officers prefer to play. Most internal recognition, including promotions, is given as a result of law enforcement activities. In a sense, a department that emphasizes the law enforcement function is creating a very heavy burden for itself. This is so because the prevention of crime is simply not exclusively a product of police efficiency. Consider the following.

1. The reasons why people commit crimes are still not understood with any degree of certainty.

2. The apparent causes of crime, such as unemployment, poor housing, and greed, are far beyond the control of the police.

3. Non-public crime such as white collar crime is not amenable to any known patrol strategies.

4. Rehabilitation of convicted criminals exists only in the theories of certain criminologists and penologists.

Nonetheless, there are police agencies that emphasize the law enforcement function, and the achievement of this function (insofar as it is possible) is facilitated by department policies and procedures that provide for:

1. Heavy reliance on the legal process with accompanying quota systems for arrests and summonses; also usually found is the existence of a detective division with its accompanying emphasis on arrests and convictions

2. A centralized organizational structure with emphasis on authority from the top

3. Narrow discretionary authority

COMMUNITY SERVICE ROLE

As its name implies, this police role emphasizes the provision of services to the public. Although in many ways the peacekeeping role and the crime-fighting role are dramatically opposed to each other, this is not true of the service role. However, the service role does seem to blend better with the peacekeeping role than it does with the crime-fighting role. In fact, many so-called peacekeeping activities are in essence service activities. When a police department operates under the philosophy that service to the community should be the most important objective of its police officers, that department emphasizes the community service role.

EXAMATOPICS ABOUT POLICE ROLES

1. The police themselves have traditionally placed major emphasis on the law enforcement role.

2. The present emphasis in progressive police departments is on the service model and the order maintenance model.

3. Police officers assigned to the detective division are most likely to view the community they come in contact with as uncooperative. This occurs mostly because detectives usually adopt the law enforcement job.

4. Police officers must be made to understand that they very often must suffer abuse because they are the visible part of a larger political system.

5. Police-community relations must be performed by all police officers receiving expert advice from specialists; therefore, police-community relations is both a line and a staff function. See the chapter on the principles of management and administration for a discussion of line and staff authority.

6. Foot patrol, because it fosters a close relationship with the community, is an important tool in departments that emphasize the maintenance of order function.

7. No matter what primary function a police department emphasizes, all police officers utilize the order maintenance role at some time.

8. Officers whose role is primarily that of crime fighters hold all community members to one standard of conduct and depend heavily on the formal legal processes of arrest and citation. The opposite is true of officers whose primary role is peacekeeping; they do not rely heavily on the formal legal process.

9. There is very often tension created by the conflicting demands of the crime-fighting role and the peacekeeping and service roles.

10. Because of the widespread use of discretionary authority inherent in the maintenance of order role, there is a high potential for corruption associated with this role.

11. The role a police officer assumes is determined by the operating philosophy of the department, by the norms and mores of society, and by the individual preference of the police officer. It is also determined by the department's organizational structure.

Community Relations Versus Public Relations

It is true that most police administrators nowadays recognize the need for police-community relations, but it is also true that the true meaning and purpose of community relations are often misunderstood. Unfortunately, many police agencies believe community relations is public relations and thereby limit their community relations activities solely to those of a public relations nature. When this occurs, the agency involved will not reap the benefits of a well-rounded community relations program.

WHAT IS PUBLIC RELATIONS AND WHAT PURPOSE DOES IT SERVE?

We have already discussed the meaning of community relations, but for comparison purposes, let us reemphasize the point that the key element in the definition of community relations is a philosophy that involves integrating certain police operations with community needs on a continuing basis in order to resolve common problems. Let us also reiterate that community relations is a two-way process, involving give and take with the community. Public relations, on the other hand, is a unidimensional process. It involves only an outward flow of information from the police to the public. There is usually no formal provision in a police public relations program for even obtaining feedback, let alone acting on the feedback. The type of information that is transmitted to the public via the public relations process is meant to enhance the image of the agency. Public relations, therefore, is an attempt to "sell" a positive police image to the community. More often than not the public relations effort will include a component that concentrates on explaining the objectives of the police agency involved and the various police tactics and programs that will be used to obtain these objectives. Also included in this component is a concerted attempt to win public support for the various tactics and programs involved. The purpose of public relations, therefore, is to achieve the following:

1. Create and sustain a working environment conducive to effective operations

2. Influence in a positive fashion the various publics the police rely upon, including the general public, elected officials, especially those who control the police agency's budget, and the courts

3. Win support for various policies and procedures

HOW IS THE PUBLIC RELATIONS FUNCTION ACCOMPLISHED?

Unlike community relations, the public relations process does not and should not permeate the entire department. It does not require significant involvement from operating personnel. On the contrary, the public relations process seems to work best when it is centralized, either by assigning responsibility for it to one person in a small agency or by establishing a separate unit to handle public relations. In either case, the most important person in the public relations effort is the public information officer. This is in contrast to community relations, in which the most important factor is the conduct of every police officer who has contact with the public. The most common ways by which public relations are performed are as follows:

1. Via agency issued press or media releases

2. Through the work of a speakers bureau

3. By the implementation of special programs such as tours of police facilities, ride-along programs, and awards by the police to concerned individuals and organizations.

EXAMATOPICS ABOUT PUBLIC RELATIONS

1. Because of the nature of the two occupations, the conflict between the police and the press can be lessened but it can never be completely eliminated.

2. The most important person in any police-public relations effort is the public information officer.

3. The involvement of the community in public relations is consciously kept to a minimum.

4. The print media focus on many issues, but their favorite topic seems to be criminal acts of violence.

5. The direction of the flow of information in a public relations program is outward, toward the public.

6. The relative importance of a public relations program can be judged by the rank of the department member in charge of the operation. The higher the rank of the commanding officer, the greater the significance the department attaches to the function.

7. Public relations is not a problem-solving mechanism of the police; problem solving is the essence of community relations.

8. A criticism of public relations is that the wrong targets are often reached. Much time and effort is often spent "winning over" citizens who actually already support the police and not enough time and effort are expended on those who are alienated from the police.

9. It is a mistake to use public relations as a method to deal with problems of a very sensitive or critical nature since public relations is not a problem-solving technique.

10. The best way to "sell" the police department to the public is through efficient and effective police work, not through the use of public relations techniques.

Community Relations Units

In recognition of the importance of community relations, most medium-sized police departments have a full-time community relations officer and virtually all large departments have established specialized units to plan, develop, and coordinate the department's community relations programs. In many small departments, the police chief performs this function. It is true that community relations activities should be controlled and coordinated by a centralized authority, but there are dangers involved in the creation of community relations specialists, very much the same dangers as when any specialist position is created.

DANGER OF CREATING COMMUNITY RELATIONS SPECIALISTS

The problems associated with specialization of the community relations function revolves around the necessity for the actual community relations work to be shared by everyone in the department, especially those who come into contact with the public. Unfortunately, however, it is a well-recognized evil of specialization that, once a specialist position or unit is established, the rest of the department believes that they no longer have responsibility for the work of the specialist. The effect of this in the area of community relations is disastrous. A good working relationship between the police and the community is hard enough to develop when everyone is striving to obtain it; it is impossible to attain if only a few specialists are working at it. This is the most important danger involved in the creation of a specialized unit, but there are other dangers:

1. The public might come to believe that only community relations personnel are interested in their problems.

2. A philosophy might develop that only the community relations specialists require specialized training in such things as human relations and problem-solving techniques, when this training is needed for all patrol personnel.

JOB OF THE COMMUNITY RELATIONS SPECIALISTS

The key to understanding the job of the community relations specialist is in understanding the nature of staff authority as explained in the chapter on the principles of management and administration. This is so because a community relations unit has staff authority over the function for the entire department. If the principles of line and staff relationships are not violated, the specialists can perform many useful and positive functions to further good, effective community relations. A listing of the duties and responsibilities of a community relations unit or a community relations officer is as follows.

1. Research, develop, recommend, and monitor agency policies and programs in the area of community relations

2. Assist line commanders in implementing new policies and programs in their commands and in improving the quality of existing programs

3. Coordinate intradepartmental programs that require the combined resources of more than one unit of the department

4. Provide staff assistance and advice for all of the department's community relations programs

This list is not meant to imply that personnel of the community relations unit do not perform a line function. Community relations officers do, in fact, become directly involved in the day-to-day operations that ensure the success of the department's community relations program. In effect, community relations specialists have both line and staff authority and responsibilities.

1. That other public agencies serve the needs of the public does not relieve the police of their responsibility to create a community relations unit.

2. An important goal of a community relations unit should be to get citizens involved with the problems of their neighbors, to overcome the problem of big city apathy.

Community Relations Programs

There are two ways by which a police-community relations program comes into existence. The first occurs when a police department unilaterally decides that a certain program should be implemented and then sets about to develop the program. After the program is fully developed, the police attempt to implement the program and act surprised, hurt, and sometimes indignant when the community doesn't totally accept and support the department's program. Unfortunately, this is the most common method used to develop and implement such programs. A preferred method is to provide for community involvement in the development and implementation of any new programs. This would include the necessary step of determining the need for the program. Advance participation by the ultimate users or implementers of a plan is good insurance that the plan will work. This is true for almost any kind of a plan.

CRIME PREVENTION AND COMMUNITY RELATIONS

In the early seventies, certain progressive police agencies experimented with blending citizen involvement, a necessary ingredient in any community relations program, with crime prevention activities. Today, crime prevention programs have become the backbone of all police-community relations efforts. Why this has happened is simple: it is a concept that works. It is generally agreed that, in the great majority of cases, before a serious crime occurs, such as burglary, automobile larceny, street mugging, or forcible rape, the criminal must have a desire to commit the crime and a belief that the opportunity exists to commit the crime successfully. There is very little the police and the community can do to reduce a person's desire to engage in criminal activity, but it has been firmly established that the police and the community, working closely together, can in fact impact on the criminal's opportunity to successfully commit the crime. In short, crime prevention, from a community relations viewpoint, means the police and the community collaborating to take away the opportunity to commit preventable crimes. The basic premise of all these programs is known as "hardening the target," or making a particular neighborhood, block, house, or auto more difficult and risky to attack criminally. A very simple example tells it best. Statistics show that about half of all automobile larcenies occur when the keys to the car are left in the ignition of an unlocked automobile. Therefore, a program that convinced car owners to lock their vehicles and take their keys with them would reduce the number of automobile larcenies, at least in the area in which the program is being conducted.

SPECIFIC EXAMPLES OF CRIME PREVENTION PROGRAMS

The following is a listing of community relations and crime prevention programs that tends to show the variety of ways the police and the community can work together to "harden the target" and thereby prevent crime.

BLOCK WATCHES OR NEIGHBORHOOD WATCHES

This program encourages community residents to watch out for their neighbor's property. Watchers are given training in what to look for and how to describe suspects. The importance of quick contact with the police via the telephone is emphasized. Provision is often made to make reports on an anonymous basis, or by using a block watcher identification number.

OPERATION IDENTIFICATION PROGRAMS

In this program the police encourage community residents, merchants, and business concerns to inscribe an identifying mark, usually a social security number or driver's license number, on various high-risk theft items, such as televisions, VCRs, DVDs, stereos, and other personal property. The number inscribed is then sometimes given to the police for ready reference, or it is reported to the police if there is a subsequent theft of any of the marked items.

SECURITY INSPECTION

This is perhaps the most popular crime prevention program. It involves a cost-free inspection of the security of premises, either commercial or residential. A trained crime prevention officer surveys the premise and makes recommendations to reduce the premise's susceptibility to criminal attack.

NEIGHBORHOOD OR TENANT PATROL

This type of program is the most controversial crime prevention program because of the strong possibility of face-to-face confrontation between the would-be criminal and the citizen volunteer. For this reason, training for participants is an essential element of any such program. The volunteers must be trained to be the eyes and ears of the police department, not modern-day vigilantes.

AUXILIARY POLICE PROGRAM

This is a sophisticated and safer option to civilian patrols, and it is also more effective. Civilian volunteers receive comprehensive police training, which includes unarmed self-defense, and are assigned to a structured auxiliary police unit under the supervision of a police officer or coordinator. Auxiliary police officers patrol in uniform, in pairs, and equipped with police department radios. They are trained to avoid confrontations and to call for assistance from the regular police at the first sign of trouble or suspicious activity.

GENERAL EDUCATION PROGRAMS

A concerted effort is made to educate everyone in the community about ways to reduce vulnerability to criminal attack. The various means used to deliver this training include seminars, radio call shows, television talk shows, and pamphlets. When planning these educational campaigns, care has to be taken to avoid making them public relations campaigns. The best way to do this is to somehow provide for a dialogue with the community so a two-way flow of information can take place. Also, if too much "image building" is built into the script, the tendency will be for the community to dismiss the program as propaganda.

REDUCING THE DESIRE TO COMMIT CRIMES

We mentioned earlier in this chapter that there is very little the police can do to reduce a person's desire to commit a crime. However, in certain limited situations, the police can engage in preventive action that can, at least in the immediate instance, reduce the desire to commit a crime. The three areas thought to be the most susceptible to such corrective treatment by the police are as follows.

WHEN INTERVENING IN FAMILY FIGHTS OR DOMESTIC DISPUTES

When properly trained in "crisis intervention" skills, which emphasize early assessment of a conflict and a prompt referral to an appropriate source of assistance, police officers can quite often prevent escalation of domestic disputes into acts of violence. It is recommended that a uniform department procedure be formulated as a guide for police officers in these situations. This procedure should emphasize the necessity to make arrests in family fights and domestic dispute calls when probable cause exists to indicate criminal activity has occurred.

WHEN INTERVENING IN A SITUATION WITH THE POTENTIAL FOR COMMUNITY CONFLICT

Advocates of conflict management training maintain that the police can prevent escalation of potentially violent confrontations through the application of conflict management techniques. Proponents of conflict management training correctly point out that quite often a well-intentioned but improperly trained police officer actually triggers the violence during community conflict situations. Emphasis on early recognition of community conflict is an important element of conflict management, as is the necessity for the police to develop close ties to the community. Situations that seem to be amenable to conflict management techniques are racial conflicts, labor disputes, neighbor-neighbor and landlord-tenant disputes, and civil demonstrations.

WHEN DEALING WITH JUVENILES

The key to reducing the desire of juveniles to commit crimes seems to be a program of diversion. The prevention of delinquency requires early identification of possible problems and appropriate referral to an appropriate helping agency.

TEAM POLICING

Team policing is a term that represents many varying attempts by police agencies to bring the police and the community closer so they can truly work together to resolve their mutual problems. Two common elements of all team policing efforts are as follows:

1. The decentralization of the police organization to provide for more responsiveness to community demands

2. A strong emphasis on community involvement

OTHER COMMUNITY RELATIONS PROGRAMS

It is true that crime prevention programs now dominate community relations agendas, but there are some non-crime prevention approaches to community relations that are still thought to be effective.

COMMUNITY COUNCILS

A community council is a group of representatives from all segments of the business and residential community. The council meets on a periodic basis, usually monthly, to discuss mutual problems with the local police and to explore possible resolutions to these problems. One of the major benefits of a community council is that it can serve as a catalyst for improved communication between the police and the public.

STOREFRONT CENTERS

This is a relatively successful program that requires the establishment of police substations in accessible areas of the community, but most especially in disadvantaged areas. The basic operating philosophy, however, is no different from any other community relations program. It is an attempt to bridge the gap between the police and the community so truly cooperative efforts can be made to increase the quality of life in the community involved. Care must be taken, however, not to let a storefront center program take on a strictly public relations stance. Two-way communication must take place.

EXAMATOPICS ABOUT COMMUNITY RELATIONS PROGRAMS

1. The radio, television, and newspaper media are a principal conduit between the police and the community.

2. In the team policing concept, the closeness of the police officers on the team brings about the community's involvement in mutual problem solving.

3. When ride-along programs involve young community members, more than one youth should participate so it will not appear to be an arrest situation.

4. A main reason the police are reluctant to accept new police-community relations programs is the natural human tendency to resist change.

5. Community relations programs should be designed to meet the needs of the entire community, not just that segment of the com-

munity that demonstrates a willingness to understand the police and cooperate with them.

6. Park, walk, and talk programs are designed to bring motorized police officers into closer contact with the public by having police officers park their patrol cars and walk a beat from time to time.

7. Community relations programs aimed at juveniles are excellent "investments" since the children of today are the public of tomorrow.

8. One of the newest ideas in community relations is the concept of encouraging citizens to engage in crime prevention activities, such as block watchers and tenant patrols.

9. The Police Speakers Bureau program, although well received, has the disadvantage of not being utilized by antagonists of the police.

10. Of all the order maintenance functions performed by the police, none requires more time than intervening in domestic disputes.

11. Intervening in family fights and domestic disputes is a very dangerous activity and accounts for a significant number of assaults on police officers.

12. Department policy covering the handling of domestic disputes must include a clear definition of what relationships are to be considered "family" relationships.

13. Many experts now believe that the greater the extent of the community involvement in a crime prevention program, the greater the likelihood of the program's success.

Advocacy Policing

A comprehensive, well-rounded community relations program should contain three components:

1. Public relations component

2. Community service component

3. Advocacy policing component

We have already discussed the public relations and community service components. Advocacy policing, the third component, is the most controversial of the three and occurs when the police act as "advocates" on behalf of the community in an attempt to win benefits for the community they seem to be unable to gain for themselves.

EXAMPLES OF ADVOCACY POLICING

Many segments of the community, especially in large cities, are not sufficiently acquainted with the workings of the government to obtain maximum service and all the benefits they are entitled to receive. Under these circumstances, when the police intervene on behalf of the community, usually through the specialized community relations units, they are engaging in advocacy policing. Many departments engage in this process without specifically or formally referring to their efforts as Advocacy Policing. This is so because the police often intervene on behalf of citizens in their dealing with other municipal agencies as part of their service function. It is merely an extension of the social work concept of police work for the police to engage in advocacy policing.

EXAMATOPICS ABOUT ADVOCACY POLICING

1. Advocacy policing is very controversial and ambitious since it operates out of the traditional mainstream of police activities.

2. Advocacy policing, like public relations, does not require agency-wide participation since it is performed best by specialists.

Impact of Discretionary Authority

No discussion of police-community relations would be complete unless it included reference to the use of discretionary authority by the police. By the use of discretionary authority we mean the selective and many times discriminatory enforcement of the law. There was a time not too long ago when police administrators refused to publicly admit the existence of police discretionary authority. This, thankfully, is no longer the case. It is now well recognized that the nature of police work demands that the police exercise discretion. When used wisely and when its use is sufficiently controlled, the use of discretion can be a positive force in developing good police-community relations. In fact, it has been stated by experts that the primary way the police can inject community expectations into the criminal law process is through the use of discretion. For example, when alternate side of the street parking regulations must be enforced to allow efficient cleaning of the streets, a policy of allowing controlled double parking on the opposite side of the street being cleaned, in violation of the strict letter of the law, is a way by which the discretionary authority of the police can be used to develop good police-community relations.

EVILS OF DISCRETION

It is well established that the average citizen often judges the quality of police service by the treatment he/she was afforded through personal involvement with a police officer. This is why we have stated so often that the most important factor in any effort to improve community relations is the individual conduct of each and every police officer who comes into contact with the public. If that contact is unpleasant, community relations suffer. The existence of discretionary authority increases the possibility of an unpleasant contact. If the police officer allows individual biases or, even worse, prejudices to influence the exercise of discretionary authority, this is when and how the inappropriate use of discretion severely damages police-community relations. Some examples of how this may occur are as follows.

1. A police officer allows a motorist who violated a traffic ordinance to proceed after oral reprimand but issues a summons to a motorist under identical circumstances simply because the second motorist is disliked by the officer.

2. A police officer utilizes discretionary authority to use physical force on someone he/she dislikes.

3. The problems involving the use of discretion by the police are compounded by the fact that, because of the unsupervised nature of the patrol officer's job, the overwhelming majority of the officer's discretionary decisions are not reviewed for appropriateness.

WHY DISCRETIONARY AUTHORITY EXISTS

As alluded to previously, police organizations are unique because the greatest amount of discretionary authority is exercised at the level of operations by the entry-level worker, the police officer. The reasons police officers absolutely must exercise discretion in their everyday decision-making process are as follows.

1. The sheer volume and breadth of laws the police are required to enforce makes selective enforcement a necessity. This is the principal reason the police engage in the use of discretion. The police, and indeed the entire criminal justice system, simply do not have the resources to adhere to a policy of full enforcement.

2. The understanding that strict enforcement of all laws, without regard to such things as wrongful intent and mitigating circumstances, would result in significant injustices.

3. Many state statutes are out of date or in existence merely to make a moral statement, such as the laws against adultery.

4. The great majority of people in the community are against enforcement of the statute in question.

5. Police officers may be able to trade off a minor violation of law to obtain information to solve a much more serious case.

6. The public itself would rebel over a policy of full enforcement.

IMPROVING THE USE OF DISCRETION

Given that the police cannot function without discretion, what can be done to ensure, insofar as possible, that discretionary authority will not be abused? The following are the most often heard recommendations to control discretionary authority.

1. The various state legislatures should officially recognize the existence of and use of discretionary authority by law enforcement officers. This would serve to legitimize the process and bring it more into the public eye.

2. Federal and state judiciaries should support and encourage the development and implementation by police administrators of administrative rules to govern the use of discretion in their agencies.

3. Police administrators should develop administrative guidelines to assist officers in the proper use of their discretionary authority. Specific examples should be included in these guidelines.

4. Extensive training should be conducted to make police officers better able to properly exercise their discretionary authority.

5. Internal control mechanisms should be developed and implemented to monitor the police use of discretion and to provide sanctions against officers who abuse their discretionary authority.

EXAMATOPICS ABOUT DISCRETIONARY AUTHORITY

1. Discretionary authority in a police department is somewhat unique because it increases as one goes down the chain of command.

2. When the police indiscriminately engage in field interrogations and frisks based on their discretionary authority to do so (and their legal authority), they often disrupt relations with the community because minority groups are so often the targets of this indiscriminate practice.

3. Some police departments control discretionary authority through selective enforcement boards, some members of the board being representatives of the community. These boards, however, do not get involved in civilian complaints against police officers.

4. The most controversial use of police discretion involves the decision to use deadly physical force, that is, discharging a firearm.

5. Virtually all police discretion is exercised in the enforcement of *mala prohibita* crimes, which are acts deemed to be criminal not because they are evil in themselves *(mala in se),* but because society, through their elected representatives, have labeled them criminal acts. Examples are gambling, prostitution, and pornography. These are called criminogenic laws because they do in a sense create criminality. We see a great deal of criminogenic law in the area of victimless crimes. The police must be careful in conducting drives to enforce these kinds of laws since tensions between the community and police are raised during these drives because it always appears that the police have unilaterally decided to clean up the town. This is why it is so important to involve the community prior to starting such a drive. Examples of *mala in se* crimes are murder, rape, robbery, and assault. The use of discretion is not often involved when *mala in se* crimes are involved.

6. The existence of discretionary authority is a definite corruption hazard, for it allows the police to release a law breaker without taking formal enforcement action.

7. The public must accept that the police legitimately have and use discretion as a mark of the profession. It should also be remembered that professional police must demonstrate a greater dedication to the service of their clientele rather than their instant employer, the police department.

Receiving Citizen Complaints

The First Amendment to the United States Constitution guarantees to the people the right to redress their grievances. Just the same, dissatisfaction with the citizen complaint procedure is a main source of hostility between the police and many of the citizens in the community. It is in the best interests of a police agency to establish a grievance procedure that is fully accessible to all the citizens in the community. In addition to being accessible, the procedure for taking citizen complaints should be acceptable to the community. Such a comprehensive system for fully recording and investigating all civilian complaints, including anonymous ones, will often serve to protect police officers from irresponsible accusations. When an investigation uncovers an abusive officer, it is in the best interests of all concerned because then and only then can corrective action be taken.

SUGGESTED GUIDELINES FOR A CITIZEN COMPLAINT PROCEDURE

Following is a listing of guidelines for the establishment of a comprehensive system for receiving, processing, and investigating civilian complaints:

1. Complaints should be received if made in person, by telephone, or through the mails.

2. Regardless of the place of occurrence, complaints should be accepted at any police facility, including the office of the chief of the department.

3. Complainants should not be treated like criminals but rather like responsible citizens trying to correct a possible injustice.

4. Insofar as possible, citizens complaints should not be investigated by the immediate supervisors of the officer about whom the complaint is being made.

5. There should be a written policy outlining the complaint procedure, and the policy should be well known inside of and outside of the agency.

6. All civilian complaint investigations should be based on sound investigative processes.

7. Where possible, a negotiated settlement should be sought that, insofar as possible, is acceptable to all concerned.

8. In all cases in which the complainant is known, the results of the investigation should be communicated to him or her.

EXAMATOPICS ABOUT HANDLING CITIZEN COMPLAINTS

1. When citizen complaints reveal a need to exercise better control of police officers, the quickest and most effective means of accomplishing the needed control is through the department's disciplinary system.

2. The use of profanity by a police officer when settling a dispute with a civilian complainant is unprofessional and reduces the chance of negotiating a solution to the conflict.

3. Since anonymous information is often quite valuable, a police agency should, insofar as possible and unless otherwise prohibited by law, fully investigate all anonymous complaints against police officers.

EXAMATOPICS ABOUT COMMUNITY RELATIONS: MISCELLANEOUS

1. Many segments of the community frown upon the police using community relations as a vehicle to gather intelligence information; the police officers themselves, however, see no problem in this.

2. Promotions in police departments are usually based on law enforcement activities, not community relations activities.

3. Not much peer approval is obtained from community relations activities.

4. Recognition from the media for the community relations activities is negligible.

5. For the police to effectively engage in community relations, they must achieve and maintain a professional status.

6. If the chief of police doesn't support community relations activities, they are doomed to failure.

7. Police officers, in their zeal to promote good community relations, should understand that it is inappropriate to get too personal too quickly with members of the community. For example, the use of first names when addressing certain citizens, especially the elderly, may be interpreted by the citizens involved as disrespectful.

8. Community councils, consisting of community residents or business people, are excellent vehicles to facilitate communication between the police and all sections of the community.

9. Training is an important and necessary ingredient in a police department's community relations program, and the value of community service should be an important theme in all such training.

10. Important training topics for improving a department's community relations are as follows:

    a. Communication skills

    b. Legal use of force, including the department's firearms policies

    c. Conflict resolution and crisis intervention

    d. Culture of minority groups

    e. Recognition of human shortcomings, such as scapegoating, which is immediately preceded by simple preferences, active biases, prejudice, and discrimination

    f. Identification of human responses to frustration, such as projection, repression, displacement, and rationalization

    g. Discovery of communication blocks, such as tabloid thinking

11. The press can be used by the police in the area of public relations. The press seeks to gain and print information about police activities. Their right to do this is guaranteed under the First Amendment to the United States Constitution. However, defendants in criminal actions also have a right to a fair trial under the Sixth Amendment of the Constitution. Often these rights find themselves in competition when the press prints information about defendants who claim that what is being printed about them limits their ability to get a fair trial. The police have attempted to minimize this conflict by setting general guidelines regarding the releasing of information to the press. Some examples of information that should *not* be given to the press include:

    a. Results of forensic examinations, such as ballistic or polygraph tests

    b. Statements made by the defendant or witnesses

    c. Identities of victims of sex crimes

On the other hand, police regulations usually allow the release of information concerning

a. The amount of bail set

b. The defendant's marital status

c. Whether a weapon was used in the crime

d. The identity of witnesses, but usually not the home addresses or telephone numbers of witnesses.

12. Specific police policy for dealing with the press differs from agency to agency. However, all doubts regarding whether information should be given the press should be resolved in favor of not giving out the information. It can always be given later, but once given it is difficult, if not impossible, to take back.

Practice Exercises

You are now ready to do some practice questions. Always try to answer the questions in the allotted time. After completing each one of the three groups of questions, make sure you thoroughly review the explanation for each answer before going to the next set of questions. This includes reviewing the explanations for all questions: those you answered correctly and those you answered incorrectly. This is done to ensure that you always arrive at the correct choice for the right reasons. Remember, now is the time to make mistakes. If you understand why you made a mistake, you should not make the same mistake on the examination, when it really counts.

GROUP ONE—10 QUESTIONS—15 MINUTES

1. Sergeant Barker is placed in charge of the department's newly formed police-community relations unit. The sergeant believes forming the unit is a good idea but that it may have some negative aspects. Which of the following most accurately describes one such negative aspect?
   A. Those officers not picked for the assignment may bear ill feelings toward those assigned to the unit.
   B. The rest of the department may believe that community relations is no longer part of their job.

C. The officers assigned to the unit may believe they are better than those officers not selected for the unit.

D. The rest of the department may try to show the newly formed unit up and indicate it was not needed.

2. It is important for the police to understand the public they serve. As the nation has moved from an agriculturally based economy to one of urban centers, certain changes have taken place. Which of the following is not one of these changes?

A. The neighborhood has come to exercise less social control.

B. In a single city, one can see high levels of wealth and poverty.

C. Those residing in the cities have come to bear with increasing frequency conflicts of a personal nature.

D. The level of involvement among neighbors has increased.

3. Sergeant Rex overhears a police officer briefly using profanity in dealing with an excited complainant in a robbery case. A short time after the incident, the sergeant admonishes the officer about his language. In this instance, the sergeant was:

A. Correct, since profanity decreased the officer's ability to negotiate

B. Incorrect, since the officer's use of profanity made it easier to hold the complainant's attention for a longer period of time

C. Correct, since profanity usually quiets people and impresses them with the authority of the police

D. Incorrect, since if the complainant expressed no dissatisfaction the sergeant should not

4. Where the final accountability for police-community relations lies must be clearly identified and understood for a successful police-community relations effort. The person or persons who have such final authority is (are):

A. Each police officer on a beat

B. All patrol supervisors

C. All commanding officers

D. The chief of the department

5. A police sergeant observes a certain police officer performing her patrol duties. Which of the following actions performed by the police officer is most likely not to promote good community relations?
   A. Greeting civilians on her post with a smile
   B. Referring a citizen to another agency regarding an inquiry about a nonpolice matter
   C. Calling a senior citizen by his first name after meeting him for the first time
   D. Taking the first step to introduce herself to merchants on her post

6. In recent years many community relations programs have taken the shape of crime prevention programs. The public has generally accepted these programs. However, not all the crime prevention programs are without controversy. Which of the following best indicates the most controversial crime prevention program?
   A. Block watcher programs in which some of the participants have wrongfully implicated innocent members of the community
   B. Tenant patrols in which tenants confront the criminal face to face, with the potentially dangerous result of vigilantism
   C. Auxiliary police programs, which are seen by the police as interfering with their jobs as police officers
   D. Security inspections in which there is the potential of receiving a "tip" for services performed

7. The police quite often get involved in nonpolice-related incidents. This accounts, in part, for the extensive amount of time the police spend delivering services to the public. Why this is so is a subject of considerable interest to many. Actually, what the police do is a product of many factors. Which of the following does not accurately describe one of these factors?
   A. The police are available twenty-four hours a day.
   B. The police react to pressures brought about by their various communities.
   C. The police have considerable legal authority to use force.
   D. The legislative mandates of elected officials are very precise.

8. Consider the following statements concerning police discretion.
   (1) The police have generally been reluctant to outwardly discuss this discretion.
   (2) As one leaves the police officer rank and ascends the hierarchy, discretion decreases until it reaches the chief of the department.
   (3) Discretion has no place in a true profession.
   Based on the above, which of the following statements is most accurate?
   A. Statements 1 and 2 are true; statement 3 is false.
   B. Statements 1 and 3 are true; statement 2 is false.
   C. Statements 2 and 3 are true; statement 1 is false.
   D. All of the statements are true.

9. For many years the practice of field stop and frisk investigations has been an irritant to members of the minority community. Which of the following is not an accurately stated reason of why this feeling exists among leaders of the minority community?
   A. These stop and frisk investigations take place indiscriminately.
   B. These stop and frisk investigations take place mostly in the poorer neighborhoods.
   C. These stop and frisk investigations are usually done in an abusive manner.
   D. These stop and frisk investigations never result in any meaningful crime reduction.

10. Consider the following concerning juvenile delinquency.
    (1) The attitude of the public of tomorrow toward the police will be influenced by the attitude of the children of today.
    (2) Because of their twenty-four-hour service, the police are in a unique position to discover conditions affecting juveniles that require attention.
    (3) The position of the police in the overall structure of government enables them to get the cooperation of appropriate groups in carrying forth delinquency prevention efforts.

Which of the following statements is most accurate?

A. Only statement 1 is true; statements 2 and 3 are not.
B. Only statements 1 and 2 are true; statement 3 is not.
C. All of the statements are true.
D. All of the statements are false.

GROUP TWO—10 QUESTIONS—15 MINUTES

11. There are at least three main components in many police-community relations programs. They are public relations, community service, and advocacy policing. Concerning these types of police-community relations programs, which of the following is most accurate?

A. Community service is the most ambitious.
B. Public relations is the most expensive.
C. Advocacy policing is the most controversial.
D. All three components are equally ambitious, controversial, and expensive.

12. The issue of selective enforcement has been a difficult area for the police. An answer to this difficulty has been the use of selective enforcement boards, with some of its members drawn from private citizens from the community. With which of the following would such a policy board usually not become involved?

A. Enforcement of gambling laws
B. Handling of family disputes
C. Civilian complaints against the police
D. Enforcement of prostitution laws

13. When the police conduct a ride-along program involving young community members, it is generally recommended that more than one youth participate in each instance, for which of the following reasons?

A. The police can reach more youths more quickly.
B. It will not look like an arrest situation, and the youths will feel more at ease while in the patrol car.

C. It prevents the police from engaging in improper patrol practices.

D. It provides the police with more witness evidence should an arrest be made.

14. If a police-community relations program is to be successful, then the police should know "Who is the community?" Which of the following best describes the community to the police?

A. Those members of the community who demonstrate an understanding of the position of the police at all times

B. Those members of the community who indicate that they are willing to cooperate with the police

C. Those members of the community who have proven to be troublesome and radicals to the police

D. All of the above

15. A line function is one that does the work of the agency directly; a staff function supports that work. Regarding police-community relations, it would be most accurate to state which of the following?

A. Police-community relations is totally a staff function.

B. Police-community relations is totally a line function.

C. Police-community relations is both a line and staff function.

D. Police-community relations is either totally a line function or totally a staff function, depending upon the size of the department.

16. The police have interceded in the dispute between the press and defendants in criminal actions by setting guidelines for dissemination of information to the press. Which of the following could be given to the press before the trial of a suspect?

A. The results of a polygraph examination of the suspect

B. A statement concerning the anticipated testimony of a witness

C. The identity of a witness

D. The results of a ballistics test concerning a firearm used during the crime

17. Most police authorities agree that, except for the smallest police agencies, a community relations unit is a necessity. However, the size of the unit is often debated. During such debates a number of factors surface to aid in solving the problem of how large a community relations unit should be. Which of the following does not accurately describe such a factor?
    A. Whether other agencies exist that were created to serve the needs of the public
    B. The kind of area (i.e., city or county) being serviced by the police
    C. The size of the department
    D. Whether any friction currently exists between the police and the community

18. Some police experts have described community relations as a tripod of sorts. They have pictured it as supported by three components. Which of the following is not one of these components?
    A. A participative climate of problem solving with the community
    B. Police work that highlights service to the public
    C. Control of the major activities of the police by the community
    D. The one-way, outward flow of information designed to present a positive police image

19. When police officers describe their job, they tend to describe it in terms of its crime-fighting aspects rather than community service. This is true for a variety of reasons. Which of the following least accurately states one such reason?
    A. The media frequently focus on crime fighting aspects but rarely on community service.
    B. With respect to career advancement, making a good arrest is on an equal plane with good community service.
    C. A good arrest record is what gets the approval and recognition of a police officer's peers.
    D. The public is most impressed by a good arrest and not by good community service.

20. The relationship between the police and the community is not as it should be. In fact, relations between the police and the community are often full of tension and conflict. The source of much of this tension and conflict arises from which of the following?
    A. The centralized command structure of most police agencies
    B. Police corruption
    C. The discretionary authority of the police
    D. The constantly changing laws the police must enforce

GROUP THREE—10 QUESTIONS— 15 MINUTES

21. The model of police service offered by a police agency certainly influences its community relations program and necessitates policies and procedures that emphasize certain traits. Which of the following is a trait of a department that emphasizes the crime-fighting role for its police officers?
    A. A loose and general surveillance of the community enabling the police to gather information about criminal conduct
    B. A specialization of duties with the resultant gains in efficiency
    C. An informal hierarchy that allows individual decision making
    D. Combatting criminal activity while adhering to the spirit rather than the letter of the law

22. Sergeant Cleaver is explaining to a group of newly assigned police officers that there is a certain direction to the flow of information in public relations. Which of the following most accurately describes this flow?
    A. Outward
    B. Inward
    C. Either outward or inward depending on the level of cooperation of the target group
    D. Both outward and inward at the same time

23. In examining the role of the police, several distinct roles emerge. Which of the following does not accurately describe one of these roles?
   A. Law enforcement role
   B. Service model role
   C. Private citizen role
   D. Order maintenance role

24. The answer to many community relations problems lies in police training. Which of the following remains a problem of such training efforts?
   A. Getting qualified trainers
   B. What is taught to the police
   C. The amount of time dedicated to training
   D. A serious commitment to understanding the need for training

25. An informed public is usually found to be a cooperative public. Concerning the function of keeping the public informed, the police should remember that greatest confusion exists in the minds of the public with respect to which of the following?
   A. Whom the police should serve
   B. Where the police should be doing their job
   C. How the police should do their job
   D. Why the police do the things they do

26. A certain police sergeant makes the statement that any conflict between the police and the media can be removed totally with the proper effort. The sergeant's statement is:
   A. True, since the problem lies solely in the minds of the police who do not understand the press
   B. False, since the police and the press serve a different purpose in our society
   C. True, since all that is required is to deal with a handful of reporters who are overly liberal in their political views
   D. False, since certain members of the community will always manipulate the press to their advantage

27. Even when there are no unusual circumstances in the community, police officers often encounter a great deal of abuse and disrespect while on post. A sergeant would be most accurate in telling officers that this happens because:

A. Unfortunately, the police must enforce the laws, which for the most part are unpopular
B. Very often the police suffer because they are the visible part of a larger political system
C. Unless the courts give the police more power, nothing will change
D. Almost all citizens resent the authority the police represent

28. Consider the following statements concerning police-public relations.
    (1) The responsibility for public relations is usually fixed in one unit of the department.
    (2) The involvement of the community in public relations is consciously kept to a minimum.
    (3) The most important person in any police-public relations effort is the public information officer.

    Based on these statements, which of the following is most accurate?
    A. All of the statements are true.
    B. All of the statements are false.
    C. Only two of the statements are true.
    D. Only two of the statements are false.

29. When the police work in an atmosphere of public hostility, several consequences result. Which of the following is not one of these consequences?
    A. The police may unnecessarily use force.
    B. Citizens may experience an increase in verbal abuse from the police.
    C. Police officers very often may abuse their authority.
    D. Police officers may quite often act too quickly in any given situation.

30. Although it is difficult to make generalizations in the area of police-community relations, certain general characteristics have been identified by experts conducting studies concerning complaints against the police. It would appear from these studies that the most important characteristics of those citizens who are critical of police service are:
    A. Political preferences and religious beliefs
    B. Area of residence and age
    C. Race and economic status
    D. Race and age

Answer Key

1. **B**	7. **D**	13. **B**	19. **B**	25. **D**
2. **D**	8. **A**	14. **D**	20. **C**	26. **B**
3. **A**	9. **D**	15. **C**	21. **B**	27. **B**
4. **D**	10. **C**	16. **C**	22. **A**	28. **A**
5. **C**	11. **C**	17. **A**	23. **C**	29. **D**
6. **B**	12. **C**	18. **C**	24. **B**	30. **D**

Answer Explanations

GROUP ONE

1. **B** This is always a danger when a specialized unit is formed. In reality, community relations is always everyone's job.

2. **D** Actually the police constantly attempt to get citizens more involved with the problems of their neighbors. This is an especially important goal of a community relations unit. Big city apathy must be overcome for a total crime prevention effort to work well.

3. **A** Profanity might temporarily get attention, but it reduces the possibility of negotiating a satisfactory resolution to the conflict at hand. Besides, the public use of profanity is extremely unprofessional.

4. **D** Many participants in the community relations process are accountable, but it is the chief who is ultimately responsible.

5. **C** Many adult citizens, especially senior citizens, would take offense to such an action and find it demeaning. There is a big difference between being friendly and helpful and getting too personal.

6. **B** The purpose of neighborhood and tenant patrols should be to serve as the eyes and ears of the police, not to confront criminals and act as vigilantes.

7. **D** If anything, the legislative mandates of the elected officials have been overgeneralized, and they are not a factor in determining how police spend their time. Of all the factors involved, it is clear that the twenty-four-hour-a-day availability of the police is the major reason they become so involved in non-law enforcement activities.

8. **A** Statement 3 is the only false statement since discretion is one of the main traits of a profession. Unfortunately, the improper use of discretionary authority is a principal source of irritation between the police and the community.

9. **D** Choices A, B, and C do clearly indicate criticism by minority leaders; choice D is strictly made up. (Also note as a test-taking technique the use of the absolute word *never*. As mentioned in Chapter 2, absolute words often offer a strong clue as to the correct answer.)

10. **C** All three choices describe reasons for police involvement in juvenile delinquency prevention. Since such a great proportion of all crimes, especially violent crimes, are committed by young adults, any youth programs of the police are "sound investments."

GROUP TWO

11. **C** Advocacy policing is the most ambitious and controversial of the three components since it involves operating out of the normal mainstream of police activities. The relative expense of each of the three components varies from jurisdiction to jurisdiction.

12. **C** A selective enforcement board should not be confused with a civilian complaint review board. A selective enforcement board would develop guidelines for police officers to follow when exercising their discretionary authority.

13. **B** Only if the youths are at ease when in the patrol car will beneficial two-way communication take place.

14. **D** The police serve the community, and agreeing with the police is not a prerequisite to being a member of the community.

15. **C** Since it is to be performed by everyone, it is a line function in that sense; however, it does on occasion facilitate other tasks.

16. **C** The identity of a witness might be given to the press, but the results of polygraph or ballistic tests would not, nor would the content of anticipated statements.

17. **A** The existence of other public agencies does not relieve the police of their responsibility for good community relations.

18. **C** Community control of police departments has very few advocates among recognized police experts, although many civil libertarians believe it is a good idea. Regarding the other choices, note that choice A highlights participation, which is obtained through two-way communication, and choice B stresses service. Choice D is nothing more than the police informing the public of who they are through one-way public relations.

19. **B** In more progressive police departments, community service accomplishments are beginning to receive the recognition they deserve. In far too many departments, however, law enforcement activities are given much higher recognition than work of a service nature.

20. **C** Discretionary authority is not only found in the law enforcement activity of the police but also in the areas of public service and order maintenance. However, the greatest amount of discretion is found in order maintenance.

GROUP THREE

21. **B** The crime-fighting role favors the use of specialists to increase their arrest efficiency. It also favors a close surveillance of the community, a formal hierarchy with considerable authority, and a literal interpretation of the letter of the law.

22. **A** The direction of the flow of information in public relations is outward. Remember, also, that public relations is a one-way process and community relations is a two-way process. Therefore, if the question had asked about the direction of flow of information in community relations, choice D would be the answer.

23. **C** It is strictly made up. Choices A, B, and D comprise the three roles of the American police.

24. **B** The problem with police training is not so much the amount of hours devoted to training but the specific content matter of the training. Remember, training should be conducted only after a need for the training is revealed (see the chapter on training and safety for a fuller explanation).

25. **D** This is where the efforts of each member of the agency can help by explaining, where appropriate, the why of an action to the citizen.

26. **B** The police must understand and accept the role of those in the media. The police are in many instances required to keep certain information confidential. Media personnel, on the other hand, see their role as getting as much information as possible in order to keep the public well informed.

27. **B** As the symbol of this system, the police must understand that they are in fact the up-front target for this dissatisfaction. The abuse should, however, not be internalized and taken personally.

28. **A** Note how each of these true statements is the direct opposite of what is true for community relations. In community relations, responsibility lies with every member of the department; the community is heavily involved; and the most important person is every officer who has contact with the public.

29. **D** Actually an atmosphere of public hostility may make police officers reluctant to act. The unfortunate fact is that this can become cyclic. That is, the police inaction then creates more hostility, which, in turn, creates more police inaction.

30. **D** It would seem to follow that most complaints would come from those with whom the police have more frequent contact, and these studies bear that out. Most citizen complaints come from minority group members and young people, two groups with whom the police have numerous contacts.

CHAPTER 9

Patrol Operations

Patrol Function

Patrol is the one police function that cannot be eliminated. The patrol division is the "backbone" of the police department. Most of the money in a police department's operating budget is earmarked for salaries, and the greatest number of officers are assigned to the patrol division. Therefore, most of the money in the budget is used to support the function. One very critical point about the patrol division is that its effectiveness impacts on the effectiveness of all other line units, including investigations, traffic, youth, and vice. The reason for this is that the police officer on patrol acts as the eyes and ears of the rest of the department. So, if the effectiveness of the patrol division decreases, as a general rule so does the effectiveness of all line divisions. There is a definite irony involved in this state of affairs. It is a fact that, although it is unanimously agreed that patrol is vital to the success of the entire department, the more experienced and qualified patrol officers are often removed from patrol duties at the peak of their careers to become specialists.

PATROL RESOURCE ALLOCATION

We have already pointed out that patrol is the most costly police function and that the most expensive patrol resources are the police officers who perform patrol duties. This makes the question of patrol resource allocation especially important. How should police officers be assigned? If the patrol division is to be efficient and effective, the answers to these questions must be given very careful consideration. Unfortunately, there is no one way to allocate patrol resources, but there are some well-established guidelines that must be followed.

PRIMARY OBJECTIVE OF PATROL ALLOCATION

The patrol force should be distributed according to demonstrated proportional need. This distribution must consider where the officers will work geographically and at what times they should work. Most departments base their patrol distribution on the basis of a formula that accounts, insofar as possible, for the major factors that have to be considered to achieve effective distribution. Although this process can admittedly be complex and time-consuming, it is a vital process. Police departments that arbitrarily distribute their labor according to some superficial process or, worse yet, by assigning equal numbers of officers to each of the three shifts are doing a disservice to themselves and their community.

The information needed to input into the patrol allocation formula comes for the most part from police records and reports. Therefore, to have an accurate distribution of personnel, the department's reporting system must be efficient. Once all the information is available, a determination of how personnel are to be distributed can be made. Remember, the goal of personnel allocation is to arrive at a distribution according to a proportional need. Thus, if one hundred officers were available to be assigned to the three shifts and it was determined that fifty percent of the need for these officers existed during the third platoon, the 4 P.M. to midnight shift, then fifty of the hundred officers should be assigned to the third platoon.

FACTORS USED IN THE DISTRIBUTION FORMULA

Choosing factors to be used in the patrol distribution formula is a subjective issue that has to be decided by the department's hierarchy. Also, a decision is needed as to the relative weight assigned to each factor. A listing of factors commonly used in the personnel distribution formula is as follows.

Volume of reported crimes. Here, some distinction is made between more serious crimes and misdemeanors and violations. Also, some departments use only quality of life crimes, such as burglary, robbery, assault, rape, larceny, and arson.

Number of arrests made. The times and places where many arrests are made require the assignment of more officers.

Number of calls for service. Obviously, the more calls for services, the greater is the need for personnel.

Tangible hazards. A police hazard is the existence of something that creates the need for police presence. Examples of hazard factors are as follows:

1. Area where prostitutes congregate

2. Amusement park

3. Drag strip where youngsters race their cars in violation of the law

4. Home for senior citizens

Please note that the formula provides for inclusion of "tangible" hazards. There are also "intangible" hazards, which can't be counted or measured. The best way to deal with intangible hazards is through routine preventive patrol, as explained later in this chapter.

Community complaints. It is generally agreed that there should be a provision for community input into the personnel allocation process. Remember, citizen involvement in police decisions is not the same as community control. Allowing citizen input into decisions makes it easier to implement the decisions.

Generalization Versus Specialization

All police departments face the problem of whether to specialize or, more appropriately, to what degree to specialize since all but the smallest departments utilize some specialization. It is said that delinquencies in the patrol function necessitate greater specialization, but it is ironic that most often the specialist is drawn from the patrol division and is usually a high performer. Therefore, the more specialization is used, the weaker the patrol division tends to become. A further disadvantage of specialization is that the more a department specializes, the less interesting the job of the generalist becomes. In other words, the more routine the patrol officer's job becomes, the more boring and uninteresting it also becomes. For this reason, many departments give the responsibility of conducting preliminary investigations of reported crimes to the patrol officers. In that manner, the officers don't view themselves as "report-taking robots" but as contributing investigators. The preliminary investigation is defined as an investigation of a recently committed crime up until the time when a postponement of the investigation to a later time will not hinder the investigation. Therefore, allowing the patrol officer to conduct the preliminary investigation serves two purposes. One is that, as stated above, it enriches and enlarges the patrol officer's job. The second purpose is that it negates the necessity for the investigator/specialist to get involved in the preliminary investigation unless specifically summoned by the patrol officer.

STEADY SHIFTS

Many police departments assign their patrol officers to steady shifts; that is, some officers perform only day tours, some only 4 P.M. to midnight tours, and the balance work steady late tours. Other departments rotate most of their patrol officers on all tours, such as one week of day tours and one week of late tours. The major advantages of a steady shift assignment are as follows.

1. It allows an officer to become familiar with conditions on the assigned shift. It is well known that different police problems occur at different times of the day and night.

2. It provides supervisors with tools to reward and punish officers through desirable or undesirable shift assignments.

3. It allows the officers to develop regular living habits and is generally conducive to better health and less stress.

4. There doesn't seem to be a major advantage to rotating shift assignments, although the following justifications are often voiced.

   ● They are established by contractual negotiations and can only be changed at the negotiating table.

   ● They are fair and impartial and eliminate charges of favoritism; everyone takes a turn at each tour of duty.

STEADY POSTS

Steady post, sector, or beat assignments are a different issue from steady shift assignments. An officer could have a steady post assignment while working either steady or rotating shifts. The major and very significant advantage of steady post assignments is that the officers so assigned can accomplish two very important objectives.

1. They can become very familiar with the hazards, conditions, and happenings on the post. Remember, in order to recognize the unusual, you must know what is usual.

2. They can, in many instances, achieve a close relationship with those on the post. This relationship fosters citizen involvement in police affairs, which is vital to improved efficiency and effectiveness.

In the recent past, there was a movement away from steady post, sector, or beat assignments due to a belief that they foster corruption. In other words, it was assumed that close ties to the community and corruption went hand in hand. The resulting loss of citizen involvement was staggering, and nowadays most progressive police administrators have renewed faith in such steady assignments, although many also have internal procedures to guard against corruption.

OBSERVATION AND PERCEPTION

Good patrol officers must develop the five senses. The ability to perform the patrol function efficiently depends on the keenness of the senses. The patrol officers' safety as well as the safety of those they are sworn to protect often depends on the officers' observation and perception skills.

As mentioned above, the success of the patrol function depends heavily upon the observation skills of the patrol officer. Please note that we refer to the ability to observe and perceive as skills. It is important for a patrol supervisor to realize that the powers to observe and perceive can be improved. Every newly appointed police officer who works a first tour with a seasoned patrol officer marvels at the veteran officer's ability to point out items of interest or to hear the police radio without ever appearing to listen to it. However, with the application of certain principles, and with practice, the rookie officer can develop those same skills. An important first step in this development is obtaining a good understanding of the process of human observation. First, however, let's understand the close relationship between *observe* and *perceive*. When we observe something, we notice or perceive it. We perceive by becoming aware of stimuli through sight, hearing, touch, taste, or smell.

HOW DOES THE PROCESS OF OBSERVATION WORK?

The process of observation involves perceiving some stimuli through one or more of the five senses, and this perception is instantaneously transmitted via the nervous system to the brain, where it is registered. It is not a photographic process. Most people never perceive what is going on around them because they are preoccupied with other thoughts. They aren't paying attention to what is going on around them. Even those stimuli that are perceived might not be perceived exactly. In accordance with what they expect to occur, people may fill in blank spots or add something to what actually happened. Again, however, the key is concentration or attention.

Now we must consider why we pay more attention to some things than we do to other things. Put another way, why do we selectively perceive things that occur around us? There are external reasons for selective perception and also internal reasons for selective perception.

EXTERNAL REASONS FOR SELECTIVE PERCEPTION

The average person tends to take greater notice of things around them because of:

Unusual size or intensity. Things that are large or loud, for example, tend to be noticed or perceived.

Closeness or proximity. The general rule is that the closer people are to something, the better the chance that they will notice it.

Repetition. Things that repeat themselves tend to be noticed. The repetition doesn't have to be immediate. For example, if every Friday between 1 and 2 P.M. a certain store owner goes to the bank, a police officer would tend to notice it. Remember, you must know the usual to recognize the unusual. If, on a given Friday, for example, the store owner didn't go to the bank, the police officer might think that something is wrong.

Movement. Things that move get our attention more than stationary objects do.

Similarity and contrast. Seeing one bald man in a restaurant by himself might not register, but a dozen bald men at one table would be noticed. That is similarity. If, however, sitting among the dozen bald men was one man with a healthy head of long hair, that would also draw attention. That is contrast.

INTERNAL REASONS FOR SELECTIVE PERCEPTION

People observe some things more than others, not only for external reasons, as discussed above, but also for internal reasons, as follows.

Personal drives. Hunger makes a person notice a restaurant or smell cooking food. Sex drives make us notice those who attract us sexually. Envy causes people to notice those who appear to be better off than they are.

Personal interests. Avid golfers never pass a golf course without noticing it. Movie lovers always notice what's playing when they pass a movie house. People naturally pay attention to what interests them.

Training. For the purposes of the patrol supervisor, training is the most important internal or external factor influencing people's perception of what's going on around them. Police officers can and must be trained or conditioned to perceive stimuli that indicate something out of the ordinary is occurring. This conditioning must involve all of the senses, but especially sight, hearing, and smell. Examples are as follows:

1. Hearing a shot being fired, or a person screaming, or glass breaking

2. Seeing a person running, or a fight occurring, or smoke coming from a building

3. Smelling a fire, a marijuana cigarette, gunpowder, or gas

SUSPICION AROUSERS

Certain things should always attract the attention of a good patrol officer. These are known as attention getters or suspicion arousers. Among the most common of these are:

1. Persons running, especially at night

2. Persons dressed improperly for weather conditions

3. Vehicles driving without lights

4. Dogs barking

5. Cars with broken windows

6. Clean cars with dirty license plates, and vice versa

7. Store owners or workers with frozen looks or who appear frozen in place

8. Cars parked with the motor running

EXAMATOPICS ABOUT THE PATROL FUNCTION

1. The effectiveness of the patrol function in any police department impacts on the effectiveness of all other line units in the department. If the patrol function is performed effectively, the work of the specialized units is facilitated.

2. The police are responsible for patrolling all public areas and cannot take it upon themselves to neglect that responsibility.

3. When establishing post, beat, or sector boundaries, a relatively unimportant concern is the special skills of the officers to be assigned since such assignments are subject to immediate and constant change but boundary lines are changed rather infrequently.

4. The process of specialization weakens the patrol force since the specialists are invariably selected from the patrol force and they are usually very proficient patrol officers.

5. It is always a good idea to involve patrol officers in the resolution of patrol problems; they often have good ideas, and such a practice motivates them to do a good job.

6. The patrol sergeant, who is the first-line supervisor, is the key figure in determining whether patrol is successful; this is actually the major responsibility of the patrol sergeant's job.

7. Patrol is a line function, as is the work of those units engaged in juvenile or youth work, traffic control, investigations, and the control of vice and public morals.

8. It is generally agreed that a good shift for newly appointed officers is the midnight to 8 A.M. shift, when the rookies will have less contact with the public and can be afforded closer supervision.

9. Bicycle patrol is very inexpensive and recommended for use in parks, playgrounds, shopping malls, and similar areas. However, bicycle patrol can be extremely tiring.

10. To the extent that the patrol division fails to do its job, specialized units are needed.

11. Of all of the five senses, sight is, of course, the patrol officer's greatest asset.

12. Human perception is conditioned to human desires, personal beliefs, and expectations. Put another way, we sense what we want to sense and what we believe to be true, and perhaps most importantly, we sense what we already expect to sense.

Kinds of Patrol

There is a common misunderstanding, especially among young police officers, and there is only one kind of patrol, the kind performed by uniformed officers on routine patrol. Although that kind of patrol, known as preventive patrol, is indeed the kind of patrol most often used, there are other kinds of patrol, each one designed to achieve a special purpose. So, if patrol supervisors have to decide what kind of patrol would be best in any given situation, they first have to be sure of the purpose the patrol is intended to serve, for example, to prevent crime, to apprehend criminals in the commission of street crimes, or to deal with a specific condition.

Before considering the various kinds of patrol, let us first define what we mean by patrol: *Patrol* is the planned presence of police officers in a certain geographic area for a specific purpose. So we can see from the definition of patrol that there are different kinds of patrol, depending on the specific purpose to be achieved. The most common kinds of patrol are as follows:

1. Preventive patrol

2. Anticrime patrol

3. Traffic patrol

4. Directed patrol

5. Vertical patrol

PREVENTIVE PATROL

Preventive patrol is the most common form of patrol used by the police. It is also steeped in controversy. Over the years various studies have been made, the results of which evaluate preventive patrol as ranging from useless to effective. Nonetheless, until something better comes along, police departments will continue to rely on preventive patrol. In fact, the terms "routine patrol" and "preventive patrol" are synonymous. They have the same meaning.

THEORY OF PREVENTIVE PATROL

Preventive patrol, and the way in which it is performed, is predicated on the following theory.

1. The great majority of criminals engage in their criminal activity because they have a desire to do so, and they also have an opportunity to do so.

2. A person's desire to commit a crime stems from such things as greed, jealousy, hate, anger, passion, and, perhaps most importantly, from various socioeconomic conditions, such as poor housing, unemployment, underemployment, and a lack of educational opportunities.

3. A person's opportunity to engage in criminal activity stems from such things as victim carelessness, citizen apathy, and a belief that detection, apprehension, and punishment can be avoided.

4. The police can do very little to eliminate or even reduce a person's desire to commit criminal acts. Therefore, to prevent crime the police must concentrate on taking away the belief that a potential criminal can commit a crime and avoid detection, apprehension, and punishment.

The purpose of preventive patrol, therefore, is to take away or significantly reduce a potential criminal's belief that a crime can be committed safely.

HOW IS PREVENTIVE PATROL PERFORMED?

The basic objective of preventive patrol is to create an impression of police "omnipresence"; or, in other words, to make people, including the potential criminal, believe that the police are everywhere and that you never can tell when a police officer will appear. Therefore, to achieve this objective of creating a feeling of omnipresence, preventive patrol must be performed in accordance with the following guidelines.

1. The police officers on preventive patrol must be readily identifiable as police officers. Therefore, they must be dressed in a conspicuous police uniform.

2. A motorized officer engaged in preventive patrol must use a conspicuously marked police vehicle immediately recognizable as an official police vehicle.

3. The pattern of patrol by a police officer engaged in preventive patrol must be one that cannot be predicted. Preventive patrol must be performed in an irregular manner but on a frequent basis. So, for example, a motorized officer on preventive patrol might pass a certain location twice in a ten-minute period and not again for thirty minutes. But it is essential that the officer be recognized as a police officer each time. This is, in theory, how the feeling of omnipresence is created.

FLAWS IN THE THEORY

Unfortunately, preventive patrol has many weaknesses, so that although in theory it sounds as if it should work well, in practice its utility is clouded. The major weaknesses of preventive patrol are as follows.

1. Even at its best, preventive patrol can only control crimes committed in public areas, that is, street crime. Obviously, the police are not authorized to patrol private areas.

2. In many departments, the volume of calls for services makes it virtually impossible to properly perform preventive patrol, since so much time is spent responding to and handling radio runs.

3. If the criminal avoids punishment for committing a crime, then detection and apprehension don't deter crime. For example, if an arrested person is sentenced to probation because there is no prison space, then what punishment was administered? Without punishment, how can there be a deterrent effect? Remember, also, that for punishment to be effective, it must be swift and certain. Severity of punishment is not necessary for deterrence.

ANTICRIME PATROL

The purpose of anticrime patrol is to apprehend criminals during or immediately after the commission of a quality of life street crime, such as robbery, rape, burglary, assault, or larceny. When statistics indicate that, despite prevention measures by the police and the community, a certain area is still rife with street crimes, a kind of patrol different from preventive patrol is needed. More often than not, the kind of patrol that is used in these circumstances is anticrime patrol.

HOW IS ANTICRIME PATROL PERFORMED?

Preventive patrol depends on the police conspicuously attempting to appear omnipresent, but the success of police officers on anticrime patrol rests upon their ability to remain anonymous. They have to blend into the area where they are working. Therefore, their appearance and dress are a product of the appearance and dress of the majority of people in the area being patrolled. For example, if anticrime officers are working a banking area, they might be dressed in business suits, but if they are working on the docks, they would be dressed to look like longshoremen. Area selection is also critical for the success of anticrime patrol, as is time selection. If a very careful analysis of the incidence of quality of life street crimes shows a pattern at certain times and in certain areas, then that area and those times are where and when anticrime personnel should patrol.

DECOY OPERATION

Some anticrime patrol operations include the use of decoys. Here, the idea is carried a step further. Instead of merely blending into a high-crime area at peak times of criminal activity and hoping to interrupt a crime in progress, the decoy operation includes an added dimension. One of the officers involved poses as an ideal target or victim for the criminal element to attack. Under the careful observation of backup officers, the decoy cop will assume the role of the typical victim in the specific area being patrolled. For example, if the purpose of the decoy operation is to arrest those who have been preying on senior citizens around a nursing home, the anticrime officer-decoy will dress up like and pose as a helpless senior citizen. When the criminal strikes, the backup team moves in and an arrest is made. Critics of anticrime tactics maintain that decoy operations engage in entrapment. However, the courts have consistently maintained that merely offering someone an opportunity to commit a crime, as a decoy officer does, is not entrapment. In order for entrapment to occur, some form of enticing or encouragement must accompany the offering of the opportunity. Just the same, the supervisor of anticrime personnel should make certain that the anticrime officers do not engage in entrapment activities.

TRAFFIC PATROL

The primary purpose of traffic patrol is to deter pedestrians and motorists from violating the traffic laws. This means that traffic law enforcement must create deterrents to traffic violations by issuing warnings and/or citations to violators. This deterrence effort is important because fewer traffic violations equals fewer vehicle accidents with their resulting injuries, deaths, and property damage. Statistics indicate that approximately 50,000 people a year die in automobile accidents, and an additional 1,800,000 people are injured every year. So many of the fatalities involve drivers who are under the influence of alcohol and/or drugs.

In addition to traffic enforcement, the police officer assigned to traffic patrol also must investigate accidents, facilitate the flow of traffic, and educate the public about traffic regulations.

TRAFFIC ENFORCEMENT

There are a number of paradoxes involved in traffic enforcement. The first is that police officers are expected to win the trust, confidence, and support of the people in the community. This, as we previously discussed, is an important community relations objective. On the other hand, the police are supposed to enforce traffic laws, including those involving stopping, standing, and parking violations. The conflict that arises is obvious. How can the police win the trust and confidence of the same members of the community against whom they must enforce the traffic laws? For this reason, it is imperative that traffic enforcement be carried out in a uniform, courteous, and professional manner. Another irony is that everyone wants the accident rate to be reduced and the "other guy" to be dealt with properly by the police, but few people readily accept enforcement action when it is directed against them.

HIDDEN ENFORCEMENT

Most experts agree that although visible traffic enforcement is one of the most effective ways of deterring violations of the traffic laws, "hidden enforcement" has very little general deterrent effect. Hidden enforcement occurs when an officer virtually hides from the motoring public in a secluded position to watch for a violation. Many subjects of hidden enforcement go away with a distinct feeling of being victimized and with a strong belief in the existence of a quota system. Hidden enforcement does have some limited usefulness but only in areas with high accident rates.

WHAT IS "TOLERANCE" IN TRAFFIC ENFORCEMENT?

Tolerance is the unofficial gap or difference between the letter of the law and what the traffic officer actually enforces. For example, if the speed limit is 55 mph and enforcement action is not taken unless a speed of 60 mph is observed, then there is a tolerance of 5 mph. Tolerance is common-sense policy, and it works well if it is properly controlled. There should be uniform tolerance levels throughout the agency, but the fixing of tolerance levels should not totally strip the officer of discretionary power. Also, when a tolerance level becomes public knowledge, the tendency is for the tolerance limit to actually become the law.

FULL ENFORCEMENT OF THE TRAFFIC LAWS

It has long been recognized that the police cannot enforce all traffic laws. Instead, the police engage in a policy of selective enforcement of the traffic laws. Selective enforcement means the enforcement of certain specific accident-causing violations at times and at locations in which a high number of vehicle accidents occur. The principle of selective enforcement also applies to the enforcement of criminal offenses. Although it is not practical for regular patrol units to engage in selective enforcement of the traffic laws, it is a good strategy for specially designated selective enforcement units. It should be noted here that it is never a good idea to "throw the book at a violator." When multiple violations are committed, only the violations that are more serious and provable should be cited.

CONFRONTING THE TRAFFIC VIOLATOR

The main obstacle to a successful traffic stop is conflict. Remember, there will always be an inevitable amount of conflict. The trick is to keep it to a minimum. Conflict can be avoided by adhering to the following traffic stop guidelines.

1. Allow a driver, especially one who is apparently accompanied by family or close friends, to save face.

2. Don't be oversensitive.

3. Don't be overtalkative.

4. Don't be abrupt or impolite.

5. Don't preach or be judgmental.

6. Don't demean a driver's ability.

7. Don't use the driver's first name.

8. Never accept a billfold or wallet; make the motorist take the documents out of them.

9. After greeting the driver, explain why you made the stop and what action you intend to take.

CAN CARS BE STOPPED AT RANDOM?

The practice of random stops by traffic officers violates the search and seizure provisions of the Fourth Amendment because they are not based on "articulable and reasonable suspicion." The U.S. Supreme Court regards the practice of random stops as leaving too much discretion with individual officers. However, stops can always be made when a violation is observed or in accordance with a systematic stopping of all or a certain percentage of all cars.

IMPORTANT CAVEAT ABOUT TRAFFIC STOPS

A good patrol supervisor should constantly remind the police officers under his/her supervision that personal safety should always be a concern in all traffic stops. A police officer can never be sure whom he/she has stopped. Relaxing during a traffic stop is truly inviting trouble.

ACCIDENT INVESTIGATION

The first concern of a police officer investigating a traffic accident should be the safety of all concerned. Medical attention must be immediately requested for injured parties, and the normal flow of traffic should be restored as soon as possible, consistent with the investigation that must always take place. The investigating officer must form an opinion of the cause of every accident he/she investigates. A very important point to emphasize to all police officers investigating a vehicle accident is to separate the motorists involved, as well as the witnesses, and keep them separated. They are to be interviewed separately.

Following are the recommended steps to follow when conducting an accident investigation.

Arrive safely at the scene. Sometimes worse accidents are caused by officers overanxious to get to the scene.

Perform first aid, and request necessary medical assistance. Make it a point to ask everyone involved if they require medical assistance. Examine the credentials of anyone who volunteers to render medical assistance.

Protect the accident scene. Put out cones, flares, and other such signals to prevent further accidents.

Separate the motorists, and obtain their credentials. Holding on to their credentials is good insurance against their leaving.

Locate witnesses, and obtain their statements. Don't make general requests to a crowd asking for witnesses. Ask the drivers whom they saw on the scene when the accident occurred or immediately after, and personally approach anyone so identified.

Check the highway and the vehicles involved. Especially check the vehicles against the story told by the drivers.

Care for the property of the injured. Remember, the police are responsible for the property of those removed to the hospital.

Request the assistance of other municipal agencies, if needed. There could be, for instance, gasoline spilled on the street, which must be washed down.

Gather evidence and determine the cause of the accident. Even though the officer didn't witness the accident, he/she must determine its cause. Sources to be used in making this determination are physical evidence, such as damage to the vehicles and skid marks, statements of the participants and witnesses, location of traffic control devices, and knowledge of the rules of the road.

DIRECTED PATROL

The purpose of directed patrol is to deal with specific police problems at specific locations. Directed patrol differs from preventive patrol in its specificity. A particular problem is dealt with at a particular location in directed patrol. A good working definition of directed patrol is as follows: *Directed patrol* is performed when a police officer is directed to deal with a certain police problem or to prevent certain criminal conduct at a certain location and during a certain time period.

The problems to be dealt with through directed patrol and the times and places involved are determined through an analysis of department records, such as complaint files and arrest reports. Another factor to be considered is community input. Directed patrol is a recommended way to deal with repeating community complaints.

VERTICAL PATROL

The purpose of vertical patrol is to deal with specific police problems in high-rise buildings, such as public housing complexes. Remember, however, that unless authorized to do so by competent authority, the police cannot perform vertical patrol in privately owned high-rise buildings. One innovation in the maintenance of order and crime prevention in these types of buildings is the use of closed-circuit television (CCTV) equipment. A problem, however, with CCTV patrol, as it has come to be known, is with vandalism. Spray painting the lens, for example, renders the equipment useless.

EXAMATOPICS ABOUT THE KINDS OF PATROL

1. Preventive patrol, to be effective, must be performed in a conspicuous manner and on a frequent but unpredictable or irregular basis.

2. Preventive patrol does not mean taking away a person's desire to commit a crime; that is far beyond the capabilities of the police. Preventive patrol attempts to take away the belief that an opportunity exists to successfully commit a crime.

3. Preventive patrol includes the development of a community attitude that is pro law enforcement and anti criminal activity.

4. Preventive patrol can only reasonably be expected to control street crimes.

5. When some motorized units are utilized specifically for preventive patrol on an exclusive basis and other units are responsible for responding to "calls for service," the patrol involved is known as "split force" patrol. This technique fixes accountability for preventive patrol.

6. Police officers who perform anticrime patrol must work in civilian clothes of a kind that allows them to blend into the area where they hope to make arrests.

7. Anticrime officers have a very high conviction rate, usually over ninety percent, since they usually arrest persons during or immediately after the commission or attempted commission of a crime.

8. The practice of "concealing" a traffic enforcement vehicle to covertly apprehend traffic violators is frowned upon by the community, mostly because it is indicative of a quota system. This practice is only justified in high-risk accident locations.

9. Enforcement action against an unintentional violator of the traffic laws is imperative since the unintentional violator is more of a hazard than the intentional violator.

10. The purpose of traffic enforcement is not to generate income but to prevent accidents through the deterrence of traffic violations.

11. The enforcement of traffic regulations for the sole purpose of obtaining a predetermined quota of enforcement actions is as repugnant as enforcement for purposes of generating income.

12. In enforcing the traffic laws, a police officer can and should exercise discretion. However, it is essential to note that the officer's decision should be based on the facts in each case, not on personal bias. The officer must be able to support his/her decision in each case. To this end, the making of notes is recommended.

13. Making a traffic stop is risky business. It is always a leading cause of police officer injuries and deaths. Care should always be exercised. Remember, the person in the car knows who you are, but you do not know who he/she is. Such persons could be wanted criminals.

14. At the scene of a vehicle accident, an investigator must check the highway, the vehicles involved, and the people involved for evidence of the cause of the accident.

15. A sketch of an accident scene is important because it can show the third dimension, whereas photographs cannot.

Before proceeding, let's summarize what we have learned. Remember, the kind of patrol it is best to use depends on the purpose to be achieved by the patrol.

PURPOSE OF PATROL	KIND OF PATROL
Prevent crime by taking away opportunity to commit crimes	Preventive patrol
Arrest perpetrators of crime during or immediately after commission of the crime	Anticrime patrol
Deter pedestrians and motorists from violating traffic laws	Traffic patrol
To deal with specific police problems at specific locations	Directed patrol
To deal with specific police problems in high-rise buildings	Vertical patrol

Types of Patrol

We will now shift our focus of attention from the various kinds of patrol in use to the various types of patrol available for use. It is very important to understand the distinction between kinds of patrol and types of patrol. The type of patrol used depends on a determination of how the patrol is to be performed. In a modern-day police department, there are many ways by which a patrol can be performed. The most common types of patrol are as follows:

1. Foot patrol

2. Automobile or motorized patrol

3. Scooter patrol

4. Motorcycle patrol

5. Canine or dog patrol

6. Mounted or horse patrol

7. Marine or boat patrol

8. Air patrol

It is important to point out that the various kinds of patrol can be performed in a number of different ways. So, each kind of patrol can utilize different types of patrol. For example, preventive patrol can be performed on foot, in an automobile or a scooter, with a dog, and so on. Of course, it doesn't hold true that any type of patrol can be used with each different kind of patrol. To cite some ludicrous examples, for purposes of understanding, a police officer couldn't perform vertical patrol in a boat or on a horse, nor could anticrime patrol be performed in a fixed-wing airplane.

For purposes of supervision and control, mostly all patrol is limited to a certain geographic area. These geographic areas of patrol are known in various police departments by different names, but the most commonly used labels are posts, beats, and sectors. *Posts* and *beats* are most often used to refer to areas patrolled on foot; *sector* quite often indicates an area patrolled by some form of motorized patrol. Remember, however, that this terminology is not universal; it differs from department to department. What is fairly universal, however, is the method used to determine the boundaries of a post, beat, or sector. This determination is usually made by considering any or all of the following factors:

1. Nature of the area to be patrolled—that is, industrial, residential, uninhabited, or recreational

2. Amount and kind of crime in the area

3. Population of the area

4. Amount of calls for service in the area

5. Existence of tangible hazards in the area (remember, intangible hazards can't be counted or otherwise accounted for)

6. Amount of inspectional duties in the area

FOOT PATROL

Foot patrol is considered to be the most expensive type of patrol. This is so because of the limited area an officer on foot can reasonably be held accountable for. For example, it might take ten foot officers to cover an area that can easily be patrolled by one or two officers assigned to an automobile. For reasons of expense, there was a definite movement away from foot patrol. However, foot patrol has made a comeback of sorts. Police administrators still recognize the relatively high cost of foot patrol, but they are also aware of the tremendous value of foot patrol in that an officer on foot can develop invaluable close ties with the people in the community. Mutual trust, confidence, and respect is quite often developed. Remember, from the chapter on community relations, how important it is to develop closer ties with the community. It is significant to note that the advent of the portable radio in police work has made the foot officer jobs safer and also made them more useful in answering calls for service. There are many such calls that can be efficiently and safely assigned to foot patrol officers. Finally, it should be noted that foot patrol is the one type of patrol that can be used to perform each of the various kinds of patrol.

FIXED POSTS

A *fixed post* is an assignment that involves such a serious or sensitive police problem that it requires the police officer assigned to stay in a very restricted area. Whatever the problem is that requires the establishment of a fixed post, it is one that must be kept constantly under police observation. Guarding a diplomatic embassy or maintaining security at the entrance to city hall are good examples of fixed posts. Insofar as possible, the number of fixed posts should be kept to a minimum, for the following reasons:

1. They are a heavy drain on police resources. This is the major criticism of the use of fixed posts.

2. They involve a high level of boredom. This problem can and must be dealt with via frequent rotation of personnel so assigned.

PURPOSE OF FOOT PATROL

Foot patrol, routine patrol, and preventive patrol are usually interchangeable terms. Unless otherwise directed, officers on routine foot post must be very conspicuous and attempt to create the impression of omnipresence. They should patrol in an unpredictable manner, that is, on a frequent but irregular basis. This is also known as conspicuous patrolling. Please note that in certain situations, foot officers might want to engage in "inconspicuous patrolling." Here, the officers briefly change the kind of patrol they are performing to anticrime patrol in an attempt to make apprehensions. Remember, however, that wearing the police uniform makes this a very difficult task. Also remember that the biggest disadvantage of foot patrol is its lack of mobility.

AUTOMOBILE PATROL

Automobile patrol as we know it today has been in use by the police in this country for over fifty years. It is by far the most common type of patrol, and it is the most economical type of patrol as well. It can be used for preventive patrol, in which case the vehicle would be conspicuously marked, and it can be used for anticrime patrol, in which case the vehicle involved would be of a kind commonly found in the area being patrolled. It can also be used to perform directed patrol and traffic patrol.

ADVANTAGES OF AUTOMOBILE PATROL

Following is a listing of the advantages of the use of an automobile on patrol.

1. It provides mobility and speed to the officer on patrol.

2. It is especially suited for preventive patrol because it can be so conspicuously marked.

3. It permits the carrying of much-needed emergency equipment.

4. It protects the assigned officer(s) from the elements.

5. It can be used to transport other officers and civilians, police dogs, and prisoners.

6. It is ideally suited for the enforcement of moving traffic violations, especially speeding.

7. It is an ideal way to respond to calls for service.

8. It can be used to establish roadblocks, although most experts agree that this should be done sparingly.

9. It is the best ground vehicle for making high-speed pursuits, although such pursuits should only be made when the danger involved with letting the criminal escape outweighs the danger to the community created by the high-speed chase.

MAJOR DISADVANTAGE OF AUTOMOBILE PATROL

Despite all of the above advantages, automobile patrol has one serious disadvantage. The use of the automobile as a patrol vehicle tends to isolate the patrol officer from the people in the community. In view of the extreme importance of citizen involvement in police work, this is a major problem. It can be alleviated considerably by requiring officers to integrate the major advantage of foot patrol, which is close contact with the community, into their automobile patrol technique. This is done by parking the vehicle occasionally during a tour and patrolling on foot. The use of the portable radio has made this strategy safer and more practical since the officer can maintain constant contact with the dispatcher when out of the vehicle.

ONE-PERSON VERSUS TWO-PERSON AUTOMOBILE PATROL

The issue of one-person versus two-person automobile patrol is controversial and emotional, but not to the degree that it was in the past. The issue, for the most part, has been resolved by recognition of the following facts.

1. It is impossible to establish the across-the-board superiority of either method of patrol, especially in large urban areas with varying population densities and neighborhood characteristics.

2. Very few police departments can afford the luxury of assigning two officers to every patrol car.

3. The answer to the dilemma is most often an intelligent and carefully planned mixture of one- and two-person patrol units.

Advantages of One-Person Patrol

It is generally agreed that the use of one-person patrol units has the following advantages.

1. In most instances, a policy of one person to each patrol unit can double the observable police presence in an area patrolled, thereby increasing the efficiency of preventive patrol by increasing the feeling of omnipresence. However, this advantage only accrues if each person removed for a two-person unit is in fact assigned to a unit of his/her own.

2. Many experts believe that an officer who is alone will devote more time to duties rather than converse with the partner.

3. Officers in one-person cars will not take as many chances knowing they are alone. Please note that, concerning the safety of the officer, guidelines requiring backup units automatically to respond to assignments known to be potentially dangerous are imperative.

4. Personality clashes between the members of two-person units are reduced.

Advantages of Two-Person Patrol

1. Two-person patrol cars offer greater safety if trouble starts because of the doubling of available firepower. For this reason, it is generally recommended that two-person patrol be utilized in areas where it is known that multiple offender arrests are made.

2. The two officers involved can share the task of driving the vehicle.

3. Two pairs of eyes and ears are available to see and hear problems of trouble.

4. One person is free to operate the police radio while the other person drives.

SCOOTER PATROL

Scooter patrol is here to stay in police work. Once police officers saw for themselves how effective scooters are in the right circumstances, the resistance to their use evaporated.

ADVANTAGES OF THE USE OF SCOOTERS ON PATROL

1. They are excellent for use in shopping areas, on beaches and in other recreational areas, and for enforcing parking regulations.

2. They increase the mobility of the officer on foot.

3. They are especially valuable on terrain found at parks and recreation areas, where the shortest distance from the officer to where the officer is needed is across a field or other unpaved terrain.

4. Scooters are very useful in crowd patrol. Using techniques similar to those used by mounted officers, an officer on a scooter or, better yet, a

team of officers on scooters can influence crowds to move in a certain direction or to disperse.

DISADVANTAGES OF THE USE OF SCOOTERS ON PATROL

1. Scooters offer very little protection from the elements, although covered three-wheel scooters do provide some protection; enclosed three-wheel scooters offer considerable protection.

2. They should not be used to pursue automobiles, as this is a very dangerous practice.

3. Scooters are dangerous to use in bad weather conditions.

MOTORCYCLE PATROL

In recent years, the use of the motorcycle as a police patrol vehicle has declined significantly. There are those who maintain that there is nothing that the police can do with a motorcycle that can't be done as well and safer with a different vehicle. The major value of motorcycles seem to center around their usefulness in traffic enforcement, parades, and escort duty. It has the major and very serious disadvantage of being involved in a disproportionately high number of very serious accidents, which often result in the disability of the motorcycle officer involved. Statistics indicate that from ten to twenty percent of automobile accidents result in death or injury, over ninety percent of accidents involving motorcycles involve death or injury. In addition, motorcycles can only be used in good weather conditions.

CANINE OR DOG PATROL

Although it took some time because of the negative associations of the use of dogs caused by their involvement in the control of the civil rights demonstrations of the sixties, the use of dogs on patrol is gaining ever-increasing popularity. This turn of events was caused by the success achieved whenever and wherever they were used. It is now known that the success of police dogs on patrol is based on the relationship between the dog and its handler, on the proper selection and training of the dog, and on the proper education of the public concerning the use of the dogs. Some departments use dogs only on an as-needed basis, but more and more departments are using them as part of their routine patrol operations.

ADVANTAGES OF USING DOGS IN POLICE WORK

The use of properly selected and trained canines in police work offers the following advantages.

1. They are expert detectors of narcotics and explosives.

2. They are extremely useful in searches, especially building searches, although the building to be searched must be empty except for the presence of uniformed police officers and, of course, the object of the search.

3. They have a psychological effect on would-be criminals, which makes them quite suitable for use in preventive patrol.

4. They are excellent apprehenders of fleeing felons.

5. They are valuable in crowd control but shouldn't be used at peaceful demonstrations.

It is important to note that, unless the public is properly prepared in advance concerning the use of dogs, their use could be damaging to overall community relations.

MOUNTED PATROL

The value of the use of the horse as a type of patrol vehicle is clouded in controversy, except in remote areas with difficult access routes. The crux of the debate centers around the fact that the main value of the horse is in an area where there is not a constant need, but the high cost of maintaining the horse is constant. There is no doubt about the horse's extreme usefulness in crowd control, but how often does that need occur?

ADVANTAGES OF THE USE OF HORSES ON PATROL

1. They are excellent for use in crowd control.

2. They can be used to facilitate the flow of traffic in congested areas.

3. They have excellent public relations value.

4. They are quite useful at parks and beaches.

DISADVANTAGES OF THE USE OF HORSES ON PATROL

1. The horse and the officer need special equipment.

2. Training needs are extensive.

3. Housing, care, and feeding of the horses are expensive.

4. Transportation of the horses from their stables to their point of use is a drain on resources.

MARINE OR BOAT PATROL

The need for marine or boat patrol, quite naturally, depends first and foremost on the amount of navigable water in any given jurisdiction. The type of craft best suited for use depends on the purpose of the marine patrol. In areas where there is a drug-smuggling problem, speedboats are used. In any case, the typical marine unit performs the following functions:

1. Enforces laws and ordinances, but usually not those under the jurisdiction of the Coast Guard

2. Performs routine preventive patrol

3. Engages in rescue and tow operations

4. Promotes water safety and conducts safety inspections

AIR PATROL

The helicopter has become the air patrol vehicle of first choice in the United States.

ADVANTAGES OF HELICOPTER PATROL

1. Better and more efficient rescue operations are possible.

2. Quicker ambulance service is afforded, especially in urban areas during times of peak traffic and in remote rural areas.

3. More efficient rooftop searches can be made.

4. High-speed automobile pursuits can be made more effectively and with increased safety.

5. Use of the helicopter results in increased crime prevention and increased apprehension potential.

6. Darkened areas can be more efficiently lit with floodlights.

7. Loudspeakers permit efficient transmittal of information over large geographic areas.

8. Improved coordination of ground units is made possible.

9. VIPs and emergency personnel can be quickly transported from place to place.

DISADVANTAGE OF HELICOPTER PATROL

1. It cannot be used in bad weather.

2. Its use requires special expertise and training.

3. Landing is not always possible, especially in urban areas.

4. There is a relatively short air time potential before refueling is necessary, although great improvements are being made in this area.

5. There is no element of surprise involved with the use of a helicopter.

6. There is a constant danger from trees, high wires, and other obstacles.

7. Flying a helicopter can be quite fatiguing.

EXAMATOPICS ABOUT THE TYPES OF PATROL

1. Conspicuously marked police vehicles are excellent for crime prevention purposes but are not recommended when the patrol objective is to detect and apprehend violators of the law, when they are performing anticrime patrol.

2. When mobility within an area is important, motorized patrol is the answer.

3. The use of one-person motorized patrol doubles the amount of observable patrol in an area but only if the amount of vehicles in use is doubled.

4. Patrol sergeants should terminate vehicle pursuits engaged in by those police units under their supervision if the danger created by the pursuit outweighs the suspect's danger to the community if not apprehended.

5. Two-person motorized patrol is thought to be necessary in areas where a large percentage of multiple offender arrests are made.

6. The advent of the portable radio made it possible for motorized officers to leave their vehicles and perform a portion of their tour on foot in an attempt to develop closer ties with the community.

7. An often stated disadvantage of one-person automobile patrol is that one officer cannot possibly observe what is going on and drive the car safely at the same time.

8. Fixed posts are sometimes required to deal with a highly sensitive or volatile issue but should be used sparingly because they create a heavy drain on overall police effectiveness. They are expensive, and they limit flexibility of assignment to meet changing needs.

9. Although it is true that walking a foot post could become boring, the boredom can be overcome through public acceptance and recognition of those on the post.

10. "Door shaking," or trying the doors of "closed businesses," is ineffective, time-consuming, and a drain on personnel.

11. Studies of foot patrol have revealed that the presence of officers on foot reduces a citizen's fear of crime, although foot patrol doesn't necessarily actually reduce the level of crime.

12. The foot patrol officer should make a conscious effort to make friends on the beat.

13. Officers on foot patrol should use all of the senses while on patrol in order to observe conditions around them.

14. Areas patrolled on foot and those patrolled by automobile should not be mutually exclusive. There is nothing wrong with including a foot post in the area covered by a radio motor patrol car; in fact, it ensures added protection and service to the community.

15. The presence of dogs on routine patrol has a definite psychological effect on would-be offenders.

16. Most police dogs can recognize all uniformed police officers but cannot recognize plainclothes officers.

17. It is not generally recommended that canines be used at the scene of a demonstration, especially if it is apparently peaceful.

18. Some jurisdictions are avoiding the high cost of horse patrol by renting their horses on an as-needed basis.

19. The use of police dogs at the scene of peaceful demonstrations is not recommended because they might polarize the crowd. Polarization occurs when a group of people have their attention focussed on a specific occurrence, such as the appearance of police dogs. When a crowd becomes polarized, it is more likely to become violent as a result of some "triggering" incident, such as someone in the crowd taking exception to the presence of police dogs.

Practice Exercises

You are now ready to do some practice questions. Always try to answer the questions in the allotted time. After completing each one of the three groups of questions, make sure you thoroughly review the explanation for each answer before going to the next set of questions. This includes reviewing the explanations for all questions: those you answered correctly and those you answered incorrectly. This is done to ensure that you always arrive at the correct choice for the right reasons. Remember, now is the time to make mistakes. If you understand why you made a mistake, you should not make the same mistake on the examination when it really counts.

GROUP ONE—10 QUESTIONS—15 MINUTES

1. Different needs call for different approaches to patrol. However, among experts in the field, it is generally agreed that the most expensive method of patrol is:
   A. Radio motor patrol
   B. Foot patrol
   C. Horse patrol
   D. Helicopter patrol

2. Many experts agree that police officers who are recently graduated from a police academy and newly assigned to a patrol precinct should be assigned to which of the following shifts?
   A. The 8 A.M. to 4 P.M. shift
   B. The 4 P.M. to midnight shift
   C. The midnight to 8 A.M. shift
   D. The shift that gives them the greatest exposure to the public

3. Faced with a series of precinct conditions that must be dealt with, a patrol sergeant must decide which would be deterred most effectively by the assignment of uniformed police officers. Which of the following would assignment of uniformed officers on patrol most effectively control?
   A. Rash of family disputes in a certain area where unemployment is high
   B. Dramatic increase of bad check passings in a commercial section
   C. Rise in the number of purse snatchings in an area around a housing project
   D. Series of confidence swindles by two men posing as bank examiners in the banking area

4. Which of the following is not generally considered a line unit of a typical police department?
   A. Youth division
   B. Detective division
   C. Traffic division
   D. Communications division

5. Sergeant Hooper decides to utilize some police officers in his squad in a high-visibility capacity. Which of the following assignments would be least representative of patrol in a high-visibility capacity?
   A. A uniform police officer on routine patrol on the beat
   B. Two police officers in a conspicuously marked patrol car patrolling their sector or post
   C. A police officer assigned to a school crossing
   D. A detective conducting a canvass for witnesses after a shooting incident

6. Proper distribution of patrol officers is an obvious task of any police department. In performing this task, determining which of the following should be done first?

A. How many police officers are available for assignment?
B. What areas of the city have the greatest need for police service?
C. During what periods of time does the greatest need for police service exist?
D. How many supervisors are available for assignment?

7. The canine and its handler have established a place in police patrol operations. However, their use would be least appropriate in which of the following situations?
A. Area where a fight between gangs of youths is rumored to take place
B. Professional sporting event where purse snatchings have occurred
C. Demonstration by community residents, which has always been peaceful in the past
D. Busy throughfare where shoppers are making last-minute purchases before Christmas

8. As crime has moved indoors and vertically upward into high-rise apartments, the police have recommended the use of closed-circuit television as a way to combat this type of criminal conduct. Which of the following is a drawback to closed-circuit television?
A. Residents object to this invasion of property.
B. The use of closed-circuit television is more expensive than patrol by police officers.
C. Closed-circuit televisions are often the object of vandalism.
D. The use of closed-circuit televisions is a drain on personnel since someone is required to constantly monitor the transmissions.

9. The functions the police perform in any given jurisdiction determine to a large extent how the police approach their job. Most police officers emphasize the law enforcement component of their job, but it is generally agreed that the amount of time the police spend performing functions of a service nature is approximately:
A. 33⅓%   C. 60%
B. 50%   D. 80%

10. In performing the patrol function, there must be an awareness that certain hazards are intangible. Which of the following methods is best when dealing with intangible hazards?
   A. Routine patrol
   B. Inspectional duties
   C. Responding to calls for service
   D. Anticrime patrol

GROUP TWO—10 QUESTIONS—15 MINUTES

11. Regarding the geographic layout of foot posts and radio motor patrol sectors, it would be most correct to state which of the following?
   A. They should be mutually exclusive to fix responsibility for the areas concerned.
   B. They should not be mutually exclusive so that coverage can be intensified.
   C. They should be mutually exclusive so that the necessity for either foot or radio motor patrol can be clearly identified.
   D. They should not be mutually exclusive because supervision would be made more difficult.

12. Police departments have long debated over and experimented with the issue of one-person versus two-person motorized patrol. Which of the following statements is not an accurately stated advantage of two-person patrol?
   A. There is less fatigue in two-person cars since one police officer is not required to drive for eight hours straight.
   B. More observation can occur in a two-person car since there are two observers.
   C. The use of two-person cars appear to double the observable police presence in the area patrolled compared with one-person cars.
   D. In a two-person car, one officer can operate the radio and receive and transmit messages while the other officer can concentrate on driving.

13. Sergeant Regal is conducting a training session in accident investigation. During the session, the sergeant states that a police officer investigating a traffic accident should form an opinion as to the cause of the accident. The sergeant's statement is:

A. Correct, since this is one of the prime responsibilities of the police in such instances
B. Incorrect, since most accidents are caused by myriad factors
C. Correct, since not to do so may indicate unethical conduct
D. Incorrect, since only the participants in the accident are totally aware of what took place

14. A certain police sergeant, after a study of speeding regulations, recommends a tolerance of 5 mph to his commanding officer. The sergeant also recommends that the public be made aware of the tolerance. The sergeant's complete recommendation is:
A. Good, since the motorists will know exactly where they stand
B. Bad, since the tolerance limit will become the law
C. Good, since the department's image will be one of fairness
D. Bad, since such tolerance can only lead to unethical practices on the part of police officers enforcing speeding regulations

15. Which of the following is a criticism of decoy operations often heard by police supervisors?
A. Decoy officers, because of their disguises, are often mistaken by members of the public for criminals.
B. There is no real way to measure the effectiveness of decoy officers.
C. Decoy officers have no real interest in preventing crime.
D. Decoy officers are a form of police entrapment.

16. Consider the following statements concerning selective perception by a police officer on patrol.
(1) Similarity and contrast are both internal reasons for selective perception.
(2) Selective perception is such a personal action that it is something that cannot be altered by training.
(3) One sure-fire method of recognizing the unusual is by learning the usual.

Which of the following most accurately classifies these statements into those that are accurate and those that are not?

A. All of the statements are accurate.

B. All of the statements are inaccurate.

C. Only two of the statements are accurate.

D. Only one of the statements is accurate.

17. Sergeant Gold is conducting a training session in traffic enforcement duties. One of the trainees asks the sergeant, "Should the unintentional violator be dealt with more leniently than the intentional violator?" According to accepted procedure the sergeant would be most correct if he stated:

A. "No, mainly because the unintentional violator is unaware of his/her driving actions and is a serious accident threat."

B. "Yes, mainly because the intentional violator has a total disregard for the law."

C. "No, mainly because the unintentional violator will soon become the intentional violator if left unchecked."

D. "Yes, mainly because the intentional violator has probably violated the traffic laws before."

18. The police are constantly striving to find new and better ways to patrol. Lately, police departments have used the concept of directed patrol more and more. This kind of patrol directs a police officer to patrol:

A. Only a certain location

B. Only during a certain time period

C. Only to prevent certain criminal conduct

D. At a certain location, during a certain time period, primarily to prevent certain criminal conduct

19. Police Officer Roe is visited on post by Sergeant Royal. The officer, who has recently completed his probationary period, asks the sergeant to explain the meaning of the "chain of custody" as it pertains to evidence. The sergeant would be most correct if she stated that the chain of custody of evidence means that evidence obtained by a police officer should:

A. Pass through the hands of as few officers as possible and never be outside the control of authorized persons

B. Be delivered immediately to a supervisor, who shall take control over the evidence

C. Be investigated to ascertain all of the previous owners of the evidence

D. Pass only through the hands of detectives assigned to the case

20. The pivotal figure in determining whether patrol is successful is the first-line supervisor. This statement is generally:

A. True, since the first-line supervisor's most important job is seeing that patrol is performed properly

B. False, since the first-line supervisor has many duties and therefore cannot be in all places at all times.

C. True, since the first-line supervisor is the one to whom the public complains.

D. False, since the first-line supervisor is no better than the officers being supervised.

GROUP THREE—10 QUESTIONS— 15 MINUTES

21. A police officer who is assigned to a patrol vehicle that is conspicuously marked by clearly recognizable color combinations and other markings and equipment usually accomplishes all of the following except:

A. Increasing the impression of police omnipresence

B. Increasing the number of traffic violations observed

C. Increasing the patrol officer's attention to and awareness of his/her duties and responsibilities

D. Decreasing the difficulty of the task of supervision

22. Police work often involves activity at crime scenes. Regarding crime scenes, it is generally agreed that the key factor that determines the success of a crime scene investigation is:

A. Efforts of the first officer at the scene

B. Investigative skill of the detective assigned to the case

C. Thoroughness of the supervisor who responds to the scene

D. Technology available to the laboratory technician at the scene

23. Consider the following statements concerning the patrol function in a police department.
    (1) The preponderance of the budget of most police departments goes into the patrol division.
    (2) As the effectiveness of the patrol force decreases, the need for more specialists is increased.
    (3) The backbone of any police department is its first-line supervisors of patrol.

    Which of the following most accurately classifies these statements into those that are accurate and those that are not?
    A. Statements 1 and 2 are accurate; statement 3 is not.
    B. Statements 1 and 3 are accurate; statement 2 is not.
    C. Statements 2 and 3 are accurate; statement 1 is not.
    D. All of the statements are accurate.

24. Consider the following statements concerning the patrol function.
    (1) Foot patrol is less expensive than automobile patrol since there is hardly any equipment to purchase and maintain.
    (2) Any assignment given to an officer on foot patrol requires that the officer be backed up by a motorized unit.
    (3) Any officer assigned to a steady foot post will usually become ineffective after a period of time because of the closeness that develops between the officer and the people on the post.

    Which of the following most accurately classifies these statements into those that are accurate and those that are not?
    A. All of the statements are accurate.
    B. All of the statements are inaccurate.
    C. Only two of the statements are accurate.
    D. Only one of the statements is accurate.

25. The necessity for patrol is obvious. It cannot, however, do all things. What is an example of something that cannot be accomplished by patrol?
    A. Reducing the criminal's opportunity to engage in criminal conduct
    B. Discover conditions that may breed crime
    C. Eliminate a potential offender's desire to commit a crime
    D. Arresting perpetrators of crimes in progress

26. It is accepted that the identification of and answer to many police problems lie with the patrol force. A knowledgeable police supervisor recognizes that this fact is true mainly because of which of the following?
    A. The patrol force serves as the eyes and ears of the department.
    B. The patrol force is the labor pool from which specialists and supervisors will be drawn.
    C. The patrol force has the greatest number of officers and logically should be able to offer the greatest number of solutions.
    D. The patrol force has the ultimate responsibility of repressing crime.

27. Consider the following statements concerning patrol.
    (1) The uniform police officer on patrol represents to the average citizen the ultimate in the decentralization of a city's services.
    (2) The need for specialists is inversely proportional to the effectiveness of the patrol force.
    (3) Most of the evils of specialization of patrol functions are found at the operating level.
    Based on these statements, which of the following is most accurate?
    A. All of the statements are false.
    B. All of the statements are true.
    C. Only two of the statements are true.
    D. Only one of the statements is true.

28. Precinct X has many teenage gangs who engage in antisocial behavior. These gangs have different neighborhoods that each gang considers its own individual territory or "turf." Sergeant Harris directs that each officer on patrol know the exact boundaries claimed by each one of these gangs. The sergeant's direction is:

A. Good, mainly because the officers can keep each gang in its own territory to prevent trouble

B. Bad, mainly because it tends to give too much authority and recognition to these gangs

C. Good, mainly because if one gang is seen going into an area claimed by another gang, it will alert the officers that there may be trouble

D. Bad, mainly because it prevents free access to all streets by all citizens

29. Sergeant Lee is instructing a group of recruits on how to conduct a preliminary investigation. As part of his instruction, he would be most accurate if he defined a preliminary investigation as the conducting of an investigation of a recently committed crime up until the time when:

A. A supervisor arrives on the scene

B. A detective arrives on the scene

C. A postponement of the investigation to a later time will not hinder the investigation

D. The point of arrest

30. Generally speaking, the use of hidden enforcement tactics by the police while enforcing traffic regulations is not recommended. Having officers concealed from public view while waiting for traffic laws to be violated serves neither the public nor the police. There is, however, one limited instance when hidden enforcement tactics would be acceptable. Which of the following illustrates that instance?

A. The suspected violation is drag racing by youths in fast cars.

B. There seem to be a high number of intentional violators.

C. There is a very high accident rate in the area where the hidden enforcement is being used.

D. There seem to be a high number of unintentional violators.

Answer Key

1. **B**	7. **C**	13. **A**	19. **A**	25. **C**
2. **C**	8. **C**	14. **B**	20. **A**	26. **A**
3. **C**	9. **D**	15. **D**	21. **B**	27. **B**
4. **D**	10. **A**	16. **D**	22. **A**	28. **C**
5. **D**	11. **B**	17. **A**	23. **A**	29. **C**
6. **C**	12. **C**	18. **D**	24. **B**	30. **C**

Answer Explanations

GROUP ONE

1. **B** Because of the limited area an officer can patrol, foot patrol is the most expensive mode of patrol.

2. **C** Here, where they have less contact with the public, these new officers can give greater attention to a lighter case load under closer supervision.

3. **C** Preventive patrol can only reasonably be expected to control street crimes.

4. **D** Generally, the line units of a police agency consist of those units engaged in youth work, patrol, traffic control, detective work, and vice control. Radio communications is considered a staff unit.

5. **D** The highest visibility occurs when an officer wears a uniform that can be seen by many citizens.

6. **C** The first step in allocating patrol officers is a determination of when the police officers are needed most, and the next step is to determine where they are needed most.

7. **C** Great thought must be given before dogs are used at any demonstration. It could have the effect of the demonstrators becoming resentful toward the police.

8. **C** Most residents do not object to this security measure, which is quite inexpensive compared with personal patrols, even if a police officer is required to constantly monitor transmissions. The overall savings are still considerable.

9. **D** Actual estimates of service time ranges from eighty to ninety percent of the patrol officer's time. This conflict between roles, law enforcement versus service, creates tensions in the job environment.

10. **A** Intangible hazards, by definition, are nondescriptive and very difficult to identify. One avowed purpose of "routine patrol" is to reduce the negative effects resulting from intangible hazards.

Group Two

11. **B** Foot posts and motorized sectors should not be mutually exclusive; they should include common areas. In that way, patrol is intensified. Regarding supervision, it would be no more or less difficult since the supervisor would of necessity be supervising the entire precinct.

12. **C** The statement in choice C actually reflects a major advantage of one-person patrol. When properly used, one-person patrol doubles the observable police presence in the area patrolled. For example, instead of having five units of two persons each on patrol, it is possible with the same personnel to put ten units on patrol of one person each.

13. **A** Determination of the cause of accidents is what traffic accident investigations are geared to accomplish.

14. **B** Although it may be proper to create such a tolerance, it should not be publicized for the reason stated in choice B; that is, publicly announced tolerances soon become the law, regardless of the wording of the statutory law.

15. **D** The police supervisor must ensure that this very real possibility of entrapment does not take place.

16. **D** Only statement 3 is accurate. Concerning statement 1, similarity and contrast are both external reasons for selective perception. Concerning statement 2, selective perception, which is caused by internal and external stimuli, can be improved by training.

17. **A** Unintentional violators should not be treated leniently because they are not aware of their actions and are therefore a serious accident risk when driving.

18. **D** Taken together, choices A, B, and C form the definition of directed patrol, as indicated in choice D. Remember that directed patrol is a kind of patrol, and it can be performed by using a number of different types of patrol, such as on foot, in an automobile and even in a helicopter.

19. **A** The chain of custody is often started by the first officer at the scene, who is quite frequently the patrol officer on post in the area. Later, in court, the officer involved with producing the evidence must be able to accurately testify about the length of and the links in the chain of custody. The chain of custody of evidence should be kept as short as possible.

20. **A** The sergeant may have many roles but the main responsibility is to see that patrol is properly performed.

GROUP THREE

21. **B** It is believed that because of the feeling of police omnipresence created by the conspicuously marked vehicle, fewer traffic violations will occur in the presence of the officers assigned to the vehicle. In addition, because of the ease with which they are identified as police officers, the assigned officers in a conspicuously marked vehicle will be more attentive to duty, and the supervisory duties of the sergeant are facilitated by the easily recognizable police car.

22. **A** Although the factors included in all of the choices impact on the quality of a crime scene investigation, if the efforts of the first officer on the scene, who is usually a uniformed patrol officer, are faulty, any evidence recovered might not be usable in court. The first officer must protect the crime scene from contamination. Otherwise, evidence will become tainted.

23. **A** The backbone of a police department is the entire patrol force upon which the rest of the department is built.

24. **B** All of the statements are inaccurate. Concerning statement 1, foot patrol is more expensive since an officer on foot can cover far less area than a motorized officer. Concerning statement 2, many assignments can be safely assigned to a foot officer, especially one equipped with a portable radio. Concerning statement 3, the true value of foot patrol stems from the trust developed between the officer and those on the post.

25. **C** Police patrol cannot remove someone's desire to commit crime. Preventive patrol is designed to take away the potential criminal's

belief in the opportunity to successfully commit a crime. It can also be used to make arrests and discover crime conditions.

26. **A** It is the patrol officers who will get the majority of the information needed to develop solutions to police problems.

27. **B** Regarding patrol specialization, the more problems the officer on patrol can successfully handle, the less there is need for specialists. Therefore, those duties not done at the operating level, like staff inspections, are acceptable functions for specialization.

28. **C** In order to know what is unusual in an assigned area, a police officer must know what is usual. And, knowing when something unusual is happening is very important because immediate corrective action can be taken, or referrals can be made. In this case, referral to the juvenile division might be appropriate. Remember, patrol acts as the eyes and ears of the specialized units.

29. **C** This is a working definition of a preliminary investigation. Remember, also, that allowing the patrol officer to conduct the preliminary investigation is a job enrichment technique that is good for the morale of the officer.

30. **C** The only possible use for hidden enforcement techniques is to combat a very high accident rate at the location where it is being used.

CHAPTER 10

Reports and Records

No matter what police line function is involved, there is nothing more important or more valuable to a police officer than information. Every working day a police officer needs access to information about people, places, causative factors, or property. The amount of information a police officer needs is staggering. Consider a partial listing (a complete list would be impossible to create) of questions.

Is this car stolen?

Is this person wanted?

Is this a missing person?

What causes traffic accidents?

Where are the most crimes committed on my post? At what times?

Now consider this question. Where does the information come from to answer these kinds of questions? The answer is simple. The information that police officers need in the field comes from information fed into the police department's information system from, for the most part, other police officers. In other words, police officers collect the information that they and other officers need to do their jobs. More often than not, it is the patrol officer who contributes the most to the department's information system. The reporting requirement of the patrol officer's position is just another example of how the patrol officer acts as the eyes and the ears of the rest of the department. In this chapter we are going to examine the three major stages by which data are transformed from isolated facts into a comprehensive information system serving the needs of the entire department and also of interest to many outside the collecting police agency. These three stages are as follows:

1. Field note taking and crime scene reporting

2. Report writing

3. Department records and the record-keeping function

Field Note Taking and Interviewing

The taking of notes in the field is perhaps the most important step in the information gathering and dissemination process. It is obvious that accuracy is the most important quality of reports and records. This much-needed accuracy depends more than anything else on the integrity of the field note-taking process. The ability of a police officer to obtain and record accurate and comprehensive informational notes is an essential skill that must be mastered.

PURPOSES OF FIELD NOTE TAKING

Obtain a permanent record of police incidents. So many things can result from incidents the police get involved with that it is essential that a permanent record is made of what happened at each such incident. Quite often the only permanent record will be the responding officer's notes. There are times, however, when the officer has to submit a report concerning the incident. Even on these occasions the officer should first record the details in the personal memorandum book or activity log. It is interesting to note that sometimes years can go by before an officer might have to present notes in court as part of a criminal or civil case. Since the officer's log is a public record, it could be placed into evidence at a trial. Or, when appropriate, the police officer who took the notes can be authorized by the judge to refresh his/her memory by reading the field notes. For these reasons, newly appointed police officers should be cautioned not to make personal entries in their official log. Remember, the log is subject to scrutiny by opposing lawyers and quite often these lawyers would use personal notations to embarrass and discredit the police officer witness.

Serve as a memory bank for the preparation of reports. Officers working in a busy command might have to handle a number of radio runs before they get an opportunity to prepare any required reports. When this happens, the field notes are referred to constantly. For this reason, it is a big mistake for an officer to delay the note-taking process. If accurate notes are available, all else can spin off them. If not, the details of the incident could be lost forever.

Evaluate an investigation. Sometimes under the pressure of a crime scene investigation, it is difficult to think through all that is happening. When this occurs, the officer involved is best advised to go through the notes carefully and obtain an insight into the overall picture. Rereading notes often makes things clearer to an investigator.

Guide to interviews and interrogations. Prior to interviewing a witness on an old case or prior to interrogating a suspect in an open case, the officer involved should always refer to the notes so that when the interview or interrogation takes place, the officer will be familiar with every piece of information about the subject and the case. Notes can also be used to guard against witnesses and suspects changing stories without detection.

ABOUT THE FIELD NOTEBOOK

A police officer's field notebook is known by various names, depending on the jargon of each particular department. It is variously called a memo book, an activity log, a field notebook, or simply a log, which is, for the sake of convenience, how we shall refer to it for the remainder of this chapter. It is very important that the police agency involved exercise tight controls, mostly through first-line supervisors, to maintain the integrity of the officer's log. If the following controls are exerted, critics of the tendency of our courts to readily accept an officer's notes into evidence can be silenced.

1. The pages of an officer's log should be consecutively numbered, and the log should be bound together so individual pages cannot be removed. All entries should be in ink.

2. The numbered pages should be lined, but only on one side. In this way, unlined space is available for diagrams and sketches.

3. Skipping lines should be prohibited.

4. Erasures should be prohibited. Errors should be corrected by drawing a line through the incorrect entry, initialing it, and writing in the correct information.

5. Each day's entries should be preceded by the day, date, and tour involved, and the last entry for the day should be followed immediately by the officer's signature.

6. The first entry in an officer's log each day should be the officer's assignment for that day.

7. On a frequent basis, usually daily, each officer's log should be inspected and signed by the immediate supervisor.

8. The first entry of each new log should be the rank and name of the supervisor who "opened" the log for the officer. That same supervisor should "close" the old log and attest to the closing by his/her signature.

9. Officers should be required to store completed logs for their entire careers.

Note that there is disagreement among experts about the style of the officer's log. Some say the notebook should be like a loose-leaf notebook with easily removed pages. Proponents of tighter control of the officer's notebook, however, opt for the bound notebook as described above.

WHEN NOTES SHOULD BE TAKEN

Although as previously mentioned an officer's note-taking responsibilities are extremely important, they should not be paramount. As a general rule, at the scene of a police incident, a police officer should not begin taking notes right away. The reasons for this are as follows.

It could be a safety hazard. An officer who is too anxious to make notes might become careless and fail to notice potential danger. A patrol supervisor should instruct subordinates not to take notes until life and property have been properly protected.

People tend to say less if they see their comments being immediately recorded. An officer who takes notes too quickly may not get the whole story. In addition, more logical notes can be taken once the officer hears the person's complete version of what happened and gets a good general impression of the entire scenario.

TECHNIQUES OF OBTAINING INFORMATION

As a general rule, people are not obligated to give information to the police. Although certain people, including most complainants, are willing to give information to the police, the police officer must often attempt to obtain information from people who are not so willing to give it. There are legitimate professional guidelines to assist an officer in this task, but extreme care must always be taken to avoid violating anyone's individual rights as set forth in the United States Constitution and the various state constitutions. Following are some techniques that are recommended for use by the patrol officer seeking to obtain information from members of the public.

Develop close ties with people on the post, beat, or sector. Patrol officers who win the trust and confidence of the people in their assigned areas will be in an excellent position to obtain information from the public. This is by far the best way to ensure obtaining information.

When dealing with a group of people, do not make a general call for witnesses. Walking up to a group of onlookers and making a general call for witnesses is foolhardy. Instead, some of the following tips might help.

1. Ask people who would benefit from locating a witness who was present when the incident occurred. This person, with the vested interest in locating witnesses, could be a complainant in a criminal case, a victim, or a person involved in a vehicle accident. The potential witness should then be approached and addressed in the following manner: "I understand you were here when the incident occurred. Would you tell me what you observed?"

2. Another tactic to try is to look for people in the crowd who seem to be explaining the incident to others. Once identified, these people should be approached and addressed in the same manner as above.

3. If an officer finds someone who witnessed a police incident, after obtaining the required information the officer should ask if that witness saw anyone else present at the time of the incident. If the witness points out someone else, the process can begin again.

4. Another very good practice to observe at the scene of police accidents, especially those that occur in the street, is for the police officer to record license plate numbers of vehicles at the scene, especially of any vehicle that leaves the scene at the same time the police arrive or shortly thereafter. If necessary, using the license plate numbers to locate them, these individuals can be contacted at a later time.

5. Finally, when dealing with large numbers of people at a very serious incident, such as a homicide, at the very least the names and addresses of everyone present should be solicited.

WHAT INFORMATION SHOULD BE INCLUDED IN AN OFFICER'S NOTES?

When an officer locates a witness, interviews a complainant, or interrogates a suspect, it is very important that all available pertinent information be obtained. Remember, the general rule is to refrain initially from taking notes. Another proven tactic, especially with a person quite willing to volunteer information, is to let the person tell the entire story. While the person is giving an account of the incident, the officer should be making mental notes of inconsistencies and other matters needing clarification or explanation. After the witness tells the story, the officer then takes charge and begins questioning. Remember, however, direct questions have a chilling effect and a concerted effort must be made to make the subject ready to cooperate before he/she is asked direct questions. When questioning begins, it is essential that the officer obtain the answers to the following questions:

```
w h e N
w h e r E
w h O
w h a T
h o W
w h Y
```

Please notice that the last letters of these six essential questions end in the well-known and often-used acronym NEOTWY. An officer conducting an interview and obtaining the answers to all the NEOTWY questions has all the needed information to prepare any police report and/or to advance any investigation.

THE NEOTWY QUESTIONS

As mentioned above, if the answers to the NEOTWY questions are obtained, the officer has obtained the needed information. However, this is not as easy as it sounds because there are many variations of each one of the six NEOTWY questions. It is up to the questioning officer to cover all of the variations involving a particular incident. In other words, the many variations of these six essential questions must be tailored to the specifics in each case.

THE WHEN QUESTION

There are many "when" questions in almost any police incident. Examples are as follows:

1. When did it happen?

2. When was it discovered?

3. When were the police notified?

4. When was anything unusual observed?

THE WHERE QUESTION

Examples of "where" questions are as follows:

1. Where did it happen?

2. Where were you when it happened?

3. Where is the suspect now?

4. Where was the forced entry into the building made?

5. Where was the victim taken?

THE WHO QUESTION

The "who" question is perhaps the most controversial, primarily for two reasons.

1. The average person is relatively unskilled at describing others. It is not unusual to obtain such varying descriptions of the same suspect from two different witnesses that one would swear the witnesses weren't describing the same person.

2. Persons who seem to be too anxious to answer the "who" question might have ulterior motives. For example, in traffic cases, a friend of one of those involved might attempt to pose as a neutral witness and convince the officer "who" caused the accident.

Typical "who" questions are as follows:

1. Who was at fault?

2. Who is the suspect?

3. Who is the victim?

4. Who had a motive?

5. Who was present?

THE WHAT QUESTION

Typical "what" questions are as follows:

1. What happened?

2. What evidence was recovered?

3. What type of weapon was involved?

4. What type of transportation was involved?

THE HOW QUESTION

The "how" question is very important because it is the modus operandi question. Criminals tend to commit their crimes in the same way each time, and this is known as their method of operation, or modus operandi. In some cases, a modus operandi is unique, so that it is like a criminal's signature at the scene of the crime. In fact, many departments have computerized the "how" of all major crimes and the modus operandi of known criminals. If the "how" of a particular crime matches the modus operandi of a known criminal, a very important investigative lead is uncovered.

THE WHY QUESTION

The "why" question is the motive question. In criminal investigations, motive is a very important factor in the investigation. Why someone would commit this crime is a question that often leads to the perpetrator. Typical "why" questions are as follows:

1. Why was the crime committed?

2. Why did you report this incident?

3. Why didn't you report it sooner?

4. Why did you do that?

5. Why did you say that?

QUALIFICATIONS OF AN INTERVIEWER

A police officer conducting an interview has to combine the talents and qualities of a salesperson, a psychologist, the clergy, a friend, and an actor. The officer must be able to converse intelligently with a learned person and also to use the jargon of the street when appropriate. It is very important that the interviewing officer establish a rapport with the subject of the interview. To accomplish this, the skilled interviewer must have a wide breadth of interests. Finding out the interests of the subject of the interview and developing a sense of mutual interest is the key to the establishment of rapport. The interviewer must also have a forceful personality. Many experts believe, in fact, that forcefulness of personality is the primary trait an interviewer must possess. It is essential to the free flow of information that the interviewer instill a sense of trust and confidence in the subject.

GENERAL QUESTIONING GUIDELINES

Following is a list of recommendations aimed at improving a police officer's questioning skills. A patrol supervisor, in the training role, should strive to develop these skills in subordinates. Remember also that direct questions should not be asked until the subject appears ready to cooperate.

Do not ask "yes" and "no" questions. These kinds of questions inhibit the free flow of information. When a subject responds with a simple "yes" or "no" answer, despite the wording of the question, the interviewer must encourage further clarification and qualification.

Only ask one question at a time. Multiple questions confuse the subject and interrupt the logical flow of an interview.

Avoid complex questions. The tendency of a person who is asked a complex question that is not understood is to reply by saying, "I don't know."

Avoid leading or implied questions. Suggesting answers via the wording of the questions is contrary to the purpose of the interview, which is to ascertain the knowledge possessed by the respondent.

Frame request questions in a positive way. Too many officers frame questions in such a way that they make it too easy for the subject to withhold information or cooperation. For example, an officer is encouraging a noncommital response by saying to a subject, "I don't suppose you could come with me to the station house to look at some mug shots?"

MECHANICS OF NOTE TAKING

Good note-taking habits are the hallmark of a competent interviewer. Following are recommended procedures for police officers to follow when engaged in field note taking.

1. Separate witnesses when taking statements from them.

2. Police notes should include a maximum of facts and a minimum amount of opinions and conclusions.

3. Err on the side of having too much detail; this is far better than not having enough detail.

4. Insofar as possible, use the exact words of the subject, and when using direct quotes, use quotation marks.

5. When taking important statements, request the subject to attest to the accuracy of the notes by signing them.

THE CRIME SCENE SKETCH

No discussion of field note taking would be complete without a mention of the crime scene sketch. It is important to note that a sketch of a crime scene is recommended even when photographs are taken. The sketch of a crime scene is a supplement to photographs and written notes. Patrol supervisors must convince their subordinates that artistic ability is not necessary to make an adequate crime scene sketch. This is so because the purpose of the crime scene sketch is to portray pertinent information present at the crime scene accurately, but not necessarily artistically. Also, it should be pointed out that the rough sketch made at the scene does not have to be drawn to scale, although it should be somewhat proportional.

ADVANTAGES OF THE CRIME SCENE SKETCH

The reason a crime scene sketch is made even if the scene is photographed is because the sketch has some decided advantages over the photograph, as follows:

1. A sketch can indicate the third dimension, thereby permitting the inclusion on the sketch of accurate measurements, which represent a tremendous investigative aid.

2. A sketch only has to include essential elements at the crime scene along with their dimensional relationship to each other. Unnecessary details are easily omitted.

3. A sketch can easily be used to show direction, such as north or south.

A MAJOR CAVEAT CONCERNING SKETCHES

It is of vital importance that measurements shown on a sketch be accurately and uniformly portrayed. If an error is discovered in court with respect to any of the measurements on the sketch, the value of the sketch would be considerably lessened, and, inferentially, the competency of the entire case would be questioned.

EXAMATOPICS ABOUT FIELD NOTE TAKING

1. A good question for a police officer to ask when deciding whether to record an incident in the notes is, "Will I be asked about this incident sometime in the future?"

2. A police agency's main source of statistical data is the police officer on patrol.

3. When collecting information about an accident that has come to the attention of the police, a vital item of information is the reporting officer's opinion about the cause of the accident.

4. Crime scene sketches are valuable because they can capture the third dimension. In other words, they are useful because they can contain accurate measurements. However, only factual information should be included on the crime scene sketch, not an investigative hunch or theory.

5. Rough sketches of crime scenes made at the scene do not necessarily have to be drawn to scale, but they should be drawn with some sense of proportion.

6. Witnesses should always be interviewed separately and in all possible privacy.

7. Police officers should be careful to avoid putting their home address and/or telephone number in the notes. In that way, they can avoid harassment should the notebook be lost or stolen.

8. Although the use of common abbreviations is a common practice when taking notes, any individual brand of shorthand is inappropriate. Not only might the note taker be unable to translate the notes at a later date, but it is also certain that no one else could. This could defeat the ends of justice.

9. Field notes must be accurate, legible, concise, relevant, understandable, and comprehensive.

10. The key to the success of a preliminary investigation is the first police officer on the scene because it is that officer who has the best opportunity to arrest the perpetrator, protect the crime scene, and locate witnesses.

11. A police officer's first concern at a crime scene is the well-being of any injured person, including suspects.

12. Whenever possible, significant statements of witnesses or suspects should be reduced to writing and signed by the person making the statement.

13. Insofar as possible, questioning about a police incident should take place as soon as possible after the occurrence of the incident.

14. Precise questioning is the key to preventing interviews from digressing too far from the focus of the interview.

15. A sympathetic approach works very well with most complainants.

16. Sketches are useful when conducting interviews and interrogations, when preparing the crime report and the investigative report, and also when testifying in court.

Report Writing

Report writing is, at the same time, one of the most important duties of a police officer and one of the least popular duties of a police officer. With this in mind, the patrol supervisor should constantly emphasize to subordinates the importance of good reports in an attempt to motivate them to produce high-quality reports. As part of this motivation effort, the patrol supervisor should point out that almost every major improvement in law enforcement has resulted from an analysis of written reports. Furthermore, a police department without a healthy circulation of the kinds of information contained in police reports is ineffective and inefficient.

DEFINITION OF A REPORT

A good working definition of a police report is that it is a verbal or written account of a police incident or a matter under investigation or it is an official statement of facts. The account may be lengthy or brief; it may be simple or complex. It must, however, contain two indispensable elements:

1. It must be accurate. Accuracy is the most important quality of a police report.

2. It must communicate what its sender intends it to communicate.

In addition to these two essential elements, reports should also be concise, clear, and complete.

ORGANIZING A REPORT

Good reports are a product of a good fact-finding effort. Poor reports are a result of poor investigations. This is why in the last section we emphasized the importance of the note-taking process and the value of interviews. A good police report is prepared, whenever possible, in chronological order. The properly prepared police incident report should always answer the six NEOTWY questions: when, where, who, what, how, and why. Remember, as previously mentioned, there are many possible variations of each of these six basic questions.

REPORT PREPARATION

A good report writer is systematic. The following is a recommended procedure to follow when preparing a report.

Gather the facts. This process is addressed in the previous section on field note taking. However, at this point, it is recommended that the spelling of all names to be included in the report be checked and that, insofar as possible, all addresses and telephone numbers be verified.

Sort the material. A decision is made at this point about what material is essential to the report. Although brevity is a desirable quality of a good report, it must not be achieved by leaving out essential information.

Outline the material. The outline should, if possible, be chronological, and the order of the material must make good sense to the writer, or the finished product will not make sense to the reader.

Prepare a rough draft. A final report of any significance should always be preceded by the preparation of a rough draft. When writing the rough draft, don't be overly concerned with punctuation or spelling. The key test of the rough draft is whether it is accurate and if it communicates the message it is intended to communicate.

Prepare the final report. Now is the time to correct all the minor problems found in the rough draft. Remember, a written report is used by readers to evaluate the competency of the writer.

STRUCTURED VERSUS NARRATIVE REPORTS

New kinds of computers are coming onto the market that are particularly well suited to police work, and they will add considerably to the efficiency and effectiveness of the police records system. These computers, however, are quite compatible with structured reports, as opposed to nonstructured or narrative reports. A structured report is easy to complete because it relies heavily on checking appropriate boxes or putting a corresponding number in an appropriate box. It requires very little prose or narrative writing. A nonstructured report, on the other hand, relies exclusively on the written word.

ADVANTAGES OF A STRUCTURED REPORT

The advantages of a structured report are as follows.

1. It is easy and quick to complete.

2. It ensures the collection of needed information.

3. It is quite easily transformed to a data base system. In fact, structured reports are usually designed to ensure compatibility with computerization.

ADVANTAGES OF A NARRATIVE REPORT

The advantages of a narrative report are as follows.

1. It is capable of being much more descriptive and comprehensive than a structured report can be.

2. It is infinitely more flexible than a structured report.

EXAMATOPICS ABOUT REPORT WRITING

1. The first paragraph of a lengthy narrative report should contain a brief synopsis of what occurred.

2. Investigative reports of a crime should not be limited to presenting facts establishing guilt. If the facts point to the innocence of a suspect, then those facts must be included in the report. Remember, an investigation is a search for the truth.

3. Oral reports have two major advantages over written reports. They can be made quickly since no time is spent writing and rewriting. Also, clarifying questions can be immediately asked and answered.

4. Police reports should contain a maximum number of facts and a minimum number of conclusions.

5. Police officers are often judged by the quality of their written reports.

6. Police reports should contain short simple sentences, since long sentences tend to confuse.

7. Wherever possible, police reports should use concise words and be written in exact terms.

8. Police reports should include all relevant details and exclude all irrelevant ones.

9. Reports are used by police administrators primarily for purposes of planning, organizing, and directing.

Department Records and the Record-Keeping Function

No police department can function effectively without some type of records division or records officer. In fact, it is this division or officer who, more than any other support unit or person, does the most to pull together and coordinate the work of the line units in the agency. It must be remembered, however, that no matter how accurately the various reports stored at the records unit are, or how much good information they contain, they are of little value if they cannot be retrieved when needed. Therefore, if department records are to have any value, they must be accurately filed. To prevent friction between personnel of the records division and operational personnel, it is imperative that a clear and definitive policy exist concerning the use of records, especially with respect to who has access to records and when.

CENTRALIZED VERSUS DECENTRALIZED RECORDS

There are so many good reasons a police department should maintain its records on a centralized basis that it is a wonder that some departments still have a decentralized record-keeping system. In the following sections we will present the advantages of a centralized system and the disadvantages of a decentralized system. As there are no generally recognized advantages of a decentralized system or disadvantages of a centralized system, none will be presented.

ADVANTAGES OF A CENTRALIZED RECORD SYSTEM

1. When records are kept on a centralized basis, then and only then is the valuable information contained in the records readily available for use by the entire department.

2. A well-kept central records system ensures coordination of effort.

3. The responsibility for the record-keeping function is fixed.

4. Responses to requests for information are processed more quickly with a centralized system.

DISADVANTAGES OF A DECENTRALIZED RECORD-KEEPING SYSTEM

1. The first and principal disadvantage of a decentralized record-keeping system lies in the possibility of less than honest reporting and record keeping. With no outside overseer, the temptation to alter records might become too great for certain weak administrators to resist.

2. The response to requests for information is slower than in a centralized system since the records of many units must be queried.

3. The advantages of specialization are not realized; that is, records experts are not developed.

INFORMATION VERSUS INTELLIGENCE

Contrary to the belief of some, information is not synonymous with intelligence. Only after a series of procedural steps does information become intelligence, which can then be circulated with a high degree of reliance concerning its reliability. These procedural steps are as follows.

1. Information is collected via overt and covert means.

2. The collected information is evaluated, with special emphasis on the reliability of the source of the information.

3. The information evaluated as reliable is then collated with other similar intelligence data.

4. The collated material is then analyzed to determine its meaning and value.

5. The analyzed intelligence is then disseminated on a need to know or right to know basis.

EXAMATOPICS ABOUT POLICE RECORDS

1. The value of police records is determined primarily by the frequency and extent of their use.

2. It is imperative to a good working relationship between operations personnel and records-keeping personnel that a clear policy concerning the use of records be established.

3. Reports concerning the times and locations of the occurrence of crimes and traffic accidents are essential to an efficient policy of selective enforcement. These reports help the police to decide when and where enforcement action should be taken.

4. Many traffic accidents are not reported to the police. The exception is accidents involving fatalities.

5. The police should always accept and follow up on anonymous tips or complaints. They often contain good information and serve to uncover serious deficiencies.

6. It is generally agreed that police records should be kept at a centralized location to increase their availability. An exception involves records kept by the vice division, since these records are quite often confidential.

7. The biggest danger of a decentralized record-keeping system is the increased potential for less than honest reporting and record keeping.

8. The National Crime Information Center (NCIC) is the FBI computerized files containing information on wanted persons, stolen and/or missing property, and criminal histories.

9. The Uniform Crime Reports are an annual compilation of crimes reported to the police, which is published by the FBI.

Practice Exercises

You are now ready to do some practice questions. Always try to answer the questions in the allotted time. After completing each one of the three groups of questions, make sure you thoroughly review the explanation for each answer before going to the next set of questions. This includes reviewing the explanations for all questions: those you answered correctly and those you answered incorrectly. This is done to ensure that you always arrive at the correct choice for the right reasons. Remember, now is the time to make mistakes. If you understand why you made a mistake, you should not make the same mistake on the examination when it really counts.

GROUP ONE—10 QUESTIONS—15 MINUTES

1. At times, a police sergeant may be required to make an oral report. Which of the following is the main advantage of an oral report?
   A. It is fast.
   B. It is accurate.
   C. It cannot be changed because once something is said it cannot be retracted.
   D. It tends to be more complete than a written report.

2. Intelligence records can greatly assist police supervisors in dealing with criminal activities. Which of the following is probably the greatest problem with intelligence records?
   A. They are not always completely accurate.
   B. They sometimes do not leave the intelligence units and reach the operating units.
   C. They are never purged; therefore they are never totally current.
   D. They never give the full story.

3. Consider the following statements concerning police report writing:
   (1) A police agency's main source of statistical data is the police officer on patrol.
   (2) An oral report has no advantages over a written report.
   (3) Intelligence should only be disseminated on a "right to know" basis.
   Which of the following most accurately classifies these statements into those that are accurate and those that are not?
   A. All of the statements are accurate.
   B. None of the statements is accurate.
   C. Only two of the statements are accurate.
   D. Only one of the statements is accurate.

4. One of the reports prepared in connection with a crime scene is the crime scene sketch. The crime scene sketch should include all of the following except:
   A. Items that may have evidentiary value
   B. Where the perpetrator stood in relation to the victim as determined by an opinion of the assigned detective
   C. The length of the walls
   D. The location and placement of the furniture

5. Sergeant Penn is preparing a narrative-style report for his commanding officer concerning a robbery. The sergeant should begin this narrative report with a:
   A. Clear statement of his conclusion
   B. Short synopsis of what occurred
   C. Complete description of all persons involved
   D. Statement indicating the source of his information

6. When records are kept centrally many advantages result. Which of the following does not accurately describe one of these advantages?
   A. A well-kept central records system ensures coordination.
   B. The responsibility for record keeping is more easily fixed when records are centralized.
   C. The information of one officer can be shared more readily with the entire department.
   D. The response to an inquiry, although a little slower than the response from a decentralized system, is more apt to be forthright and accurate.

7. One of the reports prepared at a crime scene is the crime scene sketch. Which of the following is the main advantage of such a sketch?
   A. It ensures that all items present at the scene are noted for later investigation.
   B. It can indicate dimensions.
   C. It can refresh an investigator's memory at a later date.
   D. It is always accepted in court as a full representation of the crime scene.

8. Although the requirements of good reporting are many, which of the following is considered to be the most important quality of a good report?
   A. Timeliness
   B. Accuracy
   C. Neatness
   D. Brevity

9. Sergeant Poster is explaining the main purpose of the reporting systems in the precinct to the officers in her squad. She would be most accurate if she stated which of the following?
   A. The reports we prepare are a way to document the things we do in the precinct.
   B. Each time a report is made, it provides facts that can be used to make statistical reports.
   C. Reports are the only way we can show a need for more personnel.
   D. The preparation of reports is not the objective but a tool in obtaining the objectives of the precinct.

10. Since the early days of the automobile, the police have reported and compiled data and statistics on traffic-related matters. In which of the following areas are these statistics most likely to be most accurate?
    A. Instances of persons driving while under the influence of alcohol or drugs
    B. Instances of persons exceeding the speed limit while driving
    C. Accidents involving personal injury or property damage only
    D. Accidents involving fatalities

GROUP TWO—10 QUESTIONS—15 MINUTES

11. Raw statistical data often become the basis for police reports. Which of the following best indicates a police agency's main source of this statistical data?
    A. Citizen in the community
    B. Police officer on patrol
    C. Specialized detective
    D. Expert technicians

12. The taking of statements from witnesses at the scene of an accident is a task often performed by police officers. A police supervisor should recommend which of the following to police officers performing this task?
    A. A different investigator should interview each witness separately and in private.
    B. Each witness should be interviewed alone and in private.
    C. Witnesses who agree about what took place should be interviewed as a group to avoid unnecessary duplication.
    D. All witnesses should be interviewed by the same officer.

13. No police department can function without some type of records division or records officer. Which of the following most clearly establishes the value of such a division or officer?
    A. How often and to what extent the information kept in the records is used
    B. How efficient are the forms used by the agency
    C. How long it takes to report an incident, from time of occurrence to completed report
    D. How often are mistakes uncovered by the record division or records officer

14. Police Officer Ling is recently assigned to an investigative unit under the supervision of Sergeant Gotum. The officer wishes to become a good investigator and to learn the art of interviewing. Ling asks his sergeant, "What is the primary trait of a good interviewer?" The sergeant would be most correct if he responded by saying that the primary trait of a good interviewer is:
    A. Concern
    B. Subjectivity
    C. Forcefulness of personality
    D. Alertness

15. Sergeant Leary is examining a police officer's activity/memorandum log and notices the following entry concerning an aided case: "Mary Green, of 207 Main Street, fell and injured her hip on the sidewalk." Of the following items of information not included in the above account, which one should the sergeant recognize as the most important to include in the report?

A. Any contributing factors causing Green to fall
B. Green's occupation
C. The disposition of any of Green's personal property
D. The name of the ambulance personnel who responded to the scene

16. Friction often occurs between employees assigned to an agency's record division and operational personnel. Which of the following is the first step that should be taken by an agency to overcome this friction?
A. All records should be simplified as to preparation and use.
B. All records should be made easily accessible to all operating personnel.
C. One individual should be made responsible for all record-keeping functions.
D. A clear policy concerning the use of records should be established.

17. There is no doubt that greater advantages are realized when police records are centralized. In some very limited circumstances, however, records are appropriately kept on a decentralized basis. Which of the following types of records are most appropriately kept on a decentralized basis under special circumstances?
A. Traffic division records
B. Vice division records
C. Patrol division records
D. Detective division records

18. Consider the following statements concerning an investigative report.
(1) It is a summary limited to the facts in a case that tend to prove a suspect's guilt.
(2) It contains facts that can be shared with other investigators to enable them to continue with their parts of the investigation.
(3) It is often used as a factual basis by the police to take corrective action.
Based on these statements, which of the following is most accurate?
A. Statement 1 is false; statements 2 and 3 are true.
B. Statement 2 is false; statements 1 and 3 are true.

C. Statement 3 is false; statements 1 and 2 are true.
D. All of the statements are true.

19. There has been for some time a national movement to establish standardized police reporting formats, at least within the various states. Usually, this movement has been met with resistance at the local level. The closest approach within the states to standardized police reporting formats has occurred in which of the following areas?
A. Juvenile crime
B. Organized crime
C. Traffic accidents
D. Civilian complaints of police misconduct

20. Consider the following statements concerning narrative or prose reports.
(1) They can be more descriptive than a form or a structured report.
(2) They are difficult to analyze.
(3) They are able to contain more information than a form or structured report.
Based on these statements, which of the following is most accurate?
A. Statements 1 and 3 are true; statement 2 is false.
B. Statements 1 and 2 are true; statement 3 is false.
C. Statements 2 and 3 are true; statement 1 is false.
D. All of the statements are true.

GROUP THREE—10 QUESTIONS— 15 MINUTES

21. Generally speaking, each officer on patrol is required to maintain an activity/memorandum log of daily activities. Which of the following is the best question an officer should ask in determining whether to note an incident in the log?
A. Would any other officer make a note of this incident in the log?
B. Will I be asked about this incident sometime in the future?

C. Does this information appear on some department form?

D. Will I be violating some law if I do not make a note of this incident?

22. As soon as possible after an arrest is made, a report of the arrest should be prepared. Sergeant Ketchum always advises the officers in his squad that this is a good practice because these notes are often the basis for future court appearances. The sergeant also insists that these reports contain a:

A. Maximum of conclusions and a minimum of facts

B. Minimum of conclusions and a maximum of facts

C. Minimum of conclusions and a minimum of facts

D. Maximum of conclusions and a maximum of facts

23. A police officer who maintains an activity log of her official actions is called to court to testify regarding an arrest she made. The officer asks the sergeant if she should bring the log that has entries regarding the arrest to court. The sergeant should tell the officer:

A. To bring the log only if it is subpoenaed

B. To bring the log only if the officer believes she might need it during her testimony

C. To bring the log since it is a public record that she must produce when requested

D. Not to bring the log but a written synopsis of the case instead

24. While conducting an interview of a certain witness, Sergeant D'Amato asks a rather complicated and complex question that the witness does not understand. Under most circumstances in such a situation the witness would probably respond by saying that he/she:

A. Does not know the answer to the question

B. Does not understand the question

C. Would like the question to be repeated

D. Will find out the answer to the question and get back to the interviewer at a later date

25. When reporting on a crime scene, it is recommended that the report include a sketch of the crime scene. This sketch should include moveable objects of particular investigative interest, such as a weapon or the body of a victim. These moveable objects in the sketch should be referred for measurement purposes to other objects in the room, such as:
   A. Overhead light fixtures
   B. Doors and windows
   C. Chairs
   D. Appliances

26. Records are an integral part of any police operation. Which of the following is the most important part of any record-keeping function?
   A. The records must be accurately filed.
   B. The records must be accurately completed.
   C. The records should be comprehensively completed.
   D. The records should always be signed.

27. Frequently, the police obtain information through the use of questionnaires, as opposed to direct interviews. All of the following are advantages of questionnaires except which?
   A. They are ideal for obtaining information from large numbers of people.
   B. Their results are easily interpreted.
   C. They are quite economical.
   D. No particular training is required to distribute them.

28. Consider the following statements concerning reports.
   (1) Written reports, when properly prepared, can obviate the need for any other type of reports.
   (2) Preparing an outline before writing a report reduces the danger of omitting important points.
   (3) Most reports utilized by police agencies are structured reports.
   Based on these statements, which of the following is most accurate?
   A. All of the statements are true.
   B. All of the statements are false.
   C. Only two of the statements are true.
   D. Only one of the statements is true.

29. Wherever possible, a certain police sergeant directs the police officers under his supervision to report incidents through the use of forms or structured reports. The sergeant believes the structured reports to have many advantages. Which of the following is not one of these advantages?
   A. They ensure that certain information is collected.
   B. They are easy to complete.
   C. They are easily transformed into a data base system.
   D. They are quite descriptive.

30. Most police departments require that a police sergeant review and approve all reports prepared during the sergeant's tour of duty by officers under his/her supervision. This requirement is:
   A. Good, mainly because it enables the sergeant to evaluate the work of an officer and take corrective action when appropriate
   B. Bad, mainly because the sergeant would be overwhelmed with paperwork
   C. Good, mainly because such a procedure would relieve the sergeant from having to personally observe the performance of subordinates
   D. Bad, mainly because an inept police officer will be able to conceal poor work merely by improving proficiency in report writing

Answer Key

1. A	7. B	13. A	19. C	25. B
2. B	8. B	14. C	20. D	26. A
3. D	9. D	15. A	21. B	27. B
4. B	10. D	16. D	22. B	28. C
5. B	11. B	17. B	23. C	29. D
6. D	12. B	18. A	24. A	30. A

Answer Explanations

1. **A** There is no time spent writing and rewriting. Also, clarifying questions can be immediately asked and answered.

2. **B** Intelligence records are of no use to the field if the intelligence does not reach the officers in the field.

3. **D** Statement 1 is the only accurate statement. Statement 2 is inaccurate since oral reports are quicker than written reports and the face-to-face contact involved provides an excellent opportunity for instant feedback. Statement 3 is inaccurate since intelligence can also be disseminated on a "need-to-know" basis. In other words, some people in an agency have a right to know and receive the intelligence information automatically. Others can get the information by establishing a need to have it.

4. **B** The purpose of the sketch is to factually capture the crime scene; it is not the place for opinions.

5. **B** A brief summary in the first paragraph of a narrative report helps the reader to understand the actual story as it unfolds. Remember, you are not writing the report to keep your reader in suspense.

6. **D** Responses to inquiries are not slower but quicker since there is no need to search the records of many units.

7. **B** The showing of dimensions or measurements is something that cannot be achieved by using a photograph but can be achieved by a sketch.

8. **B** If the information does not meet the requirement of being accurate, it is of little use to anyone, no matter when it is received, how neat it is, or how brief it is.

9. **D** Reports are only a means to an end. All reports should have a use that can be explained and clearly understood. Reporting requirements should be periodically reviewed to determine if any required reports have outlived their usefulness.

10. **D** There is no guarantee that each situation as reported in choices A, B, and C would necessarily come to the attention of the police. The police almost always become aware of traffic accidents involving deaths.

316   REPORTS AND RECORDS

GROUP TWO

11. B Remember the police officer is the eyes and ears of the administrator and also of the specialized units. If the police officer's notes and reports are incomplete, the entire records system will suffer.

12. B Witnesses should not be interviewed as a group. They should be interviewed separately in all possible privacy. If there are many witnesses, it may be impossible for one officer to do it all.

13. A Records exist mainly for use by operating personnel. If they are not being used, the records have little value.

14. C By utilizing a forceful personality, an interviewer can guide an interview and obtain a maximum amount of information.

15. A Part of the reporting requirements for police incidents includes a statement as to what caused the incident. Remember, the cause of accidents and other police incidents is vital information for the planning of remedial efforts.

16. D If there is a clearly understood policy, then all employees should know the rules and friction can be minimized.

17. B Records of ongoing vice division investigations can be kept on a decentralized basis because of the sensitivity and secrecy associated with vice investigations.

18. A An investigative report would also properly include facts that tend to prove a suspect's innocence as well as guilt. Statements 2 and 3 are accurately stated.

19. C Because of licensing and vehicle registration requirements, there has been some standardization of reporting formats in the area of traffic accidents.

20. D Although narrative or prose reports take longer to write, they do have the advantages noted in statements 1 and 3. Analysis, however, is more difficult with these types of reports.

GROUP THREE

21. B The activity log of a police officer can be used to refresh his/her memory in the future. Therefore, anything the officer might be asked about in the future ought to be recorded in the log.

22. **B** Police reports, especially those that might be introduced as evidence in court, should contain a maximum number of facts and a minimum number of conclusions.

23. **C** The police officer's log is a public record and a defendant has the right to examine the original document or a bona fide copy, not a synopsis of the entries.

24. **A** Rather than admit they do not understand a complex question and thereby appear ignorant, most witnesses simply indicate that they do not know the answer to the question. This wastes a question, and it also can be misleading to the interviewer. Questions, therefore, should not be complex and/or complicated.

25. **B** These objects, like a gun, are measured in a horizontal plane from a nonmoveable object, such as a door or window.

26. **A** A record can be corrected or completed only if it can be found. Besides, the functions described in choices B, C, and D are not record-keeping functions. They are more properly report-writing functions. Remember to make sure you know what the question is asking.

27. **B** The results of questionnaire surveys are not easy to interpret. The lack of face-to-face contact with the respondent eliminates the opportunity to immediately clarify unclear responses.

28. **C** Two of the statements are true. Only statement 1 is false. Written reports can never totally take the place of oral reporting.

29. **D** Structured reports usually do not contain all of the captions needed to describe an incident completely.

30. **A** Reports serve as a form of control for the sergeant. This control is quite welcome, considering the unsupervised nature of the patrol officer's job.

CHAPTER 11

Data Interpretation

Police sergeants often work with data from graphs and tables. For this reason, questions about how to interpret graphs and tables appear on many police sergeant examinations. Such questions are called data interpretation questions. When we mention this to students who are preparing to take such tests, many of them become uneasy. They erroneously believe that they must be a combination of engineer and mathematician to handle this type of question. Once we show them how simple such questions can really be, they actually gain confidence in their ability to deal with them. This is what we intend to do in this chapter. We will strip away the mask of difficulty that seems to surround these questions and help you develop the level of skill needed to answer them quickly and accurately.

The Cardinal Rule

Before discussing the major types of data interpretation questions, we discuss the cardinal rule for dealing with all such questions. The rule follows:

> The answers are somewhere in the data. Your task is to make sure that you know what the data represent and exactly what data you are looking for.

In a way, data interpretation questions are like reading comprehension questions. This is what we mean by the first half of the cardinal rule, "The answers are somewhere in the data." Just as the answers to reading comprehension questions are found solely in the written information given as part of the question, so are the answers to data interpretation questions found in the information that supports these questions. Let's explore this a little further with a simple example.

Suppose you encountered the following question on a police sergeant examination.

The percentage of persons who are arrested for driving while intoxicated and are illiterate is 15%. What percentage of persons arrested for driving while intoxicated are illiterate?

(A) 10%
(B) 15%
(C) 20%
(D) 25%

Would such a question make you feel ill at ease? Would you find such a question to be difficult? Obviously you wouldn't. Yet, this is an example of how a data interpretation question actually works. Of course, it is not as simple as we have presented it, but that is how it works.

In actuality you will get a set of data, either in graph or table form, that contains a lot of information, most of which you do not need to answer the questions. Somewhere in that data is the fact that 15% of persons who are arrested for driving while intoxicated are illiterate. Your job in this type of question, therefore, is to sift through a lot of information to find the information you are looking for.

Graphs and Tables

The data in data interpretation questions are presented either in graph or table form. Because police sergeants work much more frequently with tables than with graphs, the majority of the questions you will see on your official examination will probably involve tables.

THREE TYPES OF GRAPHS

When writing data interpretation questions involving graphs, test writers generally use one of three different types of graphs, as follows:

1. A line graph

2. A circle graph

3. A bar graph

LINE GRAPHS

A line graph similar to those typically found on police sergeant examinations is pictured here.

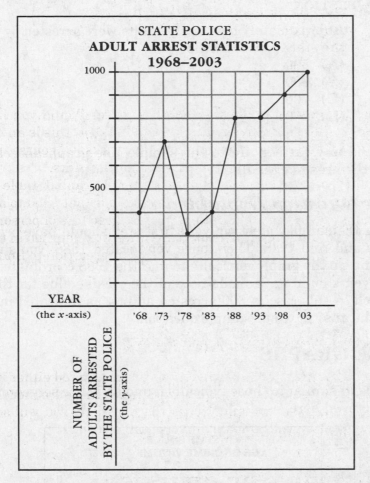

STATE POLICE
ADULT ARREST STATISTICS
1968–2003

NUMBER OF
ADULTS ARRESTED
BY THE STATE POLICE
(the *y*-axis)

YEAR
(the *x*-axis)

'68 '73 '78 '83 '88 '93 '98 '03

As a general rule, all graphs have a title. The title is very important because it usually tells you what the graph is about. The sample line graph shown is entitled "State Police, Adult Arrest Statistics, 1968–2003." Upon reading this, you know that the data involved in the questions have something to do with the number of adults arrested by the state police during the years 1968 to 2003.

Line graphs have what is known as an *x*-axis and a *y*-axis. In the sample line graph, the *x*-axis shows the years 1968 to 2003. The *x*-axis extends horizontally, from left to right. The *y*-axis shows the number of adults arrested by the state police and extends vertically from top to bottom. Although only two numbers are shown on the *y*-axis, 500 and 1000, you must count the marked increments on the *y*-axis to determine that each mark equals 100 arrested adults. The line graph itself is made up a number of coordinates, which are connected to each other with a line. The coordinates are usually shown as a dot or period. Each coordinate represents two values, the *x*-axis value and the *y*-axis value. For example, the coordinate for 1968 (the *x*-axis value) corresponds to the number 400 on the *y*-axis (the *y*-axis value), and there is an *x*-axis coordinate for 1973 that corresponds to 700 on the *y*-axis. Now, to see if you can read this graph, answer the following sample question.

SAMPLE QUESTION

> Approximately how many adults were arrested by
> the state police in 1988?
> **(A)** 500
> **(B)** 600
> **(C)** 700
> **(D)** 800

Do not read any further. Go to the sample line graph and answer the question; then resume reading.

Sample Question Explained

To answer the sample question, your first step should have been to go to the *x*-axis and find 1988. Then, once you located 1988, you should have simply gone up the graph vertically to find the 1988 coordinate. Once you found it, you should have made note of the *y*-axis value for that coordinate, which in this case is 800 arrested adults, as indicated in choice D, which is the answer to our sample question.

CIRCLE GRAPHS

A circle graph similar to those typically found on police sergeant examinations is pictured here.

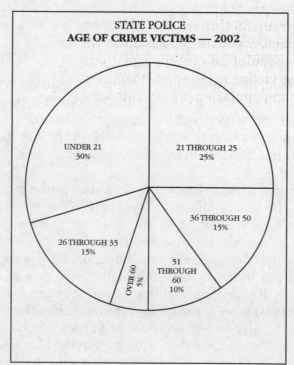

STATE POLICE
AGE OF CRIME VICTIMS — 2002

UNDER 21
30%

21 THROUGH 25
25%

36 THROUGH 50
15%

26 THROUGH 35
15%

OVER 60
5%

51
THROUGH
60
10%

Circle graphs, which are also called pie charts, are, as their name implies, circular graphs that represent data as part of the whole. As with all graphs, the first thing you should do to understand it is to read the title of the graph. In this case, the title indicates that the graph presents an analysis by the state police of the age of crime victims for the year 2002.

When working with circle graphs, you must understand that the circle itself represents 100% of whatever is being depicted. We like to tell our students to think of the circle as the whole pie. For example, the circle in the sample circle graph represents all of the crime victims during 2002. Then each segment of the circle, or each piece of the pie, represents a certain portion of that crime victim population. For example, the age group from 21 through 25 years of age represents 25% of the entire crime victim population for the year 2002. Now, to see if you can read this graph, answer the following sample question.

SAMPLE QUESTION

Together the age groups 26 through 35 years of age and 36 through 50 years of age represent:
(A) 15% of the crime victim population for 2002
(B) 20% of the crime victim population for 2002
(C) 30% of the crime victim population for 2002
(D) 40% of the crime victim population for 2002

Do not read any further. Go to the sample circle graph and answer the question; then resume reading.

Sample Question Explained

All you had to do to answer the sample question was to locate the piece of the pie that represents the age group 26 through 35 and the one that represents the age group 36 through 50, and to add together the percentages for these two groups. Since the age group 26 through 35 represents 15% of the crime victim population and the age group 36 through 50 represents 15% of the crime victim population, together they represent 30% of the entire crime victim population, as indicated in choice C.

BAR GRAPHS

A bar graph similar to those typically found on police sergeant examinations is pictured here.

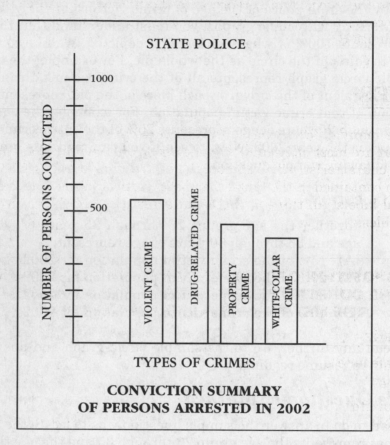

Bar graphs are, as their name implies, graphs that use bars to present data. The title of the sample bar graph reveals that it represents the conviction history of all persons arrested in 2002. A quick review of the individual bars shows that all convictions are divided into four categories: violent crime, drug-related crime, property crime, and white-collar crime. For example, the number of arrested persons who were convicted for the commission of some sort of violent crime is about 550. Now, to see if you can read this graph, answer the following sample question.

SAMPLE QUESTION

The number of persons arrested in 2002 who were convicted of property crimes is about:
(A) 400
(B) 450
(C) 500
(D) 600

Do not read any further. Go to the sample bar graph and answer the question; then resume reading.

Sample Question Explained

All that you had to do to answer our sample question was to locate the bar that represented property crimes and then measure over from the top of that bar to the *y*-axis, which represents the number of arrested persons who were convicted of a property crime. The answer is about 450, as indicated in choice B.

TABLES

There are many different ways of presenting data in table form, but the tables that are most often used on police sergeant examinations have the following characteristics in common: they have titles that describe the information contained in the table, they have vertical labels, and they have horizontal labels. All three of these characteristics are shown in the following tables.

DISPOSITION OF TRAFFIC TICKETS ISSUED DURING THE CURRENT YEAR BY POLICE OFFICERS FROM THE METROPOLIS POLICE DEPARTMENT

CHARGE	TOTAL ISSUED	GUILTY	NOT GUILTY
Unsafe lane change	123	112	11
Failure to signal	873	760	113
Following too closely	45	45	0
Failure to yield right of way	89	87	2
Speeding	1245	1201	44

As you can see, the sample table has a title that explains its contents: vertical labels, which are the various charges, and horizontal labels, which are the dispositions of the various charges. Reading the table is simple. For each charge, the vertical label, you have three pieces of information, the horizontal labels: (1) the total issued, (2) the number of guilty findings, and (3) the number of not guilty findings. For example, there were 123 tickets issued for unsafe lane changes, of which 112 were disposed of via a finding of guilty and 11 were disposed of with a finding of not guilty. Now, to see if you can read this table, answer the following sample question.

Which of the following charges resulted in the greatest number of guilty findings?
(A) Following too closely
(B) Failure to signal
(C) Unsafe lane change
(D) Speeding

Do not read any further. Go to the sample table and answer the question; then resume reading.

Sample Question Explained

All you had to do to find the answer to our sample question was look under the horizontal label "Guilty" and then proceed down and look for the largest number, which is 1201—the number of guilty findings for speeding. Having found that number you simply had to see if speeding was one of the choices. If, however, there were many more vertical labels, then it would be a better strategy to look only at the charges suggested by the choices.

Strategy for Answering Data Interpretation Questions

When you are answering data interpretation questions, the first thing you must do is to study the title of the graph or table involved and then make sure that you understand the kind of information that is presented in that graph or table. The next step is to go to the question and to make sure that you know what the question is asking. After you are familiar with the graph or table and after you know what a particular question is asking, you then go to the graph or table and search for the information you need to evaluate each choice in the question. You must remain extremely careful. Attention to detail is absolutely required to maintain a high record of success when dealing with data interpretation questions. Now, compare this strategy with our cardinal rule as it was presented earlier:

> The answers are somewhere in the data. Your task is to make sure that you know what the data represent and exactly what data you are looking for.

We hope that this cardinal rule makes much more sense to you now after our discussion.

Basic Math May Be Required

One final word about data interpretation questions is in order before you try some practice exercises. It is highly likely that arriving at some of the answers to data interpretation questions will require you to do some basic mathematics. Don't be overly concerned about this since the math involved in these questions is truly basic. It is almost always limited to addition, subtraction, multiplication, division, finding averages, determining ratios, and calculating percentages. For those who need it, we have included a comprehensive review of these mathematical skills.

ADDITION

Addition is finding the sum of numbers, and it requires two specific actions.

1. Properly line up or align the numbers to be added.

   EXAMPLE

   Add 837.68, 47, 4922.7, and 8.039.

   Remember that, when aligning numbers, 47 is the same as 47.00. So make sure that decimal points are correctly lined up. When properly aligned the numbers look like this:

$$
\begin{array}{r}
837.68 \\
47.00 \\
4922.70 \\
8.039 \\
\hline
\end{array}
$$

   Adding from the top down we get 5815.419.

2. Check the answer by adding again but this time from the bottom to the top.

SUBTRACTION

Subtraction is finding the difference between two numbers. It requires two specific actions.

1. Properly line up the numbers involved to make sure that the decimals are aligned.

Subtract 876.9 from 1289.42.

Remember, 876.9 is the same as 876.90. When properly aligned the numbers look like this:

$$
\begin{array}{r}
1289.42 \\
-876.90 \\
\hline
412.52
\end{array}
$$

2. Check your subtraction by adding. To do this add your answer 412.52 to the bottom number in your subtraction 876.90, and the sum should be 1289.42.

MULTIPLICATION

Multiplication is adding a number to itself several times. For example $4 \times 3 = 12$ is the same as adding

$$4 + 4 + 4 = 12 \text{ or } 3 + 3 + 3 + 3 = 12$$

Two specific actions required by multiplication are:

1. Align the products as you arrive at them.

and

2. If there are decimals in the numbers you are multiplying, add up the number of places to the decimal point from right to left and then count off an equal number in the answer from right to left and insert a decimal point there.

EXAMPLE

Multiply 86.2×196.47.

$$
\begin{array}{r}
196.47 \\
\times\ 86.2 \\
\hline
39294 \\
117882 \\
157176 \\
\hline
16935714
\end{array}
$$

Note how each of the numbers are aligned. The final step is to count in both numbers being multiplied, from right to left, the total number of places to the decimal point. The total number of places to the decimal point is three. Next count three places from right to left in the final product and insert a decimal in this final product. Thus the number 16935714 becomes 16,935.714, our answer.

To check a multiplication answer, merely divide the final product with one of the numbers used in the multiplication, and you should get the other number originally used in the multiplication. For example $9 \times 4 = 36$. To check the multiplication, divide 36 by 4, and you get 9.

DIVISION

Division is separating a number into a certain number of equal parts. The statement 30 divided by 5 is the same as asking how many equal parts consisting of 5 are there in 30? The answer would be 6.

Two specific actions required by division are:

1. Make sure you are dividing by the right number. When asked to divide 144 by 12 that means you must divide 12 into 144. Or how many equal parts of 12 are there in 144?

2. If the number you are dividing by has a decimal in it such as 18.37, you must first move the decimal point as many places to the right as possible. That number now becomes 1837 (you moved the decimal point two places to the right). If the number you are dividing into is, for example, 238.81, then move the decimal in the number you are dividing into an equal number of places to the right. When you do this in our example, 238.81 becomes 23881. You then divide 1837 into 23,881 and determine the answer to be 13.

   To check a division problem, simply multiply the number you divided by with the answer. If you divided correctly, you will get the number you divided into. For example, 36 divided by 3 is 12. To check it multiply 12 by 3, and you get 36.

FINDING AVERAGES

To find an average number of a group of numbers:

1. Find the sum of all the items in the group.

2. Divide by the number of items in the group.

EXAMPLE

The weights in pounds of all the prisoners in the police van are 178, 196, 231, 242, and 143. What is the average weight of the prisoners?

Adding 178, 196, 231, 242, and 143, the sum is 990. Then divide by 5, the number of prisoners, to determine the average weight, which in this case is 198 pounds.

RATIOS

A ratio is a relationship between two numbers of the same kind. When expressing a ratio, take care to compare the same kind of items.

EXAMPLE

To remove bloodstains 8 quarts of bleach were used along with 18 gallons of water. What is the ratio of bleach to water used to remove the bloodstain?

To find the ratio or relationship between the same kind of items, the number of quarts must be converted to gallons so that we can compare gallons to gallons. After converting the 8 quarts to 2 gallons (there are 4 quarts to 1 gallon), we now have 2 gallons of bleach used for every 18 gallons of water. Expressed as a ratio we would have the fraction $\frac{2}{18}$. Note that a ratio maintains its value if you multiply or divide both numbers in a ratio by the same number. In our ratio of $\frac{2}{18}$, if we divide both numbers in the ratio $\frac{2}{18}$ by 2, we get a ratio of $\frac{1}{9}$, which is the same value as $\frac{2}{18}$.

A kind of question involving ratios known as a proportion question is often asked by examiners.

EXAMPLE

If 3 police officers must be assigned for every 50 demonstrators, how many police officers must be assigned for 200 demonstrators?

Immediately set up your ratios. In this example, 3 police officers are needed for 50 demonstrators as an unknown number of police officers are needed for 200 demonstrators, or

$$\frac{3}{50} = \frac{x}{200}$$

The solution calls for cross multiplying and dividing. First cross multiply the $3 \times 200 = 600$. Then cross multiply the $50 \times x = 50x$. We now have the equation $50x = 600$. We can divide by 50 as long as we do it to both sides of our equation. Therefore,

$$\frac{50x}{50} = \frac{600}{50}$$

We are left with $x = 12$.

PERCENTAGE INCREASE OR PERCENTAGE DECREASE

Police sergeant candidates are often asked to examine a graph or a table and to correctly indicate what has been the percentage increase or decrease that has occurred from one point in time to another.

EXAMPLE

Last year the number of police officers who were injured was 150. This year 225 officers were injured. What was the percentage increase in the number of police officers who were injured?

1. Find the difference between the numbers being compared. In this case it is $225 - 150 = 75$.

2. Divide the number you just calculated, in this case 75, by the older number (that is, the number that previously existed), in this case 150. So we now have $^{75}/_{150}$ or $\frac{1}{2}$, which is 50%. The numbers increased from 150 to 225 so there has been percentage increase of 50%. Remember, in setting up this fraction, the denominator (the bottom number) will always be the older number (that is, the number that previously existed).

Practice Exercises

You are now ready to do some practice questions. Always try to answer the questions in the allotted time. After completing each of the three groups of questions, make sure you thoroughly review the explanation for each answer before going to the next set of questions. This includes reviewing the explanations for all questions, those you answered correctly and those you answered incorrectly. This is done to ensure that you always arrive at the correct choice for the right reasons. Remember, now is the time to make mistakes. If you understand why you made a mistake, you should not make the same mistake on the examination, when it really counts.

GROUP ONE—10 QUESTIONS—20 MINUTES

Answer questions 1 through 10 based on the following data.

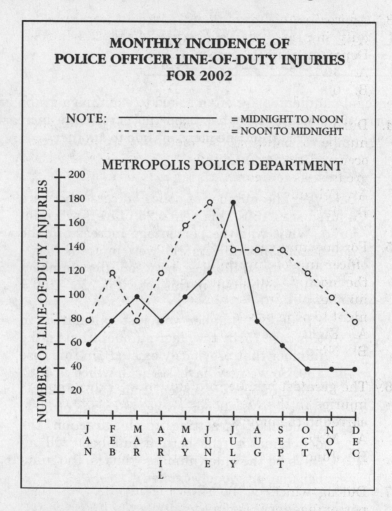

1. In what three months was the number of police officer line-of-duty injuries that occurred during midnight and noon approximately the same?
   A. July, August, and September
   B. October, November, and December
   C. January, February, and March
   D. April, May, and June

2. In what month was the number of line-of-duty injuries that occurred during midnight to noon approximately the same as the number of line-of-duty injuries that occurred during noon to midnight?
   A. April
   B. December
   C. May
   D. There was no month in 2002 when this occurred.

3. Approximately how many police officer line-of-duty injuries occurred in the Metropolis Police Department in December of 2002?
   A. 40   C. 80
   B. 60   D. 120

4. During which of the following months did the number of police officer line-of-duty injuries that occurred during midnight to noon decrease the greatest as compared to the previous month?
   A. February   C. August
   B. July   D. November

5. For how many months were the number of police officer line-of-duty injuries that occurred during the noon to midnight period greater than the number of injuries that occurred during the midnight to noon period?
   A. Eight   C. Ten
   B. Nine   D. Eleven

6. The greatest number of police officer line-of-duty injuries in the Metropolis Police Department occurred in the month of:
   A. May   C. July
   B. June   D. August

7. During which of the following months was the percentage increase in the number of line-of-duty injuries that occurred during noon and midnight the greatest when compared to the previous month?
   A. February   C. August
   B. June   D. November

8. Which of the following two-month periods ac-
   counted for the most police officer line-of-duty in-
   juries in the Metropolis Police Department?
   A. From January 1st to March 1st
   B. From May 1st to July 1st
   C. From July 1st to September 1st
   D. From October 1st to December 1st

9. Exactly how many police officer line-of-duty in-
   juries occurred in the Metropolis Police Depart-
   ment on May 28, 2002?
   A. 100
   B. 180
   C. 280
   D. Cannot be determined

10. Which of the following is the most accurate state-
    ment concerning police officer line-of-duty in-
    juries in the Metropolis Police Department during
    2002?
    A. They remained about the same for the entire
       year, although they did not remain constant.
    B. They increased during the entire year.
    C. They decreased during the entire year.
    D. They reached their peak about the middle of
       the year and then decreased.

GROUP TWO—10 QUESTIONS—20 MINUTES

Answer questions 11 through 20 based on the information presented in the following table.

ACCIDENT-PRONE LOCATIONS WITHIN JURISDIC-TION OF THE METROPOLIS POLICE DEPARTMENT

Note: A location is considered to be accident prone if a minimum of five vehicle accidents have taken place at the location in the last six months. Updating of this list takes place on the fifth day of each month.

LOCATION	PRIMARY CAUSES*	CODE**
Main Street & 14th Avenue	None	A
Elm Street & 12th Avenue	1-3-5	D
Broadway & 42nd Street	1	B
Broad Street & 10th Avenue	1	B
Park Street & 7th Avenue	1-2	E
Canal Street & 4th Avenue	1-2	C
Park Lane & 7th Avenue	6	C
Oak Street & 11th Avenue	7	D

*Primary causes are only applicable to vehicle accidents that result in the death of at least one person. They are not used for other than fatal accidents. The following are the only primary causes that apply:

1	=	Speeding
2	=	Driving while intoxicated
3	=	Following too closely
4	=	Failure to obey signal device
5	=	Failure to obey stop/yield sign
6	=	Unsafe lane change
7	=	Other than one of the above

**A code must be entered for each accident-prone location. The code is used to classify locations according to the total number of accidents in the last six months. The following are the only codes that apply.

A	=	5 to 9 accidents
B	=	10 to 14 accidents
C	=	15 to 19 accidents
D	=	20 to 24 accidents
E	=	Over 24 accidents

11. The location that has had the most vehicle acci-
    dents in the last six months is:
    A. Broadway & 42nd Street
    B. Broad Street & 10th Avenue
    C. Park Street & 7th Avenue
    D. Canal Street & 4th Avenue

12. Driving while intoxicated was a causative factor
    in a fatal accident that occurred at:
    A. Broadway & 42nd Street
    B. Broad Street & 10th Avenue
    C. Park Street & 7th Avenue
    D. Main Street & 14th Avenue

13. Of the following locations, the one that was the
    scene of the fewest accidents in the last six
    months is:
    A. Main Street & 14th Avenue
    B. Elm Street & 12th Avenue
    C. Broadway & 42nd Street
    D. Broad Street & 10th Avenue

14. Which of the following is the most common cause
    of fatal accidents in the last six months at acci-
    dent-prone locations identified by the Metropolis
    Police Department?
    A. Speeding   C. Following too closely
    B. Unsafe lane change D. Intoxicated driving

15. There were no fatal accidents in the last six
    months at:
    A. Main Street & 14th Avenue
    B. Elm Street & 12th Avenue
    C. Broadway & 42nd Street
    D. Broad Street & 10th Avenue

16. An up-to-date listing of accident-prone locations
    is available
    A. Every three months
    B. On the fifth of each month
    C. Twice a month
    D. Every Monday

17. Which of the following is the most accurate state-
    ment concerning the number of vehicle accidents
    in the last 6 months at Broadway & 42nd Street
    and Broad Street & 10th Avenue?
    A. There were more accidents at Broadway &
       42nd Street than at Broad Street & 10th Av-
       enue.
    B. There were more accidents at Broad Street &
       10th Avenue than at Broadway & 42nd
       Street.
    C. There were an equal number of accidents at
       Broad Street & 10th Avenue and Broadway &
       42nd Street.
    D. There is not enough information available to
       make specific comparisons of the number of
       accidents at those locations.

18. Which of the following was not a cause of at least
    one fatal accident in the last six months?
    A. Driving while intoxicated
    B. Following too closely
    C. Failure to obey signal device
    D. Failure to obey stop/yield sign

19. The cause of the fatal accident at Oak Street &
    11th Avenue:
    A. Was speeding
    B. Was driving while intoxicated
    C. Was unsafe lane change
    D. Cannot be determined from the available
       data

20. The number of accidents in the last six months
    that have occurred at Park Lane and 7th Avenue
    is:
    A. Over 24
    B. Between 15 and 19
    C. Either 16, 17, or 18
    D. Unknown

GROUP THREE—10 QUESTIONS—20 MINUTES

Answer questions 21 through 30 based on the following information.

CRIME STATISTICS FOR THE METROPOLIS POLICE DEPARTMENT

Note: All crimes reported in the Metropolis Police Department are given a report number starting with the number 0001 each month. Those crimes that have been cleared by arrest are marked with an asterisk.

REPORT	DATE	DAY	CRIME	TIME	LOCATION
0001	3/3	Saturday	Rape	3:00 A.M.	105 Elm Street
0005	3/7	Tuesday	Trespass	4:20 A.M.	415 Oak Street
*0009	3/7	Tuesday	Homicide	9:00 A.M.	321 Pine Street
0014	3/9	Thursday	Homicide	12:10 A.M.	203 Elm Street
0019	3/11	Saturday	Trespass	4:00 A.M.	300 Elm Street
*0023	3/11	Saturday	Rape	6:00 P.M.	439 Oak Street
0028	3/11	Saturday	Trespass	3:45 A.M.	567 Main Street
0036	3/12	Sunday	Rape	4:00 P.M.	400 Oak Street
*0043	3/16	Thursday	Rape	7:00 P.M.	387 Oak Street
0051	3/18	Saturday	Trespass	1:15 A.M.	145 Elm Street
0065	3/21	Tuesday	Homicide	7:00 A.M.	345 Pine Street
*0069	3/22	Wednesday	Homicide	1:45 A.M.	187 Elm Street
0074	3/22	Wednesday	Trespass	5:00 A.M.	535 Oak Street
0081	3/25	Saturday	Trespass	7:00 A.M.	095 Elm Street
*0083	3/26	Sunday	Rape	1:00 A.M.	310 Pine Street
0089	3/31	Saturday	Rape	4:00 P.M.	349 Pine Street

21. A police officer under your supervision would most likely be able to reduce the number of trespasses by patrolling:
    A. Elm Street between 4:00 P.M. and midnight on Tuesdays
    B. Oak Street between 1:00 P.M. and 9:00 P.M. on Mondays

C. Elm Street between midnight and 8:00 A.M. on Saturdays

D. Oak Street between midnight and 8:00 A.M. on Tuesdays

22. A police officer under your supervision would most likely be able to reduce the number of rapes by patrolling:
A. Pine Street between 4:00 P.M. and midnight, Wednesday through Sunday
B. Oak Street between 3:00 P.M. and 10:00 P.M., Tuesday through Saturday
C. Oak Street between 4:00 P.M. and midnight, Wednesday through Sunday
D. Pine Street between 1:00 P.M. and 9:00 P.M., Tuesday through Saturday

23. The day of the week that accounts for the most crime is:
A. Saturday   C. Tuesday
B. Sunday   D. Thursday

24. Which of the following is the most accurate statement?
A. All rapes are committed on Saturdays.
B. There were at least 89 crimes reported in the Metropolis Police Department during the month of March.
C. No homicides are committed in the Metropolis Police Department on Tuesdays.
D. All homicides are committed on Tuesdays.

25. How many crimes reported in the Metropolis Police Department were committed in March at exactly 4:00 P.M.?
A. At least 2   C. Exactly 4
B. Exactly 3   D. More than 4

26. A police officer under your supervision would be most likely to reduce the number of homicides by patrolling:
A. Elm Street between 11:00 P.M. and 7:00 A.M., Tuesday through Saturday
B. Pine Street between midnight and 8:00 A.M., Tuesday through Saturday
C. Oak Street between noon and 8:00 P.M., Monday through Friday
D. Main Street between midnight and 8:00 A.M., Wednesday through Sunday

27. A police officer who works on Elm Street, Oak Street, Pine Street, and Main Street should know that for the month of March the combined total of rapes, trespasses, and homicides was greatest on:
   A. Elm Street   C. Oak Street
   B. Pine Street   D. Main Street

28. Which of the following is the most accurate statement concerning the crime statistics for the Metropolis Police Department during the month of March?
   A. There were no rapes on Elm Street.
   B. There were no trespasses on Pine Street.
   C. There were no homicides on Pine Street.
   D. There were no rapes on Oak Street.

29. The day of the week with the fewest reported rapes, homicides, and trespasses is:
   A. Monday   C. Wednesday
   B. Tuesday   D. Thursday

30. How many of the reported homicides, trespasses, and rapes were cleared by arrest?
   A. 2   C. 5
   B. 3   D. Unable to determine

Answer Key

1. B	7. A	13. A	19. D	25. A
2. D	8. B	14. A	20. B	26. A
3. D	9. D	15. A	21. C	27. A
4. C	10. D	16. B	22. C	28. B
5. C	11. C	17. D	23. A	29. A
6. C	12. C	18. C	24. B	30. C

Answer Explanations

If you followed our strategy you would have taken some time before answering the questions to study the title of the graph and its contents. You should have recognized it as a line graph. Hopefully, the fact that it had two sets of lines did not confuse you. The note tells you that the solid line represents the time period from midnight to noon, and the dotted line represents the time period from noon to midnight. Then you should have observed that the x-axis represents the month of the year and the y-axis represents the number of police officer line-of-duty injuries divided into increments of 20, from 0 to 200.

1. **B** If you picked choice A, you failed to interpret the note carefully enough. The dotted line represents the time period from noon to midnight. The question involved the time period from midnight to noon.

2. **D** Graphs can also be used to indicate that something has not occurred. As in choice D, which tells us that, based on the graph, there is no month for which the number of injuries was the same for both time periods.

3. **D** In December of 2002 there were about 40 line-of-duty injuries during the midnight to noon period, and there were about 80 line-of-duty injuries during the noon to midnight period. This means that altogether there were 40 plus 80 injuries, which, of course, is 120.

4. **C** There was no need to do any math to answer this question. Concerning injuries that occurred between midnight and noon, during February, choice A, injuries increased. During July, choice B, they also increased. During November, they remained the same as the previous month. Only during August did they decrease.

5. **C** Only in March and July were the number of line-of-duty injuries that occurred during the noon to midnight period less than those that occurred during the midnight to noon period.

6. **C** In May there were about 260 line-of-duty injuries. In June there were about 300. In July, the answer, there were about 320. In August there were 220.

7. **A** In November there was a decrease in line-of-duty injuries during the noon to midnight period, and in August they remained about the same. This means that choices C and D can be eliminated. In February the number of these line-of-duty injuries went from about

80 in January to about 120. Referring to the formula you were shown above, this means that there was a 50% increase, (120 − 80 = 40; 40 ÷ 80, the old number = 50%). In June, the noon to midnight line-of-duty injuries went from about 160 to about 180, which is an increase of about 12% (180 − 160) ÷ 160, or 20/160, which is about 12%.

8. **B** Line-of-duty injuries reached their maximum incidence between May 1st and July 1st.

9. **D** If you missed this question, you probably do not understand that one cannot determine exact statistics from line graphs such as the one we used for this series of questions. These line graphs are used to show trends and not to supply specific daily statistics. To completely understand this, ask yourself this question. How would I determine exactly from the graph the point at which May 28th is represented? The answer, of course, is that you can't. Exact numbers, as you will soon find out, are presented in questions involving tables.

10. **D** The line-of-duty injuries that occurred during both time periods involved started low, reached their highest levels (in other words, they reached their peak) at about the middle of the year and then decreased.

GROUP TWO

If you followed our strategy you would have spent some time understanding the material presented in the table prior to answering the questions. Remember, one thorough review of the table is more efficient timewise than thoroughly reviewing it again and again before answering each question.

11. **C** The code for Park Street & 7th Avenue is E and that code is for locations that have been the scene of over 24 accidents in the last six months.

12. **C** Driving while intoxicated is Primary Cause #2, and it was listed as a cause of an accident that occurred at Park Street & 7th Avenue.

13. **A** Main Street & 14th Avenue is listed as a Code A location, which means that there have been no more than nine accidents at that location in the last six months.

14. **A** Speeding was a primary cause of five fatal accidents.

15. **A** The fact that there were no primary causes listed for Main Street & 14th Avenue means that there were no fatal accidents at that location.

16. B According to the note at the top of the chart, updating this list takes place on the fifth day of each month.

17. D The code for both locations is B. This means that there were between 10 and 14 accidents at both locations. More specific information is not available.

18. C The only primary cause that was not listed in the chart was number 4, and that corresponds to choice C, Failure to obey signal device.

19. D The primary cause of the fatal accident at Oak Street & 11th Avenue was listed as Primary Cause #7, which is then given as other than one of the above. This, of course, means that the primary cause of that accident cannot be determined from the available data.

20. B The code for Park Lane & 7th Avenue is C and that means that between 15 and 19 accidents have occurred at that location. If you picked choice A, you were careless and selected the number of accidents that occurred at Park Street & 7th Avenue.

GROUP THREE

21. C Of the six trespasses on the chart, three of them occurred on Elm Street between midnight and 8:00 A.M. on Saturdays. One trespass occurred on Tuesday on Oak Street, and one occurred on Wednesday on Oak Street, and one occurred on Main Street on Saturday. Clearly, the police officer involved would get the best return by patrolling on Elm Street on Saturdays between midnight and 8:00 A.M.

22. C Of the six reported rapes, three of them occurred on Oak Street between 4:00 P.M. and midnight, one occurred on Thursday, one occurred on Saturday, and one occurred on Sunday.

23. A Of the 16 crimes listed, 7 of them were committed on Saturdays.

24. B According to the note, every crime reported in the Metropolis Police Department is given a report number starting with # 0001 each month. The report number for the last crime shown on the chart is 0089.

25. A This question requires attention to detail. You must concentrate when you are doing data interpretation questions.

26. A Choices C and D are wrong because there were no reported homicides on Oak or Main Streets. Choice A is correct because there were two homicides on Elm Street between 11:00 P.M. and 7:00 A.M. from Tuesday through Saturday.

27. A Of the sixteen reported crimes, six of them took place on Elm Street.

28. B Pine Street was the scene of two homicides and two rapes but no trespasses.

29. A Monday did not appear anywhere in the table.

30. C As stated in the note, those crimes that were cleared by arrest are marked with an asterisk. There were five such crimes.

CHAPTER 12

Police Science

Policing is part art and part science. It is considered art because, of necessity, it must be practiced. At the same time it is considered science because there are certain principles that can be used by practitioners engaged in policing. As a consequence, the areas that the term *police science* encompasses can be quite broad.

Here, under the heading of police science, we have included areas that frequently serve as the subject matter of both police in-service and specialized training courses. Hence, most police practitioners have in the course of their careers had some exposure to the areas dealt with in this chapter. In addition, questions concerning these areas often find their way onto civil service police promotion examinations.

Court Testimony

Police officers quickly learn that not only must they act to enforce the law legally, but they must also be able to properly state their case in court. That means it is not enough to have acted properly, it must also be explained properly to a trier of the fact, namely the judge or jury. Stating one's case in court is what court testimony is all about.

The following are facts a police supervisor should know in connection with court testimony:

1. A police witness should begin to prepare for court testimony as soon as he/she suspects that criminal activity may be occurring.

2. A police officer should realize that the officer's notes are a public record and can be subpoenaed to court.

3. Statements made by a defendant to an officer should be recorded by the officer and reported to the prosecutor.

4. An officer's appearance and demeanor in court are important factors that can influence a jury's opinions.

5. An officer should discuss a case with the prosecutor prior to the court appearance.

6. Notes made by an officer, physical evidence, and reports prepared in connection with the case should be brought to court.

7. The presence of required witnesses should be checked.

8. The prosecutor should be consulted prior to testifying to ascertain what is to be expected while on the witness stand.

9. If elaboration of an answer is not required, yes and no answers should be used.

10. When answering a question, look directly at the person who is being addressed.

11. Refer to the defendant as Mr., Mrs., or Ms., whichever is appropriate, or as the defendant.

12. Unless a precise measurement is known, use the term approximately when describing a measurement.

13. If the answer to a question is not known, it is permissible to simply state such.

14. If it is necessary to review notes prior to answering, ask the judge for permission but do not read verbatim from notes.

15. When, as part of a question, a defense attorney repeats something previously stated and does not repeat it accurately, politely correct the attorney.

16. Before answering a defense attorney's question, pause a few seconds to give the prosecutor an opportunity to state an appropriate objection.

17. If a question is not understood, ask to have it repeated.

18. If asked about an article of physical evidence, examine the article before answering.

EXAMATOPICS ABOUT COURT TESTIMONY

1. Do not anticipate a question before it is completed nor begin answering before the attorney finishes asking the question.

2. Unless opinion is appropriate, such as in expert testimony, testify only to facts.

3. Testimony should not be memorized.

4. Testimony should be impartial, and the appearance of hostility toward the defense attorney should be avoided.

5. Police jargon not clear to a jury should be avoided.

6. If asked about any necessary force that was used, it should be readily and openly acknowledged.

7. Admit conferrals about the case that were made with a police partner or supervisor.

Evidence

Evidence covers all the information and facts which are offered to the court to prove or disprove a fact that is in issue before the court. The following are facts that a police supervisor should know in connection with evidence.

1. The evidence can be in the form of testimony by witnesses, written documents, or other things such as a painting or a revolver.

2. Real evidence is that kind of evidence from which the trier of the facts obtains knowledge by personally observing some thing or article. It is sometimes known as demonstrative evidence.

3. Direct evidence is evidence that directly establishes a fact in issue.

4. Circumstantial evidence is evidence that establishes a fact or circumstance from which the trier of the facts may infer another fact in issue.

5. Testimony consists of the oral statements of witnesses under oath.

6. Hearsay evidence is evidence that is not from the personal knowledge of the witness but from what someone else has said.

7. Evidence is relevant when it is pertinent to the facts in issue. Evidence is irrelevant when it does not influence or affect the fact in issue.

8. Evidence is material when it has a serious bearing on the issue; it must affect the issue significantly.

9. Competent evidence is evidence that is legally admissible.

10. An inference is a conclusion that can be drawn logically from other facts that have been proven.

11. Proof is the result or effect of the evidence in terms of convincing the trier of the facts.

12. A privileged communication occurs when one gives or gets information based on a confidential relationship (e.g., a lawyer and a client). Ordinarily information stemming from a privileged communication is not admissible in court.

EXAMATOPICS ABOUT EVIDENCE

1. An eyewitness account of an offense committed by a criminal is an example of direct evidence. The witness is present and describes what he/she saw.

2. When direct evidence is used to prove a fact, other evidence is not necessary to prove that particular fact.

3. Some examples of real evidence are footprints, fingerprints, bloodstains, and firearms. Real evidence includes things that are tangible.

4. The essence of circumstantial evidence is the making of an inference or conclusion that can be drawn logically from other facts which have been proven.

5. If X observes Y shoot Z, then the testimony of X about the shooting is direct evidence.

6. However, if X observes Y go into another room with Z, and then X hears a shot, sees Y running from the room with a smoking gun, and then finds Z shot, such an account of what X observed would be circumstantial evidence that Y has shot Z.

7. If X is being charged with stealing a bushel of apples, evidence introduced to show that the apples were red and not green would be immaterial.

8. If X is accused of having shot Y with a bow and arrow, evidence that showed X as an expert with a bow and arrow would be rele-

vant. It would be irrelevant to show that X was an expert pistol shot.

9. An example of hearsay evidence occurs when a witness states, "I know X robbed Y because Z told me."

10. In general hearsay evidence is not admissible. However, some exceptions to the inadmissibility of hearsay evidence include confessions, dying declarations, and spontaneous exclamations.

Firearms and Bullets

When a firearm comes into the hands of an officer during an investigation, the officer must be able to describe the firearm for future identification. As a minimum the officer must be able to identify the firearm's

Caliber (e.g., .22, .25, .32, .38)
Make—the manufacturer of the firearm
Model (e.g., "Official Police," "Military and Police")
Type—the general manner of operation (e.g., revolver, automatic, semi automatic)
Serial number—numbers located on various areas on firearms
Finish—a description of the color and surface of the firearm (e.g., nickel or blue)

Firearms identification concerns itself with two basic issues

1. Based on the bullets or cartridge cases found at the scene of a crime, what kind of firearm was used.

2. Also based on the bullets or cartridge cases found at the scene of a crime, whether a certain firearm suspected by the police is the one that was used to fire the bullets.

The answers to these questions are usually provided by police experts. However the officers at such a scene should have a clear understanding of the process and their role.

Grooves are cut into the barrel of a firearm. This produces the rifling of a firearm. The rifling can twist to the left or the right. The purpose of the rifling is to give a bullet discharged from the firearm its rotation as it moves forward.

When grooves are cut, they produce what are know as lands. The surface of these lands is the actual inside of the barrel before the grooves are cut. Thus both lands and grooves are produced as a result of the rifling of a firearm.

EXAMATOPICS ABOUT FIREARMS AND BULLETS

1. Knowing the distance from which a bullet was fired helps in distinguishing a homicide from a suicide.

2. When a firearm is difficult to identify via the usual distinguishing characteristics, such things as barrel length and overall length should be used.

3. The groove impressions produced by the rifling in a firearm are equal to the number of lands.

4. Bore diameter is the distance from land to land.

5. Groove diameter is the distance from bottom to bottom of opposite grooves.

6. The markings found on a bullet that has been fired by a firearm are caused by tiny imperfections in the barrel of the firearm. These markings are known as striae.

7. To find out if a bullet found at a crime scene has been fired from a certain suspected firearm, the investigator has another bullet fired from that suspected firearm and then has the markings on both bullets compared.

8. In the case of automatic and semiautomatic firearms, markings may also be found on the cartridge case.

9. Markings on a cartridge case may be caused by

   a. Indentations from the firing pin

   b. The breech face

   c. The extractor

   d. The ejector

10. To preserve these markings, officers should mark bullets on their base and shells on their side.

11. When a bullet is fired through a pane of glass, the following can be expected to occur:

   a. Radial fractures are formed on the side opposite from where the bullet was fired (i.e., the exit side)

b. Concentric fractures are formed on the same side as where the bullet was fired from (i.e., the entry side)

c. A crater and flaking of glass chips occur on the side opposite from where the bullet was fired (i.e., the exit side)

12. Tests used to determine if someone has recently fired a firearm include

a. The Dermal Nitrate or Paraffin Gauntlet Test

b. The Neutron Activation Analysis Test

Neither test is conclusive, however.

13. The Walker Powder Residue Test, the use of infrared photographing and the use of soft X-ray apparatus can help in determining the distance of discharge, which is often important in questionable suicide cases.

Fingerprints

Fingerprints are unique for two reasons. First, the fingerprints you are born with are those you will die with. Second, no two sets of identical fingerprints have ever been found.

Fingerprints that can be found at a crime scene can be categorized into three classes.

1. Visible fingerprints such as those left by fingers that are covered by staining materials such as blood, paint, or grease

2. Plastic fingerprints such as those left by impressions below the surface of certain substances such as soap, melted wax, putty, or tar

3. Latent fingerprints such as those which are not visible to the naked eye and a special procedure must be employed to make them visible, either utilizing special substances or lighting

CLASSIFYING FINGERPRINTS

The three main types of fingerprint patterns are:

1. Arches—the ridges of the pattern enter one side of the pattern and exit without interruption across the finger

2. Whorls—the ridges of the pattern appear to revolve around the core, or center point, of the pattern

3. Loops—the ridges enter one side of the pattern, go to the center of the pattern, curve around the core, flow in the opposite direction and then exit on the same side that they entered the pattern from

Latent fingerprints can be made visible, photographed, and then lifted by crime scene technicians. The substances used to make latent fingerprints visible include:

1. Physical or mechanical development such as:

   a. Specialized powders used to dust for prints

   b. Iodine fuming

2. Chemical techniques such as:

   c. Silver nitrate

   d. Ninhydrin

   e. Osmium tetroxide

EXAMATOPICS ABOUT FINGERPRINTS

1. Latent prints, which are extremely valuable to an investigator, should be made visible and then photographed before being lifted.

2. Latent prints have the most value for an investigator when compared to visible or plastic prints.

3. The most common type of fingerprint pattern are loops followed by whorls and then by arches.

4. Because loops are the most common pattern, they are broken down into

   a. Radial loops whose ridges start and end in the direction of the thumb of the hand by which they were made and

   b. Ulnar loops whose ridges start and end in the direction of the little finger of the hand by which they were made.

   It should be noted that it is impossible to tell whether an impression is a radial or ulnar loop unless it is known whether the impression was made by a left or right hand.

5. Deltas are triangle-shaped parts of a fingerprint pattern.

6. Arches have no deltas, loops have one delta, and whorls have two or more deltas.

7. A ridge count is established by forming an imaginary line connecting the point of a delta and the point of a core of an impression and then counting the ridges that intersect this imaginary line.

Blood and Bloodstains

Blood found at the scene of a crime can be used more to state this is not the blood of X rather than this is the blood of X. The problems posed for the investigator are:

Is there blood to be discovered at the scene?

Is what has been discovered blood?

Is it human blood?

Whose blood is it?

Finding blood at the scene is not always as easy as it seems. To the layman, blood is reddish in color and after a while develops a reddish brown color. Therefore, it is logical to look for such colored stains at the scene. However, blood can be black or even green when it is found on a wall surface whose paint has dissolved in the blood causing a color change in the blood.

In order to detect the presence of blood an investigator may

1. Use a flashlight or other artificial light source on a dark background where blood may be difficult to detect. Against a dull background, a dried bloodstain will look like glossy varnish.

2. Spray the chemical luminol over the area suspected of containing blood. It should become bluish white in color in the presence of blood, with old blood seemingly reacting better.

Field tests to answer the question "Is what has been discovered blood?" include:

1. The Benzadine Test. If there is blood, a blue or green color is produced by this test. However substances other than blood also have been known to produce the same effect. It is therefore nonspecific. Still this testing substance is somewhat easy to prepare by the field investigator.

2. The Leuco-Malachite Test. It is somewhat more specific than the Benzadine Test. Using this test, after about ten seconds maximum, a green stain appears which then becomes a dark greenish-blue after no more than one minute.

Confirming tests that are done in a lab include:

1. the Phenolphthalein Test

2. the Teichman or Hemin Crystal Test

3. the Microspectroscopic Test

To test for human blood the Precipitin Reaction Test is used. This test can distinguish between the blood of a human and that of an animal.

Human blood may be classified into four major groupings. They are known as O, A, B, and AB, with subcategories of these four basic groupings. These four major groupings are based on the ability of the blood serum of a person in one blood grouping to agglutinate or clump together the red blood cells of individuals of another grouping. The process is known as agglutination. It is for this reason that care must be taken when medical personnel give blood transfusions.

For example, in the chart below, if Yes = Agglutination occurs and No = No agglutination occurs, then

THE BLOOD SERUM OF	AGGLUTINATES WITH THE RED BLOOD CELLS OF			
	O	A	B	AB
O	No	Yes	Yes	Yes
A	No	No	Yes	Yes
B	No	Yes	No	Yes
AB	No	No	No	No

For example, the blood serum Type O agglutinates with the red blood cells of types A, B, and AB, but not with Type O.

EXAMATOPICS ABOUT BLOOD AND BLOODSTAINS

1. The blood groupings are hereditary. Also the blood grouping you are born with is that which you will die with.

2. Blood drop stains will vary according to the height from which they are dropped.

3. Blood dropped from 5–12 inches are a round circular shape.

4. Blood dropped from directly overhead from an approximate height of 12–20 inches will appear as a gearlike form with teeth.

5. Blood dropped from a height of more than 20 inches, to up to approximately 5 feet, will appear more jagged around the edges.

6. The recommended temperature to refrigerate blood at is 5 degrees centigrade or 41 degrees Fahrenheit.

7. The blood grouping of the victim of a homicide or suicide is of particular interest to an investigator and should be determined as part of the investigation.

Practice Exercises

You are now ready to do some practice questions. Always try to answer the questions in the allotted time. After completing each of the three groups of questions, make sure you thoroughly review the explanations for each answer before going to the next set of questions. This includes reviewing the explanations for all questions, those you answered correctly and those you answered incorrectly. This is done to ensure that you always arrive at the correct choice for the right reasons. Remember, now is the time to make mistakes. If you understand why you made a mistake, you should not make the same mistake on the examination, when it really counts.

GROUP ONE—10 QUESTIONS—15 MINUTES

1. Proving that an arson of a building has occurred is difficult mainly because:
   A. Arsonists are extremely clever criminals and go out of their way not to discuss their criminal activities
   B. Most police departments do not have a specialized unit to deal with such a crime
   C. Much of the evidence is consumed by the fire
   D. Firefighters of necessity unintentionally destroy the evidence while attempting to fulfill their primary duty of extinguishing the fire

2. In general the most important piece of evidence left at the scene of a robbery is:
   A. Weapons dropped by a robber
   B. The visual identification of the robber by any victims or witnesses
   C. Tire marks left by a getaway car
   D. Pieces of rope used by a robber to restrain victims

3. When a phone company's sale representative allows a potential customer to provide false identification, which is then used to activate cellular service in order to avoid payment of future bills, it is known as:
   A. Roaming fraud
   B. Subscription fraud
   C. Counterfeit fraud
   D. Network fraud

4. In police undercover buy operations of illicit drugs, which of the following would generally be least correct?
   A. The undercover police officer has more experience that the drug dealer.
   B. In such an operation, the drug dealer values drugs, money, and his/her freedom.
   C. The drug dealer wants the undercover's money more than the police want the drugs.
   D. The location of the meet with the drug dealer should be studied before the actual meet.

5. Consider the following statements concerning an undercover police operation designed to purchase illicit drugs from a drug dealer:
   (1) One of the potential risks of such an operation is an overzealous undercover officer.
   (2) An undercover officer should not enter the car of the suspect drug dealer.
   (3) A confidential informant should be allowed to do as much as possible even if it means controlling the situation.
   Which of the following choices best classifies the above statements into those which are accurate and those which are inaccurate?
   A. Statement 1 is inaccurate; statements 2 and 3 are accurate.
   B. Statement 2 is inaccurate; statements 1 and 3 are accurate.
   C. Statement 3 is inaccurate; statements 1 and 2 are accurate.
   D. All of the statements are accurate.

6. Sergeant Rems is conducting a seminar dealing with hostage situations. As part of the seminar, the sergeant compiles a list of recommendations for captives who are taken as hostages. Which of the following would be least appropriate for such a list of recommendations?

A. Be observant.
B. Initiate conversations with the captor.
C. Accept your present situation.
D. Do as directed, but no more or less.

7. When testifying in court, a police officer should recognize that his/her testimony may be judged not only on what is verbally communicated but also on what is communicated nonverbally. It is generally believed that nonverbal messages comprise approximately what percentage of a message's content?
A. 15%
B. 45%
C. 75%
D. 90%

8. A bullet has been fired through a pane of glass. The side of the glass where concentric fractures will most probably appear is:
A. On the side where the bullet exited the pane of glass
B. On the side where the bullet entered the pane of glass
C. On both the side where the bullet entered and the side where the bullet exited the pane of glass
D. On neither side of the pane of glass

9. The most common type of fingerprint pattern is the:
A. Arches
B. Whorls
C. Loops
D. Deltas

10. Sergeant Rems compares the caliber of a bullet with that of the bore of the gun from which it will be fired. In doing so the sergeant should find that typically the bullet's caliber is:
A. A little smaller than distance between the lands found in the bore of the gun
B. A little larger than the bore of the gun
C. Precisely the same as the bore of the gun
D. The same circumference as the distance between two grooves of the bore of the gun

GROUP TWO—10 QUESTIONS—15 MINUTES

11. Bullets that spin through the air after being discharged from a firearm eventually lose their velocity and ultimately their spin. When this happens they start to tumble end over end. If at this point the bullet should happen to strike a victim, the resulting wound is known as:
   A. A key hole wound
   B. A flapjack wound
   C. A head over heels wound
   D. A blunt blast wound

12. Evaluate the following statements concerning a rape homicide:
   (1) Clothing containing only semen stains may be rolled up to transport it.
   (2) Clothing containing only dried bloodstains may be rolled up to transport it.
   Which of the following is most accurate concerning the statements above?
   A. Only statement 1 is correct.
   B. Only statement 2 is correct.
   C. Both statements 1 and 2 are correct.
   D. Neither statement 1 nor 2 is correct.

13. Regarding latent fingerprints, it would be most correct to:
   A. Lift them at the same time they are photographed
   B. Lift them before they are photographed
   C. Lift them after they are photographed
   D. Not photograph them since lifting permits a more permanent record

14. When appearing as a witness for the prosecution, Police Officer June Drake makes it a practice to wait a few seconds before answering the questions of a defense attorney. This practice is:
   A. Good, mainly because it will give the jury the impression that the officer is sincerely trying to do her best when answering questions
   B. Bad, mainly because it will appear to the jury that the officer is unsure of the facts in the case

C. Good, mainly because it will provide the prosecutor an opportunity to object to a question
D. Bad, mainly because it will make the jury impatient with the officer since it will seem that the officer is intentionally wasting time

15. A bank has been robbed at gunpoint, and the robbers have fled in a late model sedan. Some distance from the scene of the robbery, the getaway car is found. The sergeant in charge of the investigation would be most correct if he directed the crime scene unit to pay particular attention to and look for fingerprint impressions:
A. On the steering wheel
B. On the rearview mirror
C. On the radio dials
D. On the outside surface of the trunk area

16. While it is extremely difficult to generalize with total accuracy about males who commit rapes of women, some fairly accurate profile information can be identified. For instance, a rapist who is somewhat narcissistic and is skillful in exploiting the generosity of female victims is most typically known as:
A. An assaultive rapist
B. A sexually inadequate rapist
C. A sadistic rapist
D. A predator rapist

17. Sergeant Hall is asked how to develop an old fingerprint that is on some paper. In this instance, the sergeant would be most correct if she recommended the use of:
A. Ninhydrin
B. Iodine fuming
C. Silver nitrate
D. Any of the above

18. Determining death is assisted by understanding a process known as rigor mortis. Sometime after death the muscles of the body stiffen and rigor mortis sets in. In connection with rigor mortis which of the following is least correct?
A. The stiffening begins in the lower extremities and works its way toward the head of the deceased.
B. Within eighteen hours after death the entire body is affected by rigor mortis.

C. It usually disappears within thirty-six hours after death.

D. Great heat can accelerate the process.

19. A dead body is found in a parked car with the motor still running and the windows closed. Carbon monoxide is suspected as contributing to the death. Such suspicions would be strengthened if the skin of the deceased was found to be:

A. A dark brown color

B. A cherry red color

C. A bruised black and blue appearance

D. A chalky white color

20. A discarded shell has been found at a crime scene by Police Officer Mark Holder. In order to maintain the chain of custody, the officer wishes to mark the shell for identification. Unsure where to mark the shell, the officer asks his supervisor Sergeant Rems. In this instance the sergeant should direct the officer to mark his initials on:

A. The base of the shell

B. The side of the shell

C. Both the side and the base of the shell

D. Either the side or the base of the shell depending on the amount of space available

GROUP THREE—10 QUESTIONS— 15 MINUTES

21. In connection with the collection and presentation of physical evidence at a criminal trial, which of the following statements is least correct?

A. Physical evidence involving different defendants should be kept separate and not comingled.

B. The admissibility of physical evidence at a criminal trial depends on an unbroken chain of custody from the arresting officer to the courtroom.

C. Physical property that is going to be introduced as evidence at a criminal trial should pass through the hands of as many people as possible.

D. If there is any doubt whether a particular piece of physical property could be evidence, it is better for the discovering officer to treat it as evidence.

22. Generally witnesses in a trial may offer facts and not opinions as part of their testimony. However, there are instances when expert opinion is admitted, and in certain restricted circumstances, even the opinion of nonexpert or lay witnesses can be admitted by the court. Which of the following best identifies an instance when the opinion of nonexpert or lay witnesses can be admitted by the court?
    A. Whether two fingerprints are the same
    B. Whether the defendant was intoxicated
    C. The chemical analysis of a drug
    D. Whether the stain found at the scene was human blood

23. Sergeant Frank Rems is instructing a group of government officials on how to behave if ever abducted as the subject of a hostage taking. The sergeant would be least correct if he suggested which of the following actions for a hostage to take?
    A. If you require medication, ask for it because a hostage may become upset with a sick captive.
    B. Try to calm the hostage taker by remaining calm.
    C. If the police break into the scene, stand up and identify yourself.
    D. Avoid becoming argumentative.

24. Several different methods can be used to search an outdoor crime scene. In connection with these various search methods, it would be least correct to state:
    A. In the strip method, the searchers slowly proceed at the same pace in parallel paths.
    B. In the spiral method, the searchers follow each other in the path of a spiral beginning at the center and spiraling toward the outside.
    C. In the wheel method, the search is conducted from a central point outwardly.
    D. In the zone method, the area to be searched is divided into quadrants.

25. Sergeant Neil Bailes has been assigned to supervise a group of police officers, both in automobiles and on foot, who will be conducting a surveillance of a subject. During his instruction, the sergeant

would be most correct if he made which of the following statements?

A. If at all possible, avoid surveillance of a subject from an automobile parked in a restricted area.

B. When two officers are conducting an extended surveillance from an automobile, both officers should remain in the front seat.

C. An officer conducting a surveillance should never give the appearance of a person who is impatiently waiting for someone.

D. If the subject of the surveillance approaches the officer, the officer should avoid looking at the subject at all costs.

26. Sergeant Jess Walker responds to a shooting. The sergeant is informed that a shot has been fired through a glass windowpane. In such an instance, the sergeant would be most likely to find on the side of the windowpane where the shot exited the windowpane all the following except:

A. A crater formed

B. Flaking of glass

C. Concentric circles

D. Radial fractures

27. At the scene of a suspected homicide, the deceased is found lying nude and face down. On the upper side of the deceased's back is evidence of post mortem lividity, a dark blue discoloration that is apparent after death. Accordingly, which of the following may NOT be properly concluded?

A. That the death occurred at least two hours in the past

B. That the body has not been moved

C. That the discoloration is probably not from bruising if the color is uniform

D. That the discoloration is probably not from bruising if there is no indication of swelling or an abrasion

28. Persons who are the subjects involved in a family dispute should be tactfully removed by the responding officers from which of the following rooms?

A. The living room

B. Any room that has a window

C. The kitchen

D. The bedroom

29. Consider the following statements concerning the use of mace.
    (1) Mace is effective in situations involving one or two subjects.
    (2) Mace is effective up to a distance of approximately twelve feet.
    (3) Mace is not intended to completely take the place of an officer's firearm.
    Which of the following choices best classifies the above statements into those which are accurate and those which are inaccurate?
    A. Statement 1 is inaccurate; statements 2 and 3 are accurate.
    B. Statement 2 is inaccurate; statements 1 and 3 are accurate.
    C. Statement 3 is inaccurate; statements 1 and 2 are accurate.
    D. All of the statements are accurate.

30. Sergeant Rems is present at the scene of a shooting. The victim is Ray who while dying makes this statement, "I know Don raped April because Joy told me." It would be most correct to consider such a statement as:
    A. A dying declaration
    B. A spontaneous declaration
    C. An example of hearsay evidence
    D. A confession

Answer Key

1. C	7. D	13. C	19. B	25. A
2. B	8. B	14. C	20. B	26. C
3. B	9. C	15. B	21. C	27. B
4. A	10. B	16. D	22. B	28. C
5. C	11. A	17. A	23. C	29. D
6. B	12. B	18. A	24. B	30. C

Answer Explanations

1. **C**   Much of the evidence is consumed by the fire, and what evidence remains goes unnoticed to all but trained arson experts.

2. **B**   While all the choices indicate important pieces of information, the fact that a robber has been visually seen by the victim is so important that it is recommended that photos be taken of the scene from the vantage of where the victims were at the time they observed the robber.

3. **B**   Roaming fraud occurs when a person uses an illegally altered cellular phone. By using something known as a tumbler phone, the illegal user can change certain code numbers at will and creates service for the fraudulent phone while an unsuspecting legitimate subscriber is billed for the phone call. Counterfeit fraud involves a duplication of the actual code numbers of a legitimate subscriber whose account is billed for all the calls made by the illegal user. The method of counterfeit fraud is easier to detect because of its immediate and discernible impact on the legitimate subscriber. Network fraud basically exists because of weaknesses in the growing industry of cellular phone use. For example, unauthorized persons often illegally use electronic serial numbers that have been created solely for testing purposes. Choice B occurs under the circumstances described in the fact pattern of this question.

4. **A**   Typically the dealer has spent 15–20 years on the street involved in such a business. The undercover officer has not. In connection with police undercover buy operations of illicit drugs, choices B, C, and D are correct statements.

5. **C**   A confidential informant, often also a criminal, should know his/her part of the plan of the operation, but no more nor no less.

6. **B**   It is recommended that a captive speak only if spoken to.

7. **D**   Dress, posture, gestures, and even eye contact all combine to form nonverbal communication.

8. **B**   Concentric fractures or circular-like cracks in the glass should form on the side where the bullet entered the pane of glass.

9. **C**   Approximately sixty percent of fingerprint patterns are categorized as loops.

10. B This is so in order to prevent gases from the explosion of the gunpowder from leaking while the bullet is moving forward inside the barrel.

GROUP TWO

11. A A large gaping wound results and is known as a key hole wound.

12. B Because semen becomes brittle when dried, it can be broken if rolled up. The full spermatozoa is needed to be preserved as evidence (that is, the head and the tail).

13. C Latent prints should be photographed first and then lifted.

14. C The defense attorney's question may be improper, and the prosecutor may be able to object. If, however, the officer blurts out a response to an improper question, regardless of whether the prosecutor objects and the judge sustains the objection, it is too late. The damage is done since the jury has already heard the answer, even if they are directed to disregard it by the judge.

15. B All areas might warrant examination for fingerprint impressions, but the rearview mirror because of its personalized adjustments by a driver should receive particular attention.

16. D This type of rapist may also have an indulgent parent or wife who may know and even support his actions.

17. A This substance, which is known to react with amino acids, can be used to develop old fingerprints, especially on paper.

18. A The stiffening begins in the upper part of the body and works its way toward the lower parts of the body.

19. B Carbon monoxide actually does not poison but asphyxiates a victim and thus causes the skin to be a cherry red color.

20. B A shell should be marked on its side while a spent bullet should be marked on its base.

GROUP THREE

21. C The chain of custody regarding physical evidence should be kept as short as possible to decrease the potential of contamination of such evidence. Thus, physical property that is going to be introduced as evidence at a criminal trial should be touched by as *few* people as possible.

22. **B** Opinion testimony by a nonexpert or lay witnesses can also be admitted by a court for such things as weights, color, emotional states, and generally things concerning subjects the average man has substantial experience with and knowledge of.

23. **C** If the police break into the scene, get down and stay on the floor.

24. **B** In the spiral method, the searchers follow each other in the path of a spiral beginning at the outside and spiraling toward the center. The other methods are correctly described.

25. **A** Choice B is incorrect because it would be better to have one officer sit in the rear seat and the other sit on the passenger side as if waiting for the driver of the vehicle to come back. Choice C is incorrect because it is not always necessary to be completely inconspicuous. Therefore, being observed as a person who is impatiently waiting for someone would not necessarily blow one's cover. Choice D is incorrect because the officer should act normally, which includes briefly looking at someone who is approaching.

26. **C** Choices A, B, and D indicate what would most likely be found on the side of the windowpane where the shot exited the windowpane.

27. **B** Post mortem lividity is caused by the blood in a dead body settling to the lowest point of the body due to its own weight. If the discoloration caused by post mortem lividity is found on the upper surface of the back of a deceased who is lying face down, it is an indication that the body was moved or at least turned over after post mortem lividity set in. Choices A, C, and D indicate proper conclusions under these circumstances.

28. **C** The kitchen is the room where potential weapons have the greatest likelihood of being found.

29. **D** All the statements are accurate.

30. **C** Hearsay evidence comes from merely repeating what a witness has heard someone else say and not from the personal knowledge of the witness. Choice A is incorrect because a dying declaration must involve the victim naming his/her killer. Choice B is incorrect because it is not a statement about a startling event, in this case a past rape, which is being made at the time of the startling event, namely the past rape. Choice D is incorrect because it is not a direct admission of guilt; rather, the statement concerns the guilt of another person.

Answer Sheet
Practice Examination One

Follow the instructions given in the text. Mark only your answers in the ovals below.

Warning: Be sure that the oval you fill is in the same row as the question you are answering. Use a No. 2 pencil (soft pencil).

Be sure your pencil marks are heavy and black. Erase completely any answer you wish to change.

Do *not* make stray pencil dots, dashes, or marks.

1 Ⓐ Ⓑ Ⓒ Ⓓ	2 Ⓐ Ⓑ Ⓒ Ⓓ	3 Ⓐ Ⓑ Ⓒ Ⓓ	4 Ⓐ Ⓑ Ⓒ Ⓓ	5 Ⓐ Ⓑ Ⓒ Ⓓ	6 Ⓐ Ⓑ Ⓒ Ⓓ
7 Ⓐ Ⓑ Ⓒ Ⓓ	8 Ⓐ Ⓑ Ⓒ Ⓓ	9 Ⓐ Ⓑ Ⓒ Ⓓ	10 Ⓐ Ⓑ Ⓒ Ⓓ	11 Ⓐ Ⓑ Ⓒ Ⓓ	12 Ⓐ Ⓑ Ⓒ Ⓓ
13 Ⓐ Ⓑ Ⓒ Ⓓ	14 Ⓐ Ⓑ Ⓒ Ⓓ	15 Ⓐ Ⓑ Ⓒ Ⓓ	16 Ⓐ Ⓑ Ⓒ Ⓓ	17 Ⓐ Ⓑ Ⓒ Ⓓ	18 Ⓐ Ⓑ Ⓒ Ⓓ
19 Ⓐ Ⓑ Ⓒ Ⓓ	20 Ⓐ Ⓑ Ⓒ Ⓓ	21 Ⓐ Ⓑ Ⓒ Ⓓ	22 Ⓐ Ⓑ Ⓒ Ⓓ	23 Ⓐ Ⓑ Ⓒ Ⓓ	24 Ⓐ Ⓑ Ⓒ Ⓓ
25 Ⓐ Ⓑ Ⓒ Ⓓ	26 Ⓐ Ⓑ Ⓒ Ⓓ	27 Ⓐ Ⓑ Ⓒ Ⓓ	28 Ⓐ Ⓑ Ⓒ Ⓓ	29 Ⓐ Ⓑ Ⓒ Ⓓ	30 Ⓐ Ⓑ Ⓒ Ⓓ
31 Ⓐ Ⓑ Ⓒ Ⓓ	32 Ⓐ Ⓑ Ⓒ Ⓓ	33 Ⓐ Ⓑ Ⓒ Ⓓ	34 Ⓐ Ⓑ Ⓒ Ⓓ	35 Ⓐ Ⓑ Ⓒ Ⓓ	36 Ⓐ Ⓑ Ⓒ Ⓓ
37 Ⓐ Ⓑ Ⓒ Ⓓ	38 Ⓐ Ⓑ Ⓒ Ⓓ	39 Ⓐ Ⓑ Ⓒ Ⓓ	40 Ⓐ Ⓑ Ⓒ Ⓓ	41 Ⓐ Ⓑ Ⓒ Ⓓ	42 Ⓐ Ⓑ Ⓒ Ⓓ
43 Ⓐ Ⓑ Ⓒ Ⓓ	44 Ⓐ Ⓑ Ⓒ Ⓓ	45 Ⓐ Ⓑ Ⓒ Ⓓ	46 Ⓐ Ⓑ Ⓒ Ⓓ	47 Ⓐ Ⓑ Ⓒ Ⓓ	48 Ⓐ Ⓑ Ⓒ Ⓓ
49 Ⓐ Ⓑ Ⓒ Ⓓ	50 Ⓐ Ⓑ Ⓒ Ⓓ	51 Ⓐ Ⓑ Ⓒ Ⓓ	52 Ⓐ Ⓑ Ⓒ Ⓓ	53 Ⓐ Ⓑ Ⓒ Ⓓ	54 Ⓐ Ⓑ Ⓒ Ⓓ
55 Ⓐ Ⓑ Ⓒ Ⓓ	56 Ⓐ Ⓑ Ⓒ Ⓓ	57 Ⓐ Ⓑ Ⓒ Ⓓ	58 Ⓐ Ⓑ Ⓒ Ⓓ	59 Ⓐ Ⓑ Ⓒ Ⓓ	60 Ⓐ Ⓑ Ⓒ Ⓓ
61 Ⓐ Ⓑ Ⓒ Ⓓ	62 Ⓐ Ⓑ Ⓒ Ⓓ	63 Ⓐ Ⓑ Ⓒ Ⓓ	64 Ⓐ Ⓑ Ⓒ Ⓓ	65 Ⓐ Ⓑ Ⓒ Ⓓ	66 Ⓐ Ⓑ Ⓒ Ⓓ
67 Ⓐ Ⓑ Ⓒ Ⓓ	68 Ⓐ Ⓑ Ⓒ Ⓓ	69 Ⓐ Ⓑ Ⓒ Ⓓ	70 Ⓐ Ⓑ Ⓒ Ⓓ	71 Ⓐ Ⓑ Ⓒ Ⓓ	72 Ⓐ Ⓑ Ⓒ Ⓓ
73 Ⓐ Ⓑ Ⓒ Ⓓ	74 Ⓐ Ⓑ Ⓒ Ⓓ	75 Ⓐ Ⓑ Ⓒ Ⓓ	76 Ⓐ Ⓑ Ⓒ Ⓓ	77 Ⓐ Ⓑ Ⓒ Ⓓ	78 Ⓐ Ⓑ Ⓒ Ⓓ
79 Ⓐ Ⓑ Ⓒ Ⓓ	80 Ⓐ Ⓑ Ⓒ Ⓓ	81 Ⓐ Ⓑ Ⓒ Ⓓ	82 Ⓐ Ⓑ Ⓒ Ⓓ	83 Ⓐ Ⓑ Ⓒ Ⓓ	84 Ⓐ Ⓑ Ⓒ Ⓓ
85 Ⓐ Ⓑ Ⓒ Ⓓ	86 Ⓐ Ⓑ Ⓒ Ⓓ	87 Ⓐ Ⓑ Ⓒ Ⓓ	88 Ⓐ Ⓑ Ⓒ Ⓓ	89 Ⓐ Ⓑ Ⓒ Ⓓ	90 Ⓐ Ⓑ Ⓒ Ⓓ
91 Ⓐ Ⓑ Ⓒ Ⓓ	92 Ⓐ Ⓑ Ⓒ Ⓓ	93 Ⓐ Ⓑ Ⓒ Ⓓ	94 Ⓐ Ⓑ Ⓒ Ⓓ	95 Ⓐ Ⓑ Ⓒ Ⓓ	96. Ⓐ Ⓑ Ⓒ Ⓓ
97 Ⓐ Ⓑ Ⓒ Ⓓ	98 Ⓐ Ⓑ Ⓒ Ⓓ	99 Ⓐ Ⓑ Ⓒ Ⓓ	100 Ⓐ Ⓑ Ⓒ Ⓓ	101 Ⓐ Ⓑ Ⓒ Ⓓ	102 Ⓐ Ⓑ Ⓒ Ⓓ
103 Ⓐ Ⓑ Ⓒ Ⓓ	104 Ⓐ Ⓑ Ⓒ Ⓓ	105 Ⓐ Ⓑ Ⓒ Ⓓ	106 Ⓐ Ⓑ Ⓒ Ⓓ	107 Ⓐ Ⓑ Ⓒ Ⓓ	108 Ⓐ Ⓑ Ⓒ Ⓓ
109 Ⓐ Ⓑ Ⓒ Ⓓ	110 Ⓐ Ⓑ Ⓒ Ⓓ	111 Ⓐ Ⓑ Ⓒ Ⓓ	112 Ⓐ Ⓑ Ⓒ Ⓓ	113 Ⓐ Ⓑ Ⓒ Ⓓ	114 Ⓐ Ⓑ Ⓒ Ⓓ
115 Ⓐ Ⓑ Ⓒ Ⓓ	116 Ⓐ Ⓑ Ⓒ Ⓓ	117 Ⓐ Ⓑ Ⓒ Ⓓ	118 Ⓐ Ⓑ Ⓒ Ⓓ	119 Ⓐ Ⓑ Ⓒ Ⓓ	120 Ⓐ Ⓑ Ⓒ Ⓓ
121 Ⓐ Ⓑ Ⓒ Ⓓ	122 Ⓐ Ⓑ Ⓒ Ⓓ	123 Ⓐ Ⓑ Ⓒ Ⓓ	124 Ⓐ Ⓑ Ⓒ Ⓓ	125 Ⓐ Ⓑ Ⓒ Ⓓ	126 Ⓐ Ⓑ Ⓒ Ⓓ
127 Ⓐ Ⓑ Ⓒ Ⓓ	128 Ⓐ Ⓑ Ⓒ Ⓓ	129 Ⓐ Ⓑ Ⓒ Ⓓ	130 Ⓐ Ⓑ Ⓒ Ⓓ	131 Ⓐ Ⓑ Ⓒ Ⓓ	132 Ⓐ Ⓑ Ⓒ Ⓓ
133 Ⓐ Ⓑ Ⓒ Ⓓ	134 Ⓐ Ⓑ Ⓒ Ⓓ	135 Ⓐ Ⓑ Ⓒ Ⓓ	136 Ⓐ Ⓑ Ⓒ Ⓓ	137 Ⓐ Ⓑ Ⓒ Ⓓ	138 Ⓐ Ⓑ Ⓒ Ⓓ
139 Ⓐ Ⓑ Ⓒ Ⓓ	140 Ⓐ Ⓑ Ⓒ Ⓓ	141 Ⓐ Ⓑ Ⓒ Ⓓ	142 Ⓐ Ⓑ Ⓒ Ⓓ	143 Ⓐ Ⓑ Ⓒ Ⓓ	144 Ⓐ Ⓑ Ⓒ Ⓓ
145 Ⓐ Ⓑ Ⓒ Ⓓ	146 Ⓐ Ⓑ Ⓒ Ⓓ	147 Ⓐ Ⓑ Ⓒ Ⓓ	148 Ⓐ Ⓑ Ⓒ Ⓓ	149 Ⓐ Ⓑ Ⓒ Ⓓ	150 Ⓐ Ⓑ Ⓒ Ⓓ

TEST YOURSELF

CHAPTER 13

Practice Examination One

The Test

100 QUESTIONS—3½ HOURS

1. Most supervisors understand that discipline is one of their primary responsibilities. However, some confusion exists among supervisors as to the primary purpose of discipline. Which of the following choices best describes the primary purpose of discipline in a police agency?
   A. To train
   B. To punish
   C. To raise public confidence in the police
   D. To reduce corruption

2. You are a sergeant charged with the responsibility of supervising a certain squad of police officers. Rumors have been circulating that two

officers in your squad do not get along. They are police officers Rex and Smith, and they are in fact constantly in conflict with each other. Finally they come to you and complain about each other. As their sergeant, you should:

A. Tell the officers to cease their conflict since their actions will ultimately affect their job performance

B. Insist that they come to you to settle any differences they may have in the future

C. Attempt to identify the reasons for their on-going conflict

D. Transfer one or both of the officers

3. At a training session for police officers who are soon to be promoted to sergeant, a trainee asks, "Is the sergeant's supervisory role any different from a supervisor in a nonpolice agency?" It would be most correct to characterize the supervision problems of a police sergeant as:

A. Slightly similar to those of most other supervisors in other jobs

B. Totally unique, since they are not experienced by nonpolice supervisors

C. Fundamentally the same as those experienced by anyone who directs people

D. Extremely different from those dealt with by nonpolice supervisors

4. Sergeant Carter seems to give the fewest orders of any of the sergeants in the precinct, yet his employees seem to get the work done satisfactorily. When asked the reasons for this situation, Sergeant Carter offers several. Which of the following would probably not be one of the reasons offered by Sergeant Carter to explain why he gives so few orders?

A. He sets loose goals for his employees and then gives them the authority required to reach these goals.

B. He introduces frequent changes in the procedures utilized by his employees in accomplishing the work.

C. He trains and encourages employees to make decisions for themselves.

D. He has established set routines for most of the jobs of his employees.

5. Sergeant Bailes gives a fairly complicated order to a police officer. The officer seems to be listening but makes no comment after the sergeant finishes explaining the order. In order to find out if the officer understands the order, the sergeant should:
   A. Ask the officer if he/she understands the order
   B. Ask the officer to repeat the order
   C. Let the officer carry out the order, and determine if he/she has understood it
   D. Immediately repeat the order and ask if there are any questions

6. Teaching aids are sometimes overrated, but they are helpful in certain types of training. In which of the following training situations would a magnetic board prove most useful?
   A. When explaining a new ordinance
   B. During a briefing on the descriptions and photographs of a gang of terrorists
   C. As part of a review of the deployment of personnel and equipment at a past hostage situation
   D. While conducting a seminar on the multifaceted causes of crime

7. It is a well-recognized fact that one of the most important duties of a police sergeant is to train subordinates so they can be more proficient at their jobs. Concerning training, a knowledgeable police sergeant should realize that:
   A. Training is always a formal process
   B. Training is always an informal process
   C. Training is sometimes a formal process and sometimes an informal process
   D. Training must always be a formal process delivered in an informal manner

8. It is an established fact that training for police officers should be an ongoing process in police agencies. Of the following, the best method to deliver this ongoing training is:
   A. By using the patrol sergeant whose daily supervisory duties include the training of subordinates
   B. By using bulletins and memos published on a daily basis and handed out to police officers during each tour of duty

C. Through the use of roll call training in the form of video cassettes on timely issues

D. By relying on each police officer to engage in personal development on his/her off duty time

9. Police departments have learned to adjust to fiscal crises. Traditionally, one of the first reactions to occur when fiscal cuts are made is best indicated by which of the following?
A. The training function suffers.
B. Police officers are laid off.
C. The salaries of all employees are immediately reduced.
D. Fewer police officers are available for patrol.

10. For an employee to be properly trained, a climate for learning must be created. Which of the following would be the best way for a supervisor to create this climate?
A. Indicate to the employee that he/she has a responsibility to the community to be well trained.
B. Clearly show the employee some personal benefit that will be gained from the intended training.
C. Motivate the employee by showing how the department needs him/her to be better trained.
D. Indicate that disciplinary action will be initiated if training efforts are resisted.

11. Generally speaking, about what part of a police department's budget is spent on other than personnel services costs?
A. 90%   C. 30%
B. 50%   D. 10%

12. Sergeant Hall conducts inspections of his unit on a periodic basis. Which of the following can the sergeant not reasonably expect to be a result of the inspection program?
A. Find out if tasks are being performed in accordance with established procedures.
B. Learn if expected results are being obtained.
C. Eliminate the need for planning in direct proportion to the quality of inspections conducted.
D. Clearly ascertain if the resources of the agency are being properly utilized for the best advantage of the agency.

13. Sergeant Kegler is in charge of a very specialized police unit. Within the unit many specialists do specific jobs with specific responsibilities. Periodically, the sergeant temporarily reassigns some of these specialists to other assignments within the unit. The most likely result of the sergeant's assignment strategy is that:
    A. Coordination of the unit will be facilitated
    B. The planning function for the unit will be facilitated
    C. It will be easier to provide training for the unit
    D. It will be easier to give directions in the unit

14. Despite the best efforts and intentions, some plans just fail. Which of the following will always render a plan useless?
    A. Failure to outline the plan in one's own mind before announcing it
    B. Failure to evaluate the plan after implementing it
    C. Not gathering enough data in the formulation stage of the plan
    D. Not effectively communicating the plan to those who will carry it out

15. Policies are plans consisting of broad-based principles that help the personnel of the agency in reaching the agency goals. Policies have all of the following characteristics except which?
    A. They evolve from experience.
    B. They evolve from the legal constraints placed on the agency.
    C. They are usually written.
    D. They are arrived at from the traditional customs of the agency.

16. In a typical police agency, which of the following is not a generally accepted function of a juvenile division?
    A. Directing the investigations of other divisions when they are investigating offenses alleged to have been committed by juveniles
    B. Surveillance of places where youths hang out
    C. Making referrals of juveniles in appropriate cases to suitable agencies
    D. Acting as a source of information regarding juvenile activities for the rest of the department

17. Police-community relations has existed in various forms and to various degrees for many years. Recently, however, a new facet has been added to police-community relations in many police departments. Which of the following best describes this new facet?
    A. Public relations
    B. Crime prevention by the community
    C. Foot patrol
    D. Increased use of anticrime patrols at the request of community leaders

18. The police must be very careful to prevent pretrial disclosure of information to the press, which might damage a defendant's chance for a fair trial. Prior to the trial of a defendant, it would not be proper for a police sergeant to allow which of the following to be disclosed to the media?
    A. The amount of bail
    B. The results of fingerprint examinations
    C. If a weapon was used in the commission of an offense
    D. The defendant's marital status

19. Team policing has been offered as having great promise for improving police-community relations. What aspect of team policing most accounts for this promise?
    A. The way the officers assigned to team policing are trained
    B. The high level of qualifications usually found in officers assigned to team policing
    C. The way the community is involved in team policing
    D. The selection system for first-line supervisors assigned to team policing

20. At times, dialogue with the community in an open community relations setting may reveal the need to control police operations. When this occurs, the quickest and most effective means of controlling police operations can be achieved through which of the following?
    A. The system of courts
    B. The community
    C. Some outside investigating body
    D. Discipline within the police agency

21. A call is received from several plainclothes officers that they are inside an otherwise empty warehouse and have a burglar trapped somewhere in the building. The patrol sergeant responds and directs that a canine and the handler search the building. The sergeant's actions are:
    A. Proper, since no number of police officers are a match for the canine's keen senses
    B. Improper, since the burglar should first be given a chance to surrender once the police presence has been established
    C. Proper, since the canine can move a lot faster than any police officer
    D. Improper, since a building that contains police officers not in uniform should not be searched by a canine

22. Veteran patrol officers believe quite correctly that they will never be able to eliminate all criminal conduct. Which of the following criminal acts is patrol least likely to prevent?
    A. Larceny of automobiles
    B. Purse snatching
    C. Homicides involving intimate relationships
    D. Robberies of liquor stores

23. A certain commanding officer gives one of his sergeants the task of recommending the deployment of the patrol force in order to cover the entire precinct, twenty-four hours a day, seven days a week. In accomplishing the task, the sergeant would be most correct if he recommended which of the following?
    A. The same number of officers should work each tour of duty.
    B. The officer should be deployed in terms of time and area according to need for service.
    C. An equal number of officers should be assigned to each squad.
    D. More officers should be assigned to areas that, according to reports, have the greatest incidence of criminal activity.

24. When police officers perform patrol duties, they are at times called on to police large crowds. One characteristic of a crowd is its polarization. The polarization of a crowd is best described by which of the following?
   A. Members of the crowd focus their attention on some event.
   B. Members of the crowd are divided by their feelings about some issue into two different subgroups.
   C. Members of the group are divided into two smaller groups by the police.
   D. Members of the group call for two opposite demands at the same time.

25. It has been stated that the quality of patrol is equally if not more important than the quantity of patrol. The quality of patrol, it has been found, varies directly for the most part with:
   A. The recruitment efforts of the department
   B. How well the officers are trained
   C. The existing crime rate
   D. The level of supervision

26. Sergeant Hall responds to a shooting of a robbery suspect by a police officer. Part of the sergeant's report on the incident includes the use of a legend in connection with the sketch of the scene. Which of the following is not an advantage of a legend on a sketch?
   A. It makes the sketch easier to understand.
   B. It forces the sketch maker to take accurate measurements.
   C. It reduces the time necessary to prepare the sketch.
   D. It reduces the need for artistic ability.

27. Sergeant Cantwell has been placed in charge of the records unit and has been mandated to revamp the presently inefficient record system by the commanding officer, Captain Ahab. On the first day of the new assignment, the sergeant calls together all six members assigned to the unit for a meeting. Which of the following would be the best way for the sergeant to explain the mandate from Captain Ahab?

A. The captain has sent me here to make some necessary changes.

B. I know you have all been working hard, but the present system is not working and I am going to change it.

C. I think the present system is working satisfactorily but the captain wants it changed.

D. I believe the current system could be better and would like your suggestions in designing a better one.

28. Police Officer Newton is performing his first tour of duty. He is unsure about how to make corrections in his activity/memorandum log. The officer asks his supervisor, Sergeant Brown. The sergeant would be most correct if he recommended which of the following?

A. Erase any entry that is mistakenly made, and rewrite it.

B. Draw a line through the incorrect entry, initial it, and then make the proper entry.

C. Remove the entire page, and then rewrite the entry correctly.

D. Call for a supervisor, and treat each case differently.

29. There are numerous kinds of orders, some more applicable in certain situations than in others. This holds true even in a quasi-military organization, such as a police department. A patrol supervisor should recognize that the best kind of order for a sensitive worker is:

A. A call for volunteers

B. An implied order

C. A request

D. A direct order

30. Sergeant Homer is consistently asked by the captain to increase productivity in all aspects of the work of the officers under the sergeant's supervision. Actually, the captain's emphasis on productivity is excessive. A knowledgeable police sergeant should realize that excessive emphasis on production produces:

A. Long-term benefits

B. Short-term benefits

C. Neither long- nor short-term benefits

D. Both long- and short-term benefits

31. In order to effectively exercise his/her supervisory functions, a police sergeant should be aware of how an individual's behavior is influenced when the individual is part of a group. Accordingly, it would be most accurate to state that as a general rule the behavior of an individual toward authority when he/she is in a group:
    A. Moves toward conformity with the group
    B. Moves away from conformity with the group
    C. Is not influenced by the consensus feelings of the group
    D. Fluctuates toward and away from conformity depending on the makeup of the group

32. If a police officer's lot is not an easy one, that of a police sergeant can from many perspectives be even more difficult. The sergeant continually runs into obstacles when supervising people. Knowledge of these obstacles is important for a police sergeant. Which of the following is not generally recognized as one of the ways to overcome these obstacles?
    A. Increased knowledge through experience
    B. Constant and close supervision of all subordinates
    C. A self-appraisal of attitudes regulating relationships with other members of the agency
    D. Obtaining further explanations of actions

33. One of the many styles of leadership is known as the "authoritarian style." Which of the following statements concerning this style of leadership is most accurate?
    A. Great reliance is placed on the informal lines of authority within the organization when the authoritarian style of leadership is utilized.
    B. There is not much individual growth in an organization under the leadership of an authoritarian leader.
    C. Each worker in an organization led by an authoritarian leader must of necessity show a lot or personal initiative.
    D. The authoritarian style of leadership never works well.

34. Being a true leader is a difficult task. Leadership is viewed differently by different people. Possibly the best view of leadership is obtained by understanding the responsibilities of leadership. Which of the following most accurately describes the responsibility of a police sergeant when acting as a leader?
    A. It consists simply and solely of accomplishing the goals of the agency through the work of subordinates.
    B. It consists simply and solely of developing the abilities of subordinates.
    C. It consists of accomplishing the goals of the agency through the work of subordinates while developing the abilities of the subordinates.
    D. It consists of being able to perform the police officer's job better than any of the subordinates being supervised.

35. Some experts believe that the morale of a police agency is enhanced by implementation of what is known as the "job enrichment" concept. This concept involves permitting wide latitude for accomplishing a given set of tasks. In such an arrangement, all of the following would result except which?
    A. Specialization would be discouraged.
    B. The level of job satisfaction would most likely increase.
    C. Centralized control would be strengthened.
    D. Individual police officers would be required to master fewer skills.

36. In conducting a training course, it is important for instructors to know if they are meeting their training objectives. During which phase or step of the instruction process can instructors determine if they are in fact meeting their training objectives?
    A. In the application step
    B. During the preparation step
    C. In the presentation step by means of the type of questions asked
    D. In the testing step

37. Consider the following statements concerning training.
    (1) Quite often an instructor assumes that trainees know less than they actually do.
    (2) The lecture method is often used excessively.
    (3) Instructional aids, no matter how innovative, do not take the place of good instructors.

    Which of the following most accurately classifies these statements into those that are accurate and those that are not?
    A. Only statement 1 is not accurate.
    B. Only statement 2 is not accurate.
    C. Only statement 3 is not accurate.
    D. All of the statements are accurate.

38. In selecting police instructors, the officer having the most expertise in a subject will always be the best instructor in the subject. This statement is:
    A. True, because the instructor will have more information to give the trainees
    B. False, because the instructor may find it difficult to see the material from the viewpoint of the trainees
    C. True, because the instructor will be able to answer any questions on the subject
    D. False, because the instructor will probably resent being taken away from operational duties that he/she more than likely enjoys

39. Fortunately, police departments have become less insular in their training. In recent years, police departments throughout the country have increased the use of outside training programs conducted at colleges and universities. Which of the following is not an advantage of this practice?
    A. Police officers can get college credits.
    B. Good relations with the academic community can be established.
    C. Police officers can improve themselves professionally as police service careerists.
    D. These college courses can totally eliminate the need for in-service and specialized training, thereby cutting costs in training.

40. The police recruits of today will become the top administrators of tomorrow's police agencies. Therefore, careful consideration should be given to the early stages of their careers. Which of the following has the greatest impact on the newly appointed police recruit?
    A. The conduct of older, more seasoned police officers
    B. The reputation of the department
    C. The content and conduct of the recruit training program
    D. The entrance salary

41. To engage in sound planning one must thoroughly understand the process. Which of the following statements is most accurate concerning the planning process?
    A. Planning is strictly a formal process.
    B. Planning is strictly an informal process.
    C. Planning is both a formal and informal process.
    D. Planning should only take place at the highest managerial levels of the agency.

42. In organizing a police department, there are at times certain diverse functions that can be placed in one division under the supervision of one commander. Which of the following best indicates paired functions that would not generally lend themselves to being combined?
    A. Patrol and traffic
    B. Youth and detective
    C. Vice and detective
    D. Records and communications

43. Work in a police organization is usually divided by using one of several bases. The work of the officers assigned on horseback in a mounted unit is an example of division of work based on:
    A. The geographic area being served
    B. Process, or how the work is to be done
    C. Clientele or population served
    D. Time, or when the work is done

44. Very often, when a police agency is reorganized, a new level of supervisory authority is added to the existing chain of command. When this takes place, all of the following occur except which?

A. The upward flow of information to the chief is impeded.
B. The downward flow of information from the chief is impeded.
C. The span of control is increased.
D. Coordination of the work of the organization is made more difficult.

45. A tall police organization is one with many layers of supervision. All of the following are characteristics of a tall organization except which?
A. Elitist groups are formed because of the high level of specialization.
B. More resourceful supervisors are developed because contact with higher ranks is not always possible.
C. The filtering process is lessened since the need for accurate information to pass over long distances is increased.
D. Training in administrative matters is more available for the department's upwardly mobile officers.

46. Many police departments maintain a speakers bureau that gives talks to various organizations in the community. Which of the following is a problem of such a service?
A. There is a lack of topics to be addressed.
B. Few organizations seek such a service.
C. Such talks usually do not reach the citizen who is not propolice.
D. Such talks are usually conducted by officers who have little or no field experience.

47. When police-community relations programs are operating soundly, observance of law follows. In such soundly operated programs, this observance of law is obtained mainly through:
A. The deterrent effect of police efforts
B. The legislative efforts on the part of the police and the community acting as one
C. The enforcement efforts targeted by the police against groups identified by the community
D. The respect for one another that develops from such programs

48. Sergeant Tully has been asked by the commanding officer to develop better communication with the community. Which of the following should be identified by the sergeant as a principal conduit between the police and the community?
   A. Selected leaders in the community
   B. The department's community relations officers
   C. The radio, television, and newspaper media
   D. Elected officials who represent the community

49. From time to time conflict arises between the press and the police. Regarding this conflict, it would be most correct to state that the conflict:
   A. Could easily be eliminated by proper guidelines for the police and the press
   B. Could be lessened but never completely eliminated
   C. Could be eliminated with appropriate legislation
   D. Can neither be eased nor eliminated

50. Public relations in a police agency is a much needed activity. Concerning public relations, which of the following statements is most accurate?
   A. There is a one-way direction to the communication process.
   B. The community joins hands with the police in this area.
   C. The responsibility is focused in many units throughout the department.
   D. The needs of the public are first identified and then met by adapting the types of service the police offer.

51. Police Officer Jenkins conducts a preliminary investigation of a crime that takes place on his foot post. All of the following are accepted reasons the officer should conduct this investigation except which?
   A. Important witnesses who might have to leave the scene can be identified for later interviews by detectives.
   B. An arrest could be effected, which is part of the preliminary investigation.
   C. The skills of specialists can be better utilized on matters requiring their particular expertise.
   D. No important evidence will be overlooked.

52. Preventive patrol has been used by police departments to reduce crime. According to the theory of preventive patrol, in which of the following situations would the police get the best crime deterrent effect?
    A. They patrol locations of low crime incidence frequently and irregularly in a fashion that does not make them conspicuous.
    B. They patrol all locations in a fashion that makes their presence inconspicuous, thereby facilitating the making of arrests.
    C. They patrol locations of high crime incidence frequently on a regular basis in a fashion that makes them conspicuous.
    D. They patrol all locations frequently on an irregular basis in a fashion that makes them conspicuous.

53. An increase in which of the following is generally not considered to be a result of the split-force patrol method.
    A. Calls for service response productivity
    B. Arrest-related duties by each member of the patrol force
    C. Police professionalism
    D. Police accountability

54. Sergeant Lynch is on patrol with a police officer. It is the police officer's first tour of duty. They notice a car parked alongside the curb with its motor running. What should the sergeant recommend that the police officer do?
    A. Immediately issue a parking summons.
    B. Make a note in the activity/memorandum log of the car and its license number and check it later.
    C. Immediately conduct an investigation.
    D. Call the radio dispatcher and ask if there have been any crimes reported in the area.

55. At times, police officers perform patrol in civilian clothes. The primary reason for this is because patrolling in civilian clothes:
    A. Enables arrests to be made more easily in most instances
    B. Increases the feeling of police omnipresence in the community

C. Facilitates the supervision of the officers involved
D. Can be used as a reward for uniformed officers who are high performers

56. A report written in a narrative style has certain distinguishable traits. Which of the following is one of these traits?
A. It is inflexible.
B. It is easily adapted for entry into a data-processing system.
C. It is adaptable to a variety of situations.
D. It is restricted in content.

57. While interviewing a witness prior to preparing a report, it is recommended that certain questions be asked. Actually there are six basic questions: when, where, who, what, how, and why. Of these six basic questions, which is generally considered to be the most controversial?
A. Who?   C. How?
B. What?   D. Why?

58. The debate in police work over whether the police should patrol in one- or two-person police cars has been long and hard. Generally, however, it is agreed that two-person patrol cars should be used in which of the following situations?
A. In an area where numerous crimes are consistently reported
B. In an area that has numerous calls for service
C. In an area where numerous multiple offender arrests are made
D. In a sector that covers a very large area

59. The movement in patrol efforts in many police departments throughout the country is seen as a substantial return to foot patrol. It is believed that foot patrol has certain benefits that make its practice advantageous. According to recent studies, which of the following most clearly indicates a recognized benefit of foot patrol?
A. Crime levels are reduced.
B. Citizen's fear of crime is reduced.
C. More police are available for service.
D. There is a greater mobility of the police because their omnipresence has been strengthened.

60. Which of the following is not a basic line function of police traffic control?
   A. Traffic direction
   B. Traffic device design
   C. Accident investigation
   D. Enforcement of traffic laws

61. A police sergeant would be most correct if she identified which of the following to be a line unit of a police agency?
   A. Vice control division
   B. Radio communications division
   C. Inspections divisions
   D. Police academy where recruit training is conducted

62. At times, proponents of the order-maintenance style of policing offer that this style of policing yields savings in police time due to fewer arrests and resulting court appearances. However, the order-maintenance role is not without expenditure of time. Of the following incidents handled via an order-maintenance style of policing, which is the most time-consuming for the police?
   A. Intervention in domestic disputes
   B. Dispersing a group of disorderly youths
   C. Settling a dispute over the payment of a taxi fare
   D. Quieting a noisy party where alcohol is being served

63. For the police to effectively engage in community relations, they must achieve and maintain a professional status. All of the following are characteristics of a profession except which?
   A. A service-oriented membership
   B. A pervasive attitude of open inquiry that constantly searches for new and better methods
   C. A stronger loyalty to the employer rather than the profession at large
   D. The compilation and utilization of specialized knowledge

64. A sergeant should guard against doing the work of subordinates. Which of the following is one of the rare occasions when it would be most appropriate for a sergeant to do the job rather than train a police officer to do it?

A. It's an important job that the sergeant can do well.
B. It's one the sergeant enjoys doing.
C. It's a job that will probably not need to be done again in the future.
D. It's one that is easy for the sergeant to do.

65. Sergeant Clark is considered an expert in fingerprint classification. When teaching the field use of the primary fingerprint classification system, the sergeant should:
   A. Progress from the complex to the simple
   B. Progress from the simple to the complex
   C. Ask the class where they wish to begin
   D. Ask other sergeants what has worked in the past

66. In order to hold an audience's interest, trainers have several available training formats. The instructional technique, whereby a discussion takes place among experts without audience participation, is known as a:
   A. Forum   C. Lecture series
   B. Panel discussion   D. Demonstration

67. Sergeant Rogers is a patrol supervisor in a certain district. A group of police officers under the supervision of Sergeant Rogers seem to perform their work well even when Sergeant Rogers is not around. The most likely reason for this is best indicated by which of the following?
   A. The officers are never sure when Sergeant Rogers may appear and therefore stay on their toes.
   B. Sergeant Rogers is probably not needed in the operation.
   C. The officers are well trained.
   D. Some units can run themselves without the intervention of a supervisor.

68. Have the police properly prioritized their training efforts? In response to this question, experts have maintained that development of continuous training for police officers at all ranks has generally:
   A. Surpassed advances in communications and scientific detection technology
   B. Stayed about even with advances in communications and scientific detection technology

C. Lagged behind advances in communications and scientific detection technology

D. Surpassed advances in communications but lagged behind scientific detection technology

69. A supervisor who is to train subordinates should realize that it is his/her job to establish the proper climate for training. To do this effectively, the supervisor must do all of the following except:

A. Be acquainted with the process of learning

B. Be aware of obstacles to efficient learning

C. Be familiar with factors that influence learning

D. Be a total expert in the job he/she is to teach

70. An informed and interested public has caused police agencies to readjust their approach to community demands. As community demands for more and improved police service have increased, the typical police agency has responded by:

A. Hiring more police and increasing the quality and quantity of training

B. Allowing the level of police service to remain static

C. Increasing only the quantity and quality of training

D. Only hiring more police officers

71. Sergeant Ward likes to be popular; therefore, he rates all of his employees higher than they actually deserve. Which of the following statements is the most accurate concerning a supervisor such as Sergeant Ward?

A. He will never rate any employee unfairly.

B. He will never give a low evaluation to an employee.

C. He will give a low evaluation to an employee if the employee does something that personally offends the sergeant.

D. His evaluations will never affect the actions of other supervisors.

72. The kind of rating error committed by a supervisor who is newly assigned to a unit and does not know subordinates well is the:

A. Association error

B. Error of leniency

C. Central tendency error

D. Error of contrast

73. When a rater is subjective and rates employees on her own view of certain traits, she is committing the rating error known as:
   A. Association
   B. Halo effect
   C. Contrast
   D. Central tendency

74. For a police organization, an employee rating system is useful as a guide in developing individual employees. It is also useful in which of the following?
   A. Public relations with the community
   B. Organizational control
   C. Fiscal planning
   D. Communications within the organization

75. The most effective way for a police supervisor to communicate with an employee who is considered by many to be a shy and somewhat retiring individual is to communicate:
   A. In a forceful manner to bring the employee out of his/her shell
   B. With a soft and tactful approach that recognizes the employee's personality
   C. Without regard to the employee's personality
   D. With that employee mainly through intermediaries

76. Consider the following statements concerning morale.
   (1) An indication of high morale is a low rate of "on the job" accidents.
   (2) A look at the absenteeism rate can give some idea of the morale of the agency.
   (3) A supervisor should only get involved in the private problems of a worker if the worker asks for help.
   Based on these statements, which of the following is most accurate?
   A. All of the statements are accurate.
   B. All of the statements are not accurate.
   C. Only two of the statements are accurate.
   D. Only two of the statements are not accurate.

77. Consider the following statements concerning grievances.
   (1) The processing of grievances should be handled formally so that all grievances are properly recorded.

     (2)   Officers who have their grievances handled by their first-line supervisors tend to become too close to those supervisors.

     (3)   Although formal grievance procedures should exist within an agency, they can foster an adversary climate.

Based on these statements, which of the following is most accurate?

A. All of the statements are accurate.
B. All of the statements are not accurate.
C. Only two of the statements are accurate.
D. Only one of the statements is accurate.

78. Police Officer Hart excitedly comes to Sergeant Green with a complaint about being selected for a certain assignment. In Sergeant Green's opinion the complaint is quite minor and not important. To Officer Green, the complaint appears to be quite important. In this case, Sergeant Green should:

A. Try to show a sense of humor about the situation by making a joke about it
B. Admonish Hart that he might be guilty of insubordination
C. Tell Hart that it is a supervisor's prerogative to make assignments
D. Let Hart continue until he is less excited, and then explain the reasons for the assignment

79. Police Officer Jones asks her sergeant when she (the police officer) can expect an answer to a grievance that the officer has made. The sergeant should:

A. Make no comment
B. Tell the officer when she can expect an answer
C. Explain to the officer that once the grievance is made it is totally in the hands of the reviewer
D. Try to find out why the officer is concerned about the time involved

80. A certain sergeant has police officers under his supervision always repeat the details of any grievances they may have. After hearing the grievance twice, the sergeant then repeats the essentials of the grievance back to the officer making the grievance. This practice is:

A. Bad, since it prolongs an uncomfortable situation for the police officer
B. Good, since the sergeant can make sure he has his facts straight
C. Bad, since it might suggest to the officer that the sergeant is not anxious to officially record the grievance
D. Good, since it gives the officer a chance to hear the complaint and evaluate its merits

81. Police work is not a single-handed operation. Which of the following is most important to the activity of coordinating the efforts of organizational units?
A. Upward communication
B. Downward communication
C. Informal communication
D. Lateral communication

82. Most experts in the field of communication believe the principal obstacle to good communications is:
A. Status differences
B. Failure to listen
C. Language barriers
D. Filtering

83. The road to becoming a skilled supervisor is long. According to experts, which of the following is the single most important skill of a supervisor?
A. Budgeting   C. Organizing
B. Communication   D. Training

84. Which of the following is considered perhaps the most important tool of a supervisor in determining if he is communicating well?
A. Obtaining feedback
B. Use of simple language
C. Setting objectives before communicating
D. Simply asking subordinates

85. When a police officer is promoted to the rank of police sergeant, he/she assumes new responsibilities. Which of the following is the most accurate statement concerning these new responsibilities?
A. The only new responsibility involved is planning.
B. The only new responsibility involved is organizing.

C. The only new responsibility involved is directing.
D. The new responsibilities include planning, organizing, and directing.

86. Captain Kornheiser tells Sergeant Goldberg to examine a certain job done by several different officers. The captain wants the sergeant to differentiate between the different performances of the different officers doing the same job. The captain is actually directing that the sergeant do a job:
A. Analysis
B. Classification
C. Description
D. Synthesis

87. Sergeant Ponds is about to give some instruction in physical defense tactics to a group of police officers in her precinct. She would be most correct if she utilized which of the following teaching sequences?
A. Moving from the difficult to the easy tactics
B. Progressing toward those tactics that are used most frequently
C. Moving toward those tactics that are used least frequently
D. Progressing from the easy to the difficult tactics

88. Police no longer deny that corruption is a hazard in police work and that proper training can reduce the danger of corruption hazards. A training program designed to deal with anticorruption measures would include all of the following except:
A. A categorizing of corrupt actions
B. Actual examples of potential corruption
C. Emphasis of the moral issues involved
D. Examination of prior corruption cases involving police officers

89. A traffic unit, if for no other reason because of its numerous contacts with the public, should be well trained. Which of the following would be least considered as a suitable part of a training course for a specialized traffic unit?
A. Pertinent court decisions concerning traffic enforcement
B. Testifying in court
C. Officer-violator relations
D. Emphasis of the full enforcement of the traffic laws

90. Unfortunately, not all police agencies have effective training in the juvenile justice system and the handling of juveniles. Which of the following police positions seems to be ignored when it comes to receiving training in the handling of juveniles?
   A. Patrol officers
   B. Detectives
   C. Command personnel
   D. Officers assigned to community relations units

91. Reprimanding an employee is one of the more difficult roles for a police sergeant. Knowing what kinds of actions to avoid when reprimanding, however, can make the process easier. When reprimanding a subordinate, a police sergeant should not:
   A. Ensure that the reprimand is warranted
   B. Give the reprimand in private
   C. Treat all subordinates equally
   D. Allow the subordinate an opportunity to respond positively

92. One of the realities of discipline is that at times punishment in the form of fines or other punitive measures must be given to employees of the organization who have been found to have acted improperly. Which of the following statements concerning punishment is inaccurate?
   A. Punishment should be certain once guilt is established.
   B. To be effective, punishment should be swiftly administered.
   C. Once good leadership and supervision are introduced in an agency, the need for punishment in that agency will disappear.
   D. A standard table of penalties should not be developed for major infractions of departmental rules and regulations.

93. The transfer of an employee can be quite upsetting to the employee. However, at times a transfer can and should be used. The transfer of an employee would be proper for all of the following reasons except which?
   A. Deal with changes in workload
   B. Reduce monotony
   C. Routinely deal with a problem employee
   D. Increase the opportunity for desirable assignments

94. Consider the following statements concerning discipline by a police sergeant in a police setting.
    (1) A police officer should be allowed to give his/her side of the story in a disciplinary situation where the sergeant has been very careful to gather all the facts.
    (2) A written reprimand can be given in greater privacy than an oral reprimand.
    (3) A supervisor should be equally as forceful in dealing with minor violations as with major violations.

    Based on these statements, which of the following is the most accurate?
    A. All of the statements are true.
    B. All of the statements are false.
    C. Only two of the statements are true.
    D. Only one of the statements is true.

95. It is the policy of a certain police department not to delegate authority to its members. Which of the following is the most likely result?
    A. The decision-making process will be centralized.
    B. The decision-making process will be decentralized.
    C. No decision making could take place in such an environment.
    D. The various units of the agency will act as fertile breeding grounds for future supervisors.

96. A sergeant delegates a job to a subordinate. During the performance of the job, the subordinate presents a problem to the sergeant. In such an instance, the sergeant can best counsel the subordinate by:
    A. Immediately providing one solution
    B. Assisting the subordinate to find his/her own solution
    C. Impressing upon the subordinate the necessity to do his/her own work
    D. Avoiding such situations so that the subordinate can learn to be independent

97. When a police officer is promoted to the rank of sergeant, he will begin engaging in what some experts refer to as a "two-way relationship." This relationship basically means that the sergeant:

A. Will act as a supervisor over the police officers while developing a relationship with his new peer group
B. Must now be responsible for his own law enforcement activities as well as those of the police officers he supervises
C. Will be responsible for the work effort of the officers he supervises while representing them to the upper echelon of the department
D. Must now act as the "carrot and the stick"

98. Some police supervisors maintain that the "trial-and-error" method of training is a proper method of training. These supervisors are wrong because the trial-and-error method is inappropriate because of all of the following reasons except that it is:
A. Slow
B. Wasteful
C. Never able to yield any results
D. Found to be more expensive than formal training

99. There are, of course, numerous methods of conducting training. Some methods seem to be utilized more than others. One such method of training that seems to get a great deal of use is the pure lecture method. The pure lecture method is greatly used due to which of the following reasons?
A. It ensures everyone will get something from the session.
B. Many instructors find it the easiest method to present material.
C. It is best for lengthy sessions.
D. It reduces wasteful comments from the trainees.

100. Certain constitutional guarantees support the rights of defendants and those of the press. What constitutional amendments are usually referred to in supporting these rights?
A. Sixth and First Amendments
B. Sixth and Fourteenth Amendments
C. Sixth and Fifth Amendments
D. Eighth and First Amendments

Answer Key

1. A	21. D	41. C	61. A	81. D
2. C	22. C	42. B	62. A	82. B
3. C	23. B	43. B	63. C	83. B
4. B	24. A	44. C	64. C	84. A
5. B	25. D	45. C	65. B	85. D
6. C	26. B	46. C	66. B	86. A
7. C	27. D	47. D	67. C	87. D
8. A	28. B	48. C	68. C	88. C
9. A	29. C	49. B	69. D	89. D
10. B	30. B	50. A	70. D	90. C
11. D	31. A	51. D	71. C	91. C
12. C	32. B	52. D	72. C	92. C
13. A	33. B	53. B	73. C	93. C
14. D	34. C	54. C	74. B	94. D
15. C	35. C	55. A	75. B	95. A
16. A	36. D	56. C	76. C	96. B
17. B	37. A	57. A	77. D	97. C
18. B	38. B	58. C	78. D	98. C
19. C	39. D	59. B	79. B	99. B
20. D	40. C	60. B	80. B	100. A

Diagnostic Chart

Insert the number of correct answers you obtained in the blank space for each section of the examination. The scale in the next column indicates how you did. The information at the bottom indicates how to correct your weaknesses.

SECTION	QUESTION NUMBERS	AREAS	YOUR NUMBER CORRECT	SCALE
1	1–5 29–35 76–80 91–97	Principles of supervision		23–24 right: excellent 21–22 right: good 19–20 right: fair Under 20 right: poor
2	6–10, 36–40, 64–70 86–90 98–100	Safety and training		24–25 right: excellent 22–23 right: good 20–21 right: fair Under 20 right: poor
3	11–15 41–45 71–75 81–85	Management		19–20 right: excellent 17–18 right: good 15–16 right: fair Under 16 right: poor
4	16–20 46–50 62–63	Community relations		12 right: excellent 11 right: good 10 right: fair Under 10 right: poor
5	21–25 51–55 58–61	Patrol operations		14 right: excellent 13 right: good 12 right: fair Under 12 right: poor
6	26–28 56–57	Report writing		5 right: excellent Under 5 right: poor

If you are weak in Section 1, then concentrate on Chapter 5.
If you are weak in Section 2, then concentrate on Chapter 6.
If you are weak in Section 3, then concentrate on Chapter 7.
If you are weak in Section 4, then concentrate on Chapter 8.
If you are weak in Section 5, then concentrate on Chapter 9.
If you are weak in Section 6, then concentrate on Chapter 10.

Note: Consider yourself weak in a section if you receive other than an excellent rating in it.

Answer Explanations

1. **A**   Discipline is both positive and negative, and the primary purpose of discipline is to train employees.

2. **C**   When an officer comes to a sergeant with a problem, it is incumbent upon the sergeant to try to find out the cause of the problem in an effort to resolve it. Remember, transferring problems seldom solves the problems.

3. **C**   The problems differ in degree but not kind. The problems of supervisors are fairly constant because they all involve dealing with people. However, remember that because of civil service constraints, a police sergeant has fewer motivating factors available, such as salary increases.

4. **B**   Every time a change is introduced, a type of order would of necessity accompany it to explain how to incorporate the change into the total effort. This would increase the number of orders given.

5. **B**   Most workers would respond in the affirmative if simply asked if they understand an order. The worker must be asked to repeat the order in his/her own words.

6. **C**   Learning is accomplished by sight as well as hearing, and being able to have an overall view of a past situation helps in improving future performance of tactical operations, such as a hostage situation.

7. **C**   Usually the choice of whether training should be formal or informal has to be made by the sergeant, who should be the one discovering the need for training.

8. **A**   The patrol sergeant has frequent daily contacts with subordinates, and it is a vital aspect of the sergeant's job to train on an ongoing basis.

9. **A**   Unfortunately, when fiscal cuts are made, the training function is one of the first areas that suffers cutbacks.

10. **B**   The best training climate exists when the employee sees that some personal gain will result from the training.

11. **D**   Expenditures other than those for personnel are about ten percent of the typical department's budget. Costs for personnel are about ninety percent.

12. **C** Inspections will not eliminate planning. They will instead identify needs, which actually is the first step in planning. Inspections will also determine if procedures are being followed, if results are being obtained, and if resources are being properly used.

13. **A** The interchange of personnel from one assignment to another for temporary periods of time facilitates the coordination process.

14. **D** The plan must be effectively communicated or no one will be able to understand its intention. Not to do so dooms a plan to failure. Choices A, B, and C all are indicative of poor planning. However, the planning deficiencies outlined in these choices will not "always" render a plan useless.

15. **C** Policies are rarely written down, but their effects are seen in other specific directives that help accomplish the goals of the organization.

16. **A** Typically, the juvenile division will not take over an investigation until the suspect has at least been positively identified as a juvenile.

17. **B** Crime prevention is a likely addition to community relations activities since it depends to a large extent on mutual cooperation and communication between the police and the community. Public relations, foot patrol, and anticrime patrols have been part of community relations activities for many years.

18. **B** Disclosure of the results of a test to the media might prevent a fair trial of a suspect.

19. **C** In team policing the closeness of the officers to the community brings about the community's involvement in mutual problem solving.

20. **D** This is the swiftest and surest method of controlling police operations.

21. **D** The dog might mistake a plainclothes officer for the burglar. The sergeant should have first ordered the plainclothes officers out of the building.

22. **C** This type of crime is done in spite of the authority of police and the potential for punishment. Besides, it is typically done on private property and usually involves people known to each other.

23. **B** Choice B is more correct because criminal activity must not be the only criterion; there are also inspectional duties, as well as calls

for service. In addition, time of occurrence must be considered along with the place of occurrence.

24. **A** The focus of the crowd may also be on some object when polarization of a crowd takes place. It is when a crowd becomes polarized that the potential for trouble increases. Apathetic crowds pose little danger.

25. **D** The patrol sergeant is the key to the success of the patrol function.

26. **B** The legend cannot force the sketch maker to take accurate measurements. The legend only reflects what has already been done.

27. **D** In order for the sergeant to have the best chance for success in carrying out the mandate, it must appear that the idea to change is the sergeant's and that the sergeant is relying on the workers to play a key part in the change process.

28. **B** Pages should not be removed nor should erasures be made in a police officer's log. Also, there should be no blank spaces.

29. **C** A request has the effect of not offending a sensitive worker. Remember, however, that request orders have limitations. They are certainly inappropriate in emergencies.

30. **B** There are some short-term benefits associated with excessive emphasis on productivity, but it is detrimental in the long run to the agency.

31. **A** A group generally influences an individual's expectations, attitudes, and perceptions of authority. Most individuals modify their behavior to conform to the predominant attitudes of the group.

32. **B** All subordinates do not need constant and close supervision. In fact, such a supervisory tactic would cause resentment among subordinates.

33. **B** When the leader "calls all of the shots," there is little room for personal growth or for personal initiative. Concerning choice D, the authoritarian style of leadership can work in an organization but it takes a leader of extraordinary ability to make it work.

34. **C** A true leader must get the job done and develop subordinates at the same time.

35. **C** When wide latitude is given to get a job done, then of necessity centralized control would be weakened, not strengthened. The con-

cept of "job enrichment" encourages the development of many skills and discourages specialization.

36. **D** Also determined in the testing step is a measure of the instructor's overall effectiveness as a teacher.

37. **A** Quite the opposite: instructors tend to believe trainees know more than they do. The problem is intensified by the fact that students are very reluctant to admit lack of assumed knowledge.

38. **B** This is often a problem when an instructor knows a field extremely well. Also, note the use of the work *always* in the stem of the question. As a general rule, things are seldom "always" true.

39. **D** The training needs of a police department cannot be totally met by a college program of study. In-service and specialized training will continue to be necessary despite the use of outside training programs.

40. **C** The initial training will determine the direction of the recruit in years to come more than other factors, such as the entrance salary, the reputation of the department, and even the conduct of older, more experienced officers.

41. **C** A plan does not always need to be written; it may be simple and only outlined mentally by a supervisor at any level. It therefore does not take place only at the highest managerial levels.

42. **B** The goal of the detective division is to arrest perpetrators; the goal of the juvenile division is to prevent delinquency by all means possible, but preferably by means other than arrest. In juvenile work, referrals often take the place of arrests.

43. **B** The mounted unit does its work on horseback, so its work is divided by process—how it is being accomplished.

44. **C** When additional supervisory levels are added to an organization, the span of control is reduced. Coordination and information flow, however, are impeded by additional levels of supervision.

45. **C** Just the opposite: a lot of filtering takes place because of the many layers of the organization in a tall police agency. The more layers of supervision a communication has to pass through, the greater is the probability that the communication will become distorted by filtering.

46. **C** Such talks are usually attended by citizens with whom the police have little or no difficulty.

47. **D** Respect, which brings with it support and confidence, is rapidly followed by better law observance. It should always be an aim of any community relations effort to develop and nurture mutual respect.

48. **C** Radio, television, and newspapers are obvious principal channels of communication between the police and the public because of their ability to reach the largest number of community members.

49. **B** It will always exist, and the police supervisor must learn how to deal with it.

50. **A** There is nothing wrong with public relations being a one-way communication effort. It only becomes a problem when public relations is not supplemented by a comprehensive community relations effort.

51. **D** Choices A, B, and C are valid reaons. However, it is impossible to guarantee that *no* important evidence will be overlooked simply because the patrol officer conducts an immediate investigation. Remember, protection of the crime scene is a very important job of the first officer on the scene.

52. **D** The elements of preventive patrol include conspicuous patrol in a frequent but irregular manner.

53. **B** Split force patrol occurs when a large portion of the patrol force is geared not toward arrest, but rather toward the prevention of crimes.

54. **C** This is an attention getter to an officer on patrol and warrants immediate attention and investigation.

55. **A** This is the essence of anticrime patrol. A patrol officer in civilian clothes in a high crime area at the peak crime times often gets the opportunity to interrupt a crime in progress. Or, the officers act as decoys and offer themselves as an easy target for criminal attack.

56. **C** Unlike a structured report or a form, the uses of a narrative report are endless. They are very flexible devices that adapt to a variety of situations.

57. **A** The "who" question is the most controversial because the average person is unskilled at describing others and because of the relative lack of reliability of eyewitness identification. Also, many people often have ulterior motives for not being truthful concerning the "who" question. Consider the deceitful witness who is attempting to prevent the police from learning the truth.

58. **C** For ease of making arrests, two officers would be required to handle multiple offenders.

59. **B** Although crime levels may not be reduced, the citizen feels safer even though there is actually no greater number of police on patrol. Regarding mobility, this gain is not obtained through foot patrol.

60. **B** Choices A, C, and D comprise the three line functions of traffic control. Traffic device design is not a basic line function of police traffic control. Remember to associate line functions with a direct exertion of authority.

61. **A** Vice control is a line function. The other choices are staff units that support line operations. In other words, staff units support the activities of the patrol divisions and other line units, such as the detective, youth, traffic, and vice units.

62. **A** Domestic disputes take up the most time because officers try to arrive at a meaningful resolution of the cause of the dispute.

63. **C** The loyalties of a true professional lie with the profession and the clientele, not the current employer. The other traits of service orientation, constantly searching for new and better methods and compiling and using specialized knowledge, are all part of a true professional.

64. **C** Even though a job is important, easy, and enjoyable or can be done well by a sergeant, he/she is not relieved of the task of training a subordinate to do the job. The exception, when a sergeant would do a job rather than train a subordinate to do it, would be when it's unlikely that the job will have to be done again in the future. In such a case, the training of a subordinate to do that job would be a waste of time and effort.

65. **B** In such a quasi-technical field, it is best to start from the simple concepts and move forward to the more complex. The instructor who is an expert in the field should not assume that everyone has interest or expertise in the subject matter.

66. **B** There is no audience participation in a panel discussion. Usually the panel is staffed with experts. The problem is that the information is limited to that which develops among the panel members. To compensate for this, those persons responsible for selecting panel members sometimes select panel members with a variety of views on the subject.

67. **C** The supervisor's role is involved with lending assistance when problems arise. If the officers are well trained, there will be fewer problems and less direct call for supervision. The notion that some units run themselves is entirely fictional. A well-trained group will reduce but not eliminate the need for supervision.

68. **C** Training at all ranks has lagged behind advances in communications as well as scientific detection technology.

69. **D** To be a good trainer, a good knowledge of the subject is needed. It is not necessary to be a total expert in the subject. The proper climate for training is created by the trainer being acquainted with the learning process, being aware of obstacles to learning, and being familiar with certain factors that influence learning, as reflected in choices A, B, and C.

70. **D** Hiring more police officers without more effective training has the potential to make things even worse.

71. **C** This type of rater will usually only give a low evaluation to an employee when the employee has done something to personally offend the rater.

72. **C** Making everyone average usually comes from not knowing the employees well. If newly assigned, the supervisor should confer with the previous supervisor to get an idea of the employee's performance. This is a legitimate effort toward objectively rating an employee. A notation of the conferral should be made on the evaluation form.

73. **C** A rater who does not objectively consider each trait being evaluated falls into this trap. The rater is examining the traits, not according to their established meanings, but instead according to how she views herself in this trait. She is considering the traits in contrast to herself. Hence, the contrast error occurs.

74. **B** An employee rating system helps the organization to see if the employees are doing their part in obtaining the goals of the agency.

75. **B** An employee's personality must be considered when communicating since it is a very personal process. A sergeant must consider not only what he/she is communicating, but also with whom he/she is communicating. Communication is a very personalized social process.

76. **C** Statement 3 is not accurate. There is one other time when a supervisor should get involved with the private problems of a worker and that occurs when the worker's private problems interfere with the quality of the work. The word *only* makes statement 3 inaccurate.

77. **D** Grievances should, if possible, be handled informally by their first-line supervisors. Statement 3 is the only correct statement. Concerning statement 1, grievances should if possible be handled informally. Concerning statement 2, officers develop a sense of trust and confidence in a supervisor who handles their grievances in a fair and impartial manner.

78. **D** A grievance, real or imagined, is always real to the person making the grievance and should be handled accordingly by the supervisor.

79. **B** If the sergeant knows he should tell the officer when the officer can expect the answer to her grievance. Also, the sergeant should see handling grievances as an integral part of the job.

80. **B** This method of taking a grievance is important since no redress can be given if the grievance is not clear and the facts are not accurately recorded.

81. **D** The heads and members of the various units of the agency must be able to talk to each other in obtaining the goals of the agency; otherwise, the chief would talk to each unit, each unit would talk to the chief, but no one would talk to each other throughout the rest of the department.

82. **B** For good communication to take place, each participant must be willing and able to listen. The other choices also describe barriers to communication, but the examiner asks for principal barrier.

83. **B** All supervisory practices depend in some way on communication. In all of the other supervisory practices, some type of message is given and received.

84. **A** Feedback must be obtained, but it cannot be expected to be obtained solely by asking one's subordinates. Other means are available, such as inspections and other control mechanisms.

85. **D** The new responsibilities of a police sergeant are often listed as planning, organizing, staffing, directing, coordinating, reporting, and budgeting.

86. **A** A good job analysis tries to identify what traits are required to do a job. Also, a job analysis is a prime requisite to conducting proper training for the job. It identifies the abilities, skills, and knowledge required to perform a specific job. It is also essential that any test on which a personnel decision is to be made be constructed from a current and accurate job analysis.

87. **D** Clearly, in self-defense, it is best to move from the easy to the difficult tactics. This not only makes understanding easier but allows confidence to be steadily built up within the student.

88. **C** The training emphasis in an anticorruption training program should be on being realistic, not on moralistic issues. It is true that there are moral issues involved, but training can more effectively deal with the realistic issues of corruption.

89. **D** Such a training program for a specialized traffic unit should emphasize discretion, not necessarily full enforcement of the traffic laws. The public neither wants nor could withstand full enforcement efforts in the area of traffic.

90. **C** It is erroneously believed that no need exists to train command personnel in the handling of juveniles. However, it is the role of command personnel to evaluate the department's overall juvenile policies. Therefore, there is a need for such training.

91. **C** When giving a reprimand, each case should be treated on its own merits. What this really means is that the total picture of the employee must be considered. That includes work performance and past disciplinary problems.

92. **C** There will always be some need for punishment in a police agency regardless of the quality of leadership and supervision. Punishment should be swift and certain following a violation. A standard table of punishments, however, should not be developed since each case is different and should be treated on a case-to-case basis.

93. **C** The answer to a problem employee is *not* to routinely use the transfer process. Some acceptable reasons for transfers are to deal with changes in workload, increase opportunities for desirable assignments, and reduce monotony.

94. **D** Only statement 1 is true. Statement 2 is false since both oral and written reprimands can be equally private. Serious violations call for a more forceful dealing to impress the violator with the seriousness of the violation; this makes statement 3 false.

95. **A** Employees throughout the department will be reluctant to make decisions without the authority to do so. Thus, authority will be centralized and so will the decision-making process. Development is not likely to occur in a department that centralizes its decision-making process.

96. **B** When a worker finds his/her own solutions to problems, the solutions will be more meaningful, and by allowing the subordinate to

work out their own problems the sergeant is providing the employee with an opportunity for self-development.

97. **C** The two-way relationship that is the ambivalent role of the first-line supervisor is described in choice C.

98. **C** Trial and error does yield limited results but is slow, wasteful, and actually more expensive than formal training. This is so because each learner must individually seek out solutions to questions instead of providing experts the solutions. Also, remember to shy away from a choice that includes the use of the word *never*.

99. **B** Unfortunately instructors overuse the lecture method. The reason for this overuse, quite simply, is that many instructors find it an extremely easy method of instruction.

100. **A** The Sixth Amendment deals with getting a fair trial; the First deals with freedom of the press. It is the clash between the rights contained in these two amendments that causes the friction between the police and the press.

Answer Sheet
Practice Examination Two

Follow the instructions given in the text. Mark only your answers in the ovals below.

Warning: Be sure that the oval you fill is in the same row as the question you are answering. Use a No. 2 pencil (soft pencil).

Be sure your pencil marks are heavy and black. Erase completely any answer you wish to change.

Do *not* make stray pencil dots, dashes, or marks.

1 Ⓐ Ⓑ Ⓒ Ⓓ	2 Ⓐ Ⓑ Ⓒ Ⓓ	3 Ⓐ Ⓑ Ⓒ Ⓓ	4 Ⓐ Ⓑ Ⓒ Ⓓ	5 Ⓐ Ⓑ Ⓒ Ⓓ	6 Ⓐ Ⓑ Ⓒ Ⓓ
7 Ⓐ Ⓑ Ⓒ Ⓓ	8 Ⓐ Ⓑ Ⓒ Ⓓ	9 Ⓐ Ⓑ Ⓒ Ⓓ	10 Ⓐ Ⓑ Ⓒ Ⓓ	11 Ⓐ Ⓑ Ⓒ Ⓓ	12 Ⓐ Ⓑ Ⓒ Ⓓ
13 Ⓐ Ⓑ Ⓒ Ⓓ	14 Ⓐ Ⓑ Ⓒ Ⓓ	15 Ⓐ Ⓑ Ⓒ Ⓓ	16 Ⓐ Ⓑ Ⓒ Ⓓ	17 Ⓐ Ⓑ Ⓒ Ⓓ	18 Ⓐ Ⓑ Ⓒ Ⓓ
19 Ⓐ Ⓑ Ⓒ Ⓓ	20 Ⓐ Ⓑ Ⓒ Ⓓ	21 Ⓐ Ⓑ Ⓒ Ⓓ	22 Ⓐ Ⓑ Ⓒ Ⓓ	23 Ⓐ Ⓑ Ⓒ Ⓓ	24 Ⓐ Ⓑ Ⓒ Ⓓ
25 Ⓐ Ⓑ Ⓒ Ⓓ	26 Ⓐ Ⓑ Ⓒ Ⓓ	27 Ⓐ Ⓑ Ⓒ Ⓓ	28 Ⓐ Ⓑ Ⓒ Ⓓ	29 Ⓐ Ⓑ Ⓒ Ⓓ	30 Ⓐ Ⓑ Ⓒ Ⓓ
31 Ⓐ Ⓑ Ⓒ Ⓓ	32 Ⓐ Ⓑ Ⓒ Ⓓ	33 Ⓐ Ⓑ Ⓒ Ⓓ	34 Ⓐ Ⓑ Ⓒ Ⓓ	35 Ⓐ Ⓑ Ⓒ Ⓓ	36 Ⓐ Ⓑ Ⓒ Ⓓ
37 Ⓐ Ⓑ Ⓒ Ⓓ	38 Ⓐ Ⓑ Ⓒ Ⓓ	39 Ⓐ Ⓑ Ⓒ Ⓓ	40 Ⓐ Ⓑ Ⓒ Ⓓ	41 Ⓐ Ⓑ Ⓒ Ⓓ	42 Ⓐ Ⓑ Ⓒ Ⓓ
43 Ⓐ Ⓑ Ⓒ Ⓓ	44 Ⓐ Ⓑ Ⓒ Ⓓ	45 Ⓐ Ⓑ Ⓒ Ⓓ	46 Ⓐ Ⓑ Ⓒ Ⓓ	47 Ⓐ Ⓑ Ⓒ Ⓓ	48 Ⓐ Ⓑ Ⓒ Ⓓ
49 Ⓐ Ⓑ Ⓒ Ⓓ	50 Ⓐ Ⓑ Ⓒ Ⓓ	51 Ⓐ Ⓑ Ⓒ Ⓓ	52 Ⓐ Ⓑ Ⓒ Ⓓ	53 Ⓐ Ⓑ Ⓒ Ⓓ	54 Ⓐ Ⓑ Ⓒ Ⓓ
55 Ⓐ Ⓑ Ⓒ Ⓓ	56 Ⓐ Ⓑ Ⓒ Ⓓ	57 Ⓐ Ⓑ Ⓒ Ⓓ	58 Ⓐ Ⓑ Ⓒ Ⓓ	59 Ⓐ Ⓑ Ⓒ Ⓓ	60 Ⓐ Ⓑ Ⓒ Ⓓ
61 Ⓐ Ⓑ Ⓒ Ⓓ	62 Ⓐ Ⓑ Ⓒ Ⓓ	63 Ⓐ Ⓑ Ⓒ Ⓓ	64 Ⓐ Ⓑ Ⓒ Ⓓ	65 Ⓐ Ⓑ Ⓒ Ⓓ	66 Ⓐ Ⓑ Ⓒ Ⓓ
67 Ⓐ Ⓑ Ⓒ Ⓓ	68 Ⓐ Ⓑ Ⓒ Ⓓ	69 Ⓐ Ⓑ Ⓒ Ⓓ	70 Ⓐ Ⓑ Ⓒ Ⓓ	71 Ⓐ Ⓑ Ⓒ Ⓓ	72 Ⓐ Ⓑ Ⓒ Ⓓ
73 Ⓐ Ⓑ Ⓒ Ⓓ	74 Ⓐ Ⓑ Ⓒ Ⓓ	75 Ⓐ Ⓑ Ⓒ Ⓓ	76 Ⓐ Ⓑ Ⓒ Ⓓ	77 Ⓐ Ⓑ Ⓒ Ⓓ	78 Ⓐ Ⓑ Ⓒ Ⓓ
79 Ⓐ Ⓑ Ⓒ Ⓓ	80 Ⓐ Ⓑ Ⓒ Ⓓ	81 Ⓐ Ⓑ Ⓒ Ⓓ	82 Ⓐ Ⓑ Ⓒ Ⓓ	83 Ⓐ Ⓑ Ⓒ Ⓓ	84 Ⓐ Ⓑ Ⓒ Ⓓ
85 Ⓐ Ⓑ Ⓒ Ⓓ	86 Ⓐ Ⓑ Ⓒ Ⓓ	87 Ⓐ Ⓑ Ⓒ Ⓓ	88 Ⓐ Ⓑ Ⓒ Ⓓ	89 Ⓐ Ⓑ Ⓒ Ⓓ	90 Ⓐ Ⓑ Ⓒ Ⓓ
91 Ⓐ Ⓑ Ⓒ Ⓓ	92 Ⓐ Ⓑ Ⓒ Ⓓ	93 Ⓐ Ⓑ Ⓒ Ⓓ	94 Ⓐ Ⓑ Ⓒ Ⓓ	95 Ⓐ Ⓑ Ⓒ Ⓓ	96. Ⓐ Ⓑ Ⓒ Ⓓ
97 Ⓐ Ⓑ Ⓒ Ⓓ	98 Ⓐ Ⓑ Ⓒ Ⓓ	99 Ⓐ Ⓑ Ⓒ Ⓓ	100 Ⓐ Ⓑ Ⓒ Ⓓ	101 Ⓐ Ⓑ Ⓒ Ⓓ	102 Ⓐ Ⓑ Ⓒ Ⓓ
103 Ⓐ Ⓑ Ⓒ Ⓓ	104 Ⓐ Ⓑ Ⓒ Ⓓ	105 Ⓐ Ⓑ Ⓒ Ⓓ	106 Ⓐ Ⓑ Ⓒ Ⓓ	107 Ⓐ Ⓑ Ⓒ Ⓓ	108 Ⓐ Ⓑ Ⓒ Ⓓ
109 Ⓐ Ⓑ Ⓒ Ⓓ	110 Ⓐ Ⓑ Ⓒ Ⓓ	111 Ⓐ Ⓑ Ⓒ Ⓓ	112 Ⓐ Ⓑ Ⓒ Ⓓ	113 Ⓐ Ⓑ Ⓒ Ⓓ	114 Ⓐ Ⓑ Ⓒ Ⓓ
115 Ⓐ Ⓑ Ⓒ Ⓓ	116 Ⓐ Ⓑ Ⓒ Ⓓ	117 Ⓐ Ⓑ Ⓒ Ⓓ	118 Ⓐ Ⓑ Ⓒ Ⓓ	119 Ⓐ Ⓑ Ⓒ Ⓓ	120 Ⓐ Ⓑ Ⓒ Ⓓ
121 Ⓐ Ⓑ Ⓒ Ⓓ	122 Ⓐ Ⓑ Ⓒ Ⓓ	123 Ⓐ Ⓑ Ⓒ Ⓓ	124 Ⓐ Ⓑ Ⓒ Ⓓ	125 Ⓐ Ⓑ Ⓒ Ⓓ	126 Ⓐ Ⓑ Ⓒ Ⓓ
127 Ⓐ Ⓑ Ⓒ Ⓓ	128 Ⓐ Ⓑ Ⓒ Ⓓ	129 Ⓐ Ⓑ Ⓒ Ⓓ	130 Ⓐ Ⓑ Ⓒ Ⓓ	131 Ⓐ Ⓑ Ⓒ Ⓓ	132 Ⓐ Ⓑ Ⓒ Ⓓ
133 Ⓐ Ⓑ Ⓒ Ⓓ	134 Ⓐ Ⓑ Ⓒ Ⓓ	135 Ⓐ Ⓑ Ⓒ Ⓓ	136 Ⓐ Ⓑ Ⓒ Ⓓ	137 Ⓐ Ⓑ Ⓒ Ⓓ	138 Ⓐ Ⓑ Ⓒ Ⓓ
139 Ⓐ Ⓑ Ⓒ Ⓓ	140 Ⓐ Ⓑ Ⓒ Ⓓ	141 Ⓐ Ⓑ Ⓒ Ⓓ	142 Ⓐ Ⓑ Ⓒ Ⓓ	143 Ⓐ Ⓑ Ⓒ Ⓓ	144 Ⓐ Ⓑ Ⓒ Ⓓ
145 Ⓐ Ⓑ Ⓒ Ⓓ	146 Ⓐ Ⓑ Ⓒ Ⓓ	147 Ⓐ Ⓑ Ⓒ Ⓓ	148 Ⓐ Ⓑ Ⓒ Ⓓ	149 Ⓐ Ⓑ Ⓒ Ⓓ	150 Ⓐ Ⓑ Ⓒ Ⓓ

CHAPTER 14

Practice Examination Two

The Test

100 QUESTIONS—3½ HOURS

1. Although there is no list long enough to totally compile all of the possible causes of employee grievances, some actions do lead the list. Of the following, the one most apt to become a prime instigator of employee grievances is:
   A. Rigid rules and regulations
   B. Inconsistent application of rules and regulations by supervisors
   C. Low pay
   D. Lack of upwardly mobile promotional opportunities

2. The existence of departmental rules is one issue; gaining compliance is another issue. A certain sergeant is trying to make the police officers under his supervision comply with certain department rules. The best way for the sergeant to do this is to:
   A. Show the purpose and worth of the rules
   B. Find ways to get the police officers to like him, especially by personal contacts
   C. Make sure the police officers follow all the technicalities of the rules
   D. Let the police officers clearly realize the consequences of their noncompliance

3. Consider the following statements concerning order giving by a police sergeant in a police agency.
   (1) A sergeant can, if his employees are capable enough, delegate away any of his responsibilities.
   (2) The first step in the preparation of an order is to establish its need.
   (3) A sergeant who fails to include detailed instructions when giving orders to inexperienced workers has to compensate by close supervision.

   Which of the following most accurately classifies these statements into those that are accurate and those that are not?
   A. Statements 1 and 2 are accurate; statement 3 is not.
   B. Statements 1 and 3 are accurate; statement 2 is not.
   C. Statements 2 and 3 are accurate; statement 1 is not.
   D. All of the statements are accurate.

4. Consider the following statements concerning "order giving" by a first-line supervisor in a police department.
   (1) Frequently issuing definite orders is the best way to have subordinates consistently work toward the goals of the organization.
   (2) When a directive or order has for its source the commanding officer of the precinct, the sergeant should make that quite clear to the officers in the squad.
   (3) When possible, the reason for an order should be explained so that the order is not viewed as arbitrary.

   Based on these statements, which of the following is most accurate?
   A. Statement 1 is accurate; statements 2 and 3 are not.
   B. Statement 2 is accurate; statements 1 and 3 are not.
   C. Statement 3 is accurate; statements 1 and 2 are not.
   D. All of the statements are accurate.

5. Order giving is not simply one person giving an order while another takes the order and follows through by completing some action. An explana-

tion of the "why" of an order ensures more enthusiasm in its being carried out and also a more receptive attitude toward the order. The kind of order in which the "why" of the order is especially significant is the:

- A. Call for volunteers
- B. Request
- C. Implied order
- D. Direct order

6. Sergeant Claron has an officer under his supervision who is quite experienced. When giving orders to this officer, the sergeant finds very often that a certain type of order works best. In general, the kind of order that is generally recommended for use when dealing with an experienced worker is:

- A. A call for volunteers
- B. An implied order
- C. A request
- D. A direct order

7. There are times when a direct order would be quite effective. The opposite of this is also true. It would not be a good idea for a police sergeant to issue a command in the form of a direct order in which of the following situations?

- A. In dealing with a reluctant worker who has a reputation for being lazy
- B. In an emergency
- C. When time is of the essence
- D. When the job is not pleasant and is considered distasteful

8. In properly supervising subordinates, a police sergeant should be aware of the difference between motives and incentives. Which of the following best describes the difference between motives and incentives?

- A. Incentives are related to motives, but incentives are much broader than motives.
- B. In general, incentives come from within an individual but motives come from outside an individual.
- C. Motives are specific ways of satisfying an incentive.
- D. Incentives are specific ways of satisfying a motive.

9. Captain Rite is addressing a number of newly promoted sergeants who have been assigned to the district. The captain tells the new sergeants that a good role model for them is Francis Parks, a veteran sergeant assigned to the district. It seems that Sergeant Parks rarely has to display his authority to the officers in his squad. The most likely reason for this is that Sergeant Parks:
   A. Gets the officers in his squad to do the job by inspiring them through his exemplary personal example
   B. Has instilled in his officers just how far they can go before he will take disciplinary action
   C. Demands that his subordinates read and understand the department's rules and regulations
   D. Makes certain that his officers are aware of the standard penalties for infractions of the rules and regulations

10. Sergeant Morris is part of a task force whose job is to evaluate the leadership climate in the department. The sergeant should be aware that a serious lack of leadership is indicated when supervisors:
    A. Rarely delegate authority to workers
    B. Refuse to delegate final responsibility for a job to a worker
    C. Are careful that authority is commensurate with responsibility
    D. Praise workers in the presence of others

11. The use of teaching aids should be employed when appropriate. Which of the following is the primary advantage in using a three-dimensional aid, such as a magnetic board?
    A. It presents a picture of what has been taught.
    B. The objects on the board are held firmly in place and cannot be moved.
    C. It requires little or no explanation.
    D. It gives the student the opportunity to deal with moveable objects.

12. Although it is true that no two trainees are the same, there are recommended approaches to the conducting of training. According to experts, which of the following methods of instruction is recommended in teaching workers how to do a job?

A. Begin with the hazardous parts of the job, which should be avoided, and then move to the nonhazardous aspects.
B. Immediately point out the complex components of a task, and then explain the more simple aspects.
C. Identify first for the workers the more difficult tasks involved in performing a job before explaining those that are simpler and easier to understand.
D. Try to connect that which a worker already knows to that which you are trying to teach.

13. "Training should be ongoing not only for the newly hired police officer, but the seasoned veteran as well." This statement is generally:
A. False, since once the recruit hits the streets, experience becomes the real trainer
B. True, since both the rookie and the veteran can learn and it should be done together as a single group
C. False, since the seasoned veteran will resent being retrained in something learned in the past
D. True, since training can be forgotten as new demands are constantly brought about by changing social conditions

14. Sergeant Bourke is asked by her commanding officer, "Which step in the instructional process controls the learning process the most?" Accordingly, the sergeant would be most correct if she answered:
A. Preparation of the student
B. Presentation of the material
C. Application of the material by the student
D. Testing of the student's knowledge of the material

15. One of the methods often used in conducting training is the use of lectures. Which of the following is not an advantage of the lecture method of training?
A. It can be attended by large numbers of trainees.
B. There can be an exchange of ideas, especially if seasoned veteran employees comprise some of those trainees in attendance.
C. It is a fairly economical method of training.
D. It can be used to cover a wide range of topics in a fairly short period of time.

16. The view of training held by the patrol sergeant sets the tone for the training of police officers. Which of the following most clearly indicates the correct view of training of subordinates for a police sergeant?
    A. It is part of the sergeant's normal supervisory activities.
    B. It is not part of the sergeant's normal supervisory activities.
    C. It is part of the sergeant's normal supervisory activities only after all other supervisory activities have been completed.
    D. It is, in the final analysis, the job of each individual employee to get training based on individual motivation.

17. Sergeant Mann believes that the most important result in his investigations of accidents involving his subordinates is to identify the employee who caused the accident. The sergeant's feeling in this matter is:
    A. Proper, mainly because the employee can then be appropriately punished
    B. Improper, mainly because it will be quite embarrassing for the employee to be singled out from among his/her peers
    C. Proper, mainly because such an employee should not be considered for any position of responsibility
    D. Improper, mainly because the focus of such investigations should be on what caused the accident and to prevent recurrences

18. One of the steps in the training process is the phase known as the "application step." Which of the following is the least accurate statement concerning the application step?
    A. During the application step, self-correction by the learner, if possible, is preferred.
    B. The application step is not the last step in the training process.
    C. It is a good practice to compliment a learner before making a correction of the learner's application of the subject matter.
    D. Errors committed by the learner during the application step always indicate that poor learning has occurred.

19. Captain King addresses a group of newly promoted sergeants. During the address, he states that training is primarily a staff function and as such should not be considered a sergeant's responsibility. The captain's statement is:
    A. Correct, since only experienced specialists can perform any meaningful training
    B. Incorrect, since training is part of the sergeant's normal role
    C. Correct, since the training division of a police agency is in the best position to know what training is needed and how to give it
    D. Incorrect, since sergeants can usually perform all the tasks of police officers better than the police officers can perform these tasks and therefore should train them

20. Training is a quite methodical and logical sequence of steps. This is also true of the development of a training program. Regarding the development of such a program, many believe that the first step is key. Which of the following best indicates the first step in developing a training program?
    A. Where the training is to take place
    B. What needs to be improved
    C. Who should conduct the training
    D. How the training should take place, that is, lecture method or seminar style

21. Sergeant Colella has been asked to prepare this year's budget for the department by the chief. The sergeant has never prepared a budget for the department previously. The best initial action for the sergeant to take in this instance would be to:
    A. Interview all commanders in the department to ascertain their needs
    B. Ask the inspections unit for a list of units that are not operating effectively
    C. Review the department's budget for last year
    D. Examine the budget of a similar police department

22. All police departments engage in some kind of inspectional process. Which of the following is most directly implemented by inspections?
    A. Command or direction
    B. Coordination
    C. Control
    D. Organizing

23. After coming to realize that coordination problems in the work effort exist between her unit and another unit of the department, Sergeant Aponte looks for a corrective course of action. Which of the following is a recommended course of action for Sergeant Aponte to take in order to increase the potential for coordination between her unit and the other unit involved?
    A. To create the potential for effective coordination and then let it happen
    B. To simply direct the members of the unit to cooperate with the other unit
    C. To request the commanding officer or the next overhead command to mandate cooperation between the units
    D. To continuously intervene personally to ensure that needed cooperation is occurring between the two units

24. Increases in specialization within a police department complicate the process of coordination. This statement is generally:
    A. True, mainly because as specialization is increased more lines of interrelations are required and this creates the potential for increased friction.
    B. False, mainly because coordination is only complicated in these instances if the number of specialists becomes greater than the overall number of generalists, and this rarely occurs
    C. True, mainly because specialists will not take orders from anyone who is not trained in their specialty
    D. False, mainly because the part of the department that is specialized is generally so small that it has very little impact on the coordination process

25. In a certain police department a central planning unit has been established. This should signify all of the following to a first-line supervisor in the department except which?
    A. Planning will be done exclusively by the central planning unit.
    B. Members of the newly formed planning unit will be available for staff assistance.

C. Members of the newly formed planning unit will probably train supervisory members of the department in planning.

D. Recommendations for future planning policies should emanate from the central planning unit.

26. The question often arises as to how much detail a police plan should contain. In a police agency, the most detailed and meticulous plans usually are needed at the:
A. Highest level of the agency
B. Middle levels of the agency
C. Lowest levels of the agency
D. Highest or middle levels of the agency depending upon ability of the planner

27. A certain police department is organized in a decentralized fashion. Throughout the city serviced by the department are numerous district stations (precinct station houses). This type of decentralized organization is primarily a:
A. Convenience to the police
B. Device to ensure quicker response to calls for service
C. Strategy to save labor and other resources
D. Technique to provide greater crime prevention

28. When an organization chart becomes outdated and no longer reflects actual changes that have been made in a police agency, certain events occur. Which of the following statements best illustrates what usually happens when an organization chart becomes outdated?
A. The chart is almost immediately updated to reflect the actual organization.
B. All work ceases without a formal organization chart indicating the lines of authority since no meaningful work can take place.
C. An informal organization develops that takes the place of the outdated organizational structure.
D. The chart is temporarily patched up by the use of dotted lines showing temporary relationships.

29. As the structure of an organization changes, the span of control of the supervisors in the organization also can change. What happens to the span of control in a department when levels of the hierarchy are removed?
   A. It increases.
   B. It decreases.
   C. It remains the same.
   D. It can either increase or decrease depending upon the type of organization.

30. Police supervisors should recognize that change or reorganization of a police department is inevitable. The question really is when and how should reorganization take place. In response to this question, a police supervisor should recognize which of the following as the best answer?
   A. Reorganization should take place regularly, approximately once every four years.
   B. Reorganization should take place only when radical changes are evidently needed.
   C. Reorganization should take place whenever a new chief is appointed so that new policies can be implemented.
   D. Reorganization should take place gradually and only after a clear need is identified.

31. Among the many roles of policing is the order-maintenance role. Which of the following is often mentioned by critics of this role of policing?
   A. It is overly harsh on the community because of the high number of arrests that result.
   B. The police are not afforded any discretion.
   C. There is an invitation for corruption.
   D. There are not enough officers assigned to foot patrol.

32. Police-community relations efforts have been ongoing for many years. Yet, police officers continue to resist the changes required by new community relations programs. This resistance stems primarily from the:
   A. Police officers' aversion to community relations
   B. Example set toward these programs by higher ranking officers
   C. Natural tendency of humans to resist change of any kind
   D. Apparent incompatibility between law enforcement and community relations

33. In recent years, the model of policing that the police of the country followed changed dramatically. Nowadays emphasis is placed on which of the following model or models of police work?
    A. Service model only
    B. Legalistic model only
    C. Order-maintenance model only
    D. Service model and the order-maintenance model

34. In the cities of urban America exists a heterogeneous society with respect to feelings about law and order. Regarding these feelings, it would be most accurate to state which of the following?
    A. There is general agreement on law but not on what constitutes order.
    B. There is general agreement on what constitutes order but not on law.
    C. There is general agreement on both what law is and what constitutes order.
    D. There is no general agreement on what law is or on what constitutes order.

35. As one goes down the chain of command in a police department, the amount of discretionary authority:
    A. Increases
    B. Decreases
    C. Stays about the same
    D. Increases or decreases, depending upon departmental rules and procedures

36. In police work, contact and cooperation with the print media are inevitable. Therefore, knowledge of what the print media covers or what have come to be the kinds of topics they focus on is important to the police. Although all of the following are issues they might focus on, which of them seems to be their favorite?
    A. Criminal acts of violence
    B. Corrupt acts of public servants
    C. Heroic acts by police and fire officers
    D. Pornography arrests

37. Although there are many factors in building a successful community relations program, there is one key factor. What is this factor?
    A. The educational level of the members of the department

B. Where the community relations unit is located in the departmental hierarchy
C. The police taking an active involvement in the community
D. An adequate budgetary allocation

38. Not all police officers view the community they deal with exactly the same. For example, officers assigned to the detective division are most likely to view the community they come in contact with as:
A. Average citizens
B. Unable to deal with their own problems
C. Uncooperative
D. Arrogant and troublesome criminals

39. Which of the following is the best example of two-way communications in police work?
A. Public relations
B. Police-community relations
C. A crime prevention program that identifies and assists those persons experiencing problems as targets of crime
D. A program that seeks to recruit qualified minorities into the police service

40. Some efforts of the police to develop viable community relations programs are not very successful. When these programs are unsuccessful, the police act quite surprised when actually they should not be surprised at all. The primary reason these programs fail is:
A. Lack of involvement of the community by the police during the planning stages of the program
B. Failure to provide sufficient personnel to the accomplishment of the goals of the program
C. Lack of first-line supervisory support
D. Rejection of any community relations program by the rank and file

41. Decoy patrol operations differ from the more traditional patrol method in several ways. Mainly the difference lies in the fact that decoy operations:
A. Act as a preventive type of patrol
B. Create a great sense of police omnipresence
C. Are more interested in immediate apprehensions than in immediate deterrence
D. Are only effective in the hours after dark

42. How to assign police officers is a question sergeants often address. Regarding this question, the issue of visibility often arises. Which of the following is the best example of an officer assigned to a high-visibility assignment?
    A. A police officer assigned to an anticrime assignment
    B. A homicide detective conducting an investigation at a crime scene
    C. A police officer directing traffic at a busy intersection
    D. A community affairs officer giving a talk on burglary prevention at a school while in uniform

43. A conspicuously marked patrol car is one that is obviously a police car. It is conspicuously painted and marked so all concerned can readily identify it as an official vehicle of the police. When the police use a conspicuously marked vehicle on patrol, all of the following occur except which?
    A. The appearance is created that patrol is intensified because of the continual viewing of an automobile obviously connected with the police.
    B. Citizens comply more readily with directions emanating from an automobile they know belongs to the police.
    C. Supervision is simplified since the officers assigned to such an automobile are less likely to engage in activities not related to their official duties.
    D. Violators of the traffic laws will be more easily detected since the violators will be quite reluctant to attempt to escape apprehension.

44. Consider the following statements concerning bicycle patrol.
    (1) Weather seriously limits bicycle patrol.
    (2) Bicycle patrol is expensive.
    (3) Bicycle patrol has been used effectively in parks, playgrounds, and shopping malls.
    Which of the following most accurately classifies these statements into those that are accurate and those that are not?
    A. Statement 1 is accurate; statements 2 and 3 are not.
    B. Statements 1 and 2 are accurate; statement 3 is not.

C. Statements 1 and 3 are accurate; statement 2 is not.
D. Statements 2 and 3 are accurate; statement 1 is not.

45. Many police departments have stopped the practice of "door shaking." All of the following are reasons for the stopping of this practice except:
A. Lack of personnel
B. Lack of effectiveness
C. Lack of demand by merchants due to the installation of iron front gates
D. It is time-consuming

46. In the past, certain police departments experimented with having the patrol sergeant assigned to supervise both radio motor patrol units and foot patrol officers while the sergeant was on foot. When such a practice is used, which of the following is most likely to result?
A. There will be better performance by officers on foot due to the closer supervision by the sergeant.
B. The officers assigned to radio motor patrol will feel more trusted and therefore perform better.
C. The officers on foot will feel resentment since they will believe they have been singled out for close supervision.
D. The officers assigned to radio motor patrol cars will not receive the proper level of supervision.

47. As police work has become more complex, more and more specialization has taken place. Which is the most negative aspect of this increased specialization?
A. The loss of prestige felt by those members of the department who are not specialists
B. The resulting weakening of the patrol force, which is traditionally the main personnel pool from which specialists are selected
C. The difficulty in properly selecting candidates to be trained as specialists
D. That the specialists know more about their specialties than the supervisors, thereby making supervision more difficult

48. In recent years, foot patrol has been used increasingly. It is sometimes boring, and officers sometimes become lethargic about it. Which of the following represents the best motivation for such officers?
    A. An increase in supervision, which stresses that an officer could be fined or even fired
    B. Acceptance and recognition from persons on the foot post
    C. Higher pay
    D. Less supervision, which enables the officer to handle a job any way he/she sees fit, even through trial and error

49. How members of the community view the police officers on patrol is extremely important because the cooperation of the public is essential for the achievement of police objectives. A knowledgeable police sergeant understands that the way in which community members view the police is primarily a product of:
    A. What is said about the police in the press, on the radio, and on television
    B. Personal contacts they or their neighbors have had with the police
    C. The opinion of the police they hear voiced by local politicians
    D. The role of the police as portrayed in the movies

50. In all police departments, there is one line division whose effectiveness impacts on all other line units. If the effectiveness of this particular division command decreases, then the workload of all other line divisions becomes more difficult. This line command that impacts on the workload of all other line commands in the department is the:
    A. Youth division
    B. Detective division
    C. Patrol division
    D. Traffic division

51. Police reporting in the form of crime statistics helps police agencies in their responsibility of crime prevention. Still, the picture of crime conditions continues to be inaccurate because it is incomplete. The primary reason for this inaccuracy is:
    A. The not-so-scrupulous efforts at data gathering by some police agencies

B. The lack of commonality between the various systems used in crime reporting

C. That the police simply do not have the needed expertise to properly gather and maintain these statistics

D. That the public does not report much of the crime that occurs

52. It is the policy of a certain police agency to accept anonymous reports of police misconduct. This practice is:
A. Good, mainly because it will encourage citizens to come forward and make complaints
B. Bad, mainly because a police officer, like a criminal, has the right to face an accuser
C. Good, mainly because investigation may reveal that the complaint is valid or that a more serious deficiency exists
D. Bad, mainly because it encourages crank complaints

53. A major purpose of preparing reports dealing with motor vehicle accidents is to reduce future accidents. In accomplishing this purpose, which of the following items of information is most important?
A. The location of the damage to the vehicles concerned
B. The age of the drivers and or pedestrians
C. The location of the accidents being reported
D. How long it took the ambulance to respond to each accident

54. Sergeant Palmer recommends to his commanding officer the "one-write" report system because of its increased efficiency and decreased costs. The sergeant explains that the "one-write" report system is basically a reporting system in which the officer:
A. Records the report on tape for a stenographer to type at a later time
B. Writes the entire report in longhand
C. Types the report directly into a digital computer
D. Dictates the report to a specially trained employee who uses speedwriting

55. Which of the following divisions in the typical police agency does the most to pull together and coordinate the work of other units in the agency?

A. Property division
B. Records division
C. Community relations division
D. Personnel division

56. As the United States continues to be a nation on wheels, the police continue to report and compile traffic statistics. What is the main purpose for this action by the police?
    A. To justify their current level of personnel commitments in this area
    B. To determine if additional police resources should be committed to traffic control
    C. To ascertain if current programs should be redesigned in the overall police effort to reduce accidents and ease traffic congestion
    D. To aid in the crime prevention effort by reducing the spiraling rate of larceny of motor vehicles

57. Police supervisors at any level or rank in the department find many similarities in their roles, but some differences do exist. Certain tasks do not accrue to the first-line supervisor. Which of the following is generally not considered to be an element of first-line supervision?
    A. Directing people
    B. Creating an environment in which the work can be accomplished efficiently and effectively
    C. Developing workers
    D. Setting broad policy guidelines

58. No two leaders are totally identical. This is probably true, but there are surely certain types of leadership styles. The leadership style that would most likely result in the emergence of unofficial leaders is the:
    A. Authoritarian style
    B. Laissez-faire style
    C. Democratic style
    D. Autocratic style

59. Part of a "prepromotion to sergeant" supervisory course given by a certain police department includes a self-appraisal component. The trainees are asked to consider positive and negative characteristics of a sergeant's supervisory behavior. Which of the following should the trainees recog-

nize as not being a negative characteristic of a police sergeant's supervisory behavior?

A. Giving unclear orders
B. Being subjective in making assignments
C. Showing a sense of humor
D. Not being consistent in dealing with subordinates

60. A feeling that the goals of the organization are worthwhile and in tune with a worker's own personal goals is an example of:

A. High job satisfaction
B. High morale
C. High productivity
D. The absence of all frustration in the work setting

61. The police sergeant plays an important role in establishing and maintaining high morale. A good example of a sergeant who helps to build high morale among subordinates occurs when a sergeant:

A. Makes any personal problems of an employee his/her personal concern
B. Encourages the elevating of the personal objectives of workers over the objectives of the agency
C. Resists increases in the workload of subordinates even for short periods of time
D. Helps to quicken the upward flow of information

62. A certain police officer brings a grievance to the attention of her sergeant. The sergeant accurately assesses the grievance to be quite minor and insignificant, and relays the assessment to the police officer. The sergeant's action was:

A. Proper, since it will prevent the police officer from taking up the sergeant's valuable time in the future with petty complaints
B. Improper, since the grievance must be important to the police officer or she would not have raised it
C. Proper, since it will indicate to the officer that the sergeant knows what is important
D. Improper, since the grievance may prove to be more serious than it appears and the sergeant will not appear competent to superiors

63. A disciplinary process that is most likely to generate grievances is one characterized by:
    A. The imposing of severe punishments
    B. Imposing swift and certain punishments
    C. Not being consistent in its application of punishment
    D. A lack of punishment sanctions

64. Sergeant Horton tells another supervisor that he (Sergeant Horton) has never had a grievance made by the officers he supervises in over five years. If this is true, then it is most probably also true that:
    A. The supervisor is seen as unapproachable by the workers
    B. There are probably no grounds for grievances
    C. Workers do not like to talk about their grievances
    D. The workers are too busy to come forward with grievances

65. After delivering the results of a grievance to the officer who made the grievance, Sergeant Rex is advised by the officer that he wants to appeal the results. The best action for the sergeant to take is to:
    A. Tell the officer how to make the appeal
    B. Remain impartial, and say nothing
    C. Ask the officer why he wants to appeal
    D. Attempt to discourage the officer from appealing since the appeal procedure is expensive and quite time-consuming

66. In training an employee to do a job, Sergeant Landau usually allows the employee to correct his own mistakes by asking the employee how he could have performed the job better. This practice is:
    A. Good, since any hint of negative confrontation should be avoided during training
    B. Bad, since there is no possible way an employee could correct himself while learning a new job
    C. Good, since the unpleasant aspects of correcting an employee are greatly reduced
    D. Bad, since it would make the employee feel inadequate

67. Among the steps in structuring a safety education drive in a police department, certain actions must precede others. The first requirement in setting up a safety education drive is to:
   A. State the goals of the drive
   B. Decide on the target audience who would benefit from the drive
   C. Determine how long the drive should last considering the exigencies of the department
   D. Select someone to be in charge of the drive, and notify the rest of the department of the selection

68. Although there is always a need for leadership training, this type of training is not always accepted. In some police agencies the resistance to leadership training most often stems from the:
   A. Lack of leadership principles on which to base the training
   B. Fact that no real merit has ever been proven to come from leadership principles
   C. Reluctance of many police supervisors to adopt leadership principles
   D. Fact that a police agency is unique so that the leadership principles appropriate for one agency do not apply to other agencies

69. Studies by law enforcement experts have long recommended that mandated training standards for police agencies exist in each state. These experts have agreed that the concept of state-mandated training standards has accomplished all of the following except which?
   A. More hours of police training
   B. Improved police training curricula
   C. Adoption of standards by many more police departments
   D. Greater use of lateral entry among police departments of different states

70. Often a job analysis is conducted prior to holding a training program for a particular job. A good job analysis accomplishes all of the following except which?
   A. The identification and removal of simpler routine tasks from the job
   B. The establishment of new, lower level positions

C. The redesign of the skilled jobs to ensure proper clustering of tasks among the skilled jobs

D. The identification of the duties of a job with a view toward establishing appropriate salaries for the job

71. Police Officers Hunt and Peck are attending a series of training lectures given by Sergeant Carter. Hunt tells Peck that Carter is not a good instructor because Carter usually begins his lectures by having one of the students capsulize the important points covered in the previous lecture. Hunt's criticism is:

A. Proper, since the student could make a mistake and confuse the rest of the group

B. Improper, since review helps learning and sets the stage for the next step

C. Proper, since the practice is very time-consuming and loses the interest of the group

D. Improper, since sometimes a student from the group can prove to have a better grasp of the material than the instructor

72. Critics of police departments have maintained that the police really fall short of true productivity efforts. Which of the following best describes the reason that training is necessary for police departments seeking to establish the productivity process in their agencies in the truest form?

A. The lack of real interest in productivity by police departments

B. The inability of police managers to develop systemwide productivity improvements

C. The lack of identifiable targets for productivity efforts

D. The absence of college-trained police officers at the managerial level

73. Not every subject can be taught in the same sequence. Regarding the giving of instruction in the use of firearms, a knowledgeable police sergeant would recognize which of the following as most accurate?

A. The instructor should first point out the hazardous aspects of the topic.

B. The instructor should first point out the safe aspects of the topic.

C. The instructor should begin where he feels most comfortable.
D. It makes no real difference where the instructor begins as long as the entire subject matter is covered.

74. Management and supervision often make not only errors of commission but also errors of omission. A vital but often neglected aspect of management and supervision is:
A. Training at the level of operations
B. Safety and accident prevention
C. Position specialization
D. Management control

75. One often-used method of training is the conference technique. Before one utilizes this technique, a full understanding of the characteristics of conference training is required. Which of the following is not a characteristic of the conference method of training?
A. It is costly.
B. It is slow.
C. It guarantees the participation of all the trainees.
D. There must be a skilled conference leader.

76. When orders are given to two different employees, the supervisor must coordinate the efforts of the two employees to ensure the accomplishment of the objectives of the agency. The coordination efforts of the supervisor in this case would be most facilitated by a:
A. Constant intervening by the supervisor
B. Sound organizational structure
C. Good information retrieval system
D. Well-established inspectional system

77. A certain task is delegated to a police officer by a police sergeant. Actually the task involves finding a solution to a rather vague problem that the police officer doesn't really understand. In this case:
A. The police officer can be held responsible since it is his job to tell the sergeant if he is unclear on any aspect of the task
B. The police officer cannot be held responsible since it is the sergeant's job to ensure that the communication was clear

C. The police officer can be held responsible since resourcefulness is an attribute a police officer must posses

D. The police officer cannot be held responsible since police officers can never be held responsible for any task that involves problem solving

78. Before conducting performance evaluations, Sergeant Larkin always checks the employee's previous performance evaluation reports. This practice is:
A. Good, since it will give him insight regarding the employee's performance capability
B. Bad, since the evaluation should be based on current performance
C. Good, since it would prevent him from rating the employee too harshly or easily
D. Bad, since the last evaluation may have been done incorrectly and therefore not indicative of past performance

79. It is well established that the evaluation process is a product of many factors. Regarding how much contact a patrol sergeant has with someone under his/her supervision, it is generally acknowledged that contacts between patrol sergeants and their subordinates are:
A. Numerous
B. Scarce
C. Either numerous or scarce depending on the style of the patrol supervisor
D. About the same in a police organization as between supervisors and subordinates in any other organization

80. Concentration is needed by a supervisor who desires to objectively rate an employee. When a supervisor performing evaluations of subordinates confuses the true meaning of certain rating traits by overlapping them, he is committing the rating error known as:
A. Leniency
B. Central tendency
C. Contrast
D. Association

81. Police Officer Colella is considered by most to be somewhat of an aggressive extrovert. In communicating with him, Sergeant De Fini, his supervisor, would do best by dealing with him by:
    A. A tactful soft approach to try to enlist his support
    B. A direct, hard approach that clearly establishes the proper relationship between the sergeant and the officer
    C. An approach that ignores the police officer's personality
    D. An approach that does not directly put the sergeant in a position that forces direct communication with the officer

82. A certain supervisor overevaluates each piece of information communicated by subordinates. As a general rule, the result of such overevaluation is that the subordinate will:
    A. Soon avoid making strong positive declarations
    B. Take extra care in preparing to speak with the supervisor to maintain the subordinate's credibility
    C. Confront the supervisor about the issue
    D. Speak directly with the supervisor's boss

83. Consider the following statements concerning guidelines for effective communication.
    (1) Before communicating, the objectives of the communications should always be considered, even if just for an instant.
    (2) The feelings and viewpoints of those being communicated with must always be considered before the communication is made.
    (3) A communicator should always include a positive aspect in the communication.
    Which of the following most accurately classifies these statements into those that are true and those that are false?
    A. All of the statements are true.
    B. All of the statements are false.
    C. Only two of the statements are true.
    D. Only one of the statements is true.

84. You are a police sergeant and a new operation is being put into effect by your unit. Although it is an unpopular procedure, experience has shown that the operation will increase efficiency. Of the following, the most proper way for you to commu-

nicate this to the police officers under your supervision is to:

A. Simply announce the new operation with no further comment

B. Tell the police officers that you realize how unpopular the new operation is but orders must be obeyed

C. Advise the police officers that the operation will not be strictly followed

D. Attempt to have the police officers recognize the benefits of the operation

85. When information is changed as it passes from one individual to another, the process is called filtering. This process takes place:

A. In downward communication only

B. In upward communication only

C. Either in downward or in upward communication

D. Only in police agencies with poor communications

86. Since community relations will be performed by the police, the kinds of candidates who become police officers are obviously important. Recruitment, therefore, plays a real role in community relations. Which of the following is not recommended as part of any police recruitment effort?

A. Attempting to recruit candidates from a wide variety of backgrounds

B. Emphasizing the more exciting and adventurous parts of police work

C. Utilizing officers of different ethnic backgrounds as recruiters

D. Stressing the service role of police as typical of the police officer's job

87. "Can the acts of the legislatures sometimes make matters worse?" Some experts claim this occurs through laws that create criminality. Which of the following laws would appear to be the most criminogenic?

A. Laws that tend to call for heavier penalties for recidivists

B. Statutes written to deal with sexual assaults

C. Those laws that deal with certain victimless crimes

D. Those laws for which someone could receive a death sentence

88. In achieving good police-community relations the need for communication is obvious. There are, however, certain communication blocks that work against good police-community relations. One such block is "tabloid thinking." Which of the following best illustrates tabloid thinking?
    A. A newspaper reporter focuses on police corruption.
    B. A member of the community tries to use political pressure to get a traffic light installed.
    C. A member of the community states that the reason for all crime is that drug addicts steal to fund their habits.
    D. A newspaper reporter tries to keep the police and the community at odds by sensationalizing reports of crimes.

89. Unfortunately, much of what the public thinks of the law enforcement community stems from how the public sees the courts and the court process. Who among the following most influences the court process?
    A. Police and district attorneys
    B. Police and defense attorneys, especially public defenders
    C. Judges and legislators through laws they pass
    D. District attorneys and judges

90. A question many newly promoted police sergeants have is as follows: "Is my job as a first-line supervisor very different from the job of a higher ranking officer in my department?" The most accurate answer to this question is that the duties and responsibilities of the first-line supervisor and those of higher ranking officers in the same department are:
    A. Exactly the same both in degree and in kind
    B. The same in kind but different in degree
    C. Different in kind but the same in degree
    D. Are different both in kind and in degree

91. Sergeant Newman has been directed by his commanding officer to reshape the configuration of two posts or beats, thereby changing the boundaries of each. In accomplishing the task, which of the following should be considered least by the sergeant?
    A. The number of inspectional duties on each post
    B. The reported number of offenses on each post

C. The individual abilities of the officers currently assigned or to be assigned to the respective posts

D. The number of calls for police service on each post for the last year

92. When a member of the community is issued a traffic summons by a police officer, quite a bit of stress exists for both the officer and the private citizen. For this reason, very specific procedures are recommended to be followed by the police officer. For example, it is recommended that the police officer clearly tell the citizen the reason for the traffic stop and what the officer intends to do. According to accepted procedure, this should be done:

A. While the police officer is still in his/her vehicle via the police loudspeaker

B. After greeting the driver and before returning to the police vehicle

C. After inspecting the driver's license

D. By showing the citizen the violation on the summons after it is completed

93. In terms of police patrol, police agencies have progressed a long way from the early days of policing in the United States. Today, there exists in the country many different kinds of patrol. Which of the following is not generally considered to be a kind of police patrol?

A. Anticrime patrol

B. Vertical patrol

C. Traffic patrol

D. Horse patrol

94. Initially, scooter patrol was not widely accepted. This has, however, changed significantly, so much so that scooter patrol now rivals foot patrol. Which of the following is not an advantage of scooter patrol over foot patrol?

A. Scooter patrol allows an officer to carry more equipment than foot patrol.

B. Scooter patrol is not as tiring as foot patrol.

C. Scooter patrol allows more mobility than foot patrol.

D. Scooter patrol enables an officer to pursue other vehicles that an officer on foot cannot pursue.

95. Sergeant Edwards tells another sergeant that he likes to let subordinates find their own way of doing things because each officer is different and works at his/her own pace. Regarding the sergeant's suggestion of a trial-and-error method of training for police officers, which of the following is most correct?
    A. Trial and error is slow and wasteful.
    B. Bad habits in work performance are able to be eliminated by trial and error.
    C. Trial and error is usually an excellent teaching mode since it immediately points out to the learner any mistakes.
    D. Emergency situations are well suited for trial and error.

96. Sergeant Clark always makes it a practice to praise subordinates in private. This practice is:
    A. Good, since the subordinate would be embarrassed if done in public
    B. Bad, since the subordinate deserves the recognition of his/her peers
    C. Good, since the subordinate can ask questions about other related items
    D. Bad, since it is too time-consuming

97. Police administrators have come to agree that police departments must be ever vigilant to combat corruption. Some question exists, however, as to who in a police agency should investigate charges of corruption. Many believe that charges of police corruption should be investigated by a staff unit of the department. This statement is generally:
    A. True, because the level of competence and expertise is always greater in a specialized staff unit
    B. False, because it is easier for a line unit closer to the officer involved to uncover the truth
    C. True, because if the line unit investigates corruption, it could be accused of a cover-up and of not being objective
    D. False, because the line unit has a better insight into the total situation

98. One of the duties of a sergeant is to skillfully handle disciplinary actions. Care must be taken so that the process is properly handled. In the instance when a sergeant is about to reprimand a

police officer for an alleged violation of department regulations, it would be most correct for the sergeant to:
- A. Refuse to listen to an explanation since the officer is probably attempting to avoid an embarrassing situation
- B. Provide the officer an opportunity to explain his/her conduct
- C. Look over the officer's past record so that a proper penalty could be given at a later time
- D. First serve the officer with a written summary of the allegation

99. Delegation is a skill a sergeant must learn if he/she is to be a successful supervisor. However, not all tasks can be delegated. Of the following, the task that should not be delegated by a supervisor to a subordinate is:
- A. Writing a response to an irate citizen complaining about the sale of marijuana in a school yard
- B. Attending a meeting with local merchants concerning burglary prevention
- C. Devising a plan to increase the police response to the larceny of automobiles
- D. Gathering information concerning fatalities arising from vehicle accidents

100. The role of the police sergeant has been described as "walking a tightrope." Which of the following most nearly indicates this description?
- A. The sergeant must sometimes "wink at" improper police conduct by the work group of which he is actually a part.
- B. The sergeant must support the policies of management, which at times are seen as bothersome by the police officers.
- C. When the work of subordinates is unsatisfactory, it is the sergeant who must make excuses for the work.
- D. The sergeant always must be aware that if he fails he could be demoted back into the group he now supervises.

Answer Key

1. **B**	21. **C**	41. **C**	61. **D**	81. **B**
2. **A**	22. **C**	42. **C**	62. **B**	82. **A**
3. **C**	23. **A**	43. **D**	63. **C**	83. **D**
4. **C**	24. **A**	44. **C**	64. **A**	84. **D**
5. **A**	25. **A**	45. **C**	65. **A**	85. **C**
6. **B**	26. **C**	46. **D**	66. **C**	86. **B**
7. **D**	27. **A**	47. **B**	67. **D**	87. **C**
8. **D**	28. **C**	48. **B**	68. **C**	88. **C**
9. **A**	29. **A**	49. **B**	69. **D**	89. **D**
10. **A**	30. **D**	50. **C**	70. **D**	90. **B**
11. **D**	31. **B**	51. **D**	71. **B**	91. **C**
12. **D**	32. **C**	52. **C**	72. **B**	92. **B**
13. **D**	33. **D**	53. **C**	73. **B**	93. **D**
14. **D**	34. **D**	54. **B**	74. **B**	94. **D**
15. **B**	35. **A**	55. **B**	75. **C**	95. **A**
16. **A**	36. **A**	56. **C**	76. **B**	96. **B**
17. **D**	37. **C**	57. **D**	77. **B**	97. **C**
18. **D**	38. **C**	58. **B**	78. **B**	98. **B**
19. **B**	39. **B**	59. **C**	79. **B**	99. **C**
20. **B**	40. **A**	60. **B**	80. **D**	100. **B**

Diagnostic Chart

Insert the number of correct answers you obtained in the blank space for each section of the examination. The scale in the next column indicates how you did. The information at the bottom indicates how to correct your weaknesses.

SECTION	QUESTION NUMBERS	AREAS	YOUR NUMBER CORRECT	SCALE
1	1–10 57–65 96–100	Principles of supervision		23–24 right: excellent 21–22 right: good 19–20 right: fair Under 20 right: poor
2	11–20 66–75 95	Safety and training		20–21 right: excellent 18–19 right: good 16–17 right: fair Under 16 right: poor
3	21–30 76–85 90	Management		20–21 right: excellent 18–19 right: good 16–17 right: fair Under 16 right: poor
4	31–40 86–89	Community relations		14 right: excellent 13 right: good 12 right: fair Under 12 right: poor
5	41–50 91–94	Patrol operations		14 right: excellent 13 right: good 12 right: fair Under 12 right: poor
6	51–56	Report writing		6 right: excellent 5 right: good Under 5 right: poor

If you are weak in Section 1, then concentrate on Chapter 5.
If you are weak in Section 2, then concentrate on Chapter 6.
If you are weak in Section 3, then concentrate on Chapter 7.
If you are weak in Section 4, then concentrate on Chapter 8.
If you are weak in Section 5, then concentrate on Chapter 9.
If you are weak in Section 6, then concentrate on Chapter 10.

Note: Consider yourself weak in a section if you receive other than an excellent rating in it.

Answer Explanations

1. **B** Here we once again see the need for objective actions on the part of the supervisor. Inconsistency almost always creates resentment and claims of favoritism.

2. **A** Once someone understands the why of an order, compliance follows more readily. Except in limited situations, such as an emergency, the purpose of orders should be explained to those who are going to carry them out.

3. **C** Establishment of need is the first step in the order-giving process. A sergeant should never delegate all responsibilities—the disciplinary maintenance role, for example—and fewer details in orders to inexperienced workers mean closer supervision is necessary.

4. **C** Overuse of definite orders creates resentment and damages morale, so statement 1 is not accurate. When a sergeant gives an order, it should seem to come from the sergeant, so statement 2 is not accurate.

5. **A** The need for the order, once clarified, generates more interest in the order, especially in a call for volunteers. Remember, however, that explaining the "why" of an order is not recommended in emergency situations when time is of the essence.

6. **B** Because of his experience, the experienced worker would know what to do. It would be unfair to give an implied order to an inexperienced worker who would not recognize what was being implied by the sergeant.

7. **D** The situation in choice D would best be handled by a call for volunteers.

8. **D** Motives are broader than incentives; usually incentives, which come from outside an individual, are used to satisfy an individual's motives, which come from inside an individual.

9. **A** Inspiring workers by personal example is the best way for a supervisor to gain compliance and thereby limit the need for displaying authority. Remember, standardized penalties are frowned upon since punishment should be levied according to the facts in each specific situation.

10. **A** A supervisor who does not delegate work is indeed a poor leader. When properly used, delegation benefits the worker, the de-

partment, and the supervisor. The actions indicated in the other choices are all indicative of good leadership.

11. **D** Three-dimensional aids are excellent in teaching field tactics and operations in the classroom. Because the objects are moveable, the individual student is given a chance to use his/her judgment or apply the principles being learned to hypothetical situations in a realistic setting.

12. **D** It builds a worker's confidence when you move from the known to the unknown and also facilitates the learning process.

13. **D** Training is ongoing, especially in the police field, where the work is influenced by the dynamic nature of society. It must be noted, however, that the training needs of rookies and veterans are different.

14. **D** There are four steps in teaching, and the testing step exerts the most control in the learning process. In sequential order the steps are:

(1) Preparation of the student
(2) Presentation of the material
(3) Application performed by the student
(4) Testing of the student by the instructor

At times the application step is performed in conjunction with the testing step. It is the testing step that tells the student and the instructor how well the student is doing.

15. **B** In a lecture, there is very little two-way communication. Conferences and seminars are where a great deal of instructor-student exchange occurs.

16. **A** Training is one of the most important supervisory activities of a patrol sergeant, and it is an ongoing responsibility, not periodic.

17. **D** The prevention of accidents is the purpose of personnel accident investigations; they are not conducted solely to blame some person.

18. **D** When a learner fails to learn, it could also indicate that poor teaching might have occurred.

19. **B** A major component of the sergeant's role is the training and development of police officers. This training can be in a formal or informal setting when the sergeant conducts it.

20. **B** The training need must clearly exist and must be addressed. This, as in planning, must exist first since if no need exists, then why should the training take place?

21. **C** A budget is a fiscal plan, but is a very personal plan. It is for and all about one agency. Looking elsewhere would uncover responses to needs your agency may not have. Other commanders could be queried, as well as staff units, such as inspections units, but that all comes later. The first step should be to look at last year's budget.

22. **C** Critically analyzing or reviewing personnel, their performance, and their use of material are the primary factors that determine if the job is being done correctly. This is the essence of the control function.

23. **A** Coordination between units cannot happen by ordering it to happen, nor by constant intervention. The supervisor's best course of action in this case is to set the tone for cooperation and then let it happen.

24. **A** When specialization occurs, members begin to feel they are not part of the department and their efforts are for their own objectives, whereas in reality their efforts must be coordinated with the rest of the department toward the achievement of common goals and objectives.

25. **A** Just because a central planning unit is formed, it doesn't relieve the first-time supervisor of planning responsibilities.

26. **C** More meticulous plans are required for personnel at the operation level, where very specific directions are needed for carrying out tasks so that the intended goals are attained.

27. **A** The use of decentralized station houses throughout a geographic area is primarily a convenience to the police; although it is an organizational arrangement that sometimes has great community relations value, this wasn't mentioned as a choice. Remember, the great majority of requests for police service are made by telephone. Most of the other requests are made through direct notification of the officer on patrol. Very few people walk into the station house to request service. Decentralized station houses require a greater expenditure of labor and other resources, not less. Finally, decentralization has little to do with response time or crime prevention.

28. **C** When workers are thwarted by an outdated organization chart, they establish informal relationships to get their jobs done. Dotted lines should never be used on an organization chart.

29. **A** The supervisor's span of control increases when levels are removed from the police organization. This is an obvious result. The operations level would never be removed, so the level removed will always be a supervisory level. With fewer supervisors, the span of control of the remaining supervisors must increase.

30. D There is no need to repair something that is working well. There should not be organizational change just for the sake of change.

31. B In the order maintenance role there are fewer arrests and large amounts of discretion and foot patrol, but because of the heavy discretionary powers the potential for corruption exists.

32. C As stated in Chapter 5, people have a natural tendency to resist change. When a new program requires organizational changes, resistance will emerge.

33. D The police have come to realize that the discretion inherent in the order maintenance model must be mixed with the service model concept.

34. D This presents a particular problem for the police, who are left to decide the norms of behavior in this setting.

35. A The police agency is one of the few organizations where this occurs. This is because the typical police officer on post works virtually alone and unsupervised and is faced with an endless array of choices in dealing with problems.

36. A Experts have indicated that violent crime is a favorite of those in the print media. This can be explained by the commercial nature of their end product. In short, sensationalism sells newspapers.

37. C There can be no community relations without the police truly getting involved in the community.

38. C Different views of the community are a function of the service provided and the problems presented. No one knows better the frustration of an uncooperative citizenry than a detective attempting to solve a case.

39. B By its very nature, police-community relations is a two-way communication process.

40. A When the police act in a vacuum and do not involve the community, then community relations will fail.

41. C Officers involved in decoy operations attempt to intercept ongoing criminal acts or those that have just been committed.

42. C The traits of high visibility are usually a distinguishable uniform, which is viewed by large numbers of people while conducting their daily routines.

43. **D** Actually, the use of a conspicuously marked police vehicle makes it more difficult to *detect* violators of the traffic laws since only the most flagrant violators will break the law when it is obvious that a police vehicle is in the vicinity. Choices A, B, and C are all accurately stated effects of the use of conspicuously marked police vehicles.

44. **C** Bicycle patrol is inexpensive and a good supplement to other forms of patrol in the areas enumerated in statement 3.

45. **C** Merchants would still enjoy this service, which represents a costly expenditure of police time and resources and is generally ineffective.

46. **D** It is unrealistic for the sergeant to supervise officers in patrol cars while on foot.

47. **B** The worst part of specialization is that it draws so much from the first line of defense, the patrol force. In addition, specialization usually takes the best officers out of patrol. Concerning choice D, it is not necessary for a supervisor to possess the same level of expertise as those he/she supervises, although a good working knowledge of the specialty area is most helpful.

48. **B** The accepted worker is a more willing worker. Although a totally negative supervisory climate is not the answer, neither is a climate of trial and error, which to say the least is extremely expensive.

49. **B** The greatest impression of all the police emanates from the result of direct contacts with individual officers.

50. **C** Remember, the patrol function is the backbone of the police operation. For one thing, patrol acts as the eyes and ears of all specialized units. If the patrol division is ineffective, all other line units suffer.

51. **D** Possibly the best example unfortunately continues to be rape, which is traditionally the most underreported index crime. People are reluctant to report crimes for a number of reasons, such as fear of reprisal, distrust of the police, the belief that there is nothing the police can do, and a reluctance to get involved in the system.

52. **C** It is the duty of an agency, although costly, to thoroughly police itself. Anonymous tips often contain good information and should be acted upon.

53. **C** By knowing the location of previous accidents, police enforcement efforts to prevent accidents can be concentrated at those locations. This is an example of selective enforcement of traffic laws.

54. **B** In the "one-write" system, the officer writes the report once in longhand. There is no retyping; hence it is quick and economical. Several police agencies are currently experimenting with this system.

55. **B** A centralized records division is not just a repository for records. It is a location where the work of the entire agency comes together and can be measured.

56. **C** The purpose of records and reports in traffic cases is to assist the police in directing traffic, investigating accidents, and enforcing laws, which are all aimed at reducing accidents and congestion.

57. **D** Broad policy guidelines are set at the top of the organization. It is the patrol supervisor's job to transform these broad policies into productive work.

58. **B** When the formal style of the official leader is laissez-faire, unofficial leaders emerge to fill the gap created by the let-alone philosophy of the official leader.

59. **C** More and more, experts are realizing the benefit of a sense of humor when engaged in the supervisory process. On the other hand, unclear orders and a lack of consistency creates confusion in the minds of subordinates. Lastly, objective assignments should be made after considering the needs of the assignment and the qualifications of the worker.

60. **B** This is a good working definition of high morale. Note that good morale and high job satisfaction do not always occur together. In addition, a work setting does not have to be free of all frustrations in order to be a setting where high morale exists.

61. **D** The pace of the upward flow of information is important to morale because management must be kept aware of the feelings and conditions at the level of operations. In this way morale will not be damaged by broad policies that are not based on accurate statements of conditions at the operating level.

62. **B** If the employee believes a grievance is important, it is important enough to be entertained.

63. **C** Employees will endure many things in connection with a disciplinary system, but they will not accept a system that is not applied consistently.

64. **A** Grievances, real or imagined, will always exist in an agency. Simply because they are not being verbalized is no proof that they do not exist; rather the boss is probably seen as having a "closed door" and "closed mind."

65. A It is part of the sergeant's job to assist an employee during the entire grievance procedure; this includes assisting an officer who wants to appeal a finding by the supervisor.

66. C It is important that the employee be put at ease during a training session. As indicated here, getting the employee to correct his own mistakes helps create a sense of control by the employee and contributes toward a more relaxed atmosphere.

67. D Only with real leadership can a safety program realize its goals; therefore, the first requirement is selecting a suitable person to be in charge. The proper selection sends a signal to the rest of the department that the drive is not just lip service to safety education. The decisions involving the goals, targets, and duration of the drive then follow.

68. C Some supervisors say if the old style was good enough to be used on me, I will use it too. They simply refuse to accept the many leadership principles which have been successfully adopted and found to be useful in both police and non-police agencies.

69. D The concept of having standards for training mandated by the individual states has led to more and improved training and the adoption of standards by many more police departments but has not led to greater use of lateral entry among police of different states.

70. D Job classifications identifies the duties of a job with an eye towards establishing appropriate salaries for the job. A job analysis, on the other hand, states the knowledge, skills and abilities necessary for the job, while also streamlining the job and removing routine tasks from it which can be given to newly created or existing lower level positions.

71. B Repetition is truly the mark of learning. Having a brief review of the previous lecture before the current lecture is a good idea.

72. B Because the top officials of a department usually move up through the ranks, few have the needed expertise for wide reaching productivity changes even though there is interest in the subject and target areas have been identified.

73. B Experts have held that in the area of firearms use, it is best to move from the safe to the hazardous aspects of the subject.

74. B While all of these aspects of management could be improved, the leading need lies with safety and accident prevention. Actually, if closely examined, it would soon become apparent that enormous gains can be achieved for the agency through a successful safety and accident prevention program.

75. C There is no guarantee that all those in attendance will participate. As a matter of fact, it calls for a skillful conference leader to attempt to gain the participation of those attending a conference.

76. B Coordination is easier in a well-structured organization. Constant supervisory intervention is not recommended because, among other things, it causes severe employee resentment.

77. B The sergeant must make sure he is understood when communicating. The point here is that if the police officer did not understand, he cannot be held responsible. It is the sergeant's job to make sure the officer understands. The best way for the sergeant to verify understanding is by having the officer paraphrase the instructions back to the sergeant.

78. B Evaluations should measure the present and not the past. If, however, a supervisor is new to the command, he should confer with the employee's previous supervisor who supervised the employee during some part of the current evaluation period.

79. B For the most part, the police officer on patrol is unsupervised. For the purpose of obtaining an accurate performance evaluation, this is unfortunate since the more contacts between a sergeant and subordinate, the better the chance for a meaningful evaluation.

80. D This occurs when a supervisor erroneously believes two different traits are the same and gives the subordinate the same rating in both these traits. He "associates" one trait with the other and commits the rating error known as association.

81. B The sergeant cannot ignore the officer nor his personality and at times a firm, direct approach is needed to set the tone for the present and, even more importantly, for future communications.

82. A Fear of criticism will motivate a subordinate to avoid making firm, positive statements. The subordinate will avoid being able to be pinned down, thereby making the supervisor's job of getting information through the communication process more difficult.

83. D This is a very difficult question. Statement 1 is true as it states accurately that the objectives of a communication must always be considered in the mind of a communicator before he/she communicates. If this was not true, then the old adage "you don't know what you are talking about" would be appropriate. Even in an emergency this guideline holds true. Of course, in an emergency, the length of the consideration would many times be "just for an instant." Contrary to the general rule, however, the feelings of the receiver of a communication do not always have to be considered, nor does a positive aspect always have to be included in a communication. An obvious exception in both of these cases would be in an emergency situation.

84. **D** If the benefits are explained and understood, compliance will follow more easily and readily. To simply announce an unpopular operation or to indicate that orders must be obeyed strongly hints that even the supervisor does not fully support the unpopular procedure.

85. **C** Filtering is a fact of communication. It can be controlled but not eliminated even in the best of police departments with the best communication processes.

86. **B** Less than ten percent of the work of the police involves activities of this type.

87. **C** For example, if there were no laws against gambling, it would not be illegal. So in a sense, the police are not making a group of people (those who gamble) potential criminals. Victimless crimes are said to be *mala prohibita* crimes, which means they are bad or evil only because they have been prohibited by society. This is in contrast to *mala in se* crimes, which are evil in themselves. Typical *mala in se* crimes are homicide, robbery, forcible rape, and assault.

88. **C** Usually with tabloid thinking, time is not spent to understand the real issues. Obviously, drug addicts are not the reason for all crime. It is very difficult to communicate facts to someone who will tend to block your communication efforts regardless of how accurate your facts may be.

89. **D** It is these two groups who dictate policy and even supervise police activities. Through the process of judicial review, the courts exercise control over police procedures.

90. **B** The first-line supervisor performs the same kinds of tasks and has the same kinds of responsibilities as any other ranking officer in the department, but there is a difference in degree, or how often they both perform each of the various supervisory functions.

91. **C** The officers involved at any given time may leave the post because of transfer or promotion, but the post remains long afterward. Choices A, B, and D all describe important factors in the development of a beat or post.

92. **B** After greeting the citizen, the officer should explain the reason for the stop and the intended action. This is to prevent irregularities and to avoid a debate between the citizen and the officer.

93. **D** Choices A, B, and C are all "kinds" of patrol that are all different in purpose. Choice D indicates horse patrol, which is a "type" of patrol and indicates how the kinds of patrol will be performed.

94. **D** Choices A, B, and C are advantages of scooter patrol over foot patrol. Choice D, however, is not an advantage. A scooter should not be used to chase other vehicles. It's too dangerous.

95. **A** Trial and error is expensive, slow, and wasteful. It should never be used in emergency situations, when there is obviously no room for error.

96. **B** Remember: praise in public; reprimand in private. At the sergeant's rank you almost certainly will get a question in this area on your examination.

97. **C** The investigation would be more objective when done by a staff unit. However, there is no guarantee that the level of competence is always greater in a staff unit.

98. **B** The sergeant should not be thinking of a penalty in this situation since it is still an alleged violation. Also, there is no need to serve a written summary since the process has not proceeded that far yet.

99. **C** The sergeant cannot delegate away the planning function. He/she can and should involve subordinates in the development of plans, but the actual planning function cannot be delegated.

100. **B** The tightrope comes from the ambivalent role of the sergeant.

Answer Sheet
Practice Examination Three

Follow the instructions given in the text. Mark only your answers in the ovals below.

Warning: Be sure that the oval you fill is in the same row as the question you are answering. Use a No. 2 pencil (soft pencil).

Be sure your pencil marks are heavy and black. Erase completely any answer you wish to change.

Do *not* make stray pencil dots, dashes, or marks.

To remove please cut along dotted line

1 Ⓐ Ⓑ Ⓒ Ⓓ	2 Ⓐ Ⓑ Ⓒ Ⓓ	3 Ⓐ Ⓑ Ⓒ Ⓓ	4 Ⓐ Ⓑ Ⓒ Ⓓ	5 Ⓐ Ⓑ Ⓒ Ⓓ	6 Ⓐ Ⓑ Ⓒ Ⓓ
7 Ⓐ Ⓑ Ⓒ Ⓓ	8 Ⓐ Ⓑ Ⓒ Ⓓ	9 Ⓐ Ⓑ Ⓒ Ⓓ	10 Ⓐ Ⓑ Ⓒ Ⓓ	11 Ⓐ Ⓑ Ⓒ Ⓓ	12 Ⓐ Ⓑ Ⓒ Ⓓ
13 Ⓐ Ⓑ Ⓒ Ⓓ	14 Ⓐ Ⓑ Ⓒ Ⓓ	15 Ⓐ Ⓑ Ⓒ Ⓓ	16 Ⓐ Ⓑ Ⓒ Ⓓ	17 Ⓐ Ⓑ Ⓒ Ⓓ	18 Ⓐ Ⓑ Ⓒ Ⓓ
19 Ⓐ Ⓑ Ⓒ Ⓓ	20 Ⓐ Ⓑ Ⓒ Ⓓ	21 Ⓐ Ⓑ Ⓒ Ⓓ	22 Ⓐ Ⓑ Ⓒ Ⓓ	23 Ⓐ Ⓑ Ⓒ Ⓓ	24 Ⓐ Ⓑ Ⓒ Ⓓ
25 Ⓐ Ⓑ Ⓒ Ⓓ	26 Ⓐ Ⓑ Ⓒ Ⓓ	27 Ⓐ Ⓑ Ⓒ Ⓓ	28 Ⓐ Ⓑ Ⓒ Ⓓ	29 Ⓐ Ⓑ Ⓒ Ⓓ	30 Ⓐ Ⓑ Ⓒ Ⓓ
31 Ⓐ Ⓑ Ⓒ Ⓓ	32 Ⓐ Ⓑ Ⓒ Ⓓ	33 Ⓐ Ⓑ Ⓒ Ⓓ	34 Ⓐ Ⓑ Ⓒ Ⓓ	35 Ⓐ Ⓑ Ⓒ Ⓓ	36 Ⓐ Ⓑ Ⓒ Ⓓ
37 Ⓐ Ⓑ Ⓒ Ⓓ	38 Ⓐ Ⓑ Ⓒ Ⓓ	39 Ⓐ Ⓑ Ⓒ Ⓓ	40 Ⓐ Ⓑ Ⓒ Ⓓ	41 Ⓐ Ⓑ Ⓒ Ⓓ	42 Ⓐ Ⓑ Ⓒ Ⓓ
43 Ⓐ Ⓑ Ⓒ Ⓓ	44 Ⓐ Ⓑ Ⓒ Ⓓ	45 Ⓐ Ⓑ Ⓒ Ⓓ	46 Ⓐ Ⓑ Ⓒ Ⓓ	47 Ⓐ Ⓑ Ⓒ Ⓓ	48 Ⓐ Ⓑ Ⓒ Ⓓ
49 Ⓐ Ⓑ Ⓒ Ⓓ	50 Ⓐ Ⓑ Ⓒ Ⓓ	51 Ⓐ Ⓑ Ⓒ Ⓓ	52 Ⓐ Ⓑ Ⓒ Ⓓ	53 Ⓐ Ⓑ Ⓒ Ⓓ	54 Ⓐ Ⓑ Ⓒ Ⓓ
55 Ⓐ Ⓑ Ⓒ Ⓓ	56 Ⓐ Ⓑ Ⓒ Ⓓ	57 Ⓐ Ⓑ Ⓒ Ⓓ	58 Ⓐ Ⓑ Ⓒ Ⓓ	59 Ⓐ Ⓑ Ⓒ Ⓓ	60 Ⓐ Ⓑ Ⓒ Ⓓ
61 Ⓐ Ⓑ Ⓒ Ⓓ	62 Ⓐ Ⓑ Ⓒ Ⓓ	63 Ⓐ Ⓑ Ⓒ Ⓓ	64 Ⓐ Ⓑ Ⓒ Ⓓ	65 Ⓐ Ⓑ Ⓒ Ⓓ	66 Ⓐ Ⓑ Ⓒ Ⓓ
67 Ⓐ Ⓑ Ⓒ Ⓓ	68 Ⓐ Ⓑ Ⓒ Ⓓ	69 Ⓐ Ⓑ Ⓒ Ⓓ	70 Ⓐ Ⓑ Ⓒ Ⓓ	71 Ⓐ Ⓑ Ⓒ Ⓓ	72 Ⓐ Ⓑ Ⓒ Ⓓ
73 Ⓐ Ⓑ Ⓒ Ⓓ	74 Ⓐ Ⓑ Ⓒ Ⓓ	75 Ⓐ Ⓑ Ⓒ Ⓓ	76 Ⓐ Ⓑ Ⓒ Ⓓ	77 Ⓐ Ⓑ Ⓒ Ⓓ	78 Ⓐ Ⓑ Ⓒ Ⓓ
79 Ⓐ Ⓑ Ⓒ Ⓓ	80 Ⓐ Ⓑ Ⓒ Ⓓ	81 Ⓐ Ⓑ Ⓒ Ⓓ	82 Ⓐ Ⓑ Ⓒ Ⓓ	83 Ⓐ Ⓑ Ⓒ Ⓓ	84 Ⓐ Ⓑ Ⓒ Ⓓ
85 Ⓐ Ⓑ Ⓒ Ⓓ	86 Ⓐ Ⓑ Ⓒ Ⓓ	87 Ⓐ Ⓑ Ⓒ Ⓓ	88 Ⓐ Ⓑ Ⓒ Ⓓ	89 Ⓐ Ⓑ Ⓒ Ⓓ	90 Ⓐ Ⓑ Ⓒ Ⓓ
91 Ⓐ Ⓑ Ⓒ Ⓓ	92 Ⓐ Ⓑ Ⓒ Ⓓ	93 Ⓐ Ⓑ Ⓒ Ⓓ	94 Ⓐ Ⓑ Ⓒ Ⓓ	95 Ⓐ Ⓑ Ⓒ Ⓓ	96 Ⓐ Ⓑ Ⓒ Ⓓ
97 Ⓐ Ⓑ Ⓒ Ⓓ	98 Ⓐ Ⓑ Ⓒ Ⓓ	99 Ⓐ Ⓑ Ⓒ Ⓓ	100 Ⓐ Ⓑ Ⓒ Ⓓ	101 Ⓐ Ⓑ Ⓒ Ⓓ	102 Ⓐ Ⓑ Ⓒ Ⓓ
103 Ⓐ Ⓑ Ⓒ Ⓓ	104 Ⓐ Ⓑ Ⓒ Ⓓ	105 Ⓐ Ⓑ Ⓒ Ⓓ	106 Ⓐ Ⓑ Ⓒ Ⓓ	107 Ⓐ Ⓑ Ⓒ Ⓓ	108 Ⓐ Ⓑ Ⓒ Ⓓ
109 Ⓐ Ⓑ Ⓒ Ⓓ	110 Ⓐ Ⓑ Ⓒ Ⓓ	111 Ⓐ Ⓑ Ⓒ Ⓓ	112 Ⓐ Ⓑ Ⓒ Ⓓ	113 Ⓐ Ⓑ Ⓒ Ⓓ	114 Ⓐ Ⓑ Ⓒ Ⓓ
115 Ⓐ Ⓑ Ⓒ Ⓓ	116 Ⓐ Ⓑ Ⓒ Ⓓ	117 Ⓐ Ⓑ Ⓒ Ⓓ	118 Ⓐ Ⓑ Ⓒ Ⓓ	119 Ⓐ Ⓑ Ⓒ Ⓓ	120 Ⓐ Ⓑ Ⓒ Ⓓ
121 Ⓐ Ⓑ Ⓒ Ⓓ	122 Ⓐ Ⓑ Ⓒ Ⓓ	123 Ⓐ Ⓑ Ⓒ Ⓓ	124 Ⓐ Ⓑ Ⓒ Ⓓ	125 Ⓐ Ⓑ Ⓒ Ⓓ	126 Ⓐ Ⓑ Ⓒ Ⓓ
127 Ⓐ Ⓑ Ⓒ Ⓓ	128 Ⓐ Ⓑ Ⓒ Ⓓ	129 Ⓐ Ⓑ Ⓒ Ⓓ	130 Ⓐ Ⓑ Ⓒ Ⓓ	131 Ⓐ Ⓑ Ⓒ Ⓓ	132 Ⓐ Ⓑ Ⓒ Ⓓ
133 Ⓐ Ⓑ Ⓒ Ⓓ	134 Ⓐ Ⓑ Ⓒ Ⓓ	135 Ⓐ Ⓑ Ⓒ Ⓓ	136 Ⓐ Ⓑ Ⓒ Ⓓ	137 Ⓐ Ⓑ Ⓒ Ⓓ	138 Ⓐ Ⓑ Ⓒ Ⓓ
139 Ⓐ Ⓑ Ⓒ Ⓓ	140 Ⓐ Ⓑ Ⓒ Ⓓ	141 Ⓐ Ⓑ Ⓒ Ⓓ	142 Ⓐ Ⓑ Ⓒ Ⓓ	143 Ⓐ Ⓑ Ⓒ Ⓓ	144 Ⓐ Ⓑ Ⓒ Ⓓ
145 Ⓐ Ⓑ Ⓒ Ⓓ	146 Ⓐ Ⓑ Ⓒ Ⓓ	147 Ⓐ Ⓑ Ⓒ Ⓓ	148 Ⓐ Ⓑ Ⓒ Ⓓ	149 Ⓐ Ⓑ Ⓒ Ⓓ	150 Ⓐ Ⓑ Ⓒ Ⓓ

CHAPTER 15

Practice Examination Three

The Test

100 QUESTIONS—3½ HOURS

1. Consider the following statements concerning the use of punishment as part of the disciplinary process:

    (1) Punishment is not an effective deterrent unless there is a feeling of certainty among employees that wrongdoing will be uncovered and those responsible will be punished appropriately.

    (2) When punishment is necessary, it must be applied swiftly.

    (3) The effectiveness of punishment is always dependent upon the severity of the punishment.

    Which of the following most correctly classifies the above statements into those which are accurate and those which are not?

    A. Statements 1 and 2 are accurate; 3 is inaccurate.
    B. Statements 1 and 3 are accurate; 2 is inaccurate.
    C. Statements 2 and 3 are accurate; 1 is inaccurate.
    D. All of the statements are accurate.

2. Which of the following supervisors is not following accepted principles of good leadership?

    A. One who always backs up his/her subordinates
    B. One who always finds time to get to know his/her subordinates
    C. One who always leads by personal example
    D. One who is always interested in developing his/her subordinates

3. A police officer approaches her supervisor and asks for counseling concerning a personal problem. In this situation, the supervisor should:
   A. Tell the officer exactly how to handle the problem
   B. Help the officer find her own solution to the problem
   C. Refuse to offer any advice since the problem is not job related
   D. Ask the officer to put her problem in writing

4. The major responsibility for administering both positive and negative discipline in a police agency belongs to:
   A. The police chief
   B. Immediate line supervisors
   C. Commanding officers
   D. Staff officers

5. The essence of positive discipline is:
   A. Punishment
   B. Training and counseling
   C. Fear
   D. Submission

6. A newly promoted sergeant approaches a veteran supervisor and asks for advice concerning what types of orders should be given to subordinates. The veteran sergeant would be most correct if he responded by saying that the type of order given to an individual should depend mostly on:
   A. The leadership style of the supervisor issuing the order
   B. The situation and on the attributes of the individual
   C. The experience of the supervisor
   D. The nature of the job to be done

7. Sergeant Rems is issuing an order to one of her subordinates. The best way for her to make sure that the order receiver understands the order is for her to:
   A. Ask the subordinate if he understands
   B. Repeat the order to the subordinate at least twice
   C. Present the order to the subordinate in writing
   D. Have the order receiver repeat the order in his own words

8. Implied orders are useful tools for:
   A. Handling emergencies
   B. Dealing with lazy workers
   C. Dealing with inexperienced officers
   D. Developing the initiative and judgment of officers

9. Sergeant Rems is approached by a subordinate who presents the sergeant with a grievance about working conditions. The sergeant believes the grievance is a trivial one and says so to the subordinate. In this situation the sergeant acted:
   A. Correctly, since valuable supervisory time should not be spent resolving trivial grievances
   B. Incorrectly, since all grievances must be handled exactly the same
   C. Correctly, since to act otherwise could prompt a flood of trivial grievances
   D. Incorrectly, since the grievance is important in the mind of the officer

10. Sergeant Rems is talking to Sergeant Ginty. Rems states that his subordinates make grievances to him on a fairly regular basis. Ginty states that his subordinates almost never bring grievances to him and adds that this means that he is doing a good job since his subordinates don't seem to have any grievances. Sergeant Ginty's statement is most probably:
    A. Correct, since a lack of grievances can always be taken as a sign of good supervision
    B. Incorrect, since supervisors who almost never have grievances brought to them are probably thought by the workers to be unapproachable
    C. Correct, since workers are reluctant to bring grievances to supervisors who they think are doing a good job
    D. Incorrect, since a lack of worker grievances is the norm

11. Which of the following is the most accurate statement concerning the delegation process?
    A. Every employee in an organization can delegate away a portion of their authority.
    B. A task must be delegated in its entirety.
    C. A first line supervisor must delegate authority in order to function effectively.
    D. Every supervisory task is amenable to the delegation process.

12. Consider the following statements concerning the delegation process:
    (1) It prevents slowdowns in services.
    (2) It allows supervisors to spend more time on such things as training and planning.
    (3) It increases the skills of subordinates.
    Which of the following most correctly classifies the above statements into those which are accurate and those which are not?
    A. Statements 1 and 2 are accurate; 3 is inaccurate.
    B. Statements 1 and 3 are accurate; 2 is inaccurate.
    C. Statements 2 and 3 are accurate; 1 is inaccurate.
    D. All of the statements are accurate.

13. When a task is delegated, the final responsibility for that task:
    A. Belongs to the person who performs the task
    B. Is shared by the person doing the task and the supervisor who made the delegation
    C. Is maintained by the supervisor who made the delegation
    D. May or may not rest with the supervisor who made the delegation

14. Supervisors must:
    A. Reduce all delegations to writing
    B. State all delegations in general terms
    C. Follow up on all delegations
    D. Delegate only to subordinates and peers

15. Which of the following is not a recommended strategy for a supervisor to follow to build and maintain worker morale?
    A. Give most work assignments primarily to willing workers
    B. Praise workers in public but criticize them in private
    C. Administer discipline in a fair and impartial manner
    D. Provide employees with an opportunity for individual growth

16. In connection with training, which of the following statements is least correct?
    A. Training is an ongoing event.
    B. Unless what is learned from training is applicable to what is required on the job, the training effort has been of little value.

C. Even though an instructor is an expert in his/her field, the trainee still must play an active role in the training for real training to take place.

D. Training does not do much to shape attitudes.

17. Which of the following is usually the result of an effective agency training program?
A. A high turnover of personnel because trained employees leave the agency to seek better jobs
B. An increase in the number of grievances filed
C. Lower morale because employees are required to learn more
D. Increased safety

18. If subordinates are well trained, then there is less need for immediate and constant supervision because:
A. Supervision is no longer needed
B. The employees will take over the supervisor's job and become the supervisor
C. The supervisor is not brought into tasks that are able to be done by subordinates
D. Supervisory tasks such as planning and following-up will be eliminated

19. Which of the following is the least accurate statement concerning training?
A. Training increases feelings of insecurity among employees because they feel pressured to learn new things.
B. Trained workers become more productive because unnecessary waste of time, effort, and materials is reduced.
C. Trained workers often become more motivated because they come to rely less and less on the agency for their self improvement.
D. Trained workers go beyond what is routinely expected from them because they become more confident in the performance of their jobs.

20. Which of the following is the first step in devising and conducting a training program?
A. Establishing the goals of the program
B. Evaluating the program
C. Discovering training needs
D. Developing the training program

21. The most serious problem associated with train-
    ing is:
    A. Trainers checking for understanding inappro-
       priately by merely asking trainees if they un-
       derstand
    B. Supervisors who maintain that training is
       not a supervisor's job, and who have no time
       for it because the department has a central
       training division
    C. Overqualified trainers who intimidate the
       students and are considered unapproachable
    D. Paranoia on the part of trainers who feel that
       if too much information is given out then the
       trainees will be able to pass the trainers in
       the organization

22. Evaluate the following statements:
    (1) Training is a process.
    (2) Training is given only for the purpose of
        helping workers in their present job.
    Which of the following is most accurate concern-
    ing the statements above?
    A. Only statement 1 is correct.
    B. Only statement 2 is correct.
    C. Both statements 1 and 2 are correct.
    D. Neither statement 1 nor 2 is correct.

23. If Sergeant Bob Rays properly conducts a training
    program, then which of the following is least
    likely to result?
    A. He will get to know his subordinates better.
    B. His potential for promotion will increase.
    C. He will be keeping abreast of the latest devel-
       opments in the area being taught.
    D. A more dangerous workplace will evolve be-
       cause workers will become overly confident in
       their work and take unnecessary chances.

24. Probably the most important trait for a supervi-
    sor to possess as a trainer is:
    A. The ability to train
    B. A status as a knowledgeable trainer
    C. Knowledge of the job
    D. A willingness to train

25. Sergeant Mary Rems wants to motivate a group
    of officers she is about to train. In such an in-
    stance, the sergeant would be most correct if she:

A. Told the officers that they should not find the training material too difficult
B. Informed the officers how the training will personally benefit them in their present jobs
C. Convinced the officers that the material about to be taught represents the latest state-of-the-art information in the field
D. Impressed the officers with her own personal credentials

26. Regarding the process of learning, which of the following is most correct?
A. People learn at different rates of speed.
B. Effective learning should require using only one of the senses.
C. Information dealing with a subject that the trainee has only slightly been exposed to will be remembered for a long period of time by the trainee.
D. The environment in which a training session takes place has little or no impact on the learning process.

27. The most common mistake made by trainers when demonstrating an operation or procedure is:
A. To assume the trainees know more than they really do
B. Not being able to think on their feet
C. Being too much of an expert to deal with the trainees
D. Not properly checking for understanding

28. There is a feeling in some police departments that because an employee passes an examination, that employee will automatically be skilled at being a supervisor. Actually nothing could be farther from the truth. Therefore in response to this situation, some enlightened police departments conduct:
A. Shift training
B. In-service training
C. Command course training
D. Specialized training

29. Sergeant Frank Rems is about to set up a training program. Regarding the goals of such a training program, it would be least correct to state that the goals of the training program should:

A. Be stated in general terms so that they may be easily reached by the trainees
B. Be identified before the program begins
C. Seek to have the trainee perform the job under conditions similar to those under which the trainee will be expected to operate
D. Include a description of what will actually constitute a satisfactory job

30. Consider the following statements:
   (1) Trial and error is a cheap method of training.
   (2) In training, application of what has been learned by a trainee is essential.
   (3) A lack of questions by trainees is a good barometer that always indicates learning has taken place.
   Which of the following choices best classifies the above statements into those which are accurate and those which are inaccurate?
   A. Statement 1 is accurate; statements 2 and 3 are inaccurate.
   B. Statement 2 is accurate; statements 1 and 3 are inaccurate.
   C. Statement 3 is accurate; statements 1 and 2 are inaccurate.
   D. None of the statements is accurate.

31. When communicating, a supervisor should empathize with the recipient of the communication. This is true in all of the following situations except:
   A. When dealing with an emergency
   B. When disciplining a subordinate
   C. When dealing with the public
   D. When counseling a worker

32. Filtering of communications occurs when a subordinate tries to shield a supervisor from negative information. Concerning the filtering process, a supervisor should:
   A. Ignore it
   B. Eliminate it
   C. Be aware that it will occur and try to minimize its frequency and impact
   D. Identify the major offenders and make sure they are appropriately disciplined

33. A newly appointed supervisor approaches Sergeant Rems, who is a veteran supervisor, and inquires as to the best way to deal with rumors.

Sergeant Rems would be most correct if he replied by saying that the remedy for rumors is
A. Discipline   C. Experience
B. Training   D. Truth

34. While clarity of communications is always a desirable goal, it is essential in written communications. This is so because:
A. Written communications are always more important than communications made orally
B. Readers often do not have the face-to-face opportunity to clarify the meaning of written communications
C. Of the permanency of written communications
D. It is so much easier to communicate in writing

35. Which of the following is the least correct statement concerning performance evaluations?
A. The rating of employees should done on a continuous basis.
B. Careless errors on performance evaluations can have serious consequences.
C. Rating traits must be job related if they are to have any validity.
D. A worker's previous evaluation should be the critical factor in a current performance evaluation.

36. The first step in the planning process is to:
A. Determine the objectives of the plan
B. Establish the need for the plan
C. Decide what resources are required
D. Implement a control mechanism

37. The principle of unity of command requires that every worker be under the direct command and supervision of only one ranking officer. If this principle is violated without justification, it results in confusion among workers and the possibility of a conflicting direction being given. A ranking officer is justified in violating the principle of unity of command in two instances. The first is when there is an emergency situation, and the second is when:
A. The reputation of the department is at stake
B. Disciplinary action is required
C. A worker has need for guidance
D. A worker has a personal problem

38. The principle of span of control refers to the number of workers that can be effectively supervised by one supervisor. Which of the following is the most accurate statement concerning the optimal span of control at the operational level in a police agency?
    A. The optimal span of control is six workers to one supervisor.
    B. The optimal span of control is eight workers to one supervisor.
    C. The optimal span of control is ten workers to one supervisor.
    D. There is no optimal span of control.

39. If there is no formal evaluation system in a police agency, supervisors in that agency:
    A. Have no personnel evaluation responsibilities
    B. Should only periodically rate subordinates
    C. Should rate subordinates on a continuous basis
    D. May or may not have personnel evaluation responsibilities

40. The tendency of a rater to evaluate personnel more favorably than deserved:
    A. Is very seldom encountered in a police agency
    B. Never occurs in a police agency
    C. Occurs only when the rater is inexperienced
    D. Is very often the most common rating error in police agencies

41. When citizens become actually involved in police matters, which of the following usually will not occur?
    A. More crime will be reported.
    B. More witnesses will come forth.
    C. More police officers will get injured because of citizens unfortunately getting in the way.
    D. More citizens will actively engage in crime prevention.

42. Officer Day tells Sergeant Rems, he feels too much of his job does not seem to involve the enforcement of the law. Sergeant Rems should:
    A. Criticize the officer since the officer is probably just not making enough arrests
    B. Send the officer to a refresher course in the law

C. Conduct an in-depth comparison of the officer's arrest activity with the arrest activity of all the other officers in the department

D. Agree with the officer by pointing out that most of the work of a police officer does not deal with the direct enforcement of the law

43. One of the reasons why the police provide social services to people is because:
A. The traditional social agencies have failed
B. The average police officer knows it is the best way to get promoted
C. The police are trained in all the social services
D. The field police officer is able to gain peer recognition by providing such services

44. The primary or superordinate goal of the police is:
A. The arrest of all felons
B. Public cooperation
C. To provide a sense of total security to all citizens
D. Public acknowledgment

45. The maintenance of order is made easier by department policies that provide for all the following except:
A. Wide discretionary authority
B. Emphasizing the importance of arrests while maintaining an absence of arrest quotas
C. Development of a close working relationship between the police and the community
D. Decentralized command authority

46. Which of the following is characteristic of community policing?
A. Problem solving by the police using exclusively the resources of the police
B. Problem solving by the police using exclusively other than police resources
C. Problem solving by a community that actually polices itself
D. Problem solving by the police by jointly using the resources of the police and other legitimate sources

47. The main justification for community relations programs aimed at juveniles is that:
    A. Juveniles often have information regarding the criminal activities of older criminals
    B. The best way to enlist the aid of the adult members of the community is through their children
    C. The children of today represent the adult community of tomorrow
    D. All juveniles enjoy the company of the police

48. Typically, which of the following is the chief drawback of a police department's speakers bureau?
    A. Never having qualified speakers
    B. Not having timely and appropriate topics to speak about
    C. Never being accepted by any other members of the department
    D. Not being used by antagonists of the police

49. Consider the following statements concerning guidelines for accepting citizen complaints against the police.
    (1) Complaints should be received only from persons who make a complaint in person.
    (2) The best person to investigate citizen complaints against a police officer is that officer's immediate supervisor.
    (3) Anonymous citizen complaints should never be investigated.
    Which of the following choices best classifies the above statements into those which are accurate and those which are inaccurate?
    A. Statement 1 is accurate; statements 2 and 3 are inaccurate.
    B. Statement 2 is accurate; statements 1 and 3 are inaccurate.
    C. Statement 3 is accurate; statements 1 and 2 are inaccurate.
    D. None of the statements is accurate.

50. It should be recognized that the use of discretion is part of a police officer's job. Which of the following is the most accurate statement concerning the use of discretion by a police officer?
    A. As one goes down the chain of command in a police department, discretion increases.
    B. The most controversial use of discretion involves the issuing of summonses.

C. Civilian complaint review boards should help establish policy statements concerning discretion.
D. The use of discretion by police officers poses little or no problems with the community.

51. Which of the following is the principal reason why the discretionary authority of the police necessitates selective enforcement?
A. The sheer volume of the laws the police are expected to enforce
B. The resistance of the public to full enforcement of every law
C. The police must be able to forego the arrest of a petty criminal for information about a criminal who commits more serious crimes
D. The existence of many statutes that are just simply out of date and exist only to make a moral statement

52. In reality, the prevention of crime is not merely a product of police efficiency. All the following correctly support such a position except:
A. The police find it difficult to discover exactly why people commit crimes
B. Many apparent causes of crime are beyond the control of the police
C. Other parts of the criminal justice system have failed when it comes to the rehabilitation of criminals
D. The crime-fighting role has not been one most police officers enjoy

53. Sergeant April Rays has been designated the public information officer for her department. As such she should recognize that:
A. Public relations calls for two-way communication
B. A good public relations program can win support for the department's various policies and procedures
C. Public relations demands a large input from the community
D. Negative as well as positive information about the department is what truly comprises effective public relations

54. The most important person in a police department's public relations effort is:
   A. The chief of the department
   B. The officer on street patrol
   C. The department's public relations officer
   D. The first line patrol supervisor

55. A certain police department creates a special unit to deal with community relations. In such a situation, all the following are likely to result except:
   A. Specialists in community relations will be developed in the newly created special unit.
   B. Training in community relations will be facilitated through the use of the newly created special unit.
   C. A high level of esprit de corps will develop by those assigned to the newly created special unit.
   D. All members of the department will begin to do more in the area of community relations based on the importance given to the newly created special unit.

56. The pattern of patrol by a police officer engaged in preventive patrol must be:
   A. Routine   C. Random
   B. Systematic   D. Regular

57. Hidden enforcement of traffic laws occurs when an officer virtually hides from the motoring public in a secluded position to watch for a violation. Most experts agree that hidden enforcement:
   A. Has great deterrent effect
   B. Has moderate deterrent effect
   C. Is the best way to deter effect
   D. Has very little deterrent effect

58. Which of the following is an appropriate guideline for a police officer to follow when making a traffic stop?
   A. Allow the driver to save face
   B. Talk as much as possible
   C. Use the driver's first name
   D. Be judgmental

59. A newly appointed police officer approaches her supervisor, Sergeant Rems. The officer asks the sergeant if it is a good idea to make random car stops for purposes of promoting safety on the highways. The sergeant would be most correct if she responded by saying that the practice of making random car stops is:
    A. Recommended, regardless of the purpose of the stop
    B. Not recommended because, although it is legal, it is not effective
    C. Recommended, but only if the purpose of the stop is to promote safety
    D. Not recommended, since random car stops have been found to be unconstitutional

60. The first concern of a police officer investigating a traffic accident should be:
    A. The movement of traffic
    B. Determining the cause of the accident
    C. Taking enforcement action against violators
    D. The safety of all concerned

61. Which of the following is not a recommended step to take when investigating a vehicle accident?
    A. Ask everyone involved if they require medical assistance
    B. Make a general request to those present asking for witnesses
    C. Separate the motorists and examine their credentials
    D. Care for the property of the injured

62. When investigating a traffic accident, the investigating police officer must make a determination of the cause of the accident:
    A. In all cases
    B. Only if the officer personally witnessed the accident
    C. Only if the officer has impartial witnesses
    D. Only if the accident involved personal injury

63. A police officer engaged in preventive patrol can only reasonably be expected to control:
    A. Violent crimes
    B. Property crimes
    C. Street crimes
    D. Victimless crimes

64. You are a sergeant on patrol when you are notified of a high-speed pursuit involving an officer under your supervision. Concerning this high-speed pursuit, you should:
   A. Terminate it immediately regardless of the situation
   B. Make a decision whether to terminate it based on your evaluation of the possibility of apprehension
   C. Make a decision whether to terminate it based on the danger created by the pursuit as compared to the danger to the community if the vehicle is not apprehended
   D. Not even consider the possibility of terminating the pursuit

65. Which of the following is the least accurate statement concerning foot patrol?
   A. It is the most expensive type of patrol.
   B. It isolates the officer from the community.
   C. It offers minimum protection from the elements.
   D. It is more tiring than automobile patrol.

66. Sergeant Rems, a veteran police supervisor, is approached by a newly appointed police officer who asks the sergeant if it is true that decoy police operations can result in entrapment. The sergeant would be most correct if he responded by saying that:
   A. It is true that all decoy operations are a form of entrapment
   B. Entrapment occurs during a decoy operation if someone is offered an opportunity to commit a crime
   C. There is no possibility that decoy operations could result in entrapment of suspects
   D. Entrapment takes place during a decoy operation if someone is encouraged or enticed to commit a crime he/she would not ordinarily commit

67. A field command post should be established when a police incident requires the need for police operations over an extended period of time. The major purpose of a field command post is to:
   A. Serve as a point of arrival and departure for officers
   B. Offer shelter to assigned officers

C. Coordinate the operation

D. Serve as a detention facility for arrested persons

68. Sergeant Rems is given an assignment by his commanding officer to resolve a patrol problem in a certain area. For Sergeant Rems to involve the patrol officers assigned to that area in the resolution of the problem is:

A. Not appropriate, since they are too close to the problem to approach it with objectivity

B. Appropriate, since they might have some very good ideas and involving them will motivate them to do a good job

C. Not appropriate, since they might feel threatened by the fact that a problem exists in their area of responsibility

D. Appropriate, since it is an absolute rule that subordinates be involved in the resolution of all problems

69. Consider the following statements concerning preventive patrol:

(1) Officers in civilian clothes have the best chance of achieving the aims of preventive patrol.

(2) Unmarked vehicles are the best ones for officers on preventive patrol to use.

(3) Preventive patrol should be predictable.

Which of the following most correctly classifies the above statements into those which are accurate and those which are not?

A. Statement 1 is accurate; 2 and 3 are inaccurate.

B. Statement 2 is accurate; 1 and 3 are inaccurate.

C. Statement 3 is accurate; 1 and 2 are inaccurate.

D. None of the statements is accurate.

70. The goal of preventive patrol is to:

A. Take away the opportunity to successfully commit crimes

B. Take away the desire of criminals to commit crimes

C. Take away the motivation of criminals to commit crimes

D. Take away the intent of criminals to commit crimes

71. Evaluate the following statements concerning the purpose of field note taking by police officers:
    (1) It can be used to obtain a permanent record of police incidents.
    (2) It can serve as a memory bank for the preparation of reports.
    Which of the following is most accurate concerning the statements above?
    A. Only statement 1 is correct.
    B. Only statement 2 is correct.
    C. Both statements 1 and 2 are correct.
    D. Neither statement 1 nor 2 is correct.

72. Which of the following is NOT a recommended practice to be followed in connection with the use of a police field notebook?
    A. The pages should be consecutively numbered.
    B. A line should be skipped between the entries of each tour of duty.
    C. Erasures should be prohibited.
    D. There should be at least a daily inspection of an officer's field notebook by a supervisor.

73. Sergeant Carter approached a group of people standing in front of a store where a robbery has taken place. The sergeant asks the group if anyone was a witness to the robbery. The sergeant's actions were:
    A. Good, mainly because the sergeant can save time and quickly find out if anyone was a witness
    B. Bad, mainly because some of the group might be connected to the robbers and intentionally provide false leads
    C. Good, mainly because if one person offers information others will surely follow
    D. Bad, mainly because many citizens are reluctant to provide information to the police in front of other citizens

74. A certain witness is being interviewed while Sergeant Hall is taking notes. The sergeant asks a complex question that the witness does not understand. In such an instance, it would be most likely that the witness would:
    A. Answer, "I don't understand."
    B. Answer, "I don't know."
    C. Answer, "Repeat the question."
    D. Remain silent

75. Sergeant Tom Walker is instructing a newly assigned police officer in report writing. The sergeant would be most correct if he instructed the officer to always include a maximum of:
    A. Facts
    B. Recommendations
    C. Conclusions
    D. Opinions

76. In connection with the records of a police department, the police officer on patrol typically stands as:
    A. The best report writer
    B. The department's main source of statistical data
    C. The worst report writer
    D. Someone interested in only making arrests and not interested at all in making reports

77. Most experts agree that the records of a police department should be centralized and kept in one location accessible to the whole department. However, an exception to such a practice would be most proper in which of the following situations?
    A. Payroll records so that personnel information regarding individual deductions is kept private
    B. Criminal histories of recent arrests
    C. Traffic accident information
    D. Vice division records

78. Consider the following statements concerning report writing:
    (1) Information is not the same as intelligence.
    (2) One purpose of taking field notes is that they can serve later as a guide to future interviews.
    (3) People tend to say less when they see that their comments are being recorded.
    Which of the following choices best classifies the above statements into those which are accurate and those which are inaccurate?
    A. Statement 1 is inaccurate; statements 2 and 3 are accurate.
    B. Statement 2 is inaccurate; statements 1 and 3 are accurate.
    C. Statement 3 is inaccurate; statements 1 and 2 are accurate.
    D. All of the statements are accurate.

79. The principal disadvantage of a decentralized record-keeping system is:
   A. It provides a slower response than a centralized record-keeping system
   B. Record-keeping experts are not developed
   C. The possibility of less than honest reporting and record keeping exists
   D. Responsibility for record keeping is not fixed

80. Evaluate the following statements:
   (1) The accuracy needed in reporting depends more than anything else on the integrity of the field note-taking process.
   (2) A sketch of a crime scene is potentially able to take the place of reports and photographs.
   Which of the following is most accurate concerning the statements above?
   A. Only statement 1 is correct.
   B. Only statement 2 is correct.
   C. Both statements 1 and 2 are correct.
   D. Neither statement 1 nor 2 is correct.

Answer questions 81 through 84 based solely on the information that follows:

FELONY ARRESTS MADE BY POLICE OFFICERS ASSIGNED TO THE METROPOLIS POLICE DEPARTMENT

POLICE OFFICER	LAST YEAR	THIS YEAR
Ginty	20	18
Baker	10	12
Rivers	26	14
Walls	17	15
Coils	18	20
Cuffs	19	14
Tock	24	15
Bell	16	12

81. Which of the following officers had the greatest percentage increase in felony arrests when comparing this year to last year arrest record?
    A. Ginty
    B. Baker
    C. Coils
    D. Bell

82. Which of the following officers had the greatest percentage decrease in felony arrests when comparing this year to last year?
    A. Bell   C. Cuffs
    B. Tock   D. Walls

83. If all the felony arrests were added up and a comparison made between this year and last year, it would be most correct to state that there has been:
    A. A twenty percent decrease
    B. A twenty-five percent decrease
    C. A thirty percent decrease
    D. Less than a ten percent decrease

84. Which of the following officers had the greatest number of felony arrests when considering this year and last year?
    A. Ginty
    B. Baker
    C. Walls
    D. Cuffs

Answer questions 85 through 90 based solely on the following data.

INFORMATION FOR POLICE OFFICERS ON PATROL

POST	LOCATION	SUSPECTED CONDITION
Post 3	*229 Elm St.	Sale of narcotics
Post 5	*453 Elm St.	Sale of narcotics
Post 7	*125 Main St.	** Sale of narcotics
Post 9	*215 Park St.	Illegal gambling
Post 15	Elm St., 10–11 Aves.	*** Prostitution
Post 19	110–118 Oak St.	Disorderly youths
Post 20	321–329 Main Ave.	** Sale of narcotics
Post 24	Oak St., 3–9 Aves.	Auto theft
Post 27	Pine St., 2–14 Aves.	+ Drag racing
Post 29	Elm St. & 14 Ave.	++ Carjacking
Post 33	Main St., 16–18 Aves.	** Sale of firearms
Post 35	*432 Main Ave.	Sale of narcotics
Post 38	Pine St., 3–5 Aves.	Prostitution
Post 40	919 Elm St.	Sale of narcotics
Post 42	545 Main St.	Sale of contraband

LEGEND

* = Inside location

** = Exercise caution, suspects may be armed

*** = Arrests of prostitutes are to be made only after conferral with a supervisor

+ = Notify Auto Squad before taking any action if condition is observed

++ = Fixed post, assigned police officer must notify supervisor before leaving post for any reason

---

85. Before leaving post, a police officer assigned to Post 29 must:
    A. Notify a supervisor
    B. Be properly relieved
    C. Obtain permission from the desk officer
    D. Notify the radio dispatcher

86. Armed suspects would most likely be encountered:
   A. Only on Post 7
   B. Only on Post 20
   C. Only on Post 33
   D. On Posts 7, 20, and 33

87. A police officer assigned to Post 27 who observes drag racing must:
   A. Notify a supervisor
   B. Notify the auto squad
   C. Arrest those responsible
   D. Obtain immediate assistance

88. Most of the posts with suspected sale of narcotics conditions are located on:
   A. Main Street
   B. Elm Street
   C. Pine Street
   D. Oak Street

89. The sale of firearms is suspected on
   A. Post 3   C. Post 33
   B. Post 20   D. Post 40

90. On which of the following posts is suspected sale of heroin taking place?
   A. Post 3
   B. Post 33
   C. Post 40
   D. It cannot be determined from the data.

91. One of the main duties of a patrol officer is to detect or observe. Which of the following statements concerning observation by a police officer is least correct?
   A. The first step in making useful observations is to learn what is considered the usual in a given area.
   B. The ability to make useful observations is totally innate.
   C. Such things as attitudes and expectations affect the way we select, interpret, and organize our perceptions.
   D. Observation skills developed through practice can be applied to crime scenes.

92. Consider the following statements.
    (1) Surveillance involves the continuous observation of persons, places, and things.
    (2) If a police officer while walking a beat sees what is believed to be a suspicious person, the officer should stop immediately.
    (3) The main purpose of a criminal surveillance is to obtain information.

    Which of the following choices best classifies the above statements into those which are accurate and those which are inaccurate?
    A. Statement 1 is inaccurate; statements 2 and 3 are accurate.
    B. Statement 2 is inaccurate; statements 1 and 3 are accurate.
    C. Statement 3 is inaccurate; statements 1 and 2 are accurate.
    D. All of the statements are accurate.

93. Sergeant Rems is instructing a newly assigned officer concerning traffic direction duties. The sergeant would be most correct if he made which of the following statements?
    A. Politely answer any request for directions from a motorist from the middle of the intersection.
    B. The best place to direct traffic from is the sidewalk.
    C. The main objective of intersection control is to avoid spillback.
    D. If necessary to turn while directing traffic, turn in the direction opposite to the direction the vehicles are moving.

94. Which of the following police actions is recommended at the scene of a labor dispute?
    A. Avoid the use of barriers since they might be seen as being overly restrictive and thus provoke the striking workers.
    B. Make a large and constant display of physical force.
    C. Avoid arrests, if possible making them only when alternative methods are not practical.
    D. Do not offer explanations for police actions taken since it tends to diminish the authority of the police in the eyes of those at the scene.

95. Sergeant Don Fields is supervising a situation where a suspect is being taken into custody by two rookie police officers. One of the two officers taking the suspect into custody asks the sergeant for direction in how to take the suspect into custody. In this instance, the sergeant would be least correct if he made which of the following statements?
   A. Demonstrating self-confidence helps to control a suspect.
   B. Handcuffs are no substitute for an officer's alertness.
   C. As soon as control of the suspect has been achieved, the suspect should be thoroughly frisked to ensure the safety of the officers.
   D. Each officer present should give orders to keep the suspect overwhelmed.

96. Sergeant June Harps is giving a training class in conducting preliminary investigations of past burglaries. The sergeant would be most correct if she made which of the following statements?
   A. It is very common to have witnesses to burglaries.
   B. One of the first pieces of information to ascertain is how entry was made.
   C. If keys were among the items taken during the burglary, it is an absolute certainty that the burglar(s) will return.
   D. Burglaries are usually committed by highly skilled and trained perpetrators.

97. Sergeant Frank Rems responds to a past assault that has just occurred. Police Officer Bonds is already on the scene. Officer Bonds asks the sergeant what should be done first? The sergeant would be most correct if he directed the officer:
   A. To check to see if the victim requires medical assistance
   B. To get a description of the perpetrator and transmit it over the portable radio
   C. To immediately pursue the suspect
   D. To find out if any weapons were used

98. The criminal action that is generally recognized as the "complete trespass" is:
   A. Having one's pocket picked
   B. Being the subject of a confidence game where one's own greed contributed to the success of the confidence artist
   C. Having one's home burglarized
   D. Being raped

99. Consider the following statements concerning fingerprints:
   (1) Visible fingerprints made by bloody hands should be photographed.
   (2) Plastic fingerprints are visible and molded into an object.
   (3) Latent fingerprints are not visible to the naked eye.
   Which of the following choices best classifies the above statements into those which are accurate and those which are inaccurate?
   A. Statement 1 is inaccurate; statements 2 and 3 are accurate.
   B. Statement 2 is inaccurate; statements 1 and 3 are accurate.
   C. Statement 3 is inaccurate; statements 1 and 2 are accurate.
   D. All of the statements are accurate.

100. Evaluate the following statements concerning the collection of evidence:
   (1) Blood should be subjected to heat to dry it.
   (2) A fan should be used to dry wet objects from which fingerprints are to be taken.
   Which of the following is most accurate concerning the statements above?
   A. Only statement 1 is correct.
   B. Only statement 2 is correct.
   C. Both statements 1 and 2 are correct.
   D. Neither statement 1 nor 2 is correct.

Answer Key

1. A	21. B	41. C	61. B	81. B
2. A	22. A	42. D	62. A	82. B
3. B	23. D	43. A	63. C	83. A
4. B	24. D	44. B	64. C	84. A
5. B	25. B	45. B	65. B	85. A
6. B	26. A	46. D	66. D	86. D
7. D	27. A	47. C	67. C	87. B
8. D	28. C	48. D	68. B	88. B
9. D	29. A	49. D	69. D	89. C
10. B	30. B	50. A	70. A	90. D
11. C	31. A	51. A	71. C	91. B
12. D	32. C	52. D	72. B	92. B
13. C	33. D	53. B	73. D	93. C
14. C	34. B	54. C	74. B	94. C
15. A	35. D	55. D	75. A	95. D
16. D	36. B	56. C	76. B	96. B
17. D	37. A	57. D	77. D	97. A
18. C	38. D	58. A	78. D	98. D
19. A	39. C	59. D	79. C	99. D
20. C	40. D	60. D	80. A	100. D

Diagnostic Chart

Insert the number of correct answers you obtained in the blank space for each section of the examination. The scale in the next column indicates how you did. The information at the bottom indicates how to correct your weaknesses.

SECTION	QUESTION NUMBERS	AREAS	YOUR NUMBER CORRECT	SCALE
1	1–15	Principles of Supervision		14–15 right: excellent 12–13 right: good 10–11 right: fair Under 11 right: poor
2	16–30	Safety and Training		14–15 right: excellent 12–13 right: good 10–11 right: fair Under 11 right: poor
3	31–40	Management		9–10 right: excellent 7–8 right: good 6 right: fair Under 6 right: poor
4	41–55	Community relations		14–15 right: excellent 12–13 right: good 10–11 right: fair Under 11 right: poor
5	56–70	Patrol operations		14–15 right: excellent 12–13 right: good 10–11 right: fair Under 11 right: poor
6	71–80	Report writing		9–10 right: excellent 7–8 right: good 6 right: fair Under 6 right: poor
7	81–90	Data interpretation		9–10 right: excellent 7–8 right: good 6 right: fair Under 6 right: poor
8	91–100	Police science		9–10 right: excellent 7–8 right: good 6 right: fair Under 6 right: poor

How to correct weaknesses:

If you are weak in Section 1, then concentrate on Chapter 5.
If you are weak in Section 2, then concentrate on Chapter 6.
If you are weak in Section 3, then concentrate on Chapter 7.
If you are weak in Section 4, then concentrate on Chapter 8.
If you are weak in Section 5, then concentrate on Chapter 9.
If you are weak in Section 6, then concentrate on Chapter 10.
If you are weak in Section 7, then concentrate on Chapter 11.
If you are weak in Section 8, then concentrate on Chapter 12.

Note: Consider yourself weak in a section if you receive other than an excellent rating in it.

Answer Explanations

1. **A** Concerning punishment, the following facts are often tested. To be effective, punishment must be swift and certain, but not necessarily severe. Punishment must also be objectively administered.

2. **A** Good leaders do not necessarily always back up their subordinates. It depends on the circumstances. If a subordinate is in the right, however, a good leader gives that worker full support.

3. **B** Counseling does not mean telling a subordinate what to do. It means helping a person find his/her own solution to a problem.

4. **B** The immediate line supervisor is the key figure in the disciplinary process.

5. **B** There are no negative connotations associated with positive discipline.

6. **B** Different situations require different types of orders. In addition, certain orders, such as an implied order, just don't work with certain individuals.

7. **D** It is the responsibility of the order giver to make sure the order receiver understands the order. It is a mistake simply to ask a subordinate if an order is misunderstood. Having the order receiver repeat the order in his/her own words is the recommended way to check understanding.

8. **D** An implied order is really a suggestion that something should be done. It is a useful tool for identifying willing workers. It is also helpful in developing the initiative, ability, and judgment of subordinates.

9. **D** No matter how trivial a grievance may appear to a supervisor, it must be treated seriously because it is very important in the mind of the worker. Even "imagined" grievances must be treated seriously since they are real in the mind of the grieving employee.

10. **B** Worker grievances are always present in the workplace. Workers bring their grievances to those supervisors they feel are approachable and, as a general rule, do not make grievances to supervisors they feel are unapproachable.

11. **C** A supervisor who is reluctant to delegate creates problems for himself, his subordinates, and his bosses. Only managers and supervisors can delegate, and a task or a part of a task can be

delegated, but some tasks, such as rewarding or punishing subordinates, should not be delegated.

12. **D** These three statements are the reasons why delegation is an essential process.

13. **C** A supervisor cannot delegate away his/her final responsibility for getting a task done.

14. **C** This required follow-up is made to ensure that the intent of the delegation was accomplished.

15. **A** Work assignments should be distributed fairly and equitably. It is an error to overload a willing worker with assignments.

16. **D** Choice D is incorrect because training shapes attitudes, imparts knowledge, and develops skills.

17. **D** Well-trained personnel tend to stay with the agency because they experience a higher level of satisfaction; they also file less grievances because they are better informed in the policies of the agency. Morale is raised not lowered because the individual goals of the worker are brought closer to the goals of the agency. Therefore choices A, B, and C are incorrect. Choice D is a result of an effective agency training program.

18. **C** Choices A, B, and D are incorrect because when a subordinate is able to proficiently do a certain task, the supervisor is able to focus on the employee and planning and following-up, instead of performing the task. This results in a lessening of immediate and constant supervision.

19. **A** Choice A is incorrect because if the department is spending its time and money in training an employee, then the department must feel good about the employee and his/her work. This would increase the worker's security, not decrease it. Choices B, C, and D are accurate statements concerning training.

20. **C** The first step in devising and conducting a training program is discovering the need for the training program. Training is expensive. If there is no need for a particular training program it should not be conducted.

21. **B** All the choices indicate problems associated with training, but choice B is the most serious problem.

22. **A** Statement 1 is correct, but statement 2 is incorrect because training can help in a present or *future* job.

23. **D** The sergeant will get to know his subordinates better, and his trained workers will perform better putting the sergeant in a better light and making him a better choice for promotion, especially since the sergeant will keep abreast of the latest developments. Choices A, B, and C are accurate. Choice D is inaccurate because the workplace actually becomes safer because sloppy and dangerous work habits are reduced.

24. **D** All are important, but the most important trait for a supervisor to possess as a trainer is a willingness to train.

25. **B** If a trainee can be shown why a subject is personally important to the trainee, the trainee will be motivated to learn the subject.

26. **A** Choice B is incorrect because using more than one of the senses makes learning more effective. Choice C is incorrect because it is information that the trainee has been previously greatly exposed to which will be remembered for a long period of time. Choice D is incorrect because, for example, being too hot or too cold in a classroom will impact on the learning process. People do, however, learn at different rates of speed.

27. **A** All are mistakes, but the most common is to assume the trainees know more than they really do.

28. **C** Choices A, B, and D are examples of training often conducted by police departments, but choice C represents the kind of training that is designed to enable a supervisor to perform appropriately in the supervisor's new job.

29. **A** Choices B, C, and D are correct. Choice A is incorrect because the goals should be specific so that it can be easily determined if the desired results of the training program are being obtained.

30. **B** Statement 1 is inaccurate; trial-and-error training is costly because it is so time-consuming. Statement 3 is inaccurate because a lack of questions on the part of the trainees is no guarantee that learning is taking place. The trainees could be intimidated either by the expertise of the trainer or because they just simply do not understand the material. Statement 2 is accurate; trainees should be allowed to apply what has just been learned.

31. **A** The guidelines for effective communications are often suspended during an emergency when there is no time for anything other than dealing with the emergency. We suggest that you develop a good understanding of empathy as it is a favorite topic of examiners.

32. C Like the grapevine, filtering of information cannot be eliminated. It must be handled as suggested in choice C.

33. D Supervisors have a responsibility to keep their subordinates as well informed as possible. It is the lack of facts (truth) that generates rumors.

34. B Oral communication is a two-way process during which the listener has an opportunity to clarify meanings.

35. D A worker's previous evaluation should not be the critical factor in a current performance evaluation.

36. B Planning should take place only after the need for a plan has been established. After that, the planner should determine the objectives of the plan, decide what resources are required, determine the methods to be used, and implement a control mechanism.

37. A The principle of unity of command can be violated when the reputation of the department is at stake, such as when an employee is engaged in a gross deviation of the rules of conduct and the worker's immediate supervisor is not readily available.

38. D Since a supervisor's effective span of control is affected by so many variables at the operational level of a police agency, it is impossible to establish an optimal span of control at that level.

39. C Every competent police supervisor rates subordinates on a continuous basis even if there is no formal rating system in the agency.

40. D The most common rater error is leniency, which is the tendency of the rater to evaluate personnel more favorably than deserved.

41. C Fewer officers are injured because they are often spared from injury due to timely citizen intervention such as calls by the public to 911 indicating that an officer may need assistance.

42. D Most of a police officer's job is involved in providing services that actually do not directly involve enforcement of laws.

43. A Choice B is incorrect because providing social services traditionally has not led to recognition for promotion. Choice C is incorrect because obviously the police are not trained in *all* the social services. Remember our earlier admonition that the use of absolute words usually indicates a wrong choice. Choice D is incorrect because it is usually the making of arrests and not the providing of social services that gains peer recognition. Choice A is correct.

44. **B** Realistically, the police could not arrest all felons, no more than they could provide total security for all citizens. Also while it is certainly helpful to have public acknowledgment, the primary goal of the police is public cooperation.

45. **B** Choices A, C, and D all indicate policies that make the maintenance of order or peacekeeping role easier. Choice B is incorrect because the importance of arrests is de-emphasized in the police role dealing with the maintenance of order. This calls for discretionary actions on the part of the police, which emphasize a host of actions other than making arrests.

46. **D** A requirement of community policing is for the police to solve problems whose solutions often lie outside of the responsibility of the police.

47. **C** The main justification for such programs aimed at juveniles is that they will mold the public opinion and cooperation of tomorrow's public.

48. **D** Those who are anti-police and whom the police would like to reach most are usually not interested in what the police might have to say.

49. **D** Statement 1 is inaccurate because complaints should be received in person, in writing, or by phone. Statement 2 is inaccurate because the immediate supervisor might be seen as not being able to be objective in investigating the complaint. Statement 3 is inaccurate because a great deal of good information is derived from an investigation of anonymous complaints.

50. **A** Choice B is incorrect because the police use of deadly physical force via firearms represents the most controversial use of discretion by police. Choice C is incorrect because selective enforcement boards, which can obtain community input, and not civilian complaint review boards help establish discretion guidelines for the police. Choice D is incorrect because the use of discretion by the police is often mistakenly seen as police corruption by the community.

51. **A** All the choices represent reasons for selective enforcement, but the principal reason for discretion and selective enforcement is as stated in choice A.

52. **D** The crime-fighting role is one that police officers enjoy. Choices A, B, and C are correct and support the position that the prevention of crime is not merely a product of police efficiency.

53. **B** Choice A is incorrect because public relations is comprised of one-way communication, outwardly from the department. Choice C is incorrect because public relations, unlike community relations, demands no input from the community. Choice D is incorrect because only positive information should find its way into a public relations program.

54. **C** Unlike community relations where the most important factor is the conduct of every police officer who comes in contact with the public, the department's public relations officer is the most important person in a police department's public relations effort.

55. **D** Choices A, B, and C represent the likely results of creating a special unit to deal with community relations. However, choice D is not correct because once such a special unit is created, many others in the department will no longer see community relations as part of their job.

56. **C** The pattern of patrol by a police officer engaged in preventive patrol must be one that cannot be predicted. Preventive patrol must be performed in an irregular manner but on a frequent basis. It must be random.

57. **D** Hidden enforcement does have some limited usefulness but only in areas with high accident rates.

58. **A** When making a traffic stop, a police officer should allow a driver, especially one who is apparently accompanied by family or close friends, to save face. This means that the officer should allow the driver to vent a little so as not to be embarrassed or belittled.

59. **D** The U.S. Supreme Court regards the making of random car stops as leaving too much discretion with individual officers. However, stops can always be made when a violation is observed or in accordance with a systematic stopping of all or a certain percentage of cars.

60. **D** This is an example of when an examiner puts the correct choice last after a series of extremely plausible choices. Make sure to read all of the choices when doing multiple-choice questions. In this case, if you got to choice D, you would have most certainly selected it as the answer. Safety in police work is always the number one concern.

61. **B** Don't make general requests to a crowd asking for witnesses. Approach potential witnesses and personally ask them if they would like to make a statement.

62. **A** Even though the officer did not witness the accident, he/she must determine its cause. Sources to be used in making this deter-

mination are physical evidence, statements of the participants and witnesses, location of traffic devices, and knowledge of the rules of the road.

63. **C** Unfortunately, preventive patrol has many weaknesses. One of its major weaknesses is that, even at its best, it can only control crimes committed in public areas, that is, street crimes. Obviously, the police generally are not authorized to patrol in private areas.

64. **C** Patrol sergeants should terminate pursuits if the danger created by the pursuit outweighs the suspect's danger to the community if not apprehended.

65. **B** The opposite is true. While automobile patrol tends to isolate the officer from the community, the officer of foot patrol has an opportunity to develop close ties to the community.

66. **D** The courts have consistently held that merely offering someone an opportunity to commit a crime is not entrapment. In order for entrapment to occur, some form of enticing or encouragement to someone who would not ordinarily commit the crime must accompany the offering of the opportunity.

67. **C** A field command post is needed to coordinate police activity at the scene of police operations that are expected to continue for an extended period of time.

68. **B** Involving subordinates, when appropriate, in the resolution of problems is a highly recommended supervisory strategy. However, this does not mean that they should be involved in the solution of all problems.

69. **D** Officers in a distinctive uniform and conspicuously marked vehicles are best suited for preventive patrol, and the patrol pattern of the officer must be unpredictable.

70. **A** We, as yet, do not know of a way to take away a criminal's desire, motivation, or intent to commit crimes. All we can do is to try to take away the opportunity to do so.

71. **C** Both can serve as purposes of field note taking.

72. **B** Choices A, C, and D indicate recommended practices. However lines should not be skipped. If lines are not completely used, they should be ruled off to prevent adding notes later on.

73. **D** Such a practice rarely will yield positive results. Instead, the sergeant should have zeroed in on persons who appeared to be ex-

plaining the incident to others and taken such persons aside and questioned them away from the others.

74. **B** If a question is too complex, a witness will usually answer, "I don't know," rather than appear less than intelligent. For this reason questions should be kept simple and understandable.

75. **A** Recommendations, conclusions, and opinions should be included only when specifically asked. However, a maximum of facts is always required.

76. **B** Choices A and C are directly opposite and usually when two opposite choices appear, one of them is the answer. However, in this instance neither is correct. Choice D is incorrect because of the use of the absolute words *only* and *at all*. But there can be no quarrel with the fact that the police officer on patrol typically stands as the department's main source of statistical data.

77. **D** Such records are quite confidential and should not be kept in a location where the entire department might have access.

78. **D** All the statements are accurate.

79. **C** While all choices indicate a disadvantage of a decentralized record-keeping system, the principal disadvantage is as stated in choice C.

80. **A** Statement 2 is not correct because a crime scene sketch is merely a supplement to reports and photographs.

81. **B** Choices A and D can be eliminated because the arrest activity of both police officers decreased. Percentage increase is found by finding the space (difference) between the two numbers being examined and then dividing by the older or previously existing number. Choice C represents about an 11% increase [$\frac{(20-18)}{18} = \frac{2}{18} = .11 = 11\%$]. Choice B or police officer Baker's arrest activity increased 20% [$\frac{(12-10)}{10} = \frac{2}{10} = .2 = 20\%$].

82. **B**

Officer	Last Year	This Year	Diff.	%Decrease
Bell	16	12	4	$\frac{4}{16} = 25\%$
Tock	24	15	9	$\frac{9}{24} = 37.5\%$
Cuffs	19	14	5	$\frac{5}{19} = 26.3\%$
Walls	17	15	2	$\frac{2}{17} = 11.8\%$

83. **A** The number of felony arrests this year was 120 compared with 150 last year. A decrease obviously occurred, and the percentage decrease was twenty percent.

$\frac{(150-120)}{120} = \frac{30}{120} = \frac{1}{4}$ or .25, which is 25%. Choice A would mistakenly be selected if instead of dividing by the old or previously existing number, this year's number or more current number of 150 had been used to divide ($\frac{30}{150} = \frac{1}{5} = .2 = 20\%$).

84. **A** Ginty had 20 + 18 = 38
Baker had 10 + 12 = 22
Walls had 17 + 15 = 32
Cuffs had 19 + 14 = 33

85. **A** As indicated by the double plus sign in the legend, a police officer assigned to Post 29 must notify the supervisor before leaving post for any reason.

86. **D** If you jumped on choice A as the answer, you probably made the mistake of not reading all the choices. Also, be careful of the word *only*. In this case, double asterisks indicate armed suspects on Posts 7, 20, and 33.

87. **B** The single plus sign next to the condition statement for Post 27, as explained in the legend, means to notify the Auto Squad before taking any action if drag racing is observed.

88. **B** If you missed this one it was because you were careless. Posts 20 and 35 are on Main Avenue and not Main Street.

89. **C** Don't look for tricks when they are not there, and don't make careless mistakes.

90. **D** Nothing in the data specifically mentions heroin. You cannot make assumptions when answering questions when the directions tell you to answer the questions solely on the basis of the information supplied.

91. **B** The ability to detect and make useful observations is not just inborn. It can be developed.

92. **B** If a police officer while walking a beat sees what is believed to be a suspicious person, the officer should continue walking and attempt to inconspicuously surveil the suspicious person.

93. **C** Choice A is incorrect because the motorist should be made to momentarily pull over safely and then be given directions by the officer when practical to do so. Choice B is incorrect because the best place to direct traffic from is the middle of the intersection where an

officer can be seen by all. Choice D is incorrect because, if necessary to turn while directing traffic, such a turn should be made in the same direction the vehicles are moving.

94. **C** Choice A is incorrect because barriers can reduce the number of officers required to police the incident. Choice B is incorrect because, even though a strong police presence is recommended, making a large and constant display of physical force could actually cause an incident. Choice D is incorrect because such explanations often serve to underscore the neutral role the police play at labor disputes.

95. **D** One officer should give orders so that the suspect can more quickly comply with the officers' wishes and be more easily taken into custody.

96. **B** Choice A is incorrect because there are seldom witnesses to a burglary. Choice C is incorrect because such burglars rarely return. Choice D is incorrect because most burglars are neither highly skilled nor highly trained.

97. **A** Even though all the choices indicate appropriate actions in such a situation, choice A indicates what should be done first.

98. **D** All choices could leave the victim feeling trespassed, but the "complete and ultimate trespass" is rape.

99. **D** All three statements are accurate.

100. **D** Blood should not be exposed to heat nor sunlight, and wet objects from which fingerprints are to be taken should be allowed to dry naturally.

PART THREE: ASSESSMENT CENTER EXERCISES

What It's About

CHAPTER 16

Practical Assessment Tests

In the recent past, more and more private and public organizations have been running to the assessment center process to select their supervisors, managers, and administrators. The principal reasons that this is occurring are as follows:

The use of assessment center-type exercises results in more accurate selection of qualified candidates. Many studies have substantiated that candidates chosen by the assessment center method are much more likely to succeed in their new positions than those promoted on the basis of more traditional selection devices.

The validity of the method. When properly prepared, assessment center exercises are extremely job related. This is very important, since non-job-related selection techniques are in violation of equal opportunity laws.

The fairness of the method. Studies have confirmed that the results of properly constructed assessment center exercises are usually equally accurate for all protected groups.

What Is an Assessment Center?

First of all, the most obvious and common misconception must be made clear. An assessment center is not a place; it is a process. It utilizes one or more forms of job-related simulations, known as "assessment center exercises." More specifically, with respect to police officers taking a sergeant's examination, it is a process in which the police officers competing for promotion participate in one or more situations that resemble, insofar as possible, what incumbents in the rank of sergeant are typically required to do in the particular police department involved. The behavior of the officers in this simulated situation is then evaluated by trained observers and each participant is given a numerical score. It is important to note that each situation is developed from a job analysis that indicates what skills are necessary to successfully perform the job for which the test is being given. Once again, we see the importance of the job analysis.

Can You Improve Your Ability to Compete in an Assessment Center Exercise?

The answer to this question is a resounding "yes!" A candidate can definitely prepare to do well on these types of exercises. Anyone who tells you otherwise is uninformed. The steps that should be followed to adequately prepare for competing on any form of assessment center exercise are as follows.

Learn as much as possible about the exercise to be used.

Basically, there are two distinct areas in which as much information as possible is needed.

1. What specific content knowledge area is going to be tested? Here there are three possibilities. Either the entire exercise will test the technical knowledge required to do the sergeant's job, it will test the generic skills necessary to do the sergeant's job, or it will test for both the technical skills and the generic skills necessary to do the sergeant's job. As mentioned in Chapter 1, technical skills include such things as statutory law, case law, procedural law, department policies, department procedures, and department regulations. Technical skills vary from department to department, and if they are included on your examination, you must study them in addition to studying this book. On the other hand, the generic skills you might be asked about are covered in Chapters 5–12 of this book and include such areas as supervision, patrol, community relations, and report writing.

2. What specific assessment center exercise will you participate in? As discussed in detail later in this text, there are a number of "exercises" that can be used to stimulate actual working conditions of your job. If you can find out ahead of time which will be used as part of your examination, it helps you to focus your preparation effort. However, even if you can't find out which will be used, you can still adequately prepare since the basic concepts are the same regardless of the type of exercise used. Three of the most commonly used exercises are covered in detail in later chapters: in-basket exercises, oral interactive interviews, and fact-finding and decision-making exercises.

Learn to behave during the exercise in a manner that will result in the highest possible score for you.

This is the area where we do not agree with most proponents of assessment center exercises. The advice most often given to candidates about to take an assessment center exercise, such as an oral interactive interview, is to act yourself. Actually, this is very good advice if you happen to be a model police supervisor who displays all of the behavioral characteristics of such a model supervisor. If not, our advice is to learn to behave during the exercise in a way that will earn you the most points from the raters. This can be done since all of the raters (or evaluators) are trained to give points to candidates who display certain behavioral dimensions and to take points away from candidates who fail to display these behavioral dimensions. These so-called behavioral dimensions are fairly standard, few in number, and amenable to natural display through understanding and practice. In other words, through hard work and effort you can make yourself into the "model" candidate your agency wants to promote. Concerning this concept that a high score on an assessment center exercise can be achieved through coaching and self-preparation, please note the following.

1. This is a very sore point with advocates of assessment centers, since one of the selling points of this selection method is that success cannot be achieved through behavior learned specifically to participate in the center.

2. Our purpose in writing this book is to help you do well on your sergeant's examination or, for that matter, in any examination that utilizes assessment center exercises. We also believe that, if you behaved in a supervisory position the same way you learn to behave in the simulated conditions created in your exercise, then you would in fact be a better supervisor. This is a matter for you to consider. Our objective is only to show you how to successfully participate in assessment center exercises.

3. "Schools" to prepare or coach those about to participate in an assessment center are springing up at a rate proportionate to the growing use of assessment center exercises as selection devices. If prepara-

tion can't help, as some would want you to believe, then why are these "schools" growing?

4. The key to learning how to successfully participate in assessment center exercises is learning how they are scored. After all, doesn't it make sense that if "experts" can be trained to identify positive and/or negative behavioral traits (or dimensions) in a candidate, then the candidates can be trained to display the traits the raters will identify as positive and to avoid the traits the raters will identify as negative?

How Are Assessment Center Exercises Developed, Administered, and Scored?

The key to successful development of the particular exercise or exercises used in your agency is a good understanding of what the first-line supervisor does in your agency. This, as previously mentioned, is why the job analysis is so important. Once the test developer understands the job, an artificial situation is created that simulates, insofar as possible, a situation that resembles quite closely one that actually occurs on the job. The next step is to find and train "experts" who will act as role players during the actual exercise, and/or observe the exercise, and/or score the exercise. To understand this, it is important to note that some assessment center exercises, such as an in-basket exercise, can be administered without the assistance of "role players" or "observers"; others, such as an oral presentation, require only observers to be present, and still others, such as an oral interactive interview, require both role players and observers. The one common element, however, is that all such exercises must be evaluated and scored. If you know the scoring criteria, you will know how to behave and what to say or do, or what not to say or do. This, again, is the key to doing well.

What Kinds of Behavior Should Be Displayed During the Exercise?

The answer to this question lies in a good understanding of the so-called behavioral dimensions or traits that evaluators are trained to identify. The most commonly used traits, along with a definition and specific examples of each trait, follow.

LEADERSHIP

Leadership is the most commonly measured behavioral trait. Many times it is labeled as "supervisory ability." It is typically defined as the ability to get the job done effectively through the appropriate use of personnel and resources. It is demonstrated through the proper direction, motivation, disciplining, monitoring, and counseling of subordinates. Also, an important component of the leadership trait is the demonstrated ability to delegate, control, and follow up.

SPECIFIC EXAMPLES OF HIGH-ABILITY LEADERSHIP BEHAVIOR

1. The delegation of a routine job to the appropriate worker, coupled with clear directions, and some provision for follow-up

2. Praising a worker in public; criticizing in private

3. The development of a specific course of action to achieve a certain objective

4. Helping a subordinate find the right way to do a particular job

5. Involving others in the decision-making process

SPECIFIC EXAMPLES OF LOW-ABILITY LEADERSHIP BEHAVIOR

1. Giving vague directions with little or no provision for follow-up or, on the other hand, overuse of the direct order

2. Overuse of negative discipline

3. Failing to provide for the personal development of subordinates

4. Failure to use subordinates to perform routine tasks

JOB KNOWLEDGE

Job knowledge and technical skills are synonymous. It is exhibited by candidates who have learned the specifics of their job and of other related content matter, such as procedural and substantive law. You must remember, however, that not all assessment center exercises tests for the behavioral dimension of job knowledge. Many times, the instructions you receive concerning the simulated role you are to assume is the key to whether you will be required to display job knowledge. If you are told you are a sergeant in a fictitious police department, often called Anytown Police Department, then you will probably only be expected to display generic skills, not technical knowledge skills. If, however, the artificial situation is created in your own police department, the New York City Police Department, for example, then you will be required to demonstrate a good working knowledge of the law, department policy and procedures, and rules and regulations in effect in your particular agency. Remember also that job knowledge includes knowing what resources are available to you to deal with job-related problems.

SPECIFIC EXAMPLES OF HIGH-ABILITY JOB KNOWLEDGE BEHAVIOR

1. Knowing the elements of specific crimes, such as robbery, burglary, and assault

2. Knowing the procedure to follow to safeguard the property of others

3. Knowing the department policy concerning off-duty employment

4. Knowing what specific department resources are available to deal with a rash of burglaries in your geographic area of responsibility

SPECIFIC EXAMPLES OF LOW-ABILITY JOB KNOWLEDGE BEHAVIOR

1. Not being familiar with the department's disciplinary or grievance procedure

2. Not being familiar with the constitutional rights of individuals

3. Not being familiar with various ways to deal with community and crime problems

PLANNING AND ORGANIZATION

This trait is displayed by establishing a course of action for yourself or your subordinates in order to accomplish a specific goal. A major component of this trait or dimension is your ability to plan proper assignments of subordinates and to make effective allocation of available resources, such as equipment. Any indication of planning gains points for you in this trait-dimension. For example, making written notes of appointments, meetings, and other important events always indicates good planning and organization skills. Giving adequate instructions to subordinates when delegating is another good indication of planning and organization skills.

SPECIFIC EXAMPLES OF HIGH-ABILITY PLANNING AND ORGANIZATION BEHAVIOR

1. Scheduling regular progress reviews with staff and other subordinates

2. Implementing controls over available resources

3. Establishing priorities for handling assignments

4. Keeping others involved in an assignment informed of developments, especially your superiors

SPECIFIC EXAMPLES OF LOW-ABILITY PLANNING AND ORGANIZATION BEHAVIOR

1. Making vague delegations

2. Operating in a vacuum

3. Failure to deal with the appropriate people in the organization

4. Wasting resources on unimportant matters or engaging in "overkill"

JUDGMENT

A candidate exhibits good judgment when he/she evaluates available information, problems, solutions, and actions and reaches logical conclusions. A major component of the trait-dimension of judgment is the developing of alternative courses of action and ordering or prioritizing them appropriately. This is the trait-dimension we refer to as the "commonsense" trait. If you consider more than one alternative way to deal with a problem and select one because it is most logical, you are displaying good judgment. Of course, never embarrass your boss, and never go over your boss's head.

SPECIFIC EXAMPLES OF HIGH-ABILITY JUDGMENT BEHAVIOR

1. Obtaining sufficient facts or data about a problem before making a decision

2. Informing your superiors about important matters

3. Always placing safety over all other considerations

4. Involving subordinates or community members in the decision-making process

SPECIFIC EXAMPLES OF LOW-ABILITY JUDGMENT BEHAVIOR

1. Delegating assignments to peers or superiors

2. Making important decisions based on surface knowledge

3. Failing to follow up on key issues

PROBLEM ANALYSIS

This dimension-trait is demonstrated by the identification of problems or potential problems, as well as developing possible solutions, and by the obtaining of relevant information. A key component of this trait-dimension is the ability to pull together related information appearing in different sources or locations. For example, if you were considering a matter concerning a particular police officer, you would get problem analysis points for giving consideration to all of the available information about the officer.

SPECIFIC EXAMPLES OF HIGH-ABILITY PROBLEM ANALYSIS BEHAVIOR

1. Requesting additional information whenever appropriate

2. Recognizing scheduling conflicts, that is, not committing oneself to two meetings at the same time

3. Considering all available information about a person, place, or thing before making a decision

4. Recognizing problems that a particular course of action might cause; also, recognizing solutions to problems

SPECIFIC EXAMPLES OF LOW-ABILITY PROBLEM ANALYSIS BEHAVIOR

1. Making decisions in a vacuum

2. Not replacing key personnel when required

3. Putting off decisions that have to be made within a specified time frame

4. Improperly interpreting an organizational chart when making assignments

MANAGEMENT CONTROL

This is the easiest dimension-trait to demonstrate, yet it is probably the most overlooked. It is based on the principle of management, which states that you cannot escape final accountability for responsibilities that belong to you. You must follow up on matters of concern to you. Management control is defined as the establishment of procedures to monitor and/or control your own activities and responsibilities as well as the activities and responsibilities of your subordinates, especially with respect to tasks you have delegated. In a written exercise, not of the multiple-choice format, management control can best be demonstrated by making written notations, usually on a calendar if one is provided, of due dates and by making notes to follow up on any delegated assignments. Another important management control technique is always to request feedback on delegated assignments and other ongoing activities. When requesting such feedback, be specific. Rather than directing a subordinate to "keep you informed," it would be better to direct the subordinate to give you status reports "every Friday." Then, make a written notation somewhere, usually on the calendar, to remind yourself to expect the status report—as a sort of "tickler" device.

SPECIFIC EXAMPLES OF HIGH-ABILITY MANAGEMENT CONTROL BEHAVIOR

1. Asking for a report on a certain date and making a written note to yourself to expect the report

2. Asking for feedback from a meeting attended by a subordinate; stipulating a specific date for the feedback, and making a note to expect the feedback

3. Making personal notes to remind yourself of things to be done or followed up on

SPECIFIC EXAMPLES OF LOW-ABILITY MANAGEMENT CONTROL BEHAVIOR

1. Delegating a task with no mention of follow-up

2. Establishing a future course of action for yourself without taking steps to make sure you follow that course of action

<u>DELEGATION</u>

Delegation is simply the art of using subordinates effectively. However, the subordinates selected to do tasks for you must be carefully selected. Although authority given to a subordinate must be commensurate with the delegated responsibility, final responsibility can never be delegated for a task you are in fact responsible for completing. Also, peers and superiors can be requested to work with you on matters of mutual concern, but you must never delegate to peers, especially to superiors. With respect to peers, sometimes by virtue of your particular assignment, delegation to a peer is appropriate. For example, a sergeant assigned to replace a lieutenant on desk duty could properly delegate a task to a patrol sergeant.

SPECIFIC EXAMPLES OF HIGH-ABILITY DELEGATION BEHAVIOR

1. Delegating a routine task to an appropriate subordinate

2. Pushing decision making down to the level of operations, when appropriate

3. Using staff to gather information for you to make an important decision

SPECIFIC EXAMPLES OF LOW-ABILITY DELEGATION BEHAVIOR

1. Delegating disciplinary matters

2. Delegating planning responsibilities

3. Personally performing routine tasks

4. Failure to delegate, to maintain, insofar as possible, an even workload among subordinates with similar responsibilities

ORGANIZATIONAL SENSITIVITY

This dimension-trait relates to being aware of the rank structure in a semimilitary organization, such as a police department. It requires that you follow the chain of command and understand your responsibility to keep your superiors informed. Also understand that organizational sensitivity and judgment often parallel each other.

SPECIFIC EXAMPLES OF HIGH-ABILITY ORGANIZATIONAL SENSITIVITY BEHAVIOR

1. Sending carbon copies of important communications to your immediate superior

2. Keeping your immediate superior informed of any direct communication to you from those on the same organizational level as your superior or, more importantly, from those higher in the chain of command than your superior

SPECIFIC EXAMPLES OF LOW-ABILITY ORGANIZATIONAL SENSITIVITY BEHAVIOR

1. Bypassing the chain of command

2. "Going over the head" of your immediate supervisor

3. Delegating tasks to peers or superiors

RESPONSIVENESS

This dimension-trait, which is also known as "sensitivity," is defined as the demonstration of due consideration for the needs and feelings of others. A major component of this dimension or trait is showing concern for others, both inside and outside the police department. A hallmark of a person with a great deal of responsiveness is the use of tact and diplomacy.

SPECIFIC EXAMPLES OF HIGH-ABILITY RESPONSIVENESS BEHAVIOR

1. Making sure all persons who send letters or otherwise communicate with the police department are contacted

2. Keeping a person who has lodged a complaint apprised of the status of the complaint

3. Keeping people who have made requests of the police department informed of the status of the request

4. Cordially greeting people at meetings

5. Sending notes of condolences to persons experiencing personal losses, such as deaths in the family

6. Being concerned about people with problems

7. Remembering the names of subordinates

SPECIFIC EXAMPLES OF LOW-ABILITY RESPONSIVENESS BEHAVIOR

1. Criticizing people in public

2. Ignoring personal grievances of employees or otherwise ignoring requests for help

3. Failing to provide for the personal development of subordinates

ARE THERE ANY OTHER BEHAVIORAL DIMENSIONS OF WHICH YOU SHOULD BE AWARE?

Yes, although the traits listed above are those most used in selecting police personnel for promotion, there are other dimension-traits you should be familiar with and exhibit, if possible, during your assessment center exercise.

Oral communication skills. This is defined as your ability to express yourself effectively during oral exchanges. It is not, however, limited to the spoken word. It includes such things as animation, enthusiasm, inflection, eye contact, and other recognized techniques of nonverbal communication, known as body language.

Oral presentation skills. In effect, this dimension or trait measures whether a candidate can make an effective, well-organized formal oral presentation. A key here is to make sure to observe any time frames and to deliver a well-organized, logically flowing discourse with an effective introduction and a definite conclusion.

Written communication skills. Can the candidate express himself/herself clearly in writing? Does the candidate avoid spelling and grammatical errors? These are two of the factors in this dimension-trait.

Stress tolerance. This dimension-trait is meant to evaluate the candidate's stability of performance under stress. This one is easy to deal with effectively. Stay calm. Don't lose your temper, especially in oral interactive interviews.

Listening ability. This dimension-trait asks the question, "Does the candidate have the ability to extract pertinent information from oral communications?"

Decisiveness. As its name implies, this dimension-trait evaluates a candidate's readiness to make decisions, render judgment, take action, or commit oneself. This dimension-trait is something of a two-edged sword, since it is not always good to make instant decisions, especially in the absence of all of the facts. Our advice is to downplay this dimension. If you pay attention to the nine major dimensions discussed above, this one will take care of itself.

Decision making. This dimension-trait is so closely related to judgment and leadership that it is subsumed by them. Exercise good judgment and leadership, and you will score well as a decision maker. For the record, decision making is defined as making sound, logical decisions based on the evidence available

HOW DO I USE THIS INFORMATION?

Although each exercise is different and, for the most part, not amenable to standard responses, you should become as familiar as possible with the dimensions or traits described above and learn to inculcate the positive aspects of each dimension-trait into as many oral and written responses as you make during the exercise. Whenever possible, ask yourself the following questions about each response you write or present.

1. Are my directions to subordinates specific enough?

2. Can I delegate this task?

3. Am I involving enough people in the decision-making process?

4. Does this response require me to include any technical skills? If so, what knowledge should I include?

5. Am I effectively using my personnel and resources?

6. Do I have sufficient information upon which to make a wise decision?

7. Is my decision logical?

8. Is there related information concerning this item anywhere else in the material?

9. Is this meeting in conflict with any others I have scheduled?

10. Do I have a way to follow up on my proposed course of action?

11. Should I inform my superior of this matter?

12. Am I following the chain of command?

13. Am I showing sufficient concern for the people involved in this matter?

A Final Thought About These Dimensions

It is now apparent to you, we hope, that these dimensions or traits are not mutually exclusive. This means that by engaging in a certain single action you can sometimes gain positive scores in more than one dimension or trait. For example, recognizing the need to notify a superior regarding a certain matter could earn you credit in both judgment and planning and organization. Also, at times, following a certain course of action could lead to a positive score in one dimension-trait and a negative score in another. Consider the supervisor who takes immediate action without getting all of the facts. He/she would earn points for decisiveness but lose points in problem analysis. Therefore, your goal should be, as we state many times, to get as many positives as possible.

Practice Exercises

The following 10 multiple-choice questions test your understanding of practical assessment tests.

1. In the recent past, more and more organizations turned to the use of assessment centers to select their supervisors. Which of the following is not an accurate statement concerning this increasing use of assessment centers?
   A. The use of assessment center exercises has resulted in valid selections being made.
   B. Assessment center exercises lead to the promotion of the more qualified candidates.

C. Assessment center exercises are extremely inexpensive to conduct.
D. Assessment center exercises have proven to be fair to all protected groups.

2. Consider the following statements concerning assessment centers.
   (1) An assessment center is a place where testing takes place; it is not a process.
   (2) Assessment center exercises can test for both technical and generic skills.
   (3) Preparation to participate in an assessment center exercise cannot help the candidate obtain a better score.
   Which of the following most accurately classifies these statements into those that are accurate and those that are not?
   A. All of the statements are accurate.
   B. None of the statements is accurate.
   C. Only one statement is accurate.
   D. Only two statements are accurate.

3. The key to learning how to participate successfully in assessment center exercises is:
   A. Learning how they are scored
   B. Talking to those who have previously taken such examinations
   C. Doing extensive research in supervisory and, administrative principles
   D. Acting completely natural during the exercises

4. The key to the successful development of a particular exercise used at an assessment center is:
   A. A comprehensive job analysis
   B. A position classification plan
   C. Studying the duties of similar positions in similar agencies
   D. Intensive training of assessment center observers

5. While participating in an assessment center exercise, a certain candidate properly delegates a routine job to an appropriate subordinate. By doing this, the candidate is exhibiting high ability in:
   A. Leadership
   B. Job knowledge
   C. Planning and organization
   D. Judgment

6. Consider the following statements concerning the behavior dimension-trait of leadership:
   (1) Low-ability leadership behavior is indicated by a supervisor who gives vague directions.
   (2) Overuse of negative discipline is indicative of low leadership ability.
   (3) Criticizing a subordinate in private, not in public, exhibits high leadership ability.

   Which of the following most accurately classifies these statements into those that are accurate and those that are not?
   A. All of the statements are accurate.
   B. All of the statements are inaccurate.
   C. Only statement 1 is accurate.
   D. Only statement 3 is inaccurate.

7. Probably the easiest dimension-trait to demonstrate in an assessment center exercise such as an in-basket exercise is:
   A. Judgment
   B. Job knowledge
   C. Management control
   D. Planning and organization

8. Which of the following choices best indicates the kind(s) of assessment center exercises most often used by police departments in selecting police supervisors?
   A. Only in-basket exercises
   B. Only oral interactive interviews
   C. Only in-basket, fact-finding, and decision-making exercises
   D. In-basket, oral interactive interviews, and fact-finding and decision-making exercises

9. Consider the following statements concerning assessment center exercises.
   (1) Engaging in a single certain action can sometimes gain positive scores in more than one dimension.
   (2) Following a certain course of action could lead to a positive score in one dimension and a negative in another.
   (3) The goal in assessment center exercises is to gain as many positives as possible.

Which of the following most accurately classifies these statements into those that are accurate and those that are not?

A. All of the statements are accurate.
B. All of the statements are inaccurate.
C. Only two of the statements are accurate.
D. Only two of the statements are inaccurate.

10. A sergeant's candidate who, during an assessment center exercise, improperly interprets an organization chart, would most likely receive a negative score in which of the following traits?

A. Management control
B. Job knowledge
C. Responsiveness or sensitivity
D. Problem analysis

Answer Key, Diagnostic Procedure, and Answer Explanations

Answer Key

1. C	3. A	5. A	7. C	9. A
2. C	4. A	6. A	8. D	10. D

Diagnostic Procedure

If you scored less than nine (9) right, it is recommended you review this chapter.

Answer Explanations

1. **C** Assessment center exercises are rather expensive to conduct compared with more traditional multiple-choice tests. Raters, observers, and role players have to be provided and trained. However, because of the results of their use as outlined in choices A, B, and D, in the long run they are thought to be cost effective.

2. **C** Only statement 2 is accurate. Statement 1 is inaccurate because an assessment center is a process, not a place. Statement 3 is inaccurate because preparation can result in a better score.

3. **A** The key is to learn the dimensions or traits used in scoring the examinations and to exhibit the kind of behavior that scores positively under these dimensions.

4. **A** The job analysis identifies the knowledge, skills, and abilities required for the position for which the examination is being conducted. The examination is then prepared to find those employees who have these skills, abilities, and knowledge. This is why it is a good idea, when possible, to obtain a copy of the job analysis before the examination.

5. **A** Proper delegation of tasks is indicative of leadership or supervisory ability.

6. **A** All three statements are accurate. In your sergeant's examination it is almost a certainty that you will see a question that tests your knowledge of praising an employee in public and criticizing in private. Therefore, make sure you understand why statement 3 is correct.

7. **C** The easiest trait to exhibit, and at times the most overlooked, is management control. Telling someone to do something is not enough. You must follow up to see that it is performed properly.

8. **D** These three types of exercises seem to be utilized most often.

9. **A** As stated in this chapter, all of these statements are accurate.

10. **D** Being able to retrieve information from maps and charts is indicative of problem analysis skills.

Prepare Yourself

CHAPTER 17

In-Basket Exercises

What Is an In-Basket Exercise?

First of all, an in-basket exercise is what is known as an "individual" exercise. That means that no role players are needed to conduct the exercise. This is a major reason it is popular when large numbers of candidates are involved, although scoring an in-basket exercise can be time-consuming and costly. In any case, an in-basket exercise is an individual exercise in which the candidate assumes the role of a person in the rank for which the test is being given; for example, a police officer assumes the role of a police sergeant. In the typical in-basket examination for the rank of sergeant, the candidate plays the role of a desk sergeant whose job, in fact, includes the processing of a large amount of information on a daily basis. This information is in the form of letters, orders, memorandums, messages, official communications, and various other written instruments. The in-basket exercise measures primarily how effectively the candidate can process the information supplied to him/her or the information that, in the hypothetical sense, is in his/her in-basket when he/she assumes command of the desk. Remember, all of your responses to the items you process will be evaluated by using the behavioral dimensions or traits discussed in the chapter on practical assessment tests.

Suppose you find a letter in the in-basket alleging that a bomb is going to explode in the station house at a certain specified time within the next few hours. Consider all the judgments that can be made about a candidate simply by evaluating how he/she handles this one item.

1. Does the candidate know the current procedure in the department concerning the handling of bomb threats? If so, the candidate earns positive points for Job Knowledge.*

2. Does the candidate outline a specific course of action to deal with the bomb scare? If so, the candidate earns positive points for Planning and Organization.

3. Does the candidate take the bomb threat seriously enough? If so, the candidate earns positive points for Judgment.

4. Does the candidate take the necessary steps to notify superiors? If so, the candidate earns positive points for Organizational Sensitivity.

5. Does the candidate utilize subordinates effectively as part of the plan of action? If so, the candidate earns positive points for Delegation.

6. Does the candidate show concern for prisoners and other civilians in or near the station house? If so, the candidate earns positive points for Responsiveness.

This example should give you a good idea of the basic concept behind the in-basket exercise, which is that you are evaluated by your written responses to the items you are required to process. The evaluation is made in terms of the behavioral dimensions or traits discussed in the chapter on practical assessment tests.

Are There Two Major Types of In-Basket Exercises?

Yes, there are two major types of in-basket exercises. Basically, the difference between the two exercises lies in the way the candidate is required to respond to the items. In the more traditional form of in-basket exercise, the candidate responds to each item by writing notes, memos, messages, or letters. We call this form of in-basket exercise a nonstructured response in-basket. In other words, the way in which the candidate responds to the items is left solely up to the candidate. The responses are not limited by the structure of the examination.

---

*We have capitalized the specific behavioral dimensions-traits discussed in Chapter 16.

The second type of in-basket exercise is what we called a "structured" in-basket because the candidate responds to the items in the in-basket by answering structured questions, which are usually asked in the form of multiple-choice questions.

Is the Manner of Response the Only Difference Between a Structured and Nonstructured In-Basket Examination?

Yes, there is a definite strategy to follow to improve your score on in-basket exercises which we will present later in this chapter, and the basic strategy is the same for both types of exercises. The primary difference is your method of response. In the structured response format you answer multiple-choice questions or respond in some other way to very specific questions. In the nonstructured response format your method of response to each item is largely left to your discretion, so long as your response is in writing. The typical response takes the form of letters, memos, notations, and reminders, in much the same manner as you would actually respond if you were in fact a sergeant in your department assigned as a desk officer.

AN EXAMPLE OF THE DIFFERENCE BETWEEN STRUCTURED AND NONSTRUCTURED RESPONSES

At this point, we would like to give you a simple example of the difference between the two types of in-basket formats. Remember, however, that for ease of understanding, the following example is an oversimplification of the in-basket process, which we offer solely to firmly establish the difference between the two types of in-basket exercises you might encounter. Once that difference is firmly established, we will address the more complex and subtle aspects of the process.

Suppose the first item in your in-basket is a message to you from your commanding officer that reads as follows:

> I (your commanding officer) have unsubstantiated information that Police Officer Jones, a member of your squad, sleeps on duty when he is assigned as the station house security officer on late tours (midnight to 0800 hours). Please advise.

STRUCTURED RESPONSE

If the in-basket exercise you were taking was one that utilizes a structured response format, you might be asked to respond to the following multiple-choice question concerning this message, which is labeled as item 1 in your in-basket.

> With respect to item 1, the message from your commanding officer about Police Officer Jones, and any other related items, which of the following is the most appropriate course of action for you to follow?
>
> A. Confront Officer Jones at your earliest opportunity and get his side of the story.
> B. Immediately initiate disciplinary action against Officer Jones.
> C. Respond back to your commanding officer indicating it is unfair to accuse an officer based on unsubstantiated information.
> D. Discreetly initiate a fact-finding effort to obtain as much information as possible about the allegation.

The correct course of action from among the four alternatives offered is, of course, the one outlined in choice D. Your response, therefore, would simply be to indicate choice D as the answer on your answer sheet.

NONSTRUCTURED RESPONSE

If the response format of the exercise was nonstructured, an appropriate response would be as follows.

1. Prepare a brief note back to your commanding officer, informing him that you have received the message and that you will have a report for him by a certain, specifically stated date.

2. Make a reminder note on your calendar of the due date of the report so you will not lose track of the commitment you made to your captain.

3. Indicate a discreet fact-finding effort, which would include a review of Officer Jones's performance evaluations, assignments, with particular attention to any indication of his activity or lack of activity on those times, if any, when he was assigned as the station house security officer on the late hour, and interviews with other supervisors who might be able to shed light on the situation.

4. After obtaining sufficient facts, if necessary, discuss the matter with Officer Jones.

5. Make a determination, and outline a remedial course of action, if necessary.

6. Report to the commanding officer as scheduled. If necessary, submit an interim report.

The response would then, in turn, result in your receiving points in the following areas.

Organizational sensitivity, for keeping your commanding officer informed

Planning and organization, for outlining a detailed course of action

Management control, for making the "tickler" or follow-up notation on your calendar

Problem analysis, for seeking additional information

Responsiveness, for indicating you would conduct a discreet investigation

Judgment, for not acting without the facts in the matter

The difference between the two types of formats is, we hope, now clear to you. Our next step is to make you familiar with the kinds of material you can expect to find in your in-basket.

A Review of Material Commonly Found in an In-Basket Exercise

No two in-basket exercises are constructed in exactly the same way, but you can expect to find the following material in most of them.

SET OF INSTRUCTIONS

The instructions governing the exercise are crucial and must be read very carefully. For one thing, you must fully understand the time allotted for completing the exercise. Time management is critical for an in-basket exercise, as it is for all examinations. We will say more about time management later. The instructions also create the artificial situation for you that you must understand. In other words, the in-basket exercise requires you to play a role. You will be given specifics about that role in the instructions. You must pay particular attention to the following.

Who you are in the exercise. You will be given a name, and you must understand that, for the purposes of the exercise, you are that artificial person. If you sign any communications, you must use your assigned name.

Where you are working. You will be told what police department you are working in for the purpose of the exercise. It might be your actual department, or it could be a ficticious police department.

The date and time. Understanding the time frames involved is critical to your success in the exercise. You will be told the specific date on which the artificial situation in the exercise is occurring. You will also be given the time of the day. Please note that all your scheduling decisions must be made from the point of reference of the particular date and time created for you by the instructions.

Who else is available to help you, and who is not available to help you. Many in-basket exercises put you in a situation in which you are isolated from any help and, quite often, a situation is created that requires you to leave town immediately after completing the exercise and that keeps you out of town, incommunicado, for a period of time. Other in-basket exercises tell you who else is working and who is not working. You are then free to utilize the services of anyone available to you. You must be sure to assume final responsibility for any delegations you make.

The scope of your authority. Many times you will be given an organization chart to help you understand who your subordinates are, who your peers are, and who your superiors are. However, even if you are not given an organization chart, the instructions will develop the scope of your authority for you. You must be careful to properly exercise that authority throughout the exercise. For example, you will be given positive points if you delegate certain tasks, but you must delegate to the appropriate person over whom you have authority. You should not delegate to those not in your chain of command.

What to base your answers on. The instructions will inform you if your exercise will test technical skills, generic skills, or both. If, for example, you were told to base your answers strictly on the information available in the packet, you are taking a generic skills exercise and will not need to use any technical skills. If you are told to base your answers on your knowledge of law and department policies, procedures, and so on, then you will be required to exhibit technical skills. If the setting for the exercise is the police agency you work for, then again, you probably will be asked to exercise technical skills. If the setting is a fictitious police department in a fictitious location, however, then you should base your answers on the information in the packet and your generic skills. If you are not certain of the distinction between generic skills and technical skills, you should review Chapter 16.

A LISTING OF PAGES IN THE PACKET

Usually the first item after the instructions is a list of pages in the packet. We refer to this page as the "index" page, and it plays a very important role in the test-taking strategy we present later in this chapter. For an example of what an index page looks like, see Chapter 21, page 571.

A CALENDAR

Most in-baskets contain a blank calendar page as part of the package. The value of the calendar is very high if the exercise is of the nonstructured response format. By making entries on the calendar concerning your schedule you earn Planning and Organization points, and entries concerning follow-up earn you Management Control points. However, in a structured response format, that is, multiple-choice questions, entries on the calendar do not earn you extra credits.

AN ORGANIZATION CHART

An organization chart is often included in the material. Remember, it may be an actual organization of the department you work in or that of the fictitious department that has been created for you in the instructions.

A MAP

Most in-basket exercises contain a map of the area or precinct you are working in according to the simulated or artificial situation. The map is often helpful in answering questions concerning the appropriate post, beat, or sector to assign to a call for assistance at a certain location.

BACKGROUND INFORMATION

Usually included in the in-basket materials packet is a host of background information on the city you work in, on the department you work in, and on the people you work with. We will emphasize this point again later in this chapter when we outline a strategy for you to follow, but it is important to point out at this time that it is a big mistake to "study" the background information unless and until you are certain you will need the information to respond to the items and/or questions about the items. Be aware that examiners love to include what they refer to as filler material. This is complex and lengthy material that although it looks important and relevant, is not used as the basis for any responses on your part. Therefore, it is a waste of time for you to study it. You only study the material when you are certain you need the information to frame an answer. *Beware of filler material!* Also, please note that this material is often referred to as "special pages" because it often has special use during the exercise.

VARIOUS ITEMS TO WHICH YOU WILL BE ASKED TO RESPOND

Following the special material itemized above, you will be given a number of letters, memos, orders, messages, and other forms of written communications you will be requested to process.

Be mindful of the following.

1. Instructions for in-basket exercises vary considerably from exercise to exercise. This is so because there is no one format for this type of exercise. Therefore, you must very carefully read the instructions as they appear on your examination. However, the general concepts are the same for all such exercises. This is why we can offer you a general strategy to follow. Your job is to understand the general concepts and strategies involved and then adapt them to the type of exercise you are given.

2. The items in your informational packet are numbered consecutively. It is our very strong advice that you do not take any items out of their numerical sequence. You must be able to find various items in the packet at various times during the exercise with a minimum of effort and as quickly as possible. The surest way of being able to do this is to keep the items in their numerical order.

A Strategy for Taking an In-Basket Test

Please note that the test-taking strategy outlined below is appropriate for use regardless of the response format of the exercise. The strategy is as follows:

Carefully read the instructions. Remember, as we emphasized above, when reading the instructions you must be certain that you know:

1. How much time you have to complete the exercise

2. The details of the role you will be playing in the exercise

3. On what knowledge, technical and/or generic, to base your responses.

4. When reading the instructions, it is often quite helpful to underline key points and also to make notes in the margin concerning what you perceive to be very important points.

Check your materials. After reading the instructions and before starting to work, you should make a quick check to make sure you have all of the materials. When there is an index page, you can use it to help you account for all of the special pages and items you should have. While making this quick check, you should determine what response format is being used—that is, structured or nonstructured.

Engage in time management. At this point you must develop a time allocation plan to follow. To develop this plan, it is important to understand that there are two separate phases involved in our strategy, as follows:

1. Reviewing and familiarizing yourself with the material in the in-basket

2. Responding to the items

A good rule of thumb when developing your time usage plan is to allow yourself enough time to adequately review the material, up to one-third of the allotted time. For example, if you are given three hours to respond to twenty items, you should use up to a maximum of one hour reviewing and becoming familiar with the material. The rest of the time is to be used responding to the items.

Familiarize yourself with the material in the in-basket. Here is without question where most untrained candidates go wrong. Their error can be summed up in one very clear mandate, as follows:

It is absolute insanity to begin to respond to items in the in-basket until you first review and become familiar with all of the material in the package. However, it is equally absurd to study the items at this time. Just become familiar with them.

The reasons this initial review of the material is important are as follows. In order to respond appropriately to some of the items, but not all of them, you must use information contained in more than one item. Therefore, before responding to any items, you must understand which items in the packet are related to each other. A simple example should make the importance of this initial review quite clear. Suppose item 3 in the in-basket was as follows:

Item 3: Invitation to attend a boy's club meeting on September 15 at 1800 hours.

Normally, such an invitation should be accepted unless there is a specific reason not to, such as another, more pressing commitment for that date and time. Now let's suppose that item 15 contained the following information.

Item 15: Direction from your commanding officer to attend a meeting with him on September 15 at 1800 hours.

If you had not reviewed the material before responding to the items, you probably would have accepted the invitation in item 3, only to realize when you came to item 15 that you must comply with your commanding officer's direction to attend the meeting on the same date and time as the scheduled boy's club meeting, which you have already accepted. This is, of course, assuming that you even spot the conflict. There is always the possibility you could mistakenly agree to attend both meetings. Therefore, the first question you must ask yourself before responding to any item is whether there are related items in the packet. In order to know the answer to that question, you must be familiar with all of the material in the packet ahead of time. It is for this reason that the "indexing" process, as explained below, is *very important*.

Another reason for reviewing and indexing the material before responding to the items is that examiners often include an item toward the end of the packet that could affect the way you must respond to many of the items coming before it. For example, suppose you are given information that the commander of the precinct detectives is a Sergeant John Harris. Then, throughout the exercise, you appropriately delegate a number of tasks to Sergeant Harris only to come upon an item near the end of the material informing you that Sergeant Harris recently took ill and is on long-term sick leave. In his place, the commanding officer has assigned a Detective Brown. Your dilemma upon learning this information is clear. Equally clear is that an initial review of the material would have prevented the dilemma.

The most important step is indexing. When you review the material in the packet prior to responding to any of the items, you must engage in a systematic review, and you must make some written notes during the review. In other words, you must index the material. By indexing we mean using the index page (mentioned above) that is usually included at the beginning of your package of material to record key information from each item in the packet. For a sample of what a blank index page looks like, see Chapter 21, page 571. If you are not supplied with an index page, simply make one yourself. Another way to view the indexing process is to think of it as a labeling process. You are going to label each item in the packet by transposing certain key information from each item on to the index sheet. The following is the kind of information that should be included on the index sheet as it relates to each item in the packet:

Brief title or label, which captures the subject matter of the item.

Pertinent dates, especially dates of meetings, events, occurrences, deadlines, due dates, transfers, and others.

Names of members of the department, complainants, victims, and others.

Important locations, but not all locations.

Cross-referencing, by indicating on the index sheet which items are related to each other. To do this properly it is necessary, of course, for you to recognize while you are indexing what interrelationships exist. The way you indicate an interrelationship between items on the index sheet is by placing the number of the related item next to the item on the sheet it relates to. This means that for every interrelationship that exists, two entries have to be made. If, for example, item 1 in the in-basket relates to item 2, we have shown below how you would show this interrelationship on the index sheet.

② Item 1:   Officer Jones requests transfer

① Item 2:   Internal Affairs investigation of P.O. Jones

Notice that the items are related since they both deal with Officer Jones. While indexing, you show this interrelationship by the circled number to the left of the word "item." For an example of a completed index sheet, see Chapter 21, page 606. Notice the circled numbers next to the items. These are the numbers that show interrelationships. Also note that it is the candidate who labels each item in his/her own handwriting, as above.

Remember that indexing material doesn't mean studying it. It is very important for you to understand that indexing the material does not mean studying the material. If you spend too much time reading items while you are indexing, you will run out of time. All that is needed initially is for you to get a working knowledge of the information in the packet and to recognize the items that are related in some way to each other. Remember, the maximum amount of time you should spend indexing is one-third the time allotted to complete the entire exercise.

Respond to the items. Once your indexing is complete, you have labeled each item on your index sheet, and you have also shown interrelationships on the index sheet as explained above, you are now ready to respond to the items. Remember, before responding to any item, check your index sheet to see if the item you are responding to is related to any other items in the exercise. If it is, consider both items when responding. Bear in mind, however, that because an item is related in some way to one or more items in the packet doesn't automatically mean you need the information from all of the related items to respond to the item in question. Nonetheless, consider all related items before responding. As a review, your response will vary according to the format of the exercise. Structured formats require objective answers to definitive questions, such as selecting an answer in a multiple-choice question. Non-structured formats require you to respond by writing memos, notes, messages, and so on.

Miscellaneous Tips and Comments

1. Efficient time management is essential to success.

2. Read your instructions very carefully.

3. Make sure you know on what to base your answers.

4. In a nonstructured response format, make planning and control entries on your calendar. Also make great use of "carbon copies" to keep your superiors informed in appropriate cases.

5. Constantly remain aware of the date and time of the simulated situation.

6. It is conceivable that the examiner could use actual forms from your department. If actual forms are used, you are responsible for making sure they are properly filled out.

7. In a structured response format, you might be asked to respond to items out of sequence. Don't let this bother you, but remember to keep your pack in numerical sequence.

8. You might be asked to do some simple arithmetic computations. They will not be difficult mathematically. Instead, the difficulty could come from making sure you are in fact making the correct computation.

9. Certain items may test your knowledge of when it is appropriate to put something off and when immediate action is necessary. Remember, items that pose a threat to someone's safety or that could damage the department's reputation should be acted upon immediately.

10. It is always a good rule to show responsiveness. That is, you should always demonstrate your concern for the feelings of others.

11. Be extremely watchful for dates that might cause a conflict for you.

12. Always seek additional information when it is possible. Always ask to be kept informed. Always indicate in writing that you are going to follow up on delegations.

13. Pay close attention to handwritten notes on items. What the notation says is very often the key to your response, especially if it is a direction from your commanding officer.

14. Be wary of complicated filler material. Don't waste time studying material you might not have to respond to.

15. If you are asked after the exercise to outline the strategy you used, always indicate that you considered the matters you thought to be important first, ahead of routine matters. In other words, in a non-structured response format, you should prioritize the items and explain why, but only if asked to do so.

16. Remember, an item can be related to more than one other item.

17. In a nonstructured response format, you will always earn Problem Analysis points by mentioning interrelationships among items.

18. In a nonstructured response, you should use short, simple sentences when writing communications, especially formal letters. Be careful of your spelling, grammar, and punctuation. In all probability your writing skill will be evaluated.

Practice Exercises

1. Which of the following is the most accurate statement concerning in-basket examinations?
   A. In-basket examinations measure traits that other assessment center exercises are not able to measure.
   B. In-basket exercises always require exceptional writing ability to score well.
   C. In-basket exercises do not require trained role players to act as examiners.
   D. In-basket exercises are not very useful because they are not capable of being job related.

2. An employee taking an in-basket examination would be faced with responding to multiple-choice type questions when taking:
   A. A structured exercise
   B. A nonstructured exercise
   C. Both structured and nonstructured exercises
   D. Neither a structured nor a nonstructured exercise

3. When taking an in-basket examination, a positive score for Management Control is obtained by:
   A. Recognizing interrelationships between the various items
   B. Making appropriate follow-up notations on a calendar
   C. Keeping your superiors informed
   D. Not acting without the facts in the matter

4. A certain candidate, while taking a nonstructured in-basket examination, outlines a detailed course of action to follow in dealing with one of the items in the exercise. The candidate would most likely receive a positive score in:
   A. Responsiveness
   B. Organizational Sensitivity
   C. Problem Analysis
   D. Planning and Organization

5. While performing an in-basket exercise a candidate properly cross-references related items. In responding to the various items, the candidate makes appropriate use of the "index." These actions would most directly result in positive scoring in the trait or dimension of:
   A. Organizational Sensitivity
   B. Planning and Organization
   C. Management Control
   D. Problem Analysis

6. Consider the following statements concerning in-basket examinations.
   (1) In-basket examinations always test for technical skills.
   (2) The instructions for an in-basket exercise usually contain a list of the items appearing on the examination.
   (3) Each item on the examination should be studied while indexing.
   Which of the following most accurately classifies these statements into those that are accurate and those that are not?
   A. All of the statements are accurate.
   B. All of the statements are inaccurate.
   C. Only two of the statements are accurate.
   D. Only one of the statements is accurate.

7. Which of the following least accurately describes what is known as a "special" in an in-basket exercise?
   A. A letter from a neighborhood merchant
   B. An organizational chart of the precinct
   C. A map of the city
   D. A calendar

8. If the allotted time for an in-basket examination is three hours, how much time should be spent on the "Indexing" effort?
   A. A maximum of thirty minutes
   B. A maximum of forty-five minutes
   C. A maximum of one hour
   D. A maximum of one-and-one-half hours

9. Consider the following statements concerning in-basket examinations.
   (1) An item can be related to more than one other item.
   (2) Examiners sometimes insert complicated filler material to see if you will waste time studying it.
   (3) In a structured response format, it may be required to respond to items out of sequence.
   Which of the following most accurately classifies these statements into those that are accurate and those that are not?
   A. All of the statements are accurate.
   B. All of the statements are inaccurate.
   C. Only statements 1 and 2 are accurate.
   D. Only statements 2 and 3 are accurate.

10. Which of the following best indicates the difference between a structured and nonstructured in-basket examination?
    A. The traits or dimensions tested are different.
    B. The difference lies in the method of response.
    C. The structured in-basket examination requires more preparation on the part of the candidate.
    D. The "indexing" effort is more important in a nonstructured examination.

Answer Key, Diagnostic Procedure, and Answer Explanations

Answer Key

1. C	3. B	5. D	7. A	9. A
2. A	4. D	6. B	8. C	10. B

Diagnostic Procedure

If you scored less than nine (9) right, it is recommended you review this chapter before taking the sample in-basket exercise in Chapter 21.

Answer Explanations

1. **C** In-basket exercises do not require role players to conduct the exercise. They are individual assessment exercises. This means they involve only the candidate. Choice C is correct. Choice A is incorrect because the traits measured by in-basket exercises can be measured by other assessment exercises. Choice B is incorrect because a structured in-basket does not require any writing at all, just a response to a multiple-choice question. Choice D is false because in-basket exercises, if properly prepared, can be very job related.

2. **A** In a structured in-basket exercise, the responses are limited by the multiple-choice format of the examination. In a nonstructured type, the employee responds to each item by writing notes, memos, letters, messages, and so on.

3. **B** Management Control is exhibited by the use of "tickler" devices or notations on a calendar to control actions taken or delegations made. Choice A is a Problem Analysis trait; choice C is a Planning and Organization trait; choice D is a Judgment trait.

4. **D** Indicating a detailed course of action for you and your subordinates gains points for Planning and Organization. If the course of action is appropriate, it could also gain credit for Judgment and Leadership.

5. **D** A key part of Problem Analysis is the ability to pull together related information appearing in different places.

6. **B** In-basket exercises test for generic and/or technical skills; the index sheet, not the instructions, lists all of the items; the items should not be studied when indexing. All that is required is enough to label each item on the index sheet. All of the choices are inaccurate.

7. **A** "Specials" are material in the packet that give you information and usually do not call for a response. They are called specials because they are often of special use in responding to the items. Choices B, C, and D are specials. Choice A is an example of an item.

8. **C** The indexing effort is extremely important. It is recommended that about one-third of the examination time be spent on it. Any more time would hurt your chances to adequately respond to the items. Also, notice we say a maximum of one hour. If you can do a good indexing job in less time, all the better.

9. **A** All of the statements are accurate. One item can be related to more than one other item, and examiners often insert lengthy material among the items to see if you are clever enough not to waste time studying the material. Finally, you are not always asked in a structured (multiple-choice) format to respond to questions about the items in sequence. You might be asked just about item 8 and about item 1.

10. **B** The only difference is the method of response (some form of multiple-choice versus written notes and memos). The traits tested are the same, as well as the preparation required. Finally, indexing is equally important in both types of formats.

CHAPTER 18

Oral Interactive Interviews

What Are They?

As the name implies, oral interactive interviews are interviews in which the participant "interacts" in some way with the interviewer or a group of interviewers. In some oral interactive interviews, you will be asked to assume a "role" or a "simulated identity." In others you will be asked direct questions that you answer without having to assume a simulated identity. Still others use a combination of questions, including some that require you to play a role and others that do not require you to role play. Additionally, in any of these interviews, the interviewers may or may not role play. Finally, some oral interactive interviews are structured so that you get material ahead of time to study, and some do not require the advance studying of material. These interviews are known by a variety of names, but for the purpose of this discussion we will title and define the most common oral interactive interviews as follows.

Straight interview: an interview in which neither the candidate nor the interviewer has to assume a role and for which no advance material is distributed for study by the candidate.

Single-role straight interview: an interview that does not involve advance material. However, the candidate has to assume a role; the interviewer does not.

Combination straight interview: an interview, not involving advance material, in which the candidate is asked a number of questions, some of which require the assumption of a role by the candidate and others that do not involve role playing by the candidate. In neither case does the interviewer assume a role.

Structured interactive interview: an interview that involves two-way role playing and is usually based primarily on material given to the candidate ahead of time. In other words, both the candidate and the interviewer assume simulated identities, and the interview concerns itself primarily with material the candidate has had the opportunity to study prior to the actual interview. In this structured type of interview the interviewer-role player asks one or more general questions, and he/she remains neutral during the candidate's response. In other words, the role player's job in this format is simply to ask the initial questions. It is therefore not a fully interactive situation.

Nonstructured interactive interview: an interview that is usually based primarily on material distributed to the candidate ahead of time and that involves continuous role playing throughout the interview by both the interviewer and the candidate. Because it is fully interactive, it is the most time-consuming and expensive interview format to prepare and administer. This is so since the interviewer-role player must be thoroughly trained as to how to respond to the candidate during the interview. This is why we call it a nonstructured interview, since the interview in effect goes wherever the candidate takes it.

The Number of Interviewers or Role Players Can Vary

In any of these interview situations, the number of interviewer-role players can be varied from one to three or more. If you hear the term "one-on-one" interview, therefore, it means an interview in which there is one interviewer-role player for one candidate. A "three-on-one" interview is one that utilizes three interviewer-role players for one candidate.

How Are These Interviews Scored?

The oral interactive type of assessment center exercises, like all other types, is scored by using the behavioral traits or dimensions we defined and explained for you in Chapter 16. If you keep these dimensions in mind when framing your answers, you will always do well. What we recommend is for you to practice structuring responses to possible questions in terms of these dimensions-traits. Remember, a candidate who demonstrates the behavioral dimensions-traits we discussed in Chapter 16 is the candidate your department believes is going to make the best supervisor. Therefore, it makes good sense to practice demonstrating these dimensions-traits when making oral or written responses to job-related questions of any kind. We recommend that you carry this "practice" over to actual performance of your job. We feel this way because we believe that the best supervisors do in fact display these dimensions-traits on the job. As previously mentioned, however, the intent of this book is to help you pass your promotion examination. It just so happens that if you do in fact behave on the job in the same manner we are suggesting you behave while taking an assessment center exercise, you will probably become a good supervisor when you get promoted. Our next step in getting you ready to participate in an oral interactive interview is to explain a little more about the specifics of each of the different interview formats mentioned above. This will be followed by a recommended strategy to follow when framing responses. After that we will conclude the chapter with a review of some typical questions you might be asked during an oral interview, and for each question we will offer a suggested response.

Always Determine Ahead of Time If You Should Include in Your Responses Any Specific Technical Knowledge About Your Own Department

The issue of "generic" responses versus "technical" responses is one you must always clear up in your mind before participating in any assessment center exercise. If you do not understand what we mean when we make this statement, then you must review that section of Chapter 16 where we discuss in detail the difference between "technical" and "generic" responses. As a brief review, a generic response would be appropriate if the role you are playing in the interview requires you to assume that you are a police supervisor working in a "typical" police department rather than the particular department in which you actually work. If this is the case, you shouldn't limit yourself to answering in terms of how things are done in your department. Instead, you should display a more "generic" knowledge of the police profession. If, on the other hand, the role you are to assume makes you a supervisor in the particular department you actually work in, then your responses should be "technical" in that you should display a good working knowledge of the resources, policies, and procedures of your department. If necessary, before the scored interview begins, you should ask the examiner for a clarification of this issue. You must know ahead of time if you are expected to include "technical" knowledge in your responses.

The Specifics of Straight Interviews

There are, as mentioned above, three types of straight interviews:

1. Straight interview

2. Single-role straight interview

3. Combination straight interview

The common threads in each of these three formats are that there is no advance material distributed and the interviewer does not play a role. You, the candidate, may or may not be expected to play a role. Remember, if you are asked to assume a role, make certain you understand if the role is in a "typical" police department or in your own police department.

HOW DO STRAIGHT INTERVIEWS WORK?

In a straight interview, you are brought into the place where the interview is going to take place at a certain predetermined time. You can expect to see one or more interviewers, a tape recorder, or equipment to videotape the interview. You will then be asked a series of job-related questions. Some or all of the questions might begin with the statement, "Assume you are a police sergeant in a police agency" or "Assume you are a police sergeant in your own police department." In many cases, you will be given a typewritten copy of the question. After the interviewer reads you the text of the question, you make your response. You do not have to respond immediately. In fact, if you are uncertain of the specifics of the question, or unsure of how to respond, you would be foolish to respond immediately.

If you are not sure of the specifics of the question and you have a copy of the question, ask permission to reread the question. It is imperative that you understand the question before you begin your response. If you don't have a copy of the question, ask for it to be repeated. If permissible, make written notes outlining points you want to make. If not, make mental notes. Remember to respond in a logical sequence. Use an introduction and a body, and end with a summary and/or a conclusion. Try to include as many facts as possible in your unprompted, initial response. Remember to think in terms of the behavioral dimensions or traits discussed in Chapter 16.

After you give your unprompted response, the interviewer may or may not question you further. Please note that just because the interviewer doesn't play a role in straight interviews doesn't necessarily mean he/she cannot ask you questions. Later in this chapter we will present a strategy for answering questions and will review typical questions and suggested responses.

After the interview is concluded, you will probably be asked if you have any comments. Although it is wise at this time to say something pleasant, you should not state that you believe the examination was fair or make any positive comments about the content matter of the examination. Making such statements could be damaging should you later want to appeal the results. We recommend, therefore, that you make a positive comment about the professional manner of the interviewers if you are asked for a comment.

A final note: unless you are specifically prohibited from doing so, we strongly urge that you seek out people who have already gone through the process on previous examinations. Try to get a good understanding of what to expect, as well as the kinds of questions you will be asked. If possible, approach someone who has already been promoted to or past the rank you are competing for. Remember that there is no guarantee that your examination will replicate previous examinations. More often than not, however, it will.

The Specifics of Interactive Interviews

Interactive interviews have the following common elements.

1. They involve two-way role playing. Both the interviewer and the candidate assume simulated identities. The candidate's role is always the same. In an examination for the rank of sergeant, the candidate would always play the role of a police sergeant. The interview-role players can act as ranking officers in the department, as subordinates, or even as members of the community.

2. Interactive interviews are almost always based on information that has been distributed in advance. It is your job to become as familiar with this information as possible before the interview. You are usually allowed to make as many notes as you wish about the information, and you may bring these notes into the examination room with you and refer to them during the interview. You can also refer to the package of material that was distributed to you.

As previously mentioned, the major difference between the structured and nonstructured interactive interviews is that in the structured interview the role player remains neutral. In other words, the role players in a structured oral interactive interview say very little after they ask their initial questions. They are told to downplay interpersonal relations. They are trained to avoid answering questions. Since they have no information that can help you, you should be alert to recognize the signs of a structured interview, and once you determined your interview to be of the structured format, avoid asking questions of the interviewer-role players and concentrate on making fully comprehensive responses to their questions.

On the other hand, the interviewer-role players in a nonstructured interview do have information that can help you, so you must intelligently interact with them. Once you see the interviewer-role players are responding to your questions with good information, you should realize you are in a nonstructured interview format and you should then probe for information.

A general rule to follow to try to get an idea ahead of time as to which format your interview will be—structured or nonstructured— is to closely analyze the instructions accompanying the advance material. Key in on the following.

With whom are you meeting? If the instructions say you are meeting with reporters, politicians, community leaders, or other persons outside the job, the interview will probably (not definitely) be structured. If you are meeting with another member of the police department, the interview will probably be nonstructured.

What are you meeting for? If you are told in the instructions that you will be asked several questions during the meeting, your interview will probably be structured. If you are told you are meeting to discuss some issues or problems, your interview will probably be nonstructured. Remember, in nonstructured interviews you should probe for information to help you make your decision.

HOW DO INTERACTIVE INTERVIEWS WORK?

In interactive interviews you must remember that both you and the interviewer(s) are playing roles, and you must play your role convincingly. You will be given a simulated identity ahead of time. When you enter the examination room you should be cordial to the "people you are meeting with" (the interviewers). You should introduce yourself, making certain to use your assigned name and make some other pertinent comment, such as, "I'm so happy to have this chance to meet with you." Also, be prepared to see recording equipment in the room.

ORAL PRESENTATIONS

Many times the instructions will inform you that you are expected to make a brief oral presentation before the questioning begins. If this is the case you will be given the subject matter of your presentation as well as the time frames involved. You should be very careful to stay within the prescribed time frames. Your presentation, which is based on the material you are given ahead of time, should be logically arranged. It should have an introduction, a body, and a conclusion. You should not simply read a prepared speech. You must make eye contact, use hand gestures, and inflect your voice.

THE QUESTIONING PERIOD

If you are asked questions during the interview, make certain you understand the question. In framing your response, think in terms of the behavioral dimensions or traits discussed in Chapter 16. Also, use the suggestions made in the strategy section later in this chapter, and review the typical questions and suggested responses that conclude this chapter.

THE DISCUSSION PERIOD

As mentioned above, fully interactive nonstructured oral interviews often involve a discussion of some kind of problem situation. In this situation you must probe the interviewer-role players for all the facts. When, and only when, you have all the facts, make a logical decision based on the facts. Be guided by the behavioral dimensions-traits discussed in Chapter 16 and the following strategy and review of typical questions and suggested responses.

A Strategy for Responding to Questions Regardless of the Content Matter of the Questions

Listed below are some general rules to follow during an oral interview, which will earn you credit regardless of the content matter of the question.

1. Always be cordial to interviewer-role players; this will earn you Responsiveness points.

2. Always show a desire to obtain as much information as possible about a problem or situation; this will earn you Problem Analysis points.

3. Always set specific due dates for completion of assignments or delegations, and make a written notation of the dates involved; this will earn you Management Control points.

4. Always be sympathetic to the plight of victims and complainants, and always make sure you do all you can to meet their needs; this will earn you Responsiveness points.

5. Always make certain to stay within the time frames of the exercise, and always make sure you respond to all questions; this will earn you Planning and Organization points.

6. Always remember to contact complainants of the results of the handling of their complaints; this will earn you Responsiveness points.

7. Always make certain you make mention of interrelated items; this will earn you Problem Analysis points.

8. Always remember to make eye contact, use gestures, and employ voice inflection when speaking, and never simply read a prepared statement; this will earn you oral Communication points.

9. When you have been given material ahead of time, wherever possible refer to information in the material when making a response; this will earn you Problem Analysis and Planning and Organization points.

10. Always try to utilize all the resources available to you when dealing with a problem situation; this will earn you Planning and Organization and Leadership points.

11. Always show a willingness to involve others in the planning process; this will earn you Planning and Organization and Leadership points.

12. Always use available statistics to guide you in the decision-making process; this will earn you Judgment and Planning and Organization points.

13. Always show great concern for the protection of life; this will earn you Judgment points.

14. Never make decisions based on insufficient facts; this will earn you Judgment points.

15. Never use jargon or shop talk when communicating with non-police personnel unless you explain your meaning; this will earn you Judgment points.

Typical Questions and Suggested Responses

A great many job-related situations lend themselves to good questions for purposes of oral interactive interviews. Also considerable are the varying specifics that can be built into each situation. Therefore, what we are going to do now is to review five typical situations you could be asked about during your promotional interview. We will then offer, in outline form, suggested responses for each situation. Your job is to become familiar with the process used to develop a response. You will see that there is a definite pattern involved. You must always go through the same steps, as follows.

1. Make sure you understand the situation.

2. Be sensitive to the feelings of everyone involved.

3. Insofar as possible, verify the information you have.

4. Consider alternatives. Good planning requires the development and consideration of alternatives.

5. Make a decision after you have all the facts.

6. Follow up on your source of action.

TYPICAL SITUATION 1

It is called to your attention that a worker with a previous good record is no longer performing up to standards. What should you do?

SUGGESTED RESPONSE

1. Consider how you found out about the problem. If someone brought it to your attention, thank him/her.

2. Verify facts. Was the worker really performing well in the past? Is the worker really performing poorly now?

3. Consider personal problems. Discreetly try to determine if the officer is experiencing some personal problems. This is often the case when a good worker goes bad.

4. Consider other reasons for problems. Has the officer recently been reassigned to new duties? Does he/she have a new supervisor?

5. Get as much background information as possible. Always look for documentation of possible problems. If possible, refer to the material you received ahead of time.

6. Meet with the officer and get his/her history. When appropriate, protect the identity of your original source of information.

7. Leave the meeting with some sort of decision made. Insofar as possible, develop a detailed plan to deal with the problem.

8. Make provisions to follow up on the matter.

TYPICAL SITUATION 2

A disciplinary problem is brought to your attention. It might involve a worker who is allegedly getting favorable treatment. What should you do? Assume that the worker is supervised by a police officer whom you supervise.

SUGGESTED RESPONSE

1. State immediately that you intend to resolve the matter since maintaining discipline is a major responsibility of the first-line supervisor.

2. Consider the source of your information. Take steps to keep the flow of information coming. If the information is anonymous, fully investigate anyway. State that anonymous information is often valuable.

3. Verify all of your facts. Get background information, including performance records.

4. If appropriate, protect the identity of the complainant.

5. Interview the supervisor involved. Remember always to follow the chain of command in these cases. Make sure you tell the supervisor your policy concerning disciplinary matters. Include a statement that rules should be applied equally to all workers and that supervisors should avoid the appearance of favoritism.

6. If a worker is to be disciplined, direct that it be done properly and in private. If appropriate, mention the prior good record of the employee. Be sensitive when disciplining.

7. Make a firm decision. Develop a firm course of action.

8. Make provisions to follow up on the matter.

TYPICAL SITUATION 3

You are informed that one of your subordinates might have a drinking or drug problem. What should you do?

SUGGESTED RESPONSE

1. State your policy in these matters immediately. Indicate that this is a serious problem. If the information is accurate, then fast action is imperative.

2. Show concern for the worker. Indicate that, although alcohol and drug abuse cannot be tolerated, such conduct is indicative of a sickness and should be handled accordingly.

3. Get background information on the worker. Talk to him or her. Get all the facts.

4. Indicate that because of possible serious ramifications of the situation, this is a top-priority matter.

5. Show an extensive knowledge of the resources available to you to assist in resolving the problem—department or municipal counselors, availability of Alcoholics Anonymous program, employee assistance programs, and others.

6. Do not rely on transfer.

7. Develop a detailed plan to deal with the situation.

8. Make provisions to follow up on the matter.

TYPICAL SITUATION 4

You are newly assigned to supervise a unit that is not performing well. What should you do?

SUGGESTED RESPONSE

1. Verify that a problem exists. Don't make immediate, rapid changes before a period of review and evaluation.

2. Gather all the facts. Meet with workers. Understand the real problem.

3. Make sure every worker knows what's expected of him or her.

4. Consider that some rules may be outdated or not known.

5. Consider the need for training. Remember, training should always be continuous.

6. Develop a detailed course of action. Involve those to be affected by the plan in the implementation of the plan.

7. Follow up on the matter. Retrain if necessary. Consider the need for disciplinary action, if appropriate, but only after positive discipline, such as training, fails.

TYPICAL SITUATION 5

A member of the community complains about conditions in the neighborhood and requests more police protection. What should you do?

SUGGESTED RESPONSE

1. Be sensitive with the complainant. Assure the complainant you will look into the matter and get back to him/her.

2. Verify the complaint. Gather facts. Analyze available statistics.

3. Find out about the complainant in a discreet manner.

4. Consider alternative ways to deal with the complainant.

5. Gain concurrences from your supervisor, if necessary. In any case, inform your supervisor.

6. Decide on a detailed course of action.

7. Inform the complainant concerning your decision.

8. Make provisions to follow up on the matter.

General Steps for Problem Solving

It should be remembered that no matter what type of problem you are confronted with during an oral interactive interview, there are some general steps you can rely on to help you decide on a course of action to deal with that problem. These general steps are as follows:

1. Clearly verify/identify the existence of the problem by
   a. interviewing the complainant, and/or,
   b. checking appropriate records, and/or,
   c. interviewing concerned parties such as witnesses, victims, and other involved persons

2. Analyze the accuracy of the details involved by
   a. considering the past reliability of all sources of information, and
   b. comparing all information concerned for consistencies and inconsistencies

3. Arrive at a course of action by
   a. utilizing all pertinent information, and,
   b. considering the needs of the public, your agency, and all involved individuals, and,
   c. where appropriate, gaining the concurrences of those concerned, such as the complainant, the subject of the complaint, your supervisor, and anyone else whose cooperation is critical to the success of your plan

4. Implement your course of action, making sure that
   a. everyone who should be notified is notified
   b. all required available resources are utilized
   c. necessary coordination of effort is accomplished
   d. responsibility is clearly fixed
   e. necessary authority is delegated to carry out responsibilities assigned

5. Follow up by
   a. conducting personal inspections
   b. requiring written reports at specified times
   c. setting due dates for accomplishments, making sure to utilize proven control techniques such as a tickler file or notations on a calendar

Practice Exercises

1. In which of the following assessment center interview exercises is the candidate usually provided with material to study in advance of the interview?
   A. Straight interview
   B. Structured interactive interview
   C. Single-role straight interview
   D. Combination straight interview

2. The type of assessment center interview exercise in which the role player's job is simply to ask the initial question is a:
   A. Structured interactive interview
   B. Nonstructured interactive interview
   C. Combination straight interview
   D. Straight interview

3. The type of interview found in assessment center exercises that is most expensive to administer is the:
   A. Nonstructured interactive interview
   B. Structured interactive interview
   C. Single-role straight interview
   D. Combination straight interview

4. All of the following interviews utilized by assessment centers do not have role players, except:
   A. Straight interviews
   B. Combination straight interviews
   C. Single-role straight interviews
   D. Nonstructured interactive interviews

5. Consider the following statements concerning the interviews conducted during assessment center exercises.
   (1) When role players are required, the number of role players is never more than two.
   (2) A special type of behavioral trait not found in other assessment center exercises is used to score interactive interviews.
   (3) Time is not an important factor and should not be considered by the candidate being interviewed.
   Which of the following most accurately classifies these statements into those that are accurate and those that are not?
   A. All of the statements are accurate.
   B. All of the statements are inaccurate.
   C. Only one of the statements is accurate.
   D. Only one of the statements is inaccurate.

6. What is the main difference between a structured interactive interview and a nonstructured interactive interview?
   A. The dimensions measured by each of these types of interviews is different.
   B. The difference lies in the fact that in one of these types of interviews advance material is provided to the candidate.
   C. The use of the role player is different in each of these types of interviews.
   D. The difference is that in only one of the interview types is time a factor to be considered by the candidate.

7. Which of the following is not a recommended strategy for responding to questions encountered by a candidate during an interview in an assessment center exercise?
   A. Setting specific due dates for completion of assignments
   B. Mentioning interrelated items
   C. Exhibiting a willingness to involve others in the planning process
   D. Utilizing as much jargon as possible in all responses

8. In which of the following situations should a candidate probe an interviewer-role player for information?
   A. Structured interactive interview
   B. Nonstructured interactive interview
   C. Both structured and nonstructured interactive interviews
   D. Neither a structured nor a nonstructured interactive interview

9. A certain sergeant's candidate, while participating in an assessment center interview exercise, is faced with the following simulated situation:
   One of the police officers whom you (the candidate) supervise is allegedly experiencing a drinking problem.
   Which of the following is not a suggested response for the candidate to offer in connection with this situation?
   A. Immediately state his/her policy in such matters
   B. Recognize that a drinking problem is indicative of illness
   C. Transfer the employee
   D. Obtain background information on the employee

10. Consider the following statements concerning interviews given to candidates during assessment center exercises.
    (1) The simulated identity of the role player with whom a candidate is to meet may indicate the type of interview to be conducted.
    (2) The purpose of the simulated meeting may indicate the type of interview to be conducted.
    (3) It is best not to read a prepared speech if asked to make an oral presentation.

Which of the following most accurately classifies these statements into those that are accurate and those that are not?
A.   All of the statements are accurate.
B.   All of the statements are inaccurate.
C.   Only two of the statements are accurate.
D.   Only two of the statements are inaccurate.

Answer Key, Diagnostic Procedure, and Answer Explanations

Answer Key

1. **B**	3. **A**	5. **B**	7. **D**	9. **C**
2. **A**	4. **D**	6. **C**	8. **B**	10. **A**

Diagnostic Procedure

If you have fewer than nine (9) right, it is recommended that you review this chapter.

Answer Explanations

1. **B**   In the interviews indicated in choices A, C, and D, the candidate is not given any advance material. Only in the structured interactive interview is the candidate provided with advance material. Can you think of another type of interview in which the candidate is provided with advance material?

2. **A**   In the structured interactive interview, the role player initially asks one or more general questions and then remains neutral. In choice B, the nonstructured interactive interview, the role player continuously responds to the candidate's questions throughout the interview. In choices C and D, the combination straight interview and straight interview, the interviewer does not engage in any role playing.

3. **A**   In the nonstructured interactive interview, the role player must be thoroughly trained as to how to respond to the candidate. This makes the process very expensive.

4. **D** A trained role player is required in the nonstructured interactive interview.

5. **B** All of the statements are inaccurate. The number of role players varies from one to three or more. The same traits we explained in Chapter 16 are used in scoring interviews, and time is certainly a factor since there is a time limit on the interview.

6. **C** The main difference between the two is that in the structured interactive interview the role player remains neutral and performs no function other than asking the initial question.

7. **D** Jargon should not be used unless explained; for example, when responding to an interviewer who is playing the role of a nonpolice person, police jargon would not be appropriate, unless explained.

8. **B** In the nonstructured interactive interview the interviewer-role player possesses many facts and it's up to the candidate to get them. It is called a nonstructured interview since the interview will go wherever the candidate takes it.

9. **C** To rely on a transfer is not recommended. It shows poor leadership since it indicates an unwillingness to deal with a problem. The other responses are recommended.

10. **A** All of the statements are accurate as stated and found in the chapter.

CHAPTER 19

Fact-Finding and Decision-Making Exercises

Fact-finding and decision-making exercises are ideal for use in promotion examinations because they measure a candidate's ability to obtain enough information about a situation to make an appropriate decision based on the facts in the matter. The candidate obtains the information via a question-and-answer session with a role player who is also known as a resource person. Many dimensions or traits can be measured by this exercise, but it is primarily used to measure problem analysis skills, decisiveness, judgment, listening, and oral presentation skills.

How Does a Fact-Finding and Decision-Making Exercise Work?

At the beginning of the exercise, the candidate is given a brief written description of the basic facts concerning a hypothetical situation similar to an actual situation that could happen to a police sergeant in the agency concerned. The candidate's task is to seek out the complete details surrounding the situation and make a decision regarding the situation. There are very specific time limits within which all this must be done.

WHO IS INVOLVED IN THE EXERCISE?

A fact-finding and decision-making exercise requires, in addition to the candidate, a minimum of two other persons. One person is, as we mentioned above, known as the resource person. The resource person has access to all of the information concerning the hypothetical situation. The candidate has a limited amount of time, usually fifteen minutes, to question the resource person and obtain enough information to make an appropriate decision regarding the situation. The resource person is specifically trained to give the candidate only the specific information the candidate requests during the questioning period. In other words, the resource person does not volunteer unsolicited information. All responsibility for staying within the prescribed time frames rests with the candidate. The third person in the process is an observer whose only responsibility is to evaluate the candidate's performance. Both the observer and the resource person must be trained, making the process somewhat expensive.

HOW DOES THE CANDIDATE LEARN ABOUT THE INSTRUCTIONS CONTROLLING THE EXERCISE?

At the start of the exercise, the resource person reads the instructions concerning the exercise to the candidate. The typical instructions include the following provisions.

1. An explanation of the purpose of the exercise, which is to test the candidate's ability to seek out information, to make decisions, and to effectively communicate and defend these decisions.

2. A statement calling the candidate's attention to the existence of a brief written description of a hypothetical situation involving some police incident.

3. Instructions to the candidate about his/her assumed identity for the exercise.

4. A direction to the candidate to investigate what actually happened in the hypothetical situation and recommend a course of action to follow to handle the situation.

5. The candidate is then told that the resource person will answer any questions the candidate asks about the situation. However, the candidate will be specifically informed that if his/her questions are too general, he/she will be instructed to make them more specific. The resource person will not respond to general questions.

6. The fact will be established that the resource person is not playing any role in the situation. The resource person is a neutral source of information, and that's all.

HOW DOES THE CANDIDATE PREPARE QUESTIONS?

After being given the instructions as outlined above, the candidate is given a brief period of time, usually five minutes, to prepare questions. Naturally, the questions should be developed from the brief written description of the incident supplied to him/her. This is an extremely important part of the exercise, and we will say more about it later.

HOW DOES THE CANDIDATE PRESENT A DECISION?

After the questioning period, which usually lasts fifteen minutes, the candidate is given a brief period of time, usually five minutes, to report his/her decision in the matter and the reasoning behind it. It should be noted that the fifteen-minute questioning period includes the time required to arrive at your decision and prepare to present it along with the reasoning behind it. In other words, the questioning period involves more than asking questions. It also involves making your decision based on the information obtained from the responses of the resource person and briefly preparing to make your preparation.

IS THE CANDIDATE QUESTIONED ABOUT THE DECISION?

Yes, after the candidate presents a decision, the resource person usually questions him/her about it. This "rebuttal" period usually lasts for ten minutes. It is imperative that the candidate understand that the resource person is trained to challenge the decision made by the candidate regardless of what decision is made. Another thing the resource person will do is bring up information about the situation that the candidate failed to uncover during the questioning period. This is done in an attempt to try to make the candidate change the decision. At the end of the "rebuttal" period, the exercise is over.

A BRIEF REVIEW OF THE PROCESS WITH <u>TYPICAL TIME FRAMES</u>

TYPICAL TIME ALLOTTED	ACTION
5 minutes	Resource person reads instructions to the candidate
5 minutes	Candidate studies summary of situation and prepares questions
15 minutes	Candidate interviews resource person to obtain information upon which to make a decision; candidate also uses this time to analyze information, to arrive at a decision, and to prepare to present the decision and defend it
5 minutes	Candidate reports the decision to the resource person; also reported is the reasoning behind the decision
10 minutes	Resource person questions the candidate concerning the decision

A Strategy to Maximize Your Score

The correct strategy to follow in a decision-making and fact-finding exercise is easier to understand when you understand how the exercise is scored. The first thing to realize is that there is no single, optimum decision for you to make. In fact, the details of the situation are such that the best decision to make is not really clear, even when you are aware of all of the details. In fact, for every good argument in favor of one position, the details provide a counterargument in favor of the opposite position. This allows the resource person to challenge the candidate's decision and rationale. You must remember, therefore, that no matter how you decide, there will be facts among the details of the story both to support your position and to undermine it. When we explain this to our students they always ask the same question:

> If there is no optimum decision, then how should I decide what to do?

The answer to this question is simple. As long as your decision doesn't result from a misinterpretation of the facts and it is consistent and logical based on the information you uncovered, then your decision is a good one. Therefore, you must uncover as many of the details in the story as you can. You must then make a logical decision using the facts you have uncovered to support that decision. You must then effectively communicate your decision and defend it by using facts, not emotion. You also must show some flexibility. If you are presented facts you did not uncover, acknowledge the logic of considering these facts, but counter them with the logic of your decision using arguments from the fact pattern.

A WORD ABOUT TIME USAGE

You will be specifically instructed as to the time frames involved in the exercise. After that, time management is your responsibility and you will be evaluated on how well you use the time available to you. Therefore, it is imperative that you have a means of keeping time. Make certain you have a good, reliable timepiece with you. Preferably, it should have a sweeping seconds hand.

DURING THE FIVE-MINUTE PLANNING PERIOD

If you fail to use the planning period effectively, you will probably not do well in the exercise. We recommend you follow the following specific strategy.

1. Use the entire time allotted. Make written notes. Keep an eye on the time. Even if you are ready, look busy right up to the end of the five-minute period. This earns you Planning and Organization points.

2. Read and thoroughly understand the brief description of the immediate circumstances concerning the situation that is given to you.

3. Make an initial listing of the alternatives available to you. This is not difficult. There are usually no more than three basic available alternatives. For example, if the situation involves, as it often does, a complaint against a police officer, your alternatives would be to

   ● Take disciplinary action against the officer

   ● Drop the complaint as unfounded

   ● Attempt a reconciliation

Of course, with regard to these three alternatives, there are many variations of each of them. For example, taking disciplinary action could range from retraining, through an oral reprimand, to fines and suspension. However, initially, only list your general alternatives. You can flesh out the one you select afterward, based on the facts you uncover.

4. Make a listing of questions you intend to ask with space between them to record the responses of the resource person.

5. Base your questions on the acronym NEOTWY, which we discussed in Chapter 10. Specifically, you want to find out the when, where, who, what, how, and why of the situation. Remember to get all of the whats, wheres, whos, and so on. For example,

- Who was involved?

- Who was a witness?

- Who was injured?

6. Just prior to the end of your five minutes, put your pencil down and announce that you are ready to begin questioning.

DURING THE FIFTEEN-MINUTE QUESTIONING AND DECISION-MAKING PERIOD

You will earn points during this period if you obtain information through an organized series of questions and/or through a logical progression of questions. In other words, you should demonstrate that you used the five-minute planning period well by having an initial group of questions to ask in a systematic way. Then, after you have obtained the information from your initial round of planned questions, you should develop questions that flow logically from the responses you have already received. As each response is given to you by the resource person, you should make brief written notes. Remember it is your responsibility to keep track of the time. Also keep in mind that you must use some of this time period to make your decision and to develop a defendable rationale. Unless the facts you have uncovered clearly indicate otherwise, do not take an extreme position when you make your decision. Concerning the rationale for your decision, you must realize that *the resource person will try to get you to change your decision after you announce it.*

The way the exercise is structured, there is a reasonable counterargument for each fact you will offer in defense of your decision. As long as your decision is in accordance with the facts you uncovered during the questioning period, stick by it. Acknowledge the reasonableness of counterarguments, but use your facts to overcome the counterarguments.

DURING YOUR FIVE-MINUTE REPORTING PERIOD

During this period, the evaluator will be rating your oral communication skills as well as the content matter of your report. Therefore, you must present your decision with its supporting rationale in a well-organized, concise, and convincing manner. Modulate your voice, and do not read your presentation. Instead, you must deliver it, making sure to make good eye contact with the resource person. Use hand gestures to emphasize important points. Don't neglect time management, and make a good summary statement when concluding.

DURING THE TEN-MINUTE PERIOD WHEN YOU ARE QUESTIONED BY THE RESOURCE PERSON

Once again, we remind you that your decision will be challenged no matter what it is. The resource person will attempt to make you change your decision. Don't be too rigid when this occurs. Don't dismiss the resource person's counterpoints out of hand. If they are reasonable points, acknowledge them as such, but use your own rationale to justify your original decision.

Practice Exercises

1. Fact-finding and decision-making exercises are ideal for use in promotion examinations because they:
    A. Are quite inexpensive
    B. Are fair since no one can prepare for them in advance
    C. Require no special training to be given to any of the examiners
    D. Can measure a candidate's ability to obtain information and make decisions

2. Fact-finding and decision-making exercises are used primarily to measure all of the following, except:
    A. Judgment
    B. Listening
    C. Oral presentation skills
    D. Writing ability skills

3. Consider the following statements concerning fact-finding and decision-making exercises.
   (1) The candidate is initially given a brief written description of the basic facts concerning a hypothetical situation.
   (2) Part of the candidate's task is to seek out the complete details surrounding the situation.
   (3) There are no time restrictions placed on the candidate.
   Which of the following most accurately classifies these statements into those that are accurate and those that are not?
   A. All of the statements are accurate.
   B. Only two of the statements are accurate.
   C. Only two of the statements are inaccurate.
   D. All of the statements are inaccurate.

4. In addition to the candidate, in a fact-finding and decision-making exercise there must be a minimum of how many other persons involved?
   A. Two
   B. Three
   C. Four
   D. No minimum number

5. Which of the following statements regarding fact-finding and decision-making exercises is least accurate?
   A. The candidate receives instructions regarding his/her assumed identity.
   B. The observer provides no information to the candidate.
   C. The candidate's best strategy is to ask general questions.
   D. The candidate should arrive at a decision during his/her questioning period.

6. In a fact-finding and decision-making exercise, who actually speaks during the rebuttal component?
   A. Only the candidate
   B. Only the candidate and the resource person
   C. Only the resource person
   D. Only the resource person and the observer

7. For which of the following components of a fact-finding and decision-making exercise is the most time allotted?
   A. Reading of the instructions
   B. The studying of the written summary of the situation by the candidate
   C. The asking of questions by the candidate
   D. The reporting of the decision by the candidate

8. In attempting to maximize his/her score in a fact-finding and decision-making exercise, a candidate should first realize that:
   A. There is no one optimum decision to make
   B. He/she should be ready to change the decision when questioned by the resource person
   C. Quickly finishing all components of the exercise scores many positive points
   D. He/she should be rigid in his/her position once a decision has been given to the resource person

9. In a fact-finding and decision-making exercise, once a decision is arrived at by a candidate, the resource person:
   A. Sometimes challenges it
   B. Always challenges it
   C. Never challenges it
   D. Assists the observer in challenging the candidate's decision

10. Consider the following statements concerning fact-finding and decision-making exercises.
   (1) The resource person engages in role playing.
   (2) The candidate is given some written materials.
   (3) The exercise can measure problem analysis skills.
   Which of the following best classifies these statements into those that are accurate and those that are not?
   A. Only statement 1 is inaccurate.
   B. Only statement 2 is inaccurate.
   C. Only statement 3 is inaccurate.
   D. All of the statements are accurate.

Answer Key, Diagnostic Procedure, and Answer Explanations

Answer Key

1. D	3. B	5. C	7. C	9. B
2. D	4. A	6. B	8. A	10. A

Diagnostic Procedure

If you scored fewer than nine (9) right, it is recommended you review this chapter.

Answer Explanations

1. **D**   Fact-finding and decision-making exercises are not inexpensive since the observer and resource person must be trained. This makes choices A and C incorrect. Also, choice B is incorrect since although these exercises are quite fair, they are exercises for which you can prepare. Choice D is correct because fact-finding and decision-making exercises do measure a candidate's ability to obtain enough information about a situation to make an appropriate decision based on the facts in the matter.

2. **D**   The little writing required in these exercises is not evaluated by the observer.

3. **B**   Statement 3 is inaccurate since there are very specific time limits the candidate must observe.

4. **A**   At a minimum, one observer and one resource person are present in addition to the candidate.

5. **C**   The resource person will not answer general questions posed by the candidate. The resource person will, instead, tell the candidate to be more specific.

6. **B**   During the rebuttal component of the exercise, the resource person questions the candidate about the candidate's decision and the candidate responds.

7. **C**   The time a candidate has to ask questions is considerably longer. This is true because during this component the candidate must also analyze information, arrive at a decision, and prepare to present and defend the decision.

8. **A**   Choice B is incorrect as well as choice D, since the candidate should advise the resource person of the decision, listen to the resource person's position, and see the merits of the resource person's position but not be swayed while also not giving the appearance of being too rigid. Choice C is incorrect since the candidate is advised to use all of the time allowed. The only correct choice is A since the exercise is not designed to arrive at any one right decision but to see if the candidate gathers enough facts and then makes an appropriate decision based on these facts.

9. **B**   The resource person always challenges the decision arrived at by the candidate.

10. **A**   Statement 1 is inaccurate since the resource person only gives information in response to the candidate's questions. The resource person plays no role.

CHAPTER 20

Report-Writing Exercises

What Are Report-Writing Exercises?

Report-Writing Exercises are assessment exercises designed to test whether a candidate for promotion to a certain civil service rank has the ability to write the kind of reports required at that rank. It follows, therefore, that the exercise must be tailored to the position for which the promotion test is being held. This "tailoring" is done via a job analysis. In theory, the examiner looks at the job analysis and designs a Report-Writing Exercise that reflects the report writing responsibilities indicated by the job analysis. There are so many variations of such exercises that it is impossible to give an all-inclusive definition of a Report-Writing Exercise.

Nonetheless, we can offer helpful information about these exercises to assist you regardless of the specific Report-Writing Exercise you take. This is what we have done in the remainder of this chapter.

Remember that the results of job analyses of a position do not usually change drastically from one year to the next. Therefore, if you can get any information about the specifics of previous Report-Writing Exercises given in your department, you can assume with a relative degree of safety that the exercise you take will be structured in a similar manner.

You should also review Chapter 10 to make sure you know what goes into a good report.

What Two Abilities Do Report-Writing Exercises Always Measure?

Report-Writing Exercises, as their name implies, are designed to measure the candidate's formal writing ability. However, we always caution our students not to be overly concerned about their level of formal writing ability. Since police reports must be accurate and easy to read and understand, it is a mistake for candidates taking Report-Writing Exercises to make their reports too complex. Take vocabulary for an example. Given a choice as to which of two words to use in a Report-Writing Exercise, the rule is simple. Use the word that is more easily understood. It is a mistake to conclude that you can earn extra points by displaying a "graduate school" vocabulary. In fact, the opposite might very well be true. We will talk more about this later in the chapter. For now, suffice it to say that if you write clearly and accurately, you can score very well on most Report-Writing Exercises.

In addition to testing formal writing ability, Report-Writing Exercises also test your ability to structure a report in the format officially accepted by your department. Therefore, it is essential to become quite familiar with your department's internal regulations concerning report writing.

What Aspects of the Candidate's Formal Writing Ability Are Usually Tested on Report-Writing Exercises?

SPELLING

As a general rule, Report-Writing Exercises test your ability to spell properly. This is an easy test to deal with. The rule is simple. Don't use any words you cannot spell. This rule does not present any difficulty with respect to scoring high on the test because the level of your vocabulary is usually not a consideration in the scoring process.

SENTENCE CONSTRUCTION

Use simple and easy-to-understand words, as opposed to more complex words, in non-technical police writing. This is a very important rule to remember. Far too many police officers think they should be expressive when writing police documents. To drive this important point home we have included the following two examples. We have obviously exaggerated to make a point, but sometimes exaggeration is useful in driving a point home.

EXAMPLE ONE:

> Police Officer Smith, allowing images of light to be transmitted to his brain by means of his optic nerve, utilized his sense of sight and thus became aware that a female, who had in the past engaged in matrimony and currently uses the surname of Green, did lash out with a container whose purpose is to transport various personalized sundries, and thus made contact with the vocal cavity of a male who resides in contiguous proximity to Green.

EXAMPLE TWO:

> Police Officer Smith saw Mrs. Green hit her neighbor Mr. Hall in the mouth with her purse.

Note that in both of the above examples we have said the same thing. Obviously, however, Example Two is the preferred approach for police report writing. We hope this extreme example will help you remember this important rule.

PUNCTUATION

Report-Writing Exercises also test your ability to punctuate properly. Here the rule is also simple. Do not write lengthy "run-on" sentences that never end. Short, simple sentences are preferred. In fact, excess wordiness is often considered a negative. In addition, if you use only simple sentences, you will probably not have punctuation problems. Remember, many short sentences ending with periods are better than long sentences that require many commas.

GRAMMAR AND SYNTAX

Proper grammar and syntax are also usually factors considered in the scoring key for a Report-Writing Exercise. However, points are usually lost in these areas only if you make consistent mistakes in any of them and to a degree that takes away from the overall effectiveness of your writing. Probably the most common error students make is failing to make sure that verbs agree with subjects. This, of course, means that singular nouns require singular verbs and plural nouns require plural verbs.

Some Rules to Follow with Respect to the Format of a Report

USE THE FORMAT ACCEPTED BY YOUR DEPARTMENT

The first and most important rule is to follow the report-writing format of the department in which you work. In particular, make sure you understand the accepted way to address a police report. For example, many departments use the "From-To-Subject" format for addressing reports.

USE THE FIRST PARAGRAPH TO INTRODUCE THE REPORT

Another format point involves the construction of the first paragraph. Unless otherwise indicated in your department regulations, the first paragraph of a police report should tell the reader why the report is being written and what is contained in the report.

INDICATE THE DISTRIBUTION OF THE REPORT

Unless prohibited by department regulations, you should indicate a distribution for the report after the signature block at the end of the report. At the very least, you should indicate that you are keeping a "cc" (carbon copy) of the report for your file.

MAKING RECOMMENDATIONS

Still another common format point involves the correct way to make recommendations. The rule is that you should not make recommendations in a vacuum. Always offer specific justification for your specific recommendations. For example, if you are recommending that directed patrol be utilized to deal with reported incidents of "larceny from auto" problem in the area of a municipal parking lot, don't write:

> My recommendation is that police resources be utilized to deal with the problem.

Instead write:

It is recommended that directed patrol be utilized in the Municipal Parking Lot because Larceny from Auto problem has been reported to exist at that location.

Other Abilities Tested in Report-Writing Exercises

Depending on the structure of the exercise, you may also be tested on:

1. Your ability to review a large batch of information and identify pertinent information

2. Your technical skills

3. Your ability to apply a set of artificial procedures or regulations to a specific incident

Examples of Report-Writing Exercises

Some examples of the way a Report-Writing Exercise may be structured follow.

EXAMPLE ONE

In the instructions for the Exercise, you are given a test packet that includes, among other things, a large batch of information about the precinct to which you are assigned. This information focuses on crime-related problems at various locations throughout the entire precinct. Also included in the test packet is a memo from your boss, which requires you to write a report. This memo is the key to the exercise because it contains specific information about exactly what should be included in the report. Typically, this memo requires a report that summarizes crime conditions at a specific location in the precinct. You must:

1. Review the entire packet of material about the command.

2. Identify crime conditions at that specific location.

3. Summarize those conditions.

4. Incorporate these findings into a report that conforms to the report-writing requirements of the department you work in.

Example One is an exercise that merely tests your ability to sift through a large batch of information and determine what is pertinent.

This type of exercise is not very common, although it is sometimes used.

EXAMPLE TWO

In the instructions for this exercise, you are given information about crime and other police-related conditions at a particular location, just as in Example One. You are then required not only to summarize those conditions, but also to offer recommendations as to how best to deal with them. This is an example of how technical skills can be introduced into the Report-Writing Exercise. It is the making of the recommendations that tests your technical skills. Therefore, before taking a Report-Writing Exercise, you should review acceptable ways to deal with various police-related conditions in your jurisdiction. Bear in mind, however, that making the best recommendation to deal with any specific condition is not the goal of this exercise. Any reasonable, commonly accepted course of action that would, in all likelihood, lead to a resolution of the problem involved will probably earn credit.

This form of Report-Writing Exercise has gained great popularity in today's promotional examinations and is increasingly being used.

EXAMPLE THREE

In the instructions, you are given a set of procedures for dealing with a particular incident, such as procedures for dealing with a hostage situation. Please note that the procedures presented do not necessarily have to be the ones presently in use in your department. For the purposes of the exercise, however, you must treat these procedures as if they were in actual use. You are then given an account of how a particular incident was handled, e.g., a hostage situation. You are asked to review the procedures, compare them with what actually occurred in the incident, and write a "critique" of the incident.

The thrust of this exercise is to test your ability to apply a set of procedures to a specific incident and analyze and assess the actions that were taken.

Do Report-Writing Exercises Usually Require You to Play a Role?

Yes. Most Report-Writing Exercises require you to function in an artificially created universe in much the same manner as many other assessment exercises. The role you play is invariably that of an incumbent in the rank you are aspiring to achieve. You are given a rank and name and some brief information about your current assignment. The assignment is usually the one held by the majority of incumbents in the rank involved. Typically, the universe created for Report-Writing Exercises also includes the following information:

1. The current date and time.

2. The specific command you are assigned to.

3. Profile information about your supervisors and subordinates.

4. Background information about your command.

It is important to note that the universe is usually constructed so that it resembles, insofar as possible, the actual universe of an incumbent. For example, at the rank of sergeant, if most of the incumbent sergeants are actually functioning as patrol supervisors, the test universe will probably place you in such a position.

Other Ways a Report-Writing Exercise Could Be Structured to Test Technical Skills As Well As Report-Writing Ability

You could be required to write a letter to a community group explaining the department's procedures for handling a specific problem, such as dealing with homeless persons. Obviously, in such a situation your formal writing ability would be tested along with your technical skills, e.g., explaining the department's procedures concerning homeless persons. Here, of course, the letter would not be written in accordance with the format rules for internal communications. Rather, you would earn points in this exercise by writing a letter that includes an introduction, a body, and a conclusion.

Another possibility involves requiring you to review a general set of guidelines for handling a specific situation, such as guidelines for protest demonstrations, and then to develop a specific plan to police a protest demonstration at a specific location.

Are Report-Writing Exercises Used Independent of Other Assessment Exercises, or Are They Used in Conjunction with Other Such Exercises?

Both. The Report-Writing Exercise can easily be structured as an independent assessment exercise. However, it is also quite common to combine the Report-Writing Exercise with some other assessment exercises, such as a Fact-Finding or In-Basket Exercise.

THE REPORT-WRITING EXERCISE AS AN INDEPENDENT EXERCISE

When the Report-Writing Exercise is used as an independent exercise, it is usually structured to require you to review a larger batch of information and summarize the relevant portions of that larger batch of information, as described above. You are given a specific period of time, usually one hour, to review the instructions, review the information, and write the report. It is important to point out that when you have only one hour, you probably will not have time to write both a draft copy of your report and a final copy. We tell our students to prepare an outline of what they intend to write while they are reviewing the information and to write their report directly from this outline. Neatness is usually not a factor in the scoring process. For example, crossing out material will not result in a lower score, unless the instructions indicate that a final copy is needed. In that case, however, more time would be provided.

THE REPORT-WRITING EXERCISE COMBINED WITH AN IN-BASKET EXERCISE

When the Report-Writing Exercise is combined with an In-Basket Exercise, it is usually structured along the following lines. One of the items in the In-Basket is a note from your boss asking you to write an internal memo, such as a training memo, or to write a formal letter, usually to a member of the community. If you see such an item on an In-Basket Exercise, you should recognize it as a mechanism to evaluate your writing ability, and you should not make the mistake of delegating to a subordinate the task of writing the report. If the item specifically directs you to write the report, then you must write the report if you want to earn maximum credit.

THE REPORT-WRITING EXERCISE COMBINED WITH A FACT-FINDING EXERCISE

The third, and least-used option, is to require you to write a report and to use the facts uncovered during a Fact-Finding Exercise as the content matter for the report. This option, although once very popular, is losing popularity because it penalizes you twice for not obtaining the facts during the Fact-Finding Exercise. Not only do you lose points in the Fact-Finding Exercise for not uncovering all the facts, but also the lack of facts means you cannot write a complete report. You are doubly penalized.

How Long Should the Report Be?

This is an extremely important point to grasp. Far too many candidates believe that the more they write, the more points they will earn. Although in certain instances this may be true, it is not always the case. The answer to the question of how much you should write is simple to understand yet vital to success. When deciding how long your report should be, you *must* comply with the instructions you have received. If, for example, the instructions tell you not to exceed a certain number of handwritten pages, *do not exceed* that number of pages. Conversely, if you are told to write a minimum number of pages, you must be certain to comply with those instructions. The answer key for Report-Writing Exercises almost always contains points for following directions concerning the length of the report.

Advance Preparation

If you know you will be taking a Report-Writing Exercise, do the following:

1. Get a good basic grammar book and brush up on the most basic rules of grammar, syntax, and sentence structure.

2. Become extremely familiar with the report-writing guidelines of your agency.

3. Review actual reports that have been written by incumbents in the rank you are aspiring to achieve. (Your training unit should be able to provide samples of these.)

4. Practice, and make sure any such practice is timed to get an idea of how much you can reasonably expect to write in certain blocks of time, e.g., one hour, an hour and a half, or two hours, which is about as long as any Report-Writing Exercise we have seen.

A Recommended Strategy for Test Day

Listed below is a general strategy to follow when participating in a Report-Writing Exercise. Bear in mind, however, that like any other assessment exercise, Report-Writing Exercises can be structured in many different ways. Therefore, you must amend this general strategy, if necessary, to conform to the requirements of the specific exercise you will be taking.

1. Make sure you understand what is expected of you before you begin to work. Far too many candidates rush into the writing of the report without understanding very clearly exactly how the exercise is structured. At a minimum, you must understand how much time you are allowed, who the report should be addressed to, and just exactly what is to be included in the report. You should also be aware of the length of the report. All of this can be accomplished by a careful reading of the instructions governing the exercise. Therefore, the cardinal rule is as follows:

BEFORE STARTING ON THE REPORT, MAKE SURE YOU UNDERSTAND THE INSTRUCTIONS CONCERNING THE EXERCISE. THE KEY WILL CONTAIN POINTS FOR FOLLOWING WHAT YOU ARE TOLD TO DO.

2. The next step is to identify the content matter for the report. As mentioned above, this most often involves going through a large batch of information and deciding what is relevant. However, it might necessitate the use of technical skills. Or it might mean using facts you have gathered from a Fact-Finding Exercise.

3. As you identify the content matter for your report, you should develop an outline for your report. Remember that the first paragraph of most police reports should tell the reader why the report is being written and what is contained in the report.

4. The next step should be the actual writing of the report from the outline. When writing an internal police memo, remember to use the officially accepted department format for such memos. If you are writing a formal letter, use a format that contains an introduction, a body, and a conclusion.

5. If required, formulate recommendations remembering to offer justification for your recommendations, as explained earlier.

Summary Checklist for Preparing to Take a Report Writing Exercise

You should ask yourself, have I ...

1. Used the proper format required by the instructions?

2. If a "From-To-Subject" is required, made the "Subject" caption concise yet descriptive?

3. Properly addressed the report?

4. Indicated the proper distribution of the report, such as a copy for file?

5. Properly introduced the subject of the report in the opening paragraph?

6. Demonstrated an understanding of the purpose of the report in the opening paragraph?

7. Dealt with only one phase of the subject in each paragraph?

8. Used clear and concise sentences?

9. Transposed factual information obtained from information provided accurately, such as addresses of incidents, badge numbers, and crime statistics?

10. Presented a professional understanding of the issues involved, such as indicating the importance or seriousness of the issues?

11. When required, accurately summarized existing problems for the reader of the report?

12. Made specific findings when required to do so by the instructions on the exercise?

13. Made specific recommendations when required to do so by the instructions on the exercise?

14. Used information contained in the material provided to base any specific recommendation upon?

15. Demonstrated the technical skills a police sergeant would be required to possess, such as indicating how to deal with a recent increase in burglaries?

16. Avoided poor grammar?

17. Avoided poor spelling?

18. Avoided excess word use?

19. Avoided poor punctuation?

20. Stayed within the required length of the report as indicated in the instructions accompanying the exercise?

For every assessment exercise, the best preparation includes taking a practice exercise. Therefore, we have included such a practice exercise in Chapter 23.

First review the summary material. Then try your hand at actually writing a report based on the instructions contained in the material. After writing the report in the time allotted, objectively use the report scoring guide to evaluate your efforts.

TEST YOURSELF

CHAPTER 21

Practice In-Basket Examination

In General

This chapter contains a practice in-basket examination including fully explained answers. We strongly recommend that you do not take this test until you read and understand the material in Chapter 17.

STRUCTURED VERSUS NONSTRUCTURED RESPONSES

As we explained in Chapter 17, in-basket tests can use a structured response format (multiple-choice) or a nonstructured response format (the writing of notes and memos). For ease of administration, we have elected to use the structured, multiple-choice format. However, in the explained answer section we address both formats. That is, the examination format is structured, but the answer explanations suggest ways each item could be dealt with if the format of the exercise were unstructured.

EXAMPLE OF A GOOD "INDEXING" EFFORT

In Chapter 17 we emphasized the importance of "indexing" prior to responding to any items. In our explained answer section we have included a sample index sheet for you to compare against the one you will prepare as part of this practice exercise.

SIMULATE EXAMINATION CONDITIONS

Do not attempt to take this test on a piecemeal basis. Insofar as possible, take this in-basket exercise under the same conditions as will exist on the day of your actual examination.

ANSWER SHEET

Use the answer sheet provided for you to get used to recording your answers in the proper manner. Remember to use the test-taking strategies outlined in Chapter 2.

TIME LIMIT

Use a maximum of three hours to take this in-basket exercise. The examination begins below.

LIST OF PAGES IN ADMINISTRATIVE TEST PACKET	
Page A	Instructions
Page B	Precinct Profile
Page C	Calendar
Page D	Map
Page E	Organization Chart of Marlboro Police Department
Page F	Organization Chart of Third Precinct
Page G	Eighth Squad Personnel Data
Page H	Marlboro Police Department Patrol Guide

Item 1	Item 15
Item 2	Item 16
Item 3	Item 17
Item 4	Item 18
Item 5	Item 19
Item 6	Item 20
Item 7	Item 21
Item 8	Item 22
Item 9	Item 23
Item 10	Item 24
Item 11	Item 25
Item 12	Item 26
Item 13	Item 27
Item 14	

INSTRUCTIONS

For the purpose of this exercise, you are Police Sergeant Robert Gifford, a patrol sergeant who is in charge of the eighth squad, and is assigned to the Third Precinct in the city of Marlboro. Today is Saturday, July 19. The time is 1600 hours. Because there is no lieutenant available for assignment, you have been assigned as the desk officer for the entire tour. There are two other sergeants working this tour of 1600 × 2400 hours. They are both patrol supervisors. Their names are John Larkin and Maria Gomez. Sergeant Gomez is assigned as your relief for meal (dinner hour) between 2100 and 2200 hours. She is in charge of a detail of five police officers at the Borough Swimming Pool.

The desk officer from the preceding tour (0800 × 1600 hours) has left you to process the following packet of letters, memos, and other administrative items. Some are addressed directly to you by name, and others are simply addressed to the precinct or the desk officer.

The precinct commanding officer, Captain Frank A. Lombardo, has left for the day, and his next scheduled tour of duty is Monday, July 21, at 0800 hours.

Your task is to answer the accompanying 25 multiple-choice questions. Base your answers on the information contained in the administrative packet, the sample patrol guide procedures, and your general knowledge of administrative and supervisory principles.

PRECINCT PROFILE

The Third Precinct station house is located at 207 Gem Street. The building is a two-story brick building with an adjacent parking lot, which is used for the parking of department vehicles and the private vehicles of department personnel. There is also a detached garage used to house the two vehicles used by the volunteer auxiliary police unit. The complement of 175 police officers and civilians assigned to the precinct occupies the first floor and basement. The second floor is occupied by the precinct detective unit and precinct anticrime unit.

Also on the second floor are two units that are not attached to the precinct. They are the department's burglary unit and the intelligence unit. Recently, a water pipe burst in front of the station house, causing the street to need repairs. This has caused extensive traffic congestion around the station house.

July

| June |
| S M T W T F S |
| 1 2 3 4 5 6 7 |
| 8 9 10 11 12 13 14 |
| 15 16 17 18 19 20 21 |
| 22 23 24 25 26 27 28 |
| 29 30 |

| August |
| S M T W T F S |
| 1 2 |
| 3 4 5 6 7 8 9 |
| 10 11 12 13 14 15 16 |
| 17 18 19 20 21 22 23 |
| 24/31 25 26 27 28 29 30 |

S	M	T	W	T	F	S
		1	2	3	4	5
6	7	8	9	10	11 (Independence Day)	12
13	14	15	16	17	18	19
20	21	22	23	24	25	26
27	28	29	30	31		

THIRD PRECINCT MAP

N
W ← → E
S

SECTOR 'A' (ADAM)

SECTOR 'B' (BAKER)

SECTOR 'C' (CHARLIE)

ALPO STREET

BAKER STREET

ARK AVE

BOG AVE

CARL STREET

DON STREET

BOROUGH SWIMMING POOL

ELM STREET

ELM STREET

FRANK STREET

FRANK STREET

ARK PLACE —

GEM STREET

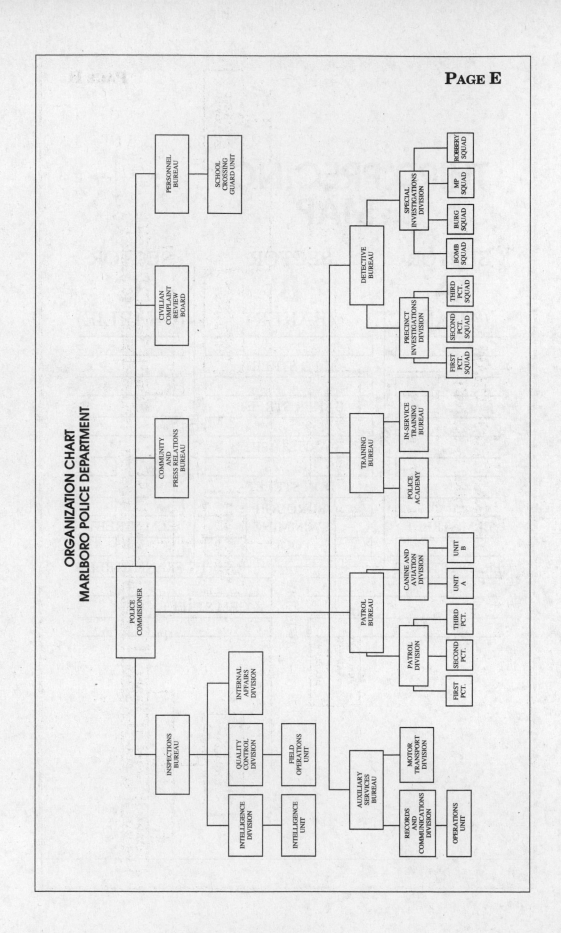

ORGANIZATION CHART
MARLBORO POLICE DEPARTMENT

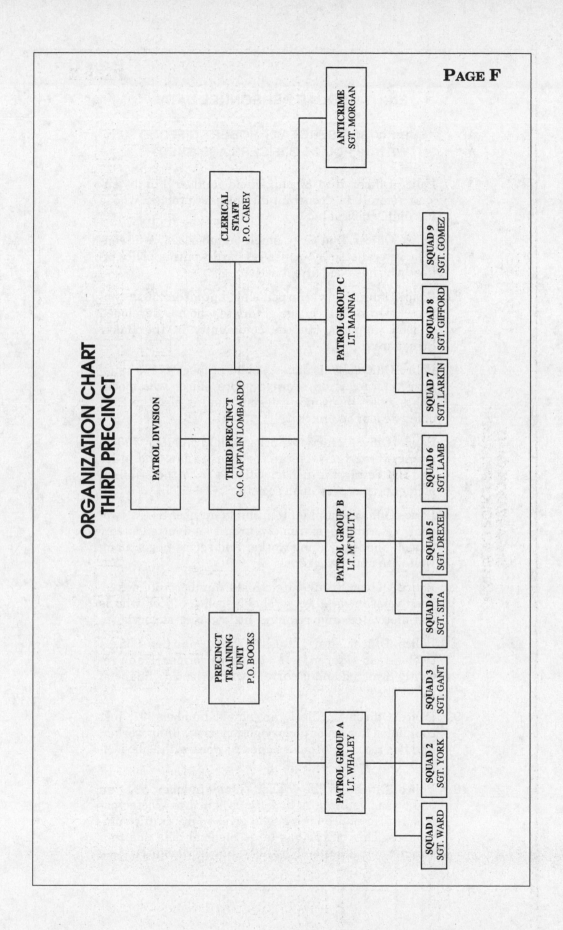

ORGANIZATION CHART
THIRD PRECINCT

PAGE F

PATROL DIVISION

THIRD PRECINCT
C.O. CAPTAIN LOMBARDO

CLERICAL STAFF
P.O. CAREY

ANTICRIME
SGT. MORGAN

PRECINCT TRAINING UNIT
P.O. BOOKS

PATROL GROUP A
LT. WHALEY

PATROL GROUP B
LT. McNULTY

PATROL GROUP C
LT. MANNA

SQUAD 1
SGT. WARD

SQUAD 2
SGT. YORK

SQUAD 3
SGT. GANT

SQUAD 4
SGT. SITA

SQUAD 5
SGT. DREXEL

SQUAD 6
SGT. LAMB

SQUAD 7
SGT. LARKIN

SQUAD 8
SGT. GIFFORD

SQUAD 9
SGT. GOMEZ

EIGHTH SQUAD PERSONNEL DATA

SUPERVISOR SERGEANT ROBERT GIFFORD
WITH 10 POLICE OFFICERS ASSIGNED

1. Police Officer Rico Firmo, shield number 170, a ten-year veteran, is a constant disciplinary problem who is not highly motivated.

2. Police Officer Tom Gray, shield number 326, a fifteen-year veteran, is a no-nonsense hard-working police officer who has good arrest activity.

3. Police Officer Daryl Harper, shield number 456, a two-year veteran, is a college graduate who has developed a good rapport with the community in the Baker Street area.

4. Police Officer Louis Jones, shield number 471, a nine-year veteran, is an average police officer who moonlights as an insurance salesman and is also the PBA delegate for the precinct.

5. Police Officer Harry Knucks, shield number 706, a twenty-three-year veteran, believes in law and order and protecting the honest citizens from the criminal elements that prey upon society.

6. Police Officer Joan Manton, shield number 841, a two-year veteran, is extremely bright and attends law school. She is a willing worker and seems to get along well with her coworkers.

7. Police Officer Frank Rite, shield number 760, a five-year veteran, is a very reliable police officer who is self-motivated and requires little direct supervision.

8. Police Officer Mario Russo, shield number 958, a twelve-year veteran, is a steady performer. He is recently divorced and is currently experiencing financial difficulties.

9. Police Officer Lucille Ryan, shield number 997, just completed her probationary period, is a willing worker, and has recently been assigned to work with Police Officer Tom Gray.

10. Police Officer Willie Wells, shield number 591, an eight-year veteran, is usually assigned to scooter patrol, a firm police officer who gives many traffic summonses. This officer has large medical bills due to a chronic illness suffered by his youngest daughter.

MARLBORO POLICE DEPARTMENT PATROL GUIDE

PROCEDURE 1: PATROL DUTIES

POLICE OFFICERS ON PATROL SHALL

1. Perform duty in uniform unless otherwise directed by competent authority.
2. Patrol post frequently and in a nonregular manner.
3. Signal the station house once each hour, unless equipped with a portable radio. (Do not signal station house if actually performing traffic post duty.)
4. Record odometer reading in activity log when assigned as an operator of a department vehicle. Said reading will be recorded at the beginning and the end of each tour of duty.
5. Not take a department vehicle out of service when assigned as an operator unless permission is obtained from the patrol supervisor.

PATROL SUPERVISOR SHALL

1. Perform duty in uniform unless otherwise directed by competent authority.
2. Visit police officers frequently and at irregular intervals while said officers are on post.
3. Indicate visits by signing rank and name in police officers' activity logs.
4. Report verbally to the station house desk officer all unusual occurrences occurring during tour of duty within the confines of the precinct.
5. Direct police officers assigned to scooter patrol to report to the desk officer for reassignment during periods of inclement weather.

THE DESK OFFICER SHALL

1. Be responsible for all police operations in the precinct during the tour of duty.
2. Supervise and be responsible for activities of patrol supervisors.

Note: Desk officers shall be of the rank of lieutenant, but on occasion these duties may be assigned to a sergeant when a lieutenant is not available for assignment.

PROCEDURE 2: AIDED CASES (DEAD HUMAN BODIES)

PURPOSE

Ensure proper police action is taken at the scene of dead human bodies, parts of dead human bodies, and human fetuses.

PROCEDURE

A police officer arrives at the scene of an apparently dead human body, a part of a dead human body, or a human fetus.

POLICE OFFICER SHALL

1. Request an ambulance and the patrol supervisor through the radio dispatcher.
2. Cover the body with opaque plastic covering (after pronounced dead by medical authorities), if exposed to public view.
3. Do not search the body until the patrol supervisor is present.

Note: Two opaque plastic coverings shall be carried in all department vehicles except the patrol supervisor's vehicle.

PATROL SUPERVISOR SHALL

1. Notify the precinct detective unit.
2. Supervise the search of the deceased's person, property, and, in appropriate cases, residence. The body of the deceased shall be searched in all cases, but any other property and his/her residence shall be searched only if:
   a. The deceased died at the residence and did not live with a competent member of his/her family
   b. No other person can establish that he/she also permanently lived at the residence
3. Direct the police officer involved to take possession of all personal property, except clothing actually worn, discovered as a result of the search.
4. Direct the police officer involved to make a record of all such property removed in the officer's activity log.
5. Sign the police officer's activity log, indicating the accuracy of the listing of property taken from the deceased.

DESK OFFICER SHALL

1. Make an appropriate entry in the command log of the event and the police action taken.
2. Notify the precinct commanding officer.

3. Notify the missing person unit if the identity of the deceased cannot be ascertained or friends or relatives cannot be notified.

   Note: The name of the department member notified at the missing person unit shall be entered in the margin of the command log entry describing the event. This entry is to be made by the desk officer.

PROCEDURE 3: SUSPECTED AND VERIFIED EXPLOSIVE DEVICES

PURPOSE Protect life and property at the scene of explosive devices.

PROCEDURE Upon arrival at the scene police officer shall

1. Evacuate the area if a device is found or if otherwise necessary.
2. When a device is found, remove all persons at least 1000 feet from the device.
3. Notify the patrol supervisor through the radio dispatcher upon arrival at the scene.

PATROL SUPERVISOR SHALL

1. If appropriate, verify that no device is present.
2. Call for the bomb squad if a suspected device is found. The bomb squad will be requested through the desk officer.
3. Direct that a search be discontinued in a vacant or evacuated building twenty minutes before a threatened time of explosion. In such cases, the search will not be continued for at least one hour after the threatened time of explosion.
4. Direct that only members of the bomb squad come in direct contact with any suspected or verified explosive device.
5. Notify the desk officer of the final disposition of the matter.

DESK OFFICER SHALL

1. Make a command log entry concerning the incident. No command log entry need be made in cases of false alarms or hoaxes.
2. Notify the operations unit only if an explosive device is found.
3. Prepare a report for the precinct commanding officer in all cases.

PROCEDURE 4: VEHICLE PURSUITS

PURPOSE　　　　　Determine the need for a vehicle pursuit involving department vehicles and the procedure to be followed for such pursuits.

PROCEDURE　　　　When unable to stop a vehicle for an investigation or suspicion of having been involved in criminal conduct

THE MEMBER OF THE DEPARTMENT INVOLVED SHALL

1. Consider the following:
   a. Reason for the stop
   b. Ability of the department vehicle
   c. Road conditions, including weather, traffic, and pedestrian density
   d. Lighting conditions

   Note: The department test to be used to determine the necessity of the pursuit is whether failure to apprehend the pursued vehicle creates a danger to the public greater than the danger to the public and the officer if the pursuit is undertaken.

2. Notify the radio dispatcher to alert the patrol supervisor that there is an active pursuit.
3. Not use the constant siren because it distorts radio transmissions and blots out the sound of oncoming vehicles.

PATROL SUPERVISOR OF THE PRECINCT OF OCCURRENCE SHALL

1. Monitor all radio transmissions.
2. Use the department test (See the above *Note*) to determine if the pursuit should be continued.
3. Allow only one department vehicle other than the originating department vehicle to directly pursue the suspect's vehicle.
4. Direct that other vehicles not form a caravan behind the pursuing vehicles.
5. Terminate the pursuit when necessary.
6. Prepare a written report of all pursuits occurring in the precinct to the precinct commanding officer.
7. Notify the desk officer of all action taken.

DESK OFFICER OF THE PRECINCT OF OCCURRENCE SHALL

1. Enter all facts in the command log.
2. Verify that required written reports are prepared and forwarded in accordance with department policy.

Note: Members involved in vehicle pursuits are reminded that

1. No ramming of vehicles shall be attempted.
2. No roadblocks are to be undertaken unless directed by a supervisor.
3. At least five car lengths' distance shall be maintained between department vehicles when engaged in a vehicle pursuit.

PROCEDURE 5: INJURY TO ON-DUTY SCHOOL CROSSING GUARD

PURPOSE

Properly handle the injury of a school crossing guard incurred in the performance of duty.

PROCEDURE

A school crossing guard is injured in the performance of duty.

POLICE OFFICER SHALL

1. Respond to the scene, give necessary first aid, and request the patrol supervisor through the radio dispatcher.
2. Call for an ambulance, if necessary.

PATROL SUPERVISOR SHALL

1. Respond to the scene or hospital.
2. Investigate the case.
3. Have the school crossing guard prepare two copies of department form AXR, if not incapacitated. Otherwise the police officer will prepare this form.
4. Have any witnesses prepare department form AXM, two copies.
5. Personally prepare a line of duty report, department form AXL, three copies, and deliver them immediately to the desk officer.

DESK OFFICER SHALL

1. Review and endorse department form AXL.
2. Forward the three copies of form AXL, as follows:
   a. The original to the personnel bureau
   b. The second copy to the school crossing guard unit
   c. The third copy to the precinct commanding officer
3. No command log entry is required.

ITEM 1: (PROPOSED) THIRD PRECINCT
MEMO 113

July ____ XXXX

To the Desk Officer 1600 x 2400 tour July 19. I'd like to get this out as soon as possible. What do you think about it? Capt. FXL

Memo from: Commanding Officer, Third Precinct

To: All Patrol Supervisors, Third Precinct

Subject: SAFETY PRECAUTIONS AT SCENE OF SUSPECTED EXPLOSIVE DEVICES

1. Effective immediately, all patrol supervisors shall strictly enforce the department regulation that mandates that all persons shall be removed a distance of at least 300 yards from a suspected explosive device.

2. For your immediate compliance.

Frank Lombardo
CAPTAIN

ITEM 2: MARLBORO POLICE DEPARTMENT

July 19, XXXX

Memo from: Captain Frank A. Lombardo

To: Sergeant Robert Gifford

Subject: POLICE OFFICER FIRMO'S FAILURE TO SIGNAL THE STATION HOUSE

1. The other day, 7/18/XX, I inspected the switchboard record. Police Officer Firmo did not signal (ring) the station house for his entire tour. I know he did not have a portable radio assigned to him because he was assigned to a traffic post for his entire tour.

2. I also see you were the patrol supervisor.

3. Please advise.

Frank A. Lombardo
Frank A. Lombardo

ITEM 3: MARLBORO POLICE DEPARTMENT
TELEPHONE MESSAGE

Sergeant Gifford
7/19/XX – 1610 hours

P.O. Jones, operator of Sector Adam, called and said
he wants to put car 1807 out of service for about 30
minutes to have a radiator hose repaired. He wants
to know what to do?

Telephone Operator
Smith

ITEM 4: BAKER STREET BLOCK
ASSOCIATION

July 16, XXXX

To the commanding officer and the other dear officers
of the third precinct, I would like to thank you for
your assistance in the recent blood donation drive
held by our block association. Your response was won-
derful. Thank you so much.

Sincerely,

Gloria Tyler

President
Baker Street
Block Association

ITEM 5

From: Precinct Anticrime Supervisor, Sergeant
Morgan

To: Commanding Officer, Third Precinct

Subject: JANUARY 1 THROUGH JUNE 30, XXXX
ARREST ACTIVITY BY ANTICRIME
UNIT

1. The chart below indicates the subject matter for
   the periods indicated.

	FELONIES	MISDEMEANORS	OTHER
Harper	15	8	3
Colon	9	16	6
Seeds	8	4	4
Hamlet	8	14	4
Jacobs	8	9	2
Neary	7	18	2
Martino	6	11	1
Marshall	6	10	1
Patterson	5	16	5
Rock	4	12	5
Fields	3	7	2

Sergeant Morgan

To Sgt. Morgan
Based on these numbers, please
recommend two officers for a
pending undercover assignment.
Capt. FAX

ITEM 6: MARLBORO POLICE DEPARTMENT
TELEPHONE MESSAGE

Sergeant Gifford
7/19/XX – 1700 hours

Sgt. Larkin called and says it's starting to rain so he reassigned Police Officer Wells from scooter patrol to the detail at the swimming pool. He just wants to let you know.

Telephone Operator
Smith

ITEM 7: MARLBORO POLICE DEPARTMENT

July 19, XXXX

Memo from: Commanding Officer, Third Precinct

To: All Supervisors

Subject: ALLEGATIONS OF UNNECESSARY FORCE USED BY MEMBERS OF THE COMMAND

1. In accordance with recently issued department order 96, any allegations received by any member of this command that allege unnecessary use of force by any member of this command will be immediately reported to the desk officer. Said desk officer will, without delay, contact the Internal Affairs Division. The Civilian Complaint Review Board will no longer be notified in these cases.

2. For immediate compliance.

Frank A. Lombardo
Frank A. Lombardo
CAPTAIN

ITEM 8: MARLBORO POLICE DEPARTMENT

July 18, XXXX

Memo from: Commanding Officer, Burglary Squad

To: Commanding Officers, All Patrol Precincts

Subject: UNUSUAL MODUS OPERANDI UTILIZED
                    BY BURGLARY PERPETRATORS

7/19/XX
Attention Desk Officers
I want these calls to be personally
made by the Desk Officer on duty
Capt. FHZ

1. In recent weeks several burglaries of commercial establishments have been perpetrated by three males who pose as building inspectors. Once inside the premises, one of the team engages the business proprietor in conversation while the other two members apparently go through the premises, taking whatever valuables are available.

2. Members of the department becoming aware of anyone using this "M.O." contact the Burglary Squad at 555-1212.

3. For your necessary attention.

Capt I. Gottum
_____
I. Gottum
CAPTAIN

ITEM 9: MARLBORO POLICE DEPARTMENT

Bob   7/19/XX

Sergeant Gifford:

I worked 0730 × 1530 hours and left before you came on duty. There's someone threatening cops. Normally we know that my squad, the Intelligence Unit, would be notified if you got information on something like this. But this particular person used the name "The Snuffer," and the boys from Internal Affairs Division think it may be a cop. Therefore, if you or anyone in the precinct get anything on this person, the desk officer is to call Internal Affairs Division right away at 555-0001.

   Let's have lunch soon.

Regards,
John Safers
_____
Lieutenant John Safers

ITEM 10: MARLBORO POLICE DEPARTMENT
TELEPHONE MESSAGE

Sergeant Gifford
7/19/XX – 1900 hours

Sergeant Larkin called. He is at a rooming house on
Alpo Street. A male, white, 80 years old, identified as
Harry Bandian, has been found dead. The landlord
says he lived alone and does not believe he has any
friends or relatives who live locally. Sergeant Larkin
will keep you informed.

*Telephone Operator
Smith*

ITEM 11: PERSONAL OBSERVATION

As you are performing desk duty, you look up and notice Police Officers Rite and Rong pass in front of you.
The officers are in the station house during their
meal (dinner hour) period, in accordance with department procedures. Officer Rite is in your squad, but
Officer Rong is in Sergeant Larkin's squad. Officer
Rite has an unauthorized holster, and Officer Rong is
inappropriately wearing a campaign button over his
badge that says "Bullmoose for Mayor."

ITEM 12: PBA—MARLBORO POLICE DEPARTMENT

July 15, XXXX

Dear Sergeant Gifford,

I would like to take this opportunity to invite you to represent the Third Precinct superior officers at our upcoming Annual PBA Dinner Dance. In years past we had made it a practice to invite the commanding officer to represent the superior officers of the precinct, but our relations in the past months with Captain Lombardo have not been good.

Please advise me if you will attend. I can be reached at 999-0001. The affair is scheduled for July 31 at 8 p.m.

Yours truly,

Fred Costello

Fred Costello
President
Patrol Benevolent
Association

ITEM 13: 300 FRANK STREET TENANT ASSOCIATION

July 17, XXXX

Dear Sergeant Gifford,

I would like to thank you for your help in organizing a tenants' patrol in our building at 300 Frank Street. You were so nice we would like to invite you to our committee brunch to say a few words. It will be on Friday, July 25, XXXX, at 10 a.m.

Please come. My phone number is 111-4708.

Regards,

Tom Thumb

Tom Thumb
President
300 Frank Street
Tenant Association

ITEM 14: MARLBORO POLICE DEPARTMENT
INTERIM ORDER

Number 77

Date 07–17-XX

TO ALL COMMANDS

SUBJECT: VENDING MACHINES IN DEPART-
MENT BUILDINGS

1. Effective immediately only the following vending
   machines will be permitted in department buildings:

   (A) Vending machines that dispense

      (1) Food
      (2) Nonalcoholic beverages
      (3) Cigarettes

2. Department regulations outlining steps for own-
   ership and installations of said authorized vending machines continue in effect.

BY DIRECTION OF THE POLICE COMMISSIONER

Sergeant Klifford
"Bob"
Two of the officers in your squad are
complaining about this order. Find out
why and report back to me.
Lt. Hanna

ITEM 15: MARLBORO POLICE DEPARTMENT

July 18, XXXX

Dear Sergeant Gifford,

I would like to speak with you privately. It is very important. Since I got to the precinct, all the male officers look at me. I know what's in their filthy minds.
The Lord does not approve of this. Even some of the
female officers lust after me. You didn't know that.

   I have always been attracted to you since I was assigned to your squad. Your character is strong, just
like my late father. Please help me; there is no one
else who can help me. I feel desperate. I'm afraid so I
took a few days off.

Please—

Police Officer Joan Manton

ITEM 16

July 18, XXXX

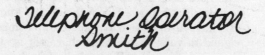

Dear Captain Lombardo,

What are you running? A mating game? I was married for ten years to Police Officer Tom Gray. Everything was fine until he started working with that slut Lucille Ryan. Now he always comes home late and says he made an arrest and had to go to court. By now the whole city of Marlboro could have been locked up by him.

My home is breaking up. We have two children. Can't something be done? If I don't hear from you, I'm going to the Police Commissioner.

Anxiously waiting,

Mrs. Irene Gray

Sgt. Gifford
Handle this one for me.
They are both in your squad.
Capt. Laz

ITEM 17: MARLBORO POLICE DEPARTMENT
TELEPHONE MESSAGE

Sergeant Gifford
7/19/XX – 1920 hours

Police Officer Russo called and said he is at the scene of a burglary on Carl Street off Bog Avenue. There's a liquor store where where three men entered and posed as building inspectors. He's investigating.

Telephone Operator Smith

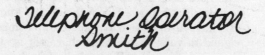

Item 18: Marlboro Police Department

Memo for: All Sergeants

There will be a meeting in my office on Friday, July 25, at 1015 hours sharp. Overtime will be granted for members on their day off. ALL sergeants *will* attend.

Frank A. Lombardo

Frank A. Lombardo
CAPTAIN

Item 19

Pigs of the 3ʳᵈ Precinct
You will have fear
As the time draws near
Like a simple puff
Officer Daryl Harper
I will snuff

the Snuffer

ITEM 20

To the Desk Officer
0800 x 1600 hours
July 20, xxxx
Call this concerned
Citizen and see what this
is all about. Advise me.
No written reports
Capt. FAL

July 18, XXXX

Captain Lombardo,

You listen to me and do something or I go to the pa-
pers. They ought to call you Captain Ostrich. You
have your head in the sand. I can tell you a lot about
what's going on in your precinct.

Call me at anytime at 900-0010.

a concerned citizen

ITEM 21

July 17, XXXX

Dear Fair Police Officers of the 3rd Precinct,

I am writing so that what happened to me doesn't
happen to others. While I was parking my car this
evening at about six o'clock, a police officer ordered
me out of my car. I asked him if anything was wrong.
He pulled me out of my car, called me a "dirtbag," and
pushed me into a hallway. He then slapped me across
the face and mumbled something about not getting
respect. He told me that if I told anyone, he would get
me. He was wearing Third precinct numerals on his
collar and his badge number was 706.

Are cops supposed to be like this?

A Terrified Citizen

ITEM 22: PRECINCT MEMO

Desk officer
1600 x 2400 hours
7/19/XX
Please see that this
gets posted on the
bulletin board
Capt. FAL

To all members:

Anyone interested in applying for possible assignment to the new Career Criminal Unit, see Lieutenant Whaley.

Frank A. Lombardo
_____
Frank A. Lombardo
CAPTAIN

ITEM 23: MARLBORO POLICE DEPARTMENT
TELEPHONE MESSAGE

Sergeant Gifford
7/19/XX – 1920 hours

The 911 Emergency Operator just received an anonymous bomb threat. The male caller said a bomb would go off at 10 p.m. tonight at the Borough Swimming Pool. No further information at this time.

Telephone Operator
Smith

ITEM 24: MARLBORO POLICE DEPARTMENT
INTERIM ORDER

Number 78

Date 07-18-XX

TO ALL COMMANDS

SUBJECT: STREET CONDITIONS REQUIRING CORRECTIVE ACTION

1. Effective 0001 hours, July 19, XXXX, any member of the department becoming aware of any of the street conditions listed below shall notify the desk officer of the precinct of occurrence without delay. The desk officer shall then ensure that the appropriate agency as indicated below is notified.

Condition	Agency to be notified
Damaged signal light	Traffic Department
Damaged parking meter	Parking Meter Bureau
Dead animal in roadway	Sanitation Department
Abandoned building	Building Department
Clogged sewer drain	Sewer Department

2. For compliance.

BY DIRECTION OF THE POLICE COMMISSIONER

July 19, XXXX

Sergeant Gifford, Bob

By now you should have been able to get through the packet I left. I tried to take care of as many as I could, but we got a little busy on the 0800 × 1600 hours tour.

There is one thing. I never got a chance to forward department forms AXL regarding a school crossing guard who was injured in the line of duty yesterday. Could you please forward them?

Thanks,

Tom L.

Sergeant Tom Lamb
DESK OFFICER
0800 × 1600 Hours
July 19, XXXX

ITEM 26: MARLBORO POLICE DEPARTMENT

Memo for: Sergeant Gifford

From: Lt. Manna

SUBJECT: SPECIAL ASSIGNMENT

1. Captain Lombardo is looking for an officer for a special assignment in the Baker Street area. It seems there was a problem with the community in that area, and the Captain wants someone to straighten things out.

2. Is there someone you would like to recommend for this assignment who you think could work with the Baker Street community?

3. There is a sense of urgency involved with this matter.

Lt Manna

Sergeant Gifford

7/19/XX – 2130 hours

Police Officer Rite called and said he was at the scene
of a vehicle accident causing minor traffic congestion
in the area of Elm Street and Ark Avenue. It seems
that a green Ford sedan swerved to avoid hitting a
dog on Elm Street and mounted the sidewalk, damaged some parking meters, and came to rest in the
yard of a building that has recently been abandoned.
Unfortunately, a car traveling behind the Ford struck
and killed the dog at the intersection of Elm and Ark.
The second car then slammed into a Sewer Department truck parked in the area.

*Telephone Operator
Smith*

Practice Questions

1. With respect to item 1, the proposed precinct memo, and any other related items, it would be most appropriate for you to do which of the following?
   A. Sign the memo for the Captain, and distribute it to the patrol supervisors after making any necessary corrections.
   B. Sign the Captain's name on the memo, and immediately distribute it to all patrol supervisors since the memo is in accordance with department procedures.
   C. Send the memo to the training officer, and direct him to review it and respond directly back to the Captain.
   D. Advise the Captain as soon as possible that the proposed memo is inaccurate, and explain why.

2. Concerning item 11 regarding Officer Rite and any other related items, which of the following actions would be most correct for you to take?
   A. Reprimand Officer Rite in front of the other officer to make your point more strongly.
   B. Call Officer Rite aside, and point out he is wearing an unauthorized holster and ask for an explanation.
   C. Call Officer Rite aside, and ask him if he has any idea what is wrong.
   D. Initiate disciplinary action against Officer Rite for violating department regulations.

3. Regarding item 13, the letter from Mr. Thumb, and any other related items, which of the following actions should you take?
   A. Direct another sergeant to attend the brunch.
   B. Call Mr. Thumb, and explain why you cannot attend.
   C. Call Mr. Thumb, and tell him you will come but can only stay a few minutes.
   D. Attend the brunch.

4. Regarding item 15, a letter from Police Officer Manton, and any other related items, your best action would be which of the following?

A. Forward a copy of her letter to the Commanding Officer, and discuss it with him the next time you are both working at the same time.

B. Try to contact Officer Manton and arrange for a face-to-face interview as soon as possible at the station house.

C. Try tactfully to find out if her allegations have any merit before speaking with her.

D. Send Sergeant Maria Gomez to interview her as soon as possible.

5. Regarding item 20, a letter from a concerned citizen, and any other related items, which of the following actions would be most appropriate?
   A. Refrain from calling the concerned citizen.
   B. Have the patrol supervisor call the citizen.
   C. Call the citizen at 900-0010, and prepare a written report for the Captain.
   D. Call the citizen at 900-0010, and make an oral report to the Captain.

6. With respect to item 10, the notification from Sergeant Larkin, and any other related items, which of the following would be correct for you to do?
   A. Notify the precinct detective unit.
   B. Sign the activity log of the police officer who conducts a search of the deceased.
   C. Make a notation in the margin of the command log of the name of a person notified at the missing person unit.
   D. Direct Sergeant Larkin to call the missing person unit.

7. Concerning item 11 with respect to Officer Rong and any other related items, which of the following actions would be most correct for you to take?
   A. In the presence of the other officer, ask Officer Rong if he is authorized to wear a campaign button while in uniform.
   B. Refer the matter of Officer Rong's campaign button to Sergeant Larkin.
   C. Privately direct Officer Rong to immediately remove the campaign button.
   D. Report the matter of the campaign button in writing to Captain Lombardo, and take no further action at the present time.

8. Regarding item 21, the letter addressed to the precinct and any other related items, it would be most correct for you to do which of the following without delay?
   A. Notify the Internal Affairs Division.
   B. Notify the commanding officer of the precinct.
   C. Notify the Civilian Complaint Review Board.
   D. Ascertain who the officer is and get his/her version of the incident.

9. With respect to item 12, the invitation from the PBA and any other related items, which of the following would be your best course of action?
   A. Ignore the invitation since it hints a broader issue may exist.
   B. Call Mr. Costello, and tell him you would be pleased to attend.
   C. Call Mr. Costello, and tell him under no circumstances will you attend.
   D. Call Mr. Costello, and suggest a meeting to discuss the invitation.

10. Regarding item 3, the request from Police Officer Jones and any other related items, you should do which of the following?
    A. Tell the telephone operator to contact Officer Jones and have him speak to you.
    B. Grant permission to Officer Jones.
    C. Tell Officer Jones to check with the patrol supervisor, Sergeant Larkin.
    D. Ask the patrol supervisor, Sergeant Larkin, if car 1807 can be spared before you respond to Jones's request.

11. Regarding item 19, the note concerning Police Officer Harper, and any other related items, which of the following should you do first?
    A. Call 555-0001 and report the incident.
    B. Notify Captain Lombardo.
    C. Call the intelligence unit.
    D. Contact Officer Harper and advise him.

12. Regarding item 6, the notification from Sergeant Larkin and any other related items, you would be most correct if you:
    A. Notified Sergeant Gomez of the addition to her detail
    B. Told Sergeant Larkin to formally notify Sergeant Gomez

C. Told Officer Wells to formally notify Sergeant Gomez

D. Advised Sergeant Larkin of the proper department procedure for future use

13. Regarding item 17, the note from telephone operator Smith and any other related items, which of the following would be most correct for you to do?
A. Have Police Officer Russo call 555-1212.
B. Have Sergeant Larkin respond to the scene, get the necessary information, and call 555-1212.
C. Personally call 555-1212.
D. Refer the matter to the precinct detective unit, and have them respond to the liquor store.

14. Regarding item 16, the letter from Mrs. Gray and any other related items, which of the following actions should you take first?
A. Call Mrs. Gray in a few days after making some discreet inquiries around the precinct.
B. Call Mrs. Gray as soon as possible and try to get more specific facts.
C. Examine the arrest statistics for the entire precinct, and see if Officer Gray does in fact make many arrests.
D. Confront Officers Ryan and Gray and ask for an explanation.

15. Regarding item 2, the note from the Captain inquiring about Officer Firmo and any other related items, it would be most appropriate for you to do which of the following?
A. Notify Officer Firmo to stop in to see the Captain as soon as possible to discuss the matter involved.
B. Direct Sergeant Larkin, the patrol supervisor, to investigate the matter and report back to the Captain.
C. Tactfully advise the Captain that, on the day in question, Officer Firmo was not required to ring, but only after you verify the officer's assignment on July 18.
D. Immediately initiate disciplinary action against Officer Firmo after you personally verify that he did not ring the station house on the day in question.

16. With respect to item 22, a note from the commanding officer and any other related items, which of the following actions would be your most appropriate first action?
    A. Prepare a list of recommendations for the commanding officer's information.
    B. Post the note on the bulletin board.
    C. Find out if the note applies to supervisors before taking any action.
    D. Have anyone interested call the career criminal unit.

17. With respect to item 23, an anonymous bomb threat and any other related items, the unit that should be initially assigned to investigate is:
    A. Sector Adam
    B. Sector Baker
    C. Sector Charlie
    D. The bomb squad

18. With respect to item 23, the anonymous bomb threat and any other related items, if the building and area involved were evacuated, a search by police personnel could be conducted between which of the following time periods?
    A. Anytime before 2130 hours and anytime after 2230 hours
    B. Anytime before 2140 hours and anytime after 2300 hours
    C. Anytime before 2145 hours and anytime after 2245 hours
    D. Anytime before 2100 hours and anytime after 2240 hours

19. With respect to item 25, the note left by the previous desk officer and any other related items, who should receive the original copy of the form that Sergeant Lamb was not able to forward?
    A. Personnel bureau
    B. School crossing guard bureau
    C. Precinct detective unit
    D. Precinct commanding officer

20. With respect to item 23, an anonymous bomb threat and any other related items, which of the following most properly indicates actions you should take if the threat proves to be a hoax?

A. Make a command log entry, notify the operations unit, and prepare a report for the commanding officer.

B. Do not make a command log entry, but notify the operations unit and prepare a report for the commanding officer.

C. Prepare a report for the commanding officer, but do not make a command log entry or notify the operations unit.

D. Do not prepare a report for the commanding officer, notify the operations unit, or make a command log entry.

21. With respect to item 4, the letter from Mrs. Tyler and any other related items, it would be most appropriate for you to do which of the following?
A. Write back to Mrs. Tyler.
B. File the letter for future reference.
C. Find out which officers she is referring to.
D. Recommend to the commanding officer that the letter be posted on the bulletin board.

22. With respect to item 5, an arrest activity report and any other related items, you would be most correct if you:
A. Checked further into the precinct records before making any recommendations
B. Forwarded the report to another sergeant who should handle making the recommendations
C. Recommended Police Officers Harper and Colon
D. Recommended Police Officers Harper and Neary

23. With respect to item 14, and any other related items it would be most proper if you do which of the following?
A. Prepare a memo to the police officers in your squad directing compliance with interim order 77.
B. Canvas the officers in your squad to find out who are the officers mentioned by the Lieutenant.
C. Ask Lieutenant Manna for more information.
D. Delegate the task to the most experienced officer in your squad.

24. With respect to item 26 and any other related items, it would be most appropriate for you to recommend to Lieutenant Manna that:
   A. Officer Knucks gets the assignment
   B. Officer Harper gets the assignment
   C. Officer Gray gets the assignment
   D. Officer Wells gets the assignment

25. With respect to item 27 and any other related items, which of the following actions are you mandated to take?
   A. Notify the Traffic Department.
   B. Notify the Traffic Department and the Parking Meter Bureau.
   C. Notify the Parking Meter Bureau, the Buildings Department, and the Sanitation Department.
   D. Notify the Buildings Department, the Parking Meter Bureau, the Sewer Department, and the Sanitation Department.

Answer Key, Diagnostic Procedure, and Answer Explanations

Structured Answer Key

1. D	6. C	11. A	16. B	21. D
2. B	7. C	12. D	17. B	22. B
3. B	8. A	13. C	18. B	23. C
4. B	9. D	14. B	19. A	24. B
5. A	10. C	15. C	20. C	25. C

Diagnostic Procedure

If you scored less than 21 correct, it is recommended that you review those parts of Chapter 16 that deal with in-basket exercises and all of Chapter 17.

Answer Explanations

GENERAL COMMENTS

Before we give you the answer explanations for your practice in-basket exercise, we would like to make a few general comments about it, as follows.

Make sure you understand the difference between a structured and a nonstructured in-basket. If you are still not certain of this distinction, review Chapter 17.

Understand that time management is a vital concern, yet so is an adequate indexing effort. The trick is to use indexing to become familiar with the information in the in-basket, but not to learn or study the material. This is so because studying the material while indexing takes up too much time.

Your ability to recognize interrelated items is critical to your success on an in-basket test. Remember, however, that many items will stand by themselves and can be responded to without referring to other items.

When responding to items in a nonstructured format, always think in terms of the key behavioral traits discussed in Chapter 17 to see if you can pick up extra points.

Immediately following these comments is a sample of what the index sheet might look like after you have finished your indexing effort. Compare the sample with your completed index sheet to see how well you indexed the material.

It is important for you to recognize that a number of questions in the exercise you just took were based on the Marlboro Police Department Patrol Guide, but on your test you could be asked procedural questions based on the actual policies and procedures in effect in your department. Remember, therefore, to read the instructions carefully, for it is in the instructions where you will be told *on what to base your answers.*

SAMPLE OF COMPLETED INDEX SHEET FOR IN-BASKET EXAMINATION

List of Pages in Administrative Test Packet

(23) Page A   (Instructions)

Page B   (Precinct Profile)

Page C   (Calendar)

(23) Page D   (Map)

Page E   (Organization Chart of Marlboro Police Department)

Page F   (Organization Chart of Third Precinct)

Page G   (Eighth Squad Personnel Data)
(2)(3)(6)(8)(9)(11)(12)
(15)(16)(21)(26)

Page H   (Marlboro P.D. Patrol Guide)
(1)(2)(3)(6)(10)(23)(25)

Item 1   *Proposed memo re:*
(H)   *Explosive Device* ASAP

Item 2   *Capt's inquiry re: P.O Firmo*
(G)(H)   *no radio on traffic post*

Item 3   *Request from P.O. Jones to put car #1809 out of service*

Item 4   *Thank You letter from Gloria Tyler*

Item 5 Anti Crime P.O.'s arrest activity with C.O.'s request to Sgt Morgan

Item 6 (G)(H) Sgt. Larkin reassigns P.O. Wells from scooter patrol to swimming pool

(21) Item 7 Captin's memo re: Unnecessary use of force

(17) Item 8 Burglary Squad's CO's memo re: Bogus Building Inspectors

(19) Item 9 Note from Lt. Safers - How to report threats by "the Snuffer"

(H) Item 10 Notification from Sgt Larkin of a dead human body on Alpo St. No relatives

(G) Item 11 P.O.'s Rite and Rong - misconduct

(G) Item 12 Invitation for July 31 PBA Dance from PBA President; CO. not invited

Item 13 (18) Invitation Frank Street Tenants' Assoc 10 AM July 25

Item 14 Lt Manna indicates problem with P.O.'s in squad re: Vending Machine Order

Item 15 (G) Letter from P.O. Manton asking for help

Item 16 (G) Complaint by P.O. Grays wife re: his partner P.O. Ryan

Item 17 (G)(8) P.O. Russo reports burglary on Carl Street by Bogus Building Inspectors

Item 18
(13) Memo from captain directing attendance at Pct. meeting July 25, at 10.15 AM

Item 19
(G)(9) Threat P.O. Harper — The Sniffer

Item 20 Anon letter with Tele # complaining re: pct. conditions

Item 21 Anon civ complaint — use of
(G)(7) force by P.O. sh # 706

Item 22 C.O. memo. Candidates for Career Criminal Unit. Post on bulletin board

Item 23 Bomb threat 10 PM, July 19, 86
(A)(D)(H) Boro Swimming Pool

Item 24 Interim Order re: Street Conditon
(27) and notifications to city agencies

Item 25 Request from previous desk
(H) officer to process form AXL re: School Cross Guard

Item 26 Special assignment in Baker
(G) Street area.

Item 27 Message re: accident on Elm
(24) Street and Ark Ave.

EXPLANATIONS

1. <u>Structured answer</u> **D**   Your indexing should have revealed a relationship between page H, the Patrol Guide procedure #3 re: explosive devices, and item 1, which is a proposed precinct memo. In the handwritten note on item 1, the precinct captain asks the desk officer what he thinks about the content matter of the proposed memo. The intent of the memo is to make certain that department guidelines are adhered to at the scene of suspected explosive devices. The problem with the memo is that the captain erroneously quotes department regulations as requiring that all persons be removed at least 300 yards from any suspected explosive device. Actually, Procedure #3 of the Patrol Guide mandates that persons be removed 1000 feet from a suspected explosive device, not 300 yards as the captain states in his proposed memo. Therefore, the proposed memo contains inaccurate information and the captain must be so informed. Choice D is the answer.

   Choice A is wrong because the captain didn't instruct you in his handwritten note to sign the memo for him. Instead, he asked you to tell him what you think. Remember handwritten notes from superiors must be complied with exactly as directed unless there is a very good reason not to do so.

   Choice B is wrong since the information in the proposed memo is not in accordance with department procedures.

   Choice C is wrong since it outlines a course of action which is contrary to the captain's written directions.

   Please note that this same type of question could be asked to test your technical knowledge of your department procedures as they actually exist. Because we are writing this test for many jurisdictions we had to create our own procedures.

   Also note that you could not have answered this question correctly unless you spotted the relationship between Page H and item 1.

   <u>Nonstructured response</u>: In this item, the examiner is testing your ability to follow instructions. You should recognize that the captain's proposed memo is incorrect by utilizing Patrol Guide Procedure #3. Recognizing this would give you a plus in Problem Analysis. Your course of action would be to send a memo back to the captain as soon as possible indicating that the proposed memo is incorrect in the most tactful way possible, a plus for Organizational Sensitivity and Judgment. Note that if you chose to correct the proposed memo and distribute it without advising the captain you would receive a plus for Decisiveness but a minus for Organizational Sensitivity and Judgment. The point, as has been mentioned in Chapter 17, is that in a nonstructured exercise there are many ways to deal with each item. The trick, obviously, is to respond in such a manner so that you receive as many plus scores as possible.

2. <u>Structured answer</u> **B** Obtaining the facts from Officer Rite before taking any action shows good Leadership and Problem Analysis ability. Doing it in private indicates high Responsiveness, and Supervisory Ability. Remember, to initiate disciplinary action without getting all of the facts is an inappropriate supervisory practice.

   <u>Nonstructured response</u>: A good way to handle item 11 would be to take immediate action to correct the situation, a plus for Decisiveness, Leadership, and Decision Making. To do it in private indicates good Judgment and Responsiveness. Your written response should also indicate that you will take some type of follow-up action to ensure that Officer Rite does not wear an unauthorized holster in the future, which would be a plus for Management Control. If in your response you also showed an awareness of Officer Rite's background as given on the personnel data sheet on page G, then you would get points for Problem Analysis. A quick comment on Management Control: when framing nonstructured responses, it is always a good idea to include some indication of follow-up when appropriate. This will always get you points for Management Control. Your intention to follow up can be shown by some written note, on your calendar if one is provided, or by a "tickler" memo to yourself.

3. <u>Structured answer</u> **B** To answer this question correctly, you would have to relate item 13 with item 18. Both of these items involve meetings on July 25 at about the same time. Since you cannot be in two places at the same time, a scheduling conflict exists. In this question the examiner is testing your Planning and Organization skills. Further, you must realize that you must respond to your superiors first, except in very extreme circumstances. Department business comes first—especially when the memo in item 18 is so strongly worded. Your Organizational Sensitivity is being tested. Finally, choice C is testing your Judgment. There is no way you can arrive at a brunch at 1000 hours, stay for awhile, and then be at the captain's meeting at 1015 hours sharp. Remember, however, that Responsiveness demands that you call Mr. Thumb and explain the situation to him.

   <u>Nonstructured response</u>: Relating items 13 and 18 would give you a plus in Problem Analysis. Making appropriate entries on a calendar or elsewhere regarding the meeting dates would be a plus for Planning and Organization. Deciding that you must attend the captain's meeting would get you a plus for Judgment and for Organizational Sensitivity. Advising Mr. Thumb that you cannot attend his brunch and explaining the reason would earn you points for Responsiveness.

4. <u>Structured answer</u> **B** In this question, the examiner is testing your Responsiveness and Judgment. Obviously, Officer Manton is upset. It would seem that she is extremely upset. She wants to speak to you. To put it off would show poor Judgment and Responsiveness. There is certainly a sense of desperation in her letter. Con-

ducting the interview at the station house shows good Judgment since this strategy reduces any possibility of future allegations against you. Choices A and C unwisely and unrealistically put the matter off. Choice D is insensitive. Officer Manton has asked to speak to you. This is part of a supervisor's responsibility, to help an employee when help is requested. To provide that help is indicative of good Leadership.

Nonstructured response: To relate item 15 with the personnel data sheet information about Officer Manton would get you a plus for Problem Analysis. That strategy would also show you that Officer Manton doesn't seem to have had any real problems in the past. Therefore, something has apparently happened to her. The situation calls for prompt, decisive, and tactful action, such as personally contacting Officer Manton as soon as possible and arranging for an interview. This would get you points for Judgment, Responsiveness, and Decision Making. Making yourself available for the interview would earn you Leadership points. The officer is in your squad and wants to speak to you. When an employee wants help or when a subordinate's personal problems interfere with his/her work, the supervisor can and should get involved. Another way to earn points on this item would be to seek the assistance of professionals, either from within the department, if available, or from some other city agency. This could earn you points for Job Knowledge, Judgment, and Planning and Organization, as well as for Responsiveness.

5. Structured answer **A**   This question highlights the importance of paying strict attention to handwritten notes on memos. A close examination of the note on item 20 reveals that the captain wants the desk officer on the 0800 × 1600 hours tour on July 20 to call the concerned citizen and then to verbally report the specifics of the call back to the captain. The only possible answer is A.

Nonstructured response: Recognizing that the note on item 20 is not meant for you would earn you points in Problem Analysis. It would be an indication of poor judgment if you were to take action in a situation contrary to the specific direction of your captain. A good idea concerning this item would be to take some steps to ensure that the item is passed along to the appropriate desk officer. This would earn you points for Planning and Organization.

6. Structured answer **C**   To correctly answer this question you must relate it to procedure 2 of the patrol guide on page H. That procedure clearly indicates that the responsibility to make the entry described in choice C belongs to the desk officer. The tasks described by choices A and B are the responsibility of the patrol supervisor. The task outlined in choice D is the responsibility of the desk officer, not the patrol supervisor. Choice C is the only correct action for the desk officer to take.

Nonstructured response: A good way to handle item 10 would be to indicate your intended actions right on the item. Your actions should include some indication of your knowledge of patrol guide procedure 2 and its interrelationship with item 10. This would earn you Problem Analysis points. Indicating that a call is needed to missing persons and that it is your responsibility to make the call and the required command log entry would get you a plus rating for Planning and Organization.

7. Structured answer **C**   Although Officer Rong is not in your squad, there is no violation of the principle of unity of command if you tell him to immediately remove the campaign button since the officer's continued wearing of the button could damage the reputation of the department. Note there is no need to first ask the officer about the button since the item tells you that Officer Rong is *inappropriately* wearing the button. To privately direct the officer to remove the button shows good Judgment and Responsiveness. Simply to refer the matter to the captain shows poor leadership.

Nonstructured response: It would be wise to indicate right on item 11 that with respect to Officer Rong you would immediately tell the officer in private to remove the button..This would earn you Judgment, Leadership, Decisiveness, and Responsiveness points. It would also be a good idea to have Sergeant Larkin notified since he is Officer Rong's immediate supervisor, and some form of follow-up with Sergeant Larkin would also be recommended. This would earn you credit for Organizational Sensitivity and Management Control.

8. Structured answer **A**   Item 21 is a letter of complaint against a police officer alleging the unnecessary use of force. A check of our index sheet reveals that item 21 is related to item 7, a memo from the captain directing that civilian complaints that allege the unnecessary use of force require an immediate notification to the Internal Affairs Division. The question exemplifies what in-basket exercises test. The examiner wants to see if you can coordinate different pieces of information and follow directions. If you properly cross-referenced your index sheet, you would have had no problem answering this question. If, however, you didn't initially spot the relationship between items 7 and 21, you should realize that you probably overlooked an interrelationship during your indexing. There is no way you could correctly answer question 8 without referring to item 7, unless you made a lucky guess.

Nonstructured response: Item 21 is a civilian complaint alleging unnecessary use of force. Therefore, while indexing, you should have related item 21 with item 7, a memo from the captain directing that such allegations of unnecessary use of force by members of the Third Precinct be referred to the Internal Affairs Unit. This would get you a plus for Problem Analysis. In practical terms, if this were a nonstructured response in-basket examination, you would go through the items while making notes and cross-referencing related items on your index sheet. When you get to item 7, the captain's memo announcing a change in procedure, there is actually little for you to do other than to be aware of the order. Your antennae should be raised because usually this is a tip-off that later there may be an item (in this case item 21) that calls for your use of the change in procedure. This should reinforce your understanding of the importance of the indexing step we talked about in Chapter 17. (In a training session we recently conducted, a question similar to this issue raised by items 21 and 7 was asked by a student. The student suggested that the officer could be identified via the personnel data, as given on page G, and interviewed by the desk officer to get the police officer's version of the incident. This would get you a plus for Problem Analysis (identifying the officer and getting facts before acts) but would get you a negative in judgment for not following departmental procedure as mandated by the captain's memo. Remember, the best response is the one that can get you the most pluses.)

9. Structured answer **D**   This is a type of in-basket question that we refer to as "generic." No specific or specialized knowledge of individual department procedures is needed. What is needed is a general knowledge of supervision and administration. The invitation cannot be ignored or rejected out of hand. Nor can it be accepted without clarification and a discussion with the captain. More information and possible compromise or negotiation are needed, which is why choice D is correct. This would especially hold true when dealing with a line organization such as the PBA.

   Nonstructured response: Regarding item 12, you should indicate the date of the dance on the calendar if one is provided. This is a plus for Planning and Organization. Some attempt to get more information (a plus for Problem Analysis) from Officer Louis Jones. If you identified him as the precinct's PBA delegate from page G you would get another plus for Problem Analysis and Planning and Organization. Then, Fred Costello should be contacted by you personally to discuss his invitation (a plus for Organizational Sensitivity) with the aim of bettering relations with the PBA. The ideal result would be to have the commanding officer represent the precinct as in past years.

10. Structured answer **C**   This is another item that requires knowledge of the procedures outlined on page H, the patrol guide, procedure 1, where it states that permission for this kind of request should come from the patrol supervisor. The other choices, A, B, and D are strictly made-up alternatives that have no basis in fact.

   Nonstructured response: In handling item 3, you would receive a plus in Problem Analysis by showing your knowledge of patrol guide procedure 1, which deals with taking a department vehicle out of service with the patrol supervisor's permission. If you decided to let Police Officer Jones take car 1807 out of service on your authority, you might get a plus for decisiveness but you would get negatives for Problem Analysis (not knowing the proper patrol guide procedure) and for Organizational Sensitivity for bypassing the patrol supervisor. (Students have asked us, "What if I just don't know how to answer a question in a nonstructured response in-basket examination or never get to a question because I run out of time?" Typically, the examiner will give you negatives in Planning and Organization (for not properly scheduling your work and running out of time) and in Judgment, Problem Analysis, and Decisiveness.)

11. <u>Structured answer</u> **A** Question 11 refers to item 19, which is a note from "the Snuffer" threatening Officer Harper's life. A check of your index sheet should reveal a relationship between items 19 and 9, which is a memo to you requesting a call to the Internal Affairs Division if any information is received about a person using the name Snuffer. Once that connection is clear, the answer to question 11 is obvious. Item 19 requires a call to phone number 555-0001, the number of Internal Affairs.

<u>Nonstructured response</u>: Noting the relationship between items 9 and 19 would give you Problem Analysis points. Indicating that you would call Internal Affairs about item 19 would give you Planning and Organization and Judgment points. Any steps you take to make the information in item 9 available to the entire precinct would earn you Judgment and Planning and Organization points. Of course, taking steps to provide for the safety of Officer Harper would earn credit for Responsiveness, Planning and Organization, Judgment, and Problem Analysis.

12. <u>Structured answer</u> **D** Procedure 1 of the patrol guide on page H is a related item needed to answer this question. That procedure directs that when inclement weather necessitates the reassignment of a scooter officer, the patrol supervisor is to direct the officer to the desk officer, who will make the reassignment. Therefore, Sergeant Larkin erred when he personally reassigned Officer Wells since it is the desk officer's job to make the reassignment and Sergeant Larkin should be so informed. Therefore, choice D is the correct choice.

<u>Nonstructured response</u>: A proper response to item 6 would be to advise the telephone operator to contact the patrol supervisor and have him call you. In a nonstructured response in-basket examination, you are provided paper and could indicate the steps you wish to be taken in a note to the telephone operator. In this case, some of the steps you plan to take should include some indication of your awareness of the proper patrol guide procedure (a plus for Problem Analysis) and some tact in dealing with another sergeant, a rank equal to yours. This would get you positives in Judgment and Organizational Sensitivity due to the fact that although in this make-believe police department you as the desk officer are apparently responsible for all police operations during the tour of duty, it is only a temporary assignment and tomorrow the other sergeant could be the desk officer. Therefore, the sergeants are actually peers.

13. <u>Structured answer</u> **C** A good indexing effort was necessary to get this question correct. Item 17, the subject of question 13, should have

been cross-referenced to item 8, which directs that a call be made to the burglary unit at 555-1212 if a burglary is attempted by three males posing as building inspectors. Item 17 concerns a burglary that did involve three men posing as building inspectors. Therefore, a call is needed to the burglary unit. However, the captain's handwritten note on item 8 requires that desk officers personally make any such calls. The only possible answer is C. Remember to carefully note all handwritten notes, especially those from superiors.

Nonstructured response: Relating items 8 and 17 would earn Problem Analysis points. Taking steps to pass on the information in item 8 so other desk officers were informed would be a plus for Planning and Organization. Concerning item 17, indicating your intention to call the burglary unit would give you credit for Judgment and Problem Analysis. Taking steps to follow up to find out the results of the investigation would earn Management Control points.

14. Structured answer **B** Facts before acts: this eliminates choice D. Waiting a few days is indicative of poor judgment since Mrs. Gray has threatened to involve the police commissioner if you don't contact her quickly. Doing as choice C suggests would be wasteful. Why examine arrest statistics for the entire precinct because of Mrs. Gray's letter? That doesn't make sense. The only course of action that would show good Judgment is choice B.

Nonstructured response: Your response to item 16 should include plans to contact Mrs. Gray as soon as possible, a plus for Responsiveness and Judgment. A discreet view of the records of the two officers to check their arrest activity would earn Problem Analysis and Planning and Organization credit. Getting more facts from Mrs. Gray when you talk to her would also yield Problem Analysis and Planning and Organization points. Confronting the officers immediately would get you negative points in Problem Analysis, Judgment, and Planning and Organization.

15. Structured answer **C** According to procedure 1 of the patrol guide, an officer on patrol who is assigned to a traffic post is not required to signal the station house every hour. If, therefore, Officer Firmo was assigned to a traffic post on July 18, he would not have been required to signal the station house at all during the tour of duty. Notice the use in choice C of the word *tactfully;* a good way to deal with superiors when informing them they are in error is to use tact. Concerning choices A and B: they could not be right since the captain has specifically instructed you to advise him of the facts. Choice D highlights that disciplinary action should never be taken without first obtaining all the facts in the case.

Nonstructured response: Item 2 measures your Problem Analysis ability by having you exhibit knowledge of the patrol guide procedure 1, which indicates that someone assigned to a traffic post need not ring (signal) the station house, regardless of whether he/she was in possession of a portable radio. A tactfully worded memo to the captain citing the fact that departmental procedures do not require signaling the station house when assigned to a traffic post would get you a plus in Organizational Sensitivity, Judgment, and Problem Analysis. If you had chosen to send Police Officer Firmo to see the captain directly, it might get you a plus for Decisiveness, but it would also get you negatives in Organizational Sensitivity since the captain told you to advise him; in Problem Analysis, since you did not show awareness of the patrol guide; and in Leadership, since the captain pointed out a possible instance of misconduct by an officer under your supervision and you are not taking any action or meaningful steps to get the facts straight before taking action. (Another word about the patrol guide beginning on page H: it obviously is strictly made up for this exercise. It should be clear to you that, in a real examination, the examiner would probably be testing you on your knowledge of your own department's patrol guide or manual of procedure. Now let's suppose you decided to check Police Officer Firmo's background, and then, after seeing that he is a disciplinary problem, you initiated immediate action against him. How would an examiner possibly score you? You could get a plus for Decisiveness and Problem Analysis (recognizing and using the personnel data of page G), but you would also get negatives for Problem Analysis for not knowing the pertinent provisions of the patrol guide and for Leadership for not interviewing the officer before initiating disciplinary action. It should be clear to you that it is entirely possible to submit a nonstructured response that could get you both a positive and a negative under the same scoring dimension at the same time. Remember, however, the goal in a nonstructured response is to get as many positives (pluses) as possible while avoiding negative scores.)

16. Structured answer **B**   Every now and then the examiner comes straight down the middle with an easy question. Don't read into it when this happens. The captain's note says post item 22 on the bulletin board. Therefore, that would be your first action.

    Nonstructured response: The captain's handwritten note on item 22 directs the desk officer on July 19, on the 1600 × 2400 hours tour, to post his memo on the bulletin board. If you recognized that you are the desk officer, you would get a plus for Problem Analysis. If you delegated the task to someone, you would get a plus for Delegation. If you followed up to make sure it was done, you would get a plus for Management Control. It should become apparent that an appropriate action you might take in a nonstructured response in-basket could get you several plus scores. Remember, when appropriate, delegate and follow up. Make plenty of notes on your calendar. Use it as a planning device and a control device.

17. Structured answer **B**   Patrol guide procedure 3 indicates the bomb squad is to be requested only if a device is found at the scene of a suspected explosive device. A look at the precinct map would indicate that the patrol car assigned to sector B covers the Borough Swimming

Pool. When you see a map, you will probably be asked a question somewhere in the examination that will test your ability to use it.

Nonstructured response: See suggested nonstructured response for question 20.

18. Structured answer **B** Patrol guide procedure 3 indicates that if a building that might contain an explosive device is evacuated, the search will be discontinued twenty minutes before, and not started again for at least one hour after, the threatened time of explosion. Therefore, if the threatened time of explosion is 10 P.M. or 2200 hours, a search would take place in the evacuated building before 2140 and after 2300 hours.

Nonstructured response: See suggested nonstructured response for question 20.

19. Structured answer **A** Unless you recognized while indexing that there was a relationship between item 25 and the patrol guide on page H, this would be an impossible question—unless you made a lucky guess. Procedure 5 of the patrol guide indicates that the desk officer is to forward the original of department from AXL to the Personnel Bureau. Therefore, A is the answer.

Nonstructured response: Recognizing the relationship between item 25 and the patrol guide procedure 5 would earn you Problem Analysis points. Complying with Sergeant Lamb's request is a positive for Organizational Sensitivity. Having someone forward it would earn Delegation points.

20. Structured answer **C** Patrol guide procedure 3, dealing with searches for explosive devices, directs that a desk officer will not make a command log entry or notify operations if no explosive device is found. However, in all cases a report will be prepared by the desk officer for the commanding officer. (*Note:* there is nothing to prohibit an in-basket examiner from basing more than one question on one item or returning to an item to ask another question based on the item.)

Nonstructured response: Concerning item 23, which contains a bomb threat, you should have based your nonstructured response on the simulated patrol guide procedure 3 we provided beginning on page H. This would have given you a plus in Problem Analysis. Particularly you should pay attention to the desk officer's duties. In every way possible, you should give this emergency matter priority (a plus for Judgment), especially if you realized there is a detail of officers assigned to the pool (a plus for Problem Analysis). Making sure you are kept notified would give you a plus for Management Control.

21. Structured answer **D** It would indicate good Judgment, Organizational Sensitivity, and Leadership to make arrangements to have Ms. Tyler's letter posted on the bulletin board. It would not be proper to write back to Ms. Tyler. There is no immediacy, and fur-

ther, the letter has not yet been seen by the commanding officer, who is the appropriate person to write a letter of acknowledgment to Ms. Tyler.

Nonstructured response: With respect to item 4, it is recommended that you route the letter to the captain through the clerical officer, Police Officer Carey. This would get you a plus in Planning and Organization and Delegation. Also, you should attach a note recommending that the members of the precinct be made aware of the letter by placing a duplicate copy on the bulletin board for all to see. This would get you a plus in Judgment, Organizational Sensitivity, and Leadership.

22. Structured answer **B** The captain's handwritten note on item 5 was not directed to you. The best you could do here is forward the report with the captain's note on it to Sergeant Morgan. The examiner, near the end of the examination, wants to see if you still can pick up details, the crux of problem analysis.

Nonstructured response: Item 5 is directed to Sergeant Morgan. You are Sergeant Gifford. If you realized this (a plus for Problem Analysis) and took steps to forward the memo to Sergeant Morgan (a plus for Planning and Organization and Judgment), then you would be evaluated as having acted properly.

23. Structured answer **C** Facts before acts. You would get a plus in Problem Analysis if you got more information from the lieutenant. It would show poor judgment to involve your entire squad for a matter that only at this point seems to involve two police officers.

Nonstructured response: Regarding item 14, you are responding to Lieutenant Manna. If you indicated your awareness that he supervises you, according to the organizational chart of the precinct, you would get a plus for Planning and Organization, Organizational Sensitivity, and Problem Analysis. Your response should include some effort to get more information from the lieutenant, at least the names of the two officers involved. This would get you additional points for Problem Analysis. If you used your calendar to remind yourself about the incident by making a calendar notation on a day during the week of July 21, you would get a plus for Management Control.

24. Structured answer **B** There is only one place you could find the information to answer this question, the personnel data sheet found on page G. If you related that source with this question, the rest was simple. It clearly states on the data sheet that Officer Harper has a good rapport with the community in the Baker Street area. It is important to point out that when you were indexing you should not have studied the information on page G, or on any of the special pages or items. All that is required is that you know what information is available in the administrative test packet and where the information can be found. After you have a need for specific information, you read the page or item more closely. Trying to learn

all of the information when you are indexing is a big mistake. It is too time-consuming.

Nonstructured response: The way to handle item 26 in a nonstructured in-basket test would be to write a quick note back to Lieutenant Manna recommending Officer Harper. This would get you points in Judgment, Problem Analysis, and Decisiveness. However, you could get additional points by noting Officer Gray's involvement in item 16, concerning the letter of complaint from his wife to the captain. Also noting Wells's propensity to give out summonses would garner points for you. Remember, the beauty of a nonstructured exercise is that you can always earn extra points by displaying a good working knowledge of all of the relevant information in the packet.

25. Structured answer C   The key to this question is relating item 27 with item 24. Once you do this, the rest should be easy. The Parking Meter Bureau is notified because of the damaged parking meters; the Buildings Department is notified because of the abandoned building; and the Sanitation Department is notified because of the dead animal in the street. These are the only mandated notifications.

Nonstructured response: We would hope that the difference between a structured and a nonstructured response is clear. In dealing with a structured response format, you merely answer each multiple-choice question. The stem of the question gives you the lead as to which item the examiner is testing. Of course, you first would have had to do your indexing to cross-reference related items. Then all you do is answer each multiple-choice question. In dealing with a nonstructured response format, there are no multiple-choice questions. After indexing, you simply respond to each item by means of notes, memos, use of the calendar, and sometimes writing directly on each item. The important thing to remember is always to consider the behavioral traits we described in Chapter 16. In dealing with item 24 in a nonstructured response in-basket format, you should read the interim order in item 24 and take steps to disseminate it to the entire precinct. Sending it to Police Officer Brooks of the precinct training unit with a recommendation that it be included in roll call training would get a plus in Planning and Organization (knowledge of the precinct organization chart) and Leadership (recognizing your training responsibilities). Advising the captain of the new interim order gets you a plus in Judgment. Putting a note on your calendar to check with Police Officer Brooks on the matter at a later date also gets you a plus in Management Control.

In dealing with item 27, an indication that notifications must be made to the Parking Meter Bureau, the Buildings Department, and the Sanitation Department would earn credits for Problem Analysis and Planning and Organization, and having someone make the notifications would earn points for Delegation.

CHAPTER 22

Practice Fact-Finding and Decision-Making Exercise

In this chapter we would like to show you what to expect when you take your fact-finding and decision-making exercise. The problem is that a resource person is needed who is willing to help you, and that resource person must be willing to spend some time preparing to administer the examination to you. This would be the ideal way for you to proceed. Find a competent person who is willing to act as your resource person. The next step is for your volunteer resource person to study the material in this chapter entitled Instructions for the Resource Person. When ready, the resource person can administer the exercise for you. At the end of the chapter we have included a scoring guide so you can get a good idea of how you did. More importantly, you will then have a good working understanding of the process. If, however, you cannot find someone to act as your resource person, you can still benefit from this chapter simply by reading and understanding the process. As mentioned in the previous chapter, the most important thing for you to realize is that *there is no optimum decision*. Just make certain the decision you make is consistent, logical, and reasonable in light of the information you uncovered.

Instructions for the Resource Person

It is very important that the resource person study and become familiar with the incident and the details of the incident that are to be used to answer the candidate's questions fairly and adequately during the fifteen-minute candidate's questioning period. The resource person should be especially familiar with the counterarguments to raise when challenging the candidate's decision and rationale. When the resource person is familiar enough with this material, the exercise can be administered.

SEQUENCE OF EVENTS DURING THE EXERCISE

The exercise begins with the resource person reading the following instructions to the candidate with the candidate reading along.

1. The purpose of this exercise is to evaluate your ability to ascertain information about a certain police incident, to arrive at a decision concerning this incident, and to present and support this decision.

2. Following these instructions is a brief description of an incident involving a civilian complaint alleging physical and verbal abuse by a police officer.

3. You, the candidate, are to play the role of a police sergeant in the Whitestone police department. Your job is to investigate the incident described below and arrive at a recommended course of action.

4. I (the resource person) have all of the information you need to reach your decision concerning this incident. You (the candidate) can obtain this information by asking me specific questions about this incident. However, I will not respond to general questions. Instead, I will ask you to make your questions more specific.

5. Please understand that I (the resource person) am a neutral party in this incident. I am not playing a role. My job is to answer your questions and then to question you (the candidate) about your decision.

6. You (the candidate) now have five minutes to study the incident presented below and prepare questions to ask me about this incident. You will then be given fifteen minutes to ask your questions, analyze the responses, and decide on a course of action. After this fifteen-minute period, you will be asked to use a maximum of five minutes to report your decision and the reasons supporting your decision. After your five-minute report, I (the resource person) will question you for ten minutes about your decision.

7. Do you have any questions?

8. Now read the incident recorded below.

Note: At this point in the actual exercise, the candidate is given a copy of the incident described below. It would be preferable if for this exercise the resource person typed the incident ahead of time and had it ready to give to the candidate at this time. Otherwise, the candidate should be allowed to read it right from this book. Also, please note that the candidate should have paper and a pencil to write questions and record responses.

9. After five minutes elapse, the resource person states that the planning period is over and that the candidate now has fifteen minutes to ask questions, arrive at a decision, and prepare a presentation.

Note: The resource person now answers the candidate's questions based on the information given to the resource person for this purpose and with which the resource person should already be familiar. If the candidate's question is too general, it is to be answered by asking for a more specific question. Information is not to be volunteered but should be freely given if specifically requested.

10. After fifteen minutes, stop answering questions and call for the candidate's decision, which must be presented within a five-minute time frame.

11. As soon as the candidate delivers the decision, it should be challenged. Attempt to make the candidate change the decision. Use the arguments in the background material to challenge the candidate's proposed course of action. Bring up information that the candidate did not uncover during the questioning period in an attempt to sway him/her. After ten minutes of questioning, the exercise is over. Dismiss the candidate in a cordial manner.

INFORMATION ABOUT THE INCIDENT GIVEN TO THE CANDIDATE

A Mr. Henry Green has made a formal civilian complaint against Police Officer John Jones. The desk officer, Lieutenant Harry Adams, has directed you to investigate the complaint and to recommend a course of action for the department to follow concerning this complaint. Police Officer Jones has made a statement concerning the incident.

INFORMATION FOR THE RESOURCE PERSON TO USE WHEN RESPONDING TO THE CANDIDATE'S QUESTIONS

Please note that on the actual examination, the candidate would not be shown the information written below.

TEXT OF COMPLAINT FROM MR. HENRY GREEN

1471 Fourteenth Avenue
Whitestone, New York

Commanding Officer
Whitestone Police Department
Whitestone, New York

Dear Captain:

Please consider this letter a formal complaint against Police Officer John Jones, Shield No. 126, which I hate to make since I am a friend of the police.

At about 2:30 a.m., on Saturday, May 31, I was unjustly issued a summons from Police Officer Jones for being drunk and disorderly in a public place. In addition to getting a summons I didn't deserve, I was also subjected by the officer to physical and verbal abuse. I am a taxpayer who should be shown more respect.

I eagerly await your decision in this matter.

Sincerely,

Henry Green

BASIC DETAILS OF THE INCIDENT

At about 2:30 a.m. on Saturday morning, May 31, Police Officer Jones was dispatched to 14th Avenue and 150th Street to investigate a disorderly person on the complaint of Ann Logan of 1419 14th Avenue, Whitestone. Upon arrival at the scene, Police Officer Jones encountered a Mr. Henry Green, and a confrontation ensued.

LOCATION OF THE INCIDENT

The incident occurred on the southeast corner of 14th Avenue and 150th Street in Whitestone. The area is a commercial one with some scattered residential apartments above the various retail establishments lining both sides of the street. Only one establishment was open at the time of occurrence. It was a local tavern called Riddlers. The only other person visible on the street at the time of occurrence was a young man waiting for a bus on the northwest corner of 14th Avenue and 150th Street. The weather was clear, and the streets in the vicinity were all well lighted.

THE LAW INVOLVED

The town of Whitestone has a local law that prohibits persons from appearing in public in an intoxicated condition if the appearance is coupled with loud and boisterous conduct that bothers or annoys others.

INFORMATION ABOUT INVOLVED PARTIES

Complainant: Mr. Henry Green

Mr. Green is a 65-year-old electrician. He is not married. He has never been convicted of a serious crime, although he has twice been found guilty of disorderly conduct. He lives at 1471 14th Avenue, Whitestone. He has no phone. He has a reputation as a "street fighter" and a "ladies man," which, at his age, gives him great pleasure.

Eye Witness: Mr. James Prissey

Mr. Prissey is a well-known local resident. He was waiting for a bus at the time of the incident since he was on his way to work as an attendant in a bath house in the city. He is 24 years old. He lives at 153 150th Street in Whitestone, and his phone number is 023-1111. He has never been arrested.

Witness: Mr. Pat Falco

Pat Falco is the bartender at the Riddlers Tavern. On the night in question, Mr. Falco, a male, white, 38 years of age, was working the late shift. He lives at 120 150th Street in Whitestone. His phone number is 023-2222. He is a former Marine. He was arrested once for attempting to bribe a police officer. The case was dismissed when the key witness was killed in a car accident.

Witness: Mrs. Ann Logan

Female, white, 54 years of age, lives at 1419 14th Avenue, Whitestone. Her phone number is 023-3333. She was the person who called the police. Mrs. Logan is a widow who lives alone. She has never had any trouble with the police.

MR. GREEN'S STATEMENT

I left my house at 1:00 a.m. on the night in question and went to visit my friend Pat Falco at Riddlers Tavern. I had two beers at the bar and was going to leave the bar when I got a call from Ann Logan, who invited me up to her house for a nightcap. I refused her invitation and left the bar to go home. When I got out in the street, Mrs. Logan, who lives adjacent to the bar, yelled an obscenity at me from her window. I was yelling back at her when this cop Jones came on the scene and told me to stop acting like a drunk S.O.B. and to act my age. He shook me by the shoulders, asked me some questions, and before I knew it, he issued me a summons. The officer should not have called me a name, and he should keep his hands to himself.

MR. PRISSEY'S STATEMENT

While I was waiting for the bus to take me to work, I heard and saw Mr. Green in front of the neighborhood bar yelling across the street, although I didn't see at whom he was yelling. Then I saw the officer arrive, and Mr. Green and the officer had words. At one point the officer grabbed Mr. Green. Then my bus came and I boarded it.

MR. FALCO'S STATEMENT

At about 1:00 a.m., Mr. Green came into the bar and stayed about one and one-half hours. Once, after I came out of the kitchen where I was making myself coffee, I saw Green on the phone. He had a couple of beers and left. That's all I know.

MRS. LOGAN'S STATEMENT

At about 2:15 a.m. I was awakened by a telephone call from Henry Green, who asked if he could come up to see me. Naturally, I refused. The next thing I knew, Henry was in the street yelling obscenities up at my window. I was quite embarrassed and called the police. Once the police came and the noise stopped, I went back to bed since I wanted to attend church early the next morning.

OFFICER JONES' STATEMENT

I was directed by the dispatcher to 14th Avenue and 150th Street to quiet a disturbance at that location. When I arrived at the scene I saw Mr. Green, in an intoxicated condition, yelling obscenities in front of the Riddler's Tavern. As I approached him, he stumbled and was falling so I grabbed him to keep him on his feet. With that, he became louder and more obnoxious. I cited him on the spot. Actually, I gave him a break. In his condition, I should have locked him up. Instead, I told him to act his age and gave him a summons. I might have called him an "old fool," but it was just to bring him to his senses. I didn't do anything wrong.

Arguments to Challenge the Candidate's Decision: For Use by the Resource Person Only

IF CANDIDATE DECIDES AGAINST THE POLICE OFFICER

1. Green certainly was acting like an "old fool."

2. Green abused Jones verbally, so he was wrong.

3. The officer didn't violently shake the complainant, he just wanted to stop him from falling.

4. Disciplinary action would not be warranted in this case; the officer was resolving a verified complaint.

5. Green was obviously drunk; how could he be believed?

6. There just aren't enough substantiated facts to warrant charging the officer.

7. Green would probably be satisfied with less severe action. He says he is a friend of the police.

8. The officer's intentions were good, so why should he be faulted?

9. Mrs. Logan's statement supports the officer.

IF CANDIDATE DECIDES TO EXONERATE OFFICER

1. The officer admits calling Green an "old fool."

2. Green couldn't be intoxicated: he only had two beers.

3. Officer Jones will now think he can freely manhandle all citizens.

4. The officer clearly abused his authority. He issued a summons when he should have made an arrest.

5. The witness Prissey verified Green's complaint about physical abuse.

6. Green will be incensed with this disposition and press his complaint to higher authorities.

7. Not taking action against Jones will put a stamp of approval on his actions.

8. The officer lost control of himself and should be disciplined for it.

IF CANDIDATE DECIDES TO ARRIVE AT SOME SORT OF NEGOTIATED SETTLEMENT

1. Officer Jones will resent this because he says he didn't do anything wrong.

2. Green will not be satisfied because he still has to deal with the summons.

3. The department will be embarrassed if Green presses his complaint further.

4. This action will not deter Jones from similar unprofessional conduct in the future.

5. The officer clearly abused his authority and should be punished.

6. Green is clearly making a baseless complaint, and the officer shouldn't have to be humiliated on Green's account.

7. Physical abuse is too serious a violation not to merit charges.

Scoring Key

In this exercise, the candidate would be given points if he/she:

1. Appeared confident throughout the exercise

2. Planned a logical series of questions

3. Stayed within the time frames

4. Obtained at least fifty percent of the details about the incident, including the statements of all the witnesses

5. Supported his/her decision with relevant information from the incident

6. Acknowledged the relevance of information contrary to his/her decision

7. Presented his/her decision in a professional manner

Final Comment

By analyzing each of the arguments listed above to assist the resource person to challenge the decision of the candidate, it should be clear to you that the actual decision in this exercise is not at all a key issue. What matters is the candidate's ability to uncover facts, make a decision based on those facts, and then to use the facts to defend the action.

CHAPTER 23

Practice Report-Writing Exercise

For ease of understanding, we have first summarized the material in the practice exercise in this chapter. Remember, however, that on the actual exercise you would not be given a summary.

Summary of Exercise

INSTRUCTIONS

Let's assume you are taking a Report-Writing Exercise for the rank of sergeant. You are given instructions that tell you who you are, your assignment, some profile information about the people you work with, and the current date and time.

PACKET OF MATERIALS

You are also given a packet of material similar to that which follows and includes:

Item 1. Information from your boss ordering you to write a three-page report for him concerning police-related conditions at the North Side Bus Terminal. More specifically, you are told to take one hour to write a report that:

1. Presents your general impression of crime and police-related conditions at the North Side Bus Terminal

2. Summarizes crime and police-related conditions thereat

In addition, the memo requires you to make recommendations as to how to deal with any crime and police-related conditions identified at the terminal. You are also told to limit the report to three pages.

Item 2. Information that outlines community complaints about a number of locations in the jurisdiction where you work. Included among these community complaints are the following specific complaints about the North Side Bus Terminal:

1. Abandoned vehicles causing a loss of revenue and safety problems

2. Homeless persons interfering with commuters

3. Youth gang members committing robberies

Items 3 and 4. Statistical data showing crime statistics regarding assaults at various locations, which shows quite clearly that there is a crime problem at the North Side Bus Terminal, i.e., numerous assaults are being reported.

Item 5. Information pointing out an increase of shoplifting at a number of commercial locations including the shops at the North Side Bus Terminal.

Item 6. Information pointing out an ongoing youth gang rivalry between two gangs, one of which frequents the North Side Bus Terminal.

NOTE: It is very important for the candidate to realize that each of the six items above contains much more information than is needed to WRITE the required report. It is your job to go through the information and identify that which is relevant according to the instructions you have received. It is for this reason that we tell our students that a Report-Writing Exercise usually measures much more than the candidate's writing skills. In other words, even if you are the best report writer in your department, you will only do well if your report contains all of the relevant material and none of the irrelevant material.

It is now time for you to take a practice Report-Writing Exercise based on the above summary. The material on the following pages is a typical Report-Writing Exercise in which the candidate has to sift through a larger batch of information, identify the relevant material, formulate recommendations to deal with any identified problems, and write a report in the appropriate format.

INSTRUCTIONS

During this exercise, you are to assume that you are Sergeant Jess Parks of the Gotham Police Department. You are assigned as a patrol sergeant in the 4th Precinct's Second Platoon. You have been assigned to the precinct for about one year and have been a sergeant for about three years, having joined the department 12 years ago. Today is September 5, XXXX, it is 0800 hours, and you are working an 0800 × 1600 hours tour. The commanding officer of the precinct is Captain Logo, and your immediate supervisor is Lieutenant Hall, who has taken an emergency day off to accompany his elderly mother to the hospital. In instances when the lieutenant is excused, it is accepted department policy to have the patrol sergeant respond directly to the precinct captain.

The 4th Precinct is approximately four-and-one-half square miles in area and has a population of 22,000 residents. It has a mix of commercial and residential areas. Generally it is considered a middle class area and its population is a blend of ethnic groups. Assigned to the precinct are 100 sworn officers, consisting of 80 police officers, 8 sergeants, 3 lieutenants, 1 detective lieutenant, 7 detectives, and 1 captain who is the precinct commander. There are also 10 civilians assigned as clerical support.

ORGANIZATION OF THE GOTHAM POLICE DEPARTMENT

The Gotham Police Department consists of six police precincts. It has 700 sworn members and 89 civilians. The department has a detective division, a city-wide uniform patrol task force, and a traffic division. It is commanded by a Chief of Police who strongly believes that staff assistance should readily be made available to line units when necessary. A Gang Intelligence unit has recently been created to help with the growing problem of youth gangs.

ORGANIZATION OF THE FOURTH PRECINCT

Commanding Officer

1 Captain

Uniform Patrol Force

0001 × 0800	0800 × 1600	1600 × 2400
First Platoon	Second Platoon	Third Platoon
1 Lieutenant	1 Lieutenant	1 Lieutenant
2 Sergeants	3 Sergeants	3 Sergeants
20 Police Officers	30 Police Officers	30 Police Officers
2 Clerical Civilians	4 Clerical Civilians	3 Clerical Civilians

Investigation Bureau

1 Lieutenant	7 Detectives	1 Clerical Civilian

Anticrime Unit

Three Police Officers from the Second Platoon and three Police Officers from the Third Platoon are detailed to civilian clothes anticrime duty.

Community Affairs Unit

Community Affairs: One Police Officer from the Second Platoon is detailed to Community Affairs duty.

September 5, XXXX

From: Commanding Officer, 4th Precinct

To: Sergeant Jess Parks

Subject: INFORMATION REQUIRED FOR A CITY HALL MEETING

1. At 1500 hours this date, I would like to see you in my office to discuss some recent evaluations of police officers of the second platoon. In addition, I would like you to prepare a report for me which I will use to assist me in a meeting I have this afternoon at 1700 hours.

2. The meeting will be with representatives of the residential and business community involved with the North Side Bus Terminal, which is located within the confines of our precinct. They want to meet with me regarding police-related conditions at the terminal. What I'd like you to do is to take one hour during your tour and have a report for me on the police-related conditions at the terminal. Once again, I need this report by 1500 hours today.

3. I have attached some pertinent information about the terminal, which I want you to go through and use in putting together your report. What I'm looking for is your overall general impression of police-related conditions at the terminal. In addition, I want you to briefly summarize the conditions at the terminal and make very specific recommendations regarding how you think we should deal with any police-related conditions you identify there.

4. Because I'm meeting with this group at 1700 hours, the time I will have to review your report is minimal. Therefore, I must insist that you write no more than three handwritten pages (letter size) when complying with the direction I have given you. You are to take no more than one hour of your tour to analyze the material I have provided for you and to write the report.

5. For your immediate attention.

Frank Logo

Frank Logo
Captain
Commanding Officer
4th Precinct

August 30, XXXX

From: Lieutenant Don Hall, Second Platoon

To: Commanding Officier, Fourth Precinct

Subject: TOWN HALL MEETING OF 08/03/XX

1. Pursuant to your direction, at 0900 hours this date I attended the Town Hall meeting held at the Gotham City Center Auditorium as your representative from the Fourth Precinct. The meeting lasted three hours beginning at 0900 and ending at 1200 hours. Attending the meeting were various local governmental officials, including a representative of our Chief of Police, as well as members of the community. The main issues discussed are as follows:

a) Complaints were aired by members of the press about the news blackout experienced by reporters assigned to cover the serial killer who has been identified as operating entirely within the confines of the Sixth Precinct. According to one reporter, his calls to the Sixth Precinct are met with either "no comment" or "leave a number and we'll get back to you." This problem was referred to the representatives of the Sixth Precinct and the Chief of Police's representatives who responded that he would recommend to the Chief that his office look into the matter but that in the interim, the Chief would issue a department bulletin, which would clarify the department's policy of appropriate access to the news by members of the press. The representative of the Sixth Precinct said that he would work closely with the Chief's office to rectify the matter.

b) Extremely harsh disapproval was voiced about the rumored fare hike for the Gotham City Subway line. The fare increase may be as much as 10 percent. Demonstrations may be held in the confines of the Third Precinct, which houses the headquarters of the Gotham City Subway Line. Representatives of the Mayor's Office indicated that round-the-clock talks are being conducted to see if the fare can be held to its present level.

c) Representatives of the business community who have businesses in and around the North Side Bus Terminal complained about cars being abandoned around the terminal. It seems that this is resulting in a loss of revenue to these business owners. In the early morning hours of 3 AM to 5 AM on weekends, cars are being abandoned in metered parking spaces in front of the stores that surround the terminal. This has resulted in an obvious loss of revenue to Gotham City of about $15,000 in parking meter fees in the last six months and also a loss in parking spaces for patrons of these stores. The store owners all agree that friends and relatives who pick up commuters at the terminal often make purchases in these stores while waiting for the commuters to arrive. It appears that now they are taking their business elsewhere, resulting in a loss of revenue to these store owners. They claim their business has dropped 10 percent in the last few months. City Councilman Harper also pointed out that the abandoned vehicles are a safety hazard to small children who frequent the area while enroute to Gotham Grade School. The principal of the school, who was also in attendance, provided statistics showing that, in the last four months, 16 injuries have been suffered by children who attended this school. All of these injuries were suffered by children under 12. It was agreed that this matter should be referred to the Police Precinct concerned to investigate and take appropriate action.

d) The Human Resources Administration of Gotham City led considerable debate on the increase of homeless persons frequenting the North Side Bus Terminal. Sentiment seemed to be divided between concern for the well being of the homeless and outright hostility towards them for the problems they create for the community in and around the terminal. Those concerned for the well being of the homeless wanted more and better outreach programs designed to identify and assist them in any way possible. However, there was larger support for dealing with the problems that have developed since the homeless began frequenting the terminal area. For instance, many of the homeless have taken to panhandling during the height of commuter rush hour at the terminal. This has impacted negatively on the quality of life in the terminal area which, the Gotham City Bus Line reports, has resulted in a decrease in ridership and accompanying revenues for Gotham City. Also as a result of the increase in homeless in the area, precinct statistics show that the homeless are often the victims of robberies and assaults by young toughs who frequent the area. This situation was also referred to the Police Precinct concerned to investigate and take appropriate action.

2. I will keep you informed of any further developments as they occur.

3. For your information.

Don Hall
Don Hall
Lieutenant

4TH PRECINCT STATISTICAL REPORT # 23

STATISTICS COMPARING REPORTED INCIDENTS OF ASSAULT AND ENFORCEMENT EFFORTS AT LOCATIONS IN THE 4TH PRECINCT FOR THE FIRST SIX MONTHS OF THIS CURRENT YEAR AS COMPARED WITH THE FIRST SIX MONTHS OF LAST YEAR.

LOCATION	ASSAULT COMPLAINTS		ASSAULT ARRESTS	
	PREV. YEAR	CURR. YEAR	PREV. YEAR	CURR. YEAR
A.	66	71	12	11
B.	33	35	22	21
C.	48	50	37	46
D.	68	75	19	38
E.	39	32	19	18
F.	64	46	58	38
G.	27	26	20	20
H.	59	99	18	17
I.	51	41	23	21
J.	48	51	38	40
K.	29	15	25	19
L.	36	35	22	20
M.	39	27	18	19
N.	42	42	17	19

Index of Locations

A. = City Hall Park
B. = Gotham Zoo
C. = Area of Gotham High School
D. = Area of Gotham Junior High School
E. = City Center Sports Arena
F. = City Center Music and Arts Center
G. = Memorial Hospital
H. = North Side Bus Terminal
I. = President Adams Museum Center
J. = Gotham Botanical Gardens
K. = Northern College Grounds
L. = Center City Shopping Mall
M. = Broadway and Main Street Shopping Mall
N. = MC Combs Park

Item 4: Gotham City
Police Department

4th Precinct Statistical Report # 24

STATISTICS COMPARING REPORTED INCIDENTS OF ASSAULT AND ENFORCEMENT EFFORTS AT LOCATIONS IN THE 4TH PRECINCT FOR THE MONTHS OF JULY AND AUGUST THIS CURRENT YEAR AS COMPARED WITH JULY AND AUGUST OF LAST YEAR.

LOCATION	ASSAULT COMPLAINTS		ASSAULT ARRESTS	
	PREV. YEAR	CURR. YEAR	PREV. YEAR	CURR. YEAR
A.	22	24	04	03
B.	11	13	07	07
C.	16	17	12	15
D.	23	25	19	38
E.	39	32	06	06
F.	21	15	19	13
G.	09	08	07	06
H.	19	33	06	05
I.	17	14	07	07
J.	16	17	13	17
K.	10	05	08	06
L.	13	12	07	07
M.	13	09	06	06
N.	14	14	06	07

Index of Locations

A. = City Hall Park
B. = Gotham Zoo
C. = Area of Gotham High School
D. = Area of Gotham Junior High School
E. = City Center Sports Arena
F. = City Center Music and Arts Center
G. = Memorial Hospital
H. = North Side Bus Terminal
I. = President Adams Museum Center
J. = Gotham Botanical Gardens
K. = Northern College Grounds
L. = Center City Shopping Mall
M. = Broadway and Main Street Shopping Mall
N. = MC Combs Park

ITEM 5: CITY OF GOTHAM
POLICE DEPARTMENT

September 3, XXXX

From: Detective Lieutenant Bob Catcher, 4th Precinct

To: Commanding Officer, 4th Precinct

Subject: INCREASE IN SHOPLIFTING THROUGHOUT THE 4TH PRECINCT

1. From January 1st of this year to date, there has been an alarming increase in shoplifting thefts from retail shops throughout our entire command. However, six specific locations are where the majority of our problem seems to lie. The six locations are:

   1. City Hall Mall Shopping Area
   2. Gotham Zoo Novelty and Gift Shops
   3. City Center Sports Arena Souvenir Shops
   4. Various Shops at the North Side Bus Terminal
   5. The Gift Shop at Memorial Hospital
   6. Center City Shopping Mall

2. With the exception of the Gotham Zoo location, all the thefts seem to be taking place on weekdays.

3. I will, of course, keep you informed of any further developments in this matter as they occur. I have checked with surrounding precincts, and they do not seem to be experiencing a similar increase. I am in the process of trying to determine why this is so.

4. Submitted for whatever action you deem appropriate.

Bob Catcher

Bob Catcher
Detective Lieutenant

September 4, XXXX

From: Margo Peoples, Community Affairs Officer, 4th Precinct

To: Commanding Officer, 4th Precinct

Subject: GANG RIVALRY WITHIN THE CONFINES OF THE 4TH
          PRECINCT

1. At 1930 hours this date, I, along with two members of the Department's Gang Intelligence Unit, interviewed several youths, known to this department, who have ties to youth gangs operating within the 4th precinct. The results of these interviews are as follows:

a. Two dominant gangs have been identified as residing and operating within this precinct. They are the Melfords and the Golden Roosters.

b. The Melfords have operated in this area for over fifteen years. Ostensibly holding themselves out to be a social club organized for sports recreation, the Melfords are believed to be prime actors in the "crack trade" that is conducted in the area of the Gotham City Housing Project where many of the members reside. Their long tenure in this precinct is a result of familial indoctrinations whereby older gang members introduce younger members of their families into the gang. In a sense gang membership is passed along from generation to generation. The active members of the gang number about 50, with ages ranging from 13 to 19 years of age. Most of the members are white.

c. The Golden Roosters are newcomers to our precinct. Mostly black and hispanic, their members range in age from 15 to 18 years of age and they are believed to have about 35 hardcore members. They reside mostly in the row houses found in the North Side Industrial Park area of Gotham City. They are involved in burglaries in their own neighborhood but are believed to be expanding into robbery. Reliable information reveals that they may be involved in the muggings of homeless persons in the North Side Bus Terminal. Further information reveals that the Golden Roosters may be attempting to set up an extortion racket in the North Side Bus Terminal, offering protection to the storeowner there in exchange for systematic payoffs.

d. It now seems as if the expansion of criminal activities by the Golden Roosters has come to the attention of the Melfords. Although the North Side Bus Terminal has always been considered among the various youth gangs as "neutral gang turf," it is the opinion of the Melfords that any expansion into the Terminal should not be engaged in by newcomers to the area such as the Golden Roosters. Rather, they believe that their "colors" should fly over the terminal, and any potential for criminal activity there belongs to them.

2. The result of this is not only the increase of crimes against persons at the Terminal but also the possibility of the eruption of an all-out gang war with the battleground being the terminal.

3. I will continue to monitor the situation as well as remaining in constant touch with members of the Gang Intelligence Unit. As developments occur, you will be informed immediately.

4. For your information.

Margo Peoples

Margo Peoples
Community Affairs Officer
4th Precinct

STOP!

**FOR MAXIMUM BENEFIT,
DO NOT PROCEED UNTIL
AFTER YOU HAVE WRITTEN
YOUR REPORT!!!**

At this time you should write your report. Remember, according to the instructions you have only one hour to complete the report. This includes the time spent reviewing the above material. When the time frames are short, you do not have the luxury of time to write a draft report and a final copy. However, please note that the key that follows does not contain points for neatness. This means that while your report must be legible, it can contain strikeovers. What we tell our students is that you should view your finished product as something that will be given to a typist for final copy.

A Representative Scoring Key

This is a sample key for the exercise. Heavily weighted items are in bold print.

POSITIVES

1. ____ Factual information, including statistics, were accurately transposed

2. ____ Brief, simple sentences were used (no run-on sentences)

3. ____ The report was properly dated

4. ____ The proper format (i.e., the one required by your department's rules) was used to address the report

5. ____ The report was addressed to the appropriate person

6. ____ The opening paragraph properly introduced the subject matter of the report

7. ____ Only one phase of the subject was covered in each paragraph

8. ____ Indication of copy for file. Also any other intended distribution other than the addressee.

9. ____ **Presented a general impression that painted a serious and/or important situation at the North Side Bus Terminal**

10. ____ **Accurately summarized the abandoned auto problem**

11. ____ **Accurately summarized the homeless persons problem**

12. ____ **Accurately summarized the youth gang robbery problem**

13. ____ **Accurately summarized the assault problem, including the use of relevant assault statistics by utilizing both charts**

14. ____ **Accurately summarized the shoplifting problem**

15. ____ **Accurately summarized the youth gang rivalry problem**

16. ____ Made appropriate recommendations for the abandoned auto problem

17. ___ Made appropriate recommendations for the homeless persons problem

18. ___ Made appropriate recommendations for the robbery problem

19. ___ Made appropriate recommendations for the assault problem

20. ___ Made appropriate recommendations for the shoplifting problem

21. ___ Made appropriate recommendations for the youth gang problem

22. ___ **Information uncovered was used to support specific recommendations**

NOTE: RECOMMENDATIONS SHOULD INCLUDE THE USE OF DEPARTMENT-WIDE RESOURCES AS WELL AS LOCAL PRECINCT RESOURCES. IN ADDITION, IN APPROPRIATE INSTANCES THE USE OF OTHER PUBLIC AGENCIES AND PRIVATE RESOURCES SUCH AS THOSE OF THE COMMUNITY SHOULD BE RECOMMENDED.

NEGATIVES

1. ___ Consistent poor grammar

2. ___ Consistent poor spelling

3. ___ Excess wordiness

4. ___ Poor punctuation

5. ___ **Uses more than three pages**

PART FOUR:
A FINAL WORD

CHAPTER 24

A Strategy for Final Preparation

The time draws near. You have waited a long time for this opportunity. You have prepared long and hard. Don't be fearful. Remember, taking the pending examination is something for which you are ready; passing it is something you can do; becoming a police sergeant is something you want.

But is there anything that should be done in the days just before the examination? How should those few days right before the examination be spent? Well, this is what we suggest for the days right before the examination and for the examination day itself.

The Final Countdown Preparation

SEVEN DAYS BEFORE THE WRITTEN EXAMINATION

Review the four practice examinations and the diagnostic charts found in Chapters 3, 13, 14, and 15 for the purposes of identifying weaknesses. Also review the questions and answers pertaining to assessment center exercises in Chapters 17, 18, and 19, if it is possible that any of these exercises will be part of your pending examination. If that's not to be included in your examination at this time, hold off on it until you are to be examined in that area. Also, sometime during this week take a trip to the examination site. If you plan to take public transportation, make sure you have the exact change, if required; know the exact train or bus to be used, the stop on the transportation route, and how to get to the site from the stop. Make sure you know the transportation schedule for the day of the examination. There's a good chance the examination will be scheduled for a weekend. You can imagine your frustration when you realize that you are waiting for a bus or a train that does not run on weekends.

If you plan to drive, make a "dry run" sometime in the week before the examination. Learn the best route to use on the day of the examination. Some candidates have even had someone drive them to the site on test day just in case the car develops problems. In that way, they could continue to the examination site on their own. If no street parking is available, make some inquiries about availability of parking on the day of the examination. We have heard horror tales about a candidate taking a promotional examination who looked up from the paper to see his new car being towed away by the traffic department because he had inadvertently parked illegally: disconcerting to say the least! You need no such distractions. Being prepared and thinking ahead translates into giving yourself every advantage.

SIX AND FIVE DAYS BEFORE THE EXAMINATION

Go over the areas in which the diagnostic charts have indicated you need help. For example, if they indicate you have had problems in the area of training and safety, then you should be reviewing Chapter 6. Be truthful with yourself. If you have had problems in a certain area, you should be working on that area. Spend these two days solely on areas that present a problem to you. Do not waste your time reviewing areas in which you are strong. You have spent enough time with them. These are two key days. Use them to tie up some loose ends.

FOUR, THREE, AND TWO DAYS BEFORE THE EXAMINATION

On each of these three days, retake one of the practice examinations found in Chapters 3, 13, 14, and 15. This will give you a chance to refamiliarize yourself with what to expect on the day of the examination. Take these tests under conditions closely duplicating those that will occur on the day of the examination. For example, sit in a room at a desk or a table. Time yourself using the time management techniques we have suggested in Chapter 2. The pressure of time, therefore, will be no stranger to you on the day of the examination. Obviously the no-smoking rule you will undoubtedly encounter on the day of the examination applies. Use the same kind of pencil you will use on examination day. Usually, you will be asked to bring a #2 lead pencil. Make sure you bring at least two. Take each of these tests in their entirety. Resist looking up answers about which you are curious. The theme is try to make everything as close to examination conditions as possible.

ONE DAY BEFORE THE EXAMINATION

Review Chapter 2, which deals with test-taking techniques. Do not review any more technical or generic skills or areas that are to appear on your examination. You are prepared. If you have faithfully used this text and studied hard, there is no need for last-minute cramming. Begin to relax. Your preparation for the examination is over.

On the evening before the examination eat a normal dinner. Get some rest and your regular amount of sleep that night. Do not take a sedative to fall asleep. It may be harmful to you the next morning.

You have taken the steps you need to be successful on the examination. Test day is just another day; nothing more needs to be done in terms of preparation.

The Day of the Examination

Wake up early enough to have a good breakfast, dress, and check over whatever test-taking material you have decided to take with you. A word about waking up: an alarm clock is adequate, but a call from a friend just to make sure is not a bad idea.

Different test takers believe in bringing different test-taking materials. We have always found the following useful:

Several sharpened pencils

A pencil sharpener

A good eraser

Several pens

Eyeglasses, if needed; a spare pair if available

Something to clean your eyeglasses

A sweater to keep you warm if the examination room is cold (you can always take it off if it's too warm or even sit on it; a desk seat can become terribly hard after awhile)

Some kind of hard candy for energy or to use if your mouth becomes dry

A wristwatch in good working order

The Examination

When you arrive at the examination site, follow the instructions of your proctors. Go to your assigned room, and be seated. Inspect your seat, and report any problems to your proctors immediately. Follow instructions to the letter. You have been exposed to several examinations in this text. You are no stranger to the process. If you have followed what we have recommended, you should be prepared to do well. Believe in your ability based upon the effort you have put into it.

You can be a sergeant. It's worth it. Good luck!